Sunil Kumar Parameswaran

Derivatives Theory and Practice

Sunil Kumar Parameswaran

Derivatives Theory and Practice

Sunil Kumar Parameswaran

Derivatives Theory and Practice

An Emerging Markets Perspective

DE GRUYTER

ISBN 978-3-11-074661-7
e-ISBN (PDF) 978-3-11-074666-2
e-ISBN (EPUB) 978-3-11-074676-1

Library of Congress Control Number: 2024941205

Bibliographic information published by the Deutsche Nationalbibliothek
The Deutsche Nationalbibliothek lists this publication in the Deutsche Nationalbibliografie; detailed bibliographic data are available on the Internet at http://dnb.dnb.de.

Cover image: Nikada/E+/Getty Images
Typesetting: Integra Software Services Pvt. Ltd.

www.degruyter.com

To my parents
Savitri Parameswaran
and
Late A.S. Parameswaran

Preface

I have been teaching MBA level courses on derivatives at various business schools in India for the past three decades. In fact, I commenced teaching the subject before the Indian securities exchanges introduced derivatives trading. This book is not strictly a textbook, nor is it a treatise written to facilitate trading by market participants. There are excellent well established textbooks like the books by John Hull, and Don Chance, and very good resources on trading aspects such as technical analysis are also available. During my teaching career, some students were of the opinion that I have the ability to make mathematical economics more comprehensible for students. Hence, this book on derivatives. My good friend and colleague, Sankarshan Basu, opined that instead of yet another conventional book on the subject, a book with a part focus on emerging markets would be more useful for readers. Thus, this book has two chapters on derivatives and emerging markets. The first chapter talks about the issues involved in setting up derivatives exchanges in emerging markets. The second looks at the Indian market for such products. The Indian market is one of the fastest growing markets, and has state-of-the-art trading and risk management systems. Foreign portfolio investors from the West are regular participants in this market. I have made a conscious decision not to reproduce statistical data on trading volumes and other related aspects. Thus, the focus is on the elucidation of concepts. Advanced mathematical issues, and technical proofs, have been kept to a bare minimum.

This book can be used by both BBA and MBA students, as well as professionals. Students may choose to use it as an accompaniment to a standard textbook. Undergraduate students of Economics and Finance will also find this book to be useful. Although the book has been written by an Indian author, the US dollar has been used throughout the manuscript, and all proper nouns are Western, in order to ensure that a global audience can relate to it.

Sunil K. Parameswaran
Director & CEO, Tarheel Consultancy Services
Manipal, Karnataka, India

https://doi.org/10.1515/9783110746662-202

Acknowledgements

I owe a tremendous debt to Sankarshan Basu of IIM Bangalore, with whom I have taught courses on derivatives at a number of leading business schools in India. The freedom to bounce ideas off him has been an invaluable asset while writing this book. I am also grateful to Banikanta Mishra, who invited me to teach this course at XIM Bhubaneshwar many years ago. Discussions with Bani on this subject have always been very stimulating and thought provoking. Shantaram Hegde, of the University of Connecticut, has also provided valuable advice and guidance over the years.

My students in India, Dubai, and Australia have contributed significantly to the expositional clarity that I believe I have been able to achieve. I must in particular mention the batches of undergraduate students at Shiv Nadar University, NOIDA, whose curiosity and inquisitiveness have been of great help.

I am grateful to the editorial team at De Gruyter, Stefan and Jaya, who have displayed immense patience, and provided enormous help and support.

Sunil K. Parameswaran

https://doi.org/10.1515/9783110746662-203

Contents

Chapter 1
Introduction to Futures

1.1 Introduction

The focus of this book is on financial derivatives, securities that have inspired fascination as well as fear. They are termed as *derivative securities*, but a more appropriate term for them would be *derivative contracts*. These contracts confer upon the parties to them, certain rights or obligations. The reason why they are termed as *derivatives*, is because they owe their existence to the presence of markets for an underlying asset or portfolio of assets, on which such agreements are written. If we consider the underlying asset to be the primary security, then these contracts which are derived from the underlying assets may be construed as derivative securities. The underlying asset may be a stock, a bond, a foreign currency, an agricultural commodity like wheat, a precious metal like gold, or an intangible asset such as a stock index. In fact, we can have derivatives on derivatives, such as options on futures contracts.

Basic derivative securities may be classified into the following categories.

1. Forward Contracts
2. Futures Contracts
3. Options Contracts
4. Swaps

The book will begin with a detailed study of forward and futures contracts. At the outset we will briefly discuss options and swaps as well, primarily to facilitate a comparison between futures and options. The latter half of this book is devoted to an in-depth study of options, and one of the final chapters contains a more elaborate exposition on swaps.

1.2 Cash/Spot versus Forward Contracts

Consider the case of a traveler who is flying from New York to Frankfurt. He may prior to his departure from JFK Airport like to convert the U.S. dollars in his possession to euros. He will therefore go to a bank and buy the required number of euros by paying the equivalent amount in dollars. In this case as soon as the deal is struck between the buyer of euros (the traveler) and the seller (the bank), the buyer has to immediately hand over the payment for the asset being bought to the seller, who in turn is required to transfer the rights to the asset to the buyer. Such a transaction is called a *cash* or *spot* transaction.

Now consider a slightly different kind of transaction, which is illustrated in Example 1.1.

https://doi.org/10.1515/9783110746662-001

Example 1.1: Mind Tech, a software firm based in California, has entered into a contract with First National Bank to acquire 200,000 euros after 60 days at an exchange rate of $1.10 per euro. Consequently, 60 days after entering into the agreement, the company is required to pay $220,000 to the bank and accept 200,000 euros in lieu. The bank, as per the contract, is obligated to accept the equivalent amount in U.S dollars and deliver the euros.

The difference in the case of such a contract, is that the actual transaction does not take place when the agreement is reached between the buyer and the seller. In such cases at the time of negotiating the deal the two parties merely agree on the terms at which they will transact at a future point in time, including the price to be paid per unit of the underlying asset. The actual transaction per se will occur only at a future date that is decided at the outset. Consequently, unlike in the case of a cash transaction, no money changes hands when the two parties enter into such a contract.

Such a transaction is termed as a *forward contract*. In foreign exchange markets, traders make a distinction between three types of transactions - *cash*, *tom*, and *spot*. A cash transaction is what we described at the beginning, where payment is made and delivery is received as soon as the deal is struck. The term *tom* stands for tomorrow. In other words, a price is fixed in advance for a transaction that is scheduled to be completed on the next business day. The term *spot* in such markets means that the terms are fixed in advance for a transaction that is scheduled to be consummated two business days later.[1] We will however use the terms *cash* and *spot* interchangeably, and by them we refer to transactions where payment and the corresponding delivery takes place as soon as a deal is negotiated between a buyer and a seller. *Futures contracts* are in many respects similar to forward contracts, although there are some key differences which we will focus upon later.

In the case of both forward as well as futures contracts, having negotiated a contract for a transaction at a future date, both parties have a binding commitment to perform. In our example, if after 60 days Mind Tech declines to acquire the euros then it would tantamount to default on its part. On the other hand, if the bank refuses to deliver the euros as per the agreed upon rate, then it would be construed as default on its part. Consequently, such instruments are known as *commitment* contracts.

1.2.1 Long and Short Positions

Both forward and futures contracts are therefore agreements for the future delivery of a good at a pre-specified price at the end of a designated period of time. Thus, there has to be a buyer of the underlying asset as well a seller of the underlying asset as per the specified terms. The party who commits itself to buy the underlying asset is said to have

---

1 The term *business days* is used, because there could be intervening market holidays.

taken a *long position* and is known as the *long*. The counterparty who is committed to sell the underlying asset is said to have taken a *short position* and he is known as the *short*.

1.3 Options

Both forward as well as futures contracts, impose an obligation on the long as well as the short. On the other hand an option gives the buyer the right, but not the obligation, to go ahead with the transaction, subsequent to entering into an agreement with the seller. The option buyer is also referred to as the long, while the seller is known as the short.[2]

The difference between a right and an obligation is that a right need be exercised only if it is in the interest of its holder, and if he deems it appropriate. Thus, the holder of an option is not obliged to go through with the transaction once he enters into such a contract. However, the counterparty, namely the short, always has an obligation. That is, if the long decides to exercise his right, the short is obliged to carry out his part of the deal.

The reader may wonder why both the long as well as the short cannot be given rights. The reason is the following. In any transaction which is scheduled for a future date, as per terms decided upon at the outset, one party will inevitably be at a loss by the time the transaction date arrives. Hence, if both parties are given rights then the party who has a loss will obviously refuse to perform. Thus, in such contracts, both the parties can have obligations imposed on them, which is what is done in the case of forward and futures contracts, or else one party can be given a right and the other party can have an obligation imposed on it, which is what is done in the case of an options contract.

1.3.1 Calls and Puts

Options give the holder the right to transact in the underlying asset. Such rights can obviously take on one of two forms. That is, the holder may be given the right to buy the underlying asset, or else he may be given the right to sell the underlying asset. An options contract which gives the holder the right, but not the obligation, to acquire the underlying asset is known as a *call* option. In such cases, the seller of the call, has the obligation to deliver the asset if the buyer chooses to exercise his right.

On the other hand, an options contract which gives the holder the right, but once again not the obligation, to sell the underlying asset is known as a *put* option. In such cases, if and when the put holder decides to exercise his option, the seller of the put has the obligation to acquire the underlying asset.

2 Option buyers are also referred to as option *holders*, while option sellers are referred to as option *writers*.

Table 1.1: Comparison of futures and forwards, and options.

Instrument	**Nature of commitment of the long**	**Nature of commitment of the short**
Forward/futures contract	Obligation to acquire the underlying asset	Obligation to sell the underlying asset
Call options	Right to acquire the underlying asset	Contingent obligation to deliver the underlying asset
Put options	Right to sell the underlying asset	Contingent obligation to accept delivery of the underlying asset

The difference between forward and futures contracts, and call and put options, can be illustrated with the help of a simple table, as depicted in Table 1.1. In the table, the short, in the case of options, is said to have a contingent obligation. The word '*contingent*' implies that he has an obligation if the long were to choose to exercise his right.

1.3.2 European and American Options

The holder of an option is given the right to transact in the underlying asset, on or before a pre-specified date. In the case of European options, the acquirer of the option can exercise it only at the time the right is scheduled to expire, which is known as the *expiration date* of the option. Obviously, if the holder were not to exercise at that point in time, then the contract itself will become null and void.

American options however, give the holder the right to transact at any point in time, between the time of acquisition of the right and the expiration date of the contract. Thus, the expiration date of the option is the *only* point in time at which a European option can be exercised, and is the *last* point in time at which an American option can be exercised.

It must be emphasized that the terms American and European have nothing to do with the respective continents. Most options contracts that are traded on organized exchanges like the Chicago Board Options Exchange (CBOE), are American in nature. However, while introducing the concept, authors initially tend to focus more on European options. The reason is that, since such options can be exercised only at expiration, one needs to consider possible cash flows only at that instant, which makes the valuation of such instruments relatively simple as compared to American options with equivalent features.

1.3.3 Option Price versus Exercise Price

In the context of options, a reader will come across the terms *option price* and *exercise price*. The term 'option price' or 'option premium' refers to the amount payable by the buyer of an option at the outset, to the writer, for permitting him to acquire the right. Thus, buyers of both call as well as put options are required to pay the writers of such options for giving them the right to transact at a subsequent point in time.

The term 'exercise price', or 'strike price', refers to the amount payable/receivable per unit of the underlying asset, if the option were to be exercised. It is the amount payable by the holder per unit of the underlying asset, if a call option were to be exercised. Equivalently, it is the amount receivable by the holder per unit of the underlying asset, if a put option were to be exercised.

The option premium may be perceived as a 'sunk cost'. For, if the transaction were not to take place subsequently, the premium cannot be recovered. The exercise price, on the other hand, is payable/receivable only if the option holder were to choose to go ahead with the transaction. Since he has a right, he may or may not wish to exercise which obviously means that the exercise price may or may not be paid/received subsequently.

Why is it that buyers of options have to pay sellers, a price for entering into such contracts? The reason is that an options contract entails the giving of a right to the holder by the writer, who in turn is taking on an obligation to perform if the buyer were to exercise the right. Rights are never given free and are always accompanied by an economic price. In other words, one has to pay to acquire them. Thus, option buyers are required to pay option writers for acquiring the right to transact in the underlying asset. Another way to appreciate this is as follows. Once an options contract is entered into, the holder may subsequently get a positive cash flow or a nil cash flow. He cannot get a negative cash flow. But the writer may get a negative or a nil cash flow subsequently. He cannot get a positive cash flow.

Futures and forward contracts are however different. Once a futures contract is entered into, either party may have to countenance a negative cash flow. Such contracts impose an equivalent obligation on both the long as well as the short. We will demonstrate subsequently, when we study the valuation of such contracts that, the futures price, which is the price at which the long is committed to acquire the underlying asset on a future date, will be set in such a way that the value of the futures contract at inception is zero, for both the long as well as the short. That is, a futures contract which entails two equivalent and opposite obligations, is structured in such a way that neither party has to pay the other at the outset.

An options contract may be perceived as an insurance contract. A party which owns an asset can protect himself from a potential price decline by acquiring a put option. For if the price were to decline subsequently, it can take advantage of the right to sell at the exercise price, which is what a put is essentially all about. Similarly, a firm that plans to buy an asset in the future can insure itself against a price rise by buying a call option. For, if the price of the asset were to increase, it can exercise its right to buy at the strike price.

Consequently, option premiums are comparable to insurance premiums. Option buyers buy protection against potential financial losses, while option writers sell insurance.

1.3.4 Illustration of a Call

Kevin Stone has taken a long position in a European call option on American Express, with an exercise price of $150, and six months to maturity. The option has been written by Kathy Scanlon, who consequently has a short position. Let's assume that the option premium is $2.75 per share. Option prices are always quoted on a per share basis, although each contract on the exchange is for 100 shares. Thus the price payable by Kevin to Kathy at the outset is $275.

If the spot price at the time of expiration of the contract, were to be greater than $150 per share, it would make sense for Kevin to exercise his right and acquire 100 shares at $150 each. Otherwise, he is in a position to buy the shares in the spot market at a price, which by assumption is lower than the exercise price. He has the freedom because he is under no compulsion to exercise the option, for it confers a right, and does not impose an obligation. It should be noted however, that the premium of $275 that he paid at the very outset cannot be recovered if the option is not exercised subsequently. Kathy, on the other hand, has a contingent obligation. If Kevin were to decide to exercise his right, she would have no choice but to deliver the shares at a price of $150 per share.

1.3.5 Illustration of a Put

Ross Taylor has bought a European put option on IBM from Mike Robbins, with an exercise price of $140 and three months to maturity. The premium on a per share basis is $2.10. Thus Ross has to pay $210 to Mike at the outset. If the spot price at the time of expiration of the contract, were to be less than $140 per share, it would make sense for Ross to exercise the option and sell the shares at $140 each. Otherwise, he could simply forget the option, and sell the shares in the spot market at a price, which by assumption is higher than the exercise price. However, if Ross were to decide to exercise his right, Mike would have no option but to accept delivery of the shares at a price of $140 per share.

1.4 Swaps

A swap is an agreement between two parties to exchange cash flows calculated on the basis of two different criteria at predefined points in time. The word *'swap'* connotes that the two parties are exchanging or swapping cash flows.

The cash flows being exchanged represent interest payments on a specified principal, computed using two different yardsticks. For instance, one interest payment may be computed using a fixed rate of interest, while the other may be based on a variable benchmark such as the London Inter Bank Offer Rate (LIBOR). Such a swap where one payment is based on a fixed rate of interest, and the other on a floating rate, is referred to as a *coupon swap*.

Swaps where both cash flows are denominated in the same currency are referred to as *interest rate swaps*. In the case of such swaps there is obviously no need to exchange the principal amount since both interest streams are computed in the same currency. Nevertheless, we need to specify a principal amount to enable the computation of interest. Thus, the underlying principal, in the case of such swaps, is referred to as a *notional principal*.

Also, in the case of interest rate swaps, a fixed rate-fixed rate swap, will amount to arbitrage. This is because the party who is required to pay a higher rate will always be paying, while the other party will always be receiving. No one will obviously agree to such a transaction. However, we can have floating rate-floating rate swaps, where each of the rates is based on a different benchmark. For instance, one leg of the swap could be based on LIBOR, while the other could be based on the U.S. T-bill rate. Such swaps are called *basis swaps*.

There do exist swaps where the two cash flows being swapped are denominated in two different currencies. These are known as *currency swaps*. In the case of such swaps, in addition to fixed-floating, and floating-floating arrangements, we could also have fixed-fixed deals. For instance one party may agree to pay 5% per annum in USD, while the counterparty may agree to pay 4.40% per annum in euros. This does not constitute an arbitrage opportunity. Such swaps entail the exchange of the principal amount, denominated in two different currencies, at expiration, and at times at inception as well.

1.5 Illustration of an Interest Rate Swap

Bank Alpha has entered into a swap contract with Bank Phi. The agreement requires Bank Alpha to make payments every quarter, for a period of one year, at a rate of 6% per annum. In return, Bank Phi is required to make payments at the same frequency, at the LIBOR prevailing at the start of the period plus 0.75%. The specified principal is one million dollars. As explained earlier, this amount does not have to be exchanged, and is consequently referred to as a notional amount.

We will assume that every quarter can be taken as 0.25 years, irrespective of the number of calendar days in the period. The payments that are required to be made by the two banks are given in Table 1.2.

Table 1.2: Illustration of an interest rate swap.

Period	LIBOR	Payment Due From Bank Alpha	Payment Due From Bank Phi
0	5.00%		
1	4.25%	$15,000	$14,375
2	5.75%	$15,000	$12,500
3	5.50%	$15,000	$16,250
4	4.75%	$15,000	$15,625

Let's interpret the third column of Table 1.2. Bank Alpha has to make payments at a constant rate of 6% per annum. Consequently its periodic payment is $15,000 per quarter. This can be derived as follows.

$$0.06 \times 0.25 \times 1{,}000{,}000 = \$15{,}000$$

The rate at which Bank Phi is required to pay is variable. Consequently its payment will usually not be the same every quarter. The start of the first quarter is what we have shown as time '0'. The LIBOR at that point in time is 5.00%. Thus Bank Phi has to make a payment at a rate of 5.75%, at the end of the first quarter. The amount due to be paid by it is therefore:

$$0.0575 \times 0.25 \times 1{,}000{,}000 = \$14{,}375$$

The remaining entries of the table can be obtained by using a similar argument.

1.6 Forward Contracts versus Futures Contracts

By now readers would have noted one obvious similarity between forward contracts and futures contracts. That is, both types of contracts require the long to acquire the underlying asset on a future date, and the short to deliver the underlying asset at the same point in time. Thus, in both cases, there is an obligation on the part of the long as well as the short. However, there is one vital difference between the two types of contracts. Futures contracts are *standardized* contracts that are traded on organized exchanges, whereas forward contracts are *customized* contracts that are traded over-the-counter (OTC).

The next issue that needs to be addressed is the clarification of the terms 'standardization' and 'customization'?

In contracts of this nature, which are based on an underlying asset, certain terms and conditions need to be clearly defined at the very beginning to avoid ambiguities and potential conflicts. The major terms which should be made explicit are the following:

1. How many units of the underlying asset is the contract based on. That is, what is the quantity that the long is required to acquire, or in other words, what is the quantity that the short has to deliver?
2. In the event of assets characterized by multiple grades, what is the acceptable grade, or in certain cases, what are the acceptable grades of the underlying asset that is/are allowable for delivery?
3. What is the specified location at which the short is required to make delivery? Is delivery allowed only at a particular location, or do one or both parties have a choice of locations?
4. What is the delivery date? Is delivery permitted only on a particular day, or is there a specified period during which it can occur?

In the case of customized contracts, the applicable terms and conditions have to be decided based on bilateral negotiations between the buyer and the seller of the contract. Thus, in such cases, the two parties are free to incorporate any features, which they can mutually agree upon. However, in the case of standardized contracts, there is a third party which will specify the allowable terms and conditions. In such cases, the long and the short have limited freedom in the sense that they can design contracts within the boundaries specified by such a third party. However, they cannot incorporate features other than those that are specifically allowed. The third party which we are referring to in the case of futures contracts is the futures exchange. A futures exchange is a securities exchange akin to a stock exchange, and is an arena where trading in futures contracts takes place.

We will illustrate the difference between customization and standardization with the help of Example 1.2.

Example 1.2: Assume that wheat futures contract are listed for trading on a US futures exchange. The terms specified by the exchange are such that each contract requires the delivery of 5,000 bushels of wheat.[3] As per the specifications, the allowable grades are No. 1 and No. 2, and the allowable locations for delivery are Kansas City, Hutchinson, Salina/Abilene, and Wichita. The exchange has stipulated that delivery can be made at any time during the expiration month.

Let's first take the case of Paul Pollock, a wholesale dealer in wheat, who wants to acquire 50,000 bushels of No. 2 wheat in Kansas City during the last week of the month. Assume that there is another party, Vince King, a farmer, who is interested in delivering 50,000 bushels of No. 2 wheat in Kansas City during the same period. In this case, the objectives of the two parties are such that the futures contracts that are listed on the exchange are suitable for both. Consequently, if they were to meet on the floor of the exchange at the same time, a trade could be negotiated between them for ten futures contracts, at a price of say \$8.95 per bushel. It must be remembered that the price that is agreed upon for the underlying asset is one feature that is not

---

3 A bushel is a unit of measure. It is used primarily as a unit of mass. A standard weight is assigned for each commodity that is measured in bushels. A bushel of wheat is 60 lb or 27.215 kilos.

specified by the exchange. This has to be negotiated between the two parties through bilateral negotiations, and is a function of demand and supply conditions.

Having demonstrated the suitability of futures contracts in the above case, let's now consider a slightly different scenario. Assume that Paul wishes to acquire 47,750 bushels of No. 2 quality wheat in Topeka during the last week of the month, and that Vince is looking to sell the same quantity of wheat in Topeka during that period. The terms of the contract that are being sought by the two parties are such that the futures contracts being traded on the exchange are not suitable for them. In this case, the quantity sought to be traded is not an integer multiple of 5,000, and obviously fractional contracts cannot be traded. Second, Topeka is not one of the specified locations for delivery. However, in principle, the two men can iron out an agreement between them which incorporates the features that they desire. Such an agreement, characterized by features arrived at by a process of consensus would be a customized agreement, that is obviously tailor made to their needs. Such an agreement is what we have been calling a forward contract.

Thus futures contracts are products that are traded on an organized exchange just like equity shares and bonds, whereas forward contracts are private contracts.

While discussing the terms that are required to be spelt out in a futures contract we have mentioned that certain contracts may permit delivery of more than one specified grade, and/or at multiple locations. In such cases the key issue is who gets to decide as to where, and what to deliver. Traditionally, the right to choose the location and the grade, has always been given to the short.

Also, the right to initiate the process of delivery, has traditionally been given to the short. That is, the delivery process will commence with the expression of the intention to deliver by a party with a short position. Thus, in practice, an investor with a long position, cannot demand delivery. What this also means is that, those investors with a long position who do not wish to take delivery, will exit the market prior to the commencement of the delivery period, by taking an opposite or offsetting position. For, once the delivery period specified by the exchange commences, they can always be called upon to take delivery without having the right to refuse.

What is offsetting? The term essentially means taking a counter-position. Thus, if a party has originally gone long, it should subsequently go short in order to offset and vice versa. The effect of offsetting is to cancel an existing long or short position in a contract.

The second difference between forwards and futures is that although both types of contracts set forth terms for delivery, futures contracts are usually not settled by delivery. Generally, only a very small percentage of outstanding contracts are delivery settled. Others are simply offset by taking counter-positions on the exchange. Forward contracts, however, are usually settled by delivery.

Third, futures contracts are *marked to market* on a daily basis, whereas forward contracts are not. What this means is that, in the case of a futures contract, the profit or loss is calculated on a daily basis, and is added to/ subtracted from the *margin account* of the trader. The margin account is one in which a trader keeps *good faith money or collateral.* Hence, futures contracts are subject to interim cash flows. In a forward contract, however, there is only one cash flow, that is, on the delivery date of the contract.

Fourth, the parties to a forward contract are exposed to *credit risk* because either party may default. In the case of futures contracts, credit risk is minimized because of the existence of an entity called a *clearinghouse* which is associated with the exchange on which the contract is traded. The clearinghouse guarantees the other side of the transaction.[4]

Finally, it is easier to offset a position in a futures contract than in a forward contract. A forward contract by definition is a customized private contract between two parties. Hence, if a party to a forward contract were to desire to exit from the original agreement, he would have to either seek out the counter-party and have the agreement canceled, or else locate a third party who would like to take over the position. This may not be easy in practice.

Canceling a futures contract is a lot easier in practice. This is because, a futures contract between two parties, say Paul and Vince, to transact in wheat at the end of a particular month, will be identical to a similar contract between two other parties, say Kathy and Pauline. This is because both the contracts would have been designed in accordance with the framework specified by the exchange. Besides, once Paul and Vince enter into a contract with each other, they have both effectively entered into a contract with the clearinghouse, and the link between them is broken. So if Paul, who has entered into a long position, wants to get out of his position, he does not need to seek out Vince. All he has to do, in practice, is to go back to the floor of the futures exchange and express his desire to take a short position in a similar contract. This time the opposite position may be taken by a new party, say Doug. Thus, by taking a long position initially with Vince, and a short position subsequently with Doug, Paul can ensure that he has a nil net position, and therefore is effectively out of the market. This would obviously mean that he has no further obligations. As far as the records of the clearinghouse are concerned, Paul would have been recorded as having bought and sold an identical futures contract, and his net position would be reflected as zero. This is the meaning of offsetting.

In practice the futures price that was prevailing when a trader enters into a position, will obviously be different from the price prevailing at the time of offsetting. Thus, offsetting will entail a profit or a loss which will be equal to the difference between the futures price that was prevailing at the time the original position was taken, and the price at the time the position is offset.

Except for these differences, we will find that the analysis of futures and forward contracts is fairly similar. Hence, we will first study the valuation of forward contracts in detail,[5] and will then apply the results to futures markets. In fact, we will state later that when the risk-less rate of interest is constant, and is the same for all maturities,

---

4 Closely related to this is the concept of margins.

5 They are easier to analyze, because there are no interim cash flows, due to the absence of the marking to market mechanism.

then, the forward price will be the same as the futures price, for contracts on a given asset, with a specified delivery date.

1.7 Standardization and the Role of the Exchange

Futures contracts are standardized instruments. When developing a new contract, the exchange must specify the following features:

1.7.1 The Underlying Asset

The asset must be clearly mentioned. That is, the contract should clearly state as to whether it is corn, or wheat, or oranges that it is based on. If there are different grades or varieties of the commodity, the contract must specify the acceptable grade or grades. In the case of contracts where the underlying asset has multiple varieties, a standard grade will be established, which will usually be the most important grade of the good traded in the spot market. This is called the *Par* grade and is deliverable at the prevailing futures price at the expiration of the contract.[6] Other grades of the commodity may be deliverable at specified premiums to or discounts from the price for the par grade. This price adjustment may be either additive or multiplicative, as we shall see later.

1.7.2 The Contract Size

The size of the contract specifies the amount of the underlying asset that has to be delivered as per the contract. Here, the exchange has to balance two factors. If the size is too large, traders who wish to transact small quantities, will be unable to do so. While, if the size is too small, more number of contracts will be required for a given trade, and trading will become more expensive due to greater transactions costs.

1.7.3 Delivery Arrangements

The contract must state the location where delivery is to be made. Sometimes, alternative locations may also be specified. The price paid by the long will be adjusted according to the location where delivery is made.

Delivery of the good is at the option of the short, with respect to the date of delivery,[7] the grade of the good delivered, and the location of delivery. That is, *the short has*

6 You will understand this as we study the delivery process in greater detail.

7 At any time during the delivery period specified by the exchange.

the option of deciding when, where, and what grade of the asset he would like to deliver. Delivery usually begins before trading ceases and continues after it has ceased.

1.7.4 The Delivery Month

A futures contract is referred to by the delivery month. For instance, a June contract, refers to a contract expiring in June.

At a given point in time, you will find that contracts are being traded for the closest delivery month and a number of subsequent delivery months. For example, most currency futures on the Chicago Mercantile Exchange have delivery months of March, June, September, and December. The exchange has to determine, as to how far into the future contracts must extend. It also has to decide as to when trading should begin in a particular contract, and has to stipulate the last day of trading as well.

The selection of the allowable expiration months varies from asset to asset. Kroll and Paulenoff (1993) give an example regarding wheat futures, which is reproduced in Example 1.3.

Example 1.3: "Futures trading in Chicago wheat is actively conducted in March, May, July, September and December. July is the first month of the new crop of Winter wheat and the July contract allows people to hedge the purchase of wheat in the spot market. The new crop of Spring wheat comes in September and can be hedged in that delivery month. The December contract facilitates hedging against grain stored during the months in which navigation is affected by frozen waterways in the Mid West of the U.S. The March contract represents the mid point between heavy winter storage and heavy spring consumption, while the May contract can reflect either old or new crop fundamentals, depending on which is more dominant during a particular year."

The fact that futures contracts are standardized, helps reduce transactions costs in such markets. The cost of negotiating a customized contract, such as a forward contract, is typically much higher. Second, as we have seen, only certain kinds of futures contracts (with the features specified by the exchange), are eligible for trading. Thus, futures markets tend to be highly liquid.

1.8 The Clearinghouse

A clearinghouse is an institution that is associated with a futures exchange.[8] The clearinghouse provides a guarantee to both parties to a contract, that they need not be concerned with the possibility of the other party defaulting. The way it achieves this in practice, is by positioning itself as the effective counter-party for each of the two original parties to the trade. In other words, once a trade is consummated, the clearinghouse

---

8 It may be a wing of the exchange or else it may be a separate corporation.

effectively becomes the buyer for the party who seeks to sell and the seller for the party that seeks to buy. Hence, the two parties need to worry only about the financial strength and integrity of the clearinghouse, and not of their respective counterparties. It must be noted that neither party actually trades with the clearinghouse. The clearinghouse enters the picture only after a trade is effected between the two parties.

For instance, assume there is a futures trade between Paul who goes long, and Vince who goes short. The moment this trade is consummated, it will be replaced by a set of equivalent trades. In the first, Paul will be designated as the long, and the clearinghouse as the short, and in the second, the clearinghouse will be designated as the long and Vince as the short. This procedure, for replacing a trade with two equivalent trades with a common counterparty, is termed as *novation*.

Why is it that the intervention of a clearinghouse is required in practice? A futures contract imposes an obligation on both parties to the trade. By the time the contract expires, depending on the movement of prices in the interim, it will be in the interest of one of the two parties to go through with the transaction. However, a price move in favor of one party would obviously be tantamount to a loss for the other. Thus, given an opportunity, one of the parties would like to default on the expiration date, although at the outset we would not know who it would be. We will illustrate this with the help of Example 1.4.

Example 1.4: Let's take the case of two traders, Paul and Keith. Assume that Paul has gone long in a futures contract to buy an asset five days hence at a price of $75, and that Keith has taken the opposite side of the transaction. We will first take the case where the spot price of the asset five days later is $80.

Consider a situation where Keith already owns the asset. As per the contract, he is obliged to deliver it for $75, thereby foregoing an opportunity to sell it in the spot market at $80. If he were not have the asset, he is required to acquire it by paying $80, and then subsequently deliver it to Paul for $75. Quite obviously, Keith will choose to default unless he has impeccable moral values.

Now let's consider a second situation where the price of the asset five days hence is $70. In this case, if Keith already has the asset, he would be perfectly willing to deliver it for $75, for the alternative scenario for him is a sale in the spot market at a price of $70. In such a situation, even if he were not to have the asset, he would be delighted to acquire it for $70 in the spot market, and deliver it to Paul in return for a payment of $75.

The problem in the second case is that Paul will refuse to pay $75 for the asset, if he can get away with it. If he were not to require the asset, taking delivery at $75 would mean a subsequent sale in the spot market at $70, and consequently a loss of $5. On the other hand, even if he were to require the asset, he would rather buy it in the spot market for $70.

The function of a clearinghouse is to ensure that such defaults are prevented. In practice, a clearinghouse ensures protection for both counterparties, by requiring them to post a performance bond or collateral called a margin. Both the long as well as the short have to deposit margins with their respective brokers, once the trade is consummated. Their brokers in turn, are required to deposit margins with the clearinghouse. The margin deposited by a broker with the clearinghouse is known as *clearing margin*. Every day, the collateral is adjusted to take into account any profit or loss for either party, as compared to the previous day, based on the price movement during the day. In the process, the clearinghouse effectively takes away the incentive for a party to default as you shall shortly see.

1.9 Margins and Marking to Market

As we have just seen, any contract requiring performance as per an agreement entered into at a prior point of time, is fraught with the possibility of default. Futures exchanges, ensure compliance by requiring both the parties to the trade to deposit collateral with their respective broker, in an account known as the *margin account*. This margin deposit is therefore a good-faith deposit or a performance guarantee.

The amount of collateral that is required to be deposited is obviously related to the potential loss that each party is likely to incur. Since both parties to a futures contract have an obligation, it is therefore necessary to collect collateral from both of them. The rationale behind requiring them to deposit such a performance guarantee is that, once such potential losses are collected, the incentive to default is effectively taken away. This is because, even if the party that ends up on the losing side were to fail to perform its obligation, the collateral collected from it would be adequate to take care of the interests of the other party.

It is important to appreciate that the loss for one of the parties or, the equivalent gain for the other, will not arise all of a sudden at the time of expiration of the contract. As the futures price fluctuates in the market from trade to trade, one of the two parties to an existing futures contract will experience a gain, while the other will experience an equivalent loss. Hence, the total loss or gain from the time of getting into a futures position till the time the position is terminated is the sum of these small losses/profits corresponding to each observed price in the interim. The point of termination of an existing contract is the time of expiration of the contract or else the time that it is offset by taking a counter-position, if that were to happen earlier,

The term 'marking to market' refers to the process of calculating the loss for one party, or equivalently the corresponding gain for the other, at specified points in time, with reference to the futures price that was prevailing at the time the contract was previously marked to market. When a futures contract is entered into, the broker will mark it to market for the first time at the end of the day. Thereafter, it will mark it to market every day until the position is either offset or else the contract itself expires. The party who has incurred a profit will have the amount credited to its margin account, while the other party, who would obviously have incurred an identical loss, will have its margin account debited. *Thus, a futures contract is effectively settled and rewritten on a daily basis. Hence a futures contract is like a series of one day forward contracts.*

Before we illustrate the marking to market mechanism, let's first define the concept of a *settlement price.*

1.9.1 Settlement Price

We have just seen that futures contracts are marked to market on a daily basis. The profit or loss is equal to difference between that day's price and the price that was used when the contract was previously marked to market. The settlement price is the price that is used to compute the daily gains and losses while marking a contract to market.

A common practice is to set the settlement price equal to the observed closing price for the day. However, due to the occurrence of heavy trading towards the close of the day, some exchanges choose to set the settlement price equal to the average of the observed futures prices, in the last half hour or hour of trading.[9] At the other extreme, if there were to be no trades at the end of the day, the exchange may set the settlement price equal to the average of the observed 'bid' and 'ask' quotes.

What do the terms 'bid' and 'ask' connote? A market maker, which is essentially a dealer who stands ready to buy and sell on its own account, will offer a two-way quote at any point in time. One side of the quote will be the price at which it is prepared to buy from a potential customer, the bid, while the other price represents the rate at which it is willing sell to a potential client, which is known as the ask. The bid will always be less than the ask,[10] for obviously the market maker will seek to buy low and sell high in order to make a profit.

In futures markets, the 'bid' represents the futures price at which a customer can take a short position, while the 'ask' is obviously the price at which he can take a long position.

We will now give a detailed illustration as to how profits and losses arise in the process of marking to market, and will highlight the way in which the corresponding changes are reflected in the margin accounts of the respective parties.

Let's take the case of Paul who has gone long in a futures contract expiring five days hence with Keith, at a futures price of $75. We will assume that the price at the expiration of the contract is $82.50, and that the prices at the end of each day prior to expiration are as shown in Table 1.3.

We will assume that as per the contract, Paul is committed to buying 100 units of the asset, and that at the time of the trade, both the parties had to deposit $1,000 as collateral in their margin accounts. The collateral that an investor is required to deposit at the time of entering into a futures contract, is referred to as the *initial margin.*

---

9 The average may be volume weighted.

10 We will discuss an exception when we study the principle of 'indirect quotes' in foreign exchange markets.

Table 1.3: End of the day futures prices.

Day	Futures Price
0	75.00
1	78.50
2	73.50
3	71.00
4	79.50
5	82.50

Day '0' denotes the time the contract was entered into, and the corresponding price is the futures price at which the deal was struck. Day 't' represents the end of that particular day, and the corresponding price is the prevailing futures price at that instant.

At the end of the first day the futures price is \$78.50. This means that if a trader were to enter into a contract at the end of the that day, the applicable price per unit of the underlying asset would be \$78.50. If Paul were to offset the position that he had entered into earlier that day, he would obviously have to do so by agreeing to sell 100 units at \$78.50 per unit. If so, he would earn a profit of \$3.50 per unit, or \$350 in all. In the process of marking Paul's position to market, the broker will behave as though he were offsetting. Thus, it would calculate his profit as \$350, and would credit this amount to his margin account. However, remember that Paul has not actually expressed a desire to offset. Consequently, taking cognizance of this fact, the broker would act as if Paul were re-entering into a long position at the prevailing futures price of \$78.50.

At the end of the second day, the prevailing futures price is \$73.50. Thus, when the contract is marked to market on this day, Paul will make a loss of \$500. It must be remembered, that his contract was re-written the previous day at a price of \$78.50, and if the broker were to now behave as if he were offsetting at \$73.50, the loss would amount to \$5 per unit, or \$500 in all. Having marked the contract to market, the broker would once again establish a new long position for Paul, this time at a price of \$73.50.

This process will continue every day either until the delivery date, when Paul will actually take possession of the asset, or until the day that he chooses to actually offset his position, if that were to happen earlier. As should be obvious from this illustration, rising futures prices lead to profits for traders with a long position, whereas falling futures prices lead to losses.

Now let's consider the situation from Keith's perspective. At the end of the first day, when the futures price is \$78.50, marking to market would mean a loss of \$350 for him. This can be understood as follows. His earlier contract to sell at \$75 will be effectively offset by making him buy at \$78.50. The corresponding loss for 100 units is \$350. Once this is done, a new short position would be established for him at $78.50. Applying the same logic, at the end of the second day, his margin account will be credited with a profit of $500. As should be obvious from Keith's perspective, rising futures prices lead to losses for traders with short positions, whereas declining futures prices lead to profits.

Thus, the profit/loss for a trader with a long position is identical to the loss/profit for one with a short position. Hence, futures contracts are called *Zero Sum Games*. One person's gain is another person's loss.

As you can see, by the time the contract expires, in this instance after five days, the loss incurred by one of the two parties, in this case the short, has been totally recovered. In our example, Paul's account would have been credited with $750. This amount represents the difference between the terminal futures price and the initial futures price, multiplied by the number of units of the underlying asset. This money would have come from Keith's account which would have been debited with $750. Thus, at expiration, if Keith were to refuse to deliver the asset, Paul would not be affected at all. Since he has already realized a profit of $750, he can take delivery in the spot market at the terminal spot price of $82.50 per unit, in lieu of taking delivery under the futures contract.[11] Thus, effectively, Paul will get possession of the asset at a price of $75 per unit, which is what had been specified as per the terms of the original futures contract.

The role of the clearinghouse in these series of transactions is essentially that of a banker. It will debit the margin account of the broker whose client has suffered a loss, and simultaneously credit the margin account of the broker whose client has made a profit. Hence, the margin accounts maintained by brokers with the clearinghouse are adjusted daily for profits and losses, in exactly the same way that a client's margin account with the broker is adjusted.

Forward contracts are different from futures contracts in this respect. That is, they are not periodically marked to market. As a consequence, both the parties to such contracts are exposed to credit risk, which is the risk that the counterparty may default. Thus, the parties to a forward contract tend to be large and well known, such as banks, financial institutions, corporate houses, and brokerage firms. The reason is that the credit worthiness of such parties is easier to appraise as compared to that of individual investors.

At the time of entering into a futures contract, both parties have to deposit a performance bond with their brokers, which we have termed as the initial margin. If the markets were to subsequently move in favor of a party to the contract, the balance in its margin account will increase, else if the market were to move against it, the balance will stand depleted. It is very important for the broker to ensure that a client always has adequate funds in his margin account. Otherwise the entire purpose of requiring clients to maintain margins can be defeated. As a consequence, the broker will specify a

---

11 You will see shortly that at the time of expiration of the contract, the futures price must be equal to the prevailing spot price.

Table 1.4: Changes in the margin account over the course of time.

Day	Futures Price	Daily Gain/Loss	Cumulative Gain/Loss	Account Balance	Margin Call
0	75.00			1,000	
1	78.50	350	350	1,350	
2	73.50	(500)	(150)	850	
3	71.00	(250)	(400)	600	400
4	79.50	850	450	1,850	
5	82.50	300	750	2,150	

Numbers in parentheses denote losses.

threshold balance for the margin account called the *maintenance margin*, which will be less than the initial margin. If due to one or more adverse price movements, the balance in the margin account were to decline below the level of the maintenance margin, the broker will immediately ask the client to deposit additional funds, to take the balance in its account back to the level of the initial margin. Such requests for more collateral are termed as *margin calls*. The additional funds deposited by a client to top up its account, in compliance with a margin call, are referred to as *variation margin*.

We will now give a detailed example to illustrate the concepts that we have just discussed. Let's once again consider the case of Paul, who went long in a contract for 100 units of the asset at a price of $75 per unit, and deposited $1,000 as collateral for the same. Let's assume that the broker fixes a maintenance margin of $750 for the contract. Assuming that the contract lasts for a period of five days, and that the futures prices on the subsequent days are as shown in Table 1.3, the effect on the margin account will be as summarized in Table 1.4.

We will analyze in detail a few of the entries in Table 1.4 to illustrate the concepts that we have expounded. Consider the second row. As compared to the time the contract was entered into, the price has increased by $3.50 per unit or $350 for 100 units. Thus, Paul, who has entered into a long position, has gained $350, which is required to be credited to his margin account. After this amount is credited, the margin account which had an opening balance of $1,000, has an end-of-the day balance of $1,350.

The settlement price at the end of the second day is $73.50. Thus, as compared to the position at the end of the previous day, Paul has suffered a loss of $5 per unit or $500 for 100 units. When this loss is debited to his margin account, the balance in the account falls to $850. The settlement price at the end of the next day is $71, which implies that Paul has suffered a further loss of $250. When this loss is factored into the margin account, by debiting it with $250, the balance in the account falls to $600, which is less than the maintenance margin requirement of $750. Therefore, at this point in time, a margin call will be issued for $400, which is the amount required to take the balance back to the initial margin level of $1,000. In response to the call, Paul will be expected to pay a variation margin of $400.

It is not necessary for every trader to meet the initial margin requirement by depositing cash. It is an acceptable practice in many markets to offer securities such as Treasury-bills and equity shares as collateral. However, the value assigned to these assets will be less than their market values at the time of submission. This is because the broker would like to protect himself against a sudden sharp decline in the value of the collateral. For instance, if the required initial margin is $90, the broker may ask the client to deposit securities with a market value of $100. Technically speaking, we would say that the broker has applied a *haircut* of 10%.

However, in practice, variation margins, must always be paid in cash. The reason for this is the following. Initial margins represent performance guarantees, and can consequently be offered in the form of cash or marketable securities. A variation margin, which is offered in response to a margin call, is however a manifestation of actual losses suffered by the client, and consequently must be paid in cash.

1.9.2 Marking to Market: A Detailed Exposition

We will now illustrate the cash flows generated due to the marking to market of futures contracts, for a trader who trades more than once on a given day. The profits/losses due to marking to market are computed by taking the difference between:

1. The trade price and the settlement price for contracts executed during the day which have not been offset
2. The previous day's settlement price and the current settlement price for contracts which have been brought forward and which have not been offset
3. The previous day's settlement price and the trade price for contracts which have been brought forward and offset during the day
4. The buy price and the sell price for contracts which have been executed during the day and which have been offset

Here are two detailed illustrations, depicted in Examples 1.5 and 1.6.

Example 1.5: Steven Saunders had a long position in 250 futures contracts as of the end of yesterday. Yesterday's settlement price was $122. Each contract is for 50 units of the underlying asset. Today Steven went long in an additional 125 contracts at a trade price of $125. 75 of these contracts were subsequently offset at a price of $127.50. Today's settlement price is $130.

The profit/loss due to marking to market may be computed as follows.

Profit/loss on account of contracts carried over from the previous day and which have not been offset is:

$$250 \times 50 \times (130 - 122) = \$100{,}000$$

Profit/loss on account of contracts entered into during the day, and which have been offset is:

$$75 \times 50 \times (127.50 - 125) = \$9{,}375$$

Profit/loss on account of contracts entered into during the day, and which have not been offset:

$$50 \times 50 \times (130 - 125) = \$12{,}500$$

Total inflow = 100,000 + 9,375 + 12,500 = $121,875

Example 1.6: Shelly Tan had a long position in 200 futures contracts as of yesterday. Yesterday's settlement price was $114. Each contract is for 50 units of the underlying asset. Today she went long in an additional 100 contracts at a trade price of $118. 125 contracts were subsequently offset at a price of $122.50. Today's settlement price is $126.

The profit/loss due to marking to market may be computed as follows.

Profit/loss on account of contracts carried over from the previous day and which have not been offset is:

$$175 \times 50 \times (126 - 114) = \$105{,}000$$

Profit/loss on account of contracts entered into during the day, and which have been offset is:

$$100 \times 50 \times (122.50 - 118) = \$22{,}500$$

Profit/loss on account of contracts carried over from the previous day, and which have been offset:

$$25 \times 50 \times (122.50 - 114) = \$10{,}625$$

Total inflow = 105,000 + 22,000 + 10,625 = $138,125

1.9.3 Value at Risk (VaR)

We have just seen that once the potential loss for the parties to a futures contract is estimated and collected in advance, the likelihood of either of them defaulting reduces considerably. In practice, if the quantum of the margin is sufficiently high, then the possibility of default is fairly remote. Thus, in order to preclude default, the margin requirement specified by the futures exchange should be based on an estimate of the potential loss.

However, no exchange can perfectly forecast as to what the magnitude of loss is likely to be from one day to the next. In practice, it can at best quantify the loss as an amount that is unlikely to be exceeded with a given level of probability. Such a forecasting approach is precisely the rationale behind the concept of Value at Risk or VaR.

The value at risk of a position may be defined as the potential loss of the asset(s) over a specified time horizon.[12] Thus, if we were to state that the 95% VaR of an asset over a one day horizon is $3,000, the implication would be that the loss in terms of the value of the asset over a one day holding period, is expected to exceed $3,000, with a probability of 5% only. The calculated VaR is a function of both the probability level as well as the holding period. Thus, in order to facilitate the interpretation of a calculated VaR number, it is necessary to specify both these parameters. For a given asset(s), changing one or both parameters, can lead to significantly different estimates of VaR.

As Darbha (2001) points out, VaR may be interpreted as *the best of the worst possible scenarios or equivalently as the worst of the best possible scenarios*. Readers should also note that the calculated VaR, does not connote the maximum possible loss that a portfolio can suffer over the holding period. In principle, the value of any asset or portfolio can always go to zero, and consequently, the maximum loss that an investor may suffer is equal to the entire portfolio value. The second feature to be noted is that the VaR does not measure the intensity of potential losses. For instance, consider two portfolios with the same 95% VaR of say $5,000. Although the VaR is identical in the two cases, the magnitude of losses in excess of the VaR on the remaining 5% of the days could be considerably different for the two portfolios.

1.9.4 The Expected Shortfall

As we just discussed, the value at risk number does not capture the magnitude of losses in excess of the VaR. Consequently, the practice is to compute the expected shortfall, which is the expected loss in excess of the estimated VaR, if there is such a loss. For instance assume that the 90% value at risk of a portfolio is $24,000. There is a probability that the loss may be $26,500 with a 3% probability; $30,000 with a 3% probability; and $36,000 with a 4% probability. The expected shortfall is

$$\frac{(26{,}500 \times 0.03 + 30{,}000 \times 0.03 + 36{,}000 \times 0.04)}{(0.03 + 0.03 + 0.04)} = \$31{,}350$$

1.9.5 Estimating the VaR in Practice

There are many different techniques for computing the value at risk of a portfolio. These include:[13]

- Historical Simulation
- Monte Carlo Simulation
- Model Building

12 See Linsmeier and Pearson (2000).

13 See Hull (2005).

We will now present a model for estimating the margin required for a long position in an index futures contract. This is based on the exponential moving average method.

Let's denote the daily volatility of an index futures contract on day 't' by σ_t. According to the exponential moving average method

$$\sigma_t^2 = \lambda\sigma_{t-1}^2 + (1-\lambda)r_t^2 \tag{1.1}$$

r_t is the return for day t, and is defined as:

$$r_t = ln\left(\frac{I_t}{I_{t-1}}\right) \tag{1.2}$$

where I_t is the index futures price at the end of day 't'. J.P. Morgan who came up with RiskMetrics, a model based approach to VaR, have recommended a value of 0.94 for λ.

If we assume that returns are normally distributed, then the probability of occurrence can be expressed in terms of the number of standard deviations from the mean. Consider the case of a short position in an index futures contract. The risk in this case is that the futures price can rise, thereby leading to a loss. From the properties of the normal distribution we know that 2.33 standard deviations encompasses 99% of the occurrences, at the loss-end, in this case the upper end, of the curve.

So if we set the anticipated return for the next day at 2.33 times the standard deviation that is calculated for that day, we get:

$$\begin{aligned} ln\left(\frac{I_{t+1}}{I_t}\right) &= 2.33\sigma_t \\ \Rightarrow I_{t+1} &= I_t e^{2.33\sigma_t} \\ \Rightarrow I_{t+1} &= I_t[1 + e^{2.33\sigma_t} - 1] \end{aligned} \tag{1.3}$$

Thus the percentage margin is $[e^{2.33\sigma_t} - 1] \times 100$. For long positions, the percentage margin will obviously be $[1 - e^{-2.33\sigma_t}] \times 100$. A computation using data is given in Example 1.7.

Example 1.7: Assume that $\sigma_{t-1} = 0.025$ and that $r_t = 0.0225$. Therefore:

$$\begin{aligned} \sigma_t &= \sqrt{[0.94 \times (0.025)^2 + (1-0.94) \times (0.0225)^2]} \\ &= 0.024857 \end{aligned}$$

Thus the percentage margin for a short position is:

$$\begin{aligned} \left[e^{2.33\sigma_t} - 1\right] \times 100 &= \left[e^{2.33\times0.024857} - 1\right] \times 100 \\ &= 5.9627\% \end{aligned}$$

Assume that the current futures price is 1,000 and that the multiplier is 250. If so, the margin for a short position in one contract will be:

$$1{,}000 \times 250 \times 0.059627 = \$14{,}906.75$$

1.9.6 Futures Commission Merchants

Futures commission merchants (FCMs) are brokers who are authorized to open trading accounts on behalf of parties who wish to take positions in futures contracts. An FCM will collect margin money from the client, and record and report all the trades routed through him. It is important to emphasize that all brokers in the futures markets cannot be categorized as FCMs. Some clients prefer to deal with *introducing brokers*. Such intermediaries, perform the function of getting a client acquainted with an FCM. However, while they are authorized to accept orders and route them through an FCM, they are not allowed to maintain margin accounts.

All FCMs need not in practice be members of the clearinghouse. Those that are, are referred to as *clearing members*. Only those FCMs who are clearing members are authorized to maintain clearing margins with the clearinghouse and clear transactions through it. Thus, if a client were to initiate a trade through a broker who is not a clearing member, the broker in turn must route the order through a clearing member. Eventually, all orders must pass through a clearing member.

1.9.7 Gross versus Net Margining

Let's assume that there are two FCMs, Alpha and Beta, and that both are authorized to clear through the clearinghouse.[14] Alpha has two clients A and B. A has a long position in 100 futures contracts while B has a short position in 80 futures contracts. Beta also has two clients C and D. C has a long position in 80 contracts while D has a short position in 100 contracts.

The FCMs have to collect margins from their clients and the clearinghouse has to collect margins from the FCMs. We will make the following assumptions.

- The clearinghouse collects margins from the clearing members on a *net* basis.
- The clearing members collect margins from their clients on a *gross* basis.[15]
- The initial margin required by the clearinghouse is $4 per contract.
- The initial margin required by the clearing members from their clients is also $4 per contract.

14 This section is based on an illustration in Edwards and Ma (1992).

15 The meanings of the terms Net and Gross will become clear to you shortly.

- Contracts are marked to market daily and variation margins are paid or withdrawn the next morning, by both clearing members (to or from the clearinghouse) as well as by the clients (to or from the clearing members).
- There is a daily price limit of $4 in either direction.

Now, what is this concept of a price limit?

Price Limits

Exchanges often impose limits on the maximum daily price change. These limits are measured from the previous day's settlement price and apply in both directions. We will clarify this with the help of an example. Let's assume that the settlement price for Soybeans is $13.60 a bushel today and that there is a limit of 60 cents on the maximum daily price change. So tomorrow's price limits will be $13.00 and $14.20. If the price moves down to the lower limit, then the contract is said to be *limit down*, whereas if it moves up to the upper limit, then it is said to be *limit up*. A move to either the upper or the lower bound, is called a *limit move*. When the price reaches one of the limits during the day, trading will slow down and may even come to a halt. Let's suppose that prices have hit limit up. It means that the buyers outnumber the sellers. If there are no sellers at the limit, then trading will cease. Sometimes, fresh news could filter in, causing prices to move up from the lower limit or down from the upper limit. If so, trading may resume. The exchange is authorized to intervene and change the limit if it deems it necessary.

It should now be obvious as to why we have assumed a $4 price limit in the above example. This is because the initial margin is $4, and we have not assumed a maintenance margin. Hence, a limit move should be such that the balance in the margin account cannot go below zero for either the long or the short.[16]

FCM Alpha will collect $400 from A and $320 from B. That is, in all it will collect $720. Similarly FCM Beta would also collect a total of $720 from its two clients. This is the meaning of *gross margin*. If the clearinghouse were also to collect margins on a gross basis, then both the FCMs would have to deposit the entire amount collected by them with the clearinghouse. In such a situation, it is obviously very likely that the FCMs will collect more than $4 per contract from their clients.

In this case the clearinghouse is collecting on a net basis. It will therefore collect $80 from Alpha and an equal amount from Beta. This is because Alpha has a net long position of 20 contracts with the clearinghouse, while Beta has a net short position of 20 contracts with it. Thus, of the total margin amount of $1,440 that is deposited by the four traders, $160 is with the clearinghouse while $640 is with each of the FCMs.

Now, suppose that the futures price rises by $4. The longs will have a profit of $4 per contract, while the shorts will have a loss of $4. FCM Alpha will require an amount

16 Remember the margin account cannot show a negative balance.

of $400 to pay client A, while FCM Beta will have to pay $320 to client C. In case the customers want to hold on to their positions,[17] then client B will have to pay $320 to FCM Alpha and client D would have to pay $400 to FCM Beta. FCM Beta will use $320 to pay client C. The balance $80 will be paid by Beta to the clearinghouse, which will pass it on to Alpha. Now, Alpha would have received $320 from client B. So in total it will collect $400, which will be just adequate for it to pay client A.

Thus, the clearing members perform a banking function, by transferring funds from one customer to another. The clearinghouse also performs a banking function by facilitating the transfer of funds from one FCM to another.

As long as the magnitude of the price change does not exceed the initial margin, the deposits held by the clearinghouse and the clearing members will be enough to protect both the buyers and the sellers. In the above case, let's first suppose that the price goes up by $4 and that the shorts are unable to pay variation margin. FCM Alpha has $640 with it. It is required to pay $800 to client A, which is the sum of the initial margin deposit made by the client and the profit from marking to market. Hence it requires an additional amount of $160, which in this case will be passed on to it by the clearinghouse. As far as FCM Beta is concerned, it too has $640. This will be adequate for it to pay client C, who has deposited $320 as the initial margin and has gained $320 from the change in the futures price.

Now let's consider the case where the price goes down by $4, and the longs are unable to pay the required variation margin. FCM Alpha needs to pay $640 to client B. This represents the sum of $320 that was initially deposited by this client, plus its profit of $320 from the market. Obviously FCM Alpha has enough money to ensure this. FCM Beta has to pay $800 to client D, which is the sum of its initial deposit and its profit. In this case FCM Beta which has $640 with it, requires an additional amount of $160, which will be passed on to it by the clearinghouse. Thus, the profits of either the longs or the shorts, are protected up to the amount of margin posted.

However take a case where the price has increased by $4 per contract, and FCM Alpha has gone bankrupt. Client A is required to be paid $800. However, in this case he is only assured of the $160 that is available with the clearinghouse. That is, since we have assumed net margining, the clearinghouse will only be in a position to pay $160 to either FCM Alpha or Beta as the case may be. The FCMs themselves are responsible for ensuring that they have adequate funds to pay the client who has made a profit. However, if the clearinghouse itself were to operate on a gross margin basis, then it could guarantee all the contracts, for it would have collected a total of $1,440 from the two FCMs.

Edwards and Ma (1992), point out that if the clearinghouse were to collect margins on a gross basis, customers would no longer be concerned with the financial health of their clearing members. This may not only reduce the credit worthiness of clearing

17 Remember the margin accounts of the shorts have gone to a zero balance level, and they must raise the balance to the initial margin level.

members, but can also lead to an increase in the cost of operations, because the clearinghouse will now have to guarantee the financial health of all its clearing members.

1.9.8 Default

Default in the case of futures contracts can manifest itself in two ways. First, the trader may not respond to a margin call issued by the FCM. Second, he may refuse to take delivery at maturity if he is a long with an open position, or else may refuse to give delivery if he is a short with an open position. Let's first consider the case where a client defaults before maturity, and illustrate it using the data in Table 1.4.

At the end of day 3, when the balance in the margin account falls to $600, a margin call will be issued for $400. If the client were to fail to respond positively by paying the required variation margin, the broker is at liberty to actually offset his position. In our example, Paul has taken a long position. Thus, an offsetting transaction initiated by the broker will entail the assumption of a short position at the prevailing market price. In our case, the price at the time the margin call was issued was $71.00. Let's assume, that by the time the broker is able to offset the contract, the price has declined further to $70.25. Paul, in this case would have incurred a further loss of $75 per contract. The broker will deduct this amount, along with any transactions charges incurred by him, from the balance of $600 that is available in Paul's margin account. The balance will be refunded to the client. Exactly the same procedure will be followed by a clearinghouse, if an FCM were to fail to respond to a margin call issued by it.

The second point in time at which default may occur is at the time of expiration of the futures contract. Let's first consider the case where the short fails to deliver the asset, which would tantamount to default on its part. In such a situation, the broker will acquire the good in the spot market and deliver it to the long. On the other hand if the default were to be on the part of the long, the broker will acquire the good from the short and sell it in the cash market. In either case, it will deduct its costs and losses from the balance in the defaulting party's margin account.

1.10 Arbitrage

Arbitrage entails the locking in of a cost-less risk-less profit by simultaneously entering into transactions in two or more markets. The key phrase here is '*cost-less and risk-less*'. The logic is as follows. If you get into a risky strategy entailing a cost, you should get a risk adjusted expected rate of return. This is the approach taken by models like the CAPM. If your strategy is risk-less but requires an initial investment, then you should get the risk-less rate of return. However, if you do not have to invest anything, and face no risk, then logically you should get no returns.[18] The presence of a positive return in such a circumstance, is referred to as an arbitrage opportunity, and the people who seek to exploit such opportunities are referred to as arbitrageurs. As the book progresses, we will see time and again, that it is the activities of arbitrageurs that keep prices in alignment and help to maintain equilibrium in the market.

The principle of arbitrage can best be explained with the help of a numerical example. Let's take the case of a share, in a hypothetical country, that trades on both the National Stock Exchange and the Union Stock Exchange. Assume that the price is $75 on the first and $80 on the second. Consider the case of an investor who is in a position to borrow $7,500,000. He is obviously in a position to acquire 100,000 shares on the National Stock Exchange. Having bought the shares, he can immediately sell them for $8,000,000 on the Union Stock Exchange. After repaying his loan, he will be left with a profit of $500,000 which was made without his having to invest any money of his own, and without taking any perceptible risks. Such a situation is essentially a manifestation of an arbitrage opportunity.

These opportunities cannot prevail for extended periods of time. Our investor is unlikely to be the only one who has detected such an opportunity. As others begin to perceive the significance of this opportunity and rush to buy shares on the National Stock Exchange, the price there will rise. At the same time, the arbitrageurs will begin to unload their shares on the Union Stock Exchange, which will cause the price there to fall. Taken together, these two factors will usually quickly eliminate any such opportunities for cost-less risk-less profits.

In our illustration we have assumed the absence of transactions costs like bid-ask spreads and brokerage fees. For retail investors, such costs will be significant in practice, and may therefore preclude them from exploiting perceived arbitrage opportunities. However, institutional investors will face much lower costs, and will consequently exploit such opportunities to the hilt. It must also be pointed out that if the two exchanges across which the arbitrage strategy is being implemented, have an identical settlement cycle, an arbitrageur will require a stockpile of shares as well as adequate cash to execute such a strategy. This is because, in such a situation, he will be unable to take delivery at an exchange early enough so as to meet the deadline for delivery at the other.

1.10.1 Arbitrage with a Forward Contract

IBM is currently trading at $140 per share on the NYSE. A bank is offered a forward contract on the stock. The contract entails the delivery of 100,000 shares of the stock at a

18 Another manifestation of arbitrage would be the existence of returns in excess of the risk-less rate for an investment that does not entail any risk.

price of $147 per share, after a period of six months. The rate of interest for borrowing/lending is 8% per annum.

The dealer in the bank decides to go short in the contract. This would therefore require him to deliver 100,000 shares after six months. In order to cover his delivery commitment he acquires 100,000 shares on the NYSE right at the outset, by investing $14 million. This purchase would obviously have to be financed. The interest cost in this case would be:

$$14{,}000{,}000 \times 0.08 \times 0.50 = \$560{,}000$$

This would be an actual cost if the dealer were to borrow in order to fund the transaction. Otherwise, if he were to deploy the funds of the bank, it would tantamount to an opportunity cost.

Six months hence, when the shares are delivered under the contract, there will be an inflow of $14.70 million for the bank. The outflow on account of the repayment of the principal borrowed, along with the interest, will be $14.56 million. Consequently there is a profit of $140,000, whose magnitude is certain right from the outset. Therefore, this is a clear case of arbitrage. In the example, the return from the stock is:

$$\frac{14{,}700{,}000}{14{,}000{,}000} - 1 = 0.05 \equiv 5\%$$

This return accrues over a period of six months. Consequently the annualized return is 10%. This is clearly greater than the borrowing rate of 8% per annum, as a result of which the dealer is able to lock in a risk-less profit of 2% per annum. However, since his strategy was devoid of risk, such a positive return is unwarranted, and is unlikely to be observed in an efficient market.

1.10.2 Arbitrage with an Options Contract

Assume as before that IBM is trading at $140 per share on the NYSE. A bank is offered a customized call options contract, which entails taking delivery of 100,000 shares at a price of $135 per share. The option is American in nature and consequently can be exercised anytime after the position is taken. The option premium is $4 per share.

If the dealer were to acquire the contract, he would have to make an investment of $400,000. He can immediately exercise the option, which would result in an inflow of:

$$100{,}000 \times (140 - 135) = \$500{,}000$$

The profit of $100,000 is once again assured right from the outset, and consequently the strategy is risk-less. Thus, the availability of the call option at the quoted price is a clear manifestation of an arbitrage opportunity.

1.11 Spot-Futures Convergence at Expiration

When a futures contract is scheduled to expire, the futures price must be the same as the spot price in order to preclude arbitrage. The rationale for this is the following. A futures position is a contract to transact at a future point in time. At the point of expiration, any futures position that it is entered into at that instant, must lead to an immediate transaction because the contract is scheduled to expire immediately. Thus, an investor who is entering into a futures contract at its point of expiration is effectively entering into a spot contract. Therefore, if the futures price at expiration were to be different from the spot price, there will be an obvious arbitrage opportunity.

Let's denote the futures price at expiration by F_T and the spot price at that point in time by S_T. To rule out arbitrage, the two need to converge, that is F_T must be equal to S_T. We will now examine strategies to realize arbitrage profits, if F_T were to be greater than S_T or if F_T were to be less than S_T. Example 1.8 depicts these two arbitrage situations.

Example 1.8:

1. $F_T > S_T$

   In such circumstances an arbitrageur will implement the following strategy. He will take a long spot position at a price of S_T and will simultaneously go short in a futures contract. Since the contract is scheduled to expire immediately, he can at once deliver for a price of F_T. Hence, the price differential, $F_T - S_T$, which by assumption is positive, is obviously an arbitrage profit for such an investor.

   Assume that the futures price of an asset at the time of expiration is \$75, whereas the spot price at the same point in time is \$72. The contract size for the futures position is 100 units. An arbitrageur will acquire 100 units of the asset in the spot market at \$72 per unit, and will immediately take a short position in a futures contract. Since the futures contract is expiring he will immediately deliver at \$75, thereby making an arbitrage profit of \$3 per unit. The total profit is \$3 × 100 = \$300.

2. $F_T < S_T$

   Now let's consider a situation where the spot price at the time of expiration is greater than the prevailing futures price. An arbitrageur will exploit this situation by taking a long position in a futures contract. Since it is about to expire, he will take immediate delivery at a price of F_T, and will then sell in the spot market for S_T. In this case, $S_T - F_T$, which by assumption is positive, represents an arbitrage profit.

   Assume that the futures price of an asset at the time of expiration is \$75, whereas the spot price is \$77.50. An arbitrageur will take a long futures position, which will entail taking immediate delivery at \$75 per unit. The acquired goods can then be sold in the spot market for a price of \$77.50 per unit. Hence, there is an arbitrage profit of \$2.50 per unit which is equivalent to a total profit of \$2.50 × 100 = \$250.

1.12 Delivery

As you would have understood by now, under a futures contract, the long has an obligation to take delivery, while the short has an obligation to make delivery. There are three ways of settling a futures contract:

- Physical Delivery
- Cash Settlement
- Exchange for Physicals

1.12.1 Physical Delivery

This is the most cumbersome way of liquidation. The period during which delivery can be made, as was explained earlier, is defined by the exchange and varies from contract to contract. The decision as to when to deliver during the delivery period is made by the short.

The actual delivery process, for commodities on US exchanges, spans a three day period. In practice, delivery will commence with an expression of a desire to deliver by the short. This is called the *position day*. At this point in time, the short's broker will convey his client's intention to the clearinghouse by giving a notice of delivery. The notice will state, as to how many contracts are being delivered, the location of delivery in case the contract permits delivery at multiple locations, and the grade of the underlying asset being delivered in the case of contracts that permit the delivery of more than one grade. On the next business day, which is known as the *notice day*, the exchange will normally select the person with the oldest outstanding long position to accept delivery.[19] Finally, on the third day, known as the *delivery day*, the long will make the required payment to the short, and in return will get a warehouse receipt granting him title to the underlying asset.

It must be noted that cessation of trading is not a pre-condition for delivery to commence. In most futures markets, the first day on which a short can indicate its intention to deliver, or the first position day is before the last day of trading, whereas the last notice day, is after the day on which trading finally ceases.

As we have mentioned, the normal practice for the exchange is to match the short who has expressed a desire to deliver with the party with the oldest outstanding long position. The rationale for this is the following. Assume that Keith traded with Paul a month ago by assuming a short position. However, today when Keith announces his intention to deliver, it is not necessary that he be in a position to deliver to the original counterparty, for Paul may have already exited from the market by taking an offsetting position. Hence, the exchange will give the notice of Keith's intention to deliver, to the party with the oldest outstanding long position.

In the case of contracts settled by delivery of the underlying asset, the price paid per unit will be the spot price prevailing at that time. We will now analyze the logic behind this. Futures contracts are subject to marking to market on every business day during their lifetime. Thus, by the time of expiration, both the long and the short would

19 The rationale for this will be explained shortly.

have realized the profit or loss from their respective positions. Therefore, in order to ensure that the long gets to acquire the asset at the price that was agreed upon at the outset, he has to be asked to pay the prevailing futures price at expiration. This price of course, due to the no-arbitrage condition, will be the same as the prevailing spot price at expiration. We will illustrate the logic using symbols, as well as with the help of a numerical example.

Let's take the case of a contract that was entered into on *day 0* at a price F_0, and which expires on *day T*. We will denote the price at expiration by F_T. Such a contract will be marked to market on days 1,2,3 . . . . up to day T. The cumulative profit or loss for the long, due to the marking to market procedure, is:

$$(F_T - F_{T-1}) + (F_{T-1} - F_{T-2}) + (F_{T-2} - F_{T-3}) \\ + ... + (F_2 - F_1) + (F_1 - F_0) = (F_T - F_0) \tag{1.4}$$

Thus, in order to ensure that the long is able to acquire the asset at the original price of F_0, which is as per the conditions of the original contract, he must be asked to pay a price P at the time of delivery, such that:

$$P - (F_T - F_0) = F_0 \\ \Rightarrow P = F_T = S_T \tag{1.5}$$

In other words, in order to ensure that the long is able to effectively take delivery at the price specified in the futures contract, he must be asked to pay the prevailing futures price, or equivalently the prevailing spot price, at the time of delivery.

Forward contracts, however, are not marked to market. Consequently there is no adjustment of profits/losses on a daily basis. Hence, in the case of such contracts, the price paid by the long, must be the same as the price that was agreed upon originally. That is:

$$P = F_0 \tag{1.6}$$

Example 1.9, depicts this difference between the two types of contracts.

Example 1.9: Consider a futures contract on corn, that was entered into at a price of $6.50 per bushel. We will assume that the contract lasts for a period of 5 days, and that the movement in the futures price over that period is as depicted in Table 1.5.

In this case, F_0 = 6.50 and F_T = 7.10. An investor who had taken a long futures position at time *0* at a price of $6.50, would have to pay the terminal futures price of $7.10 at the time of delivery. After factoring in the profit of $0.60 due to marking to market, it would have effectively paid $6.50 for the asset, which is nothing but the initial futures price.

However, an investor who takes a long forward position at $6.50, will not have its position marked to market, and consequently would have to pay $6.50 at the time of taking delivery.

Table 1.5: Marking a contract to market.

Day	Futures Price	Profit From Marking to Market
0	6.50	
1	6.25	(0.25)
2	6.00	(0.25)
3	6.30	0.30
4	6.70	0.40
5	7.10	0.40
	Total	0.60

When delivery is made, the clearinghouse will be informed and it will cancel the obligations of the corresponding FCMs on its books. The FCMs will then delete the names of the individual clients from their own books.

1.12.2 Cash Delivery

In the case of certain futures contracts, physical delivery is not permissible. What happens in such cases is that the marking to market procedure will be followed till the last day of trading, and subsequently all the positions will be declared closed. This is referred to as cash settlement. In such circumstances, therefore, both the parties to the contract will exit the market with their profit/loss. In the above example, the long would have made a profit of $0.60, and he would exit the market with this amount, but without taking delivery of the underlying asset. In principle, this is no different from delivery based settlement. This is because, if he were to desire to have physical possession of the asset, he can acquire it in the spot market for $7.10, which would effectively mean that he had paid $6.50 for the asset.

Cash settlement is the prescribed mode of settlement all over the world for stock index futures. These are futures contracts which are based on popular stock indices such as the Dow Jones Industrial Average, the Standard & Poors 500, and the Nikkei 225. In order to form a portfolio that mimics an index, known as a tracking or mimicking portfolio, the investor would have to acquire all the component securities in exactly the same proportions as they are present in the index. It should be obvious that physical delivery under such circumstances will be an extremely cumbersome affair.

In certain markets, where there is a fear of price manipulation, the regulator may specify cash delivery as the required procedure, as a mechanism to guard against the possibility of traders creating artificial shortages in the underlying asset.

1.12.3 Exchange for Physicals (EFPs)

Physical delivery, as per contract specifications, can be made only during the delivery period specified by the exchange. The short is also required to adhere to the terms and conditions specified in the contract. That is, delivery must be at one of the allowable locations, and the grade that is being delivered must be one of the permissible grades. There are times, however, when two parties with opposite positions can transact prior to the delivery period specified by the exchange. Such an arrangement is called *exchange for physicals* or EFP. Under such a procedure, a long and a short can get together and agree on a transaction that would close out their respective positions. An EFP, is an *off-the-exchange* transaction. The reason why exchanges permit EFPs is that they offer the parties greater flexibility, and make physical delivery a more attractive option. The mechanism can best be illustrated with the help of an illustration, as shown in Example 1.10.

Example 1.10: Tom King has a short position in corn futures, while Mike Casey has an equivalent long position in futures contracts on the same asset. However, the grade of corn that Tom has, is different from the grade specified in the contract. Under normal circumstances, Tom will be unable to deliver this corn, even if Mike is willing to accept it. However, under an EFP, once Tom and Mike mutually agree on a price, the two can transact in the commodity after reporting the transaction to the exchange. The exchange, in such circumstances, will simply treat the transaction, as though each party had offset his position with the other.

1.13 Trading Volume versus Open Interest

The number of futures contracts that are traded during the course of a day, on a particular underlying asset, is referred to as the trading volume for that day. There is another term used in derivative markets, namely the *open interest*. The open interest at any point in time, is the total number of outstanding contracts or the number of open positions at that point in time. Every long position must be matched by a corresponding short position. Consequently, open interest may be measured either as the number of open long positions at a point in time, or equivalently, as the number of open short positions. There is a relationship between the trading volume for a day and the change in the open interest from the close of trading on the previous day. It depends on the nature of the transactions that take place during the course of the day, and can best be illustrated with the help of an example.

Let's assume that a new futures contract on a product has just opened for trading and that five trades have taken place on the first day as depicted in Table 1.6.

The trading volume for the day is obviously 1,000 contracts. Notice that nobody has offset any contracts during the course of the day. Thus the number of open positions at the end of the day is 1,000 contracts. In other words the open interest is 1,000 contracts.

Now consider the following scenarios for the next day.

Table 1.6: Trade details for the first day.

Time	Trade	No. of Contracts
10:30 a.m	Monica goes long and Alfred goes short	150
1 p.m	Rachel goes long and Violet goes short	200
2 p.m	Paul goes long and Ross goes short	150
3 p.m.	Eric goes long and Veronica goes short	200
4 p.m.	Mike goes long and Phil goes short	300

1. **Case A**
Monica goes long in 150 contracts and Phil goes short.

Both these parties are entering into a trade that increases their open positions. As a consequence of the trade, the number of long positions has increased by 150 as has the number of short positions. The trading volume for the day is obviously 150 contracts. The number of open positions at the end of the day is 1,000 plus 150 or 1,150 contracts. Hence, the change in the open interest as compared to the previous day is +150 contracts. Thus, if a trade involves two parties who are establishing new positions by entering into a contract with each other, the open interest will rise.

2. **Case B**
Monica goes long in 150 contracts and Mike goes short.

The trading volume for the day is once again 150 contracts. But what about the open interest at the end of the day? In this case, no new positions have been created. What has happened, is that Mike who had a long position in 300 contracts has partially offset by taking a counter-position in 150 contracts, and his place has been taken by Monica. Thus, the number of long or short positions has not changed as compared to the previous day, and the number of open positions at the end of the day continues to remain at 1,000 contracts. Hence, the change in the open interest as compared to the previous day is zero. Thus, if a trade involves one party taking a counter-position by trading with another party who is opening a position, then the open interest will remain unchanged.

3. **Case C**
Monica goes short in 150 contracts and Phil goes long.

As before, the trading volume for the day is 150 contracts. The change in the open interest can be derived as follows. Monica has exited the market by going short in 150 contracts. At the same time the trade has resulted in a reduction of 150 in Phil's short position. The net result is that the number of open contracts has reduced by 150 and the change in the open interest as compared to the previous day is – 150 contracts. Consequently, the open interest at the end of the second day is only 850 contracts. Therefore, if a trade involves one party taking a counter-position by trading with another party who is also taking a counter-position, then the open interest will fall.

Trading volumes are indicators of the level of liquidity in the market. On the other hand, open interest is a barometer of future liquidity. If the open interest at the end of a day is high, it is an indication that there is more scope for counter-positions on subsequent days, and consequently it can be construed as a signal that futures volumes are likely to be high.

1.14 Conversion Factors When There Are Multiple Deliverable Grades

Certain futures contracts give the short the flexibility to deliver more than one grade of the underlying asset. Thus, the short can choose the grade that he wishes to deliver. The exchange will in such cases, designate one grade as the *par* grade. If the short were to deliver the par grade, he will receive the prevailing futures price at expiration, F_T, for reasons that we have already explained. However, if he were to deliver a more valuable grade, he will receive a premium, whereas if he were to deliver a less valuable grade, he would have to do so at a discount. There are two ways of incorporating the premium or discount for grades other than the par grade, known as *multiplicative adjustment* and *additive adjustment*. We will examine each of these techniques.

1.14.1 Multiplicative Adjustment

In the case of contracts which permit more than one grade of the underlying asset to be delivered, and which specify a multiplicative system of price adjustment, the short will receive an amount equal to a_iF_T at the time of delivery, if he were to deliver grade i. For premium grades, a_i will be greater than 1.0, whereas for discount grades, it will be less than 1.0.

We will denote the spot price of grade i at expiration by $S_{i,T}$. Hence, the profit for the short if he were to deliver grade i is:

$$a_iF_T - S_{i,T} \tag{1.7}$$

Grade i will be preferred to another grade j if

$$a_iF_T - S_{i,T} > a_jF_T - S_{j,T} \tag{1.8}$$

At expiration, in order to preclude arbitrage, the profit from delivering the most preferred grade must be zero. If we denote this grade as grade i, it must be the case that

$$\begin{aligned} a_i F_T - S_{i,T} &= 0 \\ \Rightarrow F_T &= \frac{S_{i,T}}{a_i} \end{aligned} \tag{1.9}$$

In the case of all other grades, it must be the case that

$$\begin{aligned} a_j F_T - S_{j,T} &< 0 \\ \Rightarrow F_T &< \frac{S_{j,T}}{a_j} \end{aligned} \tag{1.10}$$

Thus, the grade that will be chosen for delivery will obviously be the one for which $\frac{S}{a}$ is the lowest. Such a grade is called the *cheapest to deliver grade (CTD)* and $\frac{S}{a}$ is called the *delivery adjusted spot price*. Thus, the cheapest to deliver grade, will be the one with the lowest delivery adjusted spot price. At expiration, therefore, the futures price must converge to the delivery adjusted spot price of the cheapest to deliver grade. Example 1.11 illustrates this.

Example 1.11: Gold futures contracts allow for the delivery of gold within a certain weight range and with varying degrees of fineness.[20] The price received by the short = weight × fineness × futures price. Thus, per ounce of gold delivered, the short will receive fineness x F. The conversion factor in this case is the fineness and the par grade is 100% fine.

Assume that gold is available with either 99% fineness or with 100% fineness. Let the spot price of 99% fine gold be $1,722.60 per ounce and that of 100% fine gold be $1,750 per ounce. The delivery adjusted spot prices are $\frac{1{,}722.60}{0.99} = 1{,}740$, and $\frac{1{,}750}{1} = 1{,}750$ respectively. Thus the 99% fine gold is the cheapest to deliver grade.

1.14.2 Additive Adjustment

Now let's consider the case of contracts, which permit more than one grade to be delivered, but use an additive system of price adjustment. In the case of such contracts, the short will receive $F_T + a_i$, if he were to deliver grade *i*. For a premium grade, a_i will be positive, whereas for a discount grade, it will be negative.

The profit from delivering grade *i*, will be

$$F_T + a_i - S_{i,T} \tag{1.11}$$

20 See Siegel and Siegel (1990).

and grade i will be preferred to another grade j if

$$F_T + a_i - S_{i,T} > F_T + a_j - S_{j,T}$$
$$\Rightarrow S_{i,T} - a_i < S_{j,T} - a_j \tag{1.12}$$

Hence, the cheapest to deliver grade is the one for which $S-a$ is the lowest. That is, grade i will be the cheapest to deliver grade if

$$S_{i,T} - a_i < S_{j,T} - a_j \forall j \tag{1.13}$$

To rule out arbitrage, the profit from delivering the cheapest to deliver grade must be zero. That is

$$F_T + a_i - S_{i,T} = 0$$
$$\Rightarrow F_T = S_{i,T} - a_i \tag{1.14}$$

In this case $S - a$ is the delivery adjusted spot price, and once again, the futures price will converge to the delivery adjusted spot price of the cheapest to deliver grade.

It must be noted that irrespective of whether the multiplicative or the additive system is used, the cheapest to deliver grade need not be the one with the lowest spot price. For example, consider the data for corn, given in Table 1.7.

Table 1.7: An illustration of additive price adjustment.

Grade	Spot Price	Conversion Factor	Delivery Adjusted Spot Price
No. 1	6.51	0.015	6.495
No. 2	6.50	0	6.500
No. 3	6.49	−0.015	6.505

The par grade is obviously No. 2. But the cheapest to deliver grade is No. 1, which incidentally has the highest spot price.

1.15 Profit Profiles

Investors with long positions in futures contracts stand to gain if the futures price were to rise after they have taken a position, whereas they stand to lose if the price were to decline subsequently. For the shorts it is the opposite. That is, they profit from declining futures prices and stand to lose if the futures price were to rise.

Thus, the profit for a long futures position may be expressed as $F_T - F_t$, where t represents the point of time at which the contract is initiated, and T is the point of time at which the contract either expires, or is offset. Therefore, for every dollar increase in the terminal futures price, the profit is one dollar more, while for every dollar decrease in the terminal futures price, the profit is one dollar less.

If we plot the profit from a long position versus the terminal futures price, the graph will be linear, and upward sloping as can be seen from the depiction in Figure 1.1.

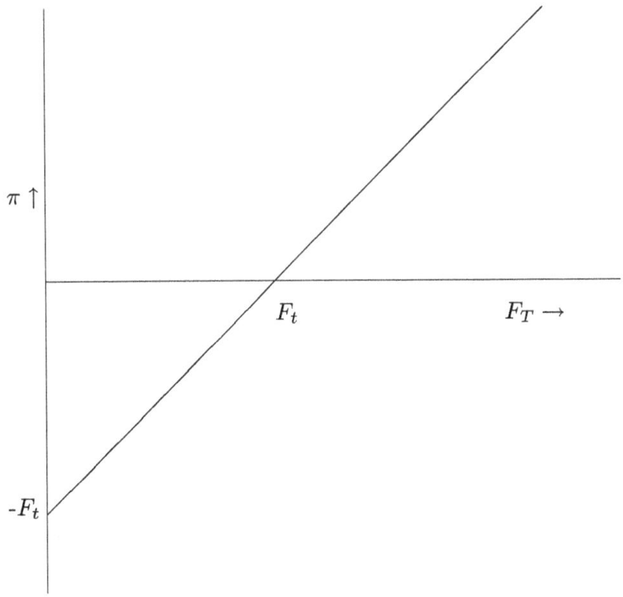

Figure 1.1: Profit profile of a long futures position.

Let's interpret the above diagram. π represents the profit, which is shown along the Y-axis. F_T is the terminal futures price which is shown along the X-axis. The maximum loss occurs when $F_T = 0$, and is equal to F_t in magnitude. The maximum profit is unlimited since F_T has no upper bound. The position breaks even if the terminal futures price is equal to the initial futures price, or in other words the price remains unchanged. Thus, holders of long positions face the specter of potentially infinite profits, but finite losses. Investors with long positions are obviously bullish about the market, for they will gain if prices were to rise.

For an investor with a short position in a futures contract, the profit may be depicted as $F_t - F_T$. The profit diagram for a short futures position is therefore also linear, but downward sloping, as depicted in Figure 1.2. In this case, the maximum profit occurs when $F_T = 0$, and is equal to F_t in magnitude. The maximum loss is obviously unlimited. Thus holders of short positions are confronted with the prospect of finite profits but infinite losses. Such investors are obviously bearish in nature, for they stand to make profits if the prices were to decline.

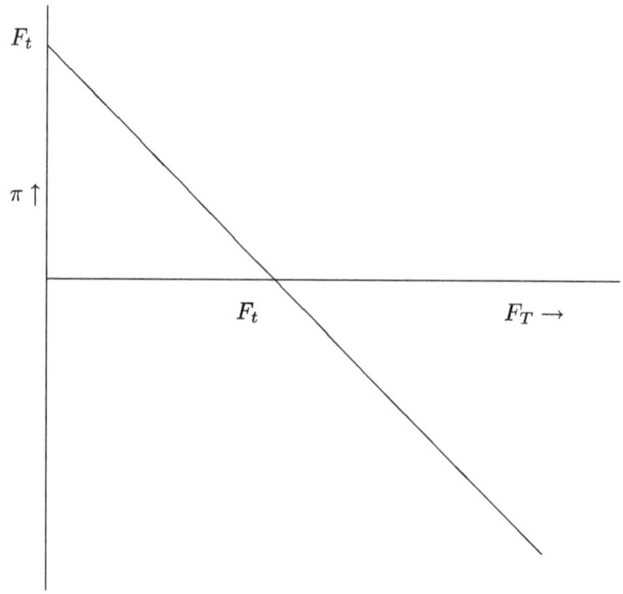

Figure 1.2: Profit profile of a short futures position.

1.16 Types of Assets Underlying Futures Contracts

On international markets, futures contracts are available on a number of assets such as food grains, oil seeds, fiber, meat, livestock, metals, petroleum, foreign currencies, stock indices, and interest rates. Until a few decades ago, most of the contracts were based on agricultural commodities. But subsequently, trading in contracts based on financial instruments such as bonds, stock indices, and foreign currencies, has outstripped the demand for commodity based contracts. One of the latest additions to the financial futures family, is *single stock* or *individual stock* futures, that is, futures contracts on the common stocks of companies.

1.17 Hedgers and Speculators

These are the two key types of players in the derivatives markets, besides arbitrageurs. They have contrasting attitudes to risk, and the active participation of both types of investors is essential for the success of a futures market. We will now define each one of them.

1.17.1 Hedgers

Hedgers are traders who seek to protect themselves against unfavorable movements in the price of the underlying asset. Obviously, a hedger already has a position in the underlying asset prior to entering the futures market. Let's consider the case of a refinery which is planning to acquire crude oil after a month. It will obviously be worried that the price of crude oil may rise during the period, and may like to lock in a price today for the commodity. *Thus, a hedger is a person whose objective is to reduce his risk.* Futures and options contracts can help such entities.

1.17.2 Speculators

Unlike a hedger who essentially wants to avoid being exposed to adverse price movements in the spot market, a speculator is an investor who deliberately wishes to take a position in the market. That is, he wants to consciously take risk hoping to profit from subsequent price changes. Such a person is either betting that the price will rise in which case we would say that he is bullish, or else he is hoping that it will fall, in which case we would categorize him as bearish. Futures and options can be used by speculators irrespective of their views about the direction of the market.

1.18 Leverage

A strategy is said to be *levered* or *geared*, if a fairly small market movement tends to have a disproportionately large impact on the funds deposited. Futures and options provide leverage to traders who take positions in them.

Consider a person who has gone long in a corn futures contract at a price of $6 per bushel, by depositing a margin of $1,000. As we have seen earlier, each contract is for 5,000 bushels. If the price were to move up to $6.15, the investor would make a profit of $750, which is 75% of the initial deposit. On the contrary, had he chosen to go long in the spot market at a price of $6 a bushel, he would have procured 5,000 bushels by paying $30,000, and a profit of $750 would have meant a return of only 2.50%. However, leverage is a double-edged sword. If the futures price were to fall to $5.85 at the end of the day, the investor would make a loss of $750, which is equivalent to a 75% erosion of his margin deposit. However, had he chosen to buy the corn in the spot market, a loss of $750 would tantamount to a loss of only 2.50% of his initial investment.

Options also similarly provide leverage. Consider a share which is selling at a price of $75. Assume, that European call options with an exercise price of $75 are available at a premium of $6. We will first consider the case where the share price at the time of expiration of the option is $82.50. If the investor were to have bought a share, he could sell it for a profit of $7.50, which is equivalent to a 10% return on investment.

On the contrary, if he had chosen to buy a call option, he would get a payoff of $7.50 by exercising, which represents a 25% return on an investment of $6. However, if the stock price at the time of expiration of the options contract were to be $67.50, the option holder would have to forego the entire premium amounting to a loss of 100%, since he will not exercise. On the contrary, had he chosen to acquire the share at the outset, he would now incur a loss of only 10%.

1.19 The Role of Futures and Options Markets

Derivative contracts can help traders in a number of ways. Some of the major benefits provided by derivatives are the following.

1.19.1 Re-allocation of Risk

All investors are not alike from the standpoint of their attitude towards risk. On one hand there is a category of traders whom we have labeled as *hedgers*. These are people who seek to avoid risk. On the other hand, we have another category of traders whom we have labeled as *speculators*. Unlike hedgers, speculators consciously seek to take calculated risks. Derivative contracts can be used to transfer or re-allocate risk from those who seek to avoid it to those who are willing to bear it. Very often, if a hedger were to take a position in a derivative security, the odds are that the counterparty is a speculator. This is however not necessarily always the case. Both parties to a contract may be hedgers or speculators, albeit with different price expectations.

1.19.2 Price Discovery

In a free market economy, fair and accurate prices are imperative for ensuring the correct allocation of resources. For, unlike in the case of a command economy, which is usually characterized by a centralized planning agency, it is the freedom to trade and the capacity of the market to correct supply-demand imbalances through the pricing mechanism, that helps resources to flow in a free and fair manner. In practice, supply and demand information tends to percolate derivative markets more easily, and consequently such markets help facilitate the dissemination of such information.

Why is it that information permeates the derivatives markets more easily? Taking a long derivatives position entails the depositing of a small margin, whereas to take a spot position the investor is required to pay the full price. Similarly, an investor who anticipates a bear market can more easily take a short position in derivatives than sell the asset short. Short selling entails the sale of an asset which the investor does not own. In practice this is achieved by borrowing it from another investor or broker. While long positions are used by bullish investors to take positions consistent with their views on prices, the freedom to short sell is critical for those with a bearish viewpoint. However, short selling is not always freely possible. Even in those markets where it is permitted, the investor is required to deposit the entire proceeds with the broker who will pay a low or nil rate of interest. Thus, from the standpoints of both the longs as well as the shorts, trading in derivatives is attractive. This has two major consequences, which further fuel the level of activity in such markets. First, transactions costs tend to be lower in derivatives markets as compared to spot markets. Second, derivatives markets are characterized by a high degree of liquidity.

Let's consider the issue of liquidity, and analyze as to why it is important. *Liquidity refers to the ability of market participants, to transact quickly at prices which are close to the true or fair value of the asset. It refers to the ability of buyers and sellers, to discover each other quickly and without having to induce a transaction by offering a large premium or discount*. Quite obviously, an investor, irrespective of his motive or market view, would like to trade without having to make major price concessions. In an illiquid market large trades can have a significant price impact. Large buy orders, placed by traders desirous of taking long positions, have the potential to send prices rising, whereas large orders to sell, placed by traders seeking to go short, can cause prices to decline rapidly. We have referred to the bid-ask spread earlier. Illiquid or thin markets are characterized by large bid-ask spreads.

1.19.3 Market Efficiency

There is obviously a relationship between the price of a futures or options contract, and the spot price of the underlying asset on which it is based.[21] Since derivatives trading is relatively easier and cheaper, the flow of new information into such markets may fleetingly manifest itself as an arbitrage opportunity between the derivatives and cash markets. Such asynchronous prices will immediately lead to the implementation of the relevant strategies by arbitrageurs. Thus, the presence of a derivatives market helps ensure an efficient spot asset market.

1.19.4 Ease of Speculation

Speculation is a sine qua non for the efficient functioning of a capital market. A market that does not facilitate speculation will not have the volumes required for it to func-

21 Readers will appreciate this better when we cover the valuation of derivatives in subsequent chapters.

tion as an efficient trading arena. Derivatives markets enable speculators to easily take positions by depositing small amounts of collateral.

1.20 Reasons for the Rapid Growth of Derivative Markets

Until the late 1960's, most of the activity in derivatives trading was restricted to commodities and to the leading capitalist economies like the U.S. Financial derivatives as a concept became significant only in the 1970's and 80's. The explosion of trading in financial futures and options has not only manifested itself by way of higher observed trading volumes in the leading markets of the world, but has lead to the establishment of newer exchanges with more sophisticated technologies, in both the developed as well as the developing world.

1. For a period of time in the last century, currencies were based on what was termed the *gold exchange standard.* In this system, every currency had a value in terms of the U.S dollar, which in turn had a value linked to gold. By the late 1960s, however, the foreign dollar liabilities of the US were much higher than its gold reserves. In 1971, this chapter of international economics came to a close. After the collapse of this system, also known as the *Bretton Woods* system, the major economies of the world switched from fixed exchange rate regimes to floating rate mechanisms. Consequently, currency risk and its management became very important, leading to growth and innovations in the market for foreign exchange derivatives.
2. There was a major war in the Middle East in 1973. After this, petroleum prices became highly volatile and unpredictable. This had far reaching effects on the prices of all commodities, since the transportation costs of all goods is directly linked to the price of crude oil. This gave a further impetus to the commodity derivatives markets. Futures contracts on crude oil, heating oil, and gasoline were introduced to facilitate the hedging of risk posed by volatile oil prices. The importance of this can be appreciated even in today's world where wildly fluctuating oil prices continue to be an issue of global concern.
3. Beginning with the U.S. Federal Reserve, major central banks began to abandon their policies of keeping interest rates stable. The focus shifted to adjustments in the levels of money supply, and interest rates became market determined. The resultant volatility in interest rates was addressed by the introduction of interest rate derivatives. Volatility of interest rates has implications for the risk of a business as a whole, since businesses thrive on borrowed money. Thus, it has ramifications not just for interest rate derivatives but for all risk management tools.
4. The three pronged strategy of 'liberalization, privatization, and globalization (LPG)' increasingly began to gain currency worldwide towards the end of the last century. Many countries across the globe began to liberalize their economies. With the removal of restrictions, capital began to move freely across borders, and markets became more integrated. Not surprisingly, risks multiplied and became a common

matter of concern, for the flow of capital is inevitably accompanied by the transmission of the attendant risks.

5. Significant market reforms were implemented in the traditionally free market economies with respect to the brokerage and banking industries. In October 1986 the London Stock Exchange (LSE) eliminated fixed brokerage commissions. This event came to be known as the 'Big Bang'. From February of the same year, the LSE had started admitting foreign brokerage firms as full members. These changes were intended to make London an attractive international financial market.[22] London is ideally located geographically, and serves as a middle link between markets in the U.S and those in the Far East, thereby facilitating 24 hours trading. Prior to World War II, London was the most active financial market in the world. However after the war, which devastated the British economy, the focus of international business shifted across the Atlantic to New York. Realizing the need for a vibrant market in London, the LSE sought to project itself as an institution of global importance.

   Similar changes were effected in the United States in 1975 and in Japan in 1999. Today, in most countries commissions are negotiable between the broker and the client. There are however countries, where government or exchange regulations specify fixed commission rates that ought to be charged by a broker. For instance, until early 2003 the minimum commission in Hong Kong was mandated to be 0.25% of the trade value.[23]

   In a deregulated brokerage industry, commissions vary substantially from broker to broker depending on the extent and quality of services provided. Prior to the regulatory changes, institutional investors were paying more than what they should have, considering the volumes of their trades, while retail investors were paying less than what was warranted. In other words, institutional investors were subsidizing the retail investors. When the brokerage industry was deregulated, retail brokerage charges initially rose sharply. However soon, a new industry called *discount broking* was born. Today, in developed markets we have three categories of brokers. On one hand, we have *full-service* brokers who charge the maximum commissions, but offer considerable value added services and investment advice. On the other hand, there exist *discount* and *deep discount* brokers who charge the least by way of commissions, but whose only function is to execute trades. In other words they do not provide research reports or other investment advice to their clients. Some of these discount brokers like Charles Schwab in the US have grown rapidly in size and are now counted among the major financial institutions. The difference between discount brokers and deep discount brokers is that while both do not offer investment advice, deep discount brokers require their clients to place orders of considerable size in order to avail of even lower brokerage rates.

22 See Resnick (1996).
23 See Harris (2003).

6. The rapid growth in *information technology* and *telecommunications* that has been witnessed over the past three decades has been a key factor in the development of derivatives exchanges. There was a time when hardware was expensive and software was primitive. Computers have now come within the reach of a middle class investor in most societies. From streamlining back-end operations in the exchanges and brokerage houses, to facilitating stock index arbitrage, computers have played a pivotal role in the growth of these markets. Similarly, modern telecommunications facilities, both voice as well as data, are indispensable for the growth of modern financial markets. Today prices and news from the leading exchanges in the world are flashed across the globe in a matter of seconds. Markets are now extremely closely linked and cross-border trading and arbitrage is an essential part of global economics. Institutions and high net worth (HNI) investors have come to realize that while it is true that one should not put all his eggs in one basket, there is no reason why the basket should be domestic. Mutual funds, pension funds, and other investors routinely diversify their wealth by investing across borders.

Suggestions for Further Reading

Chance, D.M. *An Introduction to Derivatives & Risk Management*. South Western, 2004.
Choudhry, M. *An Introduction to Value at Risk*. Securities Institute, 2002.
Edwards, F.R. and C.W. Ma *Futures and Options*. McGraw-Hill Inc., 1992.
Hull, J. *Fundamentals of Futures and Options Markets*. Prentice Hall, 2004.
Kolb, R.W. *Futures, Options, & Swaps*. Blackwell, 2003.
Kroll, S. and M.J.Paulenoff *The Business One Irwin Guide to the Futures Markets*. Business One Irwin, 1993.
Lofton, T. *Getting Started in Futures*. John Wiley, 2005.
Siegel, D.R. and D.F. Siegel *Futures Markets*. The Dryden Press, 1990.

References

Darbha, G. *Value-at-Risk and Margin Requirements – Opportunities and Pitfalls*. NSE News (June 2001).
Harris, L. *Trading and Exchanges: Market Microstructure for Practitioners*. Oxford University Press, 2003.
Linsmeier, T.J. and N.D. Pearson *Value at Risk*. *Financial Analysts Journal (March/April 2000)*.
Resnick, B.G. *The Globalization of World Financial Markets*. In P.L. Cooley (ed.), *Advances in Business Financial Management*. The Dryden Press, 1996.

Chapter 2
Valuation of Futures Contracts

2.1 Introduction to Valuation

Futures prices should accurately reflect the price of the underlying asset. The concept of arbitrage is critical for understanding as to how spot prices and futures and forward prices are linked. If the postulated relationship between the two prices is not satisfied, arbitrageurs will exploit the resulting profit opportunities until they are eliminated.

The chapter begins with a study of the pricing of contracts on assets that pay no income during the life of the contract. The analysis is subsequently extended to cover assets that pay a known cash income. The difference between financial assets and physical assets, is clearly brought out by extending the discussion to cover assets that are held for investment purposes, as well as those that are held for the convenience value that they provide. The concepts of net carry and the marginal convenience yield are introduced, and the difference between markets which are in contango and those which are in backwardation is highlighted.

Subsequently, the use of quasi-arbitrage as a strategy is brought out in detail. The chapter ends with a detailed study of arbitrage in cases where multiple grades are permitted for delivery, and demonstrates why reverse cash and carry strategies in such circumstances are best construed as risk-arbitrage.

We will now go on to analyze how forward and futures prices are related to the spot price of the underlying asset. We will first focus on forward contracts because they are much easier to analyze than futures contracts. This, as we explained earlier, is because there are no intermediate cash flows in the case of such contracts, due to the absence of the marking to market mechanism. Later on we will study that forward and futures prices will be equal, when interest rates are either constant or are a known function of time. And finally, we will analyze the consequences of relaxing this assumption.

2.2 Notation

We will use the following symbols to denote the corresponding variables:
- t ≡ the point in time at which we are standing, that is, today.
- T ≡ the point in time at which the forward contract expires.
- S_t ≡ current spot price of the asset underlying the forward contract.
- K ≡ delivery price as per the forward contract.
- F_t ≡ forward price of a contract initiated at time 't' and expiring at time 'T'.

https://doi.org/10.1515/9783110746662-002

- f ≡ current value of a long forward contract.
- r ≡ rate of interest for the period between 't' and 'T'.[1]

2.3 Assumptions

In our analysis we will make the following assumptions:

1. There are no information or transactions costs associated with buying or selling either the forward contract or the underlying asset.
2. Market participants have an unlimited ability to borrow and lend money at the rate r.
3. There is no credit risk in either forward or spot markets.
4. Commodities can be stored indefinitely without any change in their features such as quality.
5. There are no taxes.
6. Assets can be sold short with full use of proceeds.
7. Arbitrage opportunities are fully exploited as soon as they are perceived.

Let's first understand the difference between the *forward price* and the *delivery price.* The delivery price is the price that is specified in the forward contract. That is, it is the price at which the short is obliged to make delivery or equivalently it is the price at which the long is obliged to take delivery.

The forward price, at any point of time, is the applicable delivery price for a contract that is being negotiated at that particular instant. If a contract were to be sealed, based on the bilateral negotiations, the prevailing forward price would become its delivery price. However, a contract that were to be negotiated an instant later is unlikely to have the same forward price. In other words, the forward price will keep changing as new trades are negotiated.

Let's view the issue as follows. If a trader were to make a statement that she had taken a forward position at a prior point in time, the natural response would be "what was the delivery price?" and not "what was the forward price then?", although both would mean the same thing. However if we were to be confronted with an offer to get into a forward position, the question to ask would be "what is the forward price?". If the contract were to be sealed, the current forward price would become the delivery price of the contract, which would remain invariant for the life of the contract.

1 Note, this is not an annualized rate.

2.4 Forward Contracts on a Security that Provides No Income

Obvious examples of such securities are stocks that pay no dividends and zero coupon bonds. Securities that provide no income represent the simplest of assets that we will value.

2.4.1 Cash and Carry Arbitrage

From the perspective of the party who has a short position in a forward contract, it represents a commitment to make delivery. Consider the case of an investor with a short position in the contract, and who has a unit of the underlying asset with him. He would obviously have to fund the acquisition of the asset. It would entail an actual interest cost if he were to borrow the required amount, and an opportunity cost if he were to deploy his own funds. If the difference between the forward price, which is what he is scheduled to receive at expiration, and the prevailing spot price at the outset, which is the amount that he has financed, were to exceed the cost of carrying the asset until delivery, then clearly there would exist an arbitrage opportunity. In the case of an asset that pays no income, the only component of the carrying cost is the interest cost rS_t, where r is the risk-less rate of interest and S_t is the prevailing spot price at the time of entering into the contract. Hence, if the price differential were to exceed the interest cost, or

$$F_t - S_t > rS_t$$

then a person could exploit the situation by borrowing and buying the asset, and concurrently taking a short position in a forward contract.

Such a strategy, that is intended to realize an arbitrage profit, is called *cash and carry arbitrage*. Hence, to rule out such arbitrage, we require that

$$F_t - S_t \leq rS_t \Rightarrow F_t \leq S_t(1 + r) \tag{2.1}$$

Example 2.1 illustrates the implementation of a cash and carry arbitrage strategy.

Example 2.1: Assume that XYZ is currently selling for $50 per share, and as per the forecast of investors, is not expected to pay any dividends for the next six months. We will assume that the price of a forward contract for one share of the company to be delivered after six months is $54. Notice that the phrase *'security that provides no income'* refers to securities that are not expected to make any payouts during the life of the forward contract. It does not mean that the asset will never make payouts.

Let's take the case of an arbitrageur who is in a position to borrow funds at the rate of 6% per six monthly period. He can obviously borrow $50 and acquire one share of the company. Assume that at the time of the transaction, he simultaneously goes short in a forward contract to deliver the share after six months for $54. In other words he locks in the sale price of the asset at the very outset. The rate of return on his investment, for a six month horizon is:

$$\frac{(54-50)}{50} = 0.08 \equiv 8\%$$

whereas his funding cost is only 6%.

Thus, the arbitrage strategy that has been implemented is obviously a profitable proposition. This is because the forward contract is overpriced, that is:

$$F_t > S_t(1+r)$$

The rate of return for the arbitrageur in a cash and carry strategy is referred to as the *implied repo rate (IRR)*. Obviously, such an arbitrage strategy would be profitable only if the implied repo rate were to exceed the borrowing rate faced by the arbitrageur.

The net result of such a strategy may be perceived as follows. By engaging in such a transaction, the arbitrageur has ensured a payoff for himself of $54 after six months, in return for an initial investment of $50. Thus, it is as if he has bought a *zero coupon* debt security with a maturity value of $54, by paying a price of $50. Hence, a combination of a long position in the underlying asset and a short position in a forward contract is equivalent to a long position in a zero coupon security. Such a discount instrument, which is artificially generated using other assets, is referred to as a *synthetic T-bill*. Hence we can express the relationship as

$$\text{Spot} - \text{Forward} = \text{Synthetic T-bill}$$

In this expression, the negative sign in front of the forward contract denotes that the arbitrageur has taken a short position in it. Thus, an investor who has taken natural positions in any two of the three assets, can artificially create a position in the third. One significant implication of the above equation, is that although the spot and forward positions are exposed to price risk when held in isolation, their combination leads to a risk-less position.

2.4.2 Reverse Cash and Carry Arbitrage

We have just seen that cash and carry arbitrage requires a short position in a forward contract and arises if the contract were to be overpriced. That is:

$$F_t > S_t(1+r)$$

However, what if the forward price, F_t were to be less than $S_t(1+r)$, or in other words the contract were to be underpriced. It turns out that such a situation too represents an arbitrage opportunity. However, to exploit the mispricing in this case, the arbitrageur would have to take a long position in the contract. The strategy to be deployed under such circumstances requires the investor to short sell the asset and invest the proceeds at the risk-less rate of interest. He also needs to simultaneously take a long position in the forward contract.

This kind of an arbitrage strategy is called *reverse cash and carry arbitrage*, and is feasible in those circumstances where the difference between the forward price and the spot price is less than the carrying cost. In order to rule out such opportunities, we obviously require that:

$$F_t \geq S_t(1 + r) \tag{2.2}$$

Example 2.2 illustrates the implementation of a reverse cash and carry arbitrage strategy.

Example 2.2: We will assume once again that XYZ is selling for $50 per share, and that the company is not expected to pay any dividends for the next six months. We will assume that the risk-less rate of interest continues to be 6% for this period. However, the price of a forward contract for one share to be delivered after six months will be assumed to be $52.50.

Consider the following strategy which can be deployed by an arbitrageur under such circumstances. He can short sell a share at $50, invest the proceeds at a rate of 6% for six months, and simultaneously take a long position to re-acquire the share after six months at a price of $52.50.

One of the crucial assumptions that we have made in this illustration, is that the arbitrageur can lend the proceeds from the short sale at the market rate of interest. In practice, short selling entails the depositing of the proceeds with the broker. In addition, the short seller has to put up additional collateral to protect the broker against a subsequent rise in the price of the shares. The broker can obviously earn interest on the amount deposited with him. Institutional investors can, in a competitive market, demand that the broker share a part of the interest income with them. Such payments are referred to as *short interest rebates*. However, even if the broker were to pay interest to the client, the effective rate of return earned by the short seller will be lower than the prevailing market rate.

The effective cost of borrowing for the short seller in our example is:

$$\frac{(52.50 - 50.00)}{50.00} = 0.05 \equiv 5\%$$

which is less than the lending rate of 6%.

Thus, the arbitrage strategy leads to a profit for the investor. The reason why it is attractive is obviously because the contract is underpriced. That is:

$$F_t < S_t(1 + r)$$

The effective borrowing cost incurred by an arbitrageur who employs such a strategy is known as the *implied reverse repo rate (IRRR)*. Hence, reverse cash and carry arbitrage is profitable only if the implied reverse repo rate is less than the lending rate.

Let's analyze the strategy from a related perspective. By engaging in such a transaction, the investor has ensured the sale of what is akin to a zero coupon instrument with a face value of $52.50, for a price of $50. Thus, a combination of a short position in the stock and a long position in a forward contract is equivalent to a short position in an artificial zero coupon instrument, which is what we have previously termed as a synthetic T-bill. Hence we can express the relationship as:

$$-\text{Spot} + \text{Forward} = -\text{Synthetic T-bill.}$$

Cash and carry arbitrage is feasible if the contract is overpriced, that is, $F_t > S_t(1 + r)$, while reverse cash and carry arbitrage is feasible if the contract is underpriced, that is, $F_t < S_t(1 + r)$. Thus, in order to rule out both forms of arbitrage, which is an indication that the contract is fairly priced, we require that:

$$F_t = S_t(1 + r) \tag{2.3}$$

In this example therefore, the no-arbitrage forward price should be $F_t = 50 \times (1 + .06) =$ \$53.

2.4.3 The Case of Continuous Compounding

Let's re-examine the above examples on cash and carry arbitrage and reverse cash and carry arbitrage, using continuous compounding.

Consider a person who buys one share of XYZ at \$50 and enters into a forward contract to sell the share after six months. He does not have to pay anything to get into a forward contract, for its value at inception is zero. So the initial cost of this strategy is equal to the value of the share, which is \$50. Now, according to the terms of the agreement, the person will deliver the share six months later and will receive the delivery price. So all he is doing, is paying \$50 today in exchange for a cash flow, equal to the delivery price after six months. So to preclude arbitrage opportunities, the delivery price should equal \$50 compounded at the borrowing rate r.

Therefore, $K = 50e^r = 50e^{0.06} = 53.0918$

By definition, the forward price and the delivery price will be equal at inception.

Hence, $F_t = K = 53.0918$

Notice that the equilibrium forward price differs from what we got earlier because compounding continuously at 6%, differs from compounding discretely at 6%.

2.5 Repos and Reverse Repos

We have used the terms repo rate and reverse repo rate in the above discussion. These are terms that are commonly used in the money market, and we will briefly discuss them.

2.5.1 Repos

The term *repo* is a short form for a repurchase transaction, and represents collateralized borrowing by pledging securities. Using a repo, a party in need of funds, can borrow from another party who has funds to invest. A typical repo transaction is an overnight deal. That is, the borrower will sell securities to the lender at a price P_1, with a simultaneous commitment to buy them back a day later, at a higher price P_2. If we denote the overnight repo rate as R% per annum[2] then

$$P_2 = P_1 \times \left(1 + \frac{R}{360}\right) \tag{2.4}$$

The first leg of the repo is a spot transaction, while the second leg is a forward contract. Consequently, in some markets repos are known as ready-forward transactions. The difference between the price at which the securities are sold and that at which they are subsequently re-purchased, constitutes the interest for the lender.

While most repos are done on an overnight basis, there exist what are known as *term repos*, which are undertaken for longer periods. There are dealers who make a market in these transactions. They will first locate a party with a surplus, such as a corporation or a money market mutual fund, and borrow from it. The funds will subsequently be lent out to a party which has a need, and hence seeks to borrow. The majority of such transactions in global markets, are done on the strength of government securities. In the U.S. however, other money market securities such as commercial paper may also be used as collateral.

Example 2.3 demonstrates the essential features of a typical repurchase transaction.

Example 2.3: A dealer is offering a bond with a face value of $10MM to a money market mutual fund, in return for an overnight loan carrying interest at the rate of 9% per annum. The lender has decided to apply a haircut of 0.01 price points. The current market price of the bond is $102.50 per $100 of face value.

The loan amount is:

$$10{,}000{,}000 \times \left[\frac{102.50}{100} - 0.01\right] = \$10{,}150{,}000$$

The amount repayable on the following day is:

$$10{,}150{,}000\left[1 + 0.09 \times \frac{1}{360}\right] = \$10{,}152{,}537.50$$

2.5.2 Reverse Repos

A repurchase transaction is a collateralized arrangement for borrowing money. Such an agreement, as perceived from the lender's position is known as a *reverse repo*. Thus, by

2 Repo rates are quoted on a 360 day year basis, as is the norm in the money market.

employing a reverse repo, a lender will grant a loan, on the strength of the securities delivered by the borrower. The securities will obviously be returned at a higher price at the end of the period for which the funds have been loaned. The difference between the sale price and the purchase price constitutes the interest earned by the lender. Reverse repo transactions are primarily overnight deals, although dealers do undertake *term reverses*.

The nature of a given transaction depends on the motive of the dealer who undertakes it. Dealers who seek to borrow do repos, whereas those who seek to lend engage in reverses. Often a dealer will do a repo at a particular rate and will immediately follow it up with a reverse repo at a higher rate. In the process he will obviously make a spread.

2.6 Short Selling

The ability to short sell the underlying asset is critical for the execution of a reverse cash and carry arbitrage strategy. Let's therefore take a closer look at the mechanics of a short sale. Long positions in shares are taken by what we term as *bulls*. Such investors acquire shares because they foresee an increase in their value over a period of time. If their views were to turn out to be accurate, they can obviously liquidate their long positions with a profit. Thus, the ability to take long positions constitutes a speculative tool for those who are bullish about the market. The investment principle being followed in such cases is therefore, 'buy low and sell high'.

However, it is not necessary that all investors should have a bullish outlook at a given point in time. There will always be those who expect the market to decline over a period of time. Such investors are referred to as *bears*. These traders too require a tool to facilitate speculation on their part. Short selling represents such a technique.

What is short selling and how is it accomplished? A short sale is carried out by selling an asset that does not belong to the seller. Quite obviously, to do so he must borrow it from another investor. In practice investors borrow from brokers. A broker may have the shares in his personal inventory or else he may borrow it from a client such as a financial institution. The securities which are borrowed in such fashion, have obviously to be bought back and returned. The process of acquisition of shares to close out an existing short position, is called *covering the short position*. Short sellers undertake such positions in the belief that they can re-acquire the asset at a lower value at the time of closing out the position. The principle is obviously *sell high and buy low*. At times, during the period of the short sale, the asset may make a payout. In the case of equity shares the company may declare a dividend, whereas in the case of bonds the issuer may pay a coupon. The dividend or coupon in such cases will go the current owner of the security. However, from the perspective of the party who has lent the security to facilitate the short sale, he has merely lent it and not sold it. If he had not parted with the asset he would have obviously received the payment. Hence, as per the terms of the short sale agreement, the borrower of the securities is required to compensate the lender for any lost income.

Similarly, there could be other corporate actions during the period of a short sale as a stock split. If so, the short seller has to make the necessary adjustment while returning the shares. For instance, if there were to be a 5:1 split, an investor who has borrowed one share prior to the split, is responsible for returning five shares after the split.

When a trader borrows a share from a broker and sells it, he has an obligation to buy it back eventually. From the standpoint of the broker there is always a risk that the security which the short seller thinks would depreciate in value, actually ends up appreciating. Consequently, the broker needs to guard against the possibility of default. Thus, the broker in practice will retain the sale proceeds with him. Further, to protect himself against rising prices, he will require the party who is selling short to deposit additional collateral. The additional collateral as well as the sale proceeds will show up as a credit balance in the trader's account.

2.7 The Value of a Forward Contract

As we mentioned earlier, the value of a forward contract when it is first entered into is zero. Later on, it may have a positive or a negative value.

In the earlier example, the current equilibrium forward price, for a contract on XYZ, was \$53, which by definition, was equal to the delivery price of a contract being negotiated at that point in time. Let's consider another forward contract that was entered into a while earlier, with a delivery price of \$50. At that time, the forward price would have been equal to \$50. Today, say a week later, the delivery price as per the contract is still \$50, but the forward price is \$53. So the question is, what value will the old contract have today?

Consider the holder of a long forward contract with a delivery price of \$50. He will require \$50 after six months to pay and take delivery. So all he needs today, is the present value of \$50, which if invested at the prevailing rate of 6%, will be adequate for taking delivery after six months.

The present value of \$50 = $\frac{50}{1.06}$ = 47.1698. Hence, if this person has \$47.1698 plus one long forward contract, then he will be entitled to one share after six months. Now, consider another individual who pays \$50 now and buys one share in the spot market. At the end of six months, he too will be in possession of one share of the company. Thus, the portfolios held by both these persons will be worth the same at the end of six months. If the future values of these portfolios are the same, then they must have identical present values.

Let f be the value of the forward contract. Therefore

$$f + 47.1698 = 50 \Rightarrow f = 2.8302.$$

Hence, the value of a forward contract with a delivery price of $50 is $2.8302. In symbolic terms

$$f = S_t - \frac{K}{(1+r)}$$

From the no-arbitrage condition we know that

$$S_t = \frac{F_t}{(1+r)}$$

Therefore

$$f = \frac{F_t}{(1+r)} - \frac{K}{(1+r)} = \frac{(F_t - K)}{(1+r)} \tag{2.5}$$

Thus, the value of a long forward contract is the present value of the difference between the forward price and the delivery price.

Now, you are aware that forward contracts are customized contracts that are negotiated individually between the buyer and the seller. So you may be wondering how the holder of a long forward contract can possibly realize the value that we have calculated above? In order to realize the value of the above contract, all the holder has to do, is to enter into a new contract that offsets the original. We will illustrate this with the help of Example 2.4.

Example 2.4: Consider a person who is holding a long forward contract on ABC, with a delivery price of $100. In order to get out of his position, he will have to go short in a fresh contract with a current delivery price of say $105. At expiration therefore, he can buy the asset under the first contract at $100 and sell it under the second at $105. So he has a guaranteed payoff of $5 waiting for him at expiration. If we assume that the risk-less rate is 6%, then the value of his original contract is the present value of this future payoff. That is:

$$\text{Value} = \frac{5}{1.06} = 4.7170$$

2.7.1 Value of a Futures Contract

Having understood how to determine the value of a forward contract, let's now turn our attention to futures contracts. At the outset, neither the long nor the short has to pay to get into a position in either a forward or a futures contract. However, as the futures price changes subsequently, an open futures position will acquire value. There is however, a difference between forwards and futures in terms of how this value is dealt with. In the case of futures contracts, due to the marking to market mechanism, the profit/loss is calculated at the end of every day and credit/debited to the margin account. The position is then re-initialized at the settlement price that is used to mark to market at the end of that particular day. This process of marking to market, is therefore a settlement of built up value. Thus, once the profit/loss is adjusted, the value of the futures contract will once again revert back to zero. Therefore, the only time futures contracts accumulate value, is in the period between two successive settlement price calculations. Once the settlement of built up value occurs at the end of the day, the value of both long and short positions will go back to zero.

2.8 Forward Contracts on Assets that Provide a Known Cash Income

Let's now go on to consider the case of forward contracts on assets that provide a perfectly predictable cash income. Examples include stocks which pay known dividends and coupon paying bonds. If an investor were to get a cash inflow from the asset that he is holding, then he would obviously have a reduced carrying cost. The carrying cost on account of interest, as we have seen before, is rS_t. Let's denote the future value of the income from the asset, as calculated at the time of expiration of the forward contract, by I. Why do we need to calculate the future value of the income? The carrying cost is computed as at the point of expiration of the futures contract. In order to be consistent with the principles of time value of money, the value of the income too should be computed at the same point in time. Hence, if the income were to be received prior to the time that the contract matures, it has to be compounded for the remaining period using the risk-less rate of interest. Consequently, in order to rule out cash and carry arbitrage we require that

$$F_t - S_t \leq rS_t - I \Rightarrow F_t \leq S_t(1 + r) - I \tag{2.6}$$

Now let's consider a reverse cash and carry arbitrage strategy. This strategy entails a short sale, and as we have mentioned earlier, the short seller is responsible for compensating the lender of the asset for any lost income. Consequently, the effective income obtained by a short seller by investing the proceeds from the sale will be reduced by the amount of payouts from the asset. Hence, reverse cash and carry arbitrage will be profitable only if

$$F_t - S_t < rS_t - I$$

Thus to rule out reverse cash and carry arbitrage we require that

$$F_t - S_t \geq rS_t - I \Rightarrow F_t \geq S_t(1 + r) - I \tag{2.7}$$

Hence, to preclude both forms of arbitrage it must be the case that

$$F_t = S_t(1 + r) - I \tag{2.8}$$

Let's now illustrate the two arbitrage strategies in the case of forward contracts on a share that pays a known dividend. We will continue with the XYZ stock example, but will now assume that the stock will pay a dividend of \$2.50 after three months and another \$2.50 after six months. The second payment will be assumed to be made an instant prior to delivery under the forward contract. We will also assume that an arbitrageur can borrow or lend at the rate of 6% per semi-annual period.

2.8.1 Cash and Carry Arbitrage

Let the forward price be \$48.

Consider the following strategy. Buy one share of XYZ, by borrowing the \$50 required to finance the purchase. Simultaneously enter into a forward contract to sell one share after six months at \$48. During this period of six months, you will get a dividend of \$2.50 after three months, followed by another dividend of \$2.50 three months later. The first dividend can be invested until the expiry of the forward contract at 6% per six months. So at the end of six months, you will get \$48 when you deliver the share, plus interest and principal on account of the first dividend that you have invested, plus the second dividend. So the total final cash flow is

$$48 + 2.50\left(1 + \frac{1}{2} \times 0.06\right) + 2.50 = 53.075.$$

The rate of return is:

$$\frac{(53.075 - 50)}{50} \equiv 6.15\%$$

for six months. But the borrowing rate is only 6% per six-monthly period. Hence, it is obvious that there is an arbitrage opportunity. So the forward price of \$48 does not represent an equilibrium.

Let's consider another case where the forward price is \$47. The above strategy, as you can verify, will not yield arbitrage profits. But it turns out that you can make arbitrage profits by reversing the above strategy.

2.8.2 Reverse Cash and Carry Arbitrage

This strategy can be executed as follows. Short sell one share of XYZ at \$50 and go long in a forward contract to enable you to procure one share after six months. Three months later, you would require \$2.50 to compensate the person who lent you the share because he would have received a dividend equal to this amount had he not parted with the share. This amount can be borrowed at 6% per half-yearly period. Once again, by the same logic, at the end of another three months you would be required to pay \$2.50.

Thus your total outflow at the end of six months is

$$47 + 2.50\left(1 + \frac{1}{2} \times 0.06\right) + 2.50 = 52.075$$

By engaging in the above strategy, you have effectively taken a loan of \$50, and paid back \$52.075 six months later. The interest rate on your borrowing is

$$\frac{(52.075 - 50)}{50} = 4.15\%$$

However, the \$50 that you receive when you short sell the stock, can be lent at 6% for six months. Thus, there clearly exists an arbitrage opportunity.

Once again, to eliminate arbitrage profits, the IRR must equal the IRRR, which must equal the borrowing and lending rates. Let F_t be the equilibrium forward price. Then:

$$\frac{(F_t + 5.075 - 50)}{50} = 0.06 \Rightarrow F_t = 47.925$$

The amount of \$5.075 is the future value at the end of the six monthly period, of the payouts from the asset during the period, which we have denoted by I. Therefore, in symbolic terms

$$\frac{(F_t + I - S_t)}{S_t} = r \Rightarrow F_t = S_t(1 + r) - I$$

2.8.3 Value of the Forward Contract

Let the current forward price, as calculated above, be \$47.925. Consider a forward contract that was entered into a week ago, with a delivery price of \$45. A person who has a long position in one such contract and has the present value of \$45 with him, will have one share in his possession after six months. Now consider another person who owns a share and has borrowed the present value of the first dividend as well as the present value of the second dividend.[3] The borrowings can be paid back with interest when the respective dividends are received. Thus at the end of six months, this individual too will have one share with him. Since both of them will have the same terminal wealth, the present values of their portfolios must be identical.

3 The present values are calculated at the beginning of the six monthly period.

Therefore, if f is the value of the forward contract

$$f + \frac{45}{(1.06)} = 50 - \frac{2.5}{(1.03)} - \frac{2.50}{(1.06)}$$
$$\Rightarrow f = 2.7615$$

Symbolically

$$f = S_t - \frac{K}{(1+r)} - \frac{I}{(1+r)}$$
$$F_t = S_t(1+r) - I \Rightarrow S_t = \frac{F_t}{(1+r)} + \frac{I}{(1+r)}$$
$$\text{Hence, } S_t - \frac{I}{(1+r)} = \frac{F_t}{(1+r)}$$
$$\Rightarrow f = \frac{F_t}{(1+r)} - \frac{K}{(1+r)} = \frac{(F_t - K)}{(1+r)} \tag{2.9}$$

2.9 Forward Contracts on Commodities

Thus far, we have considered assets that provide no income like non dividend paying stocks and zero coupon bonds, and assets which pay a known cash income like dividend paying stocks and coupon paying bonds.

Let's now consider the case of commodities. Commodities typically do not earn any income. On the contrary, it costs money to store them and to insure them against unforeseeable events. It turns out that we must make a distinction between commodities that are held mainly as investments by most investors (typical examples are precious metals) and those that are held for consumption purposes (like agricultural commodities).

2.9.1 Restrictions on Short Sales

For the pricing relationships that we have developed thus far to hold, both cash and carry as well as reverse cash and carry arbitrage should be freely possible. Let's recapitulate these strategies. The cash and carry strategy, requires that the arbitrageur buy the asset and take a short position in the forward contract. This per se, should pose no problems. But in the reverse cash and carry arbitrage strategy, the arbitrageur is required to short sell the asset and go long in a forward contract. The problem is that there are certain assets, which are held by people for reasons other than pure investment. People who choose to hold these assets get some special benefits from them and therefore may not be willing to lend them for short sales. In such cases, reverse cash and carry arbitrage will be infeasible. We will first make a distinction between *pure* and *convenience* assets and then will go on to look at detailed examples, which will hopefully help clarify these and other related issues.

2.9.2 Pure versus Convenience Assets

What is the definition of a short sale? It is a transaction wherein you hand over an asset to a person, who immediately sells it and returns it intact to you at a future date. Any income that you would have received in the intervening period is given to you by the borrower of the asset, be it dividends or coupon payments. So, if you do not really require the asset during the period of the short sale, you are not foregoing anything.

The above argument is true if the owner of the asset is holding it for an investment purpose, that is, to earn capital gains and other income due to him. Such assets are called *pure* assets or *investment* assets. Financial assets such as stocks and bonds are examples of pure assets.

On the other hand, certain assets like wheat or rice are often held for reasons other than potential returns. Such assets are called *convenience* or *consumption* assets. The owners of such assets may not permit them to be sold short. This can best be clarified with the help of Example 2.5.

Example 2.5: Let's consider the case of wheat. As everyone is aware, prices usually rise before a harvest season and fall thereafter. A person who hoards wheat before the harvest, not only has to incur storage costs but also faces the specter of a capital loss. Thus, from an investment angle, it makes little sense for a person to hoard wheat during the harvest period. But a wheat mill owner may choose to hold the commodity for other reasons. For instance, he may want to avoid closing the mill during an unanticipated temporary shortage, which may be due to a natural calamity or a rainfall failure. The value of such potential needs is called the *convenience value*.

The holder of a convenience asset, will possibly give it up for a short sale only if he is compensated for the convenience value. Thus, you may feel that the convenience value is similar in principle to a dividend. But there are differences. First, how do you quantify a convenience value? Second, the perception of value will differ from holder to holder. That is why, we do not have markets for short selling convenience assets.

2.10 Investment Assets

We will illustrate our arguments for the pricing of such assets using gold, which is primarily held for investment purposes. To keep matters simple, let's initially assume that storage costs are zero. If so, gold is similar to an asset that pays no income. The cash and carry and reverse cash and carry arguments, can then be used to show that

$$F_t = S_t(1 + r)$$

Now let's introduce a storage cost. A cost is nothing but a negative income. For an asset which pays a known income, we have shown that

$$F_t = S_t(1 + r) - I$$

where I is the future value of payouts from the asset. Let's denote the future value of storage costs by Z. Therefore

$$F_t = S_t(1 + r) - (-Z) = S_t(1 + r) + Z \tag{2.10}$$

We will illustrate the no-arbitrage pricing condition for gold, using a suitable example. Consider Example 2.6.

Example 2.6: Let the spot price of gold be \$1,800 per ounce and the rate of interest be 7.50% per half-yearly period. We will assume that storage costs are \$10 per ounce per six monthly period, payable at the end of the period and that forward contracts are available for delivery six months into the future. If so:

$$F_t = 1{,}800 \times (1.075) + 10 = 1{,}945$$

Now let's consider mispriced forward contracts and the strategies for exploiting them.

Case A

Consider the case where F_t = \$1,960. The contract is clearly overpriced. So to exploit this opportunity, a person can engage in cash and carry arbitrage. Consider the following strategy.

Borrow \$1,800 and buy one ounce of gold. Simultaneously, go short in a forward contract to sell the gold after six months at \$1,960. Six months later, when the gold is delivered, you will receive \$1,960 and will have to pay \$10 by way of storage costs. Thus your net inflow = \$1,950. The rate of return is:

$$\frac{(1{,}950 - 1{,}800)}{1{,}800} = 0.0833 \equiv 8.33\%$$

which is greater than the borrowing rate of 7.50%. So clearly, F_t cannot be greater than $S_t(1 + r) + Z$.

Case B

Let F_t = \$1,935. The contract is underpriced. Conventional reverse cash and carry arbitrage arguments will entail the use of the following strategy.

Short sell the gold at \$1,800 per ounce and simultaneously go long in a forward contract to buy at \$1,935. The effective borrowing rate is:

$$\frac{1{,}935 - 1{,}800}{1{,}800} = 0.075 \equiv 7.50\%$$

which is the same as the lending rate. Thus, although the contract is obviously underpriced, a conventional reverse cash and carry strategy does not yield a profit. For such a strategy to yield profits to the arbitrageur, the lender of the gold would have to pass on at least a part of the storage cost saved by him, which is \$10 in this case. Let's assume that the lender does pass on \$7.50 to the arbitrageur. If so, the arbitrageur's net outflow will be \$1,927.50, which means that the implied reverse repo rate is 7.0833%, which is less than the lending rate of 7.50%.

In practice however, it is not usually possible to sell short in such a way that, the person lending the asset actually passes on the storage costs saved to the short seller. So does it mean that F_t can be less than $S_t(1 + r) + Z$, for an investment asset like gold?

The answer is no. If F_t were to be less than $S_t(1 + r) + Z$, then the mispricing can be exploited by a person who already owns gold. Consider the following strategy. A person who owns gold, but does not require it for six months, can sell it in the spot market and invest the proceeds. He can also go long in a forward contract to re-acquire the gold at the end of six months.

When he sells the gold, he will receive \$1,800. This will yield $1{,}800 \times (1.075) = \$1{,}935$ at the end of six months. He will also have an additional \$10 with him, which represents the storage costs saved. After paying \$1,935 to re-acquire the asset, he will have \$10 with him, which represents an arbitrage profit.

The arguments that we have used above, represent a strategy known as *quasi-arbitrage*. The person who engages in such a strategy has not engaged in arbitrage in the conventional sense. Rather, he has liquidated his position in the asset and has employed a strategy which effectively ensures that he gets the asset back at the end of six months. In other words, it is as if he has effectively not parted with the asset. In the parlance of derivatives, we say that he has replaced an actual spot position with a *synthetic spot* position, or to put it differently he has *sold an asset without really selling it.*[4]

Thus quasi-arbitrage will help ensure that F_t cannot be less than

$$S_t(1 + r) + Z$$

Hence, to rule out both cash and carry arbitrage, as well as reverse cash and carry quasi-arbitrage, we require that

$$F_t = S_t(1 + r) + Z$$

2.11 Consumption Assets

Let's now consider the case of wheat. If

$$F_t > S_t(1 + r) + Z$$

then the resultant arbitrage opportunity can be exploited using a cash and carry strategy. But if

$$F_t < S_t(1 + r) + Z$$

then it may not be possible to make arbitrage profits. Conventional reverse cash and carry arbitrage may not be possible because short sales may not be feasible. Reverse cash

4 We will have more to say about quasi-arbitrage and synthetic positions, a little later.

and carry quasi arbitrage may also not be possible because the person who is holding the asset may be getting a convenience value.

Consequently, it may be the case that

$$F_t < S_t(1 + r) + Z$$

and that no one is able to exploit any opportunities for making arbitrage profits.

Assets such as wheat are usually consumption assets. In the case of such assets, all that we can say by way of a no-arbitrage pricing relationship is that

$$F_t \leq S_t(1 + r) + Z \tag{2.11}$$

The marginal convenience value Y is defined to be that value which satisfies the following equation, for convenience assets

$$F_t = S_t(1 + r) + Z - Y \tag{2.12}$$

The marginal convenience value is the lowest of the convenience values, as perceived by different market participants.[5]

2.12 Net Carry

Consider the case of an asset that pays a known income. The no-arbitrage pricing relationship for such assets, states that

$$F_t = S_t(1 + r) - I$$

This implies that

$$\frac{F_t}{S_t} = 1 + r - \frac{I}{S_t} \Rightarrow \frac{(F_t - S_t)}{S_t} = r - \frac{I}{S_t}$$

The *net carry* is defined as Interest minus the Future Value of Payouts, divided by the spot price of the asset. Therefore

$$\text{net carry} = \frac{(rS_t - I)}{S_t} = r - \frac{I}{S_t}. \tag{2.13}$$

5 Remember, as we said earlier, it is not necessary that everyone should have an identical convenience value.

Hence

$$\text{net carry} = \frac{(F_t - S_t)}{S_t} \Rightarrow F_t = S_t + (\text{net carry})S_t \tag{2.14}$$

If the net carry is positive, then the forward price will exceed the spot price, else it will be less than or equal to the spot price. In the case of physical commodities which are held for investment purposes, I = −Z, where Z represents the cost of storage. Therefore

$$\text{net carry} = r - \frac{-Z}{S_t} = r + \frac{Z}{S_t} \tag{2.15}$$

which is positive. Thus, the forward price for such commodities will be greater than the spot price.

However, in the case of consumption assets, where a convenience value is involved

$$F_t = S_t + (\text{net carry})S_t - Y \tag{2.16}$$

where Y is the convenience value. In this case, the relationship between the forward price and the spot price, would depend on the relative magnitudes of the net carry and the convenience value.

If Y = 0, we say that it is a *full carry* market, whereas if the convenience value is positive, we say that the market is not at full carry.

2.13 Backwardation and Contango

If the futures price exceeds the spot price or the price of the nearby futures contract is less than that of the more distant contract, then we say that there is a *contango* market. Whereas, if the futures price is less than the spot price or the price of the nearby futures contract is more than that of the distant contract, then we say that the market is in *backwardation*. Consider Example 2.7.

Example 2.7: The data given in Tables 2.1 and 2.2 represents hypothetical prices for corn. Case A, shown in Table 2.1, illustrates a backwardation market whereas Case B, shown in Table 2.2, is an illustration of a contango market. A particular commodity, need not continuously display the characteristics of either a backwardation or a contango market. That is, the market may switch from one mode to another.

Case A: Backwardation Market

Table 2.1: Depiction of a backwardation market.

Contract	Price
Spot	6.95
March Futures	6.82
May Futures	6.65
July Futures	6.30
September Futures	6.15

Case B: Contango Market

Table 2.2: Depiction of a contango market.

Contract	Price
Spot	6.75
March Futures	6.85
May Futures	6.95
July Futures	7.10
September Futures	7.25

What could be the possible reasons for a backwardation market in corn? Quite obviously, the market is not at full carry, implying that there is a convenience yield. In other words, reverse cash and carry arbitrage is not feasible.

The most likely reason for such a scenario, is that corn is in short supply. If so, people will not be willing to lend for the purpose of a short sale, or else indulge in quasi-arbitrage themselves. Under such circumstances, they may need it for fulfilling sale contracts entered into in advance or else for their own use. In practice it has been observed that markets tend to be in backwardation when spot prices are rising. And rising spot prices are an obvious indication of impending shortages.

For financial assets, the net carry can either be positive or negative, depending on the relationship between the financing cost, rS, and the future value of the payouts from the asset, I. If the financing cost were to exceed the value of the payouts, the net carry will be positive, and we will have a contango market. Otherwise, the net carry will be negative, which will reveal itself as a market in backwardation.

In the case of physical commodities, if the market is at full carry, then we will always have a contango market. However, if the market is not at full carry, then we may either have a backwardation or a contango market. If the net carry is greater than the convenience value, there will be a contango market, else the market will be in backwardation.

2.14 Delivery Options

As you have learnt by now, futures contracts allow for the delivery of the asset at any time within a stipulated time period. As we have explained earlier, delivery can commence before the cessation of trading in the futures contract and continue after it. The option as to when to deliver during this period, is given to the short. The question that naturally arises therefore is, should a given futures contract be assumed to expire at the beginning, middle or end of the delivery period?[6]

Let's consider a futures contract on a commodity, priced at F_t, and let S_t be the corresponding spot price of the asset. We will denote the continuously compounded rate of interest by r, and the continuously compounded storage cost rate by z. It should be noted that neither r nor z represent annualized rates.

The no-arbitrage condition for a futures contract is given by:

$$\begin{aligned} F_t &\leq S_t e^{(r+z)} \\ \Rightarrow F_t e^{y} &= S_t e^{(r+z)} \end{aligned} \tag{2.17}$$

where y is the convenience value.

We have chosen to model the convenience yield as a continuously compounded variable, to be consistent with our assumptions regarding the interest rate and the storage cost. It is legitimate, since the convenience yield is nothing but a measure of an implicit dividend, that will equate the LHS and the RHS.

Let's consider the expression

$$F_t = S_t e^{(r+z-y)} = S_t e^{[r-(y-z)]}$$

For an investor with a short position, (y−z) represents the net benefit from holding the asset, while r represents the cost of financing the asset, which is either an actual interest outflow or else an opportunity cost.

In a contango market, the futures price will be greater than the spot price. This implies that $r > (y - z)$. Thus, under such conditions, the financing cost is greater than the net benefit from holding on to the asset. In such circumstances therefore, the short would like to deliver the asset as early as possible. Thus, in a contango market, the rational response for the short would be to deliver the asset right at the commencement of the delivery period.

In a backwardation market however, the futures price will be less than the spot price. This implies that $r < (y - z)$. In this situation, the financing cost is less than the net benefit from holding on to the asset. Consequently, in these circumstances, the short would like to deliver the asset as late as possible. Thus, in such a market, the rational

6 See Hull (2004) for a similar argument.

response for the short would be to deliver at the very end of the prescribed delivery period.

Our cost benefit analysis has implications for the pricing of futures contracts. The normal practice is to denote the expiration date of the futures contract by a point in time which is typically represented as T. In practice, however, for commodities, the delivery period is an interval of time and not a point in time. In such cases therefore, the issue arises as to whether the value of T that is to be used for computing the no-arbitrage price should denote the start, the middle, or the end of the prescribed delivery period. From the above arguments, we can see that futures prices in a contango market ought to be calculated under the assumption that delivery will take place right at the outset, whereas while computing the price in a backwardation market, the logical assumption ought to be that delivery will take place at the end of the delivery period.

2.15 Synthetic Securities

Let's take another look at the cash and carry arbitrage argument. According to this strategy, if we buy the good in the spot market and simultaneously go short in a forward contract, it is as if we have gone long in a T-bill. Therefore

Spot − Forward[7] = Synthetic T-bill.

The terms can be repositioned to yield the following results:

- Spot − T-bill = Synthetic Forward.
- Forward + T-bill = Synthetic Spot.

Thus, if we have any two of the assets, we can artificially create the third.

2.16 Forward Prices Versus Futures Prices

In all the cases where we have derived the pricing relationships based on the no-arbitrage arguments, we have considered forward contracts and not futures contracts. This was because as we said at the outset, forward contracts are easier to analyze since they entail only one single cash flow at the end, whereas futures contracts are marked to market daily, and consequently involve intermediate cash flows.

It can be shown that when the risk-less rate of interest is a constant, and is the same for all maturities, then the forward price for a contract on a given asset for a specified delivery date, is the same as the futures price for a contract on the same asset, for the same delivery date. Therefore, under such conditions, the relationships that we have

7 The minus sign indicates a short position.

derived for the prices of forward contracts, are equally valid for the prices of futures contracts.

2.17 Stochastic Interest Rates

In real life, interest rates are stochastic and hence forward prices need not equal futures prices. Let's consider a situation where interest rates and futures prices are positively correlated. If the futures price rises, the interest rate will also be high. When the price rises, the long will gain and in this case, will be able to invest his gains at a higher rate of interest. Correspondingly, in such a scenario, the short will be financing his losses[8] at a higher rate. Conversely, if the futures price falls, the interest rate will be low. This is a situation where the long will lose and the short will gain. Thus the long will be financing his losses at a lower rate, while the short will be investing his gains at a lower rate.

An investor with a long forward position, will however not be affected by interest rate movements in the interim, for his position will not be marked to market. Hence, an investor with a long futures position is clearly better off under such circumstances. Extending the argument along similar lines, a person with a short futures position is worse off than a person who has gone short in a forward contract. Since a long futures position is more attractive than a long forward position, the person going long in the futures contract should pay more for this advantage. In other words, the investor going short in the futures contract should receive more for this disadvantage. Hence, the futures price will exceed the forward price, when futures prices and interest rates are positively correlated.

Similar logical reasoning can be used to demonstrate that if interest rates and futures prices are negatively correlated, then the futures price will be less than the forward price.[9] These results were rigorously derived by Cox, Ingersoll and Ross (1981).

The question naturally arises as to which are the markets in which we can observe the effects predicted above. Arditti (1996) gives two examples, namely gold and T-bonds. Let's assume that interest rates rise because of higher expected inflation. We are all aware that gold is widely perceived as a hedge against inflation. So gold prices will be expected to rise if inflation is expected to rise. Hence gold prices and interest rates should be positively correlated.

Interest rates on the other hand are inversely related to bond prices. So T-bond futures prices should be negatively correlated with interest rates. Consequently we would expect a gold futures contract to be worth more than a gold forward contract and a T-bond futures contract to be worth less than a T-bond forward contract.

8 It may either be in the form of an actual borrowing or as an opportunity cost.

9 Readers should reason this out and convince themselves.

However, just because we observe differences between futures and forward prices for a particular asset, we cannot conclude that it is due to a relationship between futures prices and interest rates. There could be other important factors at work. For instance, transactions costs could be different in the two markets. Also, futures contracts have a lower risk of default than forward contracts, due to the role of the clearinghouse and the marking to market mechanism. In addition, forward markets are usually less liquid than futures markets.

So in order to test the interest rate correlation hypothesis, we must look at a market where the other factors are insignificant. It has been argued that currency markets are fairly appropriate for this purpose.

2.18 Quasi-Arbitrage

The kind of arbitrage that we have discussed thus far, in connection with the cash and carry and reverse cash and carry strategies, is called *pure arbitrage*. Arbitrageurs, who engage in pure arbitrage, are forever on the lookout for mispriced securities and will exploit the profit opportunities till equilibrium is restored.

Quasi-arbitrage[10] is engaged in by investors who are not arbitrageurs in the conventional sense. The term refers to the use of cash and carry and reverse cash and carry techniques by investors, as alternative means of establishing a desired position in the market. For, as we have discussed in the section on synthetic securities, if we have two out of three securities, we can artificially take a position in the third.

We will illustrate this concept with the help of Example 2.8.

Example 2.8: Ralph Keating, is planning to make an investment in a risk-less security for six months. One course of action that is available is to directly invest in a risk-less asset such as a T-bill. The ask price for a six month T-bill with a face value of \$100,000, is \$98,875. The brokerage fee for an investment in bills with a face value of \$100 is 12.5 cents. So for a bill with a face value of \$100,000 Ralph will have to pay a commission of \$125. The total cost of acquisition is therefore \$99,000 and the corresponding rate of return is:

$$\frac{100{,}000 - 99{,}000}{99{,}000} \equiv 1.0101\%$$

Now let's consider an arbitrage strategy. Assume that ABC shares are available at a price of \$90.25 per share. Futures contracts on the stock, maturing after six months are available for \$91.50. A pure arbitrageur can borrow at the rate of 1.25% for six months. The brokerage fees payable in the market are as follows. For every share that is bought or sold in the stock market, a commission of 12.50 cents is payable. For a transaction in futures contracts, a fee of 5 cents is payable per share. Finally, we will assume that while borrowing funds, the pure arbitrageur has to pay 12.50 cents for every share. Thus, the rate of return for a pure arbitrageur if he engages in a cash and carry strategy is

10 For an elaborate discussion of quasi-arbitrage see Siegel and Siegel (1990).

$$\frac{F_t - (S_{a,t} + C)}{(S_{a_t} + C)} = \frac{91.50 - (90.25 + 0.125 + 0.05 + 0.125)}{(90.25 + 0.125 + 0.05 + 0.125)} \equiv 1.0491\%$$

which is less than the borrowing rate of 1.25%. So clearly a pure arbitrageur cannot profitably engage in cash and carry arbitrage.[11]

But in Ralph's case, instead of investing in T-bills, he can go long in the spot market and take a short position in the futures market, thereby creating an investment in a synthetic T-bill. His transaction costs are 12.5 cents for every share that he buys and five cents for every futures contract that he goes short in.[12] Consequently, his rate of return is

$$\frac{91.50 - (90.25 + 0.175)}{(90.25 + 0.175)} \equiv 1.1888\%$$

Thus, his rate of return if he follows this strategy, will be higher than what he would get if he were to invest in T-bills. Hence, a person like Ralph who is looking for a risk-free investment, would rather engage in a cash and carry strategy to buy synthetic T-bills. This is what we mean by quasi-arbitrage.

Notice certain key features inherent in the above argument. First, although pure arbitrage is not feasible, quasi-arbitrage is profitable. Second, a pure arbitrageur will compare the implied repo rate with the borrowing rate, whereas a person like Ralph, who is contemplating a quasi-arbitrage strategy, will compare the return from this strategy with his alternative lending rate.

Finally, there is one major issue that you must understand. A pure arbitrageur will exploit a perceived arbitrage opportunity till it vanishes.[13] A quasi-arbitrageur, is however, constrained by the amount of funds at his or her disposal. In the above example, if we assume that Ralph has \$1,000,000 with him, then his ability to buy synthetic T-bills will be restricted to this amount. If he wants to invest further in the cash and carry strategy, then he would have to borrow money, which would be tantamount to pure arbitrage and therefore will not be profitable. A consequence of this is that quasi-arbitrage opportunities are likely to persist longer than pure arbitrage opportunities, since each potential quasi-arbitrageur, faces his or her own funds constraint and hence, may not be able to exploit the opportunities for profit till they are completely eliminated.

2.19 Risk and Futures Prices

We shall now address the issue of the relationship between the current futures price and today's expectation of the future spot price? Let F_t be the current futures price. Let S_T be the spot price that is expected to prevail on day T, which is the expiration date

---

11 $S_{a,t}$, is the ask price in the spot market.

12 Notice, that unlike the pure arbitrageur, he does not have to borrow.

13 Remember that we have assumed that he can borrow or lend an unlimited amount of money.

of the contract. Notice that S_T is a random variable, and cannot therefore be observed today. Consequently, we can only have an expectation of it.

Telser (1958) and Gray (1961), argued that $F_t = E(S_T)$ and that therefore, $F_t = E(F_T)$, since at expiration, $F_T = S_T$. This is called the *unbiased expectations hypothesis* or the *no risk premium hypothesis*. It says that today's futures price is nothing but the market's expectation of the future spot price.

Keynes and Hicks however, argued that most hedgers are producers and hence will hedge by going short in futures. The reason why producers will go in for a short position, is because they are long in the spot market and consequently will be apprehensive that prices will fall. If the prices fall, such people will gain in the futures market.[14] This gain will help offset the loss made by them in the spot market.

If the hedgers take a short position in the futures market, they will require others to take a long position. Such people will obviously be speculators. In order to induce speculators, who by definition are taking risk, to go long in futures, they must be compensated by a risk premium or in other words, their expected gains must be positive. The expected gains will be positive for the longs only if the futures price is expected to rise. Therefore, according to the argument advanced by Keynes and Hicks, F_t should be less than $E(F_T)$, which means that F_t should be less than $E(S_T)$. This is called the theory of *normal backwardation*. According to this theory, hedgers buy insurance from speculators by transferring their unwanted risk. For this reason, speculators are entitled to an expected profit.

On the other hand, consider the case where the majority of hedgers take a long position in the futures market.[15] In such a situation, the speculators would have to take a short position, and must therefore be suitably compensated with a risk premium. Such speculators will get an expected gain, only if the futures prices are expected to fall. Thus F_t should be greater than $E(F_T)$, which means that F_t should be greater than $E(S_T)$. Such a situation is called *normal contango*.

2.19.1 The Systematic Risk Theory

We will now focus on another explanation that has been advanced to explain the relationship between the futures price and the expected future spot price. According to this viewpoint, holders of futures contracts bear systematic risk and therefore must be suitably compensated for it.[16] The expected return demanded by the holder of the futures

14 Remember, if the price declines, investors with a short position will gain.

15 This would be the case if they were short in the spot market.

16 Those of you who are familiar with modern portfolio theory and the Capital Asset Pricing Model, will be aware of the concept of *systematic or non-diversifiable or market risk* and the logic as to why this is the only risk that is priced.

contract should therefore, be reflected by a difference between the futures price and the expected future spot price.

We have seen from the spot-futures equivalence relationship that:

$$\text{Spot} - \text{T-bill} = \text{Synthetic Futures}$$

We know that T-bills are risk-less. Hence, the risk of a futures position is equal to the risk of the underlying asset. Thus, from the above relationship, we can deduce that the expected return from a long position in a futures position is equal to the expected return from a long position in the underlying asset less the risk-less rate of return.

Why is it that a futures contract has the same inherent risk as the underlying asset, but offers a lower expected rate of return to an investor who takes a long position? The reason is the following. In order to take a long position in the underlying asset, the investor has to make an investment that is equal in magnitude to its spot price. Such an investment, which is risky in nature, must obviously earn the risk-less rate of return plus a risk premium. Futures contracts, on the contrary do not require an investment on the part of an investor who is taking a long position. Thus, the expected return on a long futures position, should be equal to the risk premium on the underlying asset.

As per the Capital Asset Pricing Model (CAPM), the expected rate of return on asset i, which we will denote by $E(r_i)$, is given by:

$$E(r_i) = r_f + \beta_i[E(r_M) - r_f] \tag{2.18}$$

where r_f is the rate of return on a risk-less asset, and r_M is the rate of return on the market portfolio. β_i is a measure of the systematic risk of asset i.

Hence a long futures position should yield an expected return of:

$$\beta_i[E(r_M) - r_f] \tag{2.19}$$

It is obvious that if the underlying asset were to have a positive beta, then a long futures position will have a positive expected return. On the other hand, in the case of short futures positions, if the beta of the asset were to be positive, then the expected return will be negative.

From the systematic risk theory, we can also conclude that the 'unbiased expectations hypothesis', will be valid only if the underlying asset were to have a zero systematic risk.

2.20 Risks Inherent in Arbitrage

Thus far, we have presented cash and carry arbitrage and reverse cash and carry arbitrage strategies, as positions designed to earn cost-less risk-less profits. In practice, however, an arbitrageur who seeks to implement such strategies will have to confront a variety of risks.

Cash and carry arbitrage requires the investor to borrow at the risk-less rate of interest in order to acquire the underlying asset. In practice, such investors may be unable to borrow at an interest rate that remains constant for the duration for which the position is in place, and hence they may have to borrow for shorter periods and roll over the loan. Therefore, the risk faced by such arbitrageurs is that interest rates may rise after they have implemented the strategy. Such risk is referred to as *financing risk*.

Second, in the case of assets which are scheduled to make payouts during the life of the contract, the potential to make arbitrage profits is critically linked to the arbitrageur's ability to forecast the payouts. If the asset does not make payouts as forecasted, then the profits that are expected at the outset may not materialize. Such risk is referred to as *payout risk* or *dividend risk*.

It should be obvious to the reader that such risks are factors in the case of reverse cash and carry arbitrage strategies as well.

2.20.1 Risk Arbitrage

Financing risk and payout risk are inherent in arbitrage strategies. However, there is a third element of risk as well, which is confronted by arbitrageurs who take long positions in contracts which specify multiple grades of the underlying asset as suitable for delivery. As we have seen, in the case of such contracts, the option as to which grade to deliver is always given to the short. The short will obviously opt to deliver the grade that is the cheapest at the time of delivery. The issue is that this grade need not correspond to the grade which has been sold short by an arbitrageur at an earlier point in time, as part of a reverse cash and carry arbitrage operation. If the grade that is delivered by the short is different from what the long requires, then the arbitrageur will have to acquire the grade which was originally short sold by him. The grade received from the short as a part of the futures contract, will obviously have to be disposed off in the spot market. The net result is that the ex-post implied reverse repo rate for the arbitrageur could be higher than the ex-ante implied reverse repo rate, and may at times be even higher than the lending rate. If so, the realized profit may be less than anticipated, or in a worse situation the arbitrageur may end up with a net loss. Hence, reverse cash and carry arbitrage under such circumstances is fraught with danger, and is more appropriately termed as *risk arbitrage*.

Before we go on to analyze the additional risk in the case of a reverse cash and carry transaction, let's first consider a cash and carry transaction. Thus far, we have assumed the arbitrageur will take a spot-futures position in the ratio of 1:1. That is, if the futures contract is for 100 units of the underlying asset, he will short sell 100 units for every contract in which he goes long. However, while this is appropriate in the case of contracts which specify only one deliverable grade, the situation is different for cases where multiple deliverable grades have been specified, and a multiplicative price adjustment method has been prescribed. Assume that the arbitrageur goes long in one unit of grade

i of the asset. We will assume that multiple grades have been specified for delivery, and that a multiplicative price adjustment system is in operation. Let's denote the required short position as h futures contracts. When he delivers the asset at expiration, he will receive $a_i F_T$. The profit from marking to market will be $h(F_t - F_T)$. For the strategy to be risk-less, we require that

$$a_i F_T + h(F_t - F_T) = a_i F_t$$
$$\Rightarrow h = a_i \quad (2.20)$$

Thus the appropriate number of futures contracts is equal to the price adjustment factor of the grade in which the arbitrageur has taken a long position. It should be noted that if an additive system of price adjustment were to be used, then the arbitrageur would require a spot futures position of 1:1. This can be demonstrated as follows:

$$F_T + a_i + h(F_t - F_T) = F_t + a_i \Rightarrow h = 1$$

The very fact that a cash and carry arbitrage strategy was initiated, signifies that the ex-ante implied repo rate is greater than the borrowing rate. That is:

$$\frac{a_i F_t - S_{i,t}}{S_{i,t}} > r \quad (2.21)$$

At the point of expiration of the futures contract, there are two possibilities. It may be the case that grade i is the cheapest to deliver grade. If so, the arbitrageur will deliver it, and his realized implied repo rate will be equal to what he has been anticipating from the very outset. However, what if, some other grade, j, has become the cheapest to deliver? If this were to be the case, the arbitrageur can sell the unit of grade i in his possession at its prevailing spot price, and acquire a_i units of grade j to deliver under the futures contract.[17]

The cash inflow will be:

$$S_{i,T} + a_i \times (a_j F_T) + a_i(F_t - F_T)$$

This represents the inflow from three sources, namely, the cash flow from the sale of grade i in the spot market, the proceeds from the delivery of grade j under the futures contract, and the cumulative profit from the marking to market mechanism. The cash outflow, on account of the acquisition of grade j will be $a_i S_{j,T}$. The net inflow will therefore be:

17 We have used the symbol $S_{i,t}$ to denote the spot price of the i th asset at time t, and $S_{i,T}$ to denote its spot price at time T. Similarly, F_t and F_T denote the futures prices at times t and T respectively.

$$
\begin{aligned}
S_{i,T} &+ a_i \times (a_j F_T) + a_i(F_t - F_T) - a_i S_{j,T} \\
&= S_{i,T} + a_i S_{j,T} + a_i(F_t - F_T) - a_i S_{j,T} \\
&= a_i F_t + a_i \left[\frac{S_{i,T}}{a_i} - \frac{S_{j,T}}{a_j} \right] \\
&> a_i F_t
\end{aligned} \tag{2.22}
$$

because if grade j is the cheapest to deliver by assumption, then its delivery adjusted spot price $\frac{S_{j,T}}{a_j}$ will be lower than that of grade i, and will be equal to the futures price, F_T. Thus, we conclude that if a cash and carry arbitrage strategy is initiated because it looks profitable at the outset, it can only lead to a greater profit, if not the anticipated profit, at the time of expiration. In other words, the ex-post implied repo rate will be greater than or equal to the ex-ante implied repo rate, which by assumption was greater than the borrowing rate. Hence, there is no risk as such.

Now let's turn our attention to a reverse cash and carry strategy. The very fact that such a strategy is being initiated, implies that:

$$
\frac{a_i F_t - S_{i,t}}{S_{i,t}} < r \tag{2.23}
$$

If the short were to deliver grade i, the grade which has been short sold by the arbitrageur, at the end, then the anticipated arbitrage profit will be realized. However, what if the arbitrageur is forced to take delivery of another grade, j, because the short finds that it is the cheapest to deliver. If so, the arbitrageur would have to sell this grade in the spot market and acquire grade i at its prevailing spot price to cover his short position.

The outflow will be:

$$
a_i(a_j F_T) + S_{i,T}
$$

This represents the outflow on account of taking delivery under the futures contract, and the cost on account of the covering of the initial short position. The inflow will be:

$$
a_i S_{j,T} + a_i(F_T - F_t)
$$

This represents the cash flow on account of the sale of grade j, as well as the cumulative cash flow due to marking to market.

The net outflow is

$$
\begin{aligned}
a_i(a_j F_T) &+ S_{i,T} - a_i S_{j,T} - a_i(F_T - F_t) \\
&= a_i S_{j,T} + S_{i,T} - a_i S_{j,T} - a_i(F_T - F_t) \\
&= a_i F_t + a_i \left[\frac{S_{i,T}}{a_i} - \frac{S_{j,T}}{a_j} \right] \\
&> a_i F_t
\end{aligned} \tag{2.24}
$$

Consequently, the ex-post implied reverse repo Rate could be greater than the ex-ante implied reverse repo rate, and perhaps even greater than the lending rate. Therefore, to reiterate, what looked like a profitable arbitrage opportunity may end up as a reduced arbitrage profit or perhaps even as a loss. Thus arbitrage, under such circumstances, is accompanied by an additional element of risk.

The same logic holds for contracts on assets where multiple grades are permissible for delivery, but an additive system of price adjustment is used. We will consider the case of cash and carry arbitrage. The extension to reverse cash and carry arbitrage is straightforward.

We know that if an additive price adjustment mechanism is in place, then an arbitrageur will use a spot futures ratio of 1:1. Once again, the very fact that a cash and carry strategy has been implemented signifies that the implied repo rate is greater than the borrowing rate. That is

$$\frac{F_t + a_i - S_{i,t}}{S_{i,t}} > r$$

If at expiration, a different grade, grade j, has become the cheapest to deliver, then the arbitrageur will sell the unit of grade i in his possession and will acquire a unit of grade j to satisfy his delivery obligations. The inflow will be

$$S_{i,T} + F_T + a_j + (F_t - F_T)$$

The outflow will be $S_{j,T}$. The net inflow will therefore be

$$\begin{aligned} & S_{i,T} + F_T + a_j + (F_t - F_T) - S_{j,T} \\ & \quad = S_{i,T} - a_i + F_t + a_i - (S_{j,T} - a_j) \\ & \quad = F_t + a_i + [(S_{i,T} - a_i) - (S_{j,T} - a_j)] \\ & \quad > F_t + a_i \end{aligned} \tag{2.25}$$

This is because, since grade j by assumption is the cheapest to deliver grade, $S_{j,T} - a_j < S_{i,T} - a_i \forall i$. Hence, if a cash and carry strategy were to be initiated, the ex-post implied repo rate will be greater than or equal to the ex-ante implied repo rate, which as per our assumption was greater than the borrowing rate. This is shown in Example 2.9.

Example 2.9: Consider a futures contract on corn, with six months till expiration. The contract size is 5,000 bushels. Two grades, that is No. 1 and No. 2, are eligible for delivery. The adjustment factor is 0.15 for No. 1 and 0.25 for No. 2, and the additive system of price adjustment is applicable. The spot price of No. 1 is $5.00 per bushel, and it is the cheapest to deliver currently. The prevailing futures price is $5.25 per bushel and the risk-less borrowing rate is 6% per six months.

The ex-ante implied repo rate for a cash and carry strategy is:

$$\frac{5.25 + 0.15 - 5.00}{5.00} = 0.08 \equiv 8\%$$

Since this is greater than the borrowing rate, cash and carry arbitrage is profitable. Fred Finley, an arbitrageur in Kansas City, decides to implement such a strategy by buying 5,000 bushels of corn and going short in one futures contract.

Now assume that six months hence, the spot price of No. 1 is \$5.75 per bushel, whereas that of No. 2 is \$5.60. The respective delivery adjusted spot prices are 5.60 and 5.35. Obviously No. 2 is the cheapest to deliver grade, and consequently the futures price will be equal to its delivery adjusted spot price of \$5.35.

Fred, who is holding 5,000 bushels of No. 1, will sell it in the spot market. He will acquire 5,000 bushels of No. 2 from the spot market and will deliver it to fulfill his obligation as per the futures contract. His net cash flow may be derived as follows.

Inflow from the spot market on account of the sale of No. 1 = 5,000 × 5.75 = \$28,750.

Cost of acquisition in the spot market of No. 2 = 5,000 × 5.60 = \$28,000.

Inflow from delivery under the futures contract = 5,000 × (5.35 + 0.25) = \$28,000.

Profit/loss from the futures market = 5,000 × (5.25 − 5.35) = −\$ 500.

Net inflow/outflow = 28,750 + 28,000 − 28,000 − 500 = \$28,250.

The ex-post implied repo rate is:

$$\frac{28{,}250 - 25{,}000}{25{,}000} = 0.13 \equiv 13\%$$

Thus the cash and carry strategy has turned out to be more profitable than anticipated.

2.20.2 Multiple Deliverable Grades and the No-arbitrage Futures Price Prior to Expiration

In the case of multiple deliverable grades, cash and carry arbitrage can be initiated with any of the allowable grades. Thus, each grade will have its own implied repo rate. Arbitrage activities will continue till there is no profit to be made from any of the deliverable grades. The cheapest to deliver grade prior to expiration will be the one that maximizes the IRR, which, in an arbitrage free setting will just equal the borrowing rate. If we call this grade, grade i then

$$\frac{F_t + a_i - S_{i,t}}{S_{i,t}} = r$$

$$\Rightarrow F_t = S_{i,t}(1 + r) - a_i \tag{2.26}$$

We will define $S_{i,t}(1 + r)$ as the no-arbitrage futures price. Thus the futures price prior to expiration will be equal to the delivery-adjusted no-arbitrage futures price of the cheapest to deliver grade.

In the case of a multiplicative system of adjustment, the equivalent condition would be

$$\frac{a_i F_t - S_{i,t}}{S_{i,t}} = r$$
$$\Rightarrow F_t = \frac{S_{i,t}(1+r)}{a_i} \tag{2.27}$$

Suggestions for Further Reading

Hull, J. *Fundamentals of Futures and Options Markets*. Prentice Hall, 2004.
Kolb, R.W. *Futures, Options, & Swaps*. Blackwell, 2003.
Siegel, D.R. and D.F. Siegel *Futures Markets*. The Dryden Press, 1990.

References

Arditti, F.D. *Derivatives*. Harvard Business School Press (1996).
Cox, J.C., J.E. Ingersoll, and S.A. Ross *The Relation Between Forward Prices and Futures Prices. Journal of Financial Economics, Vol. 9 (December 1981).*
Gray, R.W. *The Search for a Risk Premium. Journal of Political Economy, Vol. 69 (June 1961).*
Telser, L.G. *Futures Trading and the Storage of Cotton and Wheat. Journal of Political Economy, Vol. 66 (June 1958).*

Chapter 3
Hedging and Speculation

3.1 Introduction

Hedgers, by definition, are traders who seek to protect themselves from unfavourable movements in the price of an asset in which they have a commercial interest. People who seek to hedge would have already assumed a position in the underlying asset, before they attempt to implement a hedging strategy. One possibility is that the underlying asset may already be in their possession, in which case they would be said to have a long position in the spot market. In such cases, their uneasiness about unfavourable price movements, would stem from the fact that the price of the asset may decline subsequently. The other possibility is that they may have made a commitment to buy the underlying asset. Such investors would be said to have a established a short position in the spot market, and their desire to hedge may be attributed to their concern that the price of the asset may rise subsequently. In both situations, a desire to hedge demonstrates a desire on the part of the trader to avoid risk. Thus, hedgers are traders who are uncomfortable facing a risk exposure and would like to minimize if not totally eliminate uncertainty.

A short position in an asset, is by definition a commitment to acquire an asset at a future point in time, and need not always be tantamount to a short sale. As we have seen earlier, a short sale entails the borrowing of an asset by the trader in order to sell it. Quite obviously the lender of the asset would expect that the asset will be bought back and returned at a future point in time. However, the definition of a short position is broader in scope. Consider the case of an Indian company which has imported goods from Germany and is required to pay the invoice amount in euros at the end of a stated credit period. The company, being committed to acquire the euros at a future point in time, is exposed to the risk of an appreciating euro. That is, it faces the risk that the rupee price of the euro may increase by the time the foreign currency is acquired. Therefore, like the short seller, a company in such a predicament would also be worried by the specter of a rise in the price of the underlying asset. Thus, in a more general manner of speaking, a short position in an asset connotes a commitment to buy it at a future point in time, at a price that will not be revealed until the time of acquisition.

A hedging transaction helps reduce or under ideal circumstances, eliminate the price risk that an investor faces from either being long in the spot market or from being short in the spot market. The term *price risk* refers to the risk that prices will move in an adverse direction.

Thus, a hedger will simultaneously take positions in the spot as well as the futures markets. If he is long in the spot market, then he will go short in the futures market and vice versa. The main concern for a hedger is the direction of change in the price difference between the spot and futures markets. The issue is, will one's profit / loss

https://doi.org/10.1515/9783110746662-003

in the spot market, be more or less than the loss / profit in the futures market. As we shall see shortly, except in the rare case of a perfect hedge, risk cannot be completely eliminated. What a hedger does is to substitute the large and unpredictable price risk due to an open long or short position in the spot market, with a more acceptable risk of variation in the price difference between the spot price and the corresponding futures price. This price difference, called the *basis*, is the key variable of interest in hedging and we will discuss it in detail shortly.

There are two types of hedges that are possible. One is a *short hedge* or a *selling hedge* while the other is a *long hedge* or a *buying hedge*. We will discuss each one of them with the help of suitable examples.

3.2 A Selling Hedge

A short hedge requires the investor to take a short position in the futures market. A person may go in for a short hedge if he already has the asset in his possession and expects to sell it at some time in the future. Such a hedge is called an *inventory hedge*.

It works as follows. If the price in the spot market were to decline, he can still sell at the original futures price, since the other party is under an obligation to buy at this price. We will illustrate this with the help of Example 3.1.

Example 3.1: Norman Davis, a corn farmer in Iowa knows that he will have 2,500,000 bushels to sell after a month. His worry is that there may be a glut in the market, as a consequence of which the spot price at the time of sale may be substantially lower than what he is anticipating right now. We know that futures contracts on corn are available at the CME Group, and that each contract is for 5,000 bushels. If the current futures price is \$5.25 per bushel, then by going short in 500 contracts, Norman can lock in a price of \$13,125,000 for the sale that he expects to make after a month. This amount is guaranteed to be received, and is independent of the actual price of corn that is likely to prevail in the spot market one month hence. Notice that while Norman is protected against a falling market, he will be unable to take advantage of the market conditions if the price of corn were to increase, which may perhaps be due to the fact that the overall harvest was less plentiful than anticipated. This, as we will discuss in more detail shortly, is a feature of hedges implemented using futures contracts.

Short hedges can also be used by people who do not own the asset at the time of initiating the hedge but know that it will be in their possession at some time in the future. Since it is taken out in anticipation of a future event, this type of a hedge is also known as an *anticipatory hedge*. Such a hedge, is described in Example 3.2.

Example 3.2: Take the case of a company which has exported goods from India to France and knows that it will be paid in euros after 60 days. Its worry would be that the rupee may appreciate in the interim, or in other words that the rupee price of the euro may decline. Such a party may also hedge its risk by entering into a short position in a futures or a forward contract expiring after 60 days. This kind of a selling hedge is in anticipation of a future event, for the euros are not currently in stock but are expected to arrive in 60 days, and consequently is termed as an 'anticipatory hedge'.

3.3 A Buying Hedge

A long hedge requires the hedger to take a long position in the futures market. A person who needs to acquire an asset in the future and is concerned that the price will rise, will go in for such a hedge. This is another type of an anticipatory hedge. If the spot price were to rise subsequently, he can still buy at the original futures price since the other party is under an obligation to sell at this price. This is illustrated in Example 3.3.

Example 3.3: Kroger and Company has imported fruit juice worth 500,000 AUD from Golden Circle in Sydney, and is required to pay the counter-party after two months. Its worry would be that the US dollar may depreciate by then, or in other words, that the price per Australian dollar may go up. Currency futures contracts on the Australian dollar are available on the CME Group with a contract size of 100,000 AUD. The ask price for a contract, which is the relevant price for a long hedger is currently 0.6500.

If Kroger were to take a long position in five futures contracts, they can lock in a payable of $325,000.

3.4 Options and Hedging

Futures contracts are not the only derivative instruments that are suitable for hedging. Both call and put options can also be used for hedging. Call options give the holder of the option, the right to acquire the underlying asset at the exercise price. Thus, an investor with a short position in the underlying asset can protect himself against an upward movement in the spot price by buying a call. If the spot price of the underlying asset at the time of its acquisition were to exceed the exercise price, the investor can exercise the call and acquire the asset at the exercise price. However, while the option protects such a hedger against an upward price movement, it does not preclude him from taking advantage of a price decline. For, if the spot price at the time of acquisition of the asset is lower than the exercise price, the investor can simply forget the option and acquire the asset in the spot market. This is feasible, for the option confers a right and does not impose an obligation. We will illustrate this with the help of Example 3.4.

Example 3.4: Assume that Kroger, which has imported fruit juice from Australia, and consequently has a payable denominated in AUD, has bought 50 call options contracts on the Australian Dollar with an exercise price of $0.6500, where each options contract is for 10,000 AUD.

If the spot rate of exchange after two months were to be greater than $0.6500 per AUD, the company can exercise the contracts and acquire 500,000 AUD by paying $325,000. However, unlike futures contracts, which if used for hedging, entail a commitment to buy at this price, options contracts give a choice to the hedger. For, if the spot rate after two months were to be less than $0.6500 per AUD, say $0.6000 per AUD, then the required foreign currency can be bought in the spot market for a consideration of $300,000, which represents a saving of $25,000. To reiterate, this is feasible because the option confers a right and does not impose an obligation.

Put options too can be used for hedging. Consider an individual who has a long position in the underlying asset, and is consequently perturbed by the possibility of a price decline. A put option by definition gives the holder the right to sell the underlying asset at the exercise price. Consequently, if the spot price of the underlying asset were to fall and reach a level below the exercise price at the time of sale, the option can be exercised and the long position can be unwound at the exercise price. It must be remembered that a put too, like a call, confers a right on the holder. Consequently, if the spot price at the time of sale were to be higher than the exercise price, the hedger can simply allow the option to expire unexercised and dispose off the underlying asset in the spot market. We will illustrate this with the help of Example 3.5.

Example 3.5: Charles, a trader based in Chicago, owns 10,000 shares of LKP, and has bought 100 put options contracts on the stock with an exercise price of $45. Each contract is for 100 shares. Assume that Charles has an investment horizon of one month.

If the spot price of LKP after a month were to be less than $45 per share, then he can exercise the options and deliver the shares for a total consideration of $450,000. However, if the spot price at that point in time were to be more than $45 per share, say $50, then the options contracts need not be exercised. If the options are scheduled to expire at that time, then they can be allowed to do so. Else Charles can offset them by taking a counter-position at the prevailing premium. In the second instance, the effective proceeds received by him per share will be greater than the assumed spot price of $50.

3.5 Futures or Options

Futures contracts and options contracts, as we have just seen, both facilitate hedging. However they work differently, and hence cannot be said to be substitutes for each other.

Let's take the case of an investor who has a long position in the underlying asset and is contemplating the initiation of a hedge using derivative securities. If he were to use a futures contract, he would need to take a short position. On the other hand, if he were to use options, he would have to acquire a put option contract. A futures hedge would lock in a selling price for the underlying asset. Since the contract imposes an obligation on the investor he has no choice but to sell at the delivery price of the contract. Consequently, while he is protected from losses if the price of the asset were to decline subsequently, he will not be in a position to benefit from a price increase, if the price were to surge forward in the spot market. A hedging strategy using put options would however work differently. If the spot price at the time of sale were to exceed the exercise price, the asset can be sold in the spot market after allowing the options contract to expire. However, if the spot price were to have declined below the exercise price of the option, the option can be exercised and the asset can be sold at the spot price.

Hedging strategies implemented by traders with short positions in the underlying asset, can also be undertaken using futures or options. A futures hedge would entail the assumption of a long position in a futures contract. This will lock in a value for the purchase price of the asset. Thus, while the hedger would be protected from a subsequent price increase in the value of the asset, he would be precluded from taking advantage of a declining market, for he is under an obligation to buy at the original futures price. An options hedge in this case, would entail the acquisition of a call option, and would work differently. If the price of the underlying asset at the time of acquisition were to exceed the exercise price of the option, the call can be exercised and the asset can be acquired at the strike price. Thus, the maximum price payable is the exercise price of the option. On the contrary, if the price were to fall subsequently, the option can be allowed to expire and the asset can be acquired in the spot market at a price which by assumption is lower than the strike price.

Thus, futures contracts lock in the price at which an investor with a long position can sell the underlying asset, or the price at which an investor with a short position can acquire the same. However, the hedger will be unable to benefit from favourable price movements in either case. An options contract however, imposes a floor on the price at which a hedger with a long spot position can sell, and a ceiling at which an investor with a short spot position can buy.[1] Thus, if options were to be used for hedging, the hedger is very much in a position to take advantage of a favourable price movement.

Now you may wonder that if options give protection to the hedger on one side, while permitting him to take advantage of favorable price movements in the other direction, why would anyone want to use futures contracts for hedging? The rationale is as follows.

Futures contracts do not entail the payment of a price or a premium by an investor, irrespective of whether he is taking a long or a short position. Traders do have to post margins. But, a margin deposit, it must be remembered, is a performance guarantee and not a cost. Thus, the initial cost of a hedging strategy using futures contracts is nil, except of course for transactions related expenses such as brokerage fees.

However, options contracts require the payment of an option price at the outset by the buyer. Unlike a margin deposit, an option premium is an actual cost or expense and is non-refundable.

Thus, an investor who is contemplating the use of derivative securities as a part of a hedging strategy, has a choice. If he were to use a futures contract, he need not pay at the outset. However, the contract is inflexible in the sense that it locks in a price at which

1 Call options lock in a maximum purchase price, while put options lock in a minimum sale price.

he can buy or sell the underlying asset. On the other hand, if he were to use an options contract for hedging, a price would have to be paid. In this case, if the price of the underlying asset were to move in an unfavourable direction, the option can be exercised and a transaction can be effected at the exercise price. Else, if the price were to move in favor of the hedger, the option need not be exercised and a transaction can be undertaken at the prevailing spot price. It should be obvious from this line of reasoning that futures and options are not interchangeable instruments from the standpoint of hedging. The choice of the instrument would therefore depend on the personal preferences of the individual who is seeking to hedge.

Example 3.6 illustrates why a hedging strategy using futures contracts will not dominate a strategy using options and vice versa. The word *dominance* in this context means having superiority under every conceivable outcome.

Example 3.6: Let's consider the case of Kroger, which has a payable of 500,000 AUD.

The exchange rate for a two month futures contract is 0.6500 USD per AUD.[2] Call options with two months to expiration and an exercise price of 0.6500 AUD-USD are available at a premium of 0.015 USD or at 1.5 cents.

Let's first consider a hedge using futures contracts. Since Kroger has a payable in AUD it requires a long position. If the company goes long in 5 futures contracts written on Australian dollars, it is guaranteed a U.S. dollar outflow of:

$$500{,}000 \times 0.6500 = \$325{,}000$$

irrespective of the spot exchange rate prevailing at expiration.

Now let's see the difference if call options contracts were to be used for hedging. If we assume that contracts with an exercise price equal to the delivery price of the futures contracts are used, the payable in U.S. dollars will be

$$500{,}000 \times 0.6500 + 500{,}000 \times 0.015 = 325{,}000 + 7{,}500 = \$332{,}500$$

if the options are exercised, that is, the spot rate at expiration is greater than 0.6500 AUD-USD.

However, if the spot rate at expiration, S_T, were to be less than 0.6500 AUD-USD, then the firm will choose to acquire the Australian currency in the spot market, and will allow the call options to expire. In this case, it will have to pay

$$500{,}000 S_T + 7{,}500$$

If the spot exchange rate at the point of expiration of the derivative contracts were to be 0.6350 AUD-USD, then the consequences for the firm will be the same irrespective of whether it had chosen futures or options for hedging. This point of indifference can be computed by equating the outflows in both cases. That is:

$$325{,}000 = 500{,}000 S^*_T + 7{,}500 \Rightarrow S^*_T = 0.6350$$

2 The market practice is to show this as AUD-USD or AUD/USD.

If the terminal exchange rate were to be lower, then the options hedge would yield a superior outcome. However, for values of S_T greater than 0.6350 AUD-USD, the payable in terms of U.S. dollars would be less if a futures contract were to have been used for hedging.

Hence, it cannot be categorically stated that a futures hedge dominates an options hedge or vice versa. Market participants will have differing perceptions about what the spot rate is likely to be at the time of expiration of the derivative contracts. Hence, while some parties may be inclined to use options contracts for hedging, others may well prefer to use futures contracts.

3.6 Ex-post Regret

An investor who uses futures or options for hedging, may end up regretting his decision afterwards. Take the case of Kroger. If they were to have used futures contracts for hedging, they would have locked in a payable of $325,000 at the rate of $0.6500 AUD-USD. If the spot exchange rate at the end turns out to be greater than $0.6500 AUD-USD, or in other words, if the U.S. dollar depreciates, then their decision to hedge would be vindicated, for if they had chosen not to hedge, they would have ended up paying more in terms of the home currency.

However, if the dollar were to appreciate, which would mean a spot rate of less than $0.6500, then their decision to hedge would certainly be perceived as unwise. This is because they could have bought the Australian currency at a lower cost, had they decided to stay unhedged.

A priori, a party like Kroger would not know whether the price of what they are seeking to acquire, will increase or decrease. So if they were to be risk averse, that is, if they were to be uncomfortable with the prospect of a depreciating home currency in this case, then they may very well decide to hedge, despite the possibility that their decision may turn out to be unsound, when an ex-post analysis is undertaken.

Thus, traders will hedge if they are uncomfortable leaving their price exposure open, despite the specter of ex-post regret. As Parameswaran and Hegde (2007) point out, *"Hindsight as they say is a 'Perfect Science'. A normal individual cannot be expected to be prescient, and if he were, he certainly would not need derivatives in order to hedge"*.

While futures hedges can lead to ex-post regret, so can hedges that are implemented using options contracts. Let's consider the case where Kroger decides to hedge using call options with an exercise price of 0.6500 USD/AUD. The payable in terms of dollars would be

$$332{,}500 \text{ if } S_T \geq 0.6500$$

and

$$500{,}000S_T + 7{,}500 \text{ if } S_T \leq 0.6500$$

The payoff for an unhedged position would be:

$$500{,}000S_T$$

It can be demonstrated that for values of S_T less than 0.6650 USD/AUD, it would have been better if Kroger had chosen to stay unhedged. This cutoff value can be derived by equating the payoffs in the two cases.

$$332{,}500 = 500{,}000S_T \Rightarrow S_T = 0.6650$$

Once again the party cannot exactly predict the future exchange rate, which in fact is the very reason why it is contemplating a hedge. Consequently, the potential for ex-post regret is very much a factor for a hedged position that has been implemented using options contracts.

3.7 Cash versus Delivery Settlement

The above discussions have assumed that the futures contracts are settled by delivery. The reader may wonder whether our conclusions would be different if the contracts were to be cash settled. We will now demonstrate that our inferences are valid irrespective of how the contracts are settled.

Before we proceed further let's define the following variables which will be used in the ensuing discussion. Additional variables will be defined when required.

3.7.1 Notation

- T ≡ time of expiration of the futures contract used for hedging.
- t ≡ time the hedge is initiated.
- t^* ≡ time the hedge is closed out. t^* will be before T or equal to it.
- S_t ≡ spot price at the time the hedge is initiated.
- F_t ≡ futures price at the time the hedge is initiated.
- S_T ≡ spot price at the time of expiration of the contract.
- F_T ≡ futures price at the time of expiration of the contract.
- S_{t*} ≡ spot price at the time the hedge is lifted.
- F_{t*} ≡ futures price at the time the hedge is lifted.
- Q ≡ quantity of the asset that is being hedged.
- Q_f ≡ quantity of the asset, underlying the futures position that is taken.

- $b_t \equiv$ basis at the time the hedge is initiated.
- $b_T \equiv$ basis at the time of expiration of the contract.
- $b_{t*} \equiv$ basis at the time the hedge is lifted.
- $\pi \equiv$ profit

In the case of hedges created using futures contracts, the effective price that is locked in per unit of the underlying asset will be equal to the futures price prevailing at the time of initiation of the futures position. This is true for both long as well as short hedges, and is irrespective of whether the contract is delivery settled or cash settled.

Consider the case of a short hedge. If the contract is cash settled, the total profit from marking to market would be $F_t - F_T$. The underlying asset would have to be sold in the spot market at a price of S_T. The overall cash inflow will be

$$S_T + (F_t - F_T) = F_t$$

because, as we have seen earlier, at expiration the spot price must be equal to the futures price to preclude arbitrage. Notice, that we have added the profit from the futures position to the terminal spot price, in order to determine the effective inflow. This is because if the cash flow from marking to market is a positive number, that is, it actually is a profit, then it will lead to a higher effective inflow. Else if it is a negative number, or in other words is a loss, then it will lead to a lower effective inflow. Let's consider Example 3.7.

Example 3.7: Take the case of Norman Davis who went short in 500 contracts on corn. The delivery price was \$5.25. Assume that the spot price of corn at the time of expiration is \$5.40. The cumulative profit from marking to market is:

$$500 \times 5{,}000 \times (5.25 - 5.40) = -\$\,375{,}000$$

The sale proceeds is the spot market will be:

$$500 \times 5{,}000 \times 5.40 = \$13{,}500{,}000$$

The effective amount received for 2,500,000 bushels of corn is therefore:

$$13{,}500{,}000 - 375{,}000 = \$13{,}125{,}000$$

which amounts to \$5.25 per bushel, which is the initial futures price.

The same is true for a futures based long hedge. If the contract were to be cash settled, the hedger's cumulative profit from marking to market will be $F_T - F_t$. The underlying asset would have to be acquired in the spot market at a price of S_T. The overall cash outflow will be

$$-S_T + (F_T - F_t) = -F_t$$

Once again the profit from the futures position has been added to the outflow in the spot market in order to determine the effective outflow. This is because a profit, or an inflow from the futures market, will reduce the effective outflow, whereas a loss, or an outflow from the futures market, will increase the effective outflow. Let's take a look at Example 3.8.

Example 3.8: Take the case of Kroger which went long in 50 futures contracts at a price of $0.6500 per AUD. Assume that the exchange rate at expiration is $0.6750 per AUD. The cumulative profit from marking to market will be

$$50 \times 10{,}000 \times (0.6750 - 0.6500) = \$12{,}500$$

The outflow on account of the spot purchase will be:

$$500{,}000 \times 0.6750 = \$337{,}500$$

The effective outflow is therefore:

$$337{,}500 - 12{,}500 = \$325{,}000$$

which corresponds to the delivery price of 0.6500.

3.8 A Perfect Hedge

A perfect hedge is defined as one which locks in a price for the hedger with absolute certainty. If the hedge were to be perfect, a party with a long spot position would face no uncertainty with regard to his sale price, and nor will a trader with a short spot position, face any risk with respect to his cost of acquisition. In the illustrations above, Norman Davis was able to lock in a selling price of $5.25 per bushel of corn, while Kroger was able to lock in a rate of $0.6500 per AUD as its cost of acquisition of Australian dollars. Consequently, both these hedges are perfect in nature. Thus, if a hedge were to be perfect, the hedger can transform a risky spot position into a risk-free position.

3.8.1 Necessary Conditions

If a hedge is to be perfect, then the following conditions must hold.

1. The date of termination of the hedge, or in other words, the date on which the hedger wishes to buy or sell the underlying asset must coincide with the date of expiration of the futures contract that is being used for hedging.
2. The number of units of the underlying asset sought to be bought or sold by the hedger, must be an integer multiple of the contract size.
3. Futures contracts must be available on the commodity which the hedger is seeking to buy or to sell.

3.8.2 Importance of Condition-1

We will now show why it is important that the date on which the asset is bought or sold be the same as the expiration date of the futures contract, if the hedge is to be perfect. For ease of exposition, we will assume that the futures contract specifies a single delivery date.

Consider the case of a short hedger, who is desirous of selling his goods prior to the date of expiration of the futures contract. That is, he wishes to sell on day t^*, where $t < t^* < T$. Quite obviously, since the futures contract is no longer required, it would have to be offset on that day. The underlying asset will have to be disposed off in the spot market.

The cumulative profit from the short futures position due to marking to market will be $F_t - F_{t^*}$. The inflow from the spot market will be S_{t^*}. Thus the effective inflow on account of the sale transaction will be:

$$S_{t^*} + (F_t - F_{t^*}) = F_t + (S_{t^*} - F_{t^*}) \tag{3.1}$$

If the date of sale were to coincide with the contract's expiration date, that is, if t^* were to be the same as T, then S_{t^*} would be equal to F_{t^*}, due to the spot-futures convergence condition, and so the effective price received would be F_t. In other words, in such a situation, the hedge would be perfect for there would be no uncertainty regarding the effective sale price. However, if t^* were to be prior to the expiration of the futures contract, F_{t^*} will usually not be equal to S_{t^*}. In such a situation, the effective price received would depend on both F_{t^*}, the terminal futures price, and S_{t^*}, the terminal spot price. Therefore, since these are unknown variables until the end, there will always be uncertainty regarding the effective price that the hedger is likely to receive.

A similar line of argument can be advanced for long hedges. If the asset were to be bought on day t^* and the futures position were to be offset on that day, the effective outflow will be:

$$-S_{t^*} + (F_{t^*} - F_t) = -F_t - (S_{t^*} - F_{t^*}) \tag{3.2}$$

In this case too, the effective cost of acquisition of the asset will depend on both the terminal spot as well as futures prices, and consequently will be uncertain until the very end.

As can be seen, equality of spot and futures prices on the day of termination of the hedge, is imperative for there to be no prior uncertainty about the price that is being locked in. Such price convergence is assured only at the time of expiration of the futures contract, and consequently the date on which the transaction in the underlying asset takes place should be the same as the expiration date of the futures contract, if we are to ensure that the hedge is perfect.

3.8.3 Importance of Condition-2

In order for the hedge to be perfect, it is essential that the quantity being hedged should be an integer multiple of the size of the futures contract.

Assume that a farmer has 1,250 units of a commodity that he wishes to sell. Futures contracts on the commodity expiring exactly on the date of sale are available, and the contract size is 100 units. So theoretically, a short position is required in 12.50 futures contracts. This is infeasible, and in practice, the farmer will have to go short in either 12 contracts or in 13. In either case, as we demonstrate below, the effective price received per unit will be uncertain.

Case-A: The farmer uses 12 contracts

The profit from marking to market will be

$$12 \times 100 \times (F_t - F_T)$$

The inflow on account of the sale of goods in the spot market will be $1{,}250S_T$. Thus the effective price received per unit of the good will be:

$$\frac{1{,}250S_T + 1{,}200(F_t - F_T)}{1{,}250}$$
$$= \frac{50S_T + 1{,}200F_t}{1{,}250}$$

The effective price is dependent on S_T which is a random variable. Consequently the effective price that will be received per unit will be uncertain, and will be revealed only at the end. This is despite the fact that the date of termination of the hedge coincides with the expiration date of the futures contract.

Case-B: The farmer uses 13 contracts

The profit from marking to market will be

$$13 \times 100 \times (F_t - F_T)$$

The inflow from the spot market will be $1{,}250S_T$. The effective price received per unit of the good will be

$$\frac{1{,}250S_T + 1{,}300(F_t - F_T)}{1{,}250}$$
$$= \frac{1{,}300F_t - 50S_T}{1{,}250}$$

Once again there will be uncertainty regarding the effective price that is to be received.

3.8.4 Importance of Condition-3

Take the case of an investor who wishes to hedge the risk inherent in a position that he has taken in an asset on which no futures contracts are available. Quite obviously, in such cases the hedger would have no choice but to use contracts on a related commodity, assuming such contracts were to be available. The use of a futures contract on a closely related commodity for the purpose of hedging is called *cross hedging*. The term *closely related*, implies that the prices of the two assets move in tandem. In the case of such hedges, the greater the degree of positive correlation between the prices of the two assets, the greater will be the effectiveness of the hedge.

A cross-hedge cannot be perfect in practice. We will demonstrate the truth of this assertion, by considering a short hedge for the purpose of illustration.

Let S_T be the spot price of the asset that the hedger is selling on day T. There are however, no futures contracts on the asset, expiring on day T or thereafter. However, contracts are available that expire on that day, but are based on a related commodity. Let $\hat{F}_t$ be the initial futures price and $\hat{F}_T$ the terminal futures price. $\hat{S}_T = \hat{F}_T$, is the terminal spot price of the asset on which the futures contracts have been written.

On the day that the hedge is to be terminated, the hedger will obviously sell the asset in his possession at its prevailing spot price and collect his profit/loss from the futures market. The effective price received per unit will be

$$S_T + (\hat{F}_t - \hat{F}_T) = \hat{F}_t + (S_T - \hat{F}_T) \tag{3.3}$$

In this case, however, S_T or the spot price of the asset, will in general not be equal to $\hat{F}_T$ or the terminal futures price, because they represent the prices of two different commodities. Consequently, there will be uncertainty regarding the effective price that the hedger is likely to receive.

3.9 Basis Risk

One of the conditions for a perfect hedge is that the date of expiration of the futures contract should coincide with the date of sale of the underlying asset. If this condition were to be satisfied, and the position in the spot market is an integer multiple of the contract size, then the hedged position will enable the hedger to lock in the futures price that was prevailing at the inception of the hedge, assuming of course that contracts are available on the asset whose price is being sought to be hedged. In practice, even if the other required conditions are satisfied, we are unlikely to have a situation where the termination date coincides with the contract expiration date. Consequently, we would usually have to choose a futures contract that expires after the date on which we wish to terminate the hedge.[3]

We will assume that $Q = Q_f$. For instance, if $Q = 100{,}000$ bushels of wheat, and each futures contract is for 5,000 bushels, then we would use 20 contracts. We will also assume that the asset being hedged is the same as the asset underlying the futures contract.

Since by assumption, the futures contract is scheduled to expire after the transaction date, it would have to be offset on that day. For a short hedger the effective price received per unit of the underlying asset under such circumstances will be:

$$F_t + (S_{t^*} - F_{t^*})$$

The uncertainty in this case arises due to the fact that on a date prior to the expiration date of the futures contract, the spot price S_{t^*} will not in general equal the futures price F_{t^*}. A similar line of reasoning holds for long hedges. Due to this reason, in practice hedgers face what is called *basis risk*. Let's first define the basis, which is critical for understanding hedging.

Basis = Spot price of the asset being hedged – Futures price of the contract that is used for hedging, In symbolic terms, at a point in time t, the basis is given by

$$b_t = S_t - F_t \tag{3.4}$$

At the time of expiration of the futures contract, due to the no-arbitrage condition, S_T is guaranteed to equal F_T, and we can be sure that the basis will be zero. At any point prior to expiration, t^*, however, we cannot make such an assertion. Thus, a hedger who is required to offset a futures contract prior to expiration faces uncertainty regarding the basis, or what is termed as *basis risk*.

3 If we use a futures contract that expires earlier then we would subsequently have a naked or uncovered position, which would mean that we would not be hedged or protected till the transaction date.

3.9.1 Short Hedges and the Basis

Take the case of a person who has a long position in the spot market and a short position in the futures market. If this hedge is held till the expiration of the futures contract, then the profit from the spot market will be $S_T - S_t$ and the profit from the futures market will be $F_t - F_T$.

$$\text{So } \pi = (S_T - S_t) + (F_t - F_T) = (S_T - F_T) - (S_t - F_t) = b_T - b_t \tag{3.5}$$

We know that $S_T = F_T$ and therefore $b_T = 0$. So the profit from the short hedge = $-b_t$. The effective price received by the short hedger is

$$S_T + (F_t - F_T) = F_t + (S_T - F_T) = F_t + b_T = F_t \tag{3.6}$$

F_t is known at time t, when the hedge is initiated. Thus, there is no uncertainty about the effective price that will be received if the hedge is held till the date of expiration of the futures contract. In other words, risk can be completely neutralized.

Now, let's consider the case where the hedge is lifted at time t^*. The profit in this case, is

$$\pi = (S_{t^*} - S_t) + (F_t - F_{t^*}) = (S_{t^*} - F_{t^*}) - (S_t - F_t) = b_{t^*} - b_t \tag{3.7}$$

The effective price received is

$$S_{t^*} + (F_t - F_{t^*}) = F_t + b_{t^*} \tag{3.8}$$

If the basis remains unchanged, that is $b_{t^*} = b_t$, then the profit will be zero and the effective price received will be $F_t + (S_t - F_t) = S_t$. Thus, if the basis at the time the hedge is lifted is the same as the basis at the time the hedge was set up, the effective price received will be equal to the initial spot price. In general, the profit is, $b_{t^*} - b_t$. b_{t^*} is a random variable at the time the hedge is initiated and therefore there is uncertainty regarding the quantum of the profit or loss. The term *basis risk* refers to the uncertainty regarding how the basis will change. Thus, an investor who chooses to hedge replaces price risk, which is the uncertainty regarding S_{t^*}, with basis risk, which is the uncertainty regarding b_{t^*}. Consider Example 3.9.

Example 3.9: Assume that today is July 1, 20XX. Victor Yallop a wheat farmer knows that he will have 100,000 bushels of wheat ready for sale in September. Futures contracts expiring on September 15 are available and each contract is for 5,000 bushels. The futures price is $9.00 per bushel.

If the date of sale of wheat were to coincide with the date of expiration of the futures contract, then obviously the hedge would be perfect. For instance, if the spot price of wheat on September 15 is $8.75 per bushel, then Yallop can sell the wheat for $875,000. The profit from the futures market will be [9.00 – 8.75] ×

100,000 = \$25,000. The total cash inflow will be \$900,000, which means that the effective price locked in per bushel is \$9.00, which is the initial futures price.

Now let's consider a situation where Yallop decides to sell the wheat on September 2. Assume that the spot price on that day is \$8.75 per bushel, whereas the futures price for the September contract is \$8.80. The proceeds from the sale of wheat in the spot market will be \$875,000. The futures contracts will have to be offset. The profit will be [9.00 − 8.80] × 100,000 = \$20,000. The total cash inflow will be \$895,000, which means that the effective price received per bushel is \$8.95.

$$8.95 = 9.00 + (8.75 - 8.80) \equiv F_t + (S_{t^*} - F_{t^*}) = F_t + b_{t^*}$$

Thus, the effective price received is a function of the basis that is prevailing at the time of expiration of the hedge, and consequently cannot be predicted in advance. The hedge is obviously not perfect under such circumstances. The uncertainty arises due to the hedger's inability to accurately predict the value of the basis on the date of sale, which is what we have termed as basis risk.

3.9.2 A Long Hedge

Now let's take the case of a long hedger, that is a person with a short position in the spot market and a long position in the futures market. If such a hedge is held till expiration, the profit from the spot market will be $S_t - S_T$ and that from the futures market will be $F_T - F_t$. So

$$\pi = (S_t - S_T) + (F_T - F_t) = (S_t - F_t) - (S_T - F_T) = b_t - b_T \tag{3.9}$$

But $b_T = 0$, since $S_T = F_T$. Therefore, the profit from the long hedge is equal to b_t. The effective price paid by the long hedger is

$$-S_T + (F_T - F_t) = -(F_t + b_T) = -F_t \tag{3.10}$$

Why do we end up with a minus sign in front of F_t? It is because the effective price paid is an outflow. The quantum of the price paid is F_t. Thus once again, there is no uncertainty regarding the price. In other words we can completely neutralize risk and create a perfect hedge.

Let's now consider the case where the long hedge is lifted at time t^*. The profit is given by

$$\pi = (S_t - S_{t^*}) + (F_{t^*} - F_t) = (S_t - F_t) - (S_{t^*} - F_{t^*}) = b_t - b_{t^*} \tag{3.11}$$

The effective price paid is

$$-S_{t*} + (F_{t*} - F_t) = -(F_t + b_{t*}) \tag{3.12}$$

If the basis were to remain unchanged the profit will equal zero, and the effective price paid will be $F_t + (S_t - F_t) = S_t$. Once again, like in the case of the short hedge, the hedger would have locked in the initial spot price. In general, of course, the profit will be equal to the change in the basis and the hedger would once again face basis risk. Let's consider Example 3.10.

Example 3.10: Mike Saunders, an independent project consultant based in Boston, has acquired software from a party in London, and is required to pay £625,000 after one month. Assume that today is 15 November 20XX, and that futures contracts expiring a month hence are available at a price of $1.2025. Each contract is for £62,500. Consequently Mike needs to go long in 10 contracts.

First let's assume that 15 December 20XX corresponds to the expiration date of the December contract. If so, the spot price on that day will be equal to the futures price, which we will assume is $1.1750 per pound. Mike will have to acquire the pounds by paying:

$$625{,}000 \times 1.1750 = \$734{,}375$$

in the spot market.

His gain/loss from the derivatives market is:

$$(1.1750 - 1.2025) \times 62{,}500 \times 10 = (\$17{,}187.50)$$

The total cost of acquisition of £625,000 is therefore:

$$734{,}375 + 17{,}187.50 = \$751{,}562.50$$

The effective price locked in by Mike is therefore:

$$\frac{751{,}562.50}{625{,}000} = 1.2025 \text{ GBP-USD}$$

The effective price in this case is the initial futures price, which should not surprise us, for from the outset we knew that Mike had set up a perfect hedge.

Now consider the case where the expiration of the December futures contract is scheduled for 19 December 20XX, that is, four days after the date on which Mike is scheduled to acquire the British currency. Assume that the exchange rates on that day are as follows:

Spot: 1.1825

Futures: 1.1795

Mike will have to pay:

$$625{,}000 \times 1.1825 = \$739{,}062.50$$

when he acquires the pounds in the spot market. His profit/loss from the futures market is:

$$62{,}500 \times 10 \times (1.1795 - 1.2025) = (\$14{,}375)$$

The total cost of the British currency is therefore:

$$739{,}062.50 + 14{,}375 = \$753{,}437.50$$

The effective exchange rate is therefore:

$$\frac{753{,}437.50}{625{,}000} = 1.2055 \text{ GBP-USD}$$

$$1.2055 = 1.1825 - (1.1795 - 1.2025) = 1.1825 + 0.023 = 1.2025 + 0.0030$$

$$\equiv S_{t^*} - (F_{t^*} - F_t) = F_t + b_{t^*}$$

The uncertainty about the eventual exchange rate arises due to the fact that the terminal basis will not be revealed till the end. Consequently, as is to be expected, Mike faces basis risk in this case.

3.9.3 Changes in The Basis

We have defined the basis as $S_t - F_t$.[4] If the market were to be in contango, the basis as per our definition will be negative. If it were to become more negative as it evolves over time, we would say that it has widened. However, if it were to become less negative over time, it would be said to have narrowed.

On the other hand, if the market were to be in backwardation, the basis as per our definition will be positive. If it were to become more positive as it evolves over time, we would say that it has widened. However, if it were to become less positive over time, it would be said to have narrowed. Hence, the terms *widening* and *narrowing* are obviously used with reference to changes in the absolute value of the basis.

For a hedger with a short position in the futures market, the effective price received will be $F_t + b_{t^*}$. The higher the value of the basis on the date of termination, the greater will be his inflow. Thus, such hedgers will benefit from a rising basis. On the other hand, for a hedger with a long position in the futures market, the effective outflow will be $F_t + b_{t^*}$. In this case, the lower the value of the basis, the smaller is the outflow. Consequently such hedgers stand to benefit from a declining basis.

Thus, a rising basis benefits short hedgers, while a declining basis benefits long hedgers. While studying the features of long and short futures positions, we have observed that traders with long positions benefit from rising prices while those with short positions gain from declining prices. Notice, that the basis itself can be perceived as a

4 Some authors prefer to define it as the futures price minus the spot price.

synthetic price, for it is the difference of two prices. From this perspective, we can make the assertion that a short hedger is *long the basis*, while a long hedger is *short the basis*.

3.9.4 The Basis for a Cross Hedge

Thus far we have assumed that the asset whose price risk is being hedged, is the same as the asset on which the futures contracts being used are written. In the case of a cross hedge, the two assets will be different. Let S be the spot price of the asset that we wish to hedge and $\hat{S}$ the spot price of the asset underlying the futures contract that we are using. The effective price that is paid or received is

$$S_{t^*} + (\hat{F}_t - \hat{F}_{t^*}) = \hat{F}_t + (\hat{S}_{t^*} - \hat{F}_{t^*}) + (S_{t^*} - \hat{S}_{t^*}) \tag{3.13}$$

Thus, in such a case, the basis will consist of two components. The first component, $\hat{S}_{t^*} - \hat{F}_{t^*}$ is the basis that would exist, if the asset being hedged is the same as the asset underlying the futures contract. The second term, $S_{t^*} - \hat{S}_{t^*}$, is the basis that arises due the fact that the two assets are not the same.

In the case of a cross-hedge, even spot futures convergence at expiration, is inadequate to ensure a perfect hedge. For, if we set $t^* = T$ in equation 3.13, the effective price that will be paid/received by the hedger will be:

$$\hat{F}_t + (S_T - \hat{S}_T)$$

which will be revealed only at the end. Let's consider Example 3.11.

Example 3.11: Graham Stone, a farmer, wants to hedge his inventory of oats using wheat futures contracts. This is because, although futures contracts are available on oats, Graham is of the opinion that their liquidity is unsatisfactory. The current price for a wheat futures contract expiring after two months is \$9.25 per bushel, and contracts on both wheat as well as oats, are for 5,000 bushels. Graham wishes to hedge the price of 500,000 bushels of oats, and consequently decides to go short in 100 wheat futures contracts.

Let's assume that the hedge is terminated after a month, on a day on which the one month wheat futures contract is quoting at \$8.95 per bushel. The spot price of wheat is \$8.810 per bushel, while that of oats is \$3.675 per bushel.

When Graham sells the oats in the spot market, he will receive:

$$500{,}000 \times 3.675 = \$1{,}837{,}500$$

His profit/loss from the wheat futures position will be:

$$5{,}000 \times 100 \times (9.25 - 8.95) = \$150{,}000$$

The total proceeds will be:

$$1{,}837{,}500 + 150{,}000 = \$1{,}987{,}500$$

The effective price received per bushel of oats will be:

$$\frac{1{,}987{,}500}{500{,}000} = \$3.975$$

$$\begin{aligned} 3.975 &= 9.25 + (8.81 - 8.95) + (3.675 - 8.81) \\ &\equiv \hat{F}_t + (\hat{S}_{t*} - \hat{F}_{t*}) + (S_{t*} - \hat{S}_{t*}) \end{aligned} \tag{3.14}$$

3.9.5 Quantifying Basis Risk

The basis is defined as $S_t - F_t$. In Finance theory we measure risk by the variance of the random variable. So, using this yardstick

$$\sigma^2(b) = \sigma^2(S) + \sigma^2(F) - 2\rho(S,F)\sigma(S)\sigma(F) \tag{3.15}$$

where $\sigma(S)$ is the standard deviation of the spot price, $\sigma(F)$ is the standard deviation of the futures price, and $\rho(S,F)$ is the correlation coefficient between the two variables.

The critical factor is ρ. The higher the correlation, the lower will be the basis risk. Hedging as we said earlier, substitutes price risk with basis risk. Hence, an investor will find it attractive to hedge, only if the basis risk is substantially lower than the price risk.

3.10 Selecting a Futures Contract

Once a person decides to hedge, the first thing he has to do is to decide which futures contract he is going to use. This is important because basis risk would depend on the contract that is chosen. The selection of the contract would be influenced by the following factors.

In general, if the commodity that a person wishes to hedge has futures contracts written on it then he would use such a contract. This is because the futures and spot prices are likely to be highly correlated, thereby reducing basis risk. Thus, if you have a position in cocoa and cocoa futures are available, then you would use such a contract. But what if cocoa futures are not available? In such a case, you would have no choice but to select a futures contract on a different commodity. This, as we have mentioned earlier, is called cross hedging. For cross hedging to succeed, one would need to select a futures contract on an asset whose price is highly positively correlated with the price of the asset that is being hedged. For instance, if you find that coffee and cocoa prices are highly positively correlated, then you may use a coffee futures contract for hedging a position in cocoa.

However, there may be situations where you prefer to hedge cocoa using coffee futures, even though cocoa futures are available. This may be the case if cocoa futures contracts are not liquid. Liquidity is important, because when you wish to transact, you would like to both enter and exit the market quickly and at a fair price.

Another important factor to be kept in mind while selecting a contract is possible mispricing. An overpriced contract will benefit a short hedger because if prices fall subsequently he will gain. Similarly, an underpriced contract will benefit a long hedger.

The second major decision that a hedger has to take is as to which expiration month he should choose. Let's go back to our earlier example where Victor Yallop, the wheat farmer, was initiating a short hedge on July 1, 20XX. The sale of wheat was scheduled for September 20XX and hence we said that he would use the September futures contract. Let's assume that Yallop had a choice of September 20XX, December 20XX, March 20(XX+1) and May 20(XX+1) contracts.

In practice, Yallop may prefer the December 20XX contract to the September 20XX contract. There are two reasons for this. The first is that in real life, futures prices can often exhibit unusual price movements in the month in which they expire. A hedger who is trying to close out his position, would not like to be exposed to such erratic movements.

Second, consider the case of a long hedger who too plans to terminate the hedge in September and hence goes in for a September futures contract. What happens if he is chosen for delivery[5]? Let's assume that Jenner and Company, a wheat mill, are the long hedgers. Their objective may be to procure the wheat in Pittstown, where they are based. To hedge against price risk, they may use futures contracts traded on the nearest exchange, which we will assume is in Kansas City. If they are chosen for delivery, they may be asked to take delivery in Kansas City, which is the location specified in the contract. Thus, for them, taking delivery in Kansas City would entail the cost and inconvenience of taking the wheat to Pittstown. Thus, a person whose long hedge expires in September may not like to use the September contract. In this case, if Jenner and Company had hedged using December futures, they could simply offset their position in September and buy the wheat at the prevailing spot price in Pittstown.

Another factor to be kept in mind is that, in general, the basis risk will be higher, the further away the expiration month of the contract is from the date of termination of the hedge. The reason is as follows. It must be remembered that both spot as well as futures prices of a commodity, are being influenced by the same economic factors. The difference is that spot prices represent today's market price, while the futures prices represent the price for a trade at some point of time in the future. If the expiration date of the contract is close to the date on which the hedge is being terminated, then both the spot and the futures markets will be discovering the price of the commodity for virtually the same point in time and therefore the prices may be expected to converge, such that the price difference, which is the basis, is more predictable. However, if the expiration

5 Remember, the oldest outstanding long position is chosen.

date of the futures contract is much further from the date of lifting of the hedge, then the spot and futures prices are likely to be affected by different supply and demand forces, which reflect different sets of information, as a consequence of which we would expect to observe greater variability in the basis. Thus, in the case of Victor Yallop, the March 20(XX+1) contract is likely to entail greater basis risk than the December 20XX contract.[6]

Keeping these facts and factors in mind, Yallop is likely to use the December 20XX contract. *So the general rule is that the hedger should choose a contract with an expiration month that is as close as possible to the month in which the hedge is being terminated, but after it.*

However, it should be remembered that the longer the time to expiration of the contract, the less liquid it is likely to be. By less liquid, we mean that it may not be actively traded. Hence, while a hedger would generally choose an expiration month that comes after the month in which he wishes to terminate the hedge, this principle may have to be overruled due to the necessity of using a liquid contract. Thus, there may be cases where he will choose a contract with an expiration date that comes before the date on which the hedge is to be terminated. When such a contract moves into its expiration month, the futures position will be offset and a new position will be opened in the next available expiration month. Such a procedure is called *rolling the hedge forward.*

3.11 A Rolling Hedge

Let's now assume that Victor Yallop wants to sell his wheat on 15 April 20(XX+1), and not in September 20XX. In July 20XX, he has a choice of contracts with different expiration months - September 20XX, December 20XX, March 20(XX+1) and May 20(XX+1), as we have seen earlier.

Instead of using the May 20(XX+1) contract, a hedger like Yallop may decide to roll the hedge forward. In practice, he could have two possible reasons for it. Firstly, the May 20(XX+1) contract may not be liquid. Secondly, it may not even be available on July 1, 20XX, the date on which the hedge is initiated. We will now illustrate a rolling hedge with the help of Example 3.12.

Example 3.12: Let's assume that Yallop wants to hedge 100,000 bushels of wheat and that each wheat futures contract is for 5,000 bushels. So he will require 20 contracts. Let the futures price of the September 20XX contract be $9.00 per bushel, on July 1, 20XX when the hedge is initiated. Consider the following sequence of actions, shown in Table 3.1, that Yallop can take.

The reason the September contracts are offset on August 31 is that, as we said earlier, in general one would not like to hold a contract in its expiration month. The same logic applies for the other contracts. The gain in the futures market per bushel of wheat, may be calculated as follows.

---

6 See Koontz and Purcell (1999).

Table 3.1: Illustration of a rolling hedge.

Date	Action Taken
July 1, 2008	Short 20 September 20XX contracts at $9.00
August 31, 2008	Offset the September contracts at $8.75 Go short in 20 December 20XX contracts at $8.60
November 30, 2008	Offset the December contracts at $8.25 Go short in 20 March 20(XX+1) contracts at $8.15
February 28, 2009	Offset the March contracts at $8.30 Go short in 20 May 20(XX+1) contracts at $8.05
April 15, 2009	Offset the May contracts at $7.95 Sell the wheat in the spot market at $7.80

- Profit from the September contracts = (9.00 - 8.75) = 0.25.
- Profit from the December contracts = (8.60 - 8.25) = 0.35.
- Profit from the March contracts = (8.15 - 8.30) = (0.15).
- Profit from the May contracts = (8.05 - 7.95) = 0.10.
- Total profit = 0.25 + 0.35 - 0.15 + 0.10 = $0.55.

The effective price received = $7.80 + $0.55 = $8.35 per bushel.

In practice, rolling the hedge forward too frequently may be expensive because every time you close out your position and take a fresh position, you will incur transactions costs.

3.12 The Hedge Ratio

The final decision that the hedger has to take while designing his hedging strategy, is how to choose the hedge ratio. The hedge ratio refers to the futures position taken, per unit exposure in the spot market. In other words, the hedge ratio is the ratio of the size of the position taken in the futures market to the size of the exposure in the spot market. The ideal ratio should be such that the futures profit / loss, exactly matches the spot loss /profit.

In our examples thus far, we have used a hedge ratio of 1:1. For instance, to hedge 100,000 bushels of wheat, we assumed that Yallop would go short in 20 futures contracts, where each contract was for 5,000 bushels. But if the objective of the hedger is to minimize risk, then it can be demonstrated that a hedge ratio of 1:1 is not always optimal.

3.12.1 The Minimum Variance Hedge Ratio

We will denote the number of units of the underlying asset in which the investor has a long position by Q. The futures contract size will be denoted by N, and C will be used to denote the number of futures contracts that are being used for hedging. Hence, the total number of units of the underlying asset being represented by the futures position is $Q_f = NC$.

The issue is, is it always optimal to set $Q_f = Q$, or in other words should we always use a hedge ratio of 1:1.

In order to answer this question, let's look at the effective revenue for a short hedger. It can be represented as

$$R = QS_{t^*} + (F_t - F_{t^*})Q_f \tag{3.16}$$

If $t^* = T$, or in other words the termination date were to coincide with the contract expiration date, then it would be ideal to set $Q_f = Q$, so that $R = QF_t$. In this case, we would have a perfect hedge, about whose revenue there would be no uncertainty.

However, when $t^* < T$, or the hedge is terminated before the contract expiration date, then a hedge ratio of 1:1 need not be optimal.

Let's define the hedge ratio as $h = \frac{Q_f}{Q}$. If so, $Q_f = hQ$.

A short hedger will receive an amount R when the hedge is lifted, such that

$$\begin{aligned}
R &= QS_{t^*} + (F_t - F_{t^*})hQ \\
&= QS_{t^*} - (F_{t^*} - F_t)hQ \\
&= QS_t - QS_t + QS_{t^*} - (F_{t^*} - F_t)hQ \\
&= QS_t + (S_{t^*} - S_t)Q - (F_{t^*} - F_t)hQ \\
&= QS_t + \Delta SQ - \Delta FhQ \\
&= QS_t + (\Delta S - h\Delta F)Q
\end{aligned}$$

We have denoted $(S_{t^*} - S_t)$ as ΔS and $(F_{t^*} - F_t)$ as ΔF.

When the hedge is initiated, we will know only S_t and Q. The unknowns will be ΔS and ΔF. If our objective is to minimize risk, then we should minimize the variance of R, using the only variable in our control namely h.

$$\begin{aligned}
Var(R) &= Var[QS_t + (\Delta S - h\Delta F)Q] \\
&= Var[(\Delta S - h\Delta F)Q] \\
&= Q^2 Var[\Delta S - h\Delta F]
\end{aligned} \tag{3.17}$$

Let's denote $Var(\Delta S)$ by σ_s^2, $Var(\Delta F)$ by σ_f^2 and the correlation between ΔS and ΔF by ρ. Therefore

$$Var(R) = Q^2[\sigma_s^2 + h^2\sigma_f^2 - 2h\rho\sigma_s\sigma_f] \tag{3.18}$$

If we minimize the variance of R with respect to h, we will set

$$\frac{dVar(R)}{dh} = Q^2[2h\sigma_f^2 - 2\rho\sigma_s\sigma_f] = 0$$
$$\Rightarrow 2h\sigma_f^2 - 2\rho\sigma_s\sigma_f = 0$$
$$\Rightarrow h = \frac{\rho\sigma_s}{\sigma_f} \tag{3.19}$$

3.12.2 The Optimal Number of Futures Contracts

We will denote the optimal hedge ratio by h^*. We know that

$$h^* = \frac{Q_f^*}{Q}$$
$$\Rightarrow Q_f^* = h^*Q \tag{3.20}$$

Therefore, the optimal number of contracts is

$$C^* = \frac{Q_f^*}{N} = \frac{h^*Q}{N} \tag{3.21}$$

Let's assume that the optimal hedge ratio has been calculated to be 0.85. If Q = 100,000 bushels of wheat, and N = 5,000 bushels, then the optimal number of futures contracts is

$$\frac{0.85 \times 100{,}000}{5{,}000} = 17$$

3.13 Estimating the Hedge Ratio

Let's specify the following statistical relationship between the changes in the spot price of an asset and the changes in the corresponding futures price.

$$\Delta S = \alpha + \beta\Delta F + \epsilon \tag{3.22}$$

To estimate the parameters α and β, we can run a linear regression with ΔF as the independent variable and ΔS as the dependent variable. The slope coefficient β, is given by

$$\frac{Cov(\Delta S, \Delta F)}{\sigma^2(\Delta F)} = \frac{\rho\sigma_s\sigma_f}{\sigma_f^2} = \frac{\rho\sigma_s}{\sigma_f} \tag{3.23}$$

which is the minimum variance hedge ratio.

3.13.1 Hedging Effectiveness

The hedging effectiveness may be defined as:

$$1 - \frac{\sigma^2(b)}{\sigma^2(S)} \tag{3.24}$$

If the basis risk were to be equal to the price risk, then obviously there would be no risk reduction, and the hedging effectiveness will be zero. However, if the basis risk is zero, which would imply that we have a perfect hedge, the hedging effectiveness will be 1.0.

3.14 Tailing a Hedge

In all our discussions thus far, we have been treating a futures contract like a forward contract, that is, we have been ignoring the effects of marking to market. In real life, our hedging procedure should take into account this feature of futures markets. The process of adjusting the hedge ratio to take into account intermediate cash flows is called *tailing*.

Let's assume that a hedge is set up today by selling futures contracts equivalent to Q_f units, at a price F_t. The hedge will expire at time t^* and in the interim, will be marked to market at two points in time, t_1 and t_2, where $t < t_1 < t_2 < t^*$. We will assume that all intermediate gains and losses can be invested / borrowed at the risk-less rate of interest r.

At time t_1, we will get a cash flow of $(F_t - F_{t_1})Q_f$. This can be reinvested / borrowed until the expiration of the hedge at the rate r, which for expositional convenience will be assumed to be a daily rate of interest.[7] Consequently at t^*, we will get a cash flow of $(F_t - F_{t_1})Q_f(1 + r)^{t^*-t_1}$.

Similarly, when the contract is marked to market at t_2, there will be a cash flow of $(F_{t_1} - F_{t_2})Q_f$. This too will be reinvested or borrowed and will yield a corresponding cash flow of $(F_{t_1} - F_{t_2})Q_f(1 + r)^{t^*-t_2}$ at time t.

And finally, when the hedge is lifted at time t, we will receive a cash flow of $(F_{t_2} - F_{t^*})Q_f$.

7 Hence, all time periods will be measured in terms of number of days.

Thus the total cash flow at time t^* is

$$(F_t - F_{t_1})Q_f(1+r)^{t^*-t_1} + (F_{t_1} - F_{t_2})Q_f(1+r)^{t^*-t_2} + (F_{t_2} - F_{t^*})Q_f \qquad (3.25)$$

This in general, will not be equal to $(F_t - F_{t^*})Q_f$, which is what we would have received had we used a forward contract instead of a futures contract. The only way the two cash flows can be made equal is if we adjust the number of futures contracts used.

Let's now consider the following strategy. Assume that the hedge is initiated with $Q_{f1} = \frac{Q_f}{(1+r)^{t^*-t_1}}$ and that the futures position is subsequently changed as follows. At time t_1, let the number of futures contracts used be increased to $Q_{f2} = \frac{Q_f}{(1+r)^{t^*-t_2}}$. And finally, at time t_2, let the number of contracts used be increased to Q_f.

The total cash flow, at time t^* if the above procedure is used, will be

$$\begin{aligned}\frac{(F_t - F_{t_1})Q_f(1+r)^{t^*-t_1}}{(1+r)^{t^*-t_1}} &+ \frac{(F_{t_1} - F_{t_2})Q_f(1+r)^{t^*-t_2}}{(1+r)^{t^*-t_2}} + (F_{t_2} - F_{t^*})Q_f \\ &= (F_t - F_{t_1})Q_f + (F_{t_1} - F_{t_2})Q_f + (F_{t_2} - F_{t^*})Q_f \\ &= (F_t - F_{t^*})Q_f \end{aligned} \qquad (3.26)$$

which is equal to the final payoff that would have been received, had a forward contract been used.

Thus, tailing requires that the hedger adjust the number of futures contracts used or in other words the hedge ratio, every time there is an intermediate cash flow. If the number of futures contracts used were to be equivalent to Q_f units from the very beginning, then the hedger would be over-hedging.

Let's illustrate the tailing procedure, with the help of Example 3.13.

Example 3.13: Assume that Victor Yallop, wants to hedge 10,000,000 bushels of wheat. Each contract is for 5,000 bushels, so if Yallop were to use a hedge ratio of 1:1, he would use 2,000 contracts from the outset. But if Yallop were to tail his hedge, then he would proceed as follows.

Let's assume that the daily interest rate is .1% and that the hedge is kept in place for three days. So at the time of initiating the hedge, Yallop would use Q_{f1} contracts, where $Q_{f1} = \frac{10{,}000{,}000}{(1.001)^2} = 9{,}980{,}030 \cong 9{,}980{,}000 \equiv 1{,}996$ contracts. When the contract is marked to market at the end of the first day, he will change the number of contracts used to, $Q_{f2} = \frac{10{,}000{,}000}{(1.001)} = 9{,}990{,}010 \cong 9{,}990{,}000 \equiv 1{,}998$ contracts. And finally, when the contract is marked to market at the end of the second day, Yallop will short $Q_f = 10{,}000{,}000 \equiv 2{,}000$ contracts.

Consider the following hypothetical futures prices, shown in Table 3.2.

Yallop's profit / loss from his futures position, at the end of the third day, in such a scenario is

$$\begin{aligned}&(9.00 - 8.75) \times 9{,}980{,}000 \times (1.001)^2 + (8.75 - 8.50) \times 9{,}990{,}000 \times (1.001) \\ &\quad + (8.50 - 8.25) \times 10{,}000{,}000 \\ &\quad = 2{,}499{,}992.50 + 2{,}499{,}997.50 + 2{,}500{,}000 = 7{,}499{,}990 \cong \$7{,}500{,}000\end{aligned}$$

Table 3.2: Futures settlement prices.

Time	Settlement Price
0	\$9.00
1	\$8.75
2	\$8.50
3	\$8.25

Had he used a forward contract, his profit would have been the same, that is

$$(9.00 - 8.25) \times 10{,}000{,}000 = \$7{,}500{,}000$$

However, if Yallop had used a futures strategy with Q_f = 10,000,000 bushels, from the very beginning, his final payoff would have been

$$2{,}500{,}000 \times (1.001)^2 + 2{,}500{,}000 \times (1.001) + 2{,}500{,}000 = 7{,}507{,}503$$

Thus in this case, he would have over-hedged. If the futures price had consistently gone up instead of going down, over-hedging would have lead to a bigger loss.

In practice, tailing will be feasible only if you have a large futures position. For instance, if Q_f had been 10,000 in the above case, then tailing would not have been possible, because you cannot buy or sell a fraction of a contract. The difference between Q_{f1} or Q_{f2} and Q_f would depend on the time left to expiration of the hedge and on the interest rate. The longer the time left or the greater the interest rate, the more will be the required adjustment.

It must be remembered that tailing is not free of costs. Every time the number of futures contracts is adjusted, there will be transactions costs. Hence, you must weigh the pros and cons before deciding to tail. In real life, hedgers do not usually adjust their futures positions daily, that is, every time the contract is marked to market. Periodic adjustments are found to be adequate.

3.15 Delta Hedging: Futures versus Options

Before we commence our discussion of delta hedging, let's first define the term *delta*. The delta of a derivative is the rate of change of its price with respect to the price of the underlying asset, assuming that the other variables which impact the price of the derivative, are maintained at a constant level. That is:

$$\delta = \frac{\Delta F}{\Delta S}$$

where ΔF is the change in the price of the derivative, and ΔS is the change in the spot price of the underlying asset.

The value of a forward contract at time 't' is given by:

$$f = S_t - \frac{K}{(1 + r)^{T-t}} \tag{3.27}$$

Thus the rate of change of the value of a long forward contract, with respect to the spot price is 1.0. This can be perceived as follows. An increase of one dollar in the stock price will lead to an increase of $(1 + r)^{(T-t)}$ in the forward price. Thus a long forward position will have a gain of this magnitude at the point of expiration. The present value of this gain is obviously 1.0.

What about a long futures position? In this case, assuming that the underlying asset makes no payouts:

$$F_t = S_t(1 + r)^{T-t} \tag{3.28}$$

where '$T - t$' is the number of days left to expiration and 'r' is the daily risk-less rate of return. An increase of one dollar in the stock price will lead to an increase of $(1 + r)^{T-t}$ in the futures price. The holder will realize a profit of this magnitude when the contract is marked to market on the following day. The present value of this cash flow is therefore $(1 + r)^{T-t-1}$. Thus, the delta of a futures contract at time 't' is $(1 + r)^{T-t-1}$. Why is it that the futures contract has a higher delta than the forward contract, although both are based on the same asset, and represent a similar future commitment? The rationale is the following. A one dollar increase in the spot price will lead to an increase of a dollar in the value of the forward contract. However, this increase in value will be realized only when the contract expires. On the other hand, a dollar's increase in the spot price will lead to an increase in the futures price, which will manifest it self as a cash flow on the following day when the contract is market to market. Thus, the change in the value of a futures contract is greater than the corresponding change in the value of a forward contract. Therefore, unlike in the case of forward contracts, where the delta remains constant, the delta of a futures contract will steadily decline with the passage of time, assuming of course that the risk-less rate of return is constant.

Consider a portfolio consisting of a long position in a share of stock and a position in N forward contracts. The value of the portfolio is given by:

$$\pi = S_t \tag{3.29}$$

$$\Delta\pi = \Delta S + N\Delta F \tag{3.30}$$

If we make the value of the portfolio invariant to the change in price of the underlying asset, we get:

$$\Delta S + N\Delta F = 0$$
$$\Rightarrow N = -\frac{\Delta S}{\Delta F} \tag{3.31}$$

Thus we require a short position in $\frac{1}{\delta}$ forward contracts, which implies that we need a short position in one forward contract. Notice that such a hedge need not be re-balanced with the passage of time, since the delta of a forward contract is always 1.0. Consequently, such a hedging strategy may be termed as a hedge-and-forget strategy.

Now assume that we decided to hedge the value of the portfolio using futures contracts. If so:

$$N = -\frac{\Delta S}{\Delta F} = -\frac{1}{\delta} = -(1+r)^{-(T-t-1)} \tag{3.32}$$

In this case, we need to go short in $(1+r)^{-(T-t-1)}$ futures contracts. This hedge needs to be regularly re-balanced, since it is a function of the time remaining to expiration. Let's consider Example 3.14.

Example 3.14: Let's take the example of an investor who is long in 100,000,000 units in the spot market and wishes to hedge by going short in derivatives. We will first consider the implications of hedging with forward contracts. Assume that each contract is for 100 units of the underlying asset, and that the current forward price is \$100 per unit. Since the delta of a forward contract is one, the investor needs to go short in $\frac{100{,}000{,}000}{100} = 1{,}000{,}000$ contracts. This will lock in a price of \$100 per unit of the underlying asset. The total terminal value of the portfolio will be:

$$100 \times 100 \times 1{,}000{,}000 = \$10{,}000{,}000{,}000$$

The way to interpret this is as follows. An investment equivalent to the spot price of S_t has resulted in a terminal inflow of the forward price F_t. Since $F_t = S_t(1+r)^{T-t}$ the portfolio has earned the risk-less rate of return which is to be expected since we have hedged away the risk.

Now consider the case of hedging with a futures contract. Assume that there are five days left to expiration, and that the daily rate of interest is 1%. The futures price at each point in time, and the corresponding hedge ratio as well as the number of required contracts are given in Table 3.3.

Table 3.3: Futures prices and hedge ratios.

Time	Futures Price	Hedge Ratio	# of Contracts
0	100	0.960980	960,980
1	105	0.970590	970,590
2	102	0.980296	980,296
3	95	0.990099	990,099
4	103	1.0	1,000,000
5	110		

The future value of the cash flow that is generated at time 't' is:

$$(1+r)^{-(T-t-1)} \times [F_t - F_{t+1}] \times (1+r)^{(T-t-1)}$$
$$= F_t - F_{t+1}$$

Thus the cumulative cash flow at expiration in this case is:

$$[(F_0 - F_1) + (F_1 - F_2) + (F_2 - F_3) + (F_3 - F_4) + (F_4 - F_5)] = F_0 - F_5$$

The terminal futures price will be the same as the terminal spot price. So the 100,000,000 units can be sold for

$$100{,}000{,}000 \times 110 = \$11{,}000{,}000{,}000$$

The profit/loss from the futures market is:

$$100 \times 1{,}000{,}000 \times [100 - 110] = (\$\ 1{,}000{,}000{,}000)$$

The net cash flow is:

$$11{,}000{,}000{,}000 - 1{,}000{,}000{,}000 = \$10{,}000{,}000{,}000$$

Thus once again we have created a perfectly risk-less investment. Notice that delta hedging with futures contracts is exactly what we have earlier termed as *tailing a hedge*.

3.15.1 Delta Hedging with Options

Consider a portfolio consisting of a long position in N shares, and a short position in one call option. The value of the portfolio is given by:

$$\pi = NS - C \tag{3.33}$$

Therefore:

$$\frac{\partial \pi}{\partial S} = 0 \Rightarrow N = \frac{\partial C}{\partial S} \tag{3.34}$$

Thus, to hedge a short position in a call option, we need a long position in δ shares of stock. The value of an option, and consequently its delta, can be calculated only by assuming an option pricing formula. For the purpose of this illustration, we will assume that the Black-Scholes model is valid. According to this model, the delta of a call on an asset that is not scheduled to make any pay-outs during the life of the option is $N(d_1)$, where N(X) is the cumulative probability distribution function for a standard normal variable.

What is d_1? Let's first define the following variables.

- X ≡ the exercise price of the option.
- T − t ≡ time remaining in the life of the option. This is measured in years.
- σ ≡ volatility of the rate of return on the underlying asset.

From the Black-Scholes formula:

$$d_1 = \frac{ln\left(\frac{S}{X}\right) + \left(r + \frac{\sigma^2}{2}\right)(T-t)}{\sigma\sqrt{(T-t)}} \quad (3.35)$$

Thus $\delta = f(S, X, r, \sigma, T - t)$, that is, the delta of the option is a non-linear function of multiple variables. The call premium according to the Black-Scholes formula is:

$$C_t = S_t N(d_1) - Xe^{-r(T-t)} N(d_2) \quad (3.36)$$

where

$$d_2 = d_1 - \sigma\sqrt{T-t} \quad (3.37)$$

Let's consider Example 3.15.

Example 3.15: Let's assume that we wish to hedge a short position in 1,000 call options, each of which is for one unit of the underlying asset. We will assume that the exercise price is $100, and that the risk-less rate of interest is 10% per annum. The volatility of the rate of return on the underlying asset will be assumed to be 30% per annum.

Assume that the stock price follows the path described in Table 3.4, and that the option has five days left to maturity. For each value of the stock price, the table also gives the value of the call option as well as the delta of the option.

Table 3.4: Price and delta of a call option.

Period	Stock Price	Call Delta	Option Price
0	100.00	0.5226	1.4693
1	101.00	0.6434	1.8902
2	100.50	0.5899	1.4031
3	99.50	0.4247	0.6786
4	100.25	0.5731	0.7756
5	101.00	1.0000	1.0000

The number of shares required at each point in time, for a short position in 1,000 call options is given in Table 3.5.[8]

Table 3.5: # of shares and call options required.

Period	# of Calls	# of Shares
0	−1,000	523
1	−1,000	643
2	−1,000	590
3	−1,000	425
4	−1,000	573
5	−1,000	1,000

Let's analyze the hedging strategy is detail.

Time 0: We begin with an investment in 523 shares and a short position in 1,000 calls. The initial investment is:

$$100 \times 523 - 1.4693 \times 1{,}000 = \$50{,}831$$

Time 1: The value of the investment made in the previous period is:

$$101 \times 523 - 1.8902 \times 1{,}000 = \$50{,}933$$

The required investment is:

$$101 \times 643 - 1.8902 \times 1{,}000 = \$63{,}053$$

There is a deficit of:

$$63{,}053 - 50{,}933 = \$12{,}120$$

which will have to be borrowed.

Time 2: The value of the investment made in the previous period is:

$$100.50 \times 643 - 1.4031 \times 1{,}000 - 12{,}123 = \$51{,}095$$

Notice that we have to return the amount borrowed earlier with interest. For a period of one day the future value of $12,120 is approximately $12,123.

The required investment is:

$$100.50 \times 590 - 1.4031 \times 1{,}000 = \$57{,}892$$

8 We have rounded off to get the values in integers.

There is a deficit of:

$$57892 - 51{,}095 = \$6{,}797$$

which will have to be borrowed. The future value is $6,799.

Time 3: The value of the investment made in the previous period is:

$$99.50 \times 590 - 0.6786 \times 1{,}000 - 6{,}799 = \$51{,}227$$

The required investment is:

$$99.50 \times 425 - 0.6786 \times 1{,}000 = \$41{,}609$$

There is a surplus of:

$$41{,}609 - 51{,}227 = -\$\,9{,}618$$

which can be lent out. The future value is $9,621.

Time 4: The value of the investment made in the previous period is:

$$100.25 \times 425 - 0.7756 \times 1{,}000 + 9{,}621 = \$51{,}452$$

The required investment is:

$$100.25 \times 573 - 0.7756 \times 1{,}000 = \$56{,}668$$

There is a deficit of:

$$56{,}668 - 51{,}452 = \$5{,}216$$

which will have to be borrowed. The future value is $5,217.

Time 5: The value of the investment made in the previous period is:

$$101 \times 573 - 1.0 \times 1{,}000 - 5{,}217 = \$51{,}656$$

Let's interpret this result. Since the stock price at expiration is greater than the exercise price, the calls will be exercised. The inflow from 1,000 calls is:

$$1{,}000 \times 100 = \$100{,}000$$

Since the hedger already had 573 shares at the end of the previous day, he needs to acquire 427 more. The cost of acquisition is:

$$427 \times 101 = \$43{,}127$$

The net inflow is:

$$100{,}000 - 43{,}127 - 5{,}217 = \$51{,}656$$

If our initial investment had earned the risk-less rate for five days, we would have had:

$$50{,}831e^{\frac{0.10\times5}{365}} = \$50{,}901$$

Thus, the hedge is not perfect, although in this illustration it has worked to our advantage. The reason is that the delta of the call is a function of the stock price, and consequently any value that we compute is valid for only an infinitesimal change in the stock price. Since we have considered finite changes in the day to day prices, our hedge does not perform perfectly.

3.16 Speculation

Hedgers, as we have seen thus far, are investors who seek to mitigate if not eliminate price risk. Speculators, on the other hand, have a radically different attitude towards risk. Such investors, by definition, are people who consciously seek to take risk, hoping to profit from subsequent price movements. A speculator may be betting on a rising market, in which case he would be labeled as being bullish, or else he may be betting on a declining market, in which case he would be termed as being bearish. Contrary to what a lay person may believe, speculation is not tantamount to gambling.

Finance theory makes a clearcut distinction between speculation and gambling. Speculators are calculated risk takers. That is, before assuming a position in the market, such investors will evaluate the risk of an investment in its entirety, and weigh it against the anticipated return from it, prior to taking a position. Such investors will therefore take a position only if they were to be of the opinion, based on their analyses, that the anticipated return associated with the investment is adequate considering the risk that is being assumed. A gambler on the other hand will not make such an ex-ante risk-return tradeoff, and consequently is someone who takes a risk purely for the sheer thrill of taking it. The focus of such traders is solely on the associated risk, and the expected return is of no consequence while taking a decision to gamble.

Active speculation is a sine qua non for a deep and liquid market. A market characterized solely by the activities of hedgers, will in general not have the kind of trading volumes required to make it attractive. Very often, in practice, when a hedger seeks to take a position, the party taking a counter-position will be a speculator, although it must be clarified that he may also be a hedger albeit with an opposite view of the market. If a producer goes short in futures, the counterposition may be taken by a consumer, or by a bullish speculator. On the contrary, if a consumer goes long in futures, the counterposition may be taken by a producer or a bearish speculator. The success of the free market system critically hinges on the ability of market participants to actively trade based on their divergent points of view. Thus, speculators play as important a role as hedgers and arbitrageurs.

3.17 Speculation and Futures

Let's take the case of an investor who is bullish about the market and who seeks to make a profit in the event of his price expectations being realized. One way of operationalizing his views, would be by taking a long position in the spot market. If his view of the future were to be realized, he can obviously offset his spot position at a potentially handsome profit.

However, such a strategy would entail incurring substantial costs. In addition, in the case of commodities, as opposed to financial assets, the investor has to incur costs associated with storage and possibly insurance. Such expenditure can be avoided if futures contracts were to be used for speculation. If the investor were to assume a long futures position, then he can lock in a price at which he can acquire the asset. In the event of his views being vindicated, he can take delivery at expiration, and offload the asset in the spot market at a price which by assumption is higher. The advantage of using futures contracts as a vehicle for such a speculative strategy is that the entire value of the asset need not be paid at the outset. These contracts require that a relatively small margin be deposited, or in other words offer leverage to the investor. Example 3.16 demonstrates this argument.

Example 3.16: Futures contracts on corn with one month to expiration are available at a price of $5.25 per bushel. Andrew, a speculator, believes that the spot price after a month will be in excess of $5.50 per bushel. Let's assume that he chooses to speculate by going long in 100 futures contracts, each of which is for 5,000 bushels.

If his hunch is correct, and the market were to rise, he can exit with a profit. Let's assume that the spot price after a month is $5.80 per bushel. If so, Andrew can make a profit of:

$$100 \times 5{,}000 \times (5.80 - 5.25) = \$275{,}000$$

There is however a risky dimension to this strategy. What if Andrew is wrong about the future, and that the price after a month is only $4.75 per bushel. If so, he would have to acquire the corn at $5.25 per bushel and sell it in the spot market at $4.75.[9] The loss in this case will be:

$$100 \times 5{,}000 \times (4.75 - 5.25) = -\$\,250{,}000$$

Thus, speculation using futures can be extremely profitable if one were to read the future state of the market correctly. However, in the event of an error of judgment, the losses can be substantial.

Bearish investors too can speculate using futures contracts. However, they would need to take a short position in order to do so. If their hunch turns out to be correct,

9 Remember, a long futures position represents a commitment to buy.

and the market price were to decline, they can buy at the prevailing market price and sell it at the delivery price of the contract, which by assumption is higher. Let's consider Example 3.17.

Example 3.17: Unlike Andrew, Nick who is also a speculator, is of the opinion that after a month, the spot price of corn would have declined to below \$5.00 per bushel. He therefore decides to take a short position in 100 futures contracts.

If he were to be right and the market were to fall to a level of \$4.80 per bushel, he would end up making a profit of:

$$100 \times 5{,}000 \times (5.25 - 4.80) = \$225{,}000$$

However, if he were to read the market incorrectly, he faces the specter of a significant loss. Let's assume that the market price after a month is \$5.70 per bushel. In such a situation, Nick would incur a loss of:

$$100 \times 5{,}000 \times (5.25 - 5.70) = -\$\,225{,}000$$

Thus, bears, like bulls, can use futures as a tool for speculation. However, they are advised to do so after taking cognizance of the fact that in their quest for substantial gains, there is always a risk that they could make substantial losses.

3.18 Speculation and Options

Options can also be used as a speculative vehicle by investors. Bullish speculators can take a long position in call options or a short position in put options. If they were to use calls, and their hunch about the market turns out to be correct, they can exercise the options, acquire the asset at the exercise price, and sell it profitably at the prevailing market price, which by assumption is higher. If they were to use puts, and the market price at expiration were to exceed the strike price, then the counter-party will not exercise, and they can retain the premium they would have received at the outset, which constitutes the profit in this case. Consider Example 3.18.

Example 3.18: Call options on LPK expiring after one month are available with an exercise price of \$45. The premium is \$1.95 per share. Each contract is for 100 shares. Nigel is bullish about the market and consequently takes a long position in 100 call option contracts.

Let's assume that his hunch about the market is right and that the price of LPK after 30 days is \$49.50 per share. He can then exercise the options, acquire the shares at \$45 per share and immediately dispose them off for \$49.50 per share. After factoring in the premium paid at the outset, he will make a profit of

$$100 \times 100 \times (49.50 - 45) - 100 \times 100 \times 1.95 = \$25{,}500$$

It may however turn out that he has read the market incorrectly, and that the spot price after a month is $42.50 per share. In such a situation, he will simply refrain from exercising the options, since they constitute a right and not an obligation. The loss will be equal to the premium paid, which is $19,500.

Similarly, bearish investors too can use options to speculate, either by buying put options, or else by writing call options. If the market does indeed fall as anticipated, and a long position in puts has been assumed, the investor can acquire the asset at the market price, and sell it at the strike price by exercising the option, thereby making a profit. Consider Example 3.19.

Example 3.19: Put options on LPK with one month to expiration are available with an exercise price of $45 per share. Each contract, is for 100 shares and the premium is $0.90 per share. Nancy is bearish about the market and therefore decides to go long in 100 put option contracts.

If she were to read the market correctly, and the price does indeed decline to say $42 per share, she can acquire the shares in the spot market and deliver it under the contract at the exercise price of $45. After factoring in the premium, her profit would be:

$$100 \times 100 \times (45 - 42) - 100 \times 100 \times 0.90 = \$21,000$$

However, if her prediction about the market were to turn out to be wrong and the spot price after a month happens to be $48 per share, then she will simply refrain from exercising the option. In this case, the option premium of $9,000 would constitute a loss.

Another way to speculate on a bearish market is by writing call options. If the investor is correct and the market price were to fall below the exercise price, then the counter-party will not exercise and the speculator can retain the premium that he receives at the outset.

3.19 Interchangeable?

Once again a question will arise in the minds of most readers. Are futures and options similar from the standpoint of speculation? And the answer, similar to our conclusion on hedging using futures and options, is once again no. Let's first take the case of the speculator who assumes a long position in a futures contract. If he reads the market correctly, and the market does indeed rise, he can make a substantial profit as we have just seen. However, there is every possibility that he could be wrong. If the market were to actually fall, he will make a loss which may be substantial, because the futures contract imposes an obligation on him to buy the underlying asset at the delivery price, and having done so, he would have to dispose it off in the spot market at a price which could be considerably lower. Similarly, a speculator who goes short in a futures contract, also faces the possibility of incurring substantial losses if his forecast of the market turns out to be wrong. This is because if the market were to rise, he would have no choice but to acquire the asset in the spot market and deliver it at the delivery price, as per the requirements of the contract.

The payoff possibilities in the case of speculative strategies using options contracts are clearly different. An investor who chooses to speculate by going long in call options, can make substantial profits if the market were to rise. However, if he were to be wrong and the market were to fall subsequently, he can simply refrain from exercising the option and let the contract expire worthless. This is feasible, because an options contract gives a right to the holder and does not impose an obligation. In this case, his loss will be limited to the option premium that was paid at the outset. Speculating by buying put options is similar. If the speculator is right and there is a subsequent market decline, then he stands to benefit for he can acquire the asset at the spot price and sell it at the strike price. However, if it turns out that he was wrong, and the market were to subsequently rise, he can once again refrain from exercising the option.

Does this mean that all speculators will prefer to employ options to operationalize their strategies? The answer, as can be deduced from the logic presented thus far, is no. This is because, while one can speculate using futures contracts by depositing a relatively small margin, speculation using long positions in options entails the upfront payment of a premium, which is irrecoverable if the option were not to be exercised. Options and futures are thus not interchangeable from the standpoint of speculation, and we cannot state that one strategy dominates the other.

Speculation by writing calls and puts is also different from speculating using futures contracts. A speculator who chooses to write options, whether calls or puts, cannot make a profit in excess of the premium that he receives at the outset, for the best thing that can happen from his perspective is that the contracts are not exercised subsequently by the counter-party. However, the maximum loss for such strategies can be substantial, particularly in the case of short positions in calls, for the asset may have to be acquired for delivery at a price which theoretically has no upper bound.

Suggestions for Further Reading

Chance, D.M. *An Introduction to Derivatives & Risk Management*. South Western, 2004.
Edwards, F.R. and C.W. Ma *Futures & Options*. McGraw-Hill, 1992.
Hull, J. *Fundamentals of Futures and Options Markets*. Prentice Hall, 2004.
Hull, J. *Options, Futures, and other Derivatives*. Prentice Hall, 2009.
Kolb, R.W. *Futures, Options, & Swaps*. Blackwell, 2003.
Parameswaran, S.K. and S.P. Hegde *Futures Markets: 200 Questions and Answers*. John Wiley, 2007.
Siegel, D.R. and D.F. Siegel *Futures Markets*. The Dryden Press, 1990.

Chapter 4
Foreign Exchange Forwards and Futures

4.1 Introduction

The market for the sale and purchase of currencies the world over, is primarily dominated by banks. Foreign exchange is traded OTC the world over, and there is no exchange for foreign currency trading. The market is made by a network of brokers and dealers. However, futures and options on foreign currencies, are exchange traded. We will first study the spot market for foreign exchange and its related conventions in detail, following which we will go on to look at the market for forward contracts and futures contracts.

4.2 Purchase and Sale

The conversion of one currency into another, is called exchange, and the price at which the exchange takes place, is called the *exchange rate*. Thus, the exchange rate is the price of one country's currency in terms of that of another. In a free market, the exchange rate is a random variable like the stock price, and consequently fluctuates in response to factors impacting supply and demand.

In any transaction, there has to be a seller and a purchaser. *In foreign exchange transactions, the words purchase and sale are always used from the dealer's perspective.* In a purchase transaction, the dealer acquires foreign exchange from the customer and pays out the domestic currency. Thus, in the American context, acquisition of foreign currency and payment of dollars by the dealer, would constitute a purchase. On the other hand, in a sale transaction, the dealer sells foreign exchange to the customer, and acquires the domestic currency in lieu. In an American context therefore, acquisition of dollars and payment of foreign currency by the dealer would constitute a sale. Consider Example 4.1

Example 4.1: Take the case of an Indian exporter who has received US dollars from abroad. When he deposits the draft with his bank and receives rupees in lieu, it represents a purchase transaction. Similarly, if an Indian resident receives a check in Riyals from his relative in Saudi Arabia and deposits it in his bank, it would constitute a purchase.

On the other hand, an American importer who is buying machinery from Germany would have to approach his bank for a draft in euros, for which he would have to pay the equivalent amount in dollars. This would represent a sale transaction. Similarly, an outward remittance to England by an expatriate manager working in the U.S. would constitute a sale of foreign currency.

---

https://doi.org/10.1515/9783110746662-004

4.3 The Spot Market

4.3.1 Quoting Conventions

The exchange rate for a currency can be quoted in two different ways, called *direct quotes* and *indirect quotes*. We will briefly consider the indirect method because it is important that readers understand the principle. However, all our illustrations in this chapter will use the direct method.

In any quotation, a variable number of units of a currency, referred to as the *variable currency*, will be quoted in terms of a fixed number of units of another currency, referred to as the *base currency*. A quote will be given as X A/B or X A-B, where A and B are the two currencies. For instance a quote for the U.S. dollar in terms of the Indian rupee, will be given as 80.00 USD/INR or as 80.00 USD-INR. We will use the convention that the symbol for the variable currency will be on the right side, while the symbol for the base currency will be on the left side. For instance, if we were to quote the exchange rate as 80.25 USD/INR, the Indian rupee is the variable currency while the US dollar is the base currency.[1]

4.3.2 Direct Quotes

In the direct method, the foreign exchange rate is expressed, as the number of units of the domestic currency per unit of the foreign currency. Thus, the foreign currency is the base currency, while the domestic currency is the variable currency. For example, a rate of 80.80 USD/INR represents a direct quote in India. Thus, the direct method expresses the price per unit of the foreign currency in terms of the home currency.

An increase in the quoted value means that the domestic currency has depreciated and that the foreign currency has appreciated. For example, if the rate moves from 80.80 USD/INR to 81.20 USD/INR, then we would say that the rupee has depreciated and that the dollar has appreciated. On the other hand, a decline in the quoted value would mean that the domestic currency has appreciated and the foreign currency has depreciated. For example, if the rate moves to 80.20 USD/INR, it signifies an appreciation of the rupee relative to the dollar, or conversely, the depreciation of the dollar relative to the rupee.

An appreciating rupee means that fewer rupees are required to purchase a dollar or in other words that the rupee price of the dollar has gone down. Consequently, it means that imported goods will be cheaper for Indians, whereas exports from India will be costlier for foreigners. On the other hand, a depreciating rupee means that more rupees are required to acquire a dollar, which means that the price of the dollar has gone up.

1 The symbol *INR* stands for Indian Rupees and *USD* for U.S. Dollars. The symbols used for the major currencies are given in Appendix 4.1.

Consequently, it will make imported goods more expensive for Indians, but will ensure that foreigners perceive Indian imports to be more attractive.

Why do we have two methods for quoting exchange rates? Consider a daily use item like a bar of candy. Assume the price is quoted as $1.25 per bar. If we want we can quote the price as 0.80 bars per dollar. But, the universal practice is to quote the price of a good or service in terms of currency units, and not to quote the price of a currency unit in terms of a good or service. The foreign exchange market is different. Since there are two currencies involved, both methods are legitimate. Thus, the quote can be for the dollar in terms of rupees, or for the rupee in terms of dollars.

4.3.3 Bid-Ask Quotes

Let's consider the case of rupee-dollar transactions in the Indian market. From the dealer's perspective, when he is buying dollars, he would like to pay out as little as possible in rupee terms, whereas when he is selling dollars, he would like to charge as much as possible in rupee terms. Thus, the buying rate for a foreign currency in the case of the direct quotation method, will be lower than the selling rate. The differential between the buying rate, called the *bid* and the selling rate called the *ask*, is known as the *spread* and constitutes a profit for the dealer. *Thus, the maxim in the case of direct quotes is buy low and sell high.* For example, a quote of 80.35/80.65 would imply that the dealer is willing to buy dollars at the rate of rupees 80.35 per dollar, but will charge rupees 80.65 per dollar if he were to sell dollars.

4.3.4 Indirect Quotes

In the indirect method, the exchange rate is expressed as the number of units of the foreign currency per unit of the domestic currency. Thus, the domestic currency is the base currency while the foreign currency is the variable currency. For example, a rate of 1.25 USD per 100 INR represents an indirect quote in India. Thus, the indirect method expresses the price per unit of the domestic currency in terms of the foreign currency.

An increase in the quoted value means that the domestic currency has appreciated and the foreign currency has depreciated. For example, if the rate were to move from 1.25 100 INR/USD to 1.35 100 INR/USD, then we would say that the rupee has appreciated and that the dollar has depreciated. On the other hand, a decline in the quoted value means that the domestic currency has depreciated and the foreign currency has appreciated. For example, if the rate moves to 1.15 100 INR/USD, it signifies a depreciation of the rupee relative to the dollar or conversely an appreciation of the dollar relative to the rupee.

Readers may initially find this confusing, for a larger number means a depreciating rupee if the rates are quoted directly, but an appreciating rupee if they are quoted indirectly. The best way to think of it is in terms of variable and base currencies. If we quote the rate as rupees per dollar, it is a direct quote in India. A larger value would mean that the variable currency, in this case the rupee, has depreciated, whereas the base currency, in this case the dollar, has appreciated. If however, the rate were to be quoted as dollars per INR 100, it will be an indirect quote in India. In this case too, a larger value would mean that the variable currency, namely the dollar, has depreciated, whereas the base currency, the rupee, has appreciated. Similarly, in both the cases, a smaller value would signify an appreciation of the variable currency and a depreciation of the base currency.

4.3.5 Bid-Ask Quotes

Once again, let's consider the case of rupee-dollar transactions. From the dealer's perspective, when he is buying dollars he would like to buy as many dollars as he can per rupees 100, whereas when he is selling dollars, he would like to part with as few dollars as possible per rupees 100. Thus, the buying rate for foreign exchange in the case of the indirect quotation method, will be higher than the selling rate. *The maxim in the case of indirect quotes is therefore, buy high and sell low*. For example a quote of 1.35/1.25 would imply that the dealer is willing to buy dollars at the rate of 1.35 per 100 rupees, that is for every 1.35 dollars acquired by him, he will pay out 100 rupees. But, he will part with only 1.25 dollars per 100 rupees at the time of sale, if he were to sell dollars to a client.

The logic behind the bid being higher than the ask, in the case of indirect quotes, may be understood as follows. Consider a quote for an equity share, 45.25-45.40 per share in terms of dollars. The bid is for the purchase of the base item on the part of the dealer, and the ask is the rate for the sale of the base item on its part. The base item in this case is one equity share. In direct quotes in the foreign exchange market, the bid is the rate for the purchase of the base currency, from the perspective of the dealer, and the ask is the rate for the sale of the base currency. Thus, like in all the other markets, the principle while dealing with a direct foreign exchange quote is, buy low and sell high.

An indirect foreign exchange quote is however different. The bid is the rate for buying the variable currency, from the perspective of the dealer, and the ask is the rate for selling the variable currency, once again from its point of view. Consequently, we get the unusual result that the bid is higher than the ask. In a direct foreign exchange quote, if the bid were to be higher than the ask, it would represent an arbitrage opportunity. In an indirect foreign exchange quote, the norm is for the bid to be higher than the ask.

4.3.6 Converting A Direct Quote to an Indirect Quote

Consider a direct quote for the US dollar: 82.2500/82.4500 USD/INR. Let's take the bid first. A quote of 82.25 to buy U.S dollars represents a quote of $\frac{1}{82.2500}$ to sell a rupee or equivalently a rate of $\frac{100}{82.2500}$ = 1.2158 100 INR/USD to sell 100 rupees. Similarly a quote of 82.45 to sell dollars represents a quote of $\frac{100}{82.4500}$ = 1.2129 100 INR/USD to buy 100 rupees. Consequently a direct quote of 82.2500/82.4500 USD/INR in Mumbai, corresponds to an indirect quote of 1.2158/1.2129 100 INR/USD in Mumbai. Hence, to convert a direct quote to an equivalent indirect quote in the same market, we need to take reciprocals on both sides. Since, in a direct quote, the bid will be lower than the ask, when we take reciprocals, the bid will become higher than the ask.

The direct quote in Mumbai will have an equivalent direct quote in New York. The difference is that in India, the quote will be for dollars in terms of rupees, whereas in the US it will be for rupees in terms of dollars. Hence, to convert a direct quote in a country, to the equivalent direct quote in the foreign country, we need to take reciprocals on both sides and switch. Thus, the direct quote of 82.2500-82.4500 USD-INR, in Mumbai corresponds to a direct quote of 1.2129-1.2158 100 INR-USD in New York.

4.3.7 European Terms and American Terms

When an exchange rate is quoted with the US dollar as the base currency, it is referred to as a quote in European terms. For instance a quote of 0.8250 USD/EUR would be a quote as per the European convention. On the other hand, a quote with the US dollar as the variable currency is said to be a quote in American terms. For instance, a quote of 0.65 AUD/USD would be a quote as per the American convention. Thus, a direct quote for the dollar in Mumbai, is a quote as per European terms, while an indirect quote for the dollar in Mumbai, is a quote as per American terms.

4.3.8 The Big Figure and the Pips

Foreign exchange rates are normally quoted to four decimal places. The last two decimal places are called *points* or *pips*. The number in front is called the *big figure*. When dealing with each other dealers will mention only the pips on the respective sides. Thus, if the rate is 80.2125–80.2185, the dealer will simply say 25/85. However, if the dealer has to quote to a retail client, then the full rate will have to be quoted. If dealer ABC calls dealer XYZ and receives a quote, he will say 5 mine, if he wants to buy 5 million of the foreign currency, and 5 yours if he wants to sell 5 million units of the foreign currency.

4.4 Cross Rates

Consider a situation where we are given the rates for two currency pairs, A and B, as well as B and C. We can use these rates to compute the rates for the pair A and C. The method of computation depends on the way the rates are quoted, as Examples 4.2 to 4.4 will demonstrate.

Example 4.2: Consider the following spot rates:

1.1125-1.1195 EUR-USD and 80.3125-80.3205 USD-INR

We would like to compute the rates for the euro in terms of the Rupee. Let's consider the EUR-INR bid rate. That is, we would like to sell euros to the dealer and acquire rupees in lieu. We will first sell a euro in exchange for 1.1125 dollars. These dollars can then be sold for

$$1.1125 \times 80.3125 = 89.3477 \text{ INR}$$

Thus, the bid rate is 89.3477 EUR-INR.

Now let's consider the EUR-INR Ask. We can buy one euro by paying 1.1195 USD. These dollars can be acquired by paying

$$1.1195 \times 80.3205 = 89.9188 \text{ INR}$$

Hence, the ask rate is 89.9188 EUR-INR.

So if the common currency, which in this case is the USD, is base in one quote and variable in the other, we can multiply the two bids to get the cross bid, and multiply the two asks to get the cross ask.

Example 4.3: Now, consider a situation where the common currency is the base currency in both quotes.

0.8905 - 0.8985 USD-EUR and 80.3125-80.3205 USD-INR

Consider the EUR-INR bid. If we sell one Euro we can acquire $\frac{1}{0.8985}$ = 1.1130 USD. With this, we can acquire

$$1.1130 \times 80.3125 = 89.3878 \text{ INR}$$

Hence the EUR-INR bid = 89.3878 = $\frac{80.3125}{0.8985}$.

Now, consider the ask. To acquire one Euro we need $\frac{1}{0.8905}$ = 1.1230 USD. To acquire these dollars we need

$$1.1230 \times 80.3205 = 90.1999 \text{ INR}$$

Thus the EUR-INR ask = 90.1999 = = $\frac{80.3205}{0.8905}$.

Hence, if the common currency is the base currency in both the quotes, then we need to divide opposite sides of the quotes, to get the cross rates.

Example 4.4: Finally, consider a situation where the common currency is variable in both quotes.

80.3125–80.3205 USD-INR and 8.2715–8.2795 HKD-INR.

Consider the USD-HKD bid. If we sell one US dollar, we will get 80.3125 INR. To acquire one HKD we need 8.2795 INR. Hence, with 80.3125 INR, we can acquire

$$\frac{80.3125}{8.2795} = 9.7002 \text{ HKD}$$

Hence, the USD-HKD bid = 9.7002 = $\frac{80.3125}{8.2795}$.

Now, consider the USD-HKD ask. To acquire a USD we need 80.3205 INR. To acquire one rupee we need $\frac{1}{8.2715}$ HKD. Thus, to acquire 80.3205 INR we need

$$\frac{80.3205}{8.2715} = 9.7105 \text{ HKD}$$

Hence, the USD-HKD Ask = 9.7105 = $\frac{80.3205}{8.2715}$

Therefore, if the common currency, is the variable currency in both the quotes, then we need to divide opposite sides of the quotes to get the cross rates.

4.5 Appreciating and Depreciating Currencies

If the domestic currency were to appreciate with respect to a foreign currency, and the convention is to invoice all imports and exports in the foreign currency, then importers will be happy, whereas exporters would be unhappy. On the contrary, if the domestic currency were to depreciate, then exporters will be happy, whereas importers will be perturbed. A depreciating domestic currency, will make the good cheaper for foreigners, but in many cases the input costs will go up if a lot of imported components are used. A depreciating home currency is good from improving the country's balance of trade position, with respect to key trading partners.

From the standpoint of capital investments, if a foreign entity were to invest in production facilities in a country, then it would stand to gain if the currency of the country chosen for investment, were to weaken. However, if the currency were to continue weakening, the foreign company stands to lose when the funds are repatriated back on a future date. Investors who invest in foreign equities stand to gain if the domestic currency were to depreciate subsequently. The dividends received will be more in terms of the domestic currency, and the magnitude of capital gains too will be higher, when translated to the domestic currency.

4.6 Exchange Rate Regimes

What is an exchange rate regime? The term refers to a mechanism for determining the rates of exchange between currencies at a given point in time, as well as for determining the changes in such rates across time. It also encompasses the related procedures and institutional features, as well as the factors that induce changes in exchange rates.

One of the first regimes was what is referred to as the *gold standard*, which was prevalent till 1914. Under this system, a standard unit of a national currency, such as the dollar in the U.S., was expressed in terms of a fixed weight of gold. That is, although the currency in circulation consisted of paper notes and coins, the underlying edifice was gold. In the U.S., the value of gold was kept fixed at $20.67 per troy ounce.[2] Under this system, the monetary authority of a country was required to convert gold into currency units and the currency units into gold on demand, at the specified rate. The consequence of such a system was that it lead to fixed exchange rates between currencies. For instance a dollar coin with a purity of 90% had a weight of 1.672 grams of gold, whereas a coin of British currency with a purity of 91.70% had a weight of 7.988 grams. Thus the exchange rate between the two currencies was:

$$\frac{7.988 \times 0.917}{1.672 \times 0.90} = \$4.8678$$

Deviations from this rate would obviously lead to arbitrage as Example 4.5 illustrates.

Example 4.5: Assume that two countries A and B, have the franc and the dollar as their respective currencies. The franc is equivalent to 0.25 ounces of gold while the dollar is equivalent to 0.60 ounces of gold. If so, the exchange rate between the two currencies ought to be:

$$\frac{0.60}{0.25} = 2.40 \text{ francs per dollar.}$$

Let's first consider the case where the exchange rate is 2.50, or in other words the dollar is over-valued. An arbitrageur can borrow a dollar and convert it to 2.50 francs. This can be converted to 0.625 ounces of gold, which in turn can be used to acquire 1.0417 dollars. Obviously there is an arbitrage profit of 0.0417 dollars.

On the other hand if the exchange rate were to be 2.30, an arbitrageur can borrow a franc and convert it to $\frac{1}{2.30}$ dollars. This can be used to acquire 0.2609 ounces of gold which can be sold so as to yield 1.04360 francs. Once again there is an arbitrage profit of 0.04360 francs.

Strictly speaking the gold standard required a country which adopted it to adhere to the following rules.

- It ought to fix once and for all, the rate of conversion between its currency and gold.
- It ought to allow free inflows and outflows of gold.

2 See Logue (1995).

- It ought to ensure that domestic money supply was linked to the amount of gold reserves available with it. A decline in gold reserves should lead to a contraction in money supply, while an increase in gold reserves should lead to an expansion in the money supply.

At the end of World War II, an international conference was held at Bretton Woods in the U.S., to discuss ways of reforming the international monetary system.[3] The agreement that was eventually reached, stipulated the following. The dollar which was the epicenter of this system was valued at $\frac{1}{35}$th of an ounce of gold, and the U.S. government gave an undertaking to freely convert dollars to gold at this rate. Other countries agreed to fix the parities of their respective currencies with respect to the U.S. dollar. The central banks of countries other than the U.S. were required to maintain the value of their currencies vis-a-vis the dollar, within ±1% of the prescribed exchange rate. If the exchange rate were to hit the upper or lower limit, the concerned central bank was required to either buy or sell dollars as the case may be, in order to ensure that the exchange rate remained within the permissible limits.

This modified system was termed as a *gold exchange standard*, under which the key currency, namely the U.S. dollar was freely convertible to gold. It was also referred to an adjustable peg system because although the exchange rates between currencies was fixed, changes were permitted when warranted by economic circumstances. Member countries could change the par value of their currencies, up to 10% in either direction,without any external approval. If a change of a greater magnitude was sought, then approval from the IMF was required. Such approval, was contingent on determination by the IMF, that the country's balance of payments was in a *fundamental disequilibrium*. However, this concept of the balance of payments being in disequilibrium, was not formally defined. Thus, in practice, most countries resorted to changes within 10% of the prevailing rate. Any country that changed without approval, or after being denied approval, was denied access to the IMF. The Federal Reserve unlike other central banks, however did not have this freedom. In other words, the U.S had to constantly maintain the gold value of the dollar.

In 1971 the dollar was declared non-convertible since the foreign dollar liabilities of the U.S were far in excess of its reserves of gold. A fresh agreement named as the *Smithsonian Agreement* was reached, which modified the gold-dollar exchange rate to $38.02 per ounce. In other words the dollar was devalued. Central banks of countries were required to maintain the values of their currencies within a band of ±2.25% of the required parity rate with the dollar.

In 1973, the existing system was abandoned and all major currencies began to float. That is, exchange rates became market determined, based on the relative supply and

---

3 Among other outcomes of the deliberations was the birth of the International Monetary Fund (IMF), and the World Bank.

demand. In practice, the exchange rate system that prevails today is referred to as a *managed float* or a *dirty float*. That is, although rates are largely determined by free market forces, central banks tend to periodically intervene to keep rates at desirable levels. For instance, if the euro were to be constantly appreciating with respect to the USD, the Federal Reserve may sell euros from its reserves, or the ECB may buy USD to add to its reserves.

4.7 The Forward Market

The forward market allows investors to buy and sell foreign currencies for delivery at a future date. If the forward rate of a currency exceeds the spot rate, then we say that the currency is selling at a *forward premium*. For example consider the following rates.

Spot: 80.8000/81.2000 USD/INR

1 Month Forward: 81.0500/81.5000 USD/INR

In this case, the dollar is at a forward premium.

If however, the forward rate is less than the spot rate, then we say that the foreign currency is at a *forward discount*. For instance, if the one month forward rate were to be 80.5000/80.9500, then we would say that the dollar is at a forward discount.

When the spot rate is equal to the forward rate, then we say that the currency is trading *flat*.

If the forward rate is given directly, like it is above, then we call such rates as *outright forward rates*. But in practice, in the inter-bank market, only the difference between the forward rate and the spot rate, called the *forward margin or swap points* is given and we have to construct the forward rates from the spot rates.

Consider the following data.

Spot: 80.2420/80.2450 USD/INR

Forward Points: 45/72

For most currencies, a point is $\frac{1}{10{,}000}$th of the currency. Thus 45 points would imply 0.0045. For certain currencies, however, a point may connote $\frac{1}{100}$th of a unit. In the case of quotes where the price of a currency is expressed in terms of Japanese Yen, a point is 0.01 JPY.

If we look at the above data, we can see that it has not been specified as to whether the currency is at a forward premium or a discount. So the question to ask ourselves is, do we add the forward margin or do we subtract it? The thing to remember, is that the bid-ask spread will widen as we go forward. That is, the spot market will have the lowest spread. As we move forward in time, the spread will gradually increase.

Thus, if the margin is specified as *a*/*b*, where $a < b$, then adding the margin will widen the spread, and therefore, the forward margin specified indicates that it should be added. Hence, if the margin is specified as a smaller number followed by a larger number, then it signifies a forward premium and must be added. The above quotation therefore implies outright forward rates of 80.2465/80.2522. The spread in the spot market is 30 pips whereas in the forward market, it is 57 pips.

However, consider another case where the forward margin is specified as 85/40. In this case, subtracting the margin will widen the spread. Hence, if the margin is specified as a/b, where $a > b$, then the margin should be subtracted. That is, if the margin is specified as a larger number followed by a smaller number, it signifies a discount and must be subtracted. In this case, the implied outright forward rates are 80.2335/80.2410. The spread in the forward market is 75 pips, as compared to 30 pips in the spot market.

It must be remembered that the above logic is valid for direct quotes. In the case of indirect quotes, if the swap points are specified as a/b where $a < b$, then subtracting the margin will widen the spreads. Thus, a smaller number followed by a larger number, indicates a forward premium, which should be subtracted from the quoted spot rates. Similarly, if the margin is specified as a larger number followed by a smaller number, it signifies that the foreign currency is trading at a discount and hence the swap points have to be added to the quoted spot rates. Thus, the implication of a being less than b, or greater than b, remains the same, whether we are dealing with direct quotes or indirect quotes. It is the method of dealing with the margins that differs.

4.7.1 Broken-Dated Contracts

The forward margins that are observed in practice, are for standard time intervals such as one, three, and six months. However, at times a bank's client may ask for a forward contract with an odd maturity date, that is, a date that falls between two standard intervals. Such contracts are known as *broken-dated* contracts. In order to compute the applicable rate for such odd periods, a method of linear interpolation is used, as Examples 4.6 to 4.9 demonstrate.

Example 4.6: On a given day, the following rates are observed in the New York market.

Spot: 0.7250-0.7295 SGD/USD

1-M: 35/65

2-M: 50/90

Obviously the Singapore dollar is quoting at a forward premium. Assume that a client approaches a bank, seeking to buy Singapore dollars 1.6 months forward. The premium for one month is 65 points on the ask side, and 90 points for a two month contract. Thus, the additional premium for 0.6 months is

$$0.6 \times (90 - 65) = 15$$

Hence the outright ask rate for a 1.6 month contract is 0.7295 + 0.0065 + 0.0015 = 0.7375 SGD-USD. Using similar logic, the bid rate for a 1.6 months contract is

$$0.7250 + 0.0035 + 0.0009 = 0.7294 \text{ SGD-USD}$$

The spread in the spot market is 45 pips, and in the forward market it is 81 pips.

Example 4.7: On a given day, the following rates are observed in the New York market.

Spot: 0.7250-0.7295 SGD/USD
1-M: 65/35
2-M: 90/50

The Singapore dollar is at a forward discount. Consider the rates for a 1.6 months forward contract. On the ask side the discount is 35 points for a one month contract and 50 points for a two months contract. Hence, the additional discount for a month is

$$0.6 \times (50 - 35) = 9$$

Hence, the outright ask rate for a 1.6 month contract is 0.7295 − 0.0035 − 0.0009 = 0.7251 SGD-USD. Using similar logic, the bid rate for a 1.6 months contract is

$$0.7250 - 0.0065 - 0.0015 = 0.7170 \text{ SGD-USD}$$

The spread in the spot market is 45 pips, and in the forward market it is 81 pips.

Example 4.8: On a given day, the following rates are observed in the New York market.

Spot: 0.7250-0.7295 SGD/USD
1-M: 35/65
2-M: 90/50

The Singapore dollar is at a forward premium for a one month contract, and at a forward discount for two months. As we go from one month to two months on the ask side, we are going from +65 pips to -50 pips. Thus the change is -115 pips. Hence, the change for a 0.6 months contract should be

$$0.6 \times 115 = 69 \text{ pips}$$

This is obviously a discount. Hence, the outright forward rate for a 1.6 months contract is 0.7295 + 0.0065 - 0.0069 = 0.7291. Using similar logic, the bid rate for a 1.6 months contract is

$$0.7250 + 0.0035 - 0.0075 = 0.7210$$

The spread in the spot market is 45 pips, and in the forward market it is 81 pips.

Example 4.9: On a given day, the following rates are observed in the New York market.

Spot: 0.7250-0.7295 SGD/USD
1-M: 65/35
2-M: 50/90

The Singapore dollar us at a forward discount for a one month contract, and at a forward premium for two months. As we go from one month to two months on the ask side, we are going from -35 pips to +90 pips.

This the change +125 pips. Hence, the change for 0.6 months contract should be

$$0.6 \times 125 = 75 \text{ pips}$$

This is obviously a premium. Hence, the outright forward rate for a 1.6 months contract is 0.7295 - 0.0035 + 0.0075 = 0.7335. Using similar logic, the bid rate for a 1.6 months contract is

$$0.7250 - 0.0065 + 0.0069 = 0.7254$$

The spread in the spot market is 45 pips, and in the forward market it is 81 pips.

4.8 The No-Arbitrage Forward Price

We will now derive the relationship between the spot rate and the forward rate for a given maturity, using arbitrage arguments.

4.8.1 Cash and Carry Arbitrage

The spot rate for Singapore dollars in Mumbai on a given day is INR 59.2025, whereas the rate for a three month forward contract is INR 59.8075. The rate of interest for a three month loan in the Indian money market is 7.5% per annum, whereas the rate for a loan of the same tenor in the Singapore money market is 4.5% per annum.

Take the case of an arbitrageur who decides to undertake the following steps. He borrows INR 59.2025 in Mumbai and buys one Singapore Dollar. This Singapore dollar is immediately invested in the Singapore money market. This will lock in a receivable of:

$$\left(1 + \frac{0.045}{4}\right) = 1.01125 \text{ SGD}$$

after three months. The arbitrageur can lock in an equivalent amount in Indian rupees, right at the outset, by taking a short position in a forward contract.

At the end of three months, the deposit in Singapore will yield SGD 1.01125, which can be immediately sold under the forward contract to yield INR 60.4803. A part of this, that is:

$$59.2025 \times \left(1 + \frac{0.075}{4}\right) = \text{INR } 60.3125$$

will be required to pay off the loan that was taken in India. The balance of INR 0.1678, is clearly a pure arbitrage profit.

4.8.2 Reverse Cash and Carry Arbitrage

We will assume that all the other variables have the same values as in the above example, except for the forward rate, which we will assume is INR 59.3075. In such circumstances, a reverse cash and carry arbitrage strategy may be implemented as follows.

The arbitrageur can borrow a Singapore dollar in the Singapore money market, and convert it at the spot rate to INR 59.2025. This can be lent out in India at the rate of 7.5% per annum, which will lock in a receivable of INR 60.3125 after three months . Right at the outset, a long forward position can be used to ensure that the rupees can be used to acquire the following amount in Singapore currency after three months:

$$\left(1 + \frac{.045}{4}\right) = 1.01125$$

The cost in rupees will be:

$$59.3075 \times 1.01125 = \text{INR } 59.9747$$

At the end of three months, when the deposit in India matures, the arbitrageur can take delivery under the forward contract and pay off his loan in Singapore. The balance of INR 0.3378 is a clear arbitrage profit.

Let's denote the spot rate by S; the forward rate by F; the interest rate in the domestic money market by i_d; and the interest rate in the foreign market by i_f. Note we are using the direct quotation system. The no-arbitrage condition can be expressed as:

$$S(1 + i_d) = F(1 + i_f)$$

$$\Rightarrow F = S \times \frac{(1 + i_d)}{(1 + i_f)} \tag{4.1}$$

The kind of arbitrage that we have just illustrated is called *covered interest arbitrage* and the relationship that must exist if such arbitrage is to be precluded, that is:

$$\frac{F}{S} = \frac{(1 + i_d)}{(1 + i_f)}$$

is called the *interest rate parity* equation.

$$\frac{F}{S} = \frac{(1 + i_d)}{(1 + i_f)} \Rightarrow \frac{(F - S)}{S} = \frac{(i_d - i_f)}{(1 + i_f)} \tag{4.2}$$

In practice, this is often approximated as

$$\frac{(F - S)}{S} = (i_d - i_f) \tag{4.3}$$

because $1 + i_f \cong 1$, if i_f is very small.

In real life there could at times be deviations from the interest rate parity relationship, which an arbitrageur is unable to exploit. One reason is that buying and selling foreign exchange, both in the spot as well as the forward markets, entails the payment of transactions costs. Second, all countries in the world do not permit free flow of funds across their borders. Thus, if such exchange controls were to be in place, it is likely that one will observe deviations from interest rate parity that cannot be arbitraged away. In practice, it has been observed that even a perception that exchange rate controls may be imposed in the future, is adequate to preclude an investor from attempting to execute a covered interest arbitrage transaction. One final factor is that investors have to pay taxes on income and profits, which vary from country to country. Hence, the ability to make arbitrage profits on a post tax basis, is likely to depend on the investor's tax status.

4.8.3 Arbitrage in the Presence of Transactions Costs

Let's now consider a situation where both spot and forward markets, as well as the money markets, are subject to bid-ask spreads. We will denote the variables as follows:

$$\begin{aligned}\text{Spot Quote} &\equiv S_b/S_a \\ \text{Forward Quote} &\equiv F_b/F_a \\ \text{Domestic Borrowing/Lending Rates} &\equiv r_{db}/r_{dl} \\ \text{Foreign Borrowing/Lending Rates} &\equiv r_{fb}/r_{fl}\end{aligned}$$

Take the case of an investor who is contemplating a cash and carry strategy. He will have to borrow S_a units of the domestic currency to buy one unit of the foreign currency, which can be invested at r_{fl} and simultaneously enter into a forward contract at F_b to sell $(1 + r_{fl})$ units of the foreign currency. In order to preclude arbitrage, it must be that

$$\begin{aligned}(1 + r_{fl}) \times F_b &\le (1 + r_{db}) \times S_a \\ \Rightarrow F_b &\le S_a \times \frac{(1 + r_{db})}{(1 + r_{fl})}\end{aligned} \tag{4.4}$$

Now let's take the case of reverse cash and carry arbitrage. To implement this strategy, an investor must borrow one unit of the foreign currency and convert it to S_b units of the domestic currency, which can be invested at r_{dl}. He must at the same time, go long in a forward contract to acquire $(1 + r_{fb})$ units of the foreign currency at a rate F_a. In order to rule out arbitrage, it must be that

$$\begin{aligned}S_b \times (1 + r_{dl}) &\le F_a(1 + r_{fb}) \\ \Rightarrow F_a &\ge S_b \times \frac{(1 + r_{dl})}{(1 + r_{fb})}\end{aligned} \tag{4.5}$$

We will illustrate these principles with the help of Example 4.10.

Example 4.10: The following market information is available at a given instant.

Spot: 1.2015/1.2175 GBP/USD
1-Year Forward: 1.2295/1.2410 GBP/USD
Borrowing/Lending Rates in the U.S: 4.5%/4.3% per annum
Borrowing/Lending Rates in the U.K: 3.5%/3.3% per annum

We will first examine whether cash and carry arbitrage is feasible. One British Pound can be purchased by borrowing 1.2175 USD. This can be invested in the U.K to yield 1.033 GBP at maturity. If a forward contract is booked at the outset, then this amount can be sold at the rate of 1.2295 GBP/USD. The final proceeds will therefore be

$$1.033 \times 1.2295 = 1.2701 \text{ USD}$$

The repayment due on the loan taken in the U.S is

$$1.045 \times 1.2175 = 1.2723$$

Consequently, cash and carry arbitrage will not be profitable.

What about reverse cash and carry arbitrage? Consider an investor who borrows one British pound in the U.K and converts it to 1.2015 USD. This can be invested in the U.S to yield

$$1.043 \times 1.2015 = 1.2532 \text{ USD at maturity.}$$

In order to cover the loan repayment in the U.K, a forward contract will have to be booked at the outset to acquire 1.035 GBP at 1.2410 GBP/USD. The cost of acquisition will be $1.2844 USD. Hence, reverse cash and carry arbitrage is also not an attractive proposition in this case.

4.9 Option Forwards

Often, while entering into a forward contract, the client may not know the exact date on which he will complete the contract. For instance, an importer may say that he needs foreign exchange some time between one to two months from today. In such a case, he can negotiate a forward contract with an option. The option will allow him to complete the contract on any date during the stated period. The option seller, namely the dealer, will quote rates in such cases, after considering the fact that the contract may be completed on the worst possible day from his point of view. The implications of this depend on whether the dealer is buying or selling and whether the currency is at a premium or a discount, as we will illustrate with the help of Examples 4.11 to 4.16.

Example 4.11: Indian Rayon is importing machinery from the U.S and is required to make the payment between 2 to 3 months from now. However, the company is unable to specify the exact date and wants to enter into a forward contract with the option of taking delivery at any time between 2 and 3 months from today.

Assume that the following rates are prevailing in the interbank market.

Spot: 80.4500/80.8525 USD/INR

1 Month Forward: 45/85

2 Month Forward: 70/110

3 Month Forward: 110/155

The relevant base rate in this case is the selling rate. If the contract is completed at the end of two months, then the applicable premium will be 110 points, whereas if it is completed after three months, then the relevant premium is 155 points. In this case the dealer will assume that the contract will be completed after three months and charge the higher premium. Hence, the quoted forward rate will be 80.8525 + .0155 = 80.8680.

Thus the rule for a sale transaction if the currency is quoting at a premium for both maturities is, charge the higher of the two premiums.

Example 4.12: Consider the data given in Example 4.11, but assume that the dollar is trading at a forward discount and that the swap points are as follows.

1 Month Forward: 75/35

2 Month Forward: 115/75

3 Month Forward: 140/95

In this case, if the contract is completed after 2 months, then the applicable discount will be 75 points, whereas if it is completed after 3 months, then the relevant discount will be 95 points. In this case the dealer will assume that the transaction will be completed at the end of 2 months and allow the lower of the two discounts. Hence the quoted forward rate will be 85.8525 − .0075 = 80.8450.

Hence, the rule for sale transactions in the case where the currency is trading at a discount for both maturities is, allow the lower of the two discounts.

Example 4.13: Parle has exported biscuits to South Africa and will be paid in dollars sometime between one to two months from today. The current rates in the inter-bank market are as follows:

Spot: 80.3500/80.7320 USD/INR

1 Month Forward: 35/80

2 Month Forward: 65/115

The relevant spot base rate here is the buying rate of 80.3500. If the contract is completed at the end of one month, then the applicable premium is 35 points, whereas, if the party were to deliver the dollars after two months, then the premium would be 65 points. Since the bank is buying, it will take the view that the transaction may be completed at the end of one month and hence will allow a premium of only 35 points. The quoted forward rate will therefore be, 80.3500 + 0.0035 = 80.3535.

Hence, the rule for purchase transactions, in the case where the currency is trading at a premium for both maturities is, allow the lower of the two premiums.

Example 4.14: Parle has exported biscuits to South Africa and will be paid in dollars sometime between one to two months from today. The current rates in the inter-bank market are as follows:

Spot: 80.3500/80.7320 USD/INR

1 Month Forward: 80/35

2 Month Forward: 115/65

The relevant spot base rate here is the buying rate of 80.3500. If the contract is completed at the end of one month, then the applicable discount is 80 points, whereas, if the party were to deliver the dollars after two months, then the discount would be 115 points. Since the bank is buying, it will take the view that the transaction may be completed at the end of two months and hence will apply a discount of 115 points. The quoted forward rate will therefore be, 80.3500 − 0.0115 = 80.3385.

Hence, the rule for purchase transactions, in the case where the currency is trading at a discount for both maturities is, apply the higher of the two discounts.

Example 4.15: Parle has exported biscuits to South Africa and will be paid in dollars sometime between one to two months from today. The current rates in the inter-bank market are as follows:

Spot: 80.3500/80.7320 USD/INR

1 Month Forward: 35/80

2 Month Forward: 115/65

The relevant spot base rate here is the buying rate of 80.3500. If the contract is completed at the end of one month, then the applicable premium is 35 points, whereas, if the party were to deliver the dollars after two months, then the discount would be 115 points. Since the bank is buying, it will take the view that the transaction may be completed at the end of two months and hence will apply a discount of 115 points. The quoted forward rate will therefore be, 80.3500 − 0.0115 = 80.3385.

Hence, the rule for purchase transactions, in the case where the currency is trading at a discount for one maturity, and at a premium for the other is, apply the discount.

Example 4.16: Rolta has imported a machine from the US and will need to acquire dollars sometimes between one to two months from today. The current rates in the inter-bank market are as follows:

Spot: 80.3500/80.7320 USD/INR

1 Month Forward: 35/80

2 Month Forward: 115/65

The relevant spot base rate here is the selling rate of 80.7320. If the contract is completed at the end of one month, then the applicable premium is 80 points, whereas, if the party were to acquire the dollars after two months, then the discount would be 65 points. Since the bank is selling, it will take the view that the transaction may be completed at the end of one month and hence will charge a premium of 80 points. The quoted forward rate will therefore be, 80.7320 + 0.0080 = 80.7400.

Hence, the rule for sale transactions, in the case where the currency is trading at a discount for one maturity, and at a premium for the other is, charge the premium.

4.10 Non-deliverable Forwards (NDFs)

In the case of a non-deliverable forward contract, neither party buys or sells a foreign currency. If the currency which the long is required to acquire, appreciates, then the long will get a positive cash flow. Else, if the currency which the long is required to acquire, depreciates, then the long will get a negative cash flow. This can be best illustrated with the help of Examples 4.17 and 4.18.

Example 4.17: Bayer Bank in Germany has gone long in a three month NDF to acquire 50,000,000 Nigerian Niaras. The quoted rates in the forward market are 460.10–460.80 EUR-NGN. Since the bank will be acquiring Niaras the applicable rate will be 460.10.

Assume that three months hence, the spot rates are 464.25–464.95 EUR-NGN. Thus, the Niara has depreciated. So the bank will have a cash flow of

$$\frac{50{,}000{,}000}{464.95} - \frac{50{,}000{,}000}{460.10} = -1{,}133.59 \text{ EUR}$$

But what if the spot rate after three months were to have been 454.15–454.95 EUR-NGN. That is, the Niara has appreciated. If so, the bank will have a cash flow of

$$\frac{50{,}000{,}000}{454.95} - \frac{50{,}000{,}000}{460.10} = 1{,}230.16 \text{ EUR}$$

Example 4.18: Dornier Bank in Germany has gone short in a three month NDF to sell 50,000,000 Nigerian Niaras. The quoted rates in the forward market are 460.10–460.80 EUR-NGN. Since the bank will be selling Niaras the applicable rate will be 460.80.

Assume that three months hence, the spot rates are 464.25–464.95 EUR-NGN. Thus, the Niara has depreciated. So the bank will have a cash flow of

$$\frac{50{,}000{,}000}{460.80} - \frac{50{,}000{,}000}{464.25} = 806.35 \text{ EUR}$$

But what if the spot rate after three months were to have been 454.15–454.95 EUR-NGN. That is, the Niara has appreciated. If so, the bank will have a cash flow of

$$\frac{50{,}000{,}000}{460.80} - \frac{50{,}000{,}000}{454.15} = -1{,}588.84 \text{ EUR}$$

4.11 Range Forwards

A range forward contract puts an upper limit, or cap, on the exchange rate, as well as a lower limit, or floor, on it. From the long's perspective, the upper limit is the maximum rate payable, while the floor is the minimum rate payable. If the actual exchange rate, at the end, were to be in between the two limits, the actual rate will be the rate payable.

For instance, consider a range forward with a cap if 1.1250 EUR-USD, and a floor of 1.1125 EUR-USD. Assume a party has gone long in 25 contracts and that each contract is for 1,000,000 euros. If the spot rate at the time of expiration of the contract is 1.1285 EUR-USD, the euros can acquired for:

$$25 \times 1{,}000{,}000 \times 1.1250 = \$28{,}125{,}000$$

If the spot rate at the time of expiration is 1.1185 EUR-USD, the amount payable is:

$$25 \times 1{,}000{,}000 \times 1.1185 = \$27{,}962{,}500$$

Finally, what if the terminal exchange rate is 1.0005 EUR-USD? The amount payable is:

$$25 \times 1{,}000{,}000 \times 1.1125 = \$27{,}812{,}500$$

Thus, the maximum amount payable is 28.125 MM dollars and the minimum amount payable is 27.8125 MM dollars.

4.12 Exchange Margins

The inter-dealer market or the inter-bank market, is the market where dealers transact with dealers. The rates quoted by the dealer to a client, are called merchant rates. Obviously, there is a relationship between the inter-bank rates, and the merchant rates. Assume that a dealer buys a currency from a client at his bid, or the merchant bid. He is likely to subsequently sell it, in the interbank market. When he goes to sell, he is the client, and consequently the rate applicable will be the inter-bank bid. Thus, there is a relationship between the interbank bid and the merchant bid. For the dealer to make a profit, the interbank bid must be higher than the merchant bid.

Now, consider a situation where the dealer is selling a currency to a client, at the merchant ask. The chances are he would have previously acquired it in the interbank market. When the dealer seeks to buy in the interbank market, he is once again the client, and hence the rate applicable is the interbank ask. Hence, the interbank ask and the merchant ask are related. For the dealer to have a profit, the merchant ask must be greater than the interbank ask.

Since the merchant bid is lower than the interbank bid, while the merchant ask is higher than the interbank ask, the spread for the dealer will be higher than the spread in the interbank market. Consider Examples 4.19 and 4.20.

Example 4.19: The interbank rates on a given day are: 80.1255–80.1325 USD-INR. The dealer applies a profit margin, termed as the exchange margin, of 0.06% while buying, and 0.08%while selling.[4] Thus, the bid rate for the dealer is:

$$80.1255 \times (1 - 0.0006) = 80.0774$$

The ask rate is:

$$80.1325 \times (1 + 0.0008) = 80.1966$$

Hence, the interbank spread is 70 pips, while the spread for the dealer is 0.1192 rupees.

Example 4.20: The interbank rates on a given day are: 80.1255–80.1325 USD-INR. The rate for a one month forward contract is 35/75.

The dealer applies an exchange margin of 0.06% while buying, and 0.08%while selling. In this case we need the merchant bid and ask rates for a one month forward contract. The procedure is as follows.

The bid for the forward contract: (80.1255 + 0.0035) × (1 − 0.0006) = 80.0809 USD-INR

The ask for the forward contract: (80.1325 + 0.0075) × (1 + 0.0008) = 80.2041 USD-INR

4.13 Foreign Exchange Swaps

In a foreign exchange swap transaction a party will buy or sell a currency from/to another party with a simultaneous agreement to reverse the transaction at a future point in time. Thus, such a transaction may entail a spot sale and a forward purchase or a spot purchase and a forward sale.

In such a transaction, the main issue of relevance is the forward margin or swap points for the foreign currency. The spot leg may be done at the prevailing bid or the prevailing ask, or at a rate between the two. Example 4.21 should clarify the mechanics of such a transaction.

Example 4.21: First National Bank is based in Memphis. It is approached by Citibank in New York, which wishes to sell 5 million pounds after three months. The quotes in the market are as follows:

Spot: 1.2250–1.2290 GBP/USD

3-M forward: 35/75

The two banks will agree on a spot rate between 1.2250 and 1.2290. Let's assume that they agree on a rate of 1.2275. First National will deliver the pounds to Citi in exchange for $6,137,500. Citi is selling £5MM in the

4 The margin need not be identical on both sides.

second leg of the transaction. Consequently the applicable forward margin is 75 points. Thus Citi will deliver the pounds after three months, at a rate of 1.2350. This translates to a payable of $6,175,000 for First National.

4.13.1 Motives for Foreign Exchange Swaps

In Example 4.21 Citi may have a receivable in GBP after three months. To hedge, it can go short in a three month forward contract. But in the market, it is at times not easy to enter into an offsetting forward contract for the same maturity. In practice, it is easier to do a swap as described above. If the swap is undertaken Citi will deliver the pounds after three months. However, it will have an immediate receivable of £5,000,000. This can be easily sold in the spot market.

Now consider First National's perspective. It may be a speculator. Such entities, prefer to speculate with FX swaps in the foreign exchange markets, rather than outright forward contracts. The rationale may be understood as follows.

Assume the spot exchange rate for the USD is 80.2500 USD-INR. The interest rate in India us 8% per annum, while that in the US is 4% per annum. The no arbitrage six month forward rate is

$$80.25 \times \frac{1.04}{1.02} = 81.8235$$

Thus, the difference between the forward rate and the spot rate, which is the swap points, is 1.5735 Rupees.

If the spot rate changes to 80.40, then the forward rate will be

$$80.40 \times \frac{1.04}{1.02} = 81.9765$$

The difference between the spot and forward rates is 1.5765.

Thus, if the spot rate increases by 15 paise per dollar, the forward rate increases by 15.3 paise. But the difference between the spot and forward rate changes by 0.30 paise.

Now assume the interest rate in India becomes 10% per annum. The no-arbitrage six month forward rate is

$$80.25 \times \frac{1.05}{1.02} = 82.6103$$

The forward rate changes by 0.7868 Rupees. The difference between the spot and forward rates is 2.3603 INR.

Thus, if the interest rate differential changes, there is a significant impact on both the forward rate, as well as the difference between the spot and forward rates. Hence, forward rates are influenced by changes in the spot rate, as well as changes in the interest rate differential. However, the difference between the spot and forward rates is affected significantly only when there is a change in the interest rate differential. Speculators, will not like to use products which are influenced by multiple factors. Hence, speculators in the foreign exchange market, prefer FX swaps to outright forward contracts.

4.14 Hedging an Export Transaction

Merck has exported a consignment of drugs to a company in Sydney and is scheduled to receive 50MM Australian dollars after one month. The company is worried that the U.S. dollar will appreciate by then and therefore decides to hedge using three month futures contracts. Since the company will be selling Australian dollars, it requires a short hedge.[5] Since each Australian dollar futures contract is for 100,000 AUD, 500 contracts are required. We will assume that the price of the three month contract is 0.6250 AUD/USD.

Assume that the following prices prevail in the market after one month.
Spot: 0.5985 AUD/USD
2-M futures: 0.6025 AUD/USD
If Merck had not hedged, it would have received:

$$50{,}000{,}000 \times 0.5985 = \text{USD } 29{,}925{,}000$$

However, since it has hedged using the futures contracts, the effective payoff may be calculated as follows. The profit/loss from the futures market is:[6]

$$500 \times 100{,}000 \times (0.6250 - 0.6025) = \text{USD } 1{,}125{,}000$$

Therefore, the total payoff is:

$$29{,}925{,}000 + 1{,}125{,}000 = \text{USD } 31{,}050{,}000$$

The effective exchange rate is:

$$\frac{31{,}050{,}000}{50{,}000{,}000} = 0.6210 \text{AUD/USD}$$

5 The logic is that if the U.S. dollar appreciates, the U.S. dollar price of Australian dollars will fall and consequently, the short hedger will gain.
6 In this case it is a profit.

4.15 Hedging an Import Transaction

United Airlines has ordered spare parts for its aircraft from Airbus in France. The total cost is EUR 50MM and the payment is due after one month. The company is worried that the euro will appreciate, which means that the cost in dollars will go up. Since it will be buying euros, the company requires a long hedge. Assume that the current futures rate for a three month contract is 1.0325 EUR/USD.

Let's assume that the following rates prevail in the market after one month.

Spot: 1.0450 EUR/USD

2-M Futures: 1.0485 EUR/USD

If the company had not hedged, then it would have had to purchase 50MM EUR at 1.0450. This would have lead to an outflow of $52,250,000. However, since it has hedged, its effective cost can be calculated as follows.

The number of futures contracts required is:

$$\frac{50{,}000{,}000}{125{,}000} = 400$$

The profit/loss from the futures market is:[7]

$$125{,}000 \times 400 \times (1.0485 - 1.0325) = \text{USD } 800{,}000$$

The effective cost is:

$$52{,}250{,}000 - 800{,}000 = 51{,}450{,}000\ USD$$

and the effective exchange rate is:

$$\frac{51{,}450{,}000}{50{,}000{,}000} = 1.0290 \text{ EUR/USD}$$

4.16 Creating Synthetic Investments

We know that, Spot - Futures = Synthetic T-bill. Foreign exchange futures contracts can be used to make synthetic investments denominated in the domestic currency, with the help of a cash and carry arbitrage strategy. Example 4.22, is yet another manifestation of quasi-arbitrage.

7 In this case, it is once again a profit.

Example 4.22: Consider the following information. On July 11, 20XX, a portfolio manager in Sydney has 10MM AUD to invest till September 21, that is, for a period of 72 days. An investment in domestic T-bills will yield an annualized return of 7.15%. Assume that the following rates are prevalent in the foreign exchange market.

Spot: 1.5750/1.5795 USD/AUD
September 21 Futures: 1.5870/1.5920 USD/AUD
The lending rate in the U.S is 5% per annum.

It turns out that in such a situation, the manager can earn a higher rate of return without facing exchange risk, with the help of futures contracts. A cash and carry strategy would first entail the conversion of the AUD into an equivalent amount of 6,331,117.40 USD, at the ask rate of 1.5795. This amount can then be invested in the U.S at 5% per annum. Simultaneously, a short position will have to be taken in the futures contracts. The number of contracts required can be determined as follows. On September 21, the investment in the U.S will pay off

$$6{,}331{,}117.40\left[1 + 0.05 \times \frac{72}{360}\right] = 6{,}394{,}428.50 \text{ USD.}$$

In order to sell this amount on that day, the manager will require 639.4429 futures contracts, assuming that each contract is for 10,000 USD. This will lock in

$$6{,}394{,}428.50 \times 1.5870 = 10{,}147{,}958 \text{ AUD.}$$

The rate of return

$$= \frac{(10{,}147{,}958 - 10{,}000{,}000)}{10{,}000{,}000} \equiv 1.4796\%$$

$$\equiv 7.3979\% \text{ on an annualized basis,}$$

which is greater than the domestic lending rate of 7.15%.

4.17 Borrowing Funds Abroad

Just the way a cash and carry strategy can be employed to make a synthetic investment denominated in the home currency, a synthetic borrowing in the home currency can be undertaken using a reverse cash and carry strategy. The borrower would raise the funds in a foreign capital market and convert it into the domestic currency at the prevailing spot bid rate. He would simultaneously go long in futures contracts to lock in a rate for the foreign currency, in order to take care of his principal and interest payments at the time of maturity. Such quasi-arbitrage would be attractive if the domestic borrowing rate were to be higher than the synthetic borrowing rate. Example 4.23 illustrates this.

Example 4.23: A corporate treasurer is Sydney requires 10MM AUD on 11 July 20XX for a period of 72 days. One option is to borrow in the local money market at a rate of 8.25% per annum. The alternative is to borrow in the U.S., and hedge away the foreign exchange risk using futures contracts. Assume that the following rates are prevalent in the foreign exchange market.

Spot: 1.5725/1.5745 USD/AUD

September 21 Futures: 1.5785/1.5810 USD/AUD

The borrowing rate in the U.S is 5.30% per annum.

Consider the following strategy. The manager can borrow the equivalent of 10MM AUD in the U.S. money market, which at the spot bid of 1.5725 will amount to:

$$\frac{10{,}000{,}000}{1.5725} = \$6{,}359{,}300.40$$

On 21 September, this principal amount will have to be repaid with interest. The amount due will be:

$$6{,}359{,}300.40\left[1 + 0.053 \times \frac{72}{360}\right] = \$6{,}426{,}708.90$$

To lock-in the value of this in AUD the treasurer will need to go long in 642.6709 futures contracts. The payable in terms of AUD will therefore be:

$$6{,}426{,}708.90 \times 1.5810 = 10{,}160{,}626 \text{ AUD}$$

The effective borrowing cost is:

$$\frac{10{,}160{,}626 - 10{,}000{,}000}{10{,}000{,}000} \equiv 1.6063\%$$

which amounts to an annualized rate of 8.0313%. This synthetic borrowing rate is lower than the rate that is available in the local money market.

Suggestions for Further Reading

Apte, P.G. *International Financial Management*. Tata McGraw-Hill, 2006.

Chance, D.M. *An Introduction to Options & Futures*. The Dryden Press, 1991.

Edwards, F.R. and C.W. Ma *Futures & Options*. McGraw-Hill, 1992.

Logue, D.E. *The WG&L Handbook of International Finance*. South Western, 1995.

Melvin, M. *International Money and Finance*. Addison Wesley, 1997.

Mobius, M. *Foreign Exchange: An Introduction to the Core Concepts*. John Wiley, 2009.

Siegel, D.R. and D.F. Siegel *Futures Markets*. The Dryden Press, 1990.

Steiner, B. *Foreign Exchange and Money Markets*. Butterworth-Heinemann, 2002.

Appendix 4.1

Symbols for Major Currencies

Country	Currency	Symbol
Argentina	Peso	ARS
Australia	Dollar	AUD
Brazil	Real	BRL
Canada	Dollar	CAD
China	Renmimbi Yuan	CNY
Czech Republic	Koruna	CZK
Denmark	Kroner	DKK
European Monetary Union	Euro	EUR
Hong Kong	Dollar	HKD
Hungary	Forint	HUF
India	Rupee	INR
Israel	Shekel	ILS
Japan	Yen	JPY
Malaysia	Ringgit	MYR
Mexico	Peso	MXN
New Zealand	Dollar	NZD
Norway	Krone	NOK
Philippines	Peso	PHP
Poland	Zloty	PLN
Russia	Rouble	RUB
Singapore	Dollar	SGD
South Africa	Rand	ZAR
South Korea	Won	KRW
Sweden	Krona	SEK
Switzerland	Franc	CHF
Taiwan	Dollar	TWD
Thailand	Baht	THB
Turkey	Lira	TRY
U.K.	Pound Sterling	GBP
U.S.A	Dollar	USD

Chapter 5
Stock and Stock Index Futures

5.1 Introduction

Equity shares like debt securities, are a type of financial claim that are issued by companies. However, unlike debt securities, such securities confer ownership rights on the shareholders. A share of stock represents the fundamental unit of ownership of a corporation. Consequently, every firm must have at least one shareholder. On the other hand, a firm need not have a bond holder. There is however no upper limit on the number of shareholders that a firm may have, nor is there any restriction on how many shares a firm can issue to its shareholders. Every shareholder, is a part owner of the company to whose shares he has subscribed, and his stake in the company is equal to the fraction of the total share capital of the firm held by him.

When a firm seeks to reward its shareholders, it will usually pay out a percentage of its profits to them in the form of cash. This income that is received by the shareholders from the firm is called a *dividend*. Usually, a firm will not pay out the entire profits earned by it in the form of dividends. The normal practice is to plough back a part of it into the firm to meet future cash requirements. Such profits that are reinvested in the firm, are called *retained earnings*. These earnings which are retained by the firm, will manifest themselves as an increase in the *reserves and surplus* account on the balance sheet.

Shareholders are considered to be residual claimants. This perception is valid in two respects. First, they are eligible for dividends only after all payments due to the other creditors of the firm have been made. The rate of dividends is consequently not fixed, and neither is a dividend a contractual obligation. Dividend related decisions are made by the board of directors of a company, and the shareholders cannot make demands on them. However, if it were to be perceived that the directors are not acting in their interests, a group of dissident shareholders with a required majority can outvote the old director(s) and replace them with their nominees. There is another reason why shareholders are considered to be residual claimants. If the firm were to declare bankruptcy, then the shareholders would be entitled only to the residual assets, if such a residue were to be available, after the claims of all the other creditors have been met.

Unlike debt securities, which usually have a stated maturity date, equity shares never mature. That is, no founder will ever incorporate a firm with a termination date in mind. Equity shares therefore continue to be in existence as long as the firm itself continues to be in existence. A key feature of a company as opposed to a sole proprietorship or a partnership, is that shareholders have limited liability. That is, no matter how serious the financial difficulties facing a company may be, neither it nor its creditors can make financial demands on the common shareholders. On the other hand, if a partnership were to go bankrupt, its creditors can in most cases pursue the partners personally in order to recover what is owed to them. Hence, the maximum financial loss

https://doi.org/10.1515/9783110746662-005

that a shareholder may suffer is limited to the investment made by him in the process of acquisition of the shares.

5.2 Corporate Actions

5.2.1 Dividends

The shareholders of a company cannot demand dividends from it. The decision to pay dividends is entirely at the discretion of the board of directors of the company. Companies usually declare a dividend when they announce their results for a period. In the U.S., since results are typically declared on a quarterly basis, dividends are also announced every quarter. In the U.K. most companies pay their annual dividends in two stages. A dividend declaration is a statement of considerable importance. It is an affirmation by the company that its affairs are on track, and that it has adequate resources to reinvest in its operations as well as to reward its shareholders. The dividend announcement will mention a date called the *record date*. Only those shareholders, whose names appear as of the record date on the register of shareholders being maintained by the registrar, will be eligible to receive the forthcoming dividend.

Another important date in the context of dividends is known as the *ex-dividend date*. This date is specified by the exchange on which the shares are traded. If an investor were to acquire the shares on or after the ex-dividend date, then he will not be eligible to receive the forthcoming dividend. Thus, the ex-dividend date will be such that transactions prior to that date will be reflected in the register of shareholders on the record date. However, subsequent transactions will be reflected in the books only after the record date.

There is obviously a relationship between the ex-dividend date and the settlement cycle on the exchange where the shares are being traded. Assume an exchange follows a T+3 settlement cycle. Thus, if a trade occurs on day T, then delivery of shares to the buyer and payment of funds to the seller will occur three business days later. Consequently, anyone who purchases shares two business days before the record date or later will not be able to ensure that he is the owner of record as of that date. Thus, on the exchange, the ex-dividend date for an issue will be two business days prior to the record date that has been specified in the dividend announcement.

Prior to the ex-dividend date we say that the shares are being traded cum-dividend. The implication is that potential buyers will receive the forthcoming dividend. However, on the ex-dividend date the shares begin to trade ex-dividend. This signifies that a potential buyer will no longer be eligible to receive the next dividend, and that the forthcoming dividend will therefore be paid to the seller since he is the owner of record. Thus, on the ex-dividend date, the share price ought to decline by the amount of the dividend. For instance, if the cum-dividend price is \$75 per share, and the quantum of the dividend is \$2.50 per share, then in theory, the share should trade at \$72.50 ex-dividend.

5.2.2 Stock Dividends

A stock dividend is a dividend that is paid to the shareholders in the form of shares. That is, the company offers additional shares to the shareholders, without requiring them to pay any money in lieu. The issue of such shares without any monetary consideration entails the transfer of funds from the reserves and surplus account on the balance sheet to the share capital account. Such a fund transfer is known as the *capitalization of reserves*.

Irrespective of whether the funds are retained in the reserves and surplus account or transferred to the share capital account, they continue to belong to the shareholders. Thus, from a theoretical standpoint stock dividends do not create any value for the shareholders. The way to think of it is that it is as if the shareholder has two bank accounts. We are debiting one account and crediting the other. In the process, the shareholder's wealth is not affected. From the company's point of view, the issue of such additional shares does not lead to an increase in its assets. Nor does it have any implications for the earnings capacity of the firm. Consequently, following a stock dividend the share price should theoretically decline.

Assume that a firm has issued 100,000 shares and that the share price prior to the dividend announcement is \$60 per share. If the firm announces a 25% stock dividend there will be 125,000 shares outstanding after the dividends are paid. Considering that there is no change in the value of the firm, the ex-dividend price, P, should be such that:

$$60 \times 100{,}000 = P \times 125{,}000$$
$$\Rightarrow P = \$48$$

5.2.3 Splits and Reverse Splits

Unlike stock dividends which entail the capitalization of reserves, stock splits lead to a decrease in the par value of the shares, accompanied by a simultaneous increase in the number of shares outstanding. An n:1 stock split means that n new shares will be issued to the existing shareholders in lieu of one existing share. Take the case of a 5:4 split. What this means is that the holder of four shares will have five shares after the split. This is exactly analogous to a 25% stock dividend. Thus, splits and stock dividends are mathematically equivalent. However, the mechanics are different. Take the case of a company which has issued 100,000 shares with a par value of \$10 each. If it were to announce a 2:1 split, the number of shares issued will increase to 200,000. However the par value will decline to \$5. The issued capital will continue to remain at \$1,000,000.

Since a split is equivalent to a stock dividend, the share price after a split will behave in the same way as it would after an equivalent stock dividend. Assume that an investor is holding 10,000 shares worth \$60 each. The market value of the shares will be \$600,000.

If the firm were to announce a 6:5 split then he will have 12,000 shares after the split. Since the split is value neutral in theory, the post-split share price ought to be:

$$\frac{600,000}{12,000} = \$50$$

In the case of an n:m reverse split, n will be less than m. Take the case of a company which has issued 100,000 shares with a market price of $48 per share. If the firm were to announce a 4:5 reverse split, the post-reverse split price ought to be:

$$\frac{4,800,000}{80,000} = \$60.00$$

5.2.4 Pre-emptive Rights

The directors of a company must obtain the approval of existing shareholders if they wish to issue shares beyond what has been issued earlier. As per the charter of some corporations, existing shareholders must be given the first right to buy additional shares in proportion to the shares that they already own. In such cases, existing shareholders are said to have a pre-emptive right to acquire new shares as and when they are issued. That is, the existing shareholders are given an opportunity to maintain their proportionate ownership in the company.

Usually such issues are made at a price that is lower than the prevailing market price of the share. In such circumstances, the right acquires a value of its own. The existing shareholders have a choice. That is, they may either exercise their rights and acquire additional shares, or else sell they may sell the rights to another investor.

The value of a right may be determined as follows. Assume that a company has issued 100,000 shares and that it is offering its shareholders the right to purchase one share for every five shares that they are holding. The market price per share is $60 and the new shares are being offered at $48 each. The market value of the firm prior to the rights issue is:

$$100,000 \times 60 = \$6,000,000$$

The post issue theoretical value of the firm will be:

$$6,000,000 + 20,000 \times 48 = \$6,960,000$$

The ex-rights price should therefore be:

$$\frac{6,960,000}{120,000} = \$58$$

Since the shareholders are getting a share worth \$58 at \$48, the value of the right to acquire a share is \$10. Considering that the shareholder needs 5 shares to acquire the right to buy one share, the value of a right is \$2.

5.3 Adjustment of Stock Futures Contracts for Corporate Actions

In the event of certain corporate actions, the terms of a futures contract will have to be adjusted. The procedures adopted are not uniform and sometimes differ across exchanges.

5.3.1 Dividends

Usually no adjustment is made in the case of cash dividends. However, on some exchanges, a dividend may have consequences for a futures contract, if it is perceived to be extraordinary.

Exchanges which prescribe an adjustment procedure for an extraordinary cash dividend adopt the following procedure. Readers should note at the outset that for all corporate actions, changes to the futures settlement price and the contract size, will only be made at the end of the last day on which the security is traded on a cum basis, that is cum-cash dividend or cum-stock dividend. Thus, in the case of an extraordinary cash dividend, the previous day's settlement price will be reduced by the amount of the dividend, when the contract is marked to market on the ex-dividend date.

Let's assume that the settlement price on the ex-dividend date is \$120, and that the previous settlement price was \$126. Each futures contract is for 100 shares, and the dividend is \$10 per share. While marking to market on the ex-dividend date the previous day's settlement price will be taken as \$116, that is 126 − 10. Hence the profit/loss for a long position in one contract will be:

$$(120 - 116) \times 100 = \$400$$

In the case of cash dividends, there will be no adjustment made to the contract size.

5.3.2 Stock Dividends

Let's denote a stock dividend as A:B. That is, holder of B shares will have A+B shares in his possession after the dividend is declared. For a 20% stock dividend, the ratio will be 1:5. Thus the holder of 5 shares will have 6 shares after the dividend is declared. The adjustment factor in this case is $\frac{A+B}{B}$.

On the ex-dividend day the contract size will be multiplied by the adjustment factor. While marking the contract to market on the ex-dividend date, the settlement price on the previous day will be divided by the adjustment factor.

Let's consider the case of a 1:5 stock dividend. The adjustment factor is 1.20. Thus, the contract size will be adjusted from 100 to 120. Assume that the settlement price on the ex-dividend date is $108, while that on the previous day was $126. The adjusted settlement price will be $\frac{126}{1.20} = \$105$. Thus, the profit from marking to market for the holder of a long position in one contract will be:

$$120 \times (108 - 105) = \$360$$

5.3.3 Stock Splits/Reverse Splits

The adjustment for stock splits and reverse splits is very similar to the procedure that is adopted for stock dividends. Assume that a firm undergoes an A:B split or reverse split. That is, the holder of B shares will have A shares after the corporate action. The adjustment factor is therefore $\frac{A}{B}$. For instance, if a stock undergoes a 8:5 split, the adjustment factor will be 1.60.

The terms of the contract will be adjusted as follows. First, the contract size will be multiplied by the factor. Second, on the ex date, the previous day's settlement price will be divided by the factor.

In the case of an 8:5 split, the contract size will be adjusted from 100 to 160. Let's assume that the previous day's settlement price is 112 while the settlement price on the ex-date is 75. Thus the adjusted settlement price will be:

$$\frac{112}{1.60} = 70$$

Hence, the profit from marking to market for an investor with a long futures position will be:

$$160 \times (75 - 70) = \$800$$

5.3.4 Rights Issues

A company announces a 2:5 rights issue. That is, an existing shareholder is entitled to two shares for every five shares that he is holding. The right can be exercised at a price of $48 per share. At the end of the day prior to the expiry of the right, the share price is $50.80. Obviously, it is profitable to exercise the right. If the rights are exercised the value of the share will drop to:

$$\frac{5 \times 50.80 + 2 \times 48}{7} = 50$$

which represents a decline of $0.80 per share. On the next day, the settlement price for the previous day will be reduced by $0.80 while marking to market.[1] No adjustment would be made to the contract size.

5.4 Stock Indices

While tracking the stock market, it is impossible for an analyst to draw a meaningful conclusion if he is confronted with a vector of stock prices. He needs one number that is a summary measure of the performance of the market as a whole. Such a measure is termed as an index number and is intended to serve as a barometer of the performance of the stock market, or of a particular segment of the stock market. In order for the index to be a good indicator of market movements, the stocks constituting the index ought to be chosen so as to be representative of the market or of the market segment.

There are three techniques for computing a stock market index. These are:

- The price-weighted approach
- The value-weighted approach
- The equally-weighted approach

5.4.1 Price-Weighted Indices

The first step while computing an index entails the specification of the number of companies that are going to be included, and the identity of these companies. This is the case for all indices and not just those that are price weighted. In a price weighted index, the only factor that is considered is the prices of the component stocks.

To compute the index, the current prices of all the component stocks are added up and divided by a number known as the *divisor*. On the base date, or the date on which the index is being computed for the first time, the divisor can be set equal to any arbitrary value. Often, it is set equal to the number of stocks constituting the index. Subsequently, if there is a corporate action such a split/reverse split or a stock dividend, the divisor will have to be adjusted.

Let's assume that we are standing at the end of day t, and that the closing price of the i th stock on the day is $P_{i,t}$. If so, the index level I_t, is given by:

$$I_t = \sum_{i=1}^{N} \frac{P_{i,t}}{Div_t} \tag{5.1}$$

1 If the right were not to have any value on the previous day, no adjustment would be made.

where Div_t is the applicable value of the divisor for the day, and N is the number of stocks comprising the index. Example 5.1 illustrates the computation.

Example 5.1: Consider a hypothetical index consisting of four stocks. Assume that we are standing on the base date, and that the starting value of the divisor is 4.0. The closing prices of the component stocks at the end of the day are as shown in Table 5.1.

Table 5.1: Prices of the constituent stocks on the base date.

Stock	Price
ABC	40
DEF	50
XYZ	85
LKP	25
Total	200

The end of the day index value will therefore be $\frac{200}{4} = 50.00$.

5.4.2 Adjusting the Divisor

The divisor that is used to compute a price-weighted index will have to be adjusted if there is any corporate action that impacts the share price of a constituent stock. Thus, if the firm were to declare a stock dividend, a split, or a reverse split, the divisor will have to be adjusted. Second, if there is any change in the composition of the index, that is one or more of the constituent stocks are replaced by other companies, the divisor will have to be adjusted. Third, if there is a rights issue at a discount to the prevailing market price, the divisor will have to be adjusted, since the share price will be impacted.

We will now illustrate the adjustment procedure for a stock split. Assume that DEF declares a 5:4 stock split at the end of the day. The theoretical post-split value of the stock will obviously be $\frac{50 \times 4}{5} = \$40$.

The adjusted divisor should be such that the corporate action per se does not lead to a change in the level of the index. The theoretical price aggregate for the four companies, after accounting for the split is:

$$40 + 40 + 85 + 25 = \$190$$

The new divisor should be such that:

$$\frac{190}{X} = 50.00 \Rightarrow X = 3.80$$

The new divisor will be used from the following day until there is yet another corporate action for one of the constituent companies, or else there is a change in the composition of the index.

5.4.3 Value-Weighted Indices

Unlike a price-weighted index which is based solely on the prices of the component stocks, a value weighted index takes into consideration the market capitalization of the component stocks. In other words, the number of shares issued by a company is also factored in.

Assume that we are standing on day t. Let's denote the base date of the index by b. We will use $P_{i,t}$ and $P_{i,b}$ to denote the market prices of the i th stock on days t and b respectively, and $Q_{i,t}$ and $Q_{i,b}$ to denote the number of shares outstanding on those two days.

On the base date, the index can be assigned any value. We will set it as equal to 100, which is a fairly common practice. The level of the index on day t is then defined as:

$$\frac{1}{Div_t}\left(\frac{\sum_{i=1}^{N} P_{i,t}Q_{i,t}}{\sum_{i=1}^{M} P_{i,b}Q_{i,b}}\right) \times 100 \tag{5.2}$$

Div_t represents the value of the divisor on day t. The divisor is assigned a value of 1.0 on the base date. Subsequently it will be adjusted as and when required. Example 5.2 demonstrates the computation of market capitalization.

Example 5.2: We will take the same four stocks as before and use the prices shown in Table 5.1. The difference is that we will now also consider the number of shares issued by each firm.

Table 5.2: Prices, number of shares outstanding, and market capitalization of the components of a value weighted index on the base date.

Stock	Price(P)	# of Shares (Q)	Market Capitalization
ABC	40	900,000,000	36,000,000,000
DEF	50	1,250,000,000	62,500,000,000
XYZ	85	1,635,000,000	138,975,000,000
LKP	25	2,220,000,000	55,500,000,000

The total market value is

$$\sum_{i=1}^{4} P_i Q_i = 292{,}975{,}000{,}000$$

We will assign a starting value of 100 for the index. The corresponding value for the divisor is obviously 1.0.

On the following day, we will assume that the prices and number of shares outstanding are as shown in Table 5.3.

Table 5.3: Prices, number of shares outstanding, and market capitalization of the components of a value weighted index on the following day.

Stock	Price(P)	# of Shares (Q)	Market Capitalization
ABC	42.50	900,000,000	38,250,000,000
DEF	50.00	1,250,000,000	62,500,000,000
XYZ	90.00	1,635,000,000	147,150,000,000
LKP	27.50	2,220,000,000	61,050,000,000

The total market value is

$$\sum_{i=1}^{4} P_i Q_i = 308{,}950{,}000{,}000$$

The value of the index on this day is therefore

$$\frac{308{,}950{,}000{,}000}{292{,}975{,}000{,}000} \times 100 = 105.4527$$

Quite obviously, our conclusion would be that the market has moved up.

5.4.4 Adjusting the Divisor

Corporate actions such as stock splits, reverse splits, and stock dividends, are value neutral in theory. That is, there is no impact on the theoretical market value, since the change in the stock price is exactly offset by the change in the number of shares outstanding. Consequently, there is no need to adjust the divisor in the event of such an eventuality. However, the divisor will have to be adjusted if there is a change in the composition of the index. It will also have to be adjusted, if there is a rights issue, or a share buyback, since these actions will have an impact on the market capitalization. Unlike in the case of a price weighted index, the divisor will have to be adjusted even if the rights issue is at the prevailing market price. This is because, while the theoretical share price will not be impacted, the market capitalization will be.

5.4.5 Equally-Weighted Indices

An equally weighted index is also a type of barometer for tracking the performance of a portfolio of stocks. Assume that we decide to form such an index using N stocks. Just like a price weighted index, an equally weighted index too is based on the share prices and not on the market capitalization.

The value of the index on day t is defined as

$$I_t = I_{t-1} \times \frac{1}{N} \sum_{i=1}^{N} \frac{P_{i,t}}{P_{i,t-1}} \tag{5.3}$$

The ratio of the prices, $\frac{P_{i,t}}{P_{i,t-1}}$ may be expressed as $(1 + r_{i,t})$ where $r_{i,t}$ is the arithmetic rate of return on the ith stock between day t and day $t - 1$. Therefore

$$\frac{1}{N} \sum_{i=1}^{N} \frac{P_{i,t}}{P_{i,t-1}} = \frac{1}{N} \sum_{i=1}^{N} (1 + r_{i,t})$$

$$= 1 + \frac{1}{N} \sum_{i=1}^{N} r_{i,t} = 1 + \bar{r}_t \tag{5.4}$$

where $\bar{r}_t$ is the arithmetic average of the returns on all the component stocks between day $t - 1$ and day t. Thus

$$I_t = I_{t-1} \times (1 + \bar{r}_t) \tag{5.5}$$

5.4.6 Tracking Portfolios

Investors can construct portfolios that replicate the behavior of a market index. The method of construction of such a portfolio would depend on the way the underlying index has been defined.

To imitate an equally weighted index, the investor has to put an equal fraction of his wealth in all the assets that constitute the index. That is, if the underlying index consists of four stocks, he has to invest 25% of his wealth in each asset. Since the component securities will have different prices, the number of shares of each security that are required to be held will vary.

In order to track a price weighted index the investor has to hold an identical number of shares of each of the companies that are present in the index.

Forming a portfolio to track a value weighted index is the most complex task. To form such a tracking portfolio, the fraction of the investor's wealth that is invested in each asset should be equal to the ratio of the market capitalization of that stock to the total market capitalization of all the stocks that are present in the index.

Portfolios which track price and value weighted indices, have to be re-balanced whenever circumstances warrant a change in the divisor that is being used to compute the index. We have already expounded on the factors which could lead to such situations. However, a portfolio that tracks an equally weighted index will have to be re-balanced every day, for, even if one of the component stocks were to undergo a nominal price change, the portfolio will cease to be equally weighted.

5.5 Major Stock Indices

The most famous stock index is undoubtedly the Dow Jones Industrial Average (DJIA), popularly known as the *Dow*. It is a price weighted average of 30 stocks. The Nikkei Index, which is a barometer of the Japanese stock market, is also price weighted and includes 225 large Japanese companies. The Standard & Poor's 500 Index (S&P500) and the Nasdaq 100 index are both value weighted.

5.6 Pricing of Index Futures

In order to derive the expression for the no-arbitrage futures price, we will start with a numerical illustration. Let's take the case of a price weighted index that is based on five stocks. We will use the price data given in Table 5.4, and will assume that the divisor is 5.0. Since the price aggregate is 800, the index level is obviously 160.

Table 5.4: Prices of stocks.

Stock	Price
ACC	210
BD	80
CP	210
ECT	70
HUL	230
Total	800

Let's assume that today is 23 June, 20XX and that there is a futures contract based on the above index, that expires on 21 September, 20XX. We will also assume that ACC will pay a dividend of $2.40 on 23 July, that HUL will pay a dividend of $2.40 on 10 August and that CP will pay a dividend of $2.40 on 3 September. The borrowing/lending rate for all investors will be taken to be 7.2% per annum.

Consider the following strategy. Borrow money to buy one share of each of the 5 companies and simultaneously go short in an index futures contract. The cost of the portfolio will be equal to

$$(210 + 80 + 210 + 70 + 230) = 800$$

The borrowed amount will have to be repaid with interest on 21 September. The number of days between 23 June and 21 September is 90. So the amount due on 21 September is

$$800 \times \left(1 + 0.072 \times \frac{90}{360}\right) = 814.40$$

On 23 July you will get a dividend of \$2.40. This can be reinvested till 21 September to yield

$$2.40 \times \left(1 + 0.072 \times \frac{60}{360}\right) = 2.43$$

Similarly, the future values of the other two dividends, as of 21 September, are 2.42 and 2.41.

To preclude arbitrage opportunities, the futures price, in dollar terms, should be a value F such that,

$$F + 2.43 + 2.42 + 2.41 = 814.40$$
$$\Rightarrow F = \$807.14$$

However, by convention, futures prices are expressed in terms of index units and not in dollar terms. Thus, the no-arbitrage futures price should be:

$$\frac{807.14}{5} = 161.43$$

5.7 Cash and Carry Arbitrage

Let's assume that F = 163. If so, an investor can borrow \$800 to buy the five stocks and go short in one futures contract. Each dividend, when received, can be re-invested till the expiration of the futures contract at the prevailing lending rate. At expiration, the futures price will be set equal to the spot index value at that time, since *index futures contracts are always cash settled.* Thus, the arbitrageur should sell the shares at their prevailing market prices.

Let's assume that the spot prices of the shares at the time of expiration of the futures contract are as shown in Table 5.5.

Table 5.5: Prices of stocks on the expiration date.

Stock	Price
ACC	225
BD	90
CP	225
ECT	75
HUL	250
Total	865

The index value is $\frac{865}{5} = 173$. The profit/loss from the futures market is, 163–173 = (10) index points, which is equivalent in our case to 10× 5 = \$ (50). When the stocks are disposed off by the arbitrageur, there will be a cash inflow of 865. The payoffs from the reinvested dividends is:

$$2.43 + 2.42 + 2.41 = \$7.26$$

Thus, the net cash flow at expiration is:

$$865 + 7.26 - 814.40 - 50 = \$7.86$$

This value of \$7.86 is equivalent to $\frac{7.86}{5} = 1.57$ index units, which is the difference between the quoted futures price of 163 and the no-arbitrage price of 161.43. It should be noted that the profit will always be equal to the difference between the quoted price and the no-arbitrage price, and will be independent of the actual stock prices prevailing at expiration. This is because of the underlying assumption, that the arbitrageur is able to sell the shares in the market at the same prices as those used to compute the index value at expiration.

5.8 Reverse Cash and Carry Arbitrage

We will use the same information that we used for demonstrating the cash and carry arbitrage arguments. However, we will assume that the futures price is 159.

An arbitrageur can implement the following strategy. He can short sell all the five stocks which constitute the index and invest the proceeds at the lending rate of 7.2%. Simultaneously, he can take a long position in a futures contract. When the dividends are due, the arbitrageur can borrow the required amounts and pay the person(s) who have lent him the shares. At the time of expiration of the futures contract, the shares present in the index may be acquired at their prevailing spot prices and returned. The arbitrageur will also be required to repay the amounts borrowed for the dividend payments with interest. He will be entitled to the profit/loss from the futures market, and the amount invested by him at the outset, that is, the proceeds from the short sale, will now be returned to him with interest.

Therefore, the net cash flow at expiration will be:

$$-865 - 7.26 + 814.40 + 5(173 - 159) = \$12.14$$

which is equivalent to 2.43 index units. This, once again, is the difference between the futures price of 159 and the no-arbitrage price of 161.43. Once again, the profit will be independent of the stock prices prevailing at expiration.

5.9 The No-Arbitrage Equation

Let I_t be the spot value of the index on day t. Consider a futures contract maturing on day T, with a current price of F_t.[2] We will denote the borrowing/lending rate by r and the future value of the dividends paid by the component stocks between t and T, as calculated at T, by D_T, where D_T is expressed in terms of index units.[3]

The no-arbitrage equation can therefore be expressed as

$$F_t = I_t\left[1 + r\frac{(T-t)}{360}\right] - D_T \tag{5.6}$$

5.10 Index Arbitrage and Program Trading

If the observed futures price is greater than the price given by the no-arbitrage equation, then arbitrageurs will engage in cash and carry arbitrage as we have seen. On the other hand, if the observed price is less than the theoretical price, they will resort to reverse cash and carry arbitrage.

Now, unlike in the case of arbitrage using contracts on commodities or even other financial assets, index arbitrage is considerably more complex. Cash and carry index arbitrage requires the arbitrageur to buy all the stocks constituting the index simultaneously and in the same proportions in which they are present in the index, while reverse cash and carry index arbitrage requires that the arbitrageur short sell all the

2 Stock index futures prices are always in index units. They have to be multiplied by the unit size that has been specified by the exchange, in order to calculate the value of the contract in terms of the currency of the country in which they trade. The unit size for emini S&P500 is 50, for the DJIA it is 10 and for the Nikkei it is 5.

3 Each dividend is assumed to be invested at the rate r between t_i, which is the date on which the i th dividend is paid and T, the expiration date of the contract.

constituent stocks simultaneously, once again in the specified proportions. Obviously, this is the kind of task for which a *computer* is indispensable. The use of a computer program to execute large and complex stock market orders is called *program trading*. Consequently, the terms *index arbitrage* and *program trading* are used synonymously.

5.10.1 Risks Inherent In Index Arbitrage

Index arbitrage has certain underlying risks in practice.

1. Let's assume that you have analyzed the spot and futures prices and have come to the conclusion that there is money to be made through cash and carry arbitrage. To execute it, however, you need to buy the basket of securities constituting the index and sell the appropriate number of futures contracts. Let's assume that you are quickly able to take a short position in the futures market. But, how can you be sure that the prices of some of the stocks will not go up before your purchase transactions are through? If so, you may make a lower profit than anticipated or even make a loss.
2. The second problem with cash and carry arbitrage[4] is that the basket of securities has to be sold on the day of expiration at prices corresponding to those which are used to calculate the settlement price of the futures contract on that day. Why is this so?

   Remember, that since the contract is cash settled, at expiration, the futures price will be set equal to the prevailing spot index value. In order for our earlier observation, that is, that arbitrage profits are independent of the prevailing spot prices at expiration, to be true, it is necessary that we be able to sell the individual stocks at prices which correspond to those used to determine the settlement price of the index.

   In practice, the arbitrageur will issue a *market on close order*, which means that the broker has to sell the shares at the market prices prevailing at the close of trading. In real life, this can be difficult.

   The above risks are called *execution risks.*
3. The third problem with index arbitrage, is that stocks may not pay dividends as forecasted by us while identifying arbitrage opportunities. This is called *dividend risk*.
4. And finally, the interest rates that we use to calculate potential arbitrage profits at the outset may not be the same as the rates at which we are eventually able to borrow and lend. This is known as *interest rate risk*.

4 Equivalent problems will exist with reverse cash and carry arbitrage. Readers should be able to work out the logic.

5.11 Hedging with Index Futures

We will now derive the optimal number of futures contracts for a risk minimizing hedge, for hedging a portfolio P using stock index futures contracts. Let the beta of the portfolio be β_P with respect to the market portfolio. We will assume that the portfolio underlying the futures contract is a suitable proxy for the market portfolio.

The number of futures contracts required for a minimum variance hedge is given by

$$h = \frac{\text{Cov}(\Delta P, \Delta F)}{\text{Var}(\Delta F)}$$

$$\beta_P = h\frac{I_t}{P_t}$$

$$\Rightarrow h = \beta_P\frac{P_t}{I_t} \tag{5.7}$$

We will now consider an example, Example 5.3, using a futures contract on a hypothetical index. The index is value weighted and the value of the futures contract is \$ 250 per index point.

Example 5.3: Let's take the case of a portfolio manager who is handling a portfolio which is currently worth 10MM dollars. He is worried about the possibility of a market decline, and therefore decides to hedge using index futures. Quite obviously, he needs to go short in index futures.

Assume that the current value of the index is 250. The value of the index in dollar terms is therefore

$$250 \times 250 = \$62{,}500$$

Consider a futures contract with 90 days to expiration, which we will assume represents the hedging horizon of the manager. The riskless rate is assumed to be 10% per annum, and the future value of dividends in index units is assumed to be 10. If so, the no-arbitrage futures price is given by:

$$250\left[1 + 0.10 \times \frac{90}{360}\right] - 10 = 246.25$$

If the beta of the portfolio is assumed to be 1.50, then the required number of contracts for a risk minimizing hedge is:

$$1.50 \times \frac{10{,}000{,}000}{62{,}500} = 240 \text{ contracts.}$$

We will examine the performance of the hedge in two different terminal scenarios.

Case A

The index value at expiration is 275. The value of the portfolio may be deduced as follows.

The return on the index is $\frac{275 - 250}{250} \equiv 10\%$.

The dividend yield is $\frac{10 \times 250}{250 \times 250} \equiv 4\%$.

Hence, the total return on the market = 10% + 4% = 14%.

The riskless rate for 90 days is 2.50%
The portfolio return is therefore:

$$2.50 + 1.50(14 - 2.50) = 19.75\%$$

The portfolio value is therefore:

$$10(1 + 0.1975)\text{ MM} = \$11.975\text{ MM}$$

The profit/loss from the futures market is:

$$(246.25 - 275) \times 250 \times 240 = \$\,(1{,}725{,}000)$$

Thus, the net value of the investment is: 11.975 - 1.725 = $10.25 MM.

The hedged portfolio has earned a 2.50% rate of return. The rationale is as follows. The futures contract has helped remove all the inherent market risk. Therefore, the portfolio has ended up earning the riskless rate of return of 2.5% for 90 days.

Case B

Let the index value at expiration be 220.

The return on the index = $\frac{220 - 250}{250} \equiv -12\%$.
The dividend yield is 4%.
Therefore the total return on the market is -8%.
The riskless rate for 90 days is 2.50%.
Hence, the rate of return on the portfolio is:

$$2.50 + 1.50(-8 - 2.50) = -13.25\%$$

The portfolio is therefore worth $10(1 - 0.1325)$ MM = $8.675 MM

The profit/loss from the futures market is:

$$(246.25 - 220) \times 250 \times 240 = \$1{,}575{,}000$$

Thus, the net value of the investment is: 8.675 + 1.575 = $10.25 MM.

Once again, the rate of return on the hedged portfolio is 2.5%.

In practice, however, our hedge may not be perfect. The first reason is that dividends and interest rates may change over the life of the hedge. The second reason is that the return on the index over 90 days may not be perfectly correlated with the return on our portfolio.

5.12 Market Timing with Index Futures

Portfolio managers frequently use index futures contracts to engage in what are known as *market timing* strategies. These entail the movement of funds from T-bills to equities and vice versa. If the manager feels that the portfolio is going to do well, he will move funds from T-bills to equity. But, if he anticipates a bear market, then he will do the reverse.

5.12.1 Moving From Equities to T-bills

Take the case of the portfolio manager we considered in the above example on hedging. Let's assume that he is worried about a market decline and wants to shift his funds from equities to T-bills. He can use futures contracts to invest in synthetic T-bills as we have demonstrated earlier. That is, if he combines a short position in 240 futures contracts with his existing stock position, then it will be tantamount to making a riskless investment, for the overall portfolio value will be independent of the index level at expiration.

5.12.2 Moving From T-bills to Equities

Now let's consider the case of a portfolio manager who is holding T-bills worth 10MM and wants to shift to an equity portfolio with a beta of 0.80. We know that

$$\text{Futures} + \text{T-bills} = \text{Synthetic Spot.}$$

Thus, the manager needs to combine a long position in the futures contracts with his existing position in T-bills, in order to effectively take an equity position. Using the same logic as before, the number of futures contracts required is

$$0.80 \times \frac{10{,}000{,}000}{62{,}500} = 128 \text{ contracts.}$$

We will examine the performance of the overall portfolio under two different scenarios as before.

Case A: Index = 260

The value of the T-bills = $10,250,000.

The profit/loss from the futures position is

$$128 \times 250(260 - 246.25) = \$440{,}000.$$

Thus the total portfolio value is

$$10{,}250{,}000 + 440{,}000 = \$10{,}690{,}000$$

which implies a rate of return of 6.9% on the investment of 10 MM. A rate of return of 6.9% on the portfolio corresponds to a rate of return of

$$\frac{(6.9 - 2.5)}{0.80} + 2.5 = 8\%$$

on the market portfolio. Since the dividend yield is 4%, the implied return on the index is 4%, which is consistent with the observed index level of 260.

Case B: Index = 230

The value of the T-bills = $10,250,000.

The profit/loss from the futures position is

$$128 \times 250(230 - 246.25) = \$\,(520{,}000).$$

The total portfolio value is therefore

$$10{,}250{,}000 - 520{,}000 = \$9{,}730{,}000$$

which implies a rate of return of −2.7% for the portfolio, which corresponds to a return of −4% on the market. Since the dividend yield is 4%, the implied return on the index is −8%, which is consistent with an index level of 230.

5.13 Using Index Futures to Change the Beta of a Portfolio

Let's assume that we have a portfolio worth $\$P_t$, that the current index value is I_t, and that the beta of the portfolio is β^*.

Consider taking a long position in N futures contracts. If we denote our overall portfolio as o, the rate of return for this portfolio can be written as

$$r_o = \frac{\Delta P}{P_t} + N\frac{\Delta F}{P_t} \tag{5.8}$$

Therefore

$$E(r_o) = E(r_p) + \frac{N}{P_t}E(\Delta F)$$

$$= r + \beta^*[E(r_m) - r] + \frac{N}{P_t}E(\Delta F) \tag{5.9}$$

From the systematic risk explanation, we know that

$$\begin{aligned}[E(I_T) - F_t] = [E(F_T) - F_t] = E(\Delta F) &= \beta[E(r_m) - r]I_t \\ &= [E(r_m) - r]I_t \end{aligned} \tag{5.10}$$

because the beta of the futures contract can be taken to be 1.0, since it is a contract on the market portfolio. Hence

$$E(r_o) = r + \beta^*[E(r_m) - r] + \frac{N}{P_t}[E(r_m) - r]I_t \tag{5.11}$$

If we want our overall portfolio to have a beta of β_T, we should choose N such that

$$r + \beta^* [E(r_m) - r] + \frac{N}{P_t}[E(r_m) - r]I_t = r + \beta_T[E(r_m) - r]$$

$$\Rightarrow N = (\beta_T - \beta^*)\frac{P_t}{I_t} \tag{5.12}$$

Thus, if we want to increase the beta, we should go long in the required number of futures contracts, whereas if we want to decrease it, we should go short. Consider Example 5.4.

Example 5.4: A portfolio manager is holding assets worth \$30MM. The portfolio has a beta of 1.25. He is anticipating a bull market and would like to increase the beta of his portfolio to 1.50. The current value of the index is 1,200.

The dollar value of the index is therefore = 250 × 1200 = \$300,000.

Thus the number of futures contracts required is:

$$(1.50 - 1.25)\frac{30{,}000{,}000}{300{,}000} = 0.25 \times 100 = 25 \text{ contracts}$$

Obviously he needs to take a long position. We will now look at two terminal scenarios of the index in order to demonstrate that the effective portfolio beta, after the transaction, is indeed 1.50.

Assume that the futures contract has 72 days to expiration and that none of the constituent stocks are scheduled to pay a dividend. The risk-less rate of interest is 10% per annum. The no-arbitrage futures price is therefore:

$$1{,}200\left[1 + 0.10 \times \frac{72}{360}\right] = 1{,}224$$

Case-A

Let's assume that the level of the index after 72 days is 1,260. The rate of return on the market is therefore:

$$\frac{1{,}260 - 1{,}200}{1{,}200} \equiv 5\%$$

The risk-less rate of return for 72 days is obviously 2%. Thus the return on the portfolio is:

$$2 + 1.25 \times (5 - 2) = 5.75\%$$

The return in dollar terms is:

$$30{,}000{,}000 \times 0.0575 = \$1{,}725{,}000$$

The profit/loss from the futures market is:

$$25 \times 250 \times (1{,}260 - 1{,}224) = \$225{,}000$$

The effective return is therefore:

$$1{,}725{,}000 + 225{,}000 = \$1{,}950{,}000 \equiv \frac{1{,}950{,}000}{30{,}000{,}000} \times 100 = 6.50\%$$

The issue is what is the effective beta of a portfolio that would give a return of 6.50% under these circumstances. Obviously:

$$2 + \beta \times (5 - 2) = 6.50 \Rightarrow \beta = 1.50$$

Case-B

Now let's assume that the market declines and that the index is at 1,125 after 72 days. The rate of return on the market is:

$$\frac{1{,}125 - 1{,}200}{1{,}200} \equiv -6.25\%$$

Thus the return on the portfolio is:

$$2 + 1.25 \times (-6.25 - 2) = -8.3125\%$$

The return in dollar terms is:

$$30{,}000{,}000 \times -0.083125 = -\$\ 2{,}493{,}750$$

The profit/loss from the futures market is:

$$25 \times 250 \times (1{,}125 - 1{,}224) = -\$\ 618{,}750$$

The effective return is therefore:

$$-2{,}493{,}750 - 618{,}750 = \$\ -3{,}112{,}500 \equiv -\frac{3{,}112{,}500}{30{,}000{,}000} \times 100 = -10.375\%$$

The effective beta of the portfolio is therefore:

$$2 + \beta \times (-6.25 - 2) = -10.375 \Rightarrow \beta = 1.50$$

5.14 Stock Picking

Stock picking is a term used for the art of finding stocks that are underpriced or overpriced. Let's depict the rate of return for a stock, stock i, as follows.

$$r_i = r + \beta_i(r_m - r) + \epsilon_i + \alpha_i \tag{5.13}$$

ϵ_i is the unsystematic error that is, the return due to unsystematic risk. The expected value of this variable is obviously zero. The term $\beta_i(r_m - r)$ is the excess return due to the systematic or market risk of the stock. α_i is termed as the *abnormal return*, and is related to the mispricing of the stock. If the stock is correctly priced, then α_i will be zero. However, if the stock is underpriced, α_i will be positive, whereas if it is overpriced, α_i will be negative.

Stock pickers are investors who believe that they have an uncanny ability to spot underpriced and overpriced stocks, and seek to take advantage of this perceived skill. However, if an investor were to take a position in the stock because he believes that it is mispriced, without hedging against movements in the market as a whole, then there is a risk that even if the abnormal return were to be realized, the general market movement may be such that he ends up with an overall loss. This is demonstrated in Example 5.5.

Example 5.5: A stock picker believes that CP is underpriced and that he will get a positive abnormal return if he buys it. Let's assume as before that the riskless rate is 2.50% and that the beta is 1.80.

We will assume that the investor is right, and that α_i does turn out to be 0.75%. However, it so happens that there is a sharp decline in the overall market, and $r_m = -7.50\%$. If we assume that $\epsilon_i = 0$ then:

$$r_i = 2.50 + 1.8(-7.50 - 2.50) + 0.75 = -14.75\%.$$

Thus, although the investor 'backed the right horse', he ended up with a negative rate of return. This is because he was exposed to market risk. Such a situation could have been avoided, if he had chosen to hedge using stock index futures.

Let's assume that he invests $625,000 in the stock and goes short in index futures when the index level is 250. This corresponds to a futures price of 246.25. The appropriate number of futures contracts is

$$\frac{625{,}000}{250 \times 250} \times 1.8 = 18$$

Considering that the dividend yield is given to be 4%, a return of −7.50% on the market corresponds to a decline of −11.50% in the index level. Hence the corresponding index value is 221.25.

The rate of return on the stock is −14.75%, which implies that the terminal portfolio value is 625,000(1 − 0.1475) = $532,812.50

The profit/loss from the futures position is

$$18 \times 250(246.25 - 221.25) = \$112{,}500$$

The value of the portfolio after factoring in the profit/loss from the futures market is:

$$532{,}812.50 + 112{,}500 = \$645{,}312.50$$

The overall rate of return is therefore 3.25%. This value of 3.25% corresponds to the riskless rate of 2.50%, plus the abnormal return of 0.75%.

Thus, if you believe that the stock is underpriced but want to hedge yourself against market risk, you should buy the stock and go short in stock index futures. Similarly, if you believe that the stock is overpriced, short sell the stock and go long in stock index futures. Example 5.6 demonstrates the use of a perceived overpriced stock.

Example 5.6: A stock picker believes that ABC is over-valued, and that he will get a positive abnormal return of he short sells it. Assume that the risk-less rate is 2.50% and the beta is 2.0. We will assume that the investor is right and that alpha turns out to be −0.84%. However, the market goes up and return on the market is +8.4%. If we assume that $\epsilon_i = 0$ then:

$$r_i = 2.50 + 2 \times (8.40 - 2.50) - 0.84 = 13.46\%$$

Thus the return for the short-seller is −13.46%.

Let's assume that he short-sells $625,000 worth of stock and goes long in index futures when the index level is 250. This corresponds to a futures price of 246.25. The appropriate number of futures contracts is

$$\frac{625{,}000}{250 \times 250} \times 2 = 20$$

Considering that the dividend yield is given to be 4%, a return of 8.40% on the market corresponds to an increase of 4.40% in the index level. Hence the corresponding index value is 261.0. The rate of return for the short-seller is −13.46%, which means that the terminal portfolio value is

$$625{,}000 \times (1 - 0.1346) = \$540{,}875$$

The profit/loss from the futures position is

$$20 \times 250 \times (261 - 246.25) = \$73{,}750$$

The value of the portfolio after factoring in the profit/loss from the futures market is:

$$540{,}875 + 73{,}750 = \$614{,}625$$

The return obtained by investing the proceeds from the short sale is:

$$625{,}000 \times 0.025 = 15{,}625$$

The overall value is: 614,625 + 15,625 = 630,250. The rate of return is:

$$\frac{(630{,}250 - 625{,}000)}{625{,}000} \times 100 = 0.84\%$$

This value corresponds to the abnormal return of 0.84%.

5.15 Portfolio Insurance

In the section on market timing, we saw how a portfolio manager could move from an actual spot position worth 10MM dollars, to a synthetic T-bill position, by going short in futures contracts. In that case, the end result was the creation of a risk free investment, which gave the riskless rate of return.

It is not necessary that a fund manager would always like to convert his entire risky portfolio to a riskless asset. In practice, he may choose to convert a fraction of the portfolio into equivalent synthetic T-bills using futures contracts, while continuing to hold the balance in the form of the risky portfolio. The value of this risky component can at worst go to zero. However, the riskless component of the overall portfolio will continue to earn the riskfree rate of return. Thus, there is a floor on the value of the overall portfolio. The portfolio may end up earning more than the floor, but cannot earn less.

This kind of an asset allocation strategy is referred to as *portfolio insurance*. Fund managers constantly monitor the market and sell and buy futures contracts in order to move from equities to synthetic debt and vice versa. The greater the desired level of insurance, the more will be the number of futures contracts sold. This kind of asset management technique is also known as *dynamic hedging*. Consider Example 5.7.

Example 5.7: A portfolio manager is currently holding a portfolio worth \$30MM. The current value of the index is 1,200 and the contract multiplier is \$250. The risk-less rate is 10% per annum and futures contracts are available with 72 days to maturity. The portfolio has a beta of 1.50. The futures price is:

$$1{,}200 \times \left[1 + 0.10 \times \frac{72}{360}\right] = 1{,}224$$

Assume that the manager wishes hedge the value of \$15MM worth of the equity portfolio, and consequently decides to go short in index futures. The number of contracts required is:

$$1.50 \times \frac{15{,}000{,}000}{1{,}200 \times 250} = 75 \text{ contracts}$$

Consider two possible scenarios for the index after 9 days.

Case A

Assume that the index is at 1,440, that is it has increased by 20%. The corresponding futures price will be:

$$1{,}440 \times \left[1 + 0.10 \times \frac{63}{360}\right] = 1{,}465.20$$

The risk-less rate of return for 9 days is 0.25%. Thus the return on the portfolio is:

$$0.25 + 1.50 \times (20 - 0.25) = 29.875\%$$

The value of the portfolio is therefore:

$$30{,}000{,}000 \times (1 + 0.29875) = \$38{,}962{,}500$$

The profit/loss from the futures contract is:

$$250 \times 75 \times (1{,}224 - 1465.20) = -\$\,4{,}522{,}500$$

Thus the total value of the partially hedged portfolio is:

$$38{,}962{,}500 - 4{,}522{,}500 = \$34{,}440{,}000$$

If the 15MM had been perfectly hedged we would have expected a terminal value of:

$$15{,}000{,}000 \times 1.29875 + 15{,}000{,}000 \times 1.0025 = \$34{,}518{,}750$$

However, since we are terminating the hedge prior to the date of maturity of the futures contract, we are exposed to basis risk. At inception, the basis was −24. On the final day it is −25.20. We know that a short hedger is long the basis, that is he benefits from an increase in the basis. Since the basis has decreased in our case, his terminal portfolio value is lower.

Considering that the portfolio value has increased by $4.44MM, the manager may decide to increase the quantum of funds exposed to market risk. For instance, he may decide that he would like to insure the value of only $10.80MM. If so, the required number of futures contracts will be:

$$1.50 \times \frac{10{,}800{,}000}{1{,}440 \times 250} = 45 \text{ contracts}$$

Case B

Now assume that the index is at 960, that is it has decreased by 20%. The corresponding futures price will be:

$$960 \times \left[1 + 0.10 \times \frac{63}{360}\right] = 976.80$$

The risk-less rate of return for 9 days is 0.25%. Thus the return on the portfolio is:

$$0.25 + 1.50 \times (-20 - 0.25) = -30.125\%$$

The value of the portfolio is therefore:

$$30{,}000{,}000 \times (1 - 0.30125) = \$20{,}962{,}500$$

The profit/loss from the futures contract is:

$$250 \times 75 \times (1{,}224 - 976.80) = \$4{,}635{,}500$$

Thus, the total value of the partly hedged portfolio is:

$$20{,}962{,}500 + 4{,}635{,}500 = \$25{,}597{,}500$$

If the 15MM had been perfectly hedged we would have expected a terminal value of:

$$15{,}000{,}000 \times 0.69875 + 15{,}000{,}000 \times 1.0025 = \$25{,}518{,}750$$

Once again, since we are terminating the hedge prior to the date of maturity of the futures contract, we are exposed to basis risk. At inception, the basis was −24. On the final day it is −16.80. Since the basis has increased in our case, his terminal portfolio value is higher.

Considering that the portfolio value has decreased by $4.4025MM, the manager may decide to decrease the quantum of funds exposed to market risk. For instance, he may decide that he would like to insure the value of $19.20MM. If so, the required number of futures contracts will be:

$$1.50 \times \frac{19{,}200{,}000}{960 \times 250} = 120 \text{ contracts}$$

Suggestions for Further Reading

Chance, D.M. *An Introduction to Options & Futures*. The Dryden Press, 1991.
Edwards, F.R. and C.W. Ma *Futures & Options*. McGraw-Hill, 1992.
Kolb, R.W. *Futures, Options & Swaps*. Blackwell, 2000.
Siegel, D.R. and D.F. Siegel *Futures Markets*. The Dryden Press, 1990.
Stoll, H.R. and R.E. Whaley *Futures and Options: Theory and Applications*. South Western, 1993.

References

Coyle, B. *Equity Finance*. Financial World Publishing, 2002.
Geddes, H.R. *An Introduction to Corporate Finance: Transactions and Techniques*. Securities Institute, 2001.
Ross S.A., R.W. Westerfield, and Jaffe J. *Corporate Finance*. Irwin McGraw-Hill.
Scott, D.L. *How Wall Street Works*. McGraw-Hill, 1999.
Teweles, R.J and E.S. Bradley *The Stock Market*. John Wiley, 1998.
Common Stocks, Preferred Stocks - Basic Concepts. http://thismatter.com
Guide to the Markets Investors Business daily.
Subject: Stocks – Tracking Stock http://invest-faq.com
www.sec.gov
www.activefilings.com
beginnersinvest.about.com
www.mreic.com

Chapter 6
Short Term Interest Rate (STIR) Futures Contracts

6.1 Introduction

Short term debt instruments, that is assets with an original term to maturity of one year or less are referred to as *Money Market Instruments*. In the case of debt securities we must make a distinction between the original term to maturity of a security, and its actual term to maturity. The original term to maturity of an asset is the time to maturity of the instrument at the time of issue. Obviously this cannot change once the security is issued. On the other hand, the actual term to maturity is the current term to maturity of the security. With the passage of time, the actual term to maturity will keep declining. All money market securities are obviously debt securities, for equity securities do not have a maturity date.

The money market is intended for transactions to meet short-term cash needs or what are termed as *current account* transactions. It represents the arena where parties with a temporary cash surplus interact with those faced with the specter of a short-term cash deficit. The nature of transactions range from overnight deals to those with a maturity of as long as one year.

Why do we require a money market? For the majority of businesses as well as government entities, the projected inflows of cash will rarely match with the scheduled outflows. Money markets serve to bridge the gap between receipts and expenditure. Let's first take the case of a government. It will collect revenue primarily in the form of taxes. Taxes are received periodically in lumpy amounts and do not arise uniformly during the course of the financial year. However, cash disbursements have to be made throughout the year on account of expenses such as wages and salaries, office supplies and other expenses. At the time of collection of tax revenues, the government will enter the money market as a lender. At other points in time when there is a deficit, it may borrow in the money market by issuing short term debt securities. Similarly, businesses collect sales revenues at points in time that will usually not coincide with budgeted expenditure. Thus, the checking accounts of these firms will fluctuate from large credit balances to low or nil balances. Whenever there is a surplus, such firms will enter the money market to earn some returns on the surplus funds. On the other hand, firms with a temporary deficit will seek to borrow for short periods.

Money is an extremely perishable asset. When idle cash is not gainfully invested, the holder will incur an opportunity cost in the form of interest that is foregone. Such income if not earned, is lost forever. When a large amount of money is involved, the income that is lost from not profitably investing idle funds for even a day can be substantial. Take the case of an institution that has 12MM dollars available for investment overnight. If we assume that the interest rate is 12% per annum and that the year con-

https://doi.org/10.1515/9783110746662-006

sists of 360 days, which is the assumption in the case of money market securities, the loss if the funds are kept idle is:

$$12{,}000{,}000 \times 0.12 \times \frac{1}{360} = \$4{,}000$$

For a week, this amounts to $28,000 of lost income.

6.2 Eurodollars

The development of the Eurocurrency market was one of the early factors in the growth of international investment. A eurocurrency is a freely traded currency deposited in a bank outside its country of origin. For example, Eurodollar deposits are dollar denominated time deposits held by banks outside the U.S. while Euroyen are yen deposited outside Japan. These deposits are accepted by commercial banks and are not backed by any government guarantees.

6.2.1 LIBOR

LIBOR is an acronym for the *London Inter Bank Offer Rate*. It may be defined as the rate at which a bank with a high credit rating is prepared to lend to a similar bank, and is the main benchmark rate in the London inter bank market. In practice LIBOR is quoted for a number of tenors - 1 month; 2 months; 3 months; 6 months; and 12 months. Thus, there are several LIBOR rates that are quoted at any point in time, and any quotation must be prefixed by its term to maturity. Every bank in London quotes its own indicative LIBOR rate for each maturity period, but usually the rates quoted by competing banks are the same with occasional small differences of the magnitude of a few basis points. *A basis point, denoted by b.p, is one hundredth of one percent.*

6.2.2 LIBID

LIBID is an acronym for the London Inter Bank Bid Rate. It is the rate that a London bank with a good credit rating will pay on funds deposited with it by another top rated London bank. LIBID just like LIBOR is quoted for a number of tenors. While LIBOR represents the rate that banks seeking to borrow in the inter bank market might have to pay, LIBID is the rate that banks with surplus funds might have to accept on an inter bank deposit. LIBID will be lower than LIBOR. When two banks arrange an inter bank transaction, the rate that is agreed upon will often be somewhere between LIBID and LIBOR, and could possibly be an average of the two. Some banks therefore use LIMEAN, which is an arithmetic average of the LIBID and the LIBOR, as the reference rate for their inter bank transactions.

6.2.3 Floating Rate Loans and LIBOR

The growth of Eurocurrency deposits has facilitated Eurodollar loans. These are loans made on a floating rate basis, with the base rate being LIBOR. *A floating rate loan is a loan whose interest rate is linked to a base rate, and consequently is reset periodically.* The rate of interest on such loans fluctuates directly with the benchmark. That is, the higher the LIBOR, the higher will be the interest payable/receivable. Commercial loans based on LIBOR are priced at LIBOR plus a *Margin or Spread*, which would depend on the credit worthiness of the borrower.

We will illustrate such loans with the help of Example 6.1.

Example 6.1: Consider a conventional fixed rate loan of $100,000, with interest payable at the rate of 10% per annum on a semi-annual basis. The interest payable every six months would be $5,000. On the other hand, consider a floating rate loan for the same amount, with the rate being specified as LIBOR + 50 basis points. 50 basis points ≡ 0.50%. Let's assume that the interest rate is reset every six months, and that the LIBOR when the loan is made is 8%. So the interest for the first six months is:

$$0.085 \times \frac{1}{2} \times 100{,}000 = \$4{,}250$$

If at the end of the first six months, the LIBOR were to be 8.5%, then the interest for the next six months will be:

$$0.09 \times \frac{1}{2} \times 100{,}000 = \$4{,}500$$

As can be seen, the LIBOR that determines the interest rate for a six monthly period, is the rate that prevails at the start of the period. Such a system is called 'determined in advance and paid in arrears', since the LIBOR and consequently the applicable rate of interest is determined at the start of the period, but the actual interest is paid at the end of the period.

6.2.4 Day-count Conventions and Interest Computation

For inter-bank loans interest is computed on the specified principal amount, and is payable at maturity along with the corresponding principal. Certain money market securities, like Treasury bills, are however termed as discount securities. These are analogous to zero-coupon securities, for they are issued at a discount from the specified face value, and repay the principal at maturity.

For most currencies, interest on bank loans is computed under the assumption that the year has 360 days. For the purpose of interest computation the practice is to consider the actual number of days in the loan period. Consequently this day-count convention is referred to as ACT/360. Thus, for a loan in U.S. dollars, where the specified principal is \$P, and the tenor is T days, the interest payable at maturity will be:

$$P \times \frac{r}{100} \times \frac{T}{360}$$

where r is the quoted rate of interest.

However for certain currencies like the British pound, the convention is to use an ACT/365 day-count. Consequently the corresponding formula for interest computation is:

$$P \times \frac{r}{100} \times \frac{T}{365}$$

This is shown in Examples 6.2 and 6.3.

Example 6.2: A bank makes a loan of \$5 MM from 1 June until 17 September of the same year, at an interest rate of 3.25% per annum. The number of days is = 29 + 31 + 31 + 17 = 108. Notice that the start date is excluded while the end date is included. The interest is given by:

$$5{,}000{,}000 \times \frac{3.25}{100} \times \frac{108}{360} = \$48{,}750$$

Thus the amount repayable at maturity is:

$$5{,}000{,}000 + 48{,}750 = \$5{,}048{,}750$$

Example 6.3: Consider the data given in the above example, but assume that the loan is for sterling pounds, for which the applicable convention is ACT/365. The interest payable in this case will therefore be:

$$5{,}000{,}000 \times \frac{3.25}{100} \times \frac{108}{365} = £48{,}082.19$$

6.3 Transitioning Away from LIBOR

Eurodollar futures contracts, on the CME Group, were based on the three-month LIBOR. The benchmark LIBOR was the ICE LIBOR, where ICE stands for the Inter-Continental Exchange. ICE maintains a panel of banks, and for the US Dollar there are 18 banks in the panel. These banks submit rates which are then combined. Banks are required to submit rates in answer to the following question:

"At what rate could you borrow funds, were you to do so by asking for and then accepting inter-bank offers in a reasonable market size just prior to 11 A.M." The LIBOR is computed using a trimmed arithmetic mean. For the USD the top four and the bottom four quotes are excluded, and the remaining 10 are averaged.

ICE provides the LIBOR for five currencies: US Dollar (USD); British Pound (GBP); Euro (EUR); Japanese Yen (JPY); Swiss Franc (CHF).

A few years ago, market estimates showed that, on a typical day, the volume of three-month wholesale funding transactions by major global banks was about $500 million. This is much lower than the $200 trillion of financial contracts which are based on the LIBOR for the US dollar. Thus, the underlying volumes of LIBOR based contracts was much in excess of the volumes in the inter-bank market. Hence, there was a perceived need to move beyond the LIBOR. Finally, the decision was taken to retire the LIBOR, and switch to a new benchmark.

One of the reasons for switching to another reference rate, was that the LIBOR was perceived as being unreliable. Prior to the ICE LIBOR, we had the BBA LIBOR, where BBA stands for the British Bankers Association. There was a major scandal regarding this rate, about a decade ago. It was revealed that banks were rigging the rate. That is, the banks on the panel, that were being polled to compute the benchmark, were collaborating together and submitting false data. More seriously, the transactions that LIBOR was supposed to be based on, namely interbank loans, were not necessarily taking place. In other words, the banks on the panel, were merely estimating the rates at which they would hypothetically lend to one each other.

6.3.1 SOFR

The Secured Overnight Financing Rate (SOFR) is a measure of the cost of borrowing cash overnight, collateralized by Treasury securities. The SOFR includes all trades based on the General Collateral Rate (GCR). Special repo transactions are excluded from the computation. The general collateral rate is the rate that is applicable for most Treasury securities that are offered as collateral, since such securities are close substitutes for each other. However, at times a dealer may want a particular security, and to obtain it, may be willing to offer a loan at a rate that is lower than the general collateral rate. Such securities are said to be On Special.

The main difference between SOFR and LIBOR is with respect to the method with which the benchmark is arrived at. While LIBOR is based on inputs from a panel of banks, SOFR is a measure of the cost of borrowing cash overnight, collateralized by U.S. Treasury securities in the repo market. The transaction volumes underlying SOFR are around $1 trillion in terms of daily volumes. Unlike the LIBOR, it is a risk free rate, that does not include a credit risk premium.

SOFR is a weighted average of rates observed for repurchase agreements. Every morning, the New York FED publishes the rate computed by it for the previous business day. One key difference between the two benchmarks, is that SOFR is based on completed financial transactions, unlike LIBOR, which is based on quotes from commercial banks, and such quotes need not be based on actual financial transactions. Second, LIBOR is forward looking while SOFR is backward looking. The implications are that, in the case of LIBOR, banks knew the borrowing rate at the start of the period, but in the case of SOFR, they will know the amount owed only at the end of the loan.

6.3.2 An Issue with Transitioning

One of the advantages of LIBOR is that its estimates are available for seven borrowing periods, from the Inter-continental Exchange, ranging from as short as one day, to as long as 12 months. On the other hand, the SOFR represents only overnight transactions. Thus, contracts that needed to switch from LIBOR to SOFR had to be adapted. The Alternative Reference Rates Committee (ARRC), which was set up to facilitate the transition, recommended that a credit spread adjustment be added to SOFR to compensate for the difference between the two rates. After extensive deliberations, the committee, settled on using the five-year historical median difference between LIBOR and SOFR, set on March 5, 2021, and recommended the following adjustments.

- 11.448 basis points for the one-month tenor
- 26.161 basis points for the three-month tenor
- 42.826 basis points for the six-month tenor

The CME Group has determined that trading in Eurodollar futures contracts will be terminated, and all open positions will be converted on a 1:1 basis into same month CME Three-Month SOFR futures. The price adjustment will be 26.161 bp, which was recommended by the AARC.

On the CME the Eurodollar futures price has been quoted as an index, that is, 100 - Implicit Interest Rate. Since the SOFR is lower than the LIBOR, the futures price should be higher. Thus, the conversion formula is 3-Month Eurodollar futures settlement price + 26.161 basis points.

The exchange has now started trading both 3-month and 1-month SOFR based futures contracts. The final settlement price for the 1-month contract is determined by the arithmetic average of the daily SOFR during the delivery month carried out to the fourth decimal place. For the 3-month contract, the final settlement price is determined by daily compounding of the overnight SOFR rate covering the actual day count for that contract's interval.

6.4 Federal Funds

Federal funds are perhaps the most important of all money market instruments because they are the primary means of making payments in this market. The term refers to money that is available for immediate payment. In earlier years the federal funds market referred to loans made by banks with excess reserves at the Federal Reserve to banks with a need for funds. Such funds can be readily transferred in seconds by computer. These days the Fed Funds market is broader in scope. For instance, most banks maintain deposits with large correspondent banks in major financial centers. These deposits may be transferred readily from one party to another. The most important borrowers continue to be commercial banks, which use this instrument as the principal way to adjust their legal reserve account at the Federal Reserve bank in the district where they are located.

Banks and other depository institutions must hold in a reserve account, assets equal to a fraction of the funds deposited with them. Legal reserve requirements are met by holding vault cash, and reserve balances with the local Federal Reserve bank. An increase in deposits will reflect itself as an increase in reserves, while withdrawal of cash or loans granted to a borrower, will show up as a reduction in reserves. The acquisition of securities by a bank will also manifest itself as a reduction in reserves. Thus, at any point in time, some banks will be relatively flush with funds, while others will be in urgent need. Excess reserves yield nil returns, and consequently banks seek to keep such funds gainfully invested.

6.5 Forward Rate Agreements

Forward rate agreements, commonly referred to as FRAs, are OTC derivatives, which are based on a short-term interest rate. They represent an agreement between counterparties to fix an interest rate, for a transaction that is scheduled for a future date. There is no physical delivery of cash in the case of such transactions. Profits and losses are settled by way of cash settlement at the end of the contract period. In such agreements, there is a contract rate, and a market determined reference rate. If on the settlement date the FRA contract rate differs from a reference rate, then a settlement payment is made from one party to another. There is no obligation on the part of either party to borrow or lend cash.

6.5.1 Buyers and Sellers

The FRA contract rate is a fixed rate of interest, and parties who seek to pay the contract rate are said to have bought the FRA and are referred to as buyers. By buying the FRA, they can lock in a fixed rate for a payable. Parties who seek to receive the contract rate are said to have sold the FRA and are referred to as sellers. They can lock in a fixed rate for a receivable. Thus, from a hedging standpoint buyers can lock in a fixed rate for a payable, while sellers can lock in a fixed rate for a receivable. From a speculative standpoint, traders who are bullish about interest rates will buy a FRA, whereas those who are bearish about interest rates will sell a FRA. It must be remembered that since interest rates and bond prices are inversely related, a party who is bullish about interest rates, is bearish about bond prices, while a trader who is bearish about interest rates, is bullish about bond prices.

6.5.2 Terminology

FRAs are quoted with reference to two numbers, the first of which is the settlement date, while the second is the final maturity date. Standard contracts have maturities of 3, 6 or 12 months. If we have an A x B FRA, the settlement date is A months away, and the underlying loan/deposit is for B-A months. For instance, consider a 3 x 6 FRA. The settlement date is 3-months forward from the spot value date (T+2), and the maturity date is 3 months from the settlement date.

Consider a 3 x 9 FRA in the US. Assume that the trade date 26 October 20XX (WED). The spot value date will be 28 October 20XX (FRI). The settlement date will be 3 months after the spot value date, which is 28 January 20(XX+1). The maturity date will be six months after the settlement date, which is 28 July 20(XX+1).

The settlement amount, which is the only cash flow in a FRA, is due on the settlement date. It depends on the difference between the contract rate and the reference rate, and also on the notional principal and the day-count convention. There are two types of FRAs, delayed settlement and in arrears. In the case of the former the payment is due on the maturity date, whereas in the case of the latter, it is due on the settlement date. Most FRAs in the market are of the in arrears type. The difference is illustrated in Example 6.4.

Example 6.4: Consider a 3 x 9 FRA from the buyer's perspective. The notional amount is 20 MM US dollars. The contract rate is 4.80%, and the reference rate on the settlement date is 5.20%. We will assume a day-count convention of 30/360. Thus, six months corresponds to 0.50 years. In an in arrears FRA, the payment would be:

$$20{,}000{,}000 \times (0.052 - 0.048) \times 0.50 = 40{,}000$$

The buyer will receive this amount since the reference rate is higher than the contract rate. Had it been a delayed settlement FRA, this amount would be due after six months. The present value would be:

$$40{,}000/(1 + 0.052 \times 0.5) = 38{,}986.35$$

6.6 Determining the Contract Rate

If we have a process for the evolution of the reference rate, we can determine the contract rate for an FRA. Lets assume that time is measured in semi-annual periods. Six months hence, the reference rate may be 6.8915% per annum with a 50% probability, and 6.1122% per annum with an a 50% probability. Lets call the unknown contract rate as F.

At the outset, the value of a forward contract is zero. Thus:

$$0.50 \times (F - 6.8915) + 0.5 \times (F - 6.1122) = 0$$

and F = 6.5019%

Had it been a delayed settlement FRA:

$$0.50 \times (F - 6.8915)/(1 + 1.034458) + 0.50 \times (F - 6.1122)/(1 + 1.030561) = 0$$

and F = 6.5011%

6.7 SOFR Futures

SOFR futures contracts trade on the IMM in Chicago. There are contracts based on the three-month SOFR, as well as the one-month SOFR. The futures price is quoted in terms of an IMM index and implies an interest rate.

$$\text{Quoted Futures Price} = 100.00 - \text{Implicit Interest Rate}$$

The implicit interest rate in this case is however, an actual or add-on interest rate and not a discount rate as in the case of T-bills. The difference can be illustrated with the help of Example 6.5.

Example 6.5: A discount rate of 5% per annum, means that for a 90 day loan with a maturity value of 1 MM, you have to pay

$$1{,}000{,}000\left[1 - .05 \times \frac{90}{360}\right]$$
$$= \$987{,}500$$

The actual rate of return is

$$\left(\frac{1000000 - 987{,}500}{987{,}500}\right) \times \frac{360}{90}$$
$$\equiv 5.06\%$$

An add-on interest rate of 5% per annum, however, means that if you invest 1 MM for 90 days, you will get

$$1{,}000{,}000\left[1+.05\times\frac{90}{360}\right]=\$1{,}012{,}500$$

after 90 days.

6.8 Calculating Profits and Losses on STIR Futures

Let's suppose that the futures price is 96. This represents a yearly interest rate of 4% or 1% per quarter. Thus, the implied quarterly interest payment on a time deposit of 1 MM is

$$0.01\times 1{,}000{,}000=\$10{,}000$$

If the futures price were to fall to 95 at the end of the day, then it would represent a quarterly interest payment of $12,500 on a deposit of 1 MM.

Consider a person who goes long in a SOFR futures contract at 96. Such a person is agreeing to lend money at the equivalent interest rate, namely 1% per quarter.[1] If interest rates rise subsequently to 5% per annum, that is, the futures price goes down to 95 and the contract is marked to market, then the long will lose $2,500. The logic is that when the contract is marked to market, it is as if he is offsetting by going short, which in this case, means that he is agreeing to borrow at 1.25% per quarter. Thus, when the interest rates rise the longs will lose. The reverse is true for the shorts, that is, when the interest rates fall, they will lose.

You should by now be able to see the logic behind quoting futures prices in terms of an index, rather than in terms of interest rates. If futures prices were to be quoted in terms of interest rates, then the longs would gain when the futures prices fall and the shorts would gain when the futures prices rise. But in all the other markets, you have been observing that the longs gain when futures prices rise, whereas the shorts gain if futures prices fall. Thus, to make money market futures consistent with other futures markets, we do not quote futures prices in terms of interest rates, but do so in terms of an index. When the index rises, the longs will gain and when it falls, the shorts will gain.

Yet another reason for quoting futures prices in terms of an index rather than in terms of interest rates, is to ensure that the bid prices are lower than the ask. Remember, that as an investor, the borrowing rates that you will face will be typically higher than the lending rates confronted by you. Thus, the rates underlying a short position will be

1 The logic is the same as that underlying futures in the case of a debt security such as a T-bill. In the case of bills, a long position means that you are willing to buy bills at the expiration of the contract. In the case of interest rate futures, a long position means that you are willing to make a deposit of three months. In either case you are a lender.

greater than the rates underlying a long position. To be consistent with the principle that bid prices are always lower than the ask, it is necessary to convert the rates to equivalent index values.

Now consider the case where the SOFR index changes from F_0 to F_1. The profit for a long is

$$1{,}000{,}000 \times \frac{(100 - F_0)}{100} \times \frac{90}{360} - 1{,}000{,}000 \times \frac{(100 - F_1)}{100} \times \frac{90}{360}$$
$$= 1{,}000{,}000 \times \frac{(F_1 - F_0)}{100} \times \frac{90}{360}$$

6.9 The Final SOFR Settlement Rate

Let's first consider the 3-month contract. The final settlement futures price is 100 minus the SOFR rate, that has been compounded over the contract's reference quarter. For the purpose of computation, the reference quarter is defined as the interval starting from the 3rd Wednesday of the month three month's prior to the delivery month, to the third Wednesday of the delivery month. The starting Wednesday is included, while the ending Wednesday is excluded. The 3-month SOFR futures final settlement references the realized compounded values of the benchmark over a forward looking three-month period between two futures expiration months. Thus, the month symbol in the contract code refers to the beginning of the calculation period, and not the month for final settlement. The final settlement month will be three months after the month mentioned in the contract code. Thus, the final settlement for the June 20XX futures contract, will be based on the benchmark rates over the period June to September 20XX.

Now let's turn to the one month contract. The final settlement price is 100 minus the SOFR rate. This rate is an arithmetic average of the rates observed during the month. Hence, in this case, the final settlement references the realized average daily values of the benchmark over a given delivery month. Thus, the month mentioned in the contract is the delivery month for the contract. That is, the June 20XX futures will finally settle in June of that year.

6.10 Locking in a Borrowing Rate

We will first illustrate how borrowing and lending rates can be locked in using SOFR futures.

Assume that today is 15 September, 20XX. Raviola is borrowing 1 million dollars after a period of 90 days. The company is confident that given its rating, it can borrow at the SOFR. It is however worried that interest rates may rise before 15 December, which is the last day of trading for the September futures contract. The current September futures price is 94. Since the company is planning to borrow money it requires a short hedge.

Assume that Raviola goes short in one September futures contract. We will consider two different scenarios on 15 December, one where the SOFR is higher as compared to the rate implicit in the futures price, and the other where it is lower.

6.10.1 Case A: SOFR = 4%

The interest payable on the loan of 1 MM is

$$0.04 \times 1{,}000{,}000 \times \frac{90}{360}$$
$$= \$10{,}000$$

Gain/loss from the futures market is

$$1{,}000{,}000 \times \frac{(F_0 - F_1)}{100} \times \frac{90}{360}$$
$$= 1{,}000{,}000 \times \frac{(94 - 96)}{100} \times \frac{90}{360}$$
$$= (5{,}000)$$

Therefore, the effective interest paid is

$$10{,}000 + 5{,}000 = \$15{,}000$$

6.10.2 Case B: SOFR = 7%

The interest payable is

$$0.07 \times 1{,}000{,}000 \times \frac{90}{360}$$
$$= \$17{,}500$$

Profit/loss from the futures position is

$$1{,}000{,}000 \times \frac{(94 - 93)}{100} \times \frac{90}{360}$$
$$= \$2{,}500$$

Thus, the effective interest paid is

$$17{,}500 - 2{,}500 = \$15{,}000$$

Thus the company can lock in an interest payable of $15,000, irrespective of the reference rate computed on 15 December. This amount corresponds to a rate of:

$$\frac{15{,}000}{1{,}000{,}000} \times \frac{360}{90} \equiv 6\%$$

which is the rate implicit in the initial futures price.

6.11 Locking in a Lending Rate

Assume that today is 15 September, 20XX. Microsoft is planning to lend $1MM for a period of 90 days. The company is of the opinion that it can lend at the SOFR plus 75 b.p., and wants to lock in a rate using SOFR futures. 15 December is the last day of trading for the September contract, and the current futures price is 96. Since the company wishes to lock-in a lending rate, it needs to go long in futures contracts. As before, we will consider two scenarios for the terminal value of SOFR.

6.11.1 Case A: SOFR = 5.25%

The interest receivable on the loan is:

$$0.06 \times 1{,}000{,}000 \times \frac{90}{360} = \$15{,}000$$

The profit/loss from the futures position is:

$$1{,}000{,}000 \times \frac{(94.75 - 96)}{100} \times \frac{90}{360} = \$(3{,}125)$$

Thus the effective interest received is:

$$15{,}000 - 3{,}125 = \$11{,}875$$

6.11.2 Case B: SOFR = 3.25%

The interest receivable on the loan is:

$$0.04 \times 1{,}000{,}000 \times \frac{90}{360} = \$10{,}000$$

The profit/loss from the futures position is:

$$1{,}000{,}000 \times \frac{(96.75 - 96)}{100} \times \frac{90}{360} = \$1{,}875$$

Thus the effective interest received is:

$$10{,}000 + 1{,}875 = \$11{,}875$$

Thus irrespective of the scenario at expiration, the company is assured of a receivable of $11,875. The equivalent interest rate is:

$$\frac{11{,}875}{1{,}000{,}000} \times \frac{360}{90} \times 100 = 4.75\%$$

This represents the rate implicit in the initial futures price, plus the assumed spread of 75 b.p.

6.12 Hedging Rates for Periods Not Equal to 90 Days

We have seen how SOFR futures contracts can be used to lock in a borrowing rate or a lending rate for a 90 day loan. These futures can also be used to lock in rates for an N day loan if N were to be fairly close to 90. The necessary condition for such a hedge is that the interest rate for the N day loan should move closely with the rate for a 90 day loan. Before giving an illustration, we will first derive the required hedge ratio.

Assume that $d_N = \alpha + d_{90} + \epsilon$, where d_N is the annualized rate for an N day loan and d_{90} is the annualized rate for a 90 day loan. We will assume that $\epsilon = 0$. If so:

$$\Delta d_N = \Delta d_{90}$$

Take the case of a party which is raising an N day loan for Q million dollars. The change in the interest payable, due to a rate change is:

$$Q \times 1{,}000{,}000 \times \frac{\Delta d_N}{100} \times \frac{N}{360}$$

The profit/loss per contract, from the futures market is:

$$1{,}000{,}000 \times \frac{\Delta d_{90}}{100} \times \frac{90}{360}$$

The number of futures contracts, Q_f, ought to be chosen in a way such that:

$$Q \times 1{,}000{,}000 \times \frac{\Delta d_N}{100} \times \frac{N}{360} = Q_f \times 1{,}000{,}000 \times \frac{\Delta d_{90}}{100} \times \frac{90}{360}$$

Since we have assumed that $\Delta d_N = \Delta d_{90}$, we get the result that:

$$Q \times N = Q_f \times 90$$

$$\Rightarrow \frac{Q_f}{Q} = \text{the hedge ratio} = \frac{N}{90}$$

We will now illustrate as to how this hedge will perform in practice, with the help of Example 6.6.

Example 6.6: Once again assume that we are standing on 15 June, 20XX, and that Raviola is borrowing 10 MM USD on 15 September, this time for a period of 117 days. The current June futures price is 95.75.

Since Raviola is borrowing it would require a short position in SOFR futures.

$$Q_f = 10 \times \frac{117}{90} = 13$$

Let's examine the performance of this hedge.

Case A : SOFR = 4%

The actual interest paid by Raviola is:

$$0.04 \times 10{,}000{,}000 \times \frac{117}{360} = \$130{,}000$$

The profit/loss from the futures position is:

$$13 \times 1{,}000{,}000 \times \frac{(95.75 - 96)}{100} \times \frac{90}{360}$$
$$= -\$8{,}125$$

Thus, the effective interest paid by the company is $138,125.

Case B : SOFR = 4.5%

The actual interest paid by Raviola is:

$$0.045 \times 10{,}000{,}000 \times \frac{117}{360} = \$146{,}250$$

Profit/loss from the futures position is

$$13 \times 1{,}000{,}000 \times \frac{(95.75 - 95.50)}{100} \times \frac{90}{360}$$
$$= 8{,}125$$

The effective interest paid by the company is $138,125

Hence, irrespective of the SOFR on computed on 14 September, the company has locked in an interest expense of $138,125. This amount corresponds to an interest i such that

$$10{,}000{,}000\left[1 + i \times \frac{117}{360}\right] = 10{,}138{,}125$$

i is therefore equal to 4.25%, which is the rate implicit in the initial futures price.

6.13 Creating a Fixed Rate Loan

Assume that YES Bank is able to borrow money at SOFR for three month periods. Consequently the interest payable on its liability is variable. The bank however has a potential client who wishes to borrow at a fixed rate for a period of one year. Thus, the interest receivable from the proposed asset is fixed in nature. The bank would like to use futures contracts to mitigate the risk arising from the fact that it is borrowing at a floating rate, but is lending at a fixed rate. It turns out that SOFR futures contracts can be used to hedge the funding risk and determine a suitable rate that can be quoted by the bank while negotiating a fixed rate loan. We will illustrate the principle involved with the help of an example.

IT20, a company based in London, wants a loan for 100 million U.S. dollars for a period of one year from 15 June, 20XX, at a fixed interest rate. Let's assume that June, September, December, and March futures contracts, are available at 96.2, 97.1, 96.6, and 97 respectively. For ease of exposition, we will assume that the dates on which the bank will roll over its three month borrowings, namely 15 September, 15 December, and 15 March, are the same as the dates on which the futures contracts corresponding to those quarters are scheduled to expire. Each SOFR futures contract is on 1 MM USD and the bank is borrowing at a floating rate. Consequently it needs a short position in 100 each of the June, September, December and March futures contracts.

For the first quarter, the interest expense for the bank is

$$100{,}000{,}000 \times 0.038 \times \frac{90}{360} = \$950{,}000.$$

The short position in September contracts, will lock in a rate of 2.9% for a period of 90 days from September to December. This corresponds to an interest expense of

$$100{,}000{,}000 \times 0.029 \times \frac{90}{360} = \$725{,}000.$$

In a similar fashion, the short position in December contracts, will lock in

$$100{,}000{,}000 \times 0.034 \times \frac{90}{360} = \$850{,}000$$

for the 90 day period from 15 December. The March contracts will lock in the following interest amount for the last quarter.

$$100{,}000{,}000 \times 0.03 \times \frac{90}{360} = \$750{,}000$$

Hence the total interest payable by the bank for the twelve month period is:

$$950{,}000 + 725{,}000 + 850{,}000 + 750{,}000 = \$3{,}275{,}000.$$

This corresponds to an annualized interest rate of:

$$\frac{3{,}275{,}000}{100{,}000{,}000} \times 100 = 3.275\%$$

The bank can now quote a fixed rate to the client, based on this effective cost of funding, after factoring in hedging costs and a suitable profit margin.

6.13.1 Stack and Strip Hedges

We have assumed in the above illustration that the bank would use 100 futures contracts for each of the expiration months. Such a hedge, where the same number of contracts are used for each expiration month right from the outset, is called a *Strip Hedge.*

As we have seen in the chapter on hedging, when the maturity of a futures contract is very far away, the contract may not be actively traded. Such illiquidity could be a deterrent for a potential hedger, because he would seek the ability to enter and exit the market at a price that is close to the true or fair value of the asset. In this case, when the hedge is initiated in June, it is conceivable that the March futures may be illiquid. In such a situation, rather than starting with an equal number of June, September, December, and March contracts, the bank may initiate the hedge using an unequal number of September and December contracts, without taking a position in the March contract. Subsequently, when the September contracts expire, it will take a position in the March contract. Such a hedge, where the number of contracts for each maturity is not equal at the outset, is known as a *Stack Hedge*. We will illustrate the mechanics of such a hedge with the help of Example 6.7.

Example 6.7: Assume that the March futures contracts are perceived to be illiquid when the hedge is initiated. The bank therefore decides to hedge using 100 June contracts, 100 September contracts, and 200 December contracts. The position in June futures is obviously intended to lock in a rate for borrowing for the first quarter, while the September contracts, are intended to lock in a rate for the second quarter. Out of the 200 December contracts, 100 are intended to lock in a rate for the December to March quarter, while the remaining 100 are meant for hedging the March to June quarter. The inherent assumption is that on 15 September, the bank will partially offset its December position and go short in 100 March contracts, assuming that they have begun to be actively traded by then.

6.13.2 Performance: Strip versus Stack

The relative performance of a Stack Hedge vis a vis a Strip Hedge, would depend on the movement of interest rates between June and September.

Case A: The Stack Hedge is Equivalent to the Strip

Assume that the December futures price moves from 96.6 to 96 between June and September, while the March futures price moves from 97 to 96.4 during the same period.

When the 100 extra December contracts are liquidated in September, the profit from the position will be

$$100{,}000{,}000 \times \left(\frac{96.60 - 96}{100}\right) \times \frac{90}{360}$$
$$= \$150{,}000$$

The 100 March contracts which the bank will enter into at 96.4 will lock in an interest expense of

$$100{,}000{,}000 \times 0.036 \times \frac{90}{360} = \$900{,}000$$

for the last quarter. The effective interest expense for this quarter is therefore:

$$900{,}000 - 150{,}000 = \$750{,}000$$

which is the same amount that was locked in by the Strip Hedge.

Thus, if the three month SOFR rate, as contained in the December futures price, changes by the same magnitude and direction as the rate contained in the March futures price, then the Strip and Stack hedges will be equivalent. In interest rate parlance, we would say that there has been a *Parallel Shift* in the *Yield Curve*.

Case B: The Strip Outperforms

If the increase in the December rate is less than the increase in the March rate, then the Strip Hedge will outperform the Stack. For instance, assume that the December futures price moves from 96.6 to 96 whereas the March futures price moves from 97 to 96.20.

Since the futures price has declined there will be a profit when the extra December contracts are offset, which as before will be $150,000.

However, the interest expense for the last quarter will be higher. This expense will be:

$$100{,}000{,}000 \times 0.038 \times \frac{90}{360} = \$950{,}000$$

The effective interest is

$$950{,}000 - 150{,}000 = \$800{,}000$$

which is greater than the amount of 750,000 that was locked in by the Strip Hedge.

The same would be the case if the decrease in the December rate were to be more than the decrease in the March rate. In this case, there will be a loss when the December contracts are offset. However, the interest expense locked in by the March contracts will be lower. For instance assume that the December futures price moves to 96.9, whereas the March futures price moves to 97.1.

The profit from the December position will be:

$$100{,}000{,}000 \times \left(\frac{96.6 - 96.9}{100}\right) \times \frac{90}{360}$$
$$= -\$75{,}000$$

The interest expense for the last quarter, as locked in by the March contracts, will be:

$$100{,}000{,}000 \times 0.029 \times \frac{90}{360} = \$725{,}000$$

The effective interest paid is:

$$725{,}000 + 75{,}000 = \$800{,}000$$

which is greater than the amount of 750,000 that was locked in by the Strip Hedge. Clearly the gain on account of the decline in the rate implicit in the March contracts is not adequate to compensate for the loss incurred when the December contracts are offset.

Case C: The Stack Outperforms

If the increase in the December rate is more than the increase in the March rate, then the Stack Hedge will out perform the Strip. For instance, assume that the December futures price moves from 96.60 to 96, while the March futures price moves from 97 to 96.60.

The effective interest rate for the last quarter in this case is:

$$100{,}000{,}000 \times 0.034 \times \frac{90}{360} - 150{,}000$$
$$= 850{,}000 - 150{,}000$$
$$= \$700{,}000$$

The same would be true if the decrease in the December rate were to be less than the decrease in the March rate. In this case, once again there will be a loss when the December contracts are offset. However this will be more than compensated by the decline in the rate for the last quarter. For instance assume that the December futures price moves from 96.60 to 96.90, whereas the March futures price moves from 97 to 97.50.

The loss from the December position will be 75,000. The interest expense for the last quarter will be:

$$100{,}000{,}000 \times 0.025 \times \frac{90}{360} = \$625{,}000$$

The effective interest is:

$$625{,}000 + 75{,}000 = \$700{,}000$$

which is less than the amount of $750,000 that was locked in by the Strip Hedge.

6.14 Fed Funds Futures

The underlying asset is a 30-day Federal Funds loan, with a principal value of $5 million dollars. Prices are quoted as 100.00 minus the average daily Fed Funds overnight rate. At any point in time contracts for the next 24 consecutive months will be available. Contracts expire on the last business day of the delivery month, and are cash settled.

Suggestions for Further Reading

Chance, D.M. *An Introduction to Options & Futures*. The Dryden Press, 1991.
Comotto, R. *Foreign Exchange and Money Markets*. Euromoney Publications, 1998.
Coyle, B. *Money Markets*. Financial World Publishing, 2001.
Edwards, F.R. and C.W. Ma *Futures & Options*. McGraw-Hill, 1992.
Kolb, R.W. *Futures, Options, & Swaps*. Blackwell, 2000.
Marquit M. and B. Curry *Secured Overnight Financing Rate (SOFR)*.
McDonald, R.L. *Derivatives Markets*. Pearson Education, 2006.
Siegel, D.R. and D.F. Siegel *Futures Markets*. The Dryden Press, 1990.
Stigum, M. and A. Crescenzi *Stigum's Money Market*. McGraw-Hill, 2007.
Stigum, M. and F.L. Robinson *Money Market and Bond Calculations*. Irwin Professional Publishing, 1996.
Tapley, T.C. *Mathematics of Finance: Money and Time*. In D.E. Logue (ed.), *The WG&L Handbook of Financial Markets*. South Western College Publishing, 1995.

Websites

www.cmegroup.com
www.treasurydirect.gov

Chapter 7
Bond Market Futures

7.1 Introduction

Debt securities are a type of financial claim that are used by borrowing entities to raise capital. Unlike equity shares which confer ownership rights on parties who subscribe to them, a debt security merely represents the fact that the holder has lent money to the borrower, and is consequently entitled to receive interest at periodic intervals. The principal amount will be repaid at a prespecified maturity date. Such securities usually have a finite life span, unlike equity shares which do not have a stated maturity date. From the standpoint of the borrower, the interest payments on such securities are a contractual obligation. In other words, the borrowers are required to make the promised payments irrespective of the financial performance of the firm in a given time period. In contrast, a firm can always reduce the dividends on equity if it deems it necessary. In fact, there could be periods in which the firm chooses to skip the dividends entirely. Debt holders enjoy priority over shareholders in two respects. First, the interest claims of debt holders have to be satisfied before any dividends can be paid to the shareholders. Second, in the event of bankruptcy or liquidation of the firm, the proceeds from the sale of assets must be used to first settle all outstanding interest and principal that is due to the debt holders. Only the residual amount if any can be distributed among the shareholders.

Debt instruments can be *secured* or *unsecured*. In the case of secured debt, the terms of the contract will specify the assets of the firm that have been pledged as security or collateral. In the event of the company's inability to repay, the bond holders have a right over these assets. In the case of unsecured debt there is no specific pledge of collateral. In the U.S. the word 'Debenture' is specifically used to refer to unsecured debt. Debt instruments can be either *negotiable* or *non-negotiable*. Negotiable instruments are securities which can be endorsed from one party to another, and hence can be bought and sold easily in the financial markets. A non-negotiable instrument is one which cannot be transferred. Equity shares are an obvious example of a negotiable security. However, loans made by commercial banks to business firms, and savings bank accounts and time deposits of individuals, are non-negotiable in nature.

While debt is important for corporations, it is indispensable for central or federal, state, and local (municipalities) governments, for such entities obviously cannot issue equity shares. Unlike debt issued by entities in the private sector, *U.S. Treasury securities are fully backed by the federal government, and consequently have no credit risk associated with them.*[1] Thus, the interest rate on such securities becomes a benchmark

1 The term *credit risk* refers to the probability of default.

https://doi.org/10.1515/9783110746662-007

for setting the rates of returns on other, more risky, securities. The U.S. Treasury issues three categories of marketable debt instruments. Marketable securities are those that can be readily traded in the financial markets. T-bills are discount or zero coupon securities. That is, they are sold at a discount from their face value, and do not pay any interest explicitly. T-notes and T-bonds are issued at face value and are interest bearing instruments which typically make payouts at semi-annual intervals. T-bills are grouped under the category of *Money Market or Short Term Debt* instruments since they have a life span of less than one year, whereas T-notes and T-bonds are considered to be *Long Term Debt* instruments, and are consequently classified as *Capital Market* instruments. A T-note is akin to a T-bond, but has a time to maturity between 1-10 years at the time of issue, whereas T-bonds have a life span in excess of 10 years.

7.2 Fundamentals of Bond Valuation

The concepts of time value of money, can be used to value any asset, whose value is derived from future cash flows. We will see in this chapter, how these principles are applied by investors to establish the value of a bond.

An ordinary bond, also known as a *Plain Vanilla Bond*, is a fairly simple instrument.[2] It will pay interest periodically, typically every six months, and will repay the principal at maturity. *Zero Coupon* or *Deep Discount* securities, like T-bills, pay no interest. They are sold for less than the amount that is payable at maturity. The difference between the terminal payment and the issue price, constitutes the interest.

We will first take a close look at the pricing of plain vanilla bonds and attempt to understand the related principles and conventions. The following notation will be used in the course of our discussion. Additional variables will be defined as we go along.

7.2.1 Notation

- $M \equiv$ Face Value[3]
  The *Face Value* or *Par Value* is the amount that the issuer promises to pay to the lender at maturity. It is also referred to as the *Redemption Value* or *Maturity Value* or *Principal Value.*
- $T \equiv$ Term to Maturity
  A key feature of any bond is its Term to Maturity, which is the time remaining in the life of the bond. This is the period during which the borrower has to meet the

2 The most basic form of any security is referred to as the *Plain Vanilla* version. More exotic versions are said to have 'Bells and Whistles' attached.

3 The symbol ≡ stands for 'is equivalent to'.

conditions of the debt. A bond's term to maturity is the length of time after which the debt shall cease and the issuer will redeem the issue by paying the face value or principal back to the lender.[4] If we denote today as time t and the maturity date as time T, then T-t represents the term to maturity. The words Maturity, Term and Term to Maturity are used interchangeably to refer to the number of years remaining in the life of the bond.

The maturity of a bond indicates the expected life of the instrument, or the number of periods during which the holder can expect to receive the interest payments.[5] It also represents the number of periods, before the principal will be repaid.

A plain vanilla bond is a *Term Bond*, that is, it has a single maturity date which is fixed at the outset. But there can arise situations, where a bond issue can be retired early by the issuer, either in full or in part. In the case of callable bonds, the issuer can redeem the bonds by paying off the lender before the scheduled maturity date.

- $C \equiv$ Coupon
  A bond's coupon is the periodic interest payment made to the owners during the life of the bond. The coupon rate c is the rate of interest that, when multiplied by the par value, provides the dollar value of the annual coupon payment denoted by C. If the annual coupon rate is c, then the semi-annual coupon payment is $C/2$. The word 'coupon' is used because traditionally bonds were issued with a booklet of post-dated coupons. The bond holder was expected to redeem a coupon for cash at the end of every coupon period.

  Consider a bond with a face value of \$1,000, and a coupon of 10% per annum paid semi-annually. Since c = 0.10, the semi-annual interest is given by

$$\frac{C}{2} = \frac{0.10}{2} \times 1{,}000 = \$50$$

- $y \equiv$ Yield to Maturity
  The *yield to maturity* or the *YTM* is the rate of return that the buyer will get, if he buys the bond at the prevailing price and holds it to maturity. It makes an assumption that all intermediate coupon payments are reinvested at the YTM itself. Those of you who are familiar with Capital Budgeting, should note that it is similar to the concept of the *Internal Rate of Return* or *IRR* used in project appraisal.
- $N \equiv$ Number of Coupons Left in the Life of the Bond
- $k \equiv$ Time Until the Receipt of the First Coupon Expressed as a Fraction of Six Months
  If we are standing on a coupon date, then $k = 1$ else $k < 1$.

4 Remember, the issuer of the bond is the borrower and the buyer of the bond is the lender.

5 We use the phrase *Expected Life*, because bonds other than those issued by the government are subject to *Default Risk*, which means that the borrower may cease to honor his obligations before the stated time to maturity. Second, in practice many bonds are *Callable*, that is they can be recalled by the issuer well before they are due to mature.

- $P_{i,t} \equiv$ Clean Price of Bond i in the Spot Market at time t.
- $P_d \equiv$ Dirty Price
- $AI_{i,t_1,t_2} \equiv$ Accrued Interest on Bond i from t_1(the last coupon date) till t_2 (the date of valuation).

7.2.2 Valuation of a Bond as on a Coupon Date

The price of a bond as on a coupon date may be expressed by the following equation.

$$P_d = \sum_{t=1}^{N} \frac{\frac{C}{2}}{\left(1+\frac{y}{2}\right)^t} + \frac{M}{\left(1+\frac{y}{2}\right)^N} \tag{7.1}$$

A cursory glance will reveal that the price of a bond is the present value of the stream of coupon payments, which is an ordinary annuity, discounted using the YTM, plus the present value of the principal repayable at maturity. Example 7.1 illustrates the computation of the bond price on a coupon date.

Example 7.1: Let's assume that today is the 15th of August, 20XX. A Treasury Bond is available that matures on 15 August, 20(XX+20) and pays a coupon of 9% semi-annually on 15 February and 15 August every year. Unless otherwise stated the coupon rates given represent annual rates of interest. The face value is $1,000 and the yield to maturity is 8%.

The price of the bond may be calculated as follows.

We know that M = 1000, c = 9%, y = 8% and N = 40. Therefore

$$P_d = \sum_{t=1}^{40} \frac{\frac{(0.09 \times 1{,}000)}{2}}{\left(1+\frac{0.08}{2}\right)^t} + \frac{1000}{\left(1+\frac{0.08}{2}\right)^{40}}$$

$$= 890.6748 + 208.2890 = \$1098.9639$$

7.3 Valuation of a Bond Between Coupon Dates

Valuing a bond in between coupon dates is a more complex exercise. This is because the next coupon date will obviously be a fraction of a coupon period away. In practice, there is no unique way of computing this fractional period. The logically consistent way of valuing the bond would be to first price it as of the forthcoming coupon date. This price can then be discounted back for the fraction of the current coupon period that is remaining.

Assume that we are valuing the bond at a time t, such that the time till the next coupon is N_1 days, and that the current coupon period consists of N_2 days. There are N coupons remaining in the life of the bond. The cash flows remaining in the life of the bond can then be depicted as in Figure 7.1.

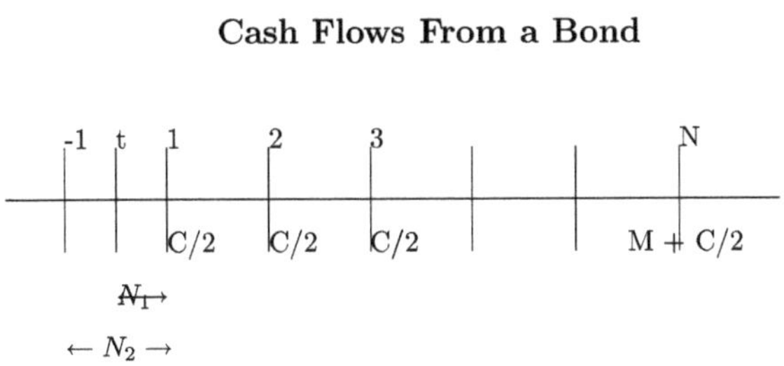

Figure 7.1: Cash Flows From a Bond.

In the above time line:
- *-1* is the date of the previous coupon
- *t* is the valuation date
- *1* is the date of the next coupon

The value of the bond at time 1, which represents the date of the next coupon, is given by:

$$\frac{C}{2} + \frac{C}{2} \times \text{PVIFA}\left(\frac{y}{2}, N-1\right) + M \times \text{PVIF}\left(\frac{y}{2}, N-1\right)$$

Thus, the value of the bond at the current point in time, *time t*, can be expressed as:

$$\frac{1}{\left(1+\frac{y}{2}\right)^k}\left[\frac{C}{2} + \frac{C}{2} \times \text{PVIFA}\left(\frac{y}{2}, N-1\right) + M \times \text{PVIF}\left(\frac{y}{2}, N-1\right)\right] \tag{7.2}$$

where PVIFA is the Present Value Interest Factor Annuity and PVIF is the Present Value Interest Factor.

$\text{PVIFA} = \frac{1}{r} \times \left[1 - \frac{1}{(1+r)^N}\right]$ and $\text{PVIF} = \frac{1}{(1+r)^N}$.

$k = \frac{N_1}{N_2}$, is the fraction of the current coupon period that is remaining.

7.3.1 Day-Count Conventions

In practice, there is no unique way of computing, k, or the fraction of the current coupon period that is remaining. There are different conventions in different markets, and sometimes for different debt securities in the same market. A day-count convention is a particular method for measuring N_1 and N_2, to enable us to compute the fractional period k. We will take a detailed look at the *Actual/Actual* method, which is the convention that is used for Treasury notes and bonds in the U.S. Example 7.2, illustrates the valuation of a US Treasury Bond between two coupon dates.

Example 7.2: Consider a Treasury bond that was issued on 15 February 20XX, and which pays coupons on 15 February and 15 August every year. The bond was issued with thirty years to maturity and has a face value of $1,000. The coupon rate is 12% per annum, and coupons are paid on a semi-annual basis. The YTM is 10% per annum. Today, the date of valuation, is 1 June 20XX.

The value of the bond as on the next coupon date will be:

$$60 + 60 \times \text{PVIFA}(5,59) + 1{,}000 \times \text{PVIF}(5,59)$$

The value of the bond today should therefore be:

$$\frac{1}{(1.05)^k}[60 + 60 \times \text{PVIFA}(5,59) + 1{,}000 \times \text{PVIF}(5,59)]$$

In the Actual-Actual method, N_1 and N_2, and consequently k, are calculated based on the actual number of days in the corresponding time periods. We have therefore to take cognizance of facts such as whether or not the year in question is a leap year. For the purpose of calculation, we are required to exclude the starting date, and include the ending date. In our case, N_1 and N_2 will be computed as shown in Tables 7.1 and 7.2.[6]

Table 7.1: Calculation of N_1.

Month	No. of Days
June	29
July	31
August	15
N_1	75

$$\text{So } k = \frac{N_1}{N_2} = \frac{75}{182} = 0.4121$$

As per this convention, N_2, or the number of days between two successive coupon dates, will always range between 181 and 184.

---

6 Assume that the current year is a leap year.

Table 7.2: Calculation of N_2.

Month	No. of Days
February	14
March	31
April	30
May	31
June	30
July	31
August	15
N_2	182

The value of the bond in this case is therefore:

$$\frac{1}{(1.05)^{0.4121}}[60 + 60 \times \text{PVIFA}(5,59) + 1{,}000 \times \text{PVIF}(5,59)] = \$1{,}223.90$$

7.3.2 Accrued Interest

Let t_1 and t_2 represent two consecutive coupon payment dates. We will denote the sale date of the bond by t, such that $t_1 < t < t_2$. On day t the seller will be giving away the right to the entire next coupon, which is due on date t_2, although he or she would have held the bond for a part of the current coupon period. This portion of the next coupon that belongs to the seller is known as the accrued interest. It may be computed as follows:

$$\text{AI} = \frac{C}{2} \times \frac{N_2 - N_1}{N_2} = \frac{C}{2} \times \left(1 - \frac{N_1}{N_2}\right) \tag{7.3}$$

The symbols N_1 and N_2 are as defined earlier. The day-count convention that is adopted for calculating the accrued interest for a bond, that is, for computing N_1 and N_2, is usually the same as the convention that is used to value the bond. Thus for T-bonds and notes, the Actual-Actual method is adopted.

In the case of the U.S. Treasury bond which was sold on 1 June 20XX, the accrued interest is:

$$\frac{120}{2} \times \frac{107}{182} = \$35.2747$$

A logical question that a reader may have, is why is there a need to consider accrued interest. Is it the case that the bond valuation equation fails to take the accrued interest into account? The bond valuation equation values the bond as the present value of all cash flows arising from it, from the point of sale onwards. This is the theoretically correct procedure for valuing any financial security. The reason why we need to take the accrued interest into account is that in practice, the quoted bond prices are reported net of accrued interest. These prices, which do not include the accrued interest, are called *Clean* or *Add-Interest* prices. Since the convention is to quote prices net of the accrued interest, the buyer needs to calculate and factor in the accrued interest in order to determine the total amount payable by him. The total price that is payable is called the *Dirty Price*, since it is contaminated with accrued interest.

We will illustrate the rationale behind this market convention with the help of an example. Take the case of the 12% Treasury bond maturing on 15 February 20(XX+30). On 1 June 20XX, the price at a YTM of 10% is $1,223.90.

Let's assume that four days hence, the YTM continues to be 10% per annum. The dirty price of the bond will be:

$$\frac{1}{(1.05)^k}[60+60 \times \text{PVIFA}(5,59) + 1{,}000 \times \text{PVIF}(5,59)]$$

$$= \frac{1}{(1.05)^{\frac{71}{182}}}[60 + 60 \times \text{PVIFA}(5,59) + 1{,}000 \times \text{PVIF}(5,59)]$$

$$= \frac{1}{(1.05)^{0.3901}}[60 + 60 \times \text{PVIFA}(5,59) + 1{,}000 \times \text{PVIF}(5,59)]$$

$$= 1{,}225.2146$$

The difference in the dirty prices is:

$$1{,}225.2146 - 1{,}223.9000 = \$1.3146$$

The accrued interest as computed on the second date is:

$$60 \times \frac{111}{182} = 36.5934$$

The change in the accrued interest during this period is therefore:

$$36.5934 - 35.2747 = 1.3187$$

which is virtually identical to the change in the dirty price. Thus, the difference in the dirty prices is almost entirely due to the increase in the accrued interest.

From the perspective of a bond analyst who is tracking the debt market, the issue of concern is the change in the required market yield. Consequently, he ought to be able to focus on yield induced price changes, without being distracted by other factors. If the price were to be quoted including the accrued interest, the effects of yield induced changes cannot be easily discerned. Hence, the practice in debt markets is to report prices net of accrued interest. If so, any observed price changes in the very short run, will be entirely yield induced.

7.3.3 Corporate Bonds

The day-count convention for corporate bonds in the U.S. is referred to as the 30/360 NASD method. As per this convention, every month is considered to have 30 days, as a consequence of which the interval between two successive coupon dates is always taken to be 180 days. N_1 for corporate bonds is computed as shown below.[7]

Define the starting date as $d_1 = (yyyy_1, mm_1, dd_1)$, and the ending date as $d_2 = (yyyy_2, mm_2, dd_2)$. N_1 may be calculated as:

$$360(yyyy_2 - yyyy_1) + 30(mm_2 - mm_1) + (dd_2 - dd_1)$$

There are three additional rules.
1. If $dd_1 = 31$, then set it equal to 30.
2. If dd_1 is the last day of February, that is 28th or 29th, then set it equal to 30.
3. If dd_1 is 30, or has been set equal to 30, then if $dd_2 = 31$, set $dd_2 = 30$.

Example 7.3 demonstrates the valuation of a corporate bond.

Example 7.3: Consider a bond that was issued by IBM on 15 February 20XX, with 30 years to maturity. The coupon dates are obviously 15 February and 15 August. The face value is \$1,000; the coupon is 12% per annum paid on a semi-annual basis; and the YTM is 10% per annum. We will once again assume that the bond is being valued on 1 June 20XX.

$$N_1 = 360(20XX - 20XX) + 30(08 - 06) + (15 - 1) = 60 + 14 = 74$$
$$k = \frac{N_1}{N_2} = \frac{74}{180} = 0.4111$$

The value of the bond is:

$$\frac{1}{(1.05)^{0.4111}}[60 + 60PVIFA(5,59) + 1{,}000PVIF(5,59)] = \$1{,}223.9593$$

The accrued interest is:

$$\frac{106}{180} \times \frac{120}{2} = \$35.3333$$

---

7 N_2 is obviously always equal to 180.

7.4 Duration

Bond market watchers have long been aware of the fact that long term bonds are more vulnerable in terms of price changes to changes in yield, than shorter term bonds. Consider the case of two bonds with a face value of $1,000 each. Let's assume that both pay a coupon of 10% per annum on a semi-annual basis, and that the YTM is 10% per annum in both cases. Bond A has a time to maturity of 10 years, while bond B has a time to maturity of 20 years. Both the bonds will obviously sell at par since the coupon rate is equal to the yield.

Let's now consider an increase of 200 b.p. in the yield, that is, assume that the YTM increases to 12% per annum. The price of bond A will decline to 885.3008, whereas that of bond B will decline to 849.5370. Thus the price of bond A will decline by 11.47%, whereas that of bond B will decline by 15.05%. Therefore, it does indeed seem to be the case that long-term bonds are impacted more by interest rate changes. What could be the rationale for this fact? We know that the present value of a cash flow is given by:

$$\frac{CF}{(1+r)^t}$$

The larger the value of t, the greater will be the impact of a change in the discount rate, for a given cash flow. A 20 year bond has a considerable amount of its cash flows coming in at later points in time as compared to a 10 year bond. Thus, it is the case that its price, which is the sum of the present values of the cash flows arising from it, is more vulnerable to changes in the interest rate.

After coming up with this explanation, it was observed that there was a related issue which too merited an explanation. Take the case of a 10 year zero coupon bond with a face value of $1,000. When the YTM is 10%, its price is:

$$\frac{1{,}000}{(1.05)^{20}} = 376.8895$$

However, when the YTM is 12%, its price is:

$$\frac{1{,}000}{(1.06)^{20}} = 311.8047$$

The corresponding decline in price is 17.2689%.

While it is understandable that a long term bond ought to be more vulnerable to interest rate changes, this fact does not explain why a 10 year zero coupon bond should be more price sensitive than a 10 year bond that pays a coupon of 10%, for after all, both have 10 years to maturity. Further reflection lead to the following explanation. A coupon paying bond is a series of cash flows arising at six monthly intervals. In other words it is a portfolio of zero coupon bonds. When we state that a bond has a maturity of N half-years, where N is the number of coupons, we are only taking cognizance of the last of the cash flows. If the bond itself is a portfolio of zero coupon components, then it is obvious that its effective time to maturity ought to be an average of the times to maturity of the component zero coupon bonds. However, a 10 year zero coupon bond will give rise to a single cash flow at maturity. In this case therefore, its stated time to maturity will be the same as its effective time to maturity. From this perspective, it is not surprising that a ten year zero coupon bond is more price sensitive, for it does have a greater effective time to maturity.

Macaulay came up with the concept of 'Duration' as a measure of the effective term to maturity of a plain vanilla bond. The duration of a bond is computed by weighting the term to maturity of each component cash flow by the fraction of the total present value of the bond that is contributed by that particular cash flow. Consider Example 7.4, where the computation is shown in Table 7.3.

Example 7.4: Consider a 5 year 10% coupon paying bond with a face value of \$1,000. If the YTM is 12% per annum, what should be the duration?

Table 7.3: Computing the Duration.

Time = t	Cash Flow = CF_t	Present Value of Cash Flow $= \frac{CF_t}{\left(1+\frac{y}{2}\right)^t}$	Weight of Cash Flow $w_t = \frac{CF_t}{P_d\left(1+\frac{y}{2}\right)^t}$	Weighted Time $w_t \times t$
1	50	47.1698	.05092	.05092
2	50	44.4998	.04804	.09608
3	50	41.9810	.04532	.13596
4	50	39.6047	.04275	.17101
5	50	37.3629	.04033	.20166
6	50	35.2480	.03805	.22829
7	50	33.2529	.03590	.25126
8	50	31.3706	.03386	.27090
9	50	29.5949	.03195	.28752
10	1,050	586.3145	.63290	6.3290
	Total	926.3991	1.00000	8.0225

The weighted average time to maturity of the component cash flows is 8.0225 semi-annual periods or 4.0113 years. For a five year zero coupon bond its weighted average time to maturity is the same as its stated time to maturity of 5 years, because it gives rise to a single cash flow. Thus, it is not really surprising, that the five year zero coupon bond is more price sensitive than the five year coupon paying bond.

7.4.1 Duration and Price Sensitivity

There is a relationship between the duration of a bond and the rate of change of the percentage change in its price with respect to a yield change. This may be expressed as:

$$\frac{\frac{dp}{P}}{dy} = -\frac{D}{\left(1+\frac{y}{2}\right)} \tag{7.4}$$

where D is the duration of the bond expressed in annual terms.

$$\frac{D}{\left(1+\frac{y}{2}\right)}$$

is called the modified duration of the bond, D_m. Thus, the rate of change of the percentage change in price with respect to the yield is equal to the modified duration of a bond, and not to its time to maturity. Therefore, it is obvious that it is the duration of a bond, and not its stated time to maturity, which accurately captures the relationship between a change in the yield and the corresponding change in its price. Thus, the duration of the bond, and not the time to maturity, is a logical measure of interest rate sensitivity.

The correct way to look at duration is as a measure of the interest rate sensitivity of the debt instrument. It cannot always be perceived as a measure of the effective average life of the instrument. As Fabozzi (1993) points out, there are certain instruments like Collateralized Mortgage Obligations(CMOs), where the instrument can have a greater duration than the underlying loan. In fact, some CMOs can have a negative duration!

7.4.2 Price Quotes

T-Bond and T-Note prices are quoted as a percentage of par plus 32^{nds}. The quotes are for a par value of $100.

Bond prices are always quoted per $100 of face value. The rationale is the following. Consider two bonds, one with a face value of $1,000 and the other with a face value of $2,000. If the prices of the two bonds are equal and are quoted as say $1,400, the implications would be very different for the two bonds. A quote of $1,400 would imply that the $1,000 face value bond is trading at a significant premium, whereas the implication would be that the $2,000 face value bond is trading at a considerable discount. However, if prices were to be quoted as per $100 of face value, a price exceeding $100.00 would signify a premium bond, whereas a price of less than $100.00 would connote a discount bond.

An actual price quote can best be illustrated with the help of Example 7.5.

Example 7.5: T-Bonds maturing on 15 August, 2021 are currently being quoted at 98 – 28. What is the corresponding price for bonds with a face value of $100,000?

98 – 28 means that the price of a bond with a face value of $100 is

$$98 + \frac{28}{32} = \$98.875$$

Thus the price of bonds with a face value of $100,000 is 98.875 × 1,000 = $98,875.

The quoted prices are always clean prices. In order to calculate the actual price that is payable, the accrued interest has to be calculated and added.

7.5 30-year T-bond Futures Contracts

The underlying asset is a T-bond with a face value of $100,000. Multiple grades are allowable for delivery. The deliverable grades must, have a maturity of at least 15 years from the first day of the delivery month, and less than 25 years as of that day. The actual futures price is subject to a conversion factor. Prices are quoted in terms of points and one half of $\frac{1}{32}$ of a point. The last trading day is the seventh business day preceding the last business day of the delivery month. Contracts are subject to delivery settlement.

7.6 Conversion Factors

As one can see from the contract specifications, a wide variety of notes and bonds with different coupons and maturity dates will be eligible for delivery under any particular futures contract. The choice as to which bond to deliver, will be made by the short and obviously the price received by him will depend on the bond that he chooses to deliver. If the short were to deliver a more valuable bond he should receive more than what he would, were he to deliver a less valuable bond. Thus, in order to facilitate comparisons between bonds, the exchange specifies a conversion factor for each bond that is eligible for delivery. This is a multiplicative price adjustment system, to facilitate comparisons between different bonds that are eligible for delivery.

The conversion factor for a bond is the value of the bond per $1 of face value, as calculated on the first day of the delivery month, using an annual YTM of 6% with semi-annual compounding. For the purpose of calculation, the life of the bond is rounded down to the nearest three months. If after rounding, the bond were to have a life that is an integer multiple of semi-annual periods, then the first coupon will be assumed to be paid after six months. However, after rounding, if the life of the bond were not to be equal to an integer multiple of half-yearly periods, then the first coupon will be assumed to be paid after three months and the accrued interest will be subtracted. We have given detailed examples, Examples 7.6 and 7.7, to illustrate these principles.

The Invoice Price, which is the price received by the short, is calculated as follows:

$$\text{Invoice Price} = \text{Invoice Principal Amount} + \text{Accrued Interest}$$

$$= CF_i \times F \times 100{,}000 + AI_i \qquad (7.5)$$

where CF_i is the conversion factor of Bond **i**, F is the quoted futures price per dollar of face value[8] and AI_i is the accrued interest.

Example 7.6: Let's assume that we are short in a September futures contract and that today is September 1, 20XX. Consider an 8% T-Bond that matures on May 15, 20(XX+20). This bond is obviously eligible for delivery under the futures contract.

On September 1, this bond has 19 years and $8\frac{1}{2}$ months to maturity. When we round off down to the nearest three months, we get a figure of 19 years and 6 months.

The first coupon is assumed to be paid after six months. The conversion factor may therefore be calculated as follows.

$$\begin{aligned} CF &= \frac{\frac{8}{2}\text{PVIFA}(3,39) + 100\text{PVIF}(3,39)}{100} \\ &= \frac{91.2329 + 31.5754}{100} \\ &= 1.2281 \end{aligned}$$

Example 7.7: Instead of the May 20(XX+20) bond, consider another bond that is maturing on February 15, 20(XX+20), with a coupon of 8%. This bond too is suitable for delivery. On September 1, 20XX, this bond has 19 years and $5\frac{1}{2}$ months to maturity. The life of the bond when we round off down to the nearest three months is 19 years and 3 months.

In this case, we assume that the first coupon is paid after three months. The CF, can be calculated in three steps as shown below.

1. First find the price of the bond three months from today, using a yield of 6% per annum.

$$\begin{aligned} P &= \frac{8}{2} + \frac{8}{2}\text{PVIFA}(3,38) + 100\text{PVIF}(3,38) \\ &= 4.00 + 89.9698 + 32.5226 \\ &= \$126.4925 \end{aligned}$$

---

8 T-Bond futures prices are quoted in the same way as the cash market prices that is, they are clean prices.

2. Discount the price gotten above for another three months.

$$\frac{126.4925}{(1.03)^{\frac{1}{2}}} = \$124.6367$$

3. Subtract the accrued interest for 3 months, from the price obtained in the second step.

$$AI = \frac{8}{2} \times \frac{1}{2} = 2$$

$$CF = \frac{124.6367 - 2}{100} = 1.2264$$

Why do we adopt two different procedures for calculating the CF? The CF is used to multiply the quoted futures price, which is a clean price. Hence the CF should not include any accrued interest. In the first example, the bond has a life that is an integer multiple of semi-annual periods after rounding. Consequently, we need not be concerned with accrued interest. However, in the second example, accrued interest for a quarter is present in the value we get in the second step. Hence, in this case, we need to subtract this interest in order to arrive at the conversion factor.

7.7 Calculating the Invoice Price for a T-bond

Assume that on September 15, 20XX the decision to deliver the 8% bond maturing on May 15, 20(XX+20), under the September futures contract, is declared by the short. The actual delivery will take place two business days later, that is, on September 17.

The invoice price may be computed as follows. The first step is to calculate the accrued interest. The last coupon would have been paid on May 15, 20XX and the next will be due on November 15, 20XX. Between the two coupon dates there are 184 days. Between the last coupon date and the delivery date, there are 125 days. The accrued interest for a T-Bond with a face value of $100,000 is:

$$AI = \frac{0.08}{2} \times \frac{125}{184} \times 100{,}000 = \$2717.3913$$

The futures settlement price[9] on September 15 is assumed to be 94–12. This corresponds to a decimal futures price per dollar of face value of

$$\frac{94 + \frac{12}{32}}{100} = 0.94375$$

9 Note that the settlement price is based on the day the intention to deliver is declared, whereas accrued interest is computed as of the Delivery Day. The reason for this is the following. Once the intention to deliver is declared, marking to market will cease and hence the futures price payable by the long will be the settlement price as of that day. However, since the long will receive the bond only on the Delivery Day, accrued interest must be computed until that day.

The conversion factor has already been calculated to be 1.2281.

$$\text{Invoice Price} = 0.94375 \times 1.2281 \times 100000 + 2{,}717.3913 = \$118{,}619.32$$

7.8 The Cheapest To Deliver Bond

The conversion factor is an example of a multiplicative adjustment, when more than one grade of the underlying asset is specified for delivery. As we have seen earlier, under such circumstances the short will choose to deliver that bond which is the cheapest to deliver. To illustrate this as well as other concepts which follow, let's depict a hypothetical situation as shown in Figure 7.2.

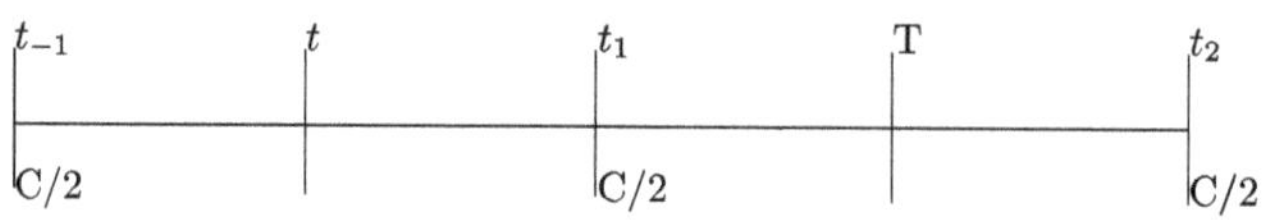

Figure 7.2: Sequence of Coupons for a Bond Being Delivered Under a T-bond Futures Contract.

t represents today. The last coupon of \$C/2 was paid at t_{-1} and the next coupon is due at time t_1. There is a T-Bond futures contract expiring at time T, which will be followed by a coupon at time t_2.

When the short delivers a particular bond, bond i, at time T, he will receive[10]
$(F_T \times CF_i + AI_{i,t_1,T}) \times 100{,}000$
The cost of acquisition of the bond in the spot market at time T is
$(P_{i,T} + AI_{i,t_1,T}) \times 100{,}000$
Thus, the profit for the short is

$$\begin{aligned}&(F_T \times CF_i + AI_{i,t_1,T}) \times 100{,}000 - (P_{i,T} + AI_{i,t_1,T}) \times 100{,}000 \\ &= (F_T \times CF_i - P_{i,T}) \times 100{,}000 \end{aligned} \tag{7.6}$$

If $F_T \times CF_i - P_{i,T}$ is to be maximized or equivalently, $CF_i\left(F_T - \frac{P_{i,T}}{CF_i}\right)$ is to be maximized, we require that $\frac{P_{i,T}}{CF_i}$ be minimized.

10 From now on, we will denote the clean price per dollar of face value by P, and the futures price per dollar of face value by F. AI will be used to denote the accrued interest per dollar of face value.

$\frac{P_{i,T}}{CF_i}$ is the *Delivery Adjusted Spot Price* in this case. Thus, as we have seen earlier, the cheapest to deliver bond is the one with the lowest delivery adjusted spot price. The delivery date spot-futures convergence will ensure that $F_T \times CF_i - P_{i,T} = 0$ that is, the quoted futures price at expiration will equal the delivery adjusted spot price of the cheapest to deliver bond.

In practice, T-Bond futures contracts give the short a number of delivery options. Consequently, the quoted futures price at expiration is usually less than the delivery adjusted spot price of the cheapest to deliver bond.

7.9 Hedging

We will first illustrate our arguments using the cheapest to deliver bond and will then discuss the case where other bond portfolios have to be hedged.

7.9.1 Hedging the Cheapest to Deliver Bond

A Naive Approach

A naive approach would take the view that for hedging Q bonds, we use Q futures contracts or in other words, that we use a hedge ratio of one. This strategy is not satisfactory, as Example 7.8 will illustrate.

Example 7.8: In our case, let's assume that the bond, which carries a coupon of 8% and matures on May 15, is the cheapest to deliver bond. Assume the spot price on August 7, is 116-17 and the corresponding futures price is 95-07.

On September 7, the settlement price is 85-18, if we assume that our bond continues to be the cheapest to deliver bond. Its spot price is 105-02, which corresponds to a YTM of 7.5% per annum.

The bond can be sold in the spot market to yield

$$\frac{105 + \frac{2}{32}}{100} \times 100{,}000 + \frac{4}{100} \times \frac{116}{184} \times 100{,}000$$
$$= \$107{,}584.23$$

The profit from the short futures position is

$$\frac{(95 + \frac{07}{32}) - (85 + \frac{18}{32})}{100} \times 100{,}000$$
$$= \$9{,}656.25$$

The total payoff is \$117,240.48.

A perfect hedge would have locked in the original futures price of 95-07 to yield

$$\frac{95 + \frac{07}{32}}{100} \times 1.2281 \times 100{,}000 + \frac{4}{100} \times \frac{116}{184} \times 100{,}000$$
$$= \$119{,}459.88$$

In this case we are clearly underhedged.

The Conversion Factor Approach

As per the conversion factor approach, the hedge ratio is given by

$$h^* = \frac{\Delta P}{\Delta F} = CF_i \tag{7.7}$$

We will examine the efficiency of this hedge using the same data as for the example on the naive hedging strategy. Consider Example 7.9.

Example 7.9: The proceeds from the spot market when the cheapest to deliver bond is sold is \$107,584.23.

Profit from the futures market = 1.2281 × 9,656.25 = \$11,858.84

The total proceeds = \$119,443.07, which is very close to the value of \$119,459.88, that is implied by the original futures price.

7.9.2 Hedging a Portfolio Other Than the CTD Bond

The naive hedging strategy has been discredited even for hedging the price of the CTD bond.[11] Hence we will not pursue it further.

Let's now analyze as to how to extend the conversion factor approach to hedge a bond other than the CTD bond.

Our hedge ratio h, should be such that $\Delta P = h\Delta F$. We know that

$$\Delta F \cong \frac{\Delta P_{CTD}}{CF_{CTD}}$$

Therefore

$$\Delta P = h\frac{\Delta P_{CTD}}{CF_{CTD}} \Rightarrow h = CF_{CTD}\frac{\Delta P}{\Delta P_{CTD}}. \tag{7.8}$$

11 CTD stands for **Cheapest to Deliver**.

Duration Based Hedging

For any bond, we know that

$$\frac{dP}{P} = \frac{-D}{\left(1+\frac{y}{2}\right)} \times dy$$

where D is the duration of the bond in annual terms.[12] Therefore

$$\frac{\Delta P}{P} \cong \frac{-D}{\left(1+\frac{y}{2}\right)} \times \Delta y$$

If we denote the bond being hedged as bond **h**, then the optimal hedge ratio is

$$\begin{aligned} & CF_{CTD}\frac{\Delta P_h}{\Delta P_{CTD}} \\ & = CF_{CTD} \times \frac{\frac{-D_h}{\left(1+\frac{y_h}{2}\right)} \times P_h \times \Delta y_h}{\frac{-D_{CTD}}{\left(1+\frac{y_{CTD}}{2}\right)} \times P_{CTD} \times \Delta y_{CTD}} \\ & = CF_{CTD} \times \frac{D_h \times P_h \times \left(1+\frac{y_{CTD}}{2}\right) \times \Delta y_h}{D_{CTD} \times P_{CTD} \times \left(1+\frac{y_h}{2}\right) \times \Delta y_{CTD}} \end{aligned} \tag{7.9}$$

If we assume that yield curve movements are parallel, that is $\Delta y_{CTD} = \Delta y_h$, then the hedge ratio will be[13]

$$CF_{CTD} \times \frac{D_h \times P_h \times \left(1+\frac{y_{CTD}}{2}\right)}{D_{CTD} \times P_{CTD} \times \left(1+\frac{y_h}{2}\right)}$$

which simplifies further to

$$CF_{CTD} \times \frac{D_h \times P_h}{D_{CTD} \times P_{CTD}}$$

12 We are assuming that the bond pays semi-annual coupons.

13 The per unit face value of the bond being hedged should be taken to be equal to the face value of the bond underlying the futures contract.

if we assume that percentage yield curve movements are parallel.[14] The number of futures contracts required is

$$\frac{\text{Face Value of Spot Exposure}}{\text{Face Value of The Bond Underlying The Futures Contract}} \times \text{h}$$

We will now illustrate this hedging technique with the help of Example 7.10.

Example 7.10: Assume that today is 7 August, 20XX. September futures contracts expire on 30 September. The cheapest to deliver bond, as we have seen earlier, is a 8% coupon bond maturing on 15 May, 20(XX+20). Its quoted price is 116-17, which corresponds to a YTM of 6.50% per annum and the conversion factor is 1.2281. The quoted futures price, as calculated before, is 95-07.

Consider a portfolio manager who is holding 25,000 ABC bonds maturing on 7 August, 20(XX+20). The face value is $100, the coupon rate is 9% per annum and the YTM is 8% per annum. The manager plans to sell the bonds on 30 September and wants to protect himself against an increase in the yield, using T-bond futures contracts.

The duration of the CTD bond on 7 August is 10.7671 years. The dirty price is 118.3721. The price of the ABC bonds is $109.8964 and the corresponding duration is 10.0623 years.

The hedge ratio is therefore

$$1.2281 \times \frac{(10.0623 \times 109.8964 \times 1.0325)}{(10.7671 \times 118.3721 \times 1.04)} = 1.0578$$

Let's assume that the YTM of the ABC bonds on 30 September is 9% per annum, and that the YTM of the CTD bond is 7.50%. The price of the ABC bond will therefore be 101.3045 and the futures price will be 85.5625. If the yield had remained at 8%, the dirty price of ABC would have been $111.1729.

The loss from the spot market is

$$25{,}000 \times (101.3045 - 111.1729) = \$(246{,}710)$$

The profit from the futures market is

$$25{,}000 \times 1.0578 \times (95.2188 - 85.5625) = \$255{,}360.85$$

The net profit is = 255,360.85 − 246,710 = $8,650.85

The tracking error = $\frac{8{,}650.85}{246{,}710} \equiv 3.51\%$

One issue that arises in the context of the duration based hedging approach, is whether we should use input values as calculated at the inception of the hedge or as determined at the point of termination. Most authors argue that we should use the expected values of the variables as of the termination date of the hedge. However, in practice, forecasting these variables is not always easy and consequently, the current values are often used as inputs. The two approaches will not yield substantially different results unless the instrument being hedged and the CTD bond are significantly different.[15]

---

14 This implies that $\frac{\Delta y_{CTD}}{(1+y_{CTD})} = \frac{\Delta y_h}{(1+y_h)}$.

15 See Daigler (1994).

7.9.3 Changing the Duration of a Portfolio of Bonds

Consider a portfolio of bonds which currently has a duration of D_h. Let's assume that we wish to change its duration to D_T, which denotes the target duration, by going long in futures contracts. The question is, what is the appropriate number of futures contracts to use? Let's denote the required hedge ratio by **h**, and the current value per unit of the bond being hedged by P_h.

If our target duration for the overall portfolio is D_T, then we should choose h such that

$$h = \frac{\dfrac{(D_T - D_h)}{\left(1 + \dfrac{y_h}{2}\right)} \times P_h}{\dfrac{D_{CTD}}{\left(1 + \dfrac{y_{CTD}}{2}\right)} \times P_{CTD}} \times CF_{CTD}$$

$$\Rightarrow h = \frac{(D_T - D_h) \times P_h \times \left(1 + \dfrac{y_{CTD}}{2}\right)}{D_{CTD} \times P_{CTD} \times \left(1 + \dfrac{y_h}{2}\right)} \times CF_{CTD} \tag{7.10}$$

The required number of futures contracts is

$$\frac{\text{Face Value of Spot Exposure}}{\text{Face Value of The Bond Underlying The Futures Contract}} \times \text{h}$$

The computation is illustrated in Example 7.11.

Example 7.11: Assume that we are on 7 August 20XX and that we wish to increase the duration of the ABC bonds from 10.0623 to 12.75. If we are holding ABC bonds with a face value of $100MM we need to go long in:

$$1.2281 \times \frac{(12.75 - 10.0623) \times 109.8964 \times 1.0325}{10.7671 \times 118.3721 \times 1.04} \times \frac{100{,}000{,}000}{100{,}000} = 0.2826 \times 1{,}000$$
$$\simeq 283 \text{ contracts.}$$

Suggestions for Further Reading

Blake, D. *Financial Market Analysis*. John Wiley, 2000.
Bodie, Z., Kane A. and Marcus A.J *Investments*. Irwin McGraw-Hill, 1996.
Chance, D.M. *An Introduction to Options & Futures*. The Dryden Press, 1991.
Edwards, F.R. and C.W. Ma *Futures & Options*. McGraw-Hill, 1992.
Kolb, R.W. *Futures, Options, & Swaps*. Blackwell, 2000.
Siegel, D.R. and D.F. Siegel *Futures Markets*. The Dryden Press, 1990.
Understanding U.S. Treasury Futures. CME Group.
U.S. Treasury Futures Delivery Process. CME Group.

References

Daigler, R.T. *Financial Futures and Options Markets: Concepts and Strategies*. Harper Collins, 1994.
Fabozzi, F.J. *Bond Markets: Analysis and Strategies*. Prentice-Hall International, 1993.
Garbade, K.D. *Fixed Income Analytics*. The MIT Press, 1996.

Chapter 8
Fundamentals of Options

8.1 Introduction

Thus far, we have covered two types of derivative securities, namely futures and forward contracts in detail. In a futures contract no money changes hands when the contract is negotiated and nor does the title to the goods. In such a contract, the buyer agrees to pay cash at a future date to the seller, who in turn agrees to transfer the ownership of the asset on that day. The buyer of a futures contract is said to have taken a *Long Position* and is known as the *Long*, while the seller is said to have taken a *Short Position* and is known as the *Short*. The important point to note is that once a futures contract is negotiated, both the long and the short have an obligation at a future date. Since both parties have an obligation, there is always a possibility that the party with a loss at the expiration of the contract may default. Compliance is ensured by requiring both the parties to deposit good faith money or collateral called *Margins* and by adjusting the profits and losses on a daily basis by a procedure known as *Marking to Market*. Forward contracts are similar to futures contracts in the sense that they too impose an obligation on the short to deliver at the time of expiration of the contract, and on the long to take delivery at that time. However, unlike futures contracts which trade on organized exchanges, and consequently have to be designed as per the terms and conditions specified by the exchange, forward contracts are Over-the-Counter contracts which are designed with mutually acceptable terms and conditions by the two parties through bilateral negotiations.

Options contracts which are the focus of this book from now on, are derivative contracts, but by design are different from futures contracts. In an options contract the buyer of the contract, also called the *Holder* or the *Long*, has a right, while the seller, also known as the *Writer* or the *Short*, has an obligation. Thus, in the case of an options contract the long has the freedom to decide whether or not he wishes to go through with the transaction, whereas the short, has no choice but to carry out his part of the agreement if and when the holder chooses to exercise his right. Therefore, unlike in the case of futures contracts, both the parties need not deposit collateral. For, if a person has a right, there is no fear of non-compliance since he will exercise his right if it is in his interest and he need not otherwise. Consequently, in the case of options contracts, only the shorts have to deposit margins.

The buyer of an option may either have the right to buy the underlying asset, or the right to sell it, depending on the terms of the agreement. Therefore, there are two types of options contracts, *Calls* and *Puts*. A call option gives the long the right to acquire the underlying asset, whereas a put option gives the long the right to sell the underlying asset. An options contract may give the long the right to transact only at a future point in time, or else it may give him the flexibility of exercising his right at any point in time,

https://doi.org/10.1515/9783110746662-008

up to and including the expiration date. Consequently, both calls and puts can be of two types, *European* and *American*. A European option gives the holder the freedom to exercise his right only at the time of expiration of the contract, while an American option may be exercised by the holder at any point in time on or before expiration. It must be noted that the terms European and American have nothing to do with geographical locations and that in practice most exchange traded contracts are American. Given the same features in all other respects, an American option will be more valuable than the corresponding European option. This is because, the holder of an American option has the flexibility to exercise early, whereas the holder of a European option does not have the freedom to exercise prior to expiration.

8.2 Options and Stocks: Similarities and Differences

Exchange traded options contracts have certain features in common with equity shares, although there are certain critical differences between the two. The trading mechanism for exchange traded options is similar to that for equity shares of listed companies. Price discovery takes place through a continuous bilateral auction procedure. However, unlike equity shares which do not have an expiry date, options have a finite life span. Besides, the supply of equity shares is limited to the quantity issued by the firm. On the other hand, the number of options contracts outstanding at any point in time, is dependent entirely on the number of buyers and sellers who have evinced a desire to buy and write options. In certain markets, equity shares are still represented by physical certificates, although with the introduction of dematerialized trading in most markets, scripless trading is fast becoming the norm. Options however are not backed by certificates of ownership. Evidence of an option position is indicated by a printed statement issued by the brokerage firm of the buyer or the writer. Finally, ownership of a company's stock confers certain privileges on the shareholders, such as the right to participate and vote in annual general meetings, and entitles them to any cash dividends declared by the company. On the other hand, options owners stand to benefit solely from the upward or downward movement of the stock price, depending on whether they own call or put options.

8.3 Common Terms Associated With Options

8.3.1 Exercise Price

This is the price which the holder of a call option has to pay to the writer, per unit of the underlying asset, if he were to decide to exercise his option. In the case of puts, it is the price which the holder of a put option will receive per unit of the underlying asset, were he to exercise. The Exercise Price is also known as the *Strike Price*.

The exercise price enters the picture only if the holder chooses to exercise the option. Since the holder has a right and not an obligation, he may or may not wish to transact, which means that the exercise price may or may not be paid/received.

8.3.2 Expiration Date

This is the point in time after which the contract becomes void. It is the only point in time at which a European option can be exercised and the last point in time at which an American option can be exercised. The Expiration Date is also known as the *Exercise Date*, or *Strike Date* or *Maturity Date*.

8.3.3 Option Premium

This is the price that the holder has to pay to the writer at the outset, in order to acquire the right to exercise. The option premium is a *'sunk cost'*. If the holder were not to exercise prior to expiration, the premium will not be refunded.

Why does the buyer of an option have to pay a premium at the outset? Options contracts entail the payment of a premium, because the buyer is acquiring a right from the writer, who is taking on an obligation to perform if the buyer were to exercise the right. Rights, it must be understood, are never free and one has to always pay a price to acquire them.

Futures and forward contracts in contrast, do not entail the payment of a premium by the long. Such contracts impose an equivalent obligation on both the long as well as the short. The futures price, which is the price at which the long will acquire the asset at the time of expiration, is set in such a way that from the standpoints of both the long as well as the short, the value of the contract at inception is zero. In other words, the two equivalent and opposite obligations ensure that neither party has to pay the other at the outset.

Another way to perceive the difference between futures and options, from the standpoint of premiums, is that, in the case of the former, both shorts and longs face the specter of a cash outflow at a subsequent point in time. In the case of options however, holders will get either a positive or a nil cash flow subsequently, whereas the writers will get a negative or a nil cash flow.

8.4 Notation

We will use the following symbols to depict the various variables.

- $t \equiv$ today, a point in time before the expiration of the options contract.
- $T \equiv$ the point of expiration of the options contract.

- S_t ≡ the stock price at time t.
- S_T ≡ the stock price at the point of expiration of the options contract.
- I_t ≡ the index value at time t.
- I_T ≡ the index value at the point of expiration of the options contract.
- X ≡ the exercise price of the option.
- C_t ≡ a general symbol for the premium of a call option at time *t*, when we do not wish to make a distinction between European and American options.
- P_t ≡ a general symbol for the premium of a put option at time *t*, when we do not wish to make a distinction between European and American options.
- C_T ≡ a general symbol for the premium of a call option at time *T*, when we do not wish to make a distinction between European and American options.
- P_T ≡ a general symbol for the premium of a put option at time *T*, when we do not wish to make a distinction between European and American options.
- $C_{E,t}$ ≡ the premium of a European call option at time *t*.
- $P_{E,t}$ ≡ the premium of a European put option at time *t*.
- $C_{A,t}$ ≡ the premium of an American call option at time *t*.
- $P_{A,t}$ ≡ the premium of an American put option at time *t*.
- $C_{E,T}$ ≡ the premium of a European call option at time *T*.
- $P_{E,T}$ ≡ the premium of a European put option at time *T*.
- $C_{A,T}$ ≡ the premium of an American call option at time *T*.
- $P_{A,T}$ ≡ the premium of an American put option at time *T*.
- r ≡ the risk-less rate of interest per annum.

Additional variables will be defined when required. Some of these variables may be redefined as we proceed. We will make the modified meanings explicit in such cases.

8.5 Exercising Call and Put Options

Exchange traded stock options are American in nature. There are two possible exercise related scenarios. The holder may choose to exercise prior to expiration or at the time of expiration. Index options may be European or American. If they were to be European in nature, they can obviously be exercised only at expiration.

When a call option is exercised before expiration the holder will receive the specified number of shares per contract that is being exercised, in return for a payment of $X per share. On the other hand if a put were to be exercised, the holder will have to deliver the specified number of shares per contract, and will receive $X per share delivered.

We will now illustrate the cash flows involved when an option is exercised. To keep matters simple we will focus on European options, although the underlying logic is the same in the case of American options. We will use stock options for the purpose of illustration, although, in principle, an options contract can be written on any asset. Consider Examples 8.1 and 8.2.

Example 8.1: Consider a person who buys a call option on ABC expiring in December, with an exercise price of \$100. Let's assume that the option premium is \$3.25 per unit of the underlying asset, which in this case is a share of ABC. Option premia are always quoted on a per share basis. The contract size for stock options, or in other words, the number of shares that the option holder can buy or sell per contract, is kept fixed at 100 in the U.S. So as soon as the deal is struck, the buyer has to pay \$3.25 × 100 = \$325 to the writer. In return, he gets the right to buy 100 shares of ABC on the expiration date at a price of \$100 per share.

When will the holder choose to exercise his right? Quite obviously, if the stock price at the time of expiration of the option is greater than \$100, then it will make sense to exercise the option and buy the shares at \$100 each. Else, it is best to let the option expire worthless. Readers encountering options for the first time, may feel that it would make sense to exercise only if the stock price at expiration were to be greater than (100 + 3.25). This viewpoint is erroneous. Assume that the terminal stock price is \$102.00. If the option is exercised, the holder can buy 100 shares for \$100 each and immediately sell them for \$102 each. After taking into account the option premium that was paid at the outset, the total profit is[1]

$$\pi = (102 - 100) \times 100 - 325 = \$(125)$$

Thus, if the holder were to exercise, he would suffer a loss of \$125 whereas if he were to allow the contract to expire worthless, he would lose the entire initial premium of \$325. This argument is an illustration of the maxim that 'sunk costs are irrelevant' while taking investment decisions.

Example 8.2: Let's reconsider the previous example, but assume that the options under consideration are put options. The question is, when will the holder choose to exercise his right? Exercise will be a profitable proposition if the terminal stock price were to be less than \$100. Else, it would be best to let the option expire worthless. Assume that the terminal stock price is \$97.50 and that the premium paid for the option is \$1.25 per share. The profit is

$$\pi = (100.00 - 97.50) \times 100 - 125 = \$125$$

8.6 Cash Settlement versus Delivery Settlement

Index options are 'cash settled'. That is, if a call holder chooses to exercise an option with an exercise price of X, at a time when the value of the underlying index is I_t, he will be paid an amount equal to $I_t - X$ times a multiplier. Similarly if a put holder were to choose to exercise he will be paid an amount equal to $X - I_t$ times a multiplier. When an index option is exercised at expiration, a call holder will receive $I_T - X$ times a multiplier, while a put holder will receive $X - I_T$ times a multiplier. Cash settlement is the universal practice for index options, for it is a cumbersome process to ensure physical delivery of

1 We will use the symbol π to denote profits and will indicate losses by putting the numbers in parentheses, after the corresponding currency symbol.

the stocks constituting an index. On the CBOE, index options on the S&P 500 index, are European in nature.

8.6.1 Payoffs and Profits: A Symbolic Representation

The payoff for a call holder at expiration is equal to $S_T - X$, if $S_T > X$, or 0 if $S_T \le X$. The payoff can therefore be represented as $\text{Max}(0, S_T - X)$.

The profit can be represented as $\text{Max}(0, S_T - X) - C_t$ where C_t is the premium paid for the call when it was acquired.

The payoff for the call writer is $-\text{Max}(0, S_T - X) = \text{Min}(0, X - S_T)$ and the profit is $\text{Min}(0, X - S_T) + C_t$.

In the case of call options therefore, the maximum profit for the holder is unlimited because the stock price at the time of exercise has no theoretical upper limit. The maximum loss is however restricted to the initial premium that is paid. From the standpoint of the call writer, the situation is just the reverse. His maximum loss is unlimited, whereas his maximum profit is the option premium that he receives at the outset.

Similarly, the payoff for a put holder is equal to $X - S_T$, if $S_T < X$, or 0 if $S_T \ge X$. The payoff can therefore be represented as $\text{Max}(0, X - S_T)$.

The profit can be represented as $\text{Max}(0, X - S_T) - P_t$ where P_t is the premium paid for the put when it was acquired.

The payoff for the put writer is $-\text{Max}(0, X - S_T) = \text{Min}(0, S_T - X)$ and the profit is $\text{Min}(0, S_T - X) + P_t$.

For a put holder therefore, the maximum profit is equal to the exercise price less the option premium, because, since stocks have limited liability the price cannot go below zero. His maximum loss is once again the option premium. For the put writer the maximum profit is equal to the premium received, whereas the maximum loss is equal to the exercise price minus the premium. Thus, irrespective of whether it is a call or a put, an option is a *Zero Sum Game*. The holder's profit is equal to the writer's loss and vice versa.

8.7 Exchange Traded Versus OTC Options

Until the introduction of options contracts by the Chicago Board Options Exchange (CBOE) in 1973, options were traded *Over The Counter (OTC)*. An OTC option is a customized agreement between the long and the short. By customized we mean that the exercise price, the date of expiration, and the contract size are negotiated between the buyer and the seller. On the other hand, options contracts traded on organized exchanges like the CBOE are standardized agreements. By standardized, we mean that the exercise prices and expiration dates for which contracts can be negotiated are specified by the exchange. Individual buyers and sellers are free to strike deals by incorporating any of the allowable exercise prices and expiration dates into the terms of the agreement, but cannot design contracts on their own terms. The contract size or the number of units of the underlying asset per contract, is also fixed by the exchange.

What are the advantages of standardization? First, since only certain exercise prices and expiration dates are permitted, the number of types of contracts available is far less than would be the case, were different individuals free to specify these features. Consequently trading volumes tend to be high and therefore, transactions costs tend to be low. High trading volumes also imply a high degree of liquidity. Second, standardized contracts can be offset easily by taking a counterposition on the floor of the exchange. The term *Counterposition* refers to the taking of a short position by a trader who had originally gone long and vice versa. We will illustrate this with the help of Example 8.3.

Example 8.3: Amy bought an options contract on ABC from Richard a week ago. The contract terms have specified an exercise price of $100 and the contract is scheduled to expire in June. Now assume that Amy wants to get out of her position. All she has to do, is to find a person on the floor of the exchange who would like to go long in a contract on ABC expiring in June, with an exercise price of $100. This person need not be Richard, the individual with whom she initially traded. Notice that to offset a position in a call option, the trader needs to take an opposite position in a call option with the same exercise price and maturity date. The same holds true for a put option.

One reason why this kind of offsetting is feasible, is because the contract is standardized. In the case of customized agreements, there is an infinite number of exercise prices and expiration dates that can be specified, as a consequence of which the odds of finding a third party who is willing to transact as per the terms of the original contract, are considerably reduced. A customized options contract, is a private contract between two parties, with terms and features that are unique to it. Consequently, such contracts can be abrogated by the long or the short, only by seeking out the other party.

The other advantage of exchange traded options, is that credit risk is minimized. Every exchange has an associated clearinghouse which enters the picture once the trade is executed.[2] Once the deal is struck, the clearinghouse positions itself between the two parties, and becomes the effective buyer for every seller and the effective seller for every buyer. In the case of futures contracts it guarantees the performance of both the parties whereas, in the case of options contracts, it need guarantee the performance of only the writer as explained earlier. The fact that the clearinghouse becomes the effective counterparty for both the parties, after the trade is consummated, is another reason why taking an offsetting position is easy. For, the link between the original long and the

---

2 The major clearinghouse in the U.S. is the Options Clearing Corporation (OCC). The OCC is a registered clearing corporation with the Securities Exchange Commission (SEC). The company has a AAA credit rating assigned by the Standard & Poor's Corporation (S&P).

short is broken, and consequently both parties need only deal with the clearinghouse subsequently.

The clearinghouse consists of members called *Clearing Firms*, who are essentially brokerage houses. All orders must eventually be routed through a clearing member. Thus, if your broker is not a clearing member, he must route your order through another member who happens to be a member of the clearinghouse. All writers have to maintain margins or collateral with their brokers. If the broker is not a clearing member, then he has to maintain a margin account with a clearing member. All clearing members have to maintain margins with the clearinghouse.

8.8 Moneyness of the Option

8.8.1 Call Options

- If $S_t > X$ the call option is said to be *In-the-money*.

  The term arises from the fact that the option holder has the right to buy the underlying asset at a price which is lower than what he would have to pay, were he to acquire it in the spot market.
- If $S_t = X$ the call option is said to be *At-the-money*.
- If $S_t < X$ the call option is said to be *Out-of-the-money*.
- If $S_t \approx X$ the call option is said to be *Near-the-money*.

Consider Examples 8.4 and 8.5.

Example 8.4: Consider a stock that is currently trading at $100. A call option with an exercise price of $100 will be said to be at-the-money. A call with a lower exercise price. say $95, will be said to be in-the-money, whereas one with a higher exercise price, say $105, will be said to be out-of-the-money. Obviously, a call option will be exercised only if it happens to be in-the-money.

8.8.2 Put Options

- If $S_t > X$ the put option is said to be *Out-of-the-money*.
- If $S_t = X$ the put option is said to be *At-the-money*.
- If $S_t < X$ the put option is said to be *In-the-money*.

  The term arises from the fact that the option holder has the right to sell the underlying asset at a price which is greater than what he would receive, were he to sell it in the spot market.
- If $S_t \approx X$ the put option is said to be *Near-the-money*.

Example 8.5: Consider a stock that is currently trading at $100. A put option with an exercise price of $100 will be said to be at-the-money. A put with a lower exercise price, say $95, will be said to be out-of-the-money, whereas one with a higher exercise price, say $105, will be said to be in-the-money. Obviously, a put option too will be exercised only if it happens to be in-the-money.

8.9 Contract Specification

Since exchange traded options are standardized agreements, the exchange will have to specify the following features before trading can commence.

8.9.1 The Underlying Asset

The assets on which contracts can be traded have to be clearly specified. In the case of stock options, this entails specifying the list of companies on whose shares contracts can be written.

8.9.2 Contract Size

The number of units of the underlying asset that are deliverable per contract has to be clearly specified. In the U.S. stock options contracts are generally for 100 shares of stock.

8.9.3 Expiration Dates

Options are referred to by the month in which they expire. For instance, when we refer to a January call, we mean a call option expiring in January.

In the U.S. stock option contracts expire on the the third Friday of the expiration month. If the third Friday of the month is an exchange holiday, the contracts will expire on the preceding Thursday.

8.9.4 Exercise Prices

The exchange also has to specify the exercise prices at which contracts can be written. There will always be an At-the-Money (ATM) or Near-the-Money contract. There will also be a number of In-the-money (ITM) and Out-of-the-Money (OTM) contracts that are eligible for trading at any point in time, depending on the rules of the exchange on which the contracts are being traded.

8.10 Choosing Expiration Months

Stock options are designed to be on *Quarterly Cycles*. A particular company could be assigned to either a January, February or a March cycle. The January cycle comprises of the following months: January, April, July and October. A February cycle comprises of February, May, August and November. And the March cycle comprises of March, June, September and December. At any point in time, the available expiration months are the *current month*, the *following month*, and the *next two* months of the cycle to which the company is assigned. We will illustrate this with the help Example 8.6.

Example 8.6: Let's assume that today is 1 September, 20XX. Consider a company that is assigned to a February cycle. Options contracts will be available with the following expiration months: September, October, November and February. Of these, September is the current month, October is the following month, and November 20XX and February 20(XX+1) are the next two months after October 20XX from the February cycle.

When the September contracts expire, options with the following expiration months will be available: October, November, February and May.

When the October options expire, the following contracts will be available: November, December, February and May.

After the expiry of the November options, the following months will be available: December, January, February and May.

And finally, after the December contracts expire, January, February, May and August will be available.

In addition to these contracts, the CBOE offers options contracts with up to *three years* to expiration. Such options are called *Long Term Equity Anticipation Securities* or *LEAPS*. LEAPS expire in January each year, on the third Friday of the expiration month.

8.11 Specification of Allowable Exercise Prices

As mentioned earlier, at any point in time, there will always be an At-the-Money or Near-the-Money contract that is available for trading. This holds true for both calls as well as puts. In addition there will be other contracts which are in-the-money or out-of-the-money to varying degrees.

When new contracts, that is, contracts with a new expiration date, are introduced, two strike prices that are closest to the stock price at that point in time will be chosen. If the stock price moves outside the price band formed by these two exercise prices, then contracts with a fresh exercise price will be introduced for trading. While fixing the exercise prices, the CBOE usually follows the rule that the strike prices be in intervals of \$2.50 if the stock price is between \$5 and \$25, in intervals of \$5 if the stock price is between \$25 and \$200, and that they be spaced \$10 apart if the stock price exceeds \$200. These rules can best be illustrated with the help of Example 8.7.

Example 8.7: Let's assume that a company XYZ is assigned to the February cycle and that the May contracts are just being introduced. We will assume that the prevailing stock price is $87.

At the outset, both call and put option contracts with exercise prices of $85 and $90 will be permitted for trading.[3] As long as the stock price remains between $85 and $90, only contracts with these two exercise prices will be allowed for trading. If the stock price were to go above $90, new call and put contracts with an exercise price of $95 will be introduced. Similarly, if the stock price were to fall below $85, new contracts with an exercise price of $80 will be permitted for trading.

At any given point in time, contracts with many different exercise prices will be trading for each of the expiration months. The number of different exercise prices that are observable at a given point in time, would depend on the movement in the price of the underlying stock from the inception of trading in contracts for that particular expiration month. Of course, not all contracts will be equally active.

All contracts on a given stock which are of the same type, that is calls or puts, are said to constitute an *Option Class*. Thus all the calls that are available on XYZ stock at a given point in time, irrespective of the exercise price or the expiration date, would be said to constitute an Option Class. Similarly, so will all the puts.

All the contracts in a given class, that is, the Call Class or the Put Class, which have the same exercise price and the same expiration date, are said to constitute an *Option Series*. Thus all call option contracts on XYZ stock with X = $75 and a time to expiration of three months would be said to belong to the same series.

8.12 Assignment of Contracts

When an option holder decides to exercise his option, it is not necessary that the writer with whom he traded initially will still be in the market, for he could have offset his position. In practice when a holder decides to exercise an option, he will have to inform his clearing firm, which will then place an exercise order with the clearinghouse. The clearinghouse will then randomly select a clearing firm through which an investor has written an option with the same features. The clearing firm that is selected, has to then choose a particular writer to deliver in the case of calls, or to accept delivery in the case of puts. The writer who is chosen is said to be *assigned*.

In order to ensure that the option is exercised on a particular day, the holder must inform his broker before the cutoff time specified by the concerned brokerage firm for accepting exercise instructions. The cutoff times for receiving such instructions can vary from broker to broker, and in the case of a particular brokerage firm, could depend on the class of options that are sought to be exercised.

3 The prevailing stock price of $87 is between $25 and $200, and so the exercise prices chosen will be $5 apart.

8.13 Adjusting for Stock Splits and Stock Dividends

Exchange traded options have to be adjusted for splits and stock dividends. Let's suppose that you own a share which is currently priced at $\$S_t$. Consider an n for m split. The new theoretical price will be $\frac{mS_t}{n}$. For instance, if there is a 5:2 split, the new price will be $\frac{2S_t}{5}$.

In the event of a split, the terms of the option contract will be adjusted as follows. For an n:m split, the exercise price of the contract will be changed from X to $\frac{mX}{n}$. And the number of shares per contract will be changed to $\frac{n}{m}\times$ number of shares per original contract. Consider Example 8.8.

Example 8.8: Consider a person who owns a call which entitles him to buy 100 shares at \$100 per share. Now, let's say the company announces a 5:2 split. The terms of the contract will be adjusted as follows. Each contract will now allow him to buy $\frac{5}{2} \times 100 = 250$ shares at an exercise price = $\frac{2\times 100}{5}$, that is at \$40.

Similar adjustments will also take place for stock dividends. Consider a 40% stock dividend. It means that you get 0.4 extra shares per share that you hold, or two extra shares for every five existing shares. Thus a 40% stock dividend is like a 7:5 split. When the contract is adjusted, the stock dividend will be treated like a 7:5 split.

8.14 The Put-Call Ratio

The put-call ratio, is the ratio of the trading volume of put options to the trading volume of call options. Changes in the ratio are interpreted as an indication of the prevailing market sentiment. An increase in the ratio, which means that the put volume is relatively higher than that of calls, is interpreted as a signal of a bear market. On the other hand, a decrease in the ratio, which means that the call volume is relatively higher than that of puts, is interpreted as a signal of a bull market.

Suggestions for Further Reading

Hull J.C. *Options, Futures, and Other Derivatives.* Prentice Hall, 2006.
Options: Essential Concepts & Trading Strategies. McGraw-Hill, 1999.

References

Long-Term Equity Anticipation Securities. The Options Clearing Corporation, 2004.
Chicago Board Options Exchange: Margin Manual. The CBOE, 2000.
Understanding Stock Options. The Options Clearing Corporation, 1994.
Understanding Index Options. The CBOE, 2001.
www.cboe.com

Chapter 9
Arbitrage Restrictions

9.1 The Absence of Arbitrage

We will now prove certain results pertaining to option prices. All option prices must satisfy these properties, or else there will be arbitrage opportunities. What do we mean by an arbitrage opportunity? *Arbitrage refers to the ability of a trader to make cost less and risk-less profits*. The phrase of significance here is *cost less and risk-less*. A costly but risky investment should yield a risk adjusted expected rate of return. A strategy that entails an investment, but is devoid of risk, should yield the risk-less rate of return. The ability of an individual to earn a return without an investment of his own, in an environment devoid of risk, is referred to as arbitrage. In other words, a strategy that yields a cash inflow at certain points in time, and a zero cash flow at other points in time, can be termed as an arbitrage strategy, because it leads to non-negative returns for the investor without requiring an investment (which would have manifested itself as a cash outflow) at any point in time. As should be obvious, an arbitrage opportunity will be exploited by anyone who perceives it, to the maximum possible extent till it is eliminated.

The following conditions must hold if arbitrage is to be ruled out. They, are however independent of the way the option prices are determined. In other words, these conditions are not specific to a particular option valuation model.

9.2 Assumptions

In order to derive the arbitrage-free properties of option prices, we will make the following assumptions.

1. Traders do not have to pay commissions or incur any form of transactions costs.
2. There are no bid-ask spreads.
3. All traders are price takers.
4. There are no taxes.
5. Traders receive the full premium on options written by them.
6. If a share is sold short, the trader is entitled to receive the full proceeds from the sale immediately.
7. Investors can trade in the stock and options markets instantaneously. If an option written by an investor is exercised, he will get immediate notice of the assignment.
8. Dividends are received on the ex-dividend date. The price decline on the ex-dividend date is exactly equal to the quantum of the dividend.

https://doi.org/10.1515/9783110746662-009

9. Investors are non-satiated. That is, they are constantly seeking opportunities to increase their wealth.
10. Arbitrage opportunities are exploited as soon as they appear, and till they cease to exist.

9.3 Non Negative Option Premia

An option cannot have a negative price. The existence of a negative price would mean that the writer is prepared to pay the holder to buy the option. If so, the holder can acquire the option, pocket the payment, and simply forget about the contract. The reason as to why the holder need not worry about further adverse consequences, or in other words, subsequent negative cash flows, is because the option is a right and not an obligation. Obviously, the presence of negative option premia would be a classic example of an arbitrage opportunity.

9.4 Properties of American Options

9.4.1 American Calls

$C_{A,t}$, should be greater than or equal to $\text{Max}[(S_t - X), 0]$.

Proof

If $S_t - X$ is less than zero, we can say that $C_{A,t} \geq 0$, since an option cannot have a negative value. However, if $S_t - X > 0$, $C_{A,t}$ must be worth at least $S_t - X$. The proof can be demonstrated as follows. Consider a case where $S_t - X > 0$ and $C_{A,t} < S_t - X$. If so, you can buy the option by paying $C_{A,t}$ and immediately exercise it. The profit of $S_t - X - C_{A,t}$ that you will get is clearly an arbitrage profit. Therefore, to preclude arbitrage, we require that

$$C_{A,t} \geq \text{Max}[(S_t - X), 0] \tag{9.1}$$

See Example 9.1.

Example 9.1: Let S_t = \$105 and X = \$100. Assume that $C_{A,t}$ = \$4.50. An arbitrageur can buy the call and immediately exercise it. This will yield an arbitrage profit of:

$$(105 - 100) - 4.50 = \$0.50$$

per share.

9.4.2 American Puts

The put price, $P_{A,t}$, should be greater than or equal to Max[$(X - S_t)$,0].

Proof
If $X - S_t$ is less than zero, we can say that $P_{A,t} \geq 0$, since an option cannot have a negative value. However, if $X - S_t > 0$, $P_{A,t}$ must be worth at least $X - S_t$. The proof can be demonstrated as follows. Consider a case where $X - S_t > 0$ and $P_{A,t} < X - S_t$. If so, you can buy the option by paying $P_{A,t}$ and immediately exercise it. The profit of $X - S_t - P_{A,t}$ that you will get is clearly an arbitrage profit. Therefore, to preclude arbitrage, we require that

$$P_{A,t} \geq \text{Max}[(X - S_t), 0] \tag{9.2}$$

See Example 9.2.

Example 9.2: Let S_t = \$100 and X = \$105. Assume that $P_{A,t}$ = \$4.50. An arbitrageur can buy the put and immediately exercise it. This will yield an arbitrage profit of:

$$(105 - 100) - 4.50 = \$0.50$$

per share.

9.5 Put-Call Parity for European Options

The Put-Call Parity theorem states that

$$C_{E,t} - P_{E,t} = S_t - \frac{X}{(1 + r)^{T-t}} \tag{9.3}$$

where $C_{E,t}$ represents the price of a European call with an exercise price of X and time to expiration equal to $T - t$ periods, and $P_{E,t}$ represents the price of a European put with the same exercise price and expiration date.

Proof
Consider the strategy and the corresponding cash flows, shown in Table 9.1.

Table 9.1: Illustration of Put-Call Parity: Strategy 1.

Action	Initial Cash Flow	Terminal Cash Flow	
		If $S_T > X$	If $S_T < X$
Buy the Stock	$-S_t$	S_T	S_T
Sell the Call	$C_{E,t}$	$-(S_T - X)$	0
Buy the Put	$-P_{E,t}$	0	$X - S_T$
Borrow the P.V. of X	$\frac{X}{(1+r)^{T-t}}$	$-X$	$-X$
Total	$-S_t + C_{E,t} - P_{E,t} + \frac{X}{(1+r)^{T-t}}$	0	0

P.V. stands for 'Present value'.

Let's analyze Table 9.1 carefully, for you will repeatedly come across such strategies in the course of your study of options. The first column in the table indicates the transactions that form components of the overall strategy. The second column indicates the initial cash flow associated with each transaction. All inflows will be positive and outflows negative. When an asset is bought there will obviously be an outflow, whereas when an asset is sold, there will be an inflow. Similarly when funds are borrowed there will be an inflow, whereas when funds are lent there will be an outflow.

The third and fourth columns represent the situation at the time of expiration of the option. Since the key variable of interest is the stock price at expiration and its level with respect to the exercise price, there are two possible situations which can arise. That is, either the stock price can be greater than the exercise price or it can be less than it. In either case the stock can be sold for its prevailing price, S_T. If the call is in the money it will be exercised by the party who has acquired it from the arbitrageur. His inflow upon exercise will be $S_T - X$, so obviously the arbitrageur's cash flow will be $-(S_T - X)$. If the put is exercised when it is in the money, the arbitrageur will receive $X - S_T$. Finally, since the present value of X has been borrowed, an amount equal to X, which represents the principal plus interest, must be repaid at expiration.

Notice that in the above table, the overall cash flow at expiration is zero, irrespective of whether the stock price at that point in time is above the exercise price or below it. Consequently, to rule out arbitrage, the initial cash flow must be non-positive, because a positive initial cash flow followed by no further outflows is a clear manifestation of arbitrage. Therefore, to rule out arbitrage, it must be the case that

$$-S_t + C_{E,t} - P_{E,t} + \frac{X}{(1+r)^{T-t}} \leq 0$$

However, we can demonstrate that it is possible to make an arbitrage profit if

$$-S_t + C_{E,t} - P_{E,t} + \frac{X}{(1+r)^{T-t}} < 0$$

This is because in such a situation, we can simply reverse the above strategy, thereby making an arbitrage profit, as shown in Table 9.2.

Table 9.2: Illustration of Put-Call Parity: Strategy 2.

Action	Initial Cash Flow	Terminal Cash Flow	
		If $S_T > X$	If $S_T < X$
Short sell the Stock	S_t	$-S_T$	$-S_T$
Buy the Call	$-C_{E,t}$	$(S_T - X)$	0
Sell the Put	$P_{E,t}$	0	$-(X - S_T)$
Lend the P.V. of X	$-\frac{X}{(1+r)^{T-t}}$	X	X
Total	$S_t - C_{E,t} + P_{E,t} - \frac{X}{(1+r)^{T-t}}$	0	0

The initial cash flow in this case will be positive if

$$-S_t + C_{E,t} - P_{E,t} + \frac{X}{(1+r)^{T-t}} < 0$$

whereas the terminal cash flows in either scenario will continue to be zero. Therefore, to preclude arbitrage, it must be the case that

$$-S_t + C_{E,t} - P_{E,t} + \frac{X}{(1+r)^{T-t}} = 0$$

$$\Rightarrow C_{E,t} - P_{E,t} = S_t - \frac{X}{(1+r)^{T-t}}$$

This relationship is known as the Put-Call parity theorem. It should be noted that it applies only to European options on stocks which do not pay a dividend during the life of the option.

We will now illustrate the potential to make arbitrage profits when put-call parity is violated. Consider Examples 9.3 and 9.4.

Example 9.3: Consider a stock which is selling for \$100. Call and put options with six months to expiration are selling for \$8 and \$3 respectively. The exercise price of the options is \$100, and the risk-less rate is 10% per annum.

$$C_{E,t} - P_{E,t} = 8 - 3 = 5$$

$$S_t - \frac{X}{(1+r)^{(T-t)}} = 100 - \frac{100}{(1.10)^{0.50}}$$
$$= 4.65$$

Thus, clearly there is a violation of put-call parity. Consider the following arbitrage strategy. Buy the stock; sell the call; buy the put; and borrow the present value of the exercise price. The initial inflow is:

$$-100 + 8 - 3 + \frac{100}{(1.10)^{0.50}} = 0.35$$

Subsequent cash flows, it can be verified will be zero, irrespective of the stock price at expiration. Thus, the initial inflow is clearly an arbitrage profit.

Example 9.4: Consider a stock which is selling for $100. Call and put options with six months to expiration are selling for $7 and $3 respectively. The exercise price of the options is $100, and the risk-less rate is 10% per annum.

$$C_{E,t} - P_{E,t} = 7 - 3 = 4$$

$$S_t - \frac{X}{(1+r)^{(T-t)}} = 100 - \frac{100}{(1.10)^{0.50}}$$
$$= 4.65$$

Thus clearly there is a violation of put-call parity. Consider the following arbitrage strategy. Short sell the stock; buy the call; sell the put; and lend the present value of the exercise price. The initial inflow is:

$$100 - 7 + 3 - \frac{100}{(1.10)^{0.50}} = 0.65$$

Subsequent cash flows, it can be verified will be zero, irrespective of the stock price at expiration. Thus, the initial inflow is clearly an arbitrage profit.

9.5.1 European Options on a Dividend Paying Stock

The put-call parity relationship for European options on a stock which pays a known dividend D at time t^*, where t^* is a point in time before the expiration of the option such that $t < t^* < T$, may be stated as:

$$C_{E,t} - P_{E,t} = S_t - \frac{D}{(1+r)^{t^*-t}} - \frac{X}{(1+r)^{T-t}} \tag{9.4}$$

Proof

Consider the strategy and the corresponding cash flows depicted in Table 9.3 below.

Table 9.3: Illustration of Put-Call Parity for a Dividend Paying Stock: Strategy 1.

Action	Initial Cash Flow	Intermediate Cash Flow	Terminal Cash Flow	
			If $S_T > X$	If $S_T < X$
Buy the Stock	$-S_t$	D	S_T	S_T
Sell the Call	$C_{E,t}$		$-(S_T - X)$	0
Buy the Put	$-P_{E,t}$		0	$X - S_T$
Borrow the P.V. of D	$\frac{D}{(1+r)^{t^*-t}}$	-D		
Borrow the P.V. of X	$\frac{X}{(1+r)^{T-t}}$		$-X$	$-X$
Total	$-S_t + C_{E,t} - P_{E,t} + \frac{D}{(1+r)^{t^*-t}} + \frac{X}{(1+r)^{T-t}}$	0	0	0

As in the case of European options on a non-dividend paying stock, the terminal payoff from the strategy is zero, irrespective of the stock price at expiration. The only difference here is that the stock will pay a dividend of $D at time t^*. Since the investor has borrowed the present value of the dividend at the outset, the net cash flow at t^* will be zero. Since the subsequent cash flows are guaranteed to be zero, that initial cash flow must be non positive. That is:

$$-S_t + C_{E,t} - P_{E,t} + \frac{D}{(1+r)^{t^*-t}} + \frac{X}{(1+r)^{T-t}} \leq 0$$

$$\Rightarrow C_{E,t} - P_{E,t} \leq S_t - \frac{D}{(1+r)^{t^*-t}} - \frac{X}{(1+r)^{T-t}}$$

However, if

$$C_{E,t} - P_{E,t} < S_t - \frac{D}{(1+r)^{t^*-t}} - \frac{X}{(1+r)^{T-t}}$$

we can as before reverse the above strategy and make arbitrage profits. Consider Table 9.4.

At t^*, the arbitrageur has to pay an amount equal to the dividend to the investor who has lent him the share to facilitate the short sale. However, since he has lent an amount equal to the present value of the dividend at the outset, he will have an inflow

Table 9.4: Illustration of Put-Call Parity for a Dividend Paying Stock: Strategy 2.

Action	Initial Cash Flow	Intermediate Cash Flow	Terminal Cash Flow	
			If $S_T > X$	If $S_T < X$
Short sell the Stock	S_t	$-D$	$-S_T$	$-S_T$
Buy the Call	$-C_{E,t}$		$(S_T - X)$	0
Sell the Put	$P_{E,t}$		0	$-(X - S_T)$
Lend the P.V. of D	$-\frac{D}{(1+r)^{t^*-t}}$	D		
Lend the P.V. of X	$-\frac{X}{(1+r)^{T-t}}$		X	X
Total	$S_t - C_{E,t} + P_{E,t} - \frac{D}{(1+r)^{t^*-t}} - \frac{X}{(1+r)^{T-t}}$	0	0	0

of \$D at t^*, which will be just adequate to pay the dividend. Once again, since all the subsequent cash flows are zero, the initial cash flow must be non-positive. That is:

$$S_t - C_{E,t} + P_{E,t} - \frac{D}{(1+r)^{t^*-t}} - \frac{X}{(1+r)^{T-t}} \leq 0$$
$$\Rightarrow C_{E,t} - P_{E,t} \geq S_t - \frac{D}{(1+r)^{t^*-t}} - \frac{X}{(1+r)^{T-t}}$$

In order for both the conditions to hold simultaneously, it must be the case that:

$$C_{E,t} - P_{E,t} = S_t - \frac{D}{(1+r)^{t^*-t}} - \frac{X}{(1+r)^{T-t}}$$

This is the put-call parity condition for European options on a stock that pays a known dividend during the life of the option.

9.6 Intrinsic Value & Time Value

The Intrinsic Value of an option is equal to the amount by which it is in the money, if it is in the money, else it is equal to zero. Therefore, the intrinsic value of a call option is

$$\text{I.V.} = \text{Max}[(S_t - X), 0] \tag{9.5}$$

and that of a put option is

$$\text{I.V.} = \text{Max}[(X - S_t), 0] \tag{9.6}$$

The difference between an option's price and its intrinsic value, is called the Time Value or the Speculative Value of the option.

Quite obviously, an option that is out of the money will have only time value, since by definition the intrinsic value of such options is zero. Since an option cannot have a negative premium, the time value of such options must be non-negative. Calls and puts which are in the money will have a positive intrinsic value. The time value of such options may or may not be positive as we shall see below.

Example 9.5: Assume that the price of a stock is \$100 and that the exercise price of a call option is \$97.50. If the call premium is \$3.50, then

$$100.00 - 97.50 = 2.50$$

is the intrinsic value of the call option, and

$$3.50 - 2.50 = 1.00$$

is its time value.

Example 9.6: Assume that the price of a stock is \$100 and that the exercise price of a put option is \$97.50. The put premium is \$1.25. In this case, the intrinsic value is zero because the put is out of the money. Therefore, the entire premium of \$1.25 is the time value of the option.

We have already shown that

$$C_{A,t} \geq \text{Max}[(S_t - X), 0] \text{ and } P_{A,t} \geq \text{Max}[(X - S_t), 0]$$

Therefore, both call as well as put options that are American in nature, must have a non-negative time value.

What about European options? From Put-Call parity, we know that

$$C_{E,t} - P_{E,t} = S_t - \frac{X}{(1+r)^{T-t}}$$

$$\Rightarrow C_{E,t} = P_{E,t} + S_t - \frac{X}{(1+r)^{T-t}}$$

$$\Rightarrow C_{E,t} = P_{E,t} + (S_t - X) + X - \frac{X}{(1+r)^{T-t}}$$

If $(S_t - X) > 0$, then $C_{E,t} \geq (S_t - X)$ because $P_{E,t} \geq 0$, since an option cannot have a negative premium and $X - \frac{X}{(1+r)^{T-t}}$ is also guaranteed to be non-negative. Hence, a European call on a non-dividend paying stock will have a non-negative time value if the option is in the money.

What if the option is out of the money? In that case, the entire premium will comprise of time value, which is guaranteed to be non-negative, since an option cannot have a negative premium. *Therefore, a European call on a non-dividend paying stock will always have a non-negative time value.*

What about European puts? From Put-Call parity, we know that

$$P_{E,t} = \frac{X}{(1+r)^{T-t}} - S_t + C_{E,t}$$

$$\Rightarrow P_{E,t} = X - S_t + \frac{X}{(1+r)^{T-t}} - X + C_{E,t}$$

If the option is out of the money, the time value cannot be negative since the premium cannot be negative. What if the option is in the money? If so, $(X-S_t)$ which is the intrinsic value will be positive. $\frac{X}{(1+r)^{T-t}} - X$ will always be less than or equal to zero. So whether or not the time value is negative, would depend on the value of $C_{E,t}$ compared to the value of $\frac{X}{(1+r)^{T-t}} - X$. Obviously, the lower the value of $C_{E,t}$, the lower will be the time value. For a given value of the exercise price, the lower the value of the stock price, the lower will the value of $C_{E,t}$. Consequently, for the European put to have a negative time value, the corresponding call must be deep out of the money, which means that the put itself must be deep in the money. *Thus, deep in the money European puts may have a negative time value.*

9.6.1 European Calls on Dividend Paying Stocks

From the put-call parity relationship for a stock paying a known dividend before expiration, we know that:

$$C_{E,t} - P_{E,t} = S_t - \frac{D}{(1+r)^{t^*-t}} - \frac{X}{(1+r)^{T-t}}$$

$$\Rightarrow C_{E,t} = P_{E,t} + (S_t - X) - \frac{D}{(1+r)^{t^*-t}} + \left[X - \frac{X}{(1+r)^{T-t}}\right]$$

If the call is substantially in the money and the magnitude of the dividend is sizeable, then it is conceivable that

$$P_{E,t} - \frac{D}{(1+r)^{t^*-t}} + \left[X - \frac{X}{(1+r)^{T-t}}\right] < 0$$

which would obviously imply a negative time value. Thus European call options on dividend paying stocks may have a negative time value.

9.7 Option Premia at Expiration

American options and European calls on non dividend paying stocks have a non-negative time value, as we have seen earlier, while European puts on non dividend paying stocks may have either a positive or a negative time value depending on the extent to which the option is in the money. At the time of expiration, the time value of an option must be zero, that is, the option premium must be equal to the intrinsic value.

Proof

Consider a call option that is in the money at expiration. Assume that the time value is positive, that is, $C_{A,T}$ or $C_{E,T}$ is greater than $S_T - X$. If so, an arbitrageur will immediately sell the call. If it is exercised, the net cash flow for him is $C_T-(S_T-X)$, which by assumption is positive. The same holds true if the option is out of the money and the time value is positive, since in this case the writer need not worry about exercise. On the other hand, if the time value were to be negative, that is, $C_{A,T}$ or $C_{E,T}$ is less than $(S_T - X)$, an arbitrageur will buy the option and immediately exercise it. The net cash flow will be $S_T - X - C_T$ which is guaranteed to be positive. Thus, to preclude arbitrage, an option must sell for its intrinsic value at expiration. The same rationale holds for put options, whether European or American.

9.8 Upper Bounds for Call Options

At any point in time, the price of a call option, whether European or American, must be less than the prevailing stock price. The rationale is simple. An option gives the holder the right to acquire a stock by paying the exercise price. If the price of the call were to exceed that of the stock, a rational investor who finds the stock to be attractive, would rather buy it directly, rather than pay a higher price for the option, which entails a further payment of the exercise price were it to be exercised subsequently.

Here is a formal proof. In proofs of this nature we will assume the converse of the proposition that we wish to prove, and take all the variables to one side so that the expression is greater than zero. In order to set up the corresponding arbitrage strategy, all variables which have a positive sign must be sold, while those with a negative sign must be bought. When it comes to borrowing and lending an amount, if the cash flow has a positive sign, it indicates that the amount must be borrowed, whereas if it has a negative sign it signifies that the amount has to be lent. If we can demonstrate that all cash flows at subsequent points in time are non-negative, then a non-negative cash flow at inception will tantamount to arbitrage. However, if the cash flow in even one of the subsequent scenarios were to be non-positive, then we will be unable to make such an assertion about the non-existence of an arbitrage opportunity.

In this case for instance, we wish to show that $C_t \leq S_t$. Assume that C_t is > S_t. Therefore $C_t - S_t > 0$. Now consider the strategy and the corresponding cash flows, shown in Table 9.5.

Table 9.5: Upper Bound for Call Options.

Action	Initial Cash Flow	Intermediate Cash Flow	Terminal Cash Flow	
		If $S_{t^*} > X$	If $S_T > X$	If $S_T < X$
Sell the Call	C_t	$-(S_{t^*} - X)$	$-(S_T - X)$	0
Buy the Stock	$-S_t$	S_{t^*}	S_T	S_T
Total	$C_t - S_t$	X> 0	X> 0	$S_T > 0$

Proof

Notice that we have incorporated an additional column in the table. This corresponds to a time t^*, where $t < t^* < T$. This is to take into account the possibility of early exercise of the option. The need for this column arises, because the proof is intended to be common for European as well as American options, and while dealing with American options we must always factor in the possibility of early exercise. Since the option that has been sold is a call, the counterparty may exercise it prematurely only if $S_{t^*} > X$.

In the above table, the initial cash flow is positive by assumption. Since the subsequent cash flows are guaranteed to be positive, it is a clear manifestation of an arbitrage opportunity. Consequently, to rule out arbitrage, we require that

$$C_t - S_t \leq 0 \Rightarrow C_t \leq S_t \tag{9.7}$$

9.9 Lower Bounds for Call Options on Non-dividend Paying Stocks

It can be demonstrated that $C_t \geq \text{Max}\left[0, S_t - \frac{X}{(1+r)^{(T-t)}}\right]$. If the expression $S_t - \frac{X}{(1+r)^{(T-t)}}$ were to be less than zero, then all that we can assert is that $C_t \geq 0$, because we know that an option cannot have a negative premium. However if the expression were to be positive, then the option premium must be greater than or equal to it to preclude arbitrage.

Proof

Assume that $C_t < S_t - \frac{X}{(1+r)^{(T-t)}} > 0$ or that $S_t - \frac{X}{(1+r)^{(T-t)}} - C_t > 0$. Consider Table 9.6. In this table the cash flow at inception is positive by assumption. The cash flows at expiration are non-negative. However, the intermediate cash flow will be negative if the call

Table 9.6: Lower Bound for Call Options.

Action	Initial Cash Flow	Intermediate Cash Flow	Terminal Cash Flow	
		If $S_{t^*} > X$	If $S_T > X$	If $S_T < X$
Short sell the Stock	S_t	$-S_{t^*}$	$-S_T$	$-S_T$
Buy the Call	$-C_t$	$(S_{t^*} - X)$	$(S_T - X)$	0
Lend the P.V. of X	$-\dfrac{X}{(1+r)^{T-t}}$	$\dfrac{X}{(1+r)^{T-t^*}}$	X	X
Total	$S_t - C_t - \dfrac{X}{(1+r)^{T-t}}$	$\dfrac{X}{(1+r)^{T-t^*}} - X < 0$	0	$X - S_T > 0$

is exercised. But, the important thing to note is that the intermediate stage will lead to a negative cash flow only if the arbitrageur exercises the option at that point in time. Since the call is under the control of the arbitrageur, he is under no compulsion to exercise, and consequently need not worry about the specter of a negative cash flow. Thus, the above strategy is guaranteed to yield non-negative cash flows subsequently, and hence the initial cash flow must be less than or equal to zero. It therefore must be the case that

$$C_t \geq S_t - \frac{X}{(1+r)^{T-t}}$$

Combining the two conditions, we can therefore state that

$$C_t \geq \text{Max}\left[0, S_t - \frac{X}{(1+r)^{T-t}}\right] \tag{9.8}$$

We know that an American call option must trade for at least its intrinsic value. That is:

$$C_{A,t} \geq \text{Max}[0, S_t - X]$$

We have just demonstrated that

$$C_{A,t} \geq \text{Max}\left[0, S_t - \frac{X}{(1+r)^{T-t}}\right]$$

because the proof that has just been presented is valid for both European as well as American calls.

The second condition gives a tighter lower bound for American calls on non-dividend paying stocks. For if $C_{A,t} \geq S_t - \frac{X}{(1+r)^{T-t}}$, then it automatically implies that $C_{A,t} \geq S_t - X$. Based on this observation, we can now draw some important conclusions about American calls on non-dividend paying stocks.

1. An in the money American call will always have a positive time value except at expiration. That is because, if $S_t > X$, then

$$C_{A,t} \geq S_t - \frac{X}{(1+r)^{T-t}} \geq S_t - X$$

2. An American call on a non-dividend paying stock will never be exercised early. If the holder chooses to exercise an in the money call, he will get the intrinsic value of the option. However, if he chooses to offset by selling an identical call, he will get the prevailing call premium which, is guaranteed to exceed the intrinsic value. Thus, an American call on a non-dividend stock would rather be offset than exercised prior to expiration.
3. An American call on a non-dividend paying stock will have the same premium as a European call on the same stock, with the same exercise price and expiration date. This is because since the American call is never going to be exercised early, the early exercise option inherent in it has no value for the holder. Consequently, the call will trade for the same premium as a European call with identical features.

9.10 Upper Bounds for Puts

Let's first consider European puts. It can be shown that $P_{E,t} \leq \frac{X}{(1+r)^{T-t}}$. To prove this, consider the strategy shown in Table 9.7.

Table 9.7: Upper Bound for European Puts.

Action	Initial Cash Flow	Terminal Cash Flow	
		If $S_T > X$	If $S_T < X$
Sell the Put	$P_{E,t}$	0	$-(X - S_T)$
Lend the P.V. of X	$-\frac{X}{(1+r)^{T-t}}$	X	X
Total	$P_{E,t} - \frac{X}{(1+r)^{T-t}}$	$X > 0$	$S_T > 0$

Proof

In order to preclude arbitrage the initial cash flow must not be positive. Therefore

$$P_{E,t} - \frac{X}{(1+r)^{T-t}} \leq 0$$

$$\Rightarrow P_{E,t} \leq \frac{X}{(1+r)^{T-t}} \tag{9.9}$$

The above proof is not however valid for American puts. For such options, we have to factor in the possibility of early exercise, and when we do so, the above strategy does not give us an explicit condition to rule out arbitrage. Consider Table 9.8.

Table 9.8: Upper Bound for American Puts: An Invalid Proof.

Action	Initial Cash Flow	Intermediate Cash Flow	Terminal Cash Flow	
		If $S_{t^*} < X$	If $S_T > X$	If $S_T < X$
Sell the Put	$P_{A,t}$	$-(X - S_{t^*})$	0	$-(X - S_T)$
Lend the P.V. of X	$-\frac{X}{(1+r)^{T-t}}$	$\frac{X}{(1+r)^{T-t^*}}$	X	X
Total	$P_{A,t} - \frac{X}{(1+r)^{T-t}}$	$S_{t^*} + \frac{X}{(1+r)^{T-t^*}} - X$	$X > 0$	$S_T > 0$

While the terminal cash flows are guaranteed to be non-negative, the sign of the intermediate cash flow is ambiguous. If it were guaranteed to be positive, we could categorically state that $P_{A,t} > \frac{X}{(1+r)^{T-t}}$ implies arbitrage. However, because of the ambiguity, we cannot make this assertion. At the same time we cannot rule out the possibility of early exercise, because we have sold the put option. In strategies that involve the acquisition of an option by the arbitrageur, a cash outflow at an intermediate stage can never arise because the option is under his control. However, the same cannot be said for strategies which entail the sale of an option by the arbitrageur.

So what is the applicable upper bound for an American put? We can demonstrate that $P_{A,t} < X$. Consider Table 9.9.

Proof

Since the subsequent cash flows are guaranteed to be non-negative, the initial cash flow must be non-positive to rule out arbitrage. Thus, we require that $P_{A,t} \leq X$.

Table 9.9: Upper Bound for American Puts: A Valid Proof.

Action	Initial Cash Flow	Intermediate Cash Flow	Terminal Cash Flow	
		If $S_{t^*} < X$	If $S_T > X$	If $S_T < X$
Sell the Put	$P_{A,t}$	$-(X - S_{t^*})$	0	$-(X - S_T)$
Lend X	-X	$X(1+r)^{(t^*-t)}$	$X(1+r)^{(T-t)}$	$X(1+r)^{(T-t)}$
Total	$P_{A,t} - X$	$S_{t^*} + X(1+r)^{(t^*-t)} - X > 0$	$X(1+r)^{(T-t)} > 0$	$S_T + X(1+r)^{(T-t)} - X > 0$

9.11 Lower Bounds for Puts

For American puts on non-dividend paying stocks, we have already demonstrated that $P_{A,t} \geq \text{Max}[0, X - S_t]$. In the case of European puts, the no-arbitrage condition is:

$$P_{E,t} \geq \text{Max}\left[0, \frac{X}{(1+r)^{(T-t)}} - S_t\right] \tag{9.10}$$

This condition can be interpreted as follows. If $\frac{X}{(1+r)^{T-t}} - S_t < 0$, then all that we can assert is that $P_{E,t} > 0$, because an option cannot have a negative premium. However, if $\frac{X}{(1+r)^{T-t}} - S_t > 0$ then we can show that $P_{E,t} \geq \frac{X}{(1+r)^{T-t}} - S_t$. To prove it, consider Table 9.10.

Table 9.10: Lower Bound for European Puts.

Action	Initial Cash Flow	Terminal Cash Flow	
		If $S_T > X$	If $S_T < X$
Buy the Put	$-P_{E,t}$	0	$(X - S_T)$
Buy the Stock	$-S_t$	S_T	S_T
Borrow the P.V. of X	$\frac{X}{(1+r)^{T-t}}$	$-X$	$-X$
Total	$\frac{X}{(1+r)^{T-t}} - P_{E,t} - S_t$	$S_T - X > 0$	0

Proof

To rule out arbitrage we require that

$$\frac{X}{(1+r)^{T-t}} - P_{E,t} - S_t \le 0$$
$$\Rightarrow \frac{X}{(1+r)^{T-t}} - S_t \le P_{E,t}$$

Although it must be the case that $P_{E,t}$ is greater than $\frac{X}{(1+r)^{T-t}} - S_t$, it is not necessary that $P_{E,t} > X - S_t$. Thus, a European option on a non-dividend paying stock can sell for less than its intrinsic value, or in other words it can have a negative time value. This of course is a possibility that we have already proved earlier.

What about American options on a non-dividend paying stock? We have already demonstrated that $P_{A,t} \ge \text{Max}[0, X - S_t]$ which obviously implies that $P_{A,t} \ge \text{Max}\left[0, \frac{X}{(1+r)^{T-t}} - S_t\right]$. Thus we get a tighter lower bound for American put options.

9.12 The Put-Call Parity Equivalent for American Options

In the case of American options, the put-call parity condition consists of two inequalities. In the case of options on a stock which is not scheduled to pay dividends during the life of the option, the condition may be stated as:

$$S_t - X \le C_{A,t} - P_{A,t} \le S_t - \frac{X}{(1+r)^{T-t}} \tag{9.11}$$

Proof

Let's first consider the R.H.S. To prove it, consider the strategy shown in Table 9.11, and the corresponding cash flows.

Since the terminal payoffs are guaranteed to be zero, the initial cash flow must be non-positive. Therefore it must be the case that:

$$-S_t + C_{A,t} - P_{A,t} + \frac{X}{(1+r)^{T-t}} \le 0$$
$$\Rightarrow S_t - \frac{X}{(1+r)^{T-t}} \ge C_{A,t} - P_{A,t}$$

One question that the reader may have is, why has the possibility of early exercise of the options not been considered. The reason is the following. The arbitrageur has sold the call. Since it is a call on a non-dividend paying stock, it will never be optimal for the counter-party to exercise early. In the case of the put, the arbitrageur has bought it. Since an American put on a non-dividend paying stock may be exercised early, it may be

Table 9.11: Illustration of Put-Call Parity for American Options on a Non-dividend Paying Stock: Strategy 1.

Action	Initial Cash Flow	Terminal Cash Flow	
		If $S_T > X$	If $S_T < X$
Buy the Stock	$-S_t$	S_T	S_T
Sell the Call	$C_{A,t}$	$-(S_T - X)$	0
Buy the Put	$-P_{A,t}$	0	$X - S_T$
Borrow the P.V. of X	$\frac{X}{(1+r)^{T-t}}$	$-X$	$-X$
Total	$-S_t + C_{A,t} - P_{A,t} + \frac{X}{(1+r)^{T-t}}$	0	0

optimal for the arbitrageur to exercise early. However, since the put is in his control, he will exercise early only if the overall payoff is guaranteed to be positive. Consequently there is no possibility of a negative cash flow at an intermediate stage. Thus, if the cash flow at inception is non-positive, then there can be no arbitrage profits.

Let's now focus on the L.H.S. Consider the strategy shown in Table 9.12 and the corresponding cash flows.

Table 9.12: Illustration of Put-Call Parity for American Options on a Non-dividend Paying Stock: Strategy 2.

Action	Initial Cash Flow	Intermediate Cash Flow	Terminal Cash Flow	
		If $S_{t^*} < X$	If $S_T > X$	If $S_T < X$
Short sell the Stock	S_t	$-S_{t^*}$	$-S_T$	$-S_T$
Buy the Call	$-C_{A,t}$	T.V.	$S_T - X$	0
Sell the Put	$P_{A,t}$	$-(X - S_{t^*})$	0	$-(X - S_T)$
Lend X	-X	$X(1+r)^{(t^*-t)}$	$X(1+r)^{(T-t)}$	$X(1+r)^{(T-t)}$
Total	$S_t - C_{A,t} + P_{A,t} - X$	$X(1+r)^{(t^*-t)} - X + T.V. > 0$	$X(1+r)^{(T-t)} - X > 0$	$X(1+r)^{(T-t)} - X > 0$

We will now analyze the entries in the above table. The overall payoff at expiration is self-explanatory, and is guaranteed to be positive. At the intermediate stage, the call will never be exercised, because it is on a non-dividend paying stock. However, the put that has been sold by the arbitrageur may be exercised early by the counterparty. The put will be exercised only if it is in the money. If the put is in the money, the call will obviously be out of the money. If so, it will have no intrinsic value, and its entire premium will consist of the time value which we have denoted by T.V. Thus if the position is unwound at an intermediate stage, the call can be sold for its time value. This explains the entries corresponding to the payoffs if the put is exercised prior to expiration. Since all subsequent cash flows are guaranteed to be positive, the initial cash flow must be non-positive.

9.13 Relationship Between European Options with Different Strikes

Consider European options on the same underlying asset and with identical terms to expiration. We will denote the premia as $C_{t,1}$ and $C_{t,2}$ for calls and $P_{t,1}$ and $P_{t,2}$ for puts. The respective exercise prices are X_1 and X_2, where $X_1 < X_2$. We will now demonstrate that:

$$C_{t,1} - C_{t,2} \leq \frac{X_2 - X_1}{(1+r)^{(T-t)}} \tag{9.12}$$

The proof is given in Table 9.13.

Table 9.13: Relationship for European Calls.

Action	Initial Cash Flow	Terminal Cash Flow		
		If $S_T < X_1$	If $X_1 < S_T < X_2$	If $S_T > X_2$
Sell the Call with $X = X_1$	$C_{t,1}$	0	$-(S_T - X_1)$	$-(S_T - X_1)$
Buy the call with $X = X_2$	$-C_{t,2}$	0	0	$(S_T - X_2)$
Lend the P.V. of $X_2 - X_1$	$-\frac{X_2 - X_1}{(1+r)^{T-t}}$	$X_2 - X_1$	$X_2 - X_1$	$X_2 - X_1$
Total	$C_{t,1} - C_{t,2} - \frac{X_2 - X_1}{(1+r)^{T-t}}$	$X_2 - X_1$	$X_2 - S_t$	0
		> 0	> 0	0

Proof

To rule out arbitrage, it must obviously the case that the initial cash flow is non-positive. Thus we require that:

$$C_{t,1} - C_{t,2} - \frac{X_2 - X_1}{(1+r)^{T-t}} \leq 0$$

$$\Rightarrow C_{t,1} - C_{t,2} \leq \frac{X_2 - X_1}{(1+r)^{T-t}}$$

It is obvious that keeping all the other variables constant, the higher the exercise price the lower must be the call option premium. Thus:

$$C_{t,1} - C_{t,2} \geq 0$$

Hence we can state that:

$$0 \leq C_{t,1} - C_{t,2} \leq \frac{X_2 - X_1}{(1+r)^{T-t}} \tag{9.13}$$

Similarly, we can show that:

$$0 \leq P_{t,2} - P_{t,1} \leq \frac{X_2 - X_1}{(1+r)^{T-t}} \tag{9.14}$$

Suggestions for Further Reading

Dubofsky D.A. *Options and Financial Futures: Valuation and Uses.* McGraw-Hill, 1992.
Figlewski S., Silber W.L., and M.G. Subrahmanyam *Financial Options: From Theory to Practice.* Irwin, 1990.

Chapter 10
Option Strategies and Profit Diagrams

10.1 Introduction

In this chapter, we will analyze various trading strategies that can be set up using call options, put options, and combinations of the two. For each strategy we will compute the payoff and profit for various scenarios at the expiration date of the options. The corresponding break even price(s) will be computed, and the profit profile will be graphically illustrated.

10.1.1 Notation

We will use the following symbols to denote the corresponding variables.

- S_T^* ≡ break even price
- S_T^{**} ≡ second break even price if there is more than one.
- C_t ≡ call option premium at time t for an option expiring at time T.
- P_t ≡ put option premium at time t for an option expiring at time T.
- r ≡ riskless rate of interest per annum
- X ≡ exercise price of the option
- π_{min} ≡ maximum loss.
- π_{max} ≡ maximum profit.

In all the graphs, the terminal stock price S_T will be plotted along the X axis, and the profit from the strategy, π will be depicted along the Y axis.

10.2 Long Call

Buying a call option is a popular strategy for bullish investors. Consider a call option with an exercise price of X, and a premium of C_t. If the stock price at expiration, $S_T \leq X$, the option will expire worthless and the investor will lose the entire premium. So for the price range, $0 \leq S_T \leq X, \pi = -C_t$, where π denotes the profit from the strategy. As the terminal stock price rises above X, for every dollar increase in the price, the investor's profit will go up by one dollar. Therefore, for the price range $S_T > X, \pi = S_T - X - C_t$. The break even price S_T^* is equal to $X+C_t$. The maximum loss, π_{min}, is obviously the premium paid at the outset. The maximum profit on the other hand is unlimited because the stock price has no upper bound.

The profits from such a strategy are depicted in Figure 10.1. Example 10.1 provides a numerical illustration.

https://doi.org/10.1515/9783110746662-010

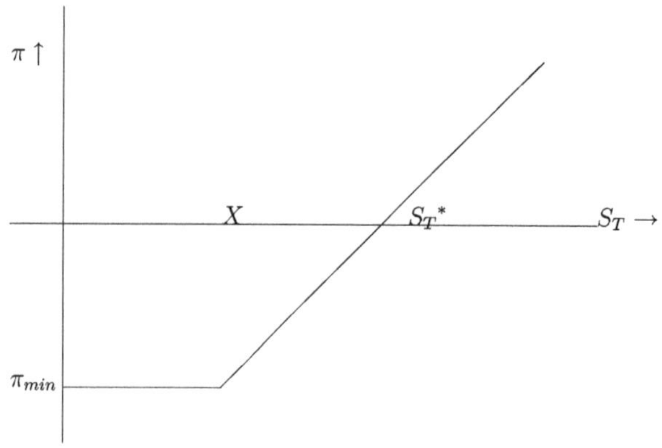

Figure 10.1: Profit Profile for a Long Call.

Example 10.1: Consider a stock whose current price is \$100. The riskless rate of interest is 10% per annum, and the volatility is 30% per annum. The premium for an option with an exercise price of \$100, and a time to expiration of six months, is \$10.91.[1]

If the stock price at expiration is less than \$100, the option will expire out of the money. The loss will be equal to the premium paid for the option which is \$10.91. As the stock price at expiration rises above \$100, for every dollar increase in the stock price, the profit from the call increases by one dollar. The break even stock price is $X + C_t = 100 + 10.91 =$ \$110.91. The maximum profit is obviously unlimited. The payoff and profit for various values of the terminal stock price are given in Table 10.1.

Table 10.1: Payoff and Profit from Long Call Position.

Terminal Stock Price	Payoff	Profit
0	0	(1,091)
25	0	(1,091)
50	0	(1,091)
75	0	(1,091)
100	0	(1,091)
110.91	1,091	0
125	2,500	1,409
150	5,000	3,909
175	7,500	6,409
200	10,000	8,909

---

1 We have used the Black-Scholes formula to compute the option prices.

10.2.1 Speculating with Calls

Andrew Smith is bullish about IBM and wants to speculate using call options. Options with an exercise price of $100 and three months to expiration are available at a premium of $8. The current stock price is $100. If we assume that Andrew goes long in one contract, his total investment is

$$8 \times 100 = \$800$$

Assume that at expiration, the price of IBM is $125. Since the option is in the money, Andrew will exercise. His profit will be

$$(125 - 100) \times 100 - 800 = \$1{,}700$$

10.2.2 The 90/10 Strategy

This strategy entails an investment of 10% of the funds at an investor's disposal in call options, and the balance 90% in a money market instrument such as a T-bill.

Assume that Andrew has $8,000 available with him for investment. He decides to buy call options with an exercise price of $100, and with three months to expiration, by paying a premium of $800, which is 10% of his wealth. He then invests the balance of $7,200 is T-bills, which we will assume yield 8% per annum.

The return from the T-bills over three months is

$$7{,}200 \times 0.08 \times 0.25 = \$144$$

The effective cost of the options contract is therefore

$$800 - 144 = \$656$$

If the stock price at expiration is less than $100, Andrew will incur a loss of $656. This is his maximum possible loss. If the terminal stock price is between $100 and $106.56, he will incur a loss which is given by

$$-656 \le \pi \le 0$$

Thus, the break even stock price is $106.56. For values of the terminal stock price in excess of $106.56, Andrew will make a profit. His maximum profit is unbounded.

10.2.3 Buying Calls to Lock in a Share Price

IBM is currently trading at $100 per share. Andrew would like to acquire 100 shares but does not have the required funds. He is however confident that he will have adequate funds in three months time. Three month options on IBM are available at a premium of $8 per share. Assume that Andrew goes long in one contract.

If the stock price after three months is $125, the options can be exercised and 100 shares of IBM can be acquired at a cost of

$$100 \times 100 + 800 = \$10,800$$

or $108 per share. The cost of the shares would have been $125 each, if Andrew had not taken a position in the options.

10.3 Long Put

Buying a put option is a strategy for bearish investors. Consider a put option with an exercise price of X, and a premium of P_t. If the stock price at expiration, $S_T \geq X$, the option will expire worthless and the investor will lose the entire premium. So for the price range $S_T \geq X, \pi = -P_t$. As the terminal stock price declines below X, for every dollar decline in the price, the investor's profit will go up by one dollar. Therefore, for the price range $0 \leq S_T < X, \pi = X - S_T - P_t$. The break even price S_T^* is equal to $X - P_t$. The maximum loss, π_{min} is obviously equal to the premium paid at the outset, which is P_t. The maximum profit, π_{max}, is equal to $X - P_t$. This is because due to the limited liability feature of stocks, the lowest possible share price is zero. The profit diagram is depicted in Figure 10.2, and a numerical illustration is provided in Example 10.2.

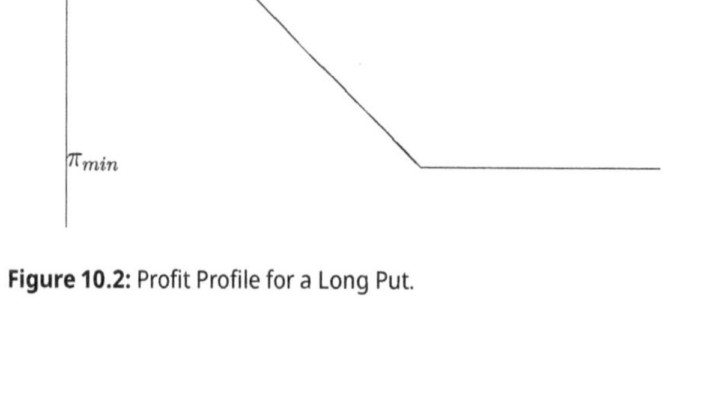

Figure 10.2: Profit Profile for a Long Put.

Example 10.2: Consider a stock whose current price is $100. The riskless rate of interest is 10% per annum, and the volatility is 30% per annum. The premium for a put option with an exercise price of $100, and a time to expiration of six months, is $6.03.

If the stock price at expiration is greater than $100, the option will expire out of the money. The loss will be equal to the premium paid for the option which is $6.03. As the stock price at expiration falls below $100, then for every dollar decrease in the stock price, the profit from the put increases by one dollar. The break even stock price is

$$X - P_t = 100 - 6.03 = \$93.97$$

The maximum profit is equal to $93.97, which corresponds to a terminal stock price of zero. The payoff and profit for various values of the terminal stock price are given in Table 10.2.

Table 10.2: Payoff and Profit from Long Put Position.

Terminal Stock Price	Payoff	Profit
0	10,000	9,397
25	7,500	6,897
50	5,000	4,397
75	2,500	1,897
93.97	603	0
100	0	(603)
125	0	(603)
150	0	(603)
175	0	(603)
200	0	(603)

10.3.1 Speculating with Puts

Mike Faye is bearish about IBM and is confident that the stock will decline in value over the next three months. One alternative is for him to short sell shares of IBM. But this strategy can give rise to unlimited losses. This is because, he will have to acquire the stock eventually to cover his short position, and the stock price has no upper bound. Besides, to establish a short position, he needs to set up a margin account, and margin calls may compel him to cover the position prematurely despite the fact that the position may still have profit potential. A long put on the other hand, allows him to speculate while restricting his maximum potential loss to the premium paid for the options.

Assume that the current stock price is $100, and that put options with an exercise price of $100 and three months to expiration, are available at a premium of $4.75 per share. If the stock price at expiration were to be \$80 per share, Mike would exercise the options. His profit will be

$$(100 - 80) \times 100 - 4.75 \times 100 = \$1{,}525$$

However, if the terminal stock price were to be \$120, Mike would refrain from exercising the options, and his loss would be the premium paid at the outset, which is \$475.

10.3.2 Buying Calls to Hedge a Short Sale

This strategy entails the purchase of one call option for every share that is sold short.

Profit from the short position in the stock = $S_t - S_T$. Profit from the call = $\text{Max}[0, S_T - X] - C_t$. The total profit is given by $\pi = S_t - S_T + \text{Max}[0, S_T - X] - C_t$.

If $S_T \leq X, \pi = S_t - S_T - C_t$. For every dollar that the stock price declines below X, the investor gains a dollar. The break even point $S_T{}^*$ is $= S_t - C_t$. The maximum profit π_{max} is $= S_t - C_t$.

If $S_T > X, \pi = S_t - X - C_t$, which is the maximum loss.

The profit diagram may be depicted as shown in Figure 10.3.

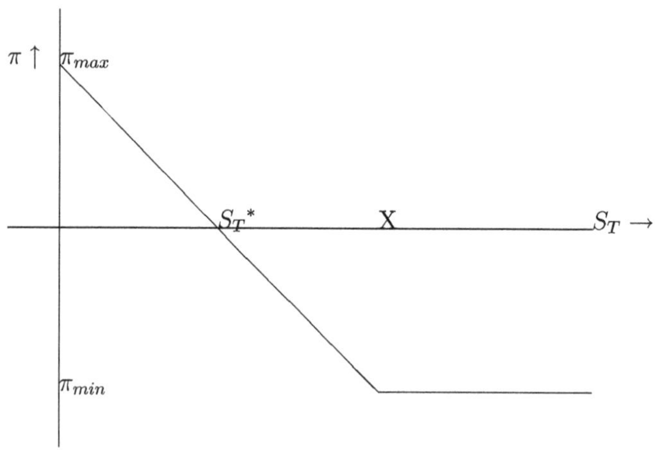

Figure 10.3: Profit Profile for a Long Call Combined with a Short Stock.

The payoff looks like the one for a long put. This is not surprising, because from put-call parity,

$$P_t - \frac{X}{(1+r)^{T-t}} = C_t - S_t$$

Thus buying a call, and shorting a share, is equivalent to buying a put and borrowing. Example 10.3 represents a numerical illustration.

Example 10.3: Andrew has short sold 100 shares of IBM at a price of $100. Quite obviously he is expecting the shares to decline in value. However, there is always a possibility that the stock may rise in value, and lead to a loss when Andrew eventually covers his short position. One way to cap the loss is to invest in call options.

Assume that call options with an exercise price of $100 and three months to expiration are available at a premium of $8, and that Andrew buys one contract. If the share price after three months is $120, it would cost Andrew $10,000 to acquire 100 shares and cover his position. After factoring in the cost of the options, his total cost will be $10,800, which amounts to $108 per share. The loss from the strategy is

$$10{,}000 - 10{,}800 = \$(800)$$

If the calls had not been acquired the loss would have been

$$(100 - 120) \times 100 = \$(2{,}000)$$

10.3.3 The Protective Put

The strategy entails buying the stock and then buying a put option on it, to gain downside protection. $\pi = S_T - S_t - P_t + \text{Max}[0, X - S_T]$. If $S_T \geq X, \pi = S_T - S_t - P_t$, while if S_T is $< X$, $\pi = X - S_t - P_t$. The maximum profit is unlimited. The maximum loss π_{max} is $X - S_t - P_t$. The break even price = $S_t + P_t$.

The profit diagram may be depicted as shown in Figure 10.4.

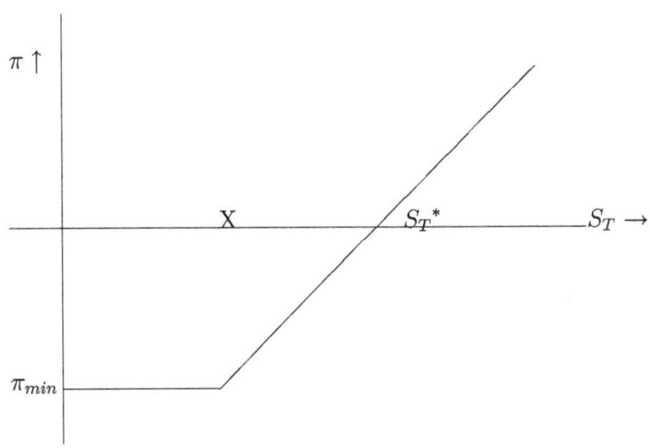

Figure 10.4: Profit Profile for a Protective Put.

For obvious reasons, the profit diagram resembles that of a long call.

In this case the put acts like an insurance policy. By buying the option with an exercise price of X, the investor ensures that he will not have to sell the stock at a lower price. The higher the exercise price, the greater will be the floor for the stock price. However, the higher the exercise price, the greater will be the option premium, and consequently the higher will be the break even point. Thus, an in the money put offers greater downside protection, but requires a larger increase in the stock price for the strategy to turn profitable. Example 10.4 provides a numerical illustration.

Example 10.4: Larry King owns 100 shares of IBM that are currently trading at \$100. Put options with six months to expiration are available. An option with an exercise price of \$90 is available at a premium of \$2.65, while an option with an exercise price of \$110 is available for \$11.16.

If Larry acquires a contract with X = \$90, his maximum loss will be

$$90 - 100 - 2.65 = \$\,(12.65)$$

and the break even stock price will be \$102.65. On the contrary if Larry were to acquire a contract with X = \$110, his maximum loss will be

$$110 - 100 - 11.16 = \$\,(1.16)$$

However the break even in this case will be \$111.16.

Thus the greater downside protection comes with a cost. And the cost is that the investor will have to give up more of the upside gains, if the stock were to go up in value.

10.4 Writing a Naked Call

This strategy requires the investor to sell call options without taking a position in the underlying stock. Consider a call with an exercise price of X and a premium of C_t. If the stock price at expiration, $S_T \le X$, the call will expire worthless and the profit for the call writer will be the premium received at the outset. So if $0 \le S_T \le X, \pi = C_t$. As the terminal stock price rises above X, for every dollar increase in the stock price, the profit will decline by a dollar. Therefore, for the price range $S_T > X, \pi = -(S_T - X) + C_t$. The break even price is, S_T^* equal to $X + C_t$. The maximum profit is the premium received at the outset. The maximum loss is unbounded.

The profit diagram may be depicted as shown in Figure 10.5. Example 10.5 provides a numerical illustration.

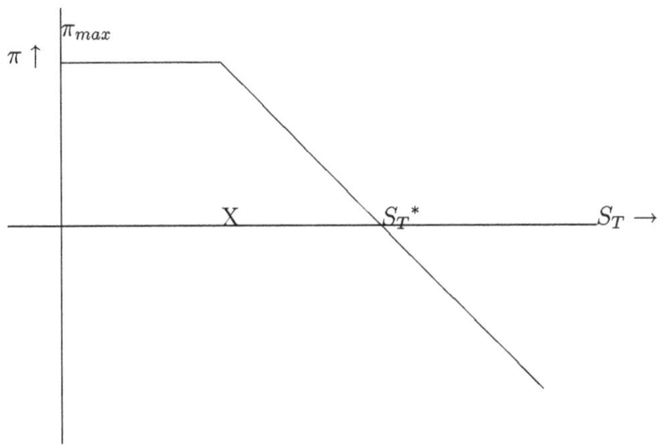

Figure 10.5: Profit Profile for a Short Call.

Example 10.5: Consider a stock which is currently trading at $100. The riskless rate of interest is 10% per annum, and the volatility is 30% per annum. The premium for a call option with an exercise price of $100, and three months to expiration, is $7.22.

If the stock price at expiration is less than the exercise price of $100, the option will expire out of the money, and the profit for the writer is the premium received at the outset which is $7.22 \times 100 = \$722$ per contract. This represents the maximum profit for the writer. As the stock price rises above $100, for every dollar increase in the price, the profit declines by one dollar. The break even stock price is $X + C_t = 100 + 7.22 = \$107.22$. The maximum loss is unlimited. The payoff and profit for various values of the terminal stock price are depicted in Table 10.3.

Table 10.3: Payoff and Profit from Short Call Position.

Terminal Stock Price	Payoff	Profit
0	0	722
25	0	722
50	0	722
75	0	722
100	0	722
107.22	(722)	0
125	(2,500)	(1,778)
150	(5,000)	(4,278)
175	(7,500)	(6,778)
200	(10,000)	(9,278)

10.4.1 In the Money versus Out of the Money Calls

Consider the following data for call options with various exercise prices. The current stock price is \$100. The prices of options with varying exercise prices is shown in Table 10.4.

Table 10.4: Call Options with Varying Exercise Prices.

Exercise Price	Premium	Break even Price
\$90	\$17.03	\$107.03
\$100	\$10.91	\$110.91
\$110	\$6.52	\$116.52

The at the money call yields the maximum profit if the terminal stock price, S_T is equal to \$100. The option also yields a positive profit in the range, $100 \leq S_T \leq 110.91$, since the break even price is \$110.91. The out of the money option has the lowest premium, which is \$6.52 in this case. The profit for the call writer is less, but he gets greater protection against a rising stock price, since the terminal stock price must exceed \$110 in order for exercise to be a worthwhile proposition for the buyer. The in the money option has the highest premium. If the stock price remains at \$100, the profit from the position is

$$-(100 - 90) + 17.03 = \$7.03$$

In order for the writer to realize the maximum profit from this option, the stock price must decline from its current level of \$100 to \$90 or below. Thus, the sale of an in the money option represents a more bearish strategy than the sale of an at the money or out of the money option.

10.5 Writing a Put

Consider a put option with an exercise price of X, and a premium of P_t. If the stock price at expiration, $S_T \geq X$, the option will expire worthless, and the profit for the writer will be P_t. So in the price range, $S_T \geq X, \pi_{max} = P_t$. As the terminal stock price declines below X, the writer's profit will decline dollar for dollar. Thus, for the price range, $0 \leq S_T \leq X, \pi = -(X - S_T) + P_t$. The break even price S_T^* is equal to $X - P_t$. The maximum profit is obviously the premium that is received at the outset. The magnitude of the maximum loss is $X - P_t$, because the stock price has a lower bound of zero.

The profit diagram may be depicted as shown in Figure 10.6. Example 10.6 provides a numerical illustration.

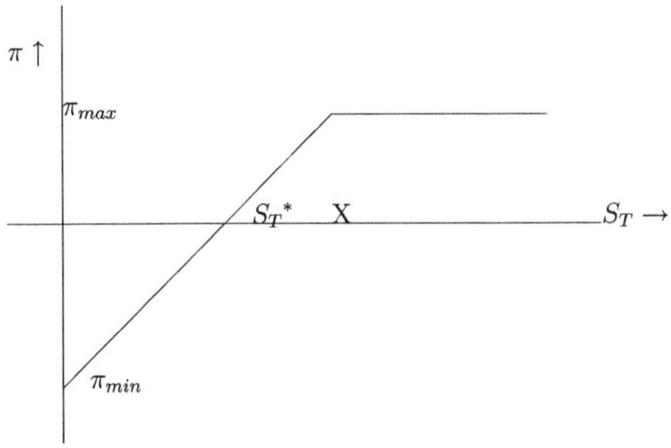

Figure 10.6: Profit Profile for a Short Put.

Example 10.6: Consider a stock which is currently trading at \$100. The riskless rate of interest is 10% per annum, and the volatility is 30% per annum. The premium for a put option with an exercise price of \$100, and three months to expiration, is \$4.75.

If the stock price at expiration is greater than the exercise price of \$100, the option will expire out of the money, and the profit for the writer is the premium received at the outset which is 4.75 × 100 = \$475 per contract. This represents the maximum profit for the writer. As the stock price declines below \$100, for every dollar decrease in the price, the profit declines by one dollar. The break even stock price is $X - P_t = 100 - 4.75 =$ \$95.25. The maximum loss is \$95.25, which will arise if the stock price were to attain a value of zero. The payoff and profit for various terminal values of the stock price are depicted in Table 10.5.

Table 10.5: Payoff and Profit from Short Put Position.

Terminal Stock Price	Payoff	Profit
0	(10,000)	(9,525)
25	(7,500)	(7,025)
50	(5,000)	(4,525)
75	(2,500)	(2,025)
95.25	(475)	0
100	0	475
125	0	475
150	0	475
175	0	475
200	0	475

10.5.1 Short Put Combined With Short Stock

This strategy entails the sale of a put option for every share that is sold short. The profit from the short stock is $S_t - S_T$, while that from the put is $P_t - \text{Max}[0, X - S_T]$. Thus the total profit from the strategy is

$$\pi = P_t - \text{Max}[0, X - S_T] + S_t - S_T \tag{10.1}$$

$$\text{If } S_T \leq X, \pi = S_t + P_t - X, \text{ whereas if } S_T > X, \pi = P_t + S_t - S_T$$

The maximum loss is unlimited because the stock has no upper bound. The break even price is, S_T^*, is $P_t + S_t$. The maximum profit is equal to $S_t + P_t - X$.

The profit diagram may be depicted as shown in Figure 10.7. Example 10.7 provides a numerical illustration.

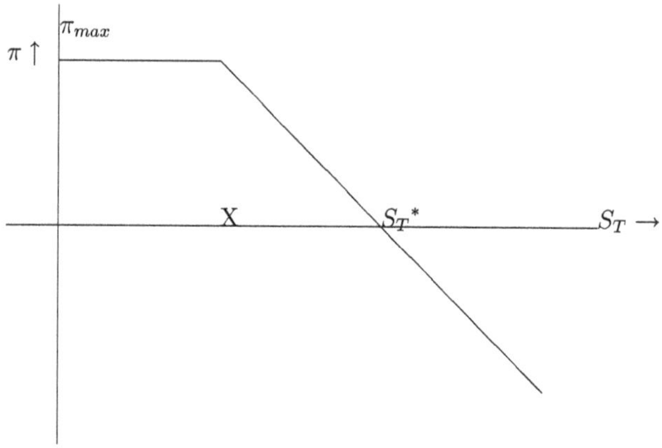

Figure 10.7: Profit Profile for a Short Put Combined with a Short Stock.

Example 10.7: Bob Harris has sold short 100 shares of IBM at a price of \$100. Put options with three months to expiration, and an exercise price of \$100 are available at a premium of \$10.16 per share. Let's consider the terminal profit from the investment if Bob writes one put contract.

If the terminal stock price exceeds \$100, the puts will not be exercised. Bob's profit from the short stock position will be $(100 - S_T) \times 100$. After factoring in the premium for the options, the overall profit will be

$$\pi = (100 - S_T) \times 100 + 10.16 \times 100$$

The break even stock price is 100 + 10.16 = \$110.16. The maximum loss is unbounded. If the terminal stock price, S_T, is less than \$100, the puts will be exercised. The profit from the strategy will be

$$\pi = (10.16 + 100 - 100) \times 100 = \$1{,}016$$

This represents the maximum profit.

10.6 Writing a Covered Call

This strategy entails the sale of a call option for every share that is owned by the investor. There are two possibilities. The calls can be sold at the time of acquisition of the shares. Or else, the purchase of the shares can precede the sale of the options. The first strategy is called 'Buy-writing', while the second is termed as 'Over-writing'.

The profit from the long stock is $S_T - S_t$, while that from the call is $C_t - \text{Max}[0, S_T - X]$. Thus the total profit from the strategy is

$$S_T - S_t + C_t - \text{Max}[0, S_T - X] \tag{10.2}$$

$$\text{If } S_T \geq X, \pi = X - S_t + C_t, \text{ whereas if } S_T < X, \pi = S_T - S_t + C_t$$

As the terminal stock price goes below X, the profit declines dollar for dollar. The maximum loss occurs when the terminal stock price is zero, and is equal to $C_t - S_t$. The break even price is $S_t - C_t$. The maximum profit is equal to $X - S_t + C_t$.

The profit diagram may be depicted as shown in Figure 10.8. See Example 10.8 for a numerical illustration.

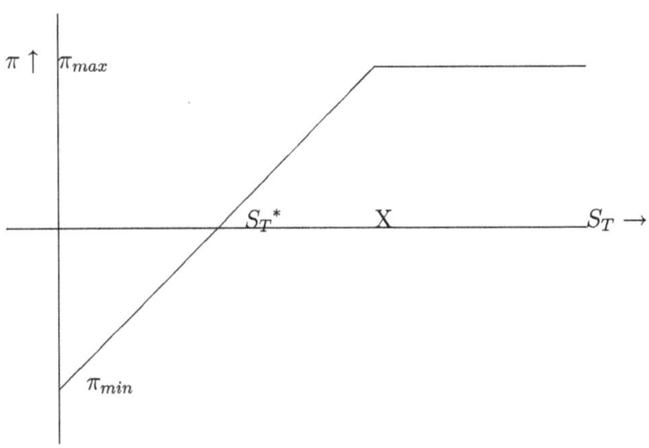

Figure 10.8: Profit Profile for a Covered Call.

Notice that the profit diagram looks like the one for a put writer.

Example 10.8: Maureen Smith owns 100 shares of IBM which she acquired at a price of \$100. She has simultaneously sold a call options contract with an exercise price of \$100, and three months to expiration, for a premium of \$7.22 per share. The profit from the stock position is $S_T - 100$, while that from the call is

$7.22 - \text{Max}[0, S_T - 100]$. If the terminal stock price is below \$100, the counterparty will not exercise the calls. The profit for Maureen in this scenario will therefore be

$$\pi = (S_T - 100) \times 100 + 7.22 \times 100$$

The range for the profit on a per share basis is

$$-92.78 \leq \pi \leq 7.22$$

If S_T were to be greater than \$100, the share will be called away, and the profit for Maureen will be capped at \$7.22 per share. If Maureen had not sold the calls, the profit would have been $S_T - 100$. If the stock price were to exceed \$107.22 or $X + C_t$, she will regret the fact that she had sold the calls. Thus $X + C_t$ is called the 'point of regret'.

Consider the maximum profit for the strategy which is $X - S_t + C_t$. However high the stock price may rise, this represents the maximum profit from the strategy. Thus, in exchange for the option premium, the call writer accepts an upper limit on the profit. The option premium however serves to reduce the magnitude of the loss if the stock price were to decline, as compared to a stand alone long stock position.

The profit from the position for various values of the terminal stock price is depicted in Table 10.6.

Table 10.6: Profit from the Covered Call for Various Values of the Terminal Stock Price.

Stock Price	Payoff From Call	Profit/Loss From Call	Profit/Loss From Stock	Total Profit/Loss
80	0	722	(2,000)	(1,278)
85	0	722	(1,500)	(778)
90	0	722	(1,000)	(278)
95	0	722	(500)	222
100	0	722	0	722
101	(100)	622	100	722
105	(500)	222	500	722
107.22	(722)	0	722	722
110	(1,000)	(278)	1,000	722
115	(1,500)	(778)	1,500	722
120	(2,000)	(1,278)	2,000	722

As can be seen, below a stock price of \$100, the loss from the stock is reduced by \$722 due to the receipt of the premium from the call. As the call goes into the money, the stock is called away and the total profit is \$722, which is the premium received from the call. The point of regret is \$107.22. Beyond this stock price the investor will regret the fact that he wrote the call, since he will be unable to realize the profit from the stock.

10.6.1 In the money, At the Money, and Out of the Money

Assume that the initial stock price is $100. Consider three call options with three months to expiration, and exercise prices of $90, $100, and $110 respectively. The corresponding premia are $13.71, $7.22, and $3.22. This is shown in Table 10.7. Let's consider covered call strategies with each of these contracts.

Table 10.7: Option Premia for Varying Degrees of Moneyness.

Exercise Price	Maximum Profit
$90	$3.71
$100	$7.22
$110	$13.22

An at the money option would be favoured by a neutral investor, because the maximum return is obtained if the stock price were to remain at its initial level. A strategy with an out of the money option, is bullish by design, because the maximum profit is realized if the stock price rises above its current level to reach a value equal to the exercise price.

In the above illustration, the stock price must rise from a current level of $100 to reach the exercise price of $110, in order for the investor to obtain the maximum profit. The total profit for 100 shares is $1,322, if the stock price rises to $110. Out of this $1,000 arises from the stock component, and $322 from the option component. While the maximum profit from the out of the money call is the greatest, there is a trade off if the stock price were to decline. This is because, the out of the money call has the smallest premium, and consequently provides the least protection if the share were to fall in value. In our illustration, the at the money call provides a protection of $7.22 per share in a declining market, whereas the out of the money call gives a protection of only $3.22 per share.

10.7 Spreads

A spread is a strategy that involves taking a position in two or more options of the same type. That is all the options must be calls, or all of them should be puts.

10.7.1 Vertical Spreads

To create a vertical spread the investor must buy an option with one exercise price, and sell another with a different exercise price. Both the options must have the same time to expiration. Vertical spreads are also known as *Strike* or *Money* or *Price* spreads.

10.7.2 Horizontal Spreads

To create this kind of a spread, the investor must buy an option with a given exercise price and expiration month, and sell another option with the same exercise price, but with a different expiration month. Horizontal spreads are also known as *Time* or *Calendar* spreads.

10.7.3 Diagonal Spreads

These are strategies where you buy an option with a given exercise price and time to maturity, and sell another option with a different exercise price and time to maturity.

We will focus only on vertical spreads.

10.8 Bull Spreads

10.8.1 With Calls

To create a bull spread with calls, the investor has to buy a call option with an exercise price = X_1, and sell a call on the same asset with an exercise price = X_2, where $X_1 < X_2$. Let $C_{t,1}$ be the premium for the first option, and $C_{t,2}$, the premium for the second. Since $X_1 < X_2$, $C_{t,1}$ must be > $C_{t,2}$.

The initial cash flow = $-C_{t,1} + C_{t,2}$ which is < 0. Thus a bull spread with calls involves a net investment.

Let's consider the payoff from a bull spread at expiration, as shown in Table 10.8.

Table 10.8: Payoffs from a Bull Spread With Calls.

Terminal Price Range	Payoff From Long Call	Payoff From Short Call	Total Payoff
$S_T < X_1$	0	0	0
$X_1 < S_T < X_2$	$S_T - X_1$	0	$S_T - X_1$
$S_T > X_2$	$S_T - X_1$	$-(S_T - X_2)$	$X_2 - X_1$

To calculate the profit in each scenario, we must subtract the initial investment from the payoff. The maximum payoff is obviously $X_2 - X_1$. The minimum payoff = 0. Thus, the maximum profit is $X_2 - X_1 - C_{t,1} + C_{t,2}$, and the maximum loss is $-C_{t,1} + C_{t,2}$. A bull spread, therefore, limits the upside potential while putting a limit on the downside risk. The break even stock price is given by,

$$\pi = S_T^* - X_1 - C_{t,1} + C_{t,2} = 0$$
$$\Rightarrow S_T^* = X_1 + C_{t,1} - C_{t,2} \tag{10.3}$$

The profit diagram is depicted in Figure 10.9. See Example 10.9 for a numerical illustration.

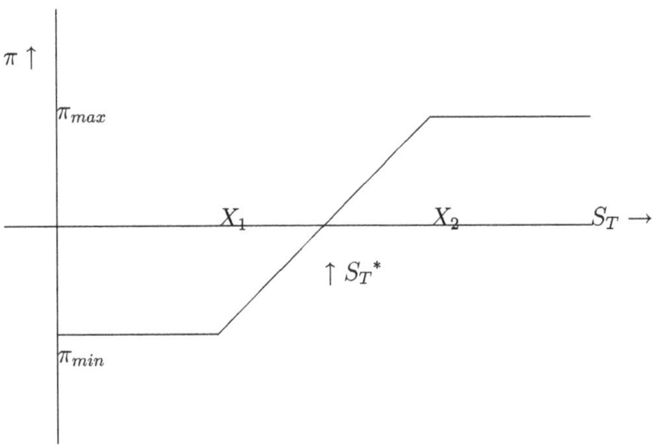

Figure 10.9: Profit Profile for a Bull Spread.

Example 10.9: Amy Hepburn has bought a call option with an exercise price of \$90 at a premium of \$13.71, and sold a call option with the same maturity, but with a higher exercise price of \$110, for a premium of \$3.22. The position obviously represents a bull spread. The initial investment is \$13.71 – \$3.22 = \$10.49. This is also the maximum loss from the strategy. The break even point is given by

$$S_T^* - 90 - 10.49 = 0 \Rightarrow S_T^* = 100.49$$

The maximum payoff from the spread is the difference between the two exercise prices, which is \$20 in this case. The maximum profit is \$20 – \$10.49 = \$9.51. The maximum profit is obtained for all values of the terminal stock price equal to or greater than \$110. The profit and payoff for various terminal stock price values is shown in Table 10.9.

Table 10.9: Profit from the Bull Spread for Various Values of the Terminal Stock Price.

Stock Price	Payoff From Long Call	Payoff From Short Call	Payoff From The Spread	Total Profit/Loss
80	0	0	0	(1,049)
85	0	0	0	(1,049)
90	0	0	0	(1,049)
95	500	0	500	(549)
100	1,000	0	1,000	(49)
100.49	1,049	0	1,049	0
105	1,500	0	1,500	451
110	2,000	0	2,000	951
115	2,500	(500)	2,000	951
120	3,000	(1,000)	2,000	951

The maximum loss is $1,049 which is the net premium paid for the spread. $100.49 is the break even point. The maximum profit from the spread is $951, which is equal to the difference between the two exercise prices, less the net premium paid. That is $ 951 = 100 × (110 − 90 − 10.49).

Bull Spread or Long Call

A long call position limits the investor's loss to the premium that is paid at the outset, without imposing an upper bound on the profit from the strategy. The question naturally arises as to what makes an investor like Amy prefer a bull spread to a long call, considering that the spread can yield only a limited profit.

Let's take Amy's example. If she had bought a call option with X = $90, she would have made an investment of $13.71 per share. The bull spread however limits her investment to $10.49 per share, because there is an inflow from the option that is sold. An investor like Amy may be bullish, but may not consider the additional investment to be warranted, considering her expectations from the stock.

10.8.2 With Puts

To create a bull spread with puts, the investor has to buy a put option with an exercise price equal to X_1, and sell a put on the same asset with an exercise price equal to X_2, where $X_1 < X_2$. Let $P_{t,1}$ be the premium for the first option, and $P_{t,2}$ the premium for the second. Since $X_1 < X_2$, $P_{t,1}$ must be less than $P_{t,2}$.

The initial cash flow = $-P_{t,1} + P_{t,2}$ which is greater than zero. Thus a bull spread with puts leads to an inflow at inception.

Let's analyze the payoff from the spread at expiration, depicted in Table 10.10.

Table 10.10: Payoffs from a Bull Spread with Puts.

Terminal Price Range	Payoff From Long Put	Payoff From Short Put	Total Payoff
$S_T < X_1$	$X_1 - S_T$	$-(X_2 - S_T)$	$X_1 - X_2$
$X_1 < S_T < X_2$	0	$-(X_2 - S_T)$	$S_T - X_2$
$S_T > X_2$	0	0	0

To calculate the profit in each scenario, we must add the initial inflow to the payoff. The minimum payoff is obviously $X_1 - X_2$. The maximum payoff is zero. Thus the maximum loss is $X_1 - X_2 - P_{t,1} + P_{t,2}$, and the maximum profit is $-P_{t,1} + P_{t,2}$. As is to be expected, the upside potential is limited, as is the downside risk. The break even stock price is given by

$$S_T^* - X_2 - P_{t,1} + P_{t,2} = 0$$
$$\Rightarrow S_T^* = X_2 + P_{t,1} - P_{t,2} \tag{10.4}$$

Example 10.10 provides a numerical illustration.

Example 10.10: Stacey Smith has bought a put option with an exercise price of \$90 at a premium of \$1.49, and sold a put option with the same maturity, but with a higher exercise price of \$110, for a premium of \$10.51. The initial inflow is \$10.51 − \$1.49 = \$9.02. This represents the maximum profit from the strategy. The break even point is given by

$$S_T^* - 110 - 1.49 + 10.51 = 0 \Rightarrow S_T^* = \$100.98$$

The minimum payoff from the strategy is 90−110 = −\$ 20. The maximum loss is therefore −20+9.02 = −\$ 10.98.

10.9 Bear Spreads

10.9.1 With Calls

To create a bear spread with calls, the investor has to sell a call option with an exercise price of X_1, and buy a call on the same asset with an exercise price of X_2, where $X_1 < X_2$. Let the respective prices of the options be $C_{t,1}$ and $C_{t,2}$. We know that $C_{t,1} > C_{t,2}$.

The initial cash flow = $-C_{t,2} + C_{t,1}$, which is > 0. Thus a bear spread with calls leads to an inflow at inception.

Let's consider the payoff from the spread at expiration, as shown in Table 10.11.

Table 10.11: Payoffs from a Bear Spread with Calls.

Terminal Price Range	Payoff From Long Call	Payoff From Short Call	Total Payoff
$S_T < X_1$	0	0	0
$X_1 < S_T < X_2$	0	$-(S_T - X_1)$	$X_1 - S_T$
$S_T > X_2$	$S_T - X_2$	$-(S_T - X_1)$	$X_1 - X_2$

The maximum payoff is obviously zero. The minimum payoff is $X_1 - X_2$. Thus, the maximum profit is $C_{t,1} - C_{t,2}$, while the maximum loss is $X_1 - X_2 + C_{t,1} - C_{t,2}$. Thus, just like the bull spread, the bear spread limits the upside potential while putting a limit on the downside risk. The break even stock price is given by

$$\pi = X_1 - S_T^* + C_{t,1} - C_{t,2} = 0 \Rightarrow S_T^* = X_1 + C_{t,1} - C_{t,2} \tag{10.5}$$

The profit diagram is depicted in Figure 10.10. See Example 10.11 for a numerical illustration.

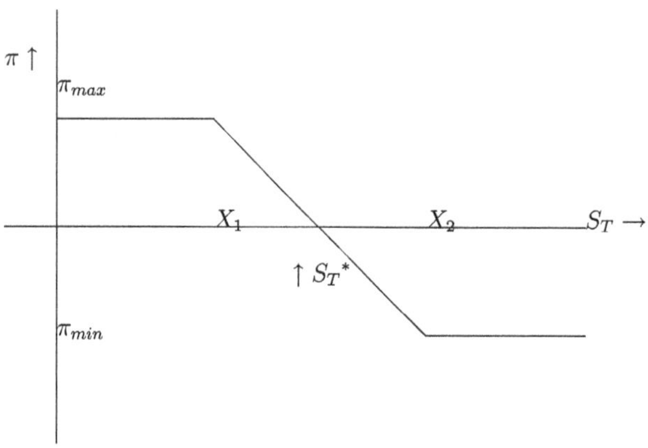

Figure 10.10: Profit Profile for a Bear Spread.

Example 10.11: Kevin Long has sold a call option with an exercise price of \$90 at a premium of \$13.71, and bought a call with the same maturity, but with an exercise price of \$110, for a premium of \$3.22. The initial cash inflow is \$ 13.71 – \$3.22 = \$10.49. This is also the maximum profit from the strategy. The break even point is given by

$$90 - S_T^* + 10.49 = 0 \Rightarrow S_T^* = \$100.49$$

The minimum payoff from the strategy is the difference between the two exercise prices which is –\$ 20 in this case. The maximum loss is therefore \$ 10.49 – \$20 = –\$ 9.51. The maximum loss occurs for all values of the stock price equal to greater than \$110. Table 10.12 shows the payoff and profit for various values of the terminal stock price.

Table 10.12: Profit from the Bear Spread for Various Values of the Terminal Stock Price.

Stock Price	Payoff From Long Call	Payoff From Short Call	Payoff From The Spread	Total Profit/Loss
80	0	0	0	1,049
85	0	0	0	1,049
90	0	0	0	1,049
95	0	(500)	(500)	549
100	0	(1,000)	(1,000)	49
100.49	0	(1,049)	(1,049)	0
105	0	(1,500)	(1,500)	(451)
110	0	(2,000)	(2,000)	(951)
115	500	(2,500)	(2,000)	(951)
120	1,000	(3,000)	(2,000)	(951)

10.9.2 With Puts

To create a bear spread with puts, the investor has to sell a put option with an exercise price of X_1 and buy a put on the same asset with an exercise price of X_2, where $X_1 < X_2$. Let $P_{t,1}$ be the price of the first option, and $P_{t,2}$ the price of the second. Since $X_1 < X_2, P_{t,1} < P_{t,2}$. The initial cash flow = $-P_{t,2} + P_{t,1}$, which is less than zero. Thus the strategy entails a cash outflow at inception.

Let's analyze the payoff from the spread at expiration, as shown in Table 10.13. See Example 10.12 for a numerical illustration.

Table 10.13: Payoffs from a Bear Spread with Puts.

Terminal Price Range	Payoff From Long Put	Payoff From Short Put	Total Payoff
$S_T < X_1$	$X_2 - S_T$	$-(X_1 - S_T)$	$X_2 - X_1$
$X_1 < S_T < X_2$	$(X_2 - S_T)$	0	$X_2 - S_T$
$S_T > X_2$	0	0	0

The minimum payoff is obviously zero, while the maximum payoff is $X_2 - X_1$. Thus the maximum loss is $P_{t,1} - P_{t,2}$, while the maximum profit is $X_2 - X_1 + P_{t,1} - P_{t,2}$. The break even stock price is given by

$$X_2 - S_T^* - P_{t,2} + P_{t,1} = 0$$
$$\Rightarrow S_T^* = X_2 - P_{t,2} + P_{t,1} \quad (10.6)$$

Example 10.12: Shirlene Kennedy has sold a put option with an exercise price of \$90 at a premium of \$1.49, and bought a put option with an exercise price of \$110, for a premium of \$10.51. The initial investment is \$ 10.51 − \$1.49 = \$9.02. This also represents the maximum loss from this strategy. The break even point is given by

$$110 - S_T^* - 9.02 = 0 \Rightarrow S_T^* = \$100.98$$

The maximum payoff from the strategy is \$20. Consequently the maximum profit is 20 − 9.02 = \$10.98.

10.10 The Convexity Property

Before we go on to analyze the next strategy, we need to establish an important result that must be satisfied by both call and put options.

Consider three exercise prices $X_1, X_2,$ and X_3 such that $X_1 < X_2 < X_3$. Let $X_2 = wX_1 + (1-w)X_3$. That is, X_2 is a weighted average of the other two exercise prices. If $C_{t,1}, C_{t,2},$ and $C_{t,3}$ represent the prices of the corresponding calls, we can show that

$$C_{t,2} \leq wC_{t,1} + (1-w)C_{t,3} \quad (10.7)$$

A similar condition must hold for put options.

10.11 Butterfly Spread

10.11.1 With Calls

This strategy requires the investor to take a position in four options, with three different exercise prices. A long butterfly spread with calls requires the investor to buy an in the money as well as an out of the money call, and sell two calls which are at the money. Let's denote the exercise prices by $X_1, X_2,$ and X_3, where $X_1 < X_2 < X_3$. The exercise prices are usually chosen such that $X_2 = \frac{(X_1+X_3)}{2}$. If we denote the corresponding option prices by $C_{t,1}, C_{t,2},$ and $C_{t,3}$, then from the convexity property

$$C_{t,2} < \frac{(C_{t,1} + C_{t,3})}{2} \Rightarrow 2C_{t,2} < C_{t,1} + C_{t,3}$$

Thus a long butterfly entails a net investment equal to $C_{t,1} + C_{t,3} - 2C_{t,2}$.

Let's consider the payoffs from the strategy at expiration, as shown in Table 10.14.

Table 10.14: Payoffs from a Long Butterfly Spread.

Terminal Price Range	**Payoff From Call With $X = X_1$**	**Payoff From Call With $X = X_3$**	**Payoff From Calls With $X = X_2$**	**Total Payoff**
$S_T < X_1$	0	0	0	0
$X_1 < S_T < X_2$	$S_T - X_1$	0	0	$S_T - X_1$
$X_2 < S_T < X_3$	$S_T - X_1$	0	$-2(S_T - X_2)$	$X_3 - S_T$
$S_T > X_3$	$S_T - X_1$	$S_T - X_3$	$-2(S_T - X_2)$	0

The minimum payoff is zero, which is realized if the terminal stock price is either below the lowest of the three exercise prices, or above the highest. In these scenarios the profit is equal to the initial investment, that is

$$\pi_{min} = 2C_{t,2} - C_{t,1} - C_{t,3} \tag{10.8}$$

This amount represents the maximum loss from the strategy.

$$\text{If } X_1 < S_T < X_2, \pi = S_T - X_1 + 2C_{t,2} - C_{t,1} - C_{t,3}$$
$$\text{If } X_2 < S_T < X_3, \pi = X_3 - S_T + 2C_{t,2} - C_{t,1} - C_{t,3}$$

The maximum profit is realized when $S_T = X_2$, and is equal to

$$X_2 - X_1 + 2C_{t,2} - C_{t,1} - C_{t,3} \text{ or } X_3 - X_2 + 2C_{t,2} - C_{t,1} - C_{t,3}$$

There are two break even prices $S_T{}^*$ and $S_T{}^{**}$

$$S_T{}^* = X_1 - 2C_{t,2} + C_{t,1} + C_{t,3} \tag{10.9}$$
$$S_T{}^{**} = X_3 + 2C_{t,2} - C_{t,1} - C_{t,3} \tag{10.10}$$

The profit diagram is depicted in Figure 10.11. See Example 10.13 for a numerical illustration.

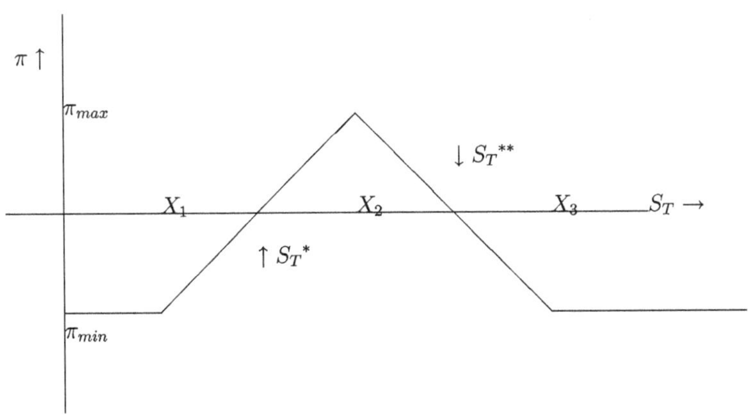

Figure 10.11: Profit Profile for a Butterfly Spread.

Example 10.13: Caroline Jones has decided to take a long position in a butterfly spread. She wants to sell two options on IBM with an exercise price of $100, and buy two options on the same stock with exercise prices of $90 and $110 respectively. All the options have three months to expiration. The premia of the options are listed in Table 10.15.

Table 10.15: Premia for Call Options with Varying Exercise Prices.

Exercise Price	Call Premium
$90	$13.71
$100	$7.22
$110	$3.20

The initial investment is 13.71+3.20−2×7.22 = $2.47. This is also the maximum possible loss from the strategy. The maximum profit is obtained at a terminal stock price of $100, and is given by

$$100 - 90 + 2 \times 7.22 - 13.71 - 3.2 = \$7.53$$

There are two break even prices:

$$S_T^{*} = 90 + 2.47 = \$92.47 \text{ and } S_T^{**} = 110 - 2.47 = \$107.53$$

The payoff and profit for various values of the terminal stock price is shown in Table 10.16.

Table 10.16: Profit from the Butterfly Spread for Various Values of the Terminal Stock Price.

Stock Price	Payoff From Long Call with X = 90	Payoff From Long Call with X = 110	Payoff From Short Calls with X = 100	Total Profit/Loss
80	0	0	0	(247)
85	0	0	0	(247)
90	0	0	0	(247)
92.47	247	0	0	0
95	500	0	0	253
100	1,000	0	0	753
105	1,500	0	(1,000)	253
107.53	1,753	0	(1,506)	0
110	2,000	0	(2,000)	(247)
115	2,500	500	(3,000)	(247)
120	3,000	1,000	(4,000)	(247)

The maximum loss is equal to the net premium paid, which is 100 × 2.47 = $247. There are two break even prices, $92.47 and $107.53.

10.11.2 With Puts

A long butterfly spread can also be set up using put options. The investor should buy puts with exercise prices of X_1 and X_3, and sell two puts with an exercise price of X_2, where $X_1 < X_2 < X_3$ and $X_2 = \frac{(X_1+X_3)}{2}$. If we denote the corresponding option prices by $P_{t,1}, P_{t,2}$, and $P_{t,3}$, then from the convexity property

$$2P_{t,2} < P_{t,1} + P_{t,3}$$

Thus the strategy entails a net initial investment. The magnitude of this investment represents the maximum loss from the position, which arises if the terminal stock price is either below the lowest exercise price, or above the highest exercise price.

The maximum profit $= X_2 - X_1 + 2P_{t,2} - P_{t,1} - P_{t,3}$ or $X_3 - X_2 + 2P_{t,2} - P_{t,1} - P_{t,3}$. The break even stock prices are

$$\begin{aligned} S_T^* &= X_1 - 2P_{t,2} + P_{t,1} + P_{t,3} \text{ and} \\ S_T^{**} &= X_3 + 2P_{t,2} - P_{t,1} - P_{t,3} \end{aligned} \tag{10.11}$$

10.12 The Condor

This strategy also entails the assumption of positions in four options. Consider four options with exercise prices X_1, X_2, X_3, and X_4, such that $X_1 < X_2 < X_3 < X_4$. Let $X_2 = \frac{(X_1+X_3)}{2}$ and $X_3 = \frac{(X_2+X_4)}{2}$. To set up a long condor, the investor has to buy two call options with exercise prices of X_1 and X_4 respectively, and sell two call options with exercise prices of X_2 and X_3 respectively.

The initial cash flow is $C_{t,2} + C_{t,3} - C_{t,1} - C_{t,4}$. From the convexity property of options

$$\begin{aligned} &C_{t,2} < \frac{(C_{t,1} + C_{t,3})}{2} \text{ and} \\ &C_{t,3} < \frac{(C_{t,2} + C_{t,4})}{2} \\ &\Rightarrow 2C_{t,2} + 2C_{t,3} < C_{t,1} + C_{t,3} + C_{t,2} + C_{t,4} \\ &\Rightarrow C_{t,2} + C_{t,3} - C_{t,1} - C_{t,4} < 0 \end{aligned} \tag{10.12}$$

Thus the long condor requires a net initial investment. Let's consider the payoffs from the strategy at expiration, as shown in Table 10.17.

Table 10.17: Payoffs from a Long Condor.

Terminal Price Range	Payoff From Call With $X = X_1$	Payoff From Call With $X = X_4$	Payoff From Call With $X = X_2$	Pay off From Call With $X = X_3$	Total Payoff
$S_T < X_1$	0	0	0	0	0
$X_1 < S_T < X_2$	$S_T - X_1$	0	0	0	$S_T - X_1$
$X_2 < S_T < X_3$	$S_T - X_1$	0	$-(S_T - X_2)$	0	$X_2 - X_1$
$X_3 < S_T < X_4$	$S_T - X_1$	0	$-(S_T - X_2)$	$-(S_T - X_3)$	$X_4 - S_T$
$S_T > X_4$	$S_T - X_1$	$S_T - X_4$	$-(S_T - X_2)$	$-(S_T - X_3)$	0

The minimum payoff from the position is zero, which occurs if $S_T < X_1$ or if $S_T > X_4$. Consequently the maximum loss is equal to the initial investment, which is $C_{t,2} + C_{t,3} - C_{t,1} - C_{t,4}$. The maximum payoff is $X_2 - X_1$, and thus the maximum profit is

$$X_2 - X_1 + C_{t,2} + C_{t,3} - C_{t,1} - C_{t,4} \tag{10.13}$$

There are two break even points, given by

$$S_T^* = X_1 - C_{t,2} - C_{t,3} + C_{t,1} + C_{t,4} \text{ and} \tag{10.14}$$

$$S_T^{**} = X_4 + C_{t,2} + C_{t,3} - C_{t,1} - C_{t,4} \tag{10.15}$$

The profit diagram is depicted in Figure 10.12. See Example 10.14 for a numerical illustration.

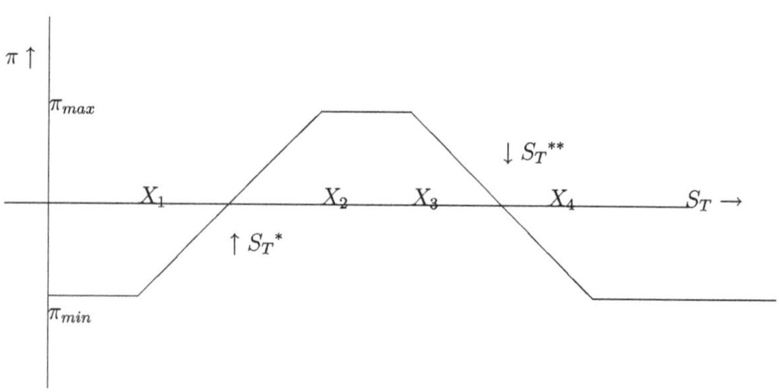

Figure 10.12: Profit Profile for a Condor.

Example 10.14: Andy Hunt has taken a long position in a condor by buying two call options on IBM with exercise prices of \$95 and \$110 respectively, and selling two call options with exercise prices of \$100 and \$105 respectively. All the options have three months to expiration. The premia of the options are listed in Table 10.18.

Table 10.18: Premia for Call Options with Varying Exercise Prices.

Exercise Price	Call Premium
\$95	\$10.16
\$100	\$7.22
\$105	\$4.92
\$110	\$3.20

The initial investment is 10.16 + 3.20 − 7.22 − 4.92 = \$1.22. This is also the maximum possible loss from the strategy. The maximum profit is obtained in the price range $100 \le S_T \le 105$, and is equal to 105 − 100 − 1.22 = \$3.78. There are two break even prices:

$$S_T^* = 95 + 1.22 = \$96.22 \text{ and } S_T^{**} = 110 - 1.22 = \$108.78$$

10.12.1 With Puts

A long condor can also be set up using put options. Consider four options with exercise prices such X_1, X_2, X_3, and X_4, such that $X_1 < X_2 < X_3 < X_4$. Let $X_2 = \frac{(X_1 + X_3)}{2}$ and $X_3 = \frac{(X_2 + X_4)}{2}$. To set up a long condor, the investor has to buy two put options with exercise prices of X_1 and X_4 respectively, and sell two put options with exercise prices of X_2 and X_3 respectively.

10.13 Combinations

Combinations are strategies that involve taking positions in both calls and puts on the same stock.

10.13.1 The Straddle

A long straddle requires the investor to buy a call as well as a put option on a stock, with the same exercise price and expiration date. The position will yield a profit if the stock goes up or down substantially. The long call will pay off if the stock goes up in value, while the long put will pay off if the stock declines in value. The position is suitable for an investor who is anticipating a large price move, but is unsure about its direction.

The initial investment, which is the sum of the premia, is $C_t + P_t$.

Let's consider the payoff table, shown in Table 10.19.

Table 10.19: Payoffs from a Long Straddle.

Terminal Price Range	Payoff From Call	Payoff From Put	Total Payoff
$S_T < X$	0	$X - S_T$	$X - S_T$
$S_T > X$	$S_T - X$	0	$S_T - X$

If $S_T > X, \pi = S_T - X - P_t - C_t$. Thus the maximum profit is unlimited in this region. If $S_T < X, \pi = X - S_T - P_t - C_t$. The maximum profit in this region is $X - P_t - C_t$, which arises if the stock price declines to zero. Above X, the profit increases dollar for dollar with the stock price. Below X, as S_T goes from X to zero, the profit increases dollar for dollar. The maximum loss occurs at $S_T = X$, and is equal to $-(P_t + C_t)$. There are two break even points:

$$X - S_T^* - P_t - C_t = 0$$

$$\Rightarrow S_T^* = X - P_t - C_t, \text{ and} \tag{10.16}$$

$$S_T^{**} - X - P_t - C_t = 0$$

$$\Rightarrow S_T^{**} = X + P_t + C_t \tag{10.17}$$

The profit diagram is depicted in Figure 10.13. See Example 10.15 for a numerical illustration.

Example 10.15: Mathew Henderson has bought a call option and a put option on IBM. Both options have an exercise price of \$100, and have three months to expiration. The premium for the call is \$7.22, while that for the put is \$4.75. Thus the initial investment is 7.22 + 4.75 = \$11.97. This amount represents the maximum potential loss from the strategy. If the stock price rises above the exercise price, the profit increases dollar for dollar. The profit for this price range is given by:

$$S_T - 100 - 11.97 = S_T - 111.97$$

The maximum profit is obviously unbounded.

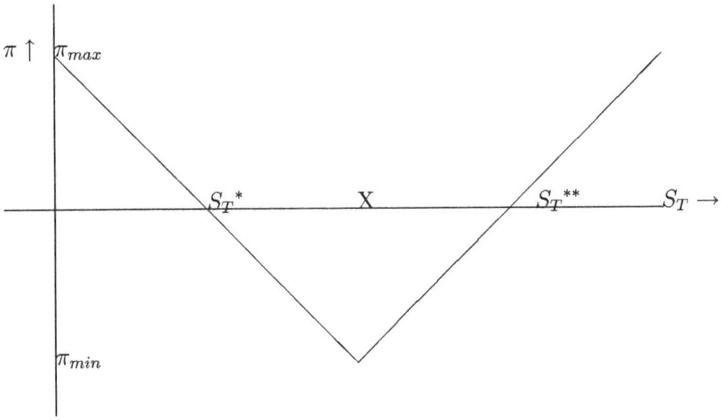

Figure 10.13: Profit Profile for a Straddle.

If the terminal stock price declines below the exercise price, the profit again increases dollar for dollar. The profit in this price range is given by:

$$100 - S_T - 11.97 = 88.03 - S_T.$$

The maximum profit is obviously \$88.03. There are two break even points, $S_T{}^* = \$111.97$, and $S_T{}^{**} = \$88.03$. The payoff and profit for various values of the terminal stock price are shown in Table 10.20.

Table 10.20: Profit from the Straddle for Various Values of the Terminal Stock Price.

Stock Price	Payoff From Long Call	Payoff From Long Put	Total Payoff	Total Profit/Loss
80	0	2,000	2,000	803
85	0	1,500	1,500	303
88.03	0	1,197	1,197	0
90	0	1,000	1,000	(197)
95	0	500	500	(697)
100	0	0	0	(1,197)
105	500	0	500	(697)
110	1,000	0	1,000	(197)
111.97	1,197	0	1,197	0
115	1,500	0	1,500	303
120	2,000	0	2,000	803

The maximum loss occurs at a stock price of \$100 and is equal to the premium paid for the two options, that is 100 × (7.22 + 4.75). There are two break even prices, \$88.03 and \$111.97.

10.14 The Strangle

This strategy, once again, requires the investor to buy a call and a put on the same stock. However, although the two options must have the same time to expiration, their exercise prices should be different. Let the call have an exercise price = X_1, and the put, an exercise price = X_2. There are two possibilities, $X_1 > X_2$, and $X_1 < X_2$. Consequently we have two types of strangles, called out-of-the money strangles and in-the-money strangles respectively. The initial cash flow, which is the sum of the premia, is given by $-(P_t + C_t)$.

10.14.1 An Out-of-the-money Strangle

Let's consider the payoff table for an out-of-the-money strangle, as shown in Table 10.21.

Table 10.21: Payoffs from an Out-of-the-money Long Strangle.

Terminal Price Range	Payoff From Call	Payoff From Put	Total Payoff
$S_T < X_2$	0	$X_2 - S_T$	$X_2 - S_T$
$X_2 < S_T < X_1$	0	0	0
$S_T > X_1$	$S_T - X_1$	0	$S_T - X_1$

If $S_T < X_2, \pi = X_2 - S_T - P_t - C_t$. The maximum profit in this region = $X_2 - P_t - C_t$. If $X_2 < S_T < X_1, \pi = -(P_t + C_t)$. If $S_T > X_1, \pi = S_T - X_1 - P_t - C_t$. The maximum profit in this region is unbounded. The maximum loss is $(P_t + C_t)$, which occurs in the region $X_2 < S_T < X_1$. There are two break even prices:

$$X_2 - S_T^* - P_t - C_t = 0$$

$$\Rightarrow S_T^* = X_2 - P_t - C_t \tag{10.18}$$

$$S_T^{**} - X_1 - P_t - C_t = 0$$

$$\Rightarrow S_T^{**} = X_1 + P_t + C_t \tag{10.19}$$

The profit diagram is depicted in Figure 10.14. See Example 10.16 for a numerical illustration.

Example 10.16: Ruth Kelly has bought a put option on IBM with an exercise price of \$95, and a call option on the same stock with an exercise price of \$105. The stock is currently priced at \$100, and both options have three months to expiration. The put premium is \$2.81 and the call premium is \$4.92. The initial investment is 2.81 + 4.92 = \$7.73, which is also the maximum potential loss. The position leads to a loss equal in magnitude to this amount, if the stock price at expiration is between \$95 and \$105. As the stock price declines below \$95,

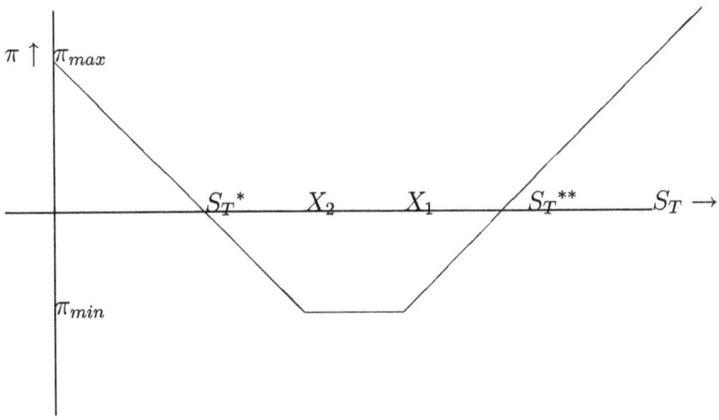

Figure 10.14: Profit Profile for a Strangle.

the profit increases dollar for dollar. The profit in this price range is given by $95 - S_T - 7.73 = \$87.27 - S_T$. The maximum profit in this price range is $87.27 which corresponds to a stock price of zero. The break even stock price is $87.27.

As the stock price increases above $105, the profit once again increases dollar for dollar. The profit in this price range is given by $S_T - 105 - 7.73 = S_T - 112.73$. The maximum profit is obviously unbounded. The break even stock price is $112.73. The payoff and profit for various stock prices, are depicted in Table 10.22.

Table 10.22: Profit from the OTM Strangle for Various Values of the Terminal Stock Price.

Stock Price	Payoff From Long Call	Payoff From Long Put	Total Payoff	Total Profit/Loss
80	0	1,500	1,500	727
85	0	1,000	1,000	227
87.27	0	773	773	0
90	0	500	500	(273)
95	0	0	0	(773)
100	0	0	0	(773)
105	0	0	0	(773)
110	500	0	500	(273)
112.73	773	0	773	0
115	1,000	0	1,000	227
120	1,500	0	1,500	727

10.14.2 An In-the-Money Strangle

Let's consider the payoff table for an in-the-money strangle, shown in Table 10.23. See Example 10.17 for a numerical illustration.

Table 10.23: Payoffs from an In-of-the-money Long Strangle.

Terminal Price Range	Payoff From Call	Payoff From Put	Total Payoff
$S_T < X_1$	0	$X_2 - S_T$	$X_2 - S_T$
$X_1 < S_T < X_2$	$S_T - X_1$	$X_2 - S_T$	$X_2 - X_1$
$S_T > X_2$	$S_T - X_1$	0	$S_T - X_1$

If $S_T < X_1, \pi = X_2 - S_T - P_t - C_t$. The maximum profit in this region = $X_2 - P_t - C_t$. If $X_1 < S_T < X_2, \pi = X_2 - X_1 - (P_t + C_t)$. If $S_T > X_2, \pi = S_T - X_1 - P_t - C_t$. The maximum profit in this region is unbounded. The maximum loss is $(X_2 - X_1) - (P_t + C_t)$, which occurs in the region $X_1 < S_T < X_2$. There are two break even prices:

$$X_2 - S_T^* - P_t - C_t = 0$$

$$\Rightarrow S_T^* = X_2 - P_t - C_t \tag{10.20}$$

$$S_T^{**} - X_1 - P_t - C_t = 0$$

$$\Rightarrow S_T^{**} = X_1 + P_t + C_t \tag{10.21}$$

Example 10.17: Anne Smith has bought a call option on IBM with an exercise price of \$95, and a put option with an exercise price of \$105. The stock is currently priced at \$100, and both the stocks have three months to expiration. The call premium is \$10.16 and the put premium is \$7.33. The initial investment is 10.16 + 7.33 = \$17.49. The maximum possible loss is:

$$105 - 95 - 17.49 = -\$\,7.49$$

As the stock price declines below \$95, the profit increases dollar for dollar. The profit in this price range is given by $105 - S_T - 17.49 = \$87.51 - S_T$. The maximum profit in this price range is \$87.51 which corresponds to a stock price of zero. The break even stock price is \$87.51.

As the stock price increases above \$105, the profit once again increases dollar for dollar. The profit in this price range is given by $S_T - 95 - 17.49 = S_T - 112.49$. The maximum profit is obviously unbounded. The break even stock price is \$112.49.

The profit diagram is identical to that for an out-of-the-money strangle.

10.15 A Strap

To go long in a strap, the investor needs to acquire calls and puts with the same exercise price and expiration date. The difference between a straddle and a strap is that, in the case of a strap,for every put that the investor buys, he needs to buy two calls. The initial investment is $2C_t + P_t$.

Let's consider the payoff table, as shown in Table 10.24.

Table 10.24: Payoffs From a Long Strap.

Terminal Price Range	Payoff From Calls	Payoff From Put	Total Payoff
$S_T < X$	0	$X - S_T$	$X - S_T$
$S_T > X$	$2(S_T - X)$	0	$2(S_T - X)$

If $S_T < X, \pi = X - S_T - 2C_t - P_t$. The maximum profit in this region = $X - 2C_t - P_t$. If $S_T > X, \pi = 2S_T - 2X - 2C_t - P_t$. The maximum profit in this region is unlimited. The maximum loss occurs when $S_T = X$, and is equal to $-2C_t - P_t$, which is nothing but the initial investment. There are two break even points:

$$S_T^* = X - 2C_t - P_t$$
$$S_T^{**} = X + C_t + \frac{P_t}{2} \tag{10.22}$$

Consider the profit diagram, as shown in Figure 10.15. Example 10.18 provides a numerical illustration.

As compared to a straddle, the upside break even stock price is easier to reach, and the downside break even stock price is harder to reach. Thus by increasing the bet on a bull market, the payoff in a bull market is higher, but the payoff in a bear market is lower. Investors who use straps consider an increase in price to be more likely than a decrease.

Example 10.18: Mitch Andrews has bought two call options and a put option on IBM. Both options have an exercise price of $100, and have three months to expiration. The premium for the call is $7.22, while that for the put is $4.75. Thus the initial investment is $2 \times 7.22 + 4.75 =$ $19.19. This amounts to the maximum potential loss from the strategy. If the stock price rises above the exercise price, the profit increases dollar for dollar. The profit for this price range is given by:

$$2S_T - 200 - 19.19 = 2S_T - 219.19$$

The maximum profit is obviously unbounded.

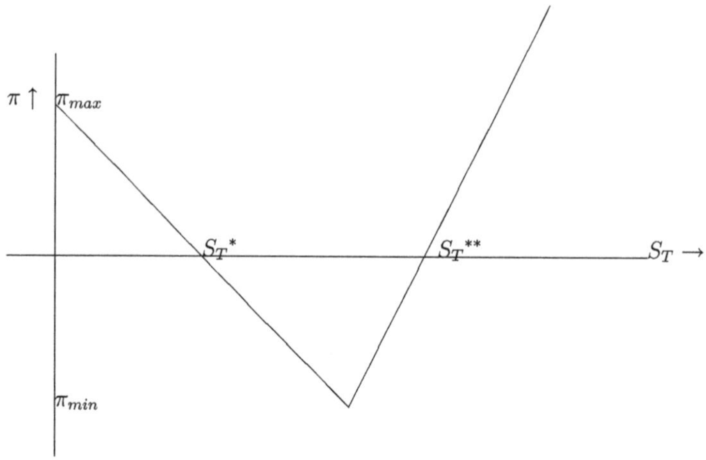

Figure 10.15: Profit Profile for a Strap.

If the terminal stock price declines below the exercise price, the profit again increases dollar for dollar. The profit in this price range is given by:

$$100 - S_T - 19.19 = 80.81 - S_T$$

The maximum profit is obviously \$80.81. There are two break even points, $S_T^* = \$109.595$, and $S_T^{**} = \$80.81$

10.16 A Strip

A strip requires the investor to buy two puts and a call, with the same exercise price and time to expiration. Thus it tantamounts to a bigger bet on a bear market. The initial investment is $C_t + 2P_t$.

Let's consider the payoff table, as shown in Table 10.25.

Table 10.25: Payoffs from a Long Strip.

Terminal Price Range	Payoff From Call	Payoff From Puts	Total Payoff
$S_T < X$	0	$2(X - S_T)$	$2(X - S_T)$
$S_T > X$	$S_T - X$	0	$S_T - X$

If $S_T < X, \pi = 2X - 2S_T - 2P_t - C_t$. The maximum profit in this region $= 2X - 2P_t - C_t$. If $S_T > X, \pi = S_T - X - 2P_t - C_t$. The maximum profit in this region is unlimited. The maximum loss occurs when $S_T = X$, and is equal to $-2P_t - C_t$, which is nothing but the initial investment. There are two break even prices.

$$S_T^{*} = X - P_t - \frac{C_t}{2} \tag{10.23}$$
$$S_T^{**} = X + 2P_t + C_t$$

The profit diagram is shown in Figure 10.16. Example 10.19 provides a numerical illustration.

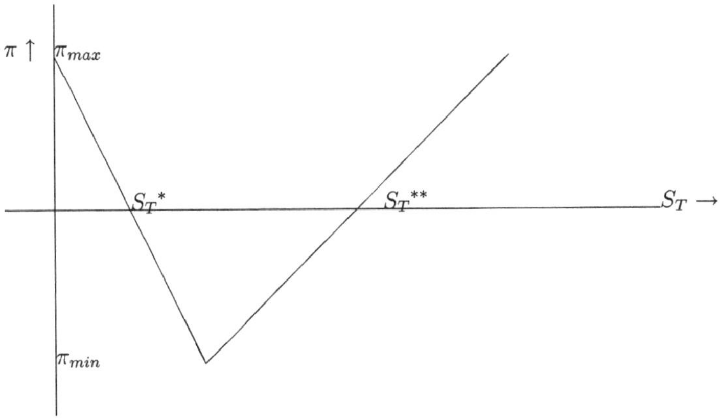

Figure 10.16: Profit Profile for a Strip.

As compared to a straddle, the upside break even stock price is harder to reach, and the downside break even stock price is easier to reach. Thus by increasing the bet on a bear market, the payoff in a bear market is higher, but the payoff in a bull market is lower. Investors who use straps consider a decrease in price to be more likely than an increase.

Example 10.19: Alice Keaton has bought two put options and a call option on IBM. Both options have an exercise price of \$100, and have three months to expiration. The premium for the call is \$7.22, while that for the put is \$4.75. Thus the initial investment is $7.22 + 2 \times 4.75$ = \$16.72. This amounts to the maximum potential loss from the strategy. If the stock price rises above the exercise price, the profit increases dollar for dollar. The profit for this price range is given by:

$$S_T - 100 - 16.72 = S_T - 116.72$$

The maximum profit is obviously unbounded.

If the terminal stock price declines below the exercise price, the profit again increases dollar for dollar. The profit in this price range is given by:

$$200 - 2S_T - 16.72 = 183.28 - 2S_T$$

The maximum profit is obviously \$183.28. There are two break even points, S_T^{*} = \$116.72, and S_T^{**} = \$91.64.

10.17 Box Spreads

A box spread is a combination of a bull spread with calls, and a bear spread with puts. Consider two exercise prices X_1 and X_2, such that $X_1 < X_2$. The strategy requires the investor to buy a call with an exercise price of X_1, and sell a call with an exercise price of X_2. It requires him to simultaneously sell a put with $X = X_1$, and buy a put with $X = X_2$. The initial cash flow is:

$$-C_{t,1} + C_{t,2} + P_{t,1} - P_{t,2} < 0 \tag{10.24}$$

because $C_{t,1} > C_{t,2}$ and $P_{t,1} < P_{t,2}$.

Let's consider the payoff from the position at expiration, as shown in Table 10.26.

Table 10.26: Payoffs from a Box Spread.

Terminal Price Range	Payoff From Call With $X = X_1$	Payoff From Call With $X = X_2$	Payoff From Put With $X = X_1$	Pay off From Put With $X = X_2$	Total Payoff
$S_T < X_1$	0	0	$-(X_1 - S_T)$	$X_2 - S_T$	$X_2 - X_1$
$X_1 < S_T < X_2$	$S_T - X_1$	0	0	$X_2 - S_T$	$X_2 - X_1$
$S_T > X_2$	$S_T - X_1$	$-(S_T - X_2)$	0	0	$X_2 - X_1$

As can be seen the payoff from the spread is independent of the terminal stock price. Thus the spread represents a riskless investment, and if it is correctly priced, the present value of the payoff at expiration discounted at the riskless rate, should equal the initial investment. If the present value exceeds the initial investment, the box spread will lead to an arbitrage profit. On the other hand, if the present value were to be less than the initial investment, an arbitrageur can make a riskless gain by reversing the positions, that is, by executing a short box spread. The payoff diagram is shown in Figure 10.17, and Example 10.20 provides a numerical illustration.

Example 10.20: Ralph Fleming has bought a call option with X = \$100, and a put option with X = \$110. He has simultaneously sold a call option with X = \$110, and a put option with X = \$100. The initial investment is:

$$-7.22 + 3.22 - 10.51 + 4.75 = -\$\,9.76$$

The terminal payoff is 110 − 100 = \$10. The rate of return is given by:

$$10 = 9.76e^{.25r} \Rightarrow r = 4[ln(10) - ln(9.76)] = .10 \equiv 10\%$$

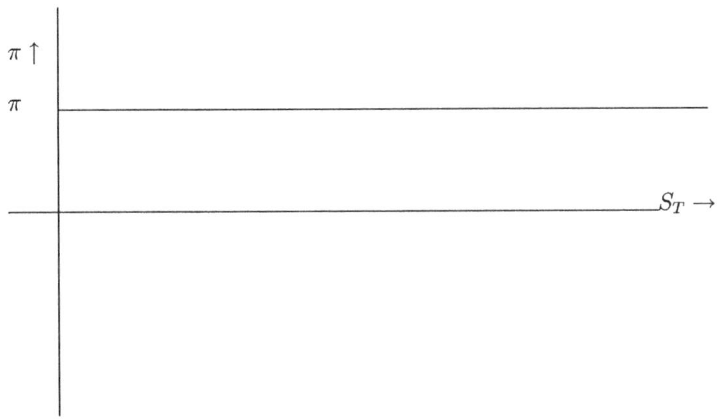

Figure 10.17: Profit Profile for a Box Spread.

The rate of return of 10% is the value that we had used to obtain the option prices using the Black-Scholes formula. Since the options are fairly priced, it is but obvious that the box spread will yield the riskless rate that was assumed.

Suggestions for Further Reading

Chance D.M. *An Introduction to Derivatives & Risk Management.* Thomson;South-Western, 2004.
Dubofsky D.A. *Options and Financial Futures: Valuation and Uses.* McGraw-Hill, 1992.
Figlewski S., Silber W.L., and M.G. Subrahmanyam *Financial Options: From Theory to Practice.* Irwin, 1990.
Options: Essential Concepts & Trading Strategies. McGraw-Hill, 1999.
Understanding Stock Options. The Options Clearing Corporation, 1994.

Chapter 11
Valuation of Options

A futures contract, which entails an obligation on the part of both the long as well as the short, is relatively easy to price as compared to an option. The value of a futures contract in an arbitrage free setting can be derived by ruling out the profitability of *Cash and Carry* and *Reverse Cash and Carry* strategies. Let's recapitulate these strategies.

11.1 Cash and Carry and Reverse Cash and Carry Arbitrage Strategies

Consider a futures contract on an asset which has a current spot price of S_t. Let the riskless rate of interest be r, for the period during which the arbitrage strategy is in place. That is, r is not an annualized rate. If the futures price is greater then $S_t(1 + r)$, then an arbitrageur can profit by engaging in a cash and carry strategy. This would entail borrowing \$ S_t and buying the stock in the spot market and simultaneously going short in the futures market to sell the asset at a future date for a price of F_t. Since by assumption, $F_t > S_t(1 + r)$, where $S_t(1 + r)$ represents the amount that has to be repaid by the arbitrageur at maturity, this strategy would clearly lead to an arbitrage profit.

On the other hand, if $F_t < S_t(1 + r)$, then a *reverse cash and carry* arbitrage strategy would yield a profit. This would entail short selling the stock and lending out the proceeds and simultaneously going long in a futures contract to reacquire the asset subsequently at a price F_t, in order to cover the short position. Since by assumption $S_t(1+r)$, which is what the arbitrageur will get when the amount lent by him is repaid, is greater than F_t, this strategy would give rise to an arbitrage profit.

Consequently, in order to preclude arbitrage, it must be the case that

$$F_t = S_t(1 + r)$$

In our analysis, we have assumed that there is no risk of default. In practice, the integrity of both the parties is ensured by imposing margins and marking the contract to market on a daily basis. Notice that nowhere in the above argument, did we have to make an assumption regarding the process of evolution of the stock price across time. The only two variables of interest were the current stock price and the riskless rate of interest.

In the case of an option however, the holder or the long has a right and not an obligation. The attractiveness of the option would therefore depend on his perception of the probability of his being able to exercise having entered into the contract, and the corresponding payoff. From the writer's standpoint, what is of consequence is the possibility of the holder not exercising the option and therefore of his being able to retain the premium.

https://doi.org/10.1515/9783110746662-011

To see why a typical cash and carry strategy does not yield an explicit price for an option, consider the case of an arbitrageur who borrows and buys a stock worth S_t, and a European put option worth $P_{E,t}$. At expiration there are two possibilities, namely $S_T > X$, that is the put is out of the money, or else $S_T < X$, that is the put is in the money.

The terminal payoff for the arbitrageur after repaying the loan with interest is

$$S_T - (S_t + P_{E,t})(1 + r)$$

if the put is out of the money, and

$$X - (S_t + P_{E,t})(1 + r)$$

if the put is in the money. To rule out arbitrage, we require that

$$X - (S_t + P_{E,t})(1 + r) \leq 0$$
$$\Rightarrow \frac{X}{(1 + r)} - S_t \leq P_{E,t} \tag{11.1}$$

which is a condition that is required as the lower bound for a European put. However, this strategy does not yield a precise expression for the put premium, in terms of the dependent variables.

Hence in the case of an options contract, valuation entails the postulation of a process for the evolution of the stock price through time. Corresponding to every hypothesis that we make about the price process, we will get an option price. In some cases we will be able to derive precise formulae for the price or closed-form solutions, while in other cases we will have to make do with numerical approximations.

11.2 Using Options to Create a Forward Contract

Consider European call and put options on the same asset, with identical exercise prices and expiration dates. Let the exercise price be equal to the prevailing forward price for the underlying asset. Take a look at the strategy depicted in Table 11.1

Table 11.1: Replicating a Forward Contract Using Options.

Action	**Initial Cash Flow**	**Terminal Cash Flow**	
		If $S_T > F$	If $S_T < F$
Buy the call	$-C_{E_t}$	$S_T - F$	0
Sell the put	$P_{E,t}$	0	$-(F - S_T)$
Total	$-C_{E,t} + P_{E,t}$	$S_T - F$	$S_T - F$

The payoff is equal to that of a long forward contract. Thus a long position in a European call coupled with a short position in a European put, is equivalent to a long forward contract on the underlying asset, if the exercise prices of the two options are equal to the prevailing forward price.

We know that the initial investment for a long forward position must be zero. In this case, the initial investment is:

$$\begin{aligned} P_{E,t} - C_{E,t} &= \frac{X}{(1+r)^{(T-t)}} - S_t \\ &= \frac{S_t(1+r)^{(T-t)}}{(1+r)^{(T-t)}} - S_t = 0 \end{aligned}$$

Thus the replicating portfolio that is required to mimic a forward contract can be set up at zero cost, as is to be expected.

11.3 Variables of Interest

The Current Stock Price

The prevailing stock price would obviously be a major factor in determining the value of an option. Everything else remaining constant, the higher the current stock price, the greater will be the value of a call option and the lower will be the value of a put option.

The Exercise Price

As one would expect, the higher the exercise price, for a given set of values for the other variables, the lower will be the value of a call option and the higher will be the value of a put option.

Dividends

A dividend payout will lead to a drop in the stock price as the stock goes ex-dividend. Consequently, dividends which are paid out during the life of the option will lead to a reduction in call values and an increase in put values. *Exchange traded options are usually not payout protected from the standpoint of cash dividends.* That is, the terms of the original option contract will not be modified were the underlying stock to pay a dividend subsequently. The terms of the agreement will however be changed in the event of stock splits or stock dividends.

Volatility

Modern finance theory is based on the assumption that all investors are risk averse. Consequently an increase in the volatility, as measured by the variance of the rate of return of the stock, will be perceived negatively and will therefore lead to a higher risk premium being demanded.

In the case of an options contract however, the holder is protected on one side, since his maximum loss is limited to the initial premium paid by him. Therefore, an increase in the volatility will be perceived positively, although it signals a greater probability of higher stock prices as well as lower stock prices. Hence, an increase in the volatility of the rate of return on the underlying asset will lead to an increase in the value of both call as well as put options.

Time to Maturity

American options and European calls on non dividend paying stocks have a non-negative time value while European puts may have either a positive or a negative time value depending on the extent to which the option is in the money.

At the time of expiration, the time value of an option as we have seen earlier must be zero, that is, the option premium must be equal to the intrinsic value. Therefore, everything else remaining constant, the value of an option will generally decline with the passage of time. We use the word 'generally', because certain European puts which are deep in the money may have a negative time value which will approach zero at expiration. Hence, options are also known as *Wasting Assets*, because they experience a decline in value with the passage of time.

Riskless Rate of Interest

Let's take the case of an investor who is contemplating the purchase of a stock. One alternative would be to buy a call instead, which can be subsequently exercised if he so desires. We know that the price of a call must be less than the prevailing stock price.

So if a person who has an amount equal to the value of the stock with him, were to decide to buy the call instead of the stock, then he can invest the difference at the riskless rate of interest. Everything else being the same, the higher the rate of interest, the more attractive will be the strategy of buying the call and investing the surplus. Therefore, it follows that the higher the interest rate, the more will be the price of the call.

What about puts? Consider the case of a person who already owns the stock and is contemplating selling it. One alternative would be to buy a put, which would ensure that he will receive a minimum price of $X for it subsequently.The higher the interest rate the more attractive will be the alternative of selling immediately in the spot market, rather than buying a put. Consequently, everything else being the same, the higher the interest rate, the less attractive will be the put option. Hence, put prices will decline as interest rates rise.

11.4 The Binomial Model

We will now go on to study theoretical pricing models for call and put options. The first model, which we will study is called the Binomial Option Pricing Model(*BOPM*). Subsequently we will study the famous *Black-Scholes* model(*BSOPM*).

The binomial model assumes that given the current stock price, during the next period the price can either change by X% or by Y%, where X and Y are specified. Since the stock price can take on only two possible values at the end of the period, the model is called *Binomial*. A realistic portrayal of the behaviour of a stock would require the specification of Y as a negative number.

11.4.1 Assumptions

The assumptions underlying the model are the following.

1. There are no frictions in the market such as transactions costs or taxes.
2. There are no margin requirements.
3. The investor is entitled to use the full proceeds from a short sale, if an asset is sold short.
4. Securities are infinitely divisible, that is investors can trade in fractions of securities.
5. Every investor is a price taker. There is a single riskless rate of return in the economy and everyone can borrow or lend unlimited amounts at this rate.
6. Investors are never satiated from the standpoint of wealth acquisition. Consequently, arbitrage opportunities if any will be fully exploited till they cease to exist.

11.5 The One Period Model

In the one period case, we consider only two points in time. These are, the present time $(T-1)$, and the expiration time of the option T.

Let the current stock price be S_t. The stock price at the end of the period can take on only the following values.

$$S_T = S_t\left(1 + \frac{X}{100}\right) = uS_t \tag{11.2}$$

where $u = \left(1 + \frac{X}{100}\right)$, and stands for the *Up State*, or

$$S_T = S_t\left(1 + \frac{Y}{100}\right) = dS_t \tag{11.3}$$

where $d = \left(1 + \frac{Y}{100}\right)$, and stands for the *Down State*. Y, in this case, is a negative number.

The price tree is depicted in Figure 11.1.

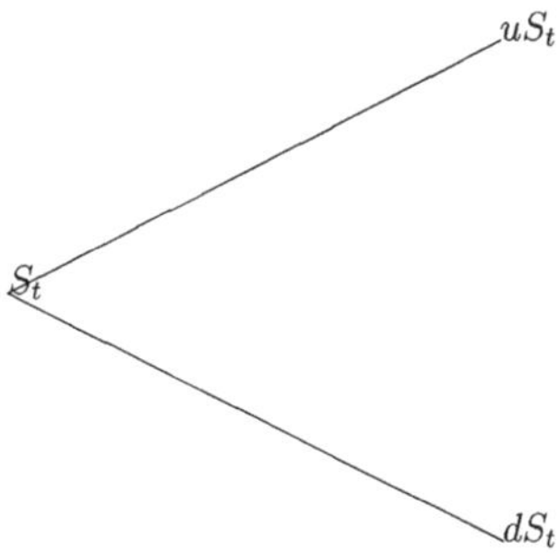

Figure 11.1: Stock Price Tree for the One Period Case.

Now, the call value at expiration will be $\text{Max}[0, uS_t - E]$, if the up state is reached, or $\text{Max}[0, dS_t - E]$, if the down state is reached. We are going to use the symbol 'E' to denote the exercise price, since the symbol 'X' has already been used to denote the extent of an up movement.

Let $C_u = \text{Max}[0, uS_t - E]$

and $C_d = \text{Max}[0, dS_t - E]$

C_u is the call value at expiration if the up state is reached, and C_d is the call value at expiration if the down state is reached.

Our objective is to find the value of the call today, that is, C_t.

Consider the following strategy. Let's buy α shares of stock and write one call option. The current value of this portfolio will be $\alpha S_t - C_t$.

If the up state is reached, the portfolio will have a value = $\alpha uS_t - C_u$, while if the downstate is reached, it will have a value = $\alpha dS_t - C_d$.

Now let's make this portfolio riskless by choosing α, such that

$$\alpha uS_t - C_u = \alpha dS_t - C_d$$

$$\Rightarrow \alpha S_t(u - d) = C_u - C_d$$

$$\Rightarrow \alpha = \frac{C_u - C_d}{S_t(u - d)} \tag{11.4}$$

α is known as the hedge ratio.

This portfolio is riskless because the payoff is independent of the state of nature at time T. Since our portfolio by design is riskless, it must earn the riskless rate of return to preclude arbitrage. Therefore,

$$auS_t - C_u = adS_t - C_d = (aS_t - C_t)r$$

where $r = 1 + $ *riskless rate of interest*. The symbol 'r' is often used to denote the riskless rate of interest per annum. In the binomial model, 'r' represents the riskless rate per period, and is defined as one plus the periodic interest rate.

We will typically assume that the parameters u and d, as well as the riskless rate of return r are constant. However, while this is done in order to simplify the calculations, this is not a necessary condition. The model merely requires that these variables be deterministic, that is they are known with certainty to all investors.

$$\text{Thus, } auS_t - C_u = (aS_t - C_t)r$$

$$\Rightarrow \left(\frac{C_u - C_d}{S_t(u-d)}\right) \times uS_t - C_u = \left(\frac{C_u - C_d}{S_t(u-d)}\right) \times rS_t - C_t r$$

$$\Rightarrow \left(\frac{C_u - C_d}{u-d}\right) \times (u - r) - C_u = -C_t r$$

$$\Rightarrow C_t = \left(\frac{C_u\left(\frac{r-d}{u-d}\right) + C_d\left(\frac{u-r}{u-d}\right)}{r}\right) \tag{11.5}$$

$$\text{Let } \frac{r-d}{u-d} = p. \text{ Therefore, } \frac{u-r}{u-d} = 1 - p$$

$$\Rightarrow C_t = \left(\frac{pC_u + (1-p)C_d}{r}\right) \tag{11.6}$$

This is the one period binomial call option pricing formula.[1] See Example 11.1 for a numerical illustration.

Example 11.1: Let $S_t = 100$, and $X = 100$. $u = 1.2, d = .80, r = 1.05$

$$C_u = \text{Max}[0, 1.2 \times 100 - 100] = 20$$

$$C_d = \text{Max}[0, 0.8 \times 100 - 100] = 0$$

$$p = \frac{r-d}{u-d} = \frac{1.05 - .80}{1.2 - .80} = .625$$

$$1 - p = .375$$

$$\text{The hedge ratio} = \frac{C_u - C_d}{S_t(u-d)} = \frac{20 - 0}{100(1.2 - .80)} = .5$$

1 We will interpret 'p' later. Notice that it seems to be some kind of probability.

That is, we have to buy .5 shares for every call that we write, in order to form a riskless portfolio.

$$C_t = \frac{.625 \times 20 + .375 \times 0}{1.05} = 11.9048$$

It can be shown that $u > r > d$, that is, p and (1-p) should both be positive. Otherwise, one can make arbitrage profits. The proof follows.

11.5.1 Proof

Case A

Suppose $u > d > r$. Consider the following strategy.

At time 'T-1', borrow \$ S_t for one period at the riskless rate, and buy a share of stock. At time 'T', you will get uS_t if the up state occurs. After repaying rS_t, you will get a net profit of $(u - r)S_t$ which is > 0. Similarly, if the down state occurs, you will get $(d - r)S_t$ which is > 0. Hence to preclude arbitrage opportunities, we require that r be > d.

Case B

Suppose $r > u > d$. Consider the following strategy.

Short sell the stock at '$T - 1$', and deposit S_t at the riskless rate. At time 'T', you will get rS_t. If the up state occurs, you will have to buy back the stock at uS_t. This will lead to a profit of $(r - u)S_t$, which is > 0. Similarly, in the down state, you will get $(r - d)S_t$, which is > 0. Hence, we require that u be > r.

Combining the two conditions, we get the requirement that $u > r > d$.

11.6 Pseudo Probabilities & Risk Neutrality

p and (1-p) are referred to as the pseudo probabilities of the call having a value of C_u and C_d respectively.

Let the actual probability of the stock being in the up state be 'q', and the probability of it being in the down state be '1-q'. As you can see, q does not appear anywhere in the pricing equation. Thus different people may disagree on the probabilities of the stock being in the up and down states, and yet agree on the call price.

You will also notice that risk preferences of individual investors do not appear in the pricing equation.[2] So people with different levels of risk aversion, can agree on the option price.

2 We have made no reference to utility functions.

So what is p? Now, if risk aversion levels are irrelevant for pricing, everyone including risk neutral investors, will agree on the call price calculated above. Consider a risk neutral investor. He will accept any risky investment which offers an expected rate of return equal to the riskless rate.

For the sake of argument, let's consider a world full of risk neutral investors. Let the probability of an up move be q, and that of a down move be (1-q). The expected rate of return on the stock in this scenario, will be equal to the riskless rate. Therefore,

$$\frac{quS_t + (1-q)dS_t - S_t}{S_t} = \frac{rS_t - S_t}{S_t}$$
$$\Rightarrow q = \frac{r-d}{u-d} \tag{11.7}$$

which is the same as our p. Thus p is the probability of an up move, in a world full of risk neutral investors.

How would a risk neutral person value the call option? He would calculate the expected value of the terminal payoff, and then discount it at the riskless rate. So, for such an investor

$$C_t = \frac{qC_u + (1-q)C_d}{r}$$
$$= \frac{pC_u + (1-p)C_d}{r}$$

So to value an option using the binomial model, we can act as if everyone were risk neutral, and use p as the probability of an up move.[3]

11.7 A Replicating Portfolio

As we have seen, a portfolio of α shares of stock and a short position in a call option yields the riskless rate of return. Thus the portfolio is equivalent to an investment of \$B in a riskless asset. Therefore

$$\alpha S_t - C_t = B$$
$$\Rightarrow \alpha S_t - B = C_t \tag{11.8}$$

3 We are not saying that everyone is risk neutral. What we are saying is that we can pretend as if everyone is risk neutral. It is in this sense, that p is a pseudo probability.

Thus an investment in a call option is equivalent to buying a shares of stock and borrowing an amount of \$B at the riskless rate.

$$a = \frac{C_u - C_d}{S_t(u - d)}$$

This will be non-negative since $C_u \geq C_d$ and $u > d$.

$$\begin{aligned}
B &= aS_t - C_t \\
&= \frac{C_u - C_d}{u - d} - \frac{pC_u + (1 - p)C_d}{r} \\
&= \frac{rC_u - rC_d - [p(u - d)C_u + (1 - p)(u - d)C_d]}{r(u - d)} \\
&= \frac{[(rC_u - rC_d) - (r - d)C_u - (u - r)C_d]}{r(u - d)} \\
&= \frac{dC_u - uC_d}{r(u - d)}
\end{aligned} \tag{11.9}$$

In our example, $a = 0.50$. $B = \dfrac{(0.8 \times 20 - 1.2 \times 0)}{(1.05)(1.2 - 0.8)} = \$38.10$. The value of the replicating portfolio is

$$0.5 \times 100 - 38.10 = \$11.90$$

which is the value that we obtained for the call. If the up state is reached, the payoff from the portfolio will be

$$0.5 \times 120 - 38.10 \times 1.05 = \$20$$

If the down state is reached the payoff will be

$$0.5 \times 80 - 38.10 \times 1.05 = 0$$

In both cases the payoff from the replicating portfolio is identical to that of the call.

11.8 The Two Period Case

Thus far, we have assumed that the option has only one period left to expiration. In general, the stock price will move many times between the date of valuation and the expiration date. In the multi period case also, the same arguments will hold.

Let the stock price two periods before the expiration date be S_t. The stock price tree, may then be depicted as shown in Figure 11.2. See Example 11.2 for a numerical illustration.

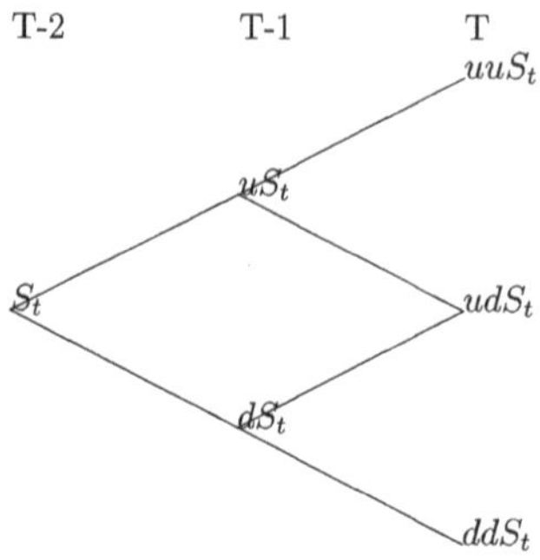

Figure 11.2: Stock Price Tree for the Two Period Case.

At T−1, there is only one period left to expiration, and so, we can apply the one period model to get C_u and C_d at T−1.

$$C_u = \frac{pC_{uu} + (1-p)C_{ud}}{r}$$
$$C_d = \frac{pC_{ud} + (1-p)C_{dd}}{r}$$

We know C_{uu}, C_{ud}, and C_{dd} because they represent terminal values of the option.

C_{uu} is the option price at T, if there are two upticks in the stock price.

C_{ud} is the option price at T, if there is an uptick followed by a downtick or vice versa.

C_{dd} is the option price at T, if there are two downticks in the stock price.

Once we find C_u and C_d, we can work backwards to find C_t.

$$C_t = \frac{pC_u + (1-p)C_d}{r}$$
$$= \frac{p^2C_{uu} + 2p(1-p)C_{ud} + (1-p)^2C_{dd}}{r^2} \quad (11.10)$$

Using the same iterative process, we can work backwards, moving one period at a time, to solve the 'N' period case.

Example 11.2: Let's use the same data as in the earlier example.

$S_t = X = 100, u = 1.2, d = 0.8, r = 1.05.$

First, let's draw the price tree, as shown in Figure 11.3.

$$p = .625, (1-p) = 0.375$$
$$C_{uu} = \text{Max}[0, 144 - 100] = 44$$
$$C_{ud} = \text{Max}[0, 96 - 100] = 0$$
$$C_{dd} = \text{Max}[0, 64 - 100] = 0$$
$$C_u = \frac{.625 \times 44 + .375 \times 0}{1.05} = 26.1905$$

$$C_d = \frac{.625 \times 0 + .375 \times 0}{1.05} = 0$$

$$C_t = \frac{.625 \times 26.1905 + .375 \times 0}{1.05} = 15.5896$$

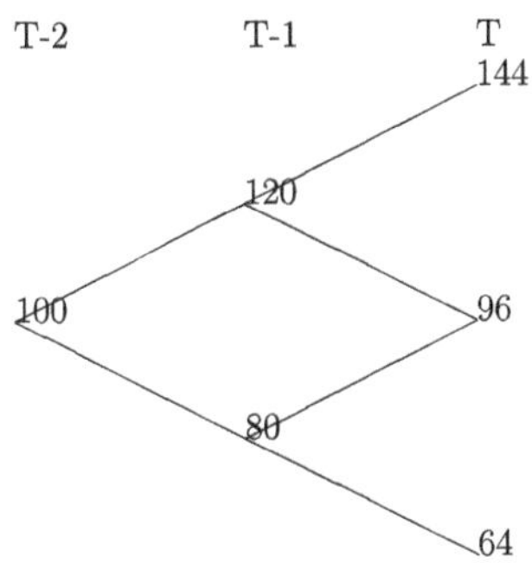

Figure 11.3: Stock Price Tree For The Two Period Example.

11.8.1 The Self-Financing Property

As we have seen a call option can be replicated by buying α shares of stock and borrowing \$B at the riskless rate. The hedge ratio at time T-2 is given by

$$\alpha_{T-2} = \frac{26.1905 - 0}{100 \times (1.2 - 0.80)} = 0.6548$$

$$B = \frac{0.80 \times 26.1905 - 1.20 \times 0}{(1.05)(1.2 - 0.80)} = 49.89$$

Thus we need to invest \$65.48 in the stock and borrow \$49.89 at the riskless rate of interest.

This portfolio has to be rebalanced at time T-1, irrespective of whether the upstate or the downstate is reached. If the upstate is reached, the new hedge ratio is given by

$$\alpha_{u,T-1} = \frac{44 - 0}{120 \times (1.20 - 0.80)} = 0.9167$$

The new value of B is given by

$$\frac{0.80 \times 44 - 1.20 \times 0}{(1.05)(1.20 - 0.80)} = 83.81$$

The additional investment required in the stock is

$$(0.9167 - 0.6548) \times 120 = \$31.43$$

The amount borrowed in the previous period was \$49.89. This would have grown to

$$49.89 \times 1.05 = \$52.38$$

The additional amount that has to be borrowed is

$$83.81 - 52.38 = \$31.43$$

which is exactly equal to the additional investment in the stock.

If the down state is reached, the new hedge ratio is given by

$$\alpha_{d,T-1} = \frac{0 - 0}{80 \times (1.20 - 0.80)} = 0$$

The new value of B is given by

$$\frac{0.80 \times 0 - 1.20 \times 0}{(1.05)(1.20 - 0.80)} = 0$$

Thus we need to sell off 0.6548 units of the stock. This will lead to an inflow of

$$0.6548 \times 80 = 52.38$$

This will be exactly adequate to pay off the amount borrowed in the previous period with interest. Thus if we start with a replicating portfolio, subsequent changes required in the composition of the portfolio are self-financing. That is the outflow/inflow due to investment/divestment in the stock is exactly equal to the amount that has to be borrowed/repaid at the riskless rate. We will demonstrate later, that the self-financing property of the replicating portfolio breaks down in cases where it is optimal to exercise an option before expiration.

11.9 The Multi Period Case

If there are 'N' periods left to expiration

$$C_t = \frac{1}{r^N}\sum_{k=0}^{N}\left[\frac{N!}{(N-k)!k!}p^k(1-p)^{N-k}\text{Max}(0, u^k d^{N-k}S_0 - X)\right] \tag{11.11}$$

11.10 Binomial Pricing for European Puts

Consider the one period case. The put value at expiration is $\text{Max}[0, E - uS_t]$ if the up state is reached, or is $\text{Max}[0, E - dS_t]$ if the down state is reached. Therefore,

$$P_u = \text{Max}[0, E - uS_t]$$
$$\text{and } P_d = \text{Max}[0, E - dS_t]$$

Using arguments similar to what we used for the call, it can be shown that

$$P_t = \frac{pP_u + (1 - p)P_d}{r} \tag{11.12}$$

where, p and (1-p) are as defined before. See Example 11.3 for a numerical illustration.

Example 11.3: We will use the same data that we used for the call. That is, $S_t = X = 100$, $u = 1.2$, $d = .8$, $r = 1.05$.

$$P_u = \text{Max}[0{,}100 - 120] = 0$$
$$P_d = \text{Max}[0{,}100 - 80] = 20$$
$$P_t = \frac{.625 \times 0 + .375 \times 20}{1.05} = 7.1429$$

11.11 Replicating Portfolio

Consider a portfolio consisting of a shares of stock and \$B in the riskless asset. The payoff from the portfolio will be:

$$auS_t + Br \text{ if the upstate is reached}$$
$$\text{and } adS_t + Br \text{ if the downstate is reached.}$$

Equating the payoffs from the portfolio to the payoff from the option, we get

$$auS_t + Br = P_u \text{ and}$$
$$adS_t + Br = P_d$$
$$\Rightarrow a(u - d)S_t = P_u - P_d$$
$$\Rightarrow a = \frac{P_u - P_d}{S_t(u - d)} \leq 0 \tag{11.13}$$

since $P_u \leq P_d$.

$$\begin{aligned} Br &= P_u - auS_t \\ &= P_u - u\frac{(P_u - P_d)}{(u-d)} \\ &= \frac{P_u(u-d) - u(P_u - P_d)}{(u-d)} \\ \Rightarrow B &= \frac{uP_d - dP_u}{r(u-d)} \end{aligned} \tag{11.14}$$

Thus, the replicating portfolio entails the short selling of a shares of stock and an investment of \$B in the riskless asset.

11.12 Valuing European Calls on Dividend Paying Stocks

Consider the data given in the earlier examples. Assume that the option has three periods left to maturity. When there is one period left to go for expiration, the stock pays a dividend of \$16. That is, if the option expires at T, then, at T-1 the stock trades ex-dividend. In other words, an instant before it trades at T-1, a dividend is paid.[4]

Let's first model the stock price tree, as shown in Figure 11.4.

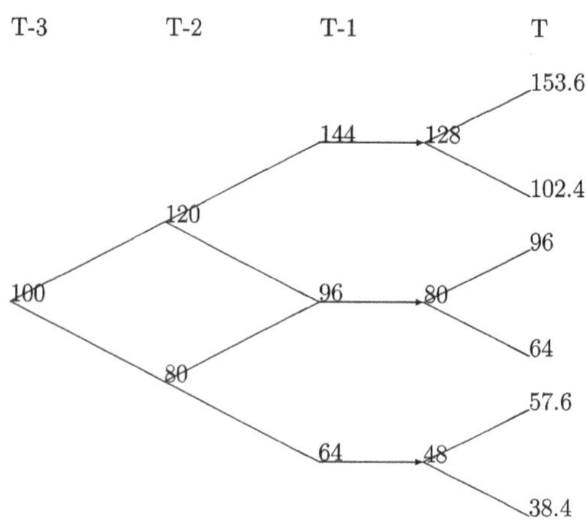

Figure 11.4: Stock Price Tree Corresponding to a Discrete Dividend.

4 When valuing options on dividend paying stocks, it is critical to know as to when exactly the dividend will be paid.

Notice that because of the dividend, you get additional branches at time T.

$$C_{uu} = \frac{.625 \times 53.6 + .375 \times 2.4}{1.05} = 32.7619$$

C_{uu} is the value of the call at 'T-1', if there are two upticks, that is, the node corresponding to an ex-dividend price of 128.

$$C_{ud} = \frac{.625 \times 0 + .375 \times 0}{1.05} = 0$$
$$C_{dd} = \frac{.625 \times 0 + .375 \times 0}{1.05} = 0$$

Using C_{uu}, C_{ud}, and C_{dd} we can work backwards to calculate, C_u and C_d.

$$C_u = \frac{.625 \times 32.7619 + .375 \times 0}{1.05} = 19.5011$$
$$C_d = \frac{.625 \times 0 + .375 \times 0}{1.05} = 0$$

Therefore,

$$C_t = \frac{.625 \times 19.5011 + .375 \times 0}{1.05} = 11.6078$$

11.13 Valuing American Calls on Dividend Paying Stocks

Consider the stock price tree given in Figure 11.4. The only difference while valuing American calls is that at each node of the stock price tree, we have to check as to whether the option will be exercised early(killed), or kept alive.

If there are two upticks, C_{uu} = 32.7619. If the option is exercised, the payoff is (128 − 100) = 28, which is less. So the option will not be exercised early.

If there is an uptick and a downtick, C_{ud} = 0 The option is out of the money, so there is no question of early exercise.

Finally, in the case of two downticks, C_{dd} = 0 The option is out of the money. So there is no need to consider the possibility of early exercise.

C_u = 19.5011 If exercised early, the payoff = 20. So the option will be exercised at this stage.

C_d = 0 The option is out of the money. So there is no possibility of early exercise.

The difference between European options, and American options, is that at each node, you have to take the greater of the model value and the payoff if exercised early, in order to work backwards.

Thus at 'T-3' C_t is calculated as follows.

$$\frac{.625 \times 20 + .375 \times 0}{1.05} = 11.9048$$

As you can see, the American call is more valuable than the corresponding European call. But this is not all. You have to compare 11.9048 with the intrinsic value at T-3 which in this case is 0. If the intrinsic value is greater, then the call must sell for the intrinsic value. In this case however, the call will sell for the model price, which is 11.9048.

11.14 Rationale for Early Exercise

If the value of the option at a particular node as determined from the model is lower than its intrinsic value then a rational investor will choose to exercise early. If he does not wish to continue to hold the option, then obviously early exercise will occur. Offsetting the option is not a worthwhile proposition, because a potential buyer will not pay more than the model value since he can always replicate the option at that value. Consequently the holder stands to benefit more by exercising. Even if the holder were to desire to continue holding the option, it would be more beneficial for him to exercise the option and replicate it at a cost which is lower than the intrinsic value.

11.15 The Breakdown of the Self-Financing Property

At time 'T-3'

$$\alpha = \frac{C_u - C_d}{S_{T-3}(u-d)} = \frac{20 - 0}{100 \times (1.20 - 0.80)} = 0.50$$

$$B = \frac{0.80 \times 20 - 1.20 \times 0}{1.05 \times (1.20 - 0.80)} = \$38.10$$

If the upstate is reached, the new hedge ratio is given by

$$\alpha_{u,T-2} = \frac{32.7619 - 0}{120 \times (1.20 - 0.80)} = 0.6825$$

$$B = \frac{0.80 \times 32.7619 - 0}{1.05 \times (1.20 - 0.80)} = \$62.40$$

The additional investment in the stock = (0.6825 − 0.50) × 120 = \$21.90 The additional amount to be borrowed = 62.40 − 38.10 × 1.05 = \$22.40. Clearly the replicating portfolio is not self-financing at a node where early exercise of the option is optimal.

11.16 European versus American Puts

Consider the data used in the earlier examples. We will assume that the stock pays no dividends.

Let's look at a put option with three periods to expiration. The stock price tree is depicted in Figure 11.5.

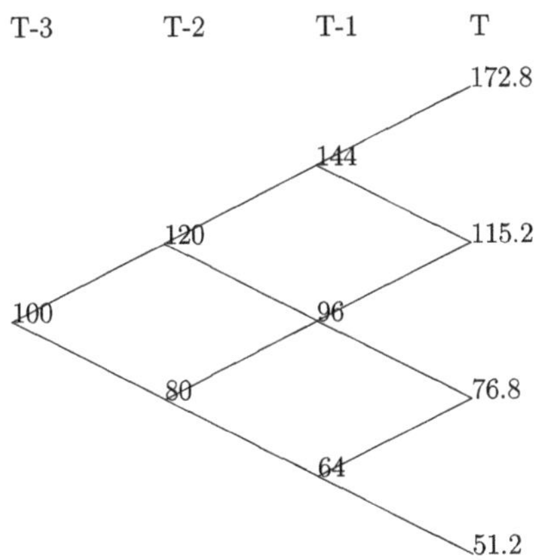

Figure 11.5: Stock Price Tree for the Three Period Case.

11.16.1 Valuing a European Put

To value the option, we will proceed backwards as follows.

$$P_{uu} = \frac{.625 \times 0 + .375 \times 0}{1.05} = 0$$

$$P_{ud} = \frac{.625 \times 0 + .375 \times 23.20}{1.05} = 8.2857$$

$$P_{dd} = \frac{.625 \times 23.2 + .375 \times 48.8}{1.05} = 31.2381$$

$$P_u = \frac{.625 \times 0 + .375 \times 8.2857}{1.05} = 2.9592$$

$$P_d = \frac{.625 \times 8.2857 + .375 \times 31.2381}{1.05} = 16.0884$$

$$P_t = \frac{.625 \times 2.9592 + .375 \times 16.0884}{1.05} = 7.5073$$

11.16.2 Valuing an American Put

For American puts, we have to, at each node, compare the value obtained from the model with the intrinsic value. If the intrinsic value is greater, we have to use it for subsequent calculations.

At uuS_t, the value according to our previous calculations is 0. The intrinsic value is also 0.

At udS_t, the model price is 8.2857, and the intrinsic value is 4, which is less.

Thus P_u will have the same value for an American put.

But at ddS_t the model price is 31.2381, while the intrinsic value is 36. So we will calculate P_d as follows.

$$P_d = \frac{.625 \times 8.2857 + .375 \times 36}{1.05} = 17.7891$$

The intrinsic value at the node corresponding to a stock price of dS_t is 20, which is greater than 17.7891.

So we will calculate P_t as follows.

$$P_t = \frac{.625 \times 2.9592 + .375 \times 20}{1.05} = 8.9043$$

This is not the final step however. You must compare 8.9043 with the intrinsic value at T-3 which in this case is 0. Thus the option will sell for 8.9043.

As you can see, the American put is priced higher than the European put. This is because early exercise is optimal at an intermediate stage.

11.17 Another Approach to Dividends

Consider a case where the stock pays a constant dividend yield of 10% per period. Thus each time the stock price moves to a new value, it immediately declines by 10% as it goes ex-dividend.

Let's consider a two period call option on this stock. Except for the dividend yield, other variables have the same value as before. Consider the stock price tree, shown in Figure 11.6.

$$C_{uu} = 16.64, C_{ud} = 0, \text{ and } C_{dd} = 0$$

$$C_u = \frac{.625 \times 16.64 + .375 \times 0}{1.05} = 9.9048$$

The intrinsic value = 8.

$$C_d = \frac{.625 \times 0 + .375 \times 0}{1.05} = 0$$

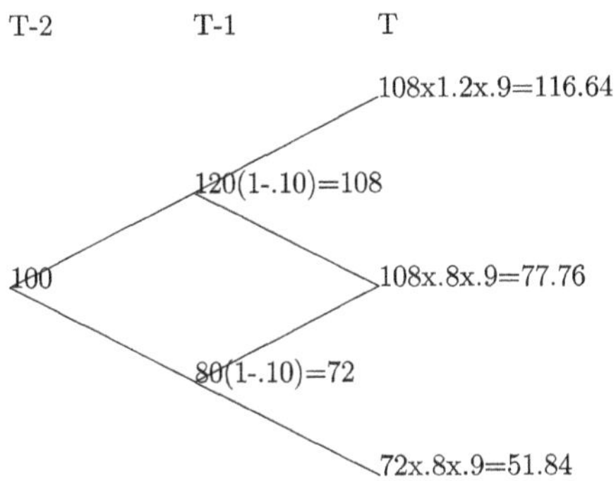

Figure 11.6: Stock Price Tree in the case of a Constant Dividend Yield.

The intrinsic value = 0.

$$C_t = \frac{.625 \times 9.9048 + .375 \times 0}{1.05} = 5.8957$$

11.18 The Black-Scholes Model

A variable is said to follow a stochastic process, if its value changes over time in an unpredictable way. As you may have guessed, a stock price is an obvious candidate. Stochastic processes may be either of the discrete time variety, or of the continuous time type. A discrete time process is used to represent variables which can take on values only at certain fixed points in time. On the other hand, variables which are described using continuous time processes, can take on values at any point in time. A stochastic process may be of the continuous state space variety, or of a discrete state space type. If the state space is discrete, the variable can take on only certain discrete values, whereas if the state space in continuous, it can take on any value in a specified range.

To describe stock prices, Black-Scholes assumed a continuous time, continuous state space process. The process assumed by them may be described as follows.

$$\frac{dS}{S} = \mu dt + \sigma dZ \tag{11.15}$$

Thus the rate of return on the stock as per this model, consists of a deterministic component as well as a random component. μdt is the deterministic component. μ is a measure of the average return per unit time, and is called the 'drift' of the process. The second term σdZ captures the random component of the return. σ is referred to as the volatility of the rate of return, and is measured as a percentage per annum.

dZ is referred to as a Wiener process. It may be expressed as

$$dZ = \epsilon \sqrt{dt} \tag{11.16}$$

where ϵ is a number drawn from a standard normal distribution, that is, a normal distribution with a mean of zero and a variance of one.

It has the following properties.

1. The expectation of dZ is zero.

$$dZ = \epsilon\sqrt{dt} \Rightarrow E[dZ] = E[\epsilon\sqrt{dt}] = \sqrt{dt}E[\epsilon] = 0 \tag{11.17}$$

2. The variance of dZ is dt.

$$\begin{aligned}\text{Var}(dZ) &= E[\epsilon\sqrt{dt}]^2 - \{E[\epsilon\sqrt{dt}]\}^2 \\ &= dtE[\epsilon]^2 = dt\end{aligned} \tag{11.18}$$

3. The values of ΔZ for any two non-overlapping short intervals of time Δt are independent.

   Let the change in Z over a period of time T, be Z(T) - Z(0). T can be divided into N non-overlapping intervals of Δt. Therefore

$$\begin{aligned}Z(T) - Z(0) &= [Z(T) - Z(T-1)] + [Z(T-1) - Z(T-2)] + \ldots.. \\ &= \sum_{i=1}^{N} \epsilon_i\sqrt{\Delta t}\end{aligned} \tag{11.19}$$

$$\begin{aligned}E[Z(T) - Z(0)] &= \sqrt{\Delta t}\sum_{i-1}^{N} E(\epsilon_i) = 0 \\ \Rightarrow E[Z(T)] &= Z(0)\end{aligned} \tag{11.20}$$

$$\begin{aligned}Var[Z(T) - Z(0)] &= \sum_{i=1}^{N} Var[\epsilon_i\sqrt{\Delta t}] \\ &= \Delta t\sum_{i=1}^{N} 1.0 = N\Delta t = T\end{aligned} \tag{11.21}$$

11.18.1 An Ito Process

Consider the process

$$dS = \mu Sdt + \sigma SdZ \tag{11.22}$$

This is a process of the form

$$dS = a(S,t)dt + b(S,t)dZ \tag{11.23}$$

That is, the drift and volatility of the process are a function of the variable itself and time. Such a process is known as an Ito process.

Ito's Lemma

Assume that a variable X follows an Ito process. That is

$$dX = a(X, t) + b(X, t)dZ \tag{11.24}$$

Define G as a function of X and time. That is, G = G(X,t). According to Ito's lemma

$$dG = \left(\frac{\partial G}{\partial X}a + \frac{\partial G}{\partial t} + \frac{1}{2}\frac{\partial^2 G}{\partial X^2}b^2 \right) dt + \frac{\partial G}{\partial X}bdZ \tag{11.25}$$

In other words, G also follows an Ito process with a drift of

$$\left(\frac{\partial G}{\partial X}a + \frac{\partial G}{\partial t} + \frac{1}{2}\frac{\partial^2 G}{\partial X^2}b^2 \right)$$

and a variance rate of $\left(\frac{\partial G}{\partial X}b \right)^2$.

11.18.2 The Lognormal Property of Stock Prices

Let the stock price S follow an Ito process, such that

$$dS = \mu Sdt + \sigma SdZ$$

Consider a function G, where G = lnS. Therefore

$$\frac{\partial G}{\partial S} = \frac{1}{S};\ \frac{\partial G}{\partial t} = 0;\ \frac{\partial^2 G}{\partial S^2} = -\frac{1}{S^2}$$

Thus, according to Ito's lemma

$$\begin{aligned} dG &= \left(\frac{1}{S}\mu S + 0 - \frac{1}{2} \times \frac{1}{S^2}\sigma^2 S^2 \right) dt + \frac{1}{S}\sigma SdZ \\ &= (\mu - \frac{\sigma^2}{2})dt + \sigma dZ \end{aligned} \tag{11.26}$$

Over a discrete time interval from t to T, we can state that

$$\begin{aligned} lnS_T - lnS_t &\sim N\left[\left(\mu - \frac{\sigma^2}{2} \right)(T - t), \sigma^2(T - t) \right] \\ \Rightarrow lnS_T &\sim N\left[lnS_t + \left(\mu - \frac{\sigma^2}{2} \right)(T - t), \sigma^2(T - t) \right] \end{aligned} \tag{11.27}$$

Thus the logarithm of S follows a normal distribution which implies that S itself follows a lognormal distribution. The process $dS = \mu Sdt + \sigma SdZ$ is referred to as a lognormal random walk.

11.19 Estimating Volatility From Historical Data

To estimate the volatility of returns using past data, we have to observe the stock prices at fixed intervals in time. Consider the case where we have 'n+1' observations of the stock price S. That is S can take on the values S_0 to S_n. Define $u_i = ln\left(\frac{S_i}{S_{i-1}}\right)$. That is, u_i is the continuously compounded rate of return.[5] An unbiased estimate of the variance of the returns is given by

$$\hat{s}^2 = \frac{1}{(n-1)}\sum_{i=1}^{n}(u_i - \bar{u})^2$$

$$\Rightarrow \hat{s}^2 = \frac{1}{(n-1)}\sum_{i=1}^{n}u_i^2 - \frac{1}{n(n-1)}\left(\sum_{i=1}^{n}u_i\right)^2 \tag{11.28}$$

We know that $lnS_T - lnS_t \sim N\left[\left(\mu - \frac{\sigma^2}{2}\right)(T-t), \sigma^2(T-t)\right]$

Therefore, our variance estimate $\hat{s}^2$ is an estimate of $\sigma^2(T-t)$. Thus $\frac{\hat{s}^2}{(T-t)}$ is an estimate of σ^2, or in other words, $\frac{s}{\sqrt{(T-t)}}$ is an estimate of σ. One of the key issues in estimating σ, is choosing the appropriate value for n. The more data we use, the more accurate our estimate is likely to be. However, in practice, it has been found that σ changes over time, and hence very old data cannot be used for predicting the future. In real life, people often use daily closing prices over the most recent 3 to 6 months.[6]

In the definition of 'u' given above, we have excluded dividends. However, if day 'j' is an ex-dividend day, we have to define u_j as,

$$u_j = ln\left(\frac{S_j + D}{S_{j-1}}\right) \tag{11.29}$$

where D is the quantum of the dividend. For all the other days, we will use

$$u_i = ln\left(\frac{S_i}{S_{i-1}}\right)$$

Example 11.4 shows the computation of volatility.

5 It is not an annualized rate.

6 See Hull(2005).

Example 11.4: Consider the vector of daily stock prices shown in Table 11.2. We have converted the prices to price relatives and then taken the natural logarithm of the price relatives to compute the rates of return. Finally we have computed the standard deviation of the vector of returns.

Table 11.2: Computing the Standard Deviation of Returns.

Day	Price	$\frac{S_t}{S_{t-1}}$	$ln\left(\frac{S_t}{S_{t-1}}\right) = r_t$
1	102.26		
2	108.95	1.065398273	0.027511988
3	102.12	0.937330735	−0.028107142
4	106.76	1.045470920	0.019311957
5	101.13	0.947185443	−0.023564985
6	103.00	1.018561154	0.007987109
7	107.22	1.040898150	0.017408237
8	109.58	1.022091327	0.009489703
9	101.03	0.921966616	−0.035284804
10	109.25	1.081311631	0.033950874
11	100.48	0.919746755	−0.036331736
12	104.50	1.039975114	0.017022947
13	102.84	0.984092982	−0.006963865
14	107.93	1.049526378	0.020993358
15	106.89	0.990350224	−0.004211196
16	108.46	1.014760684	0.006363632
17	103.29	0.952300156	−0.021226144
18	101.93	0.986826706	−0.005759106
19	108.68	1.066218662	0.02784628
20	107.31	0.987365741	−0.005521946
21	102.19	0.952325088	−0.021214774
22	109.50	1.071572170	0.030021426
23	100.58	0.918497328	−0.036922103
24	108.66	1.080299943	0.033544353
25	108.66	1.000054576	2.37013E−05
26	106.90	0.983789929	−0.007097628
27	107.92	1.009547820	0.004126895
28	101.95	0.944641661	−0.024732905
29	107.65	1.055971567	0.023652225
30	107.82	1.001507445	0.000654182
31	101.59	0.942217809	−0.025848691

$$\hat{s}^2 = 0.00050881 \Rightarrow \hat{s} = 0.02255683$$

If we assume that there are 252 trading days in a year, the time period in years is $\frac{1}{252}$. Thus

$$\sigma = \hat{s}\sqrt{252} = 0.358079 \equiv 35.8079\% \text{ per annum}$$

11.20 The Distribution of Discretely Compounded versus Continuously Compounded Rates of Return

Consider the process

$$\frac{dS}{S} = \mu dt + \sigma dZ$$

Thus the rate of return in a discrete time interval is given by

$$\frac{\Delta S}{S} \sim N\left[\mu(T-t), \sigma^2(T-t)\right]$$

However we know that

$$dlnS \sim N\left[\left(\mu - \frac{\sigma^2}{2}\right)(T-t), \sigma^2(T-t)\right]$$

If we define

$$S_T = S_t e^{i(T-t)}, \text{ then}$$
$$lnS_T = lnS_t + i(T-t)$$
$$\Rightarrow ln\frac{S_T}{S_t} = i(T-t)$$

i is the annual continuously compounded rate of return.

So is the expected rate of return per annum μ or is it $\mu - \frac{\sigma^2}{2}$. The answer is that it depends on how we define the rate of return. If the return is continuously compounded then the expected return per annum is $\mu - \frac{\sigma^2}{2}$. However if the return is computed in a discrete fashion as $\frac{(S_T - S_0)}{S_0}$, then the mean rate of return per annum is μ.

11.21 The Black-Scholes Differential Equation

Black and Scholes derived a partial differential equation which must be satisfied by the price of any derivative security whose value depends on that of a non dividend paying stock. The assumptions underlying the Black-Scholes model are as follows.

1. There are no frictions in the market such as transactions costs or taxes.
2. There are no margin requirements.
3. The investor is entitled to use the full proceeds from a short sale, if an asset is sold short.
4. Securities are infinitely divisible, that is investors can trade in fractions of securities.
5. Every investor is a price taker. There is a single riskless rate of return in the economy and everyone can borrow or lend unlimited amounts at this rate. This rate is a constant and is the same for all maturities.
6. Investors are never satiated from the standpoint of wealth acquisition. Consequently, arbitrage opportunities if any will be fully exploited till they cease to exist.
7. No dividends are paid on the underlying asset during the life of the derivative security.
8. All securities are traded continuously.
9. The stock price can be described by the Ito process with μ and σ being constant.

11.21.1 Derivation

Assume that the stock price follows an Ito process. Therefore,

$$dS = \mu S dt + \sigma S dZ$$

Let F be the price of a derivative security, which is a function of S and t. By Ito's Lemma,

$$dF = \left(\frac{\partial F}{\partial S} \mu S + \frac{\partial F}{\partial t} + \frac{1}{2} \times \frac{\partial^2 F}{\partial S^2} \sigma^2 S^2 \right) dt + \frac{\partial F}{\partial S} \sigma S dZ \tag{11.30}$$

Now, the Wiener process underlying S and F is the same. That is, $dZ = \epsilon\sqrt{dt}$ is the same for both the equations. Black and Scholes designed a portfolio using the stock and the derivative asset in a manner which eliminated the Wiener process.

Consider a portfolio which is long in $\frac{\partial F}{\partial S}$ units of the stock, and short in one unit of the derivative security. Let π be the value of this portfolio. Therefore

$$\pi = \frac{\partial F}{\partial S} S - F \tag{11.31}$$

The change in the value of this portfolio during a time interval of Δt, is

$$\begin{aligned}\Delta\pi &= \frac{\partial F}{\partial S}\Delta S - \Delta F \\ &= \left(-\frac{\partial F}{\partial t} - \frac{1}{2}\frac{\partial^2 F}{\partial S^2}\sigma^2 S^2\right)\Delta t\end{aligned} \tag{11.32}$$

Notice that this equation does not involve ΔZ. Hence it must be riskless during the time interval Δt. If it is riskless, it must earn the riskless rate of return during this period to preclude arbitrage.[7]

Therefore

$$\Delta\pi = r\pi\Delta t \tag{11.33}$$

where r is the riskless rate of interest. Hence,

$$\begin{aligned}&\left(-\frac{\partial F}{\partial t} - \frac{1}{2}\frac{\partial^2 F}{\partial S^2}\sigma^2 S^2\right)\Delta t \\ &= r\left(-F + \frac{\partial F}{\partial S}S\right)\Delta t\end{aligned}$$

$$\Rightarrow \frac{\partial F}{\partial t} + rS\frac{\partial F}{\partial S} + \frac{1}{2}\frac{\partial^2 F}{\partial S^2}\sigma^2 S^2 - rF = 0 \tag{11.34}$$

This the Black-Scholes partial differential equation. This equation has many different solutions which correspond to the various derivative securities which can be defined with the stock price as the underlying variable. The solution obtained will depend on the *boundary conditions* which are specified. Boundary conditions are the values of the derivative security at the boundaries of the possible values that S and t can take.

Boundary Conditions for European Calls and Puts

One of the boundary conditions for a European call option is $C(S,T) = Max(0, S_T - X)$. The analogous condition for a European put is $P(S,T) = Max(0, X - S_T)$. These conditions arise from the fact that an option must be worth its intrinsic value at expiration. If the stock price goes to zero, then the change in price dS is also zero. Consequently if the stock were to ever attain a value of zero then it would stay there. The call option would therefore become worthless in such a situation, irrespective of the time left to maturity. Thus C(0,t) = 0 for calls. On the other hand, if the stock price were to attain a value of zero, a European put is guaranteed to be exercised at expiration. Hence its present value must be the discounted value of the exercise price. That is P(0,t) = $Xe^{-r(T-t)}$. Finally as the

7 It must be remembered that our portfolio is not permanently riskless. As S and t change, $\frac{\partial F}{\partial S}$ will also change. Hence to keep the portfolio riskless, it must be continuously rebalanced.

stock price tends to infinity it is increasingly likely that the call will be exercised and the magnitude of the exercise price becomes more and more insignificant. Thus the call will tend to behave like the stock in such circumstances and we can state that $C(S,t) \to S$ as $S \to \infty$. Similarly if the stock price tends towards infinity it is increasingly unlikely that a European put will be exercised. Consequently $P(S,t) \to 0$ as $S \to \infty$.

11.22 Risk Neutral Valuation

When we studied the binomial model, we dealt with pseudo probabilities and risk neutral valuation. Similar principles are applicable here.

Let's consider the partial differential equation used by Black and Scholes. Notice that it does not contain any variables which pertain to the risk preferences of individuals. For instance, μ, the expected rate of return, is conspicuous by its absence. If μ were to be present, the equation would not be independent of risk preferences.[8]

Considering this fact, we can use the following argument. If risk aversion measures are absent, then we can assume any kind of risk preferences while valuing the option, since it will not affect the solution. To keep matters simple, therefore, we can assume that everyone is risk neutral.

Now, in a risk neutral world, the expected rate of return on all securities will be the riskless rate r.[9] And, the value of any cash flow can be gotten by discounting its expected value using the riskless rate.

This assumption of risk neutrality considerably simplifies option pricing. We can now assume that the expected rate of return on the stock is r, and can then calculate the expected value of the option at time T. This expected value can then be discounted back using r, to get the option price.

Remember once again that we are not saying everyone is risk neutral. By assuming that everyone is risk neutral, we are only trying to simplify the analysis. The final solution is valid for all investors, irrespective of their risk preferences.

11.23 The Black-Scholes Formula

Black and Scholes obtained exact formulae for valuing call and put options on non-dividend paying stocks, by assuming that stock prices follow a lognormal process. The formulae obtained by them are:

$$C_{E,t} = S_t N(d_1) - Xe^{-r(T-t)} N(d_2) \tag{11.35}$$

8 The more risk averse the investor, the greater will be the value of μ.

9 This is because risk neutral investors do not require a premium to induce them to take risks.

and

$$P_{E,t} = Xe^{-r(T-t)}N(-d_2) - S_tN(-d_1) \tag{11.36}$$

where

$$d_1 = \frac{ln\left(\frac{S_t}{X}\right) + \left(r + \frac{\sigma^2}{2}\right)(T-t)}{\sigma\sqrt{(T-t)}} \tag{11.37}$$

and

$$d_2 = d_1 - \sigma\sqrt{(T-t)} \tag{11.38}$$

N(X) is the cumulative probability distribution function for a standard normal variable, and σ is the standard deviation of the rate of return on the stock. Example 11.5 shows the computation of the option premium using the Black-Scholes formula.

Example 11.5: Consider a stock which is currently selling for \$100. Call and put options are available with X = 100, and time to expiration = 6 months.

The riskless rate of interest = 10% per annum, and the volatility is 30% per annum. So, S_t = X = 100; T-t = .5 years; r = 10% ≡ .10; σ = 30% ≡ .30

Let's consider the call first.

$$d_1 = \frac{ln\left(\frac{100}{100}\right) + \left(.10 + \frac{(.30)^2}{2}\right).5}{.3\sqrt{.5}}$$
$$= \frac{.0725}{.2121} = .3418$$
$$d_2 = .3418 - .2121 = .1297$$

N(d_1) and N(d_2) have to be calculated using interpolation, or using the NORMSDIST function in Excel. N(.34) = .6331. N(.35) = .6368. Therefore if we set:

$$\frac{N(.35) - N(.34)}{N(.35) - N(.3418)} = \frac{0.6368 - 0.6331}{0.6368 - X} = \frac{.35 - .34}{.35 - .3418}$$

we get N(.3418) = .6338

Similarly, since N(.12) = .5478. N(.13) = .5517, we get N(.1297) = .5516.

$$C_{E,t} = 100 \times .6338 - 100e^{-.10\times.5} \times .5516$$
$$= 10.9102$$
$$P_{E,t} = 100e^{-.10\times.5}N(-.1297) - 100N(-.3418)$$

Now, N(-X) = 1 - N(X). So, N(-.1297) = 1-.5516 = .4484, and N(-.3418) = .3662. Thus, $P_{E,t}$ = 6.0331.

11.24 Put-Call Parity

We will now show that the Black-Scholes formula satisfies put-call parity.

11.24.1 Proof

$$\begin{aligned} C_{E,t} &= S_t N(d_1) - Xe^{-r(T-t)} N(d_2) \\ &= S_t[1 - N(-d_1)] - Xe^{-r(T-t)}[1 - N(-d_2)] \\ &= Xe^{-r(T-t)} N(-d_2) - S_t N(-d_1) + S_t - Xe^{-r(T-t)} \\ &= P_t + S_t - Xe^{-r(T-t)} \end{aligned}$$

11.25 Interpretation of $N(d_1)$ and $N(d_2)$

The Black-Scholes formula for call options states that

$$C_{E,t} = S_t N(d_1) - Xe^{-r(T-t)} N(d_2)$$

The option premium is invariant to the risk preferences of investors and is consequently valid in a world characterized by risk neutrality. A risk neutral investor would value the option as the discounted value of its expected payoff. Consequently, since

$$C_{E,t} = e^{-r(T-t)}[S_t e^{r(T-t)} N(d_1) - XN(d_2)]$$

it is obvious that

$$[S_t e^{r(T-t)} N(d_1) - XN(d_2)]$$

is the expected payoff from the option from the perspective of a risk neutral investor.

$S_t e^{r(T-t)} N(d_1)$ is the expected value of a variable in a risk neutral world, that is equal to S_T if the option is exercised, and is equal to zero otherwise. $N(d_2)$ is the probability that the option will be exercised in a risk neutral world. If the option is exercised there will be an outflow of X else the outflow will be zero. Consequently, $XN(d_2)$ is the expected outflow on account of the exercise price.

The formula for puts states that

$$\begin{aligned} P_{E,t} &= Xe^{-r(T-t)} N(-d_2) - S_t N(-d_1) \\ \Rightarrow &= e^{-r(T-t)}[XN(-d_2) - S_t e^{r(T-t)} N(-d_1)] \end{aligned}$$

If $N(d_2)$ is the probability that a call option with an exercise price of X is exercised in a risk neutral world then $1 - N(d_2)$ or $N(-d_2)$ is the probability that a put with the same exercise price will be exercised. Thus $XN(-d_2)$ is the expected inflow on account of the exercise price. $S_t e^{r(T-t)} N(-d_1)$ is the expected value of a variable that will be equal to S_T if the option is exercised and is equal to zero otherwise.

11.26 Additional Insights Into the Derivation of the Black-Scholes Formula

We know that if the stock price were to follow an Ito process then:

$$\Rightarrow lnS_T \sim N\left[lnS_t + \left(\mu - \frac{\sigma^2}{2}\right)(T-t), \sigma^2(T-t)\right]$$

In a risk-neutral world:

$$E[ln(S_T)] = ln(S_t) + r(T-t) - \frac{1}{2}\sigma^2(T-t)$$

and $\text{Var}[ln(S_T)] = \sigma^2(T-t)$.

The probability that $S_T > X$ is equal to the probability that $ln(S_T) > lnX$. If we denote the mean of $ln[S_T]$ by M, and its variance by V, we can state that:

$$P\left[ln(S_T) > lnX\right] = P\left[\frac{ln(S_T) - M}{\sqrt{(V)}} > \frac{lnX - M}{\sqrt{(V)}}\right]$$

Since $\frac{ln(S_T) - M}{\sqrt{(V)}}$ is a standard normal variable,

$$P\left[\frac{ln(S_T) - M}{\sqrt{(V)}} > \frac{lnX - M}{\sqrt{(V)}}\right] = 1 - N\left[\frac{lnX - M}{\sqrt{(V)}}\right]$$
$$= N\left[\frac{M - lnX}{\sqrt{(V)}}\right]$$

$$M - lnX = ln(S_t) + r(T-t) - \frac{1}{2}\sigma^2(T-t) - lnX = ln\left(\frac{S_t}{X}\right) + \left(r - \frac{1}{2}\sigma^2\right)(T-t)$$

Therefore the probability that $S_T > X$, is nothing but $N(d_2)$.

$$E[S_T - X | S_T > X] = E[S_T | S_T > X] - E[X | S_T > X] = E[S_T | S_T > X] - X$$

It can be shown that if $ln(S_T)$ is normally distributed, then:

$$E[S_T \mid S_T > X] = E(S_T)\frac{N(d_1)}{N(d_2)}$$

where d_1 and d_2 have the usual definitions.

Thus

$$E[S_T - X \mid S_T > X] = E(S_T)\frac{N(d_1)}{N(d_2)} - X = e^{r(T-t)}S_t\frac{N(d_1)}{N(d_2)} - X$$

since in a risk-neutral world $E[S_T] = S_t e^{r(T-t)}$. We know that the value of the option is the discounted value of the expected payoff at expiration, in a risk-neutral world. Thus:

$$\begin{aligned} C_t &= e^{-r(T-t)}E[Max(0, S_T - X)] \\ &= e^{-r(T-t)}E[S_T - X \mid S_T > X]N(d_2) \\ &= e^{-r(T-t)}\left[e^{r(T-t)}S_t\frac{N(d_1)}{N(d_2)} - X\right]N(d_2) \\ &= S_tN(d_1) - Xe^{-r(T-t)}N(d_2) \end{aligned}$$

11.27 Implied Volatility

Of all the variables required to estimate the option premia using the Black-Scholes formula, the most difficult to obtain is an estimate of the volatility. The stock price and the riskless rate can be deduced from market data, and the exercise price and time to maturity are known from the terms of the option contract. One way of estimating the volatility is using a vector of historical stock price data, as we have seen above. Another way is to estimate the volatility implicit in the option prices that are observed in the market.

Let C_i, i ranging from 1 to N be a vector of option prices that are obtained from the market. Estimate the vector of option prices for an assumed value of σ using the Black-Scholes formula, for a given set of other variables. Let's denote the model values by M_i, i ranging from 1 to N. The error for the ith observation is given by $e_i = C_i - M_i$. The optimal estimate of σ is the value that minimizes the sum of squared errors for the series of data. That is, the optimal estimate $\hat{\sigma}$ is the one that minimizes

$$\sum_{i=1}^{N}[C_i - M_i]^2$$

The volatility that is obtained in this manner is referred to as the implied volatility.

If the Black-Scholes model is strictly valid, then all options on a given stock, which have the same time to expiration, should give an identical implied volatility. However, very often it is observed in practice that at-the-money options give the lowest implied volatility, while deep-in-the-money and deep-out-of-the-money options give the highest volatility.

When the implied volatility is plotted against the exercise price, for options with the same time to expiration, we get a u-shaped pattern that is referred to as the *Volatility Smile*. The very fact that we observe such patterns tells us that the Black-Scholes model does not fully capture all the facets of option pricing. Options with higher implied volatilities are obviously more expensive than those with lower implied volatilities, a phenomenon that the Black-Scholes formula is unable to explain.

11.28 European Options on Dividend Paying Stocks

For the ensuing analysis, we will assume that we can predict with certainty the dividends that will be paid during the life of the option.[10]

We will assume that the stock price at a given point in time is the sum of two components. There is a component that grows at the riskless rate of return, which will be used to pay the dividends during the life of the option. In addition, there is a risky component.

The value of the riskless component is the present value of all dividends during the life of the option. The difference between the total stock price S_t and the present value of the riskless component, is the value of the risky component S_t^*. The Black-Scholes formula can then be applied using S_t^* instead of S_t. Example 11.6 shows the computation of the option price, when there is a known dividend during the life of the option.

Example 11.6: Consider the same data we just used. Assume that a dividend of $5 is paid after 3 months.

$S_t^* = 100 - 5e^{-.10 \times .25} = 95.1235.$

$$d_1 = \frac{ln\left(\frac{95.1235}{100}\right) + \left(.10 + \frac{(.30)^2}{2}\right).5}{.3\sqrt{.5}}$$

$$= .1061$$

$d_2 = .1061 - .2121 = -.1060$

N(.1061) = .5422; N(−.1060) = .4578

$$C_{E,t} = 95.1235 \times .5422 - 100e^{-.10 \times .5} \times .4578 = 8.0287$$

$$P_{E,t} = 100e^{-.10 \times .5} \times .5422 - 95.1235 \times .4578 = 8.0281$$

As you can see, due to the dividend, the call price has come down, while the put price has gone up.

---

10 This may not be unreasonable for short term options.

11.29 Using the Binomial Model in Practice

While illustrating the binomial model, we chose the parameters u and d in a rather arbitrary fashion. In practice, the parameters u, d, and p, are chosen in such a way that the moments of the discrete time stock price process being modeled correspond to the moments of the lognormal distribution of stock prices, which is the assumption underlying the Black-Scholes model. We will now illustrate two approaches to estimating the parameters in practice.

11.29.1 Method-A

Given the current price S_t, the price next period, S_T, can be either uS_t where u represents the up state, or dS_t where d represents the down state. The expected value of S_T given S_t is

$$puS_t + (1-p)dS_t \tag{11.39}$$

In a risk neutral world we know that for a lognormal distribution

$$E(S_T) = S_t e^{r(T-t)} \tag{11.40}$$

If we equate the two, we get

$$\begin{aligned} pu + (1-p)d &= e^{r(T-t)} \\ \Rightarrow p &= \frac{e^{r(T-t)} - d}{u - d} \end{aligned} \tag{11.41}$$

If we denote T-t as Δt, we can state the risk neutral probability of an up move as $p = \frac{e^{r\Delta t} - d}{u-d}$. The variance of S_T from the binomial process is

$$\begin{aligned} &pu^2 S_t^2 + (1-p)d^2 S_t^2 - [puS_t + (1-p)dS_t]^2 \\ &= [pu^2 + (1-p)d^2 - e^{2r\Delta t}]S_t^2 \end{aligned} \tag{11.42}$$

The variance of S_T from the lognormal distribution is

$$e^{2r\Delta t}[e^{\sigma^2 \Delta t} - 1]S_t^2$$

If we equate the two, we get

$$pu^2 + (1-p)d^2 = e^{(2r+\sigma^2)\Delta t} \tag{11.43}$$

We now have two equations in three unknowns. The third condition that is normally imposed is $u = \frac{1}{d}$. The system of equations can now be solved to yield the following values for the three parameters.[11]

$$p = \frac{e^{r\Delta t} - d}{u - d} \tag{11.44}$$
$$u = A + \sqrt{A^2 - 1} \text{ and } d = A - \sqrt{A^2 - 1}$$

where

$$A = \frac{1}{2}\left[e^{-r\Delta t} + e^{(r+\sigma^2)\Delta t}\right] \tag{11.45}$$

11.29.2 Method-B

Another approach is to specify the following values for u and d.[12]

$$u = e^{\sigma\sqrt{\Delta t}} \text{ and } d = e^{-\sigma\sqrt{\Delta t}}$$

Obviously d is the reciprocal of u. The variance of the binomial process is given by

$$pu^2 + (1 - p)d^2 - [pu + (1 - p)d]^2$$
$$= e^{r\Delta t}(u + d) - ud - e^{2r\Delta t}$$

Using the result that $e^x = 1 + x + \frac{x^2}{2!} + \frac{x^3}{3!} + ...$ and discarding terms with Δt^2 and higher powers of Δt, it can be shown that the variance of the binomial process tends towards $\sigma^2(T - t)$ as $T - t = \Delta t \to 0$.

See Example 11.7 for a numerical illustration.

Example 11.7: Take the case of a stock which is currently priced at $100. Consider a one year call option with an exercise price of $100 and one year to expiration. Let the riskless rate be 10% per annum, and the volatility be 30% per annum. If we model the stock price process as a two period model, we will get the following parameters.

$$u = e^{0.30\sqrt{0.5}} = 1.2363;\ d = 0.8089;\ p = \frac{e^{0.10\times0.5} - 0.8089}{1.2363 - 0.8089} = 0.5671$$

11 See Wilmott et. al. (1999).

12 See Hull (2005).

The variance of the binomial process is

$$
\begin{aligned}
e^{r\Delta t}(u+d) - ud - e^{2r\Delta t} \\
&= e^{0.10\times0.5}(1.2363 + 0.8089) - 1.0 - e^{2\times0.10\times0.5} \\
&= 0.044889
\end{aligned}
$$

The variance of the continuous time process is

$$0.3 \times 0.3 \times 0.5 = 0.045$$

The approximation is excellent.

11.30 An Introduction to the Greeks

We have discussed the variables which influence the option premium, and their relationship with the price of an option. The rate of change of the option price with respect to these variables is denoted by various Greek symbols, and consequently this area of option theory is often referred to as 'The Greeks'.

Delta

Delta represents the rate of change of the option premium with respect to the price of the underlying asset, keeping all the other variables constant. In other words, delta is the partial derivative of the option price with respect to the price of the underlying asset. The delta of a call option will always lie between zero and one. For deep out of the money options, delta will be close to zero, whereas for options that are very deep in the money, the delta will be close to one. It must be remembered that delta represents the change in the option price for an infinitesimal change in the asset price. Consequently, as the asset price changes, so will the delta. Thus, while we may interpret a delta value of say 0.45 to mean that for a one dollar move in the asset price, the option premium will move by 45 cents, it must be remembered that this is accurate only for an infinitesimal change in the asset price.

Even if the asset price were to remain constant, the delta of an option will change with the sheer passage of time. As the call option approaches maturity, the delta will tend towards one if the option were to be in the money, whereas it will tend towards zero, if the option were to be out of the money.

For put options, quite obviously delta will be between 0 and −1.

Gamma

The rate of change of delta with respect to the asset price is called the Gamma of the option. Gamma will always be positive and tends to be at its peak when the option is near the money.

Vega

Vega is the derivative of the option price with respect to the volatility or the standard deviation of the rate of return of the underlying asset. The vega will be positive for both call and put options, as should be obvious from the arguments presented earlier.

Theta

As we have discussed earlier, options are wasting assets. That is, with everything else remaining constant, their values decline with the passage of time. Theta is a measure of the time decay of the option premium. It is expressed as the negative of the rate of change of the option premium with respect to the time to maturity. For European and American calls, theta will always be negative, indicating that option premia decline with time. The same is true for American puts. For European puts theta is usually negative. However, for certain deep in the money puts, theta can be positive.

Rho

Rho represents the rate of change of the option premium with respect to the riskless rate of interest. For call options rho will be positive, whereas for put options it will be negative.

11.30.1 The Black-Scholes Formula and the Greeks

Delta

The delta for a European call option is equal to $N(d_1)$ and that for a European put option is equal to $-N(-d_1)$. As we would expect the delta for a call is positive, while that for a put is negative.

Gamma

The gamma for both European call and put options is equal to $\frac{n(d_1)}{S_t\sigma\sqrt{T-t}}$. Thus gamma is positive for both calls as well as puts.

Vega

The vega for European call and put options is equal to $S_t n(d_1)\sqrt{T-t}$. As we would expect, vega is positive for both calls as well as puts.

Theta

Theta is defined as the negative of the rate of change of the option premium with respect to the time to maturity. For European call options

$$\text{Theta} = -rXe^{-r(T-t)}N(d_2) - S_t n(d_1)\frac{\sigma}{2\sqrt{T-t}}$$

while for European puts it is

$$rXe^{-r(T-t)}N(-d_2) - S_t n(d_1)\frac{\sigma}{2\sqrt{T-t}}$$

For call options theta is negative, which is consistent with the fact that ceteris paribus, call premiums decline with the passage of time. For puts theta may be either positive or negative. As we have seen earlier, certain deep in the money puts can have a negative time value. In such cases the option premium will actually increase with the passage of time, if all other variables were to remain constant.

Rho

For a European call option

$$\text{Rho} = X(T-t)e^{-r(T-t)}N(d_2)$$

while for European put options

$$\text{Rho} = -X(T-t)e^{-r(T-t)}N(-d_2)$$

As we would expect, for call options, rho is positive, while for put options it is negative.

Sensitivity with Respect to the Exercise Price

$$\frac{\partial C}{\partial X} = -e^{-r(T-t)}N(d_2)$$
$$\frac{\partial P}{\partial X} = e^{-r(T-t)}N(-d_2)$$

Thus the call option premium declines with an increase in the exercise price, keeping all the other variables constant, while the put option premium increases with an increase in the exercise price.

11.30.2 Computing the Delta for Varying Degrees of Moneyness

Consider the following data. The exercise price is equal to \$100. The riskless rate is 10% per annum and the volatility is 30% per annum. The options have six months to maturity. Table 11.3 lists the values of delta for both European calls and puts for stock prices ranging from \$5 to \$150 in increments of \$5.

Table 11.3: Call and Put Option Deltas For Various Stock Prices.

Stock Price	Call Delta	Put Delta
5	0	−1.0
10	0	−1.0
15	0	−1.0
20	2.17×10^{-14}	−1.0
25	2.96×10^{-10}	−1.0
30	4.82×10^{-08}	−1.0
35	2.04×10^{-06}	−0.999998
40	3.48×10^{-05}	−0.999965
45	0.00031	−0.99969
50	0.001718	−0.998282
55	0.006635	−0.993365
60	0.019410	−0.980599
65	0.045613	−0.954387
70	0.090186	−0.909814
75	0.155201	−0.844799
80	0.238808	−0.761192
85	0.335654	−0.664346
90	0.438448	−0.561552
95	0.539816	−0.460184
100	0.633737	−0.366263
105	0.71626	−0.28374
110	0.785547	−0.214453
115	0.841493	−0.158507
120	0.885171	−0.114829
125	0.918292	−0.081708
130	0.942782	−0.057218
135	0.960496	−0.039504
140	0.973067	−0.026933
145	0.98184	−0.01816
150	0.987875	−0.012125

11.30.3 Creating a Delta Neutral Position

Consider a portfolio of N_1 shares and N_2 call options. The delta for a call is $\frac{\partial C}{\partial S}$, while the delta for a stock is one. If we denote the value of the portfolio as π

$$\frac{\partial \pi}{\partial S} = N_1 + N_2 \frac{\partial C}{\partial S} \tag{11.46}$$

If the portfolio is to be delta neutral, N_1 and N_2 must be chosen in such a way that

$$\frac{\partial \pi}{\partial S} = 0$$

$$\Rightarrow N_1 = -\frac{\partial C}{\partial S} N_2 \tag{11.47}$$

Consider an investor who has sold 50 call options contracts, each of which is for 100 shares. Let the delta of the option be 0.6337. In order to make the position delta neutral, he needs to go long in

$$0.6337 \times 50 \times 100 = 3{,}168.50 \text{ shares}$$

If the stock price were to go up by $1, he would gain $3,168.50 from the shares. However, a dollar's increase in the stock price would lead to an increase of 0.6337 in the option premium. Thus the short position in the option would lead to a loss of $3,168.50.

It must be remembered that delta is a function of the stock price, and hence will change as the stock price changes. Consequently, in order to maintain the neutrality of the position, it must be periodically rebalanced.

The delta of a put option is negative. Hence to hedge a short position in puts, the investor needs to go short in the required number of shares.

11.31 Put-Call Parity and the Greeks

We have observed that both Gamma and Vega are identical for European calls and puts which are valued using the Black-Scholes model. This is not a coincidence. We know from put call parity that:

$$C_{E,t} - P_{E,t} = S_t - Xe^{-r(T-t)}$$

$$\text{Thus } \frac{\partial C}{\partial S} - \frac{\partial P}{\partial S} = 1$$

We have seen in the case of the Black-Scholes model that $\frac{\partial C}{\partial S} = N(d_1)$ and that $\frac{\partial P}{\partial S} = -N(-d_1)$. Obviously the sum of the call delta and the put delta is equal to 1.0.

$$\frac{\partial^2 C}{\partial S^2} = \frac{\partial^2 P}{\partial S^2}$$

Thus Gamma is identical for call and put-options, irrespective of the valuation model that is used.

$$\frac{\partial C}{\partial \sigma} = \frac{\partial P}{\partial \sigma}$$

Therefore Vega is also equal for call and put options irrespective of the pricing model used.

Similarly from put-call parity, we know that:

$$\frac{\partial C}{\partial X} - \frac{\partial P}{\partial X} = -e^{-r(T-t)}$$

$$\frac{\partial C}{\partial r} - \frac{\partial P}{\partial r} = (T-t)Xe^{-r(T-t)} \text{ and}$$

$$\frac{\partial C}{\partial (T-t)} - \frac{\partial P}{\partial (T-t)} = rXe^{-r(T-t)}$$

It can be easily shown that the Black-Scholes formula satisfies these conditions.

Suggestions for Further Reading

Chance D.M. *An Introduction to Derivatives & Risk Management.* Thomson;South-Western, 2004.

Dewynne J., Howison S., and P. Wilmott *The Mathematics of Financial Derivatives: A Student Introduction.* Cambridge University Press, 1999.

Hull J.C. *Options, Futures, and Other Derivatives.* Prentice Hall of India, 2005.

Kolb R.W. *Futures, Options, & Swaps.* Blackwell, 1999.

Rubinstein M. *Rubinstein on Derivatives: Futures, Options and Dynamic Strategies.* Risk Books, 2005.

References

www.ivolatility.com

www.optiontradingpedia.com

www.sitmo.com

Chapter 12
Options on Stock Indexes, Foreign Currencies, Futures Contracts, and Volatility Indexes

12.1 The Merton Model

Before we go on to analyze options on stock indexes, foreign currencies, and futures contracts, let's first derive an equivalent of the Black-Scholes formula for a stock that pays a continuous dividend yield. This model was derived by Merton and has implications for option pricing models for other financial assets such as stock indexes and foreign currencies.

Take the case of a stock that evolves from a current price of S_t to a value of S_T by time T. If this stock were to pay a continuous dividend yield at the rate of δ, the dividend can be construed as a leakage of value from it. Thus, if it were to pay such a dividend it would evolve to a value of $S_T e^{-\delta(T-t)}$ by time T. This price movement is identical to what a non-dividend paying stock which is currently priced at $S_t e^{-\delta(T-t)}$ would experience. Thus the Black-Scholes formula can be applied to the stock paying a continuous yield of δ, if we replace its price S_t with $S_t e^{-\delta(T-t)}$.

We know that for a non-dividend paying stock

$$C_{E,t} = S_t N(d_1) - Xe^{-r(T-t)} N(d_2) \tag{12.1}$$

where

$$d_1 = \frac{ln\left(\frac{S_t}{X}\right) + \left(r + \frac{\sigma^2}{2}\right)(T-t)}{\sigma\sqrt{(T-t)}} \tag{12.2}$$

and

$$d_2 = d_1 - \sigma\sqrt{(T-t)} \tag{12.3}$$

If we substitute S_t with $S_t e^{-\delta(T-t)}$ we get

$$C_{E,t} = S_t e^{-\delta(T-t)} N(d_1) - Xe^{-r(T-t)} N(d_2) \tag{12.4}$$

where

$$d_1 = \frac{ln\left(\frac{S_t}{X}\right) + \left(r - \delta + \frac{\sigma^2}{2}\right)(T-t)}{\sigma\sqrt{(T-t)}} \tag{12.5}$$

https://doi.org/10.1515/9783110746662-012

and

$$d_2 = d_1 - \sigma\sqrt{(T-t)} \tag{12.6}$$

The corresponding formula for European puts on a stock that pays a continuous dividend yield is

$$P_{E,t} = Xe^{-r(T-t)}N(-d_2) - S_t e^{-\delta(T-t)}N(-d_1) \tag{12.7}$$

where d_1 and d_2 are as defined for the call options.

12.1.1 The Underlying Rationale

We defined the Ito process for the stock price of a non-dividend paying stock as

$$dS = \mu Sdt + \sigma SdZ \tag{12.8}$$

The equivalent process for a stock that pays a continuous dividend yield is

$$dS = (\mu - \delta)Sdt + \sigma SdZ \tag{12.9}$$

Consider a derivative security F that is a function of S and t.

$$dF = \left[\frac{\partial F}{\partial S}(\mu - \delta)S + \frac{\partial F}{\partial t} + \frac{1}{2} \times \frac{\partial^2 F}{\partial S^2}\sigma^2 S^2\right]dt + \frac{\partial F}{\partial S}\sigma SdZ \tag{12.10}$$

Let π be the value of a portfolio that is long in $\frac{\partial F}{\partial S}$ units of the stock and short in one unit of the derivative.

$$\pi = \frac{\partial F}{\partial S}S - F \tag{12.11}$$

The change in π over a small interval of time Δt is given by

$$\begin{aligned}\Delta\pi &= \frac{\partial F}{\partial S}[\Delta S + \delta S\Delta t] - \Delta F \\ &= \left[-\frac{\partial F}{\partial t} - \frac{1}{2}\frac{\partial^2 F}{\partial S^2}\sigma^2 S^2 + \frac{\partial F}{\partial S}\delta S\right]\Delta t\end{aligned} \tag{12.12}$$

Since this portfolio by construction is instantaneously riskless

$$\Delta\pi = r\pi\Delta t$$

where r is the riskless rate of interest. Hence

$$\left[-\frac{\partial F}{\partial t}-\frac{1}{2}\frac{\partial^2 F}{\partial S^2}\sigma^2 S^2+\frac{\partial F}{\partial S}\delta S\right]\Delta t = r\left(-F+\frac{\partial F}{\partial S}S\right)\Delta t$$

$$\Rightarrow \frac{\partial F}{\partial t}+(r-\delta)S\frac{\partial F}{\partial S}+\frac{1}{2}\frac{\partial^2 F}{\partial S^2}\sigma^2 S^2 - rF = 0 \tag{12.13}$$

The Merton model is the solution to this equation by applying the relevant boundary conditions. For a European call option, the conditions are:

- $C(S, T) = Max[0, S_T - X]$
- $C(0, t) = 0$
- $C(S, t) \sim Se^{-\delta(T-t)}$ as $S \to \infty$

The first two conditions are identical to those for a non-dividend paying stock. The third condition is however different, and reflects the fact that there is leakage of value from the stock price. Example 12.1 shows the valuation of an option on a stock paying a continuous dividend.

Example 12.1: Consider a stock that is currently priced at $100. Call and put options with an exercise price of $100 and six months to maturity are available. The riskless rate of interest is 10% per annum and the volatility of stock returns is 30% per annum. The stock pays a continuous dividend yield of 5% per annum.

$$d_1 = \frac{ln\left(\frac{100}{100}\right)+\left(0.10-0.05+\frac{0.30\times 0.30}{2}\right)0.50}{0.30\sqrt{0.50}}$$

$$= 0.2240$$

$$d_2 = 0.2240 - .2121 = 0.0119$$

$$N(d_1) = 0.5886 \text{ and } N(d_2) = 0.5047$$

$$C_{E,t} = 100e^{-.05\times 0.5}\times 0.5886 - 100e^{-.10\times 0.5}\times 0.5047$$

$$= \$9.3982$$

$$P_{E,t} = 100e^{-.10\times 0.5}\times 0.4953 - 100e^{-.05\times 0.5}\times 0.4114$$

$$= \$6.9902$$

Applying the Binomial Model for a Given Value of Sigma

The Binomial model can be used to value options on a stock paying a continuous dividend yield. The parameters are typically defined as follows.

$$u = e^{\sigma\sqrt{\Delta t}} \tag{12.14}$$

$$d = e^{-\sigma\sqrt{\Delta t}} \tag{12.15}$$

The risk neutral probabilities can be derived as follows. Consider a portfolio consisting of α units of the stock and \$B of riskless debt. Assume that the stock pays a dividend at a rate of δ% per annum and that the dividends are re-invested in the stock. Let's choose α and B such that:

$$\alpha u S_t e^{\delta\Delta t} + Be^{r\Delta t} = C_u \tag{12.16}$$

$$\text{and } \alpha d S_t e^{\delta\Delta t} + Be^{r\Delta t} = C_d \tag{12.17}$$

$$\text{So } \alpha = \frac{C_u - C_d}{S_t(u-d)} e^{-\delta\Delta t} \tag{12.18}$$

$$\text{and } B = [C_u - \alpha u S_t e^{\delta\Delta t}]e^{-r\Delta t}$$

$$= [C_u - \frac{u(C_u - C_d)}{u-d}]e^{-r\Delta t} \tag{12.19}$$

$$\alpha S_t + B = C_t. \text{ Therefore}$$

$$\frac{C_u - C_d}{(u-d)} e^{-\delta\Delta t} + [C_u - \frac{u(C_u - C_d)}{u-d}]e^{-r\Delta t} = C_t$$

$$\Rightarrow \frac{C_u - C_d}{(u-d)} e^{(r-\delta)\Delta t} + [C_u - \frac{u(C_u - C_d)}{u-d}] = C_t e^{r\Delta t}$$

$$\Rightarrow C_u\left[\frac{e^{(r-\delta)\Delta t} - d}{u-d}\right] + C_d\left[\frac{u - e^{(r-\delta)\Delta t}}{u-d}\right] = C_t e^{r\Delta t}$$

$$\Rightarrow C_t = \left\{C_u\left[\frac{e^{(r-\delta)\Delta t} - d}{u-d}\right] + C_d\left[\frac{u - e^{(r-\delta)\Delta t}}{u-d}\right]\right\}e^{-r\Delta t} \tag{12.20}$$

This is of the form $C_t = [pC_u + (1-p)C_d]e^{-r\Delta t}$ where $p = \left[\frac{e^{(r-\delta)\Delta t} - d}{u-d}\right]$.

12.1.2 Arbitrage Restrictions

12.2 Lower Bound for European Call Options

It can be demonstrated that $C_{E,t} \geq \text{Max}\left[0, S_t e^{-\delta(T-t)} - Xe^{-r(T-t)}\right]$. If the expression $S_t e^{-\delta(T-t)} - Xe^{-r(T-t)}$ were to be less than zero, then all that we can assert is that $C_{E,t} \geq 0$, because we know that an option cannot have a negative premium. However, if the expression were to be positive, then the option premium must be greater than or equal to it to preclude arbitrage.

12.2.1 Proof

Assume that $C_{E,t} < S_t e^{-\delta(T-t)} - Xe^{-r(T-t)} > 0$ or that $S_t e^{-\delta(T-t)} - Xe^{-r(T-t)} - C_t > 0$. Consider Table 12.1.

Table 12.1: Lower Bound for a European Call Option.

Action	Initial Cash Flow	Terminal Cash Flow	
		If $S_T > X$	If $S_T < X$
Short sell $e^{-\delta(T-t)}$ units of the Stock	$S_t e^{-\delta(T-t)}$	$-S_T$	$-S_T$
Buy the Call	$-C_{E,t}$	$(S_T - X)$	0
Lend the P.V. of X	$-Xe^{-r(T-t)}$	X	X
Total	$S_t e^{-\delta(T-t)} - Xe^{-r(T-t)} - C_{E,t}$	0	$X - S_T > 0$

The initial strategy entails the short sale of $e^{-\delta(T-t)}$ units of the stock. If the lender had not parted with the stock he could have reinvested the dividends in the stock itself, and consequently would have had one unit of the stock at the time of expiration of the option. Consequently the short seller must return one share of the stock to cover his short position, which explains the outflow of S_T at time T.

In this table the cash flow at inception is positive by assumption. The cash flows at expiration are non-negative. Thus this table reflects an arbitrage opportunity. To preclude it, it therefore must be the case that

$$S_t e^{-\delta(T-t)} - Xe^{-r(T-t)} - C_{E,t} \leq 0$$
$$\Rightarrow C_{E,t} \geq S_t e^{-\delta(T-t)} - Xe^{-r(T-t)} \tag{12.21}$$

12.3 Lower Bound for European Put Options

In the case of European puts, the no-arbitrage condition is:

$$P_{E,t} \geq \text{Max}[0, Xe^{-r(T-t)} - S_t e^{-\delta(T-t)}]$$

This condition can be interpreted as follows. If $Xe^{-r(T-t)} - S_t e^{-\delta(T-t)} < 0$, then all that we can assert is that $P_{E,t} > 0$, because an option cannot have a negative premium. However, if $Xe^{-r(T-t)} - S_t e^{-\delta(T-t)} > 0$ then we can show that $P_{E,t} \geq Xe^{-r(T-t)} - S_t e^{-\delta(T-t)}$. To prove it, consider the following strategy, shown in Table 12.2.

Table 12.2: Lower Bound for a European Put Option.

Action	Initial Cash Flow	Terminal Cash Flow	
		If $S_T > X$	If $S_T < X$
Buy the Put	$-P_{E,t}$	0	$(X - S_T)$
Buy the $e^{-\delta(T-t)}$ units of the Stock	$-S_t e^{-\delta(T-t)}$	S_T	S_T
Borrow the P.V. of X	$Xe^{-r(T-t)}$	$-X$	$-X$
Total	$Xe^{-r(T-t)} - P_{E,t} - S_t e^{-\delta(T-t)}$	$S_T - X > 0$	0

To rule out arbitrage we require that.

$$Xe^{-r(T-t)} - P_{E,t} - S_t e^{-\delta(T-t)} \leq 0$$

$$\Rightarrow P_{E,t} \geq Xe^{-r(T-t)} - S_t e^{-\delta(T-t)} \tag{12.22}$$

12.3.1 Put Call Parity for European Options

The put-call parity condition for European options on a stock paying a continuous dividend yield is:

$$C_{E,t} - P_{E,t} = S_t e^{-\delta(T-t)} - Xe^{-r(T-t)}$$

The proof is given in Table 12.3.

Table 12.3: Put Call Parity for European Options.

Action	Initial Cash Flow	Terminal Cash Flow	
		If $S_T > X$	If $S_T < X$
Sell the Call	$C_{E,t}$	$-(S_T - X)$	0
Buy the Put	$-P_{E,t}$	0	$(X - S_T)$
Buy $e^{-\delta(T-t)}$ units of the Stock	$-S_t e^{-\delta(T-t)}$	S_T	S_T
Borrow the P.V. of X	$Xe^{-r(T-t)}$	$-X$	$-X$
Total	$C_{E,t} + Xe^{-r(T-t)} - P_{E,t} - S_t e^{-\delta(T-t)}$	0	0

The initial cash flow has to be less than or equal to zero to preclude arbitrage. However, if it were to be less, then we could reverse the above strategy and make arbitrage profits. Consequently to rule out any form of arbitrage, the initial cash flow must be zero. This implies that

$$C_{E,t} - P_{E,t} = S_t e^{-\delta(T-t)} - Xe^{-r(T-t)} \tag{12.23}$$

12.3.2 The Greeks for European Options on a Stock Paying a Continuous Dividend Yield

Delta

For a European call: Delta = $e^{-\delta(T-t)}N(d_1)$
For a European put: Delta = $-e^{-\delta(T-t)}N(-d_1)$

Gamma

Gamma for both calls and puts is given by: $\dfrac{e^{-\delta(T-t)}n(d_1)}{S_t\sigma\sqrt{T-t}}$

Vega

Vega for both calls and puts is given by: $e^{-\delta(T-t)}S_t n(d_1)\sqrt{T-t}$

Theta

For a European call:

Theta $= \delta e^{-\delta(T-t)}S_t N(d_1) - rXe^{-r(T-t)}N(d_2) - \dfrac{e^{-\delta(T-t)}S_t\sigma n(d_1)}{2\sqrt{T-t}}$

For a European put:

Theta $= -\delta e^{-\delta(T-t)}S_t N(-d_1) + rXe^{-r(T-t)}N(-d_2) - \dfrac{e^{-\delta(T-t)}S_t\sigma n(d_1)}{2\sqrt{T-t}}$

Rho

For a European call: Rho = $e^{-r(T-t)}X(T-t)N(d_2)$
For a European put: Rho = $-e^{-r(T-t)}X(T-t)N(-d_2)$

12.4 Index Options

Options on prominent stock indices are traded in venues across the globe.

Consider European index options. The contracts are cash settled and the multiplier is \$100. Thus if a call option is exercised,the holder will receive \$ $100 \times (I_T - X)$, whereas if a put is exercised he will receive \$ $100 \times (X - I_T)$. I_T is the index level at the time of exercise/expiration. Example 12.2 illustrates the computation of the premium of an index option.

Example 12.2: European call options on the index are available with an exercise price of 700, and six months to expiration. The riskless rate is 6% per annum and the volatility is 20% per annum. The dividend yield is 4% per annum and the current level of the index is 700.

The option price can be calculated using the Merton model.

$$d_1 = \frac{\left(0.06 - 0.04 + \frac{0.2 \times 0.2}{2}\right)0.5}{0.2 \times \sqrt{0.5}} = 0.1414$$

$$d_2 = 0.1414 - 0.2 \times \sqrt{0.5} = 0$$

$$N(d_1) = 0.5562 \text{ and } N(d_2) = 0.5000$$

$$C_{E,t} = 700 \times e^{-0.04 \times 0.5} \times 0.5562 - 700 \times e^{-0.06 \times 0.5} \times 0.5000$$

$$= 381.6306 - 339.6559 = 41.9747$$

The premium per contract is 100 × 41.9747 = \$4,197.47.

12.5 Foreign Currency Options

Foreign currency options are traded on a number of exchanges. The Philadelphia Stock Exchange (PHLX) is the world's leading platform for exchange traded currency options. The exchange currently lists options contracts on seven foreign currencies. These currencies and the contract sizes for the respective options are given in the table below. The options are European style. At any point in time, contracts are available for the four quarterly months, March, June. September and December, and for the two nearest calendar months. Contracts expire on the third Friday of the expiration month. Exercise prices are expressed in terms of U.S. cents per unit of foreign currency. For instance a call option on British pounds with an exercise price of \$135 would give the option buyer the right to buy pounds at \$1.35 per pound. Premiums for options are quoted in U.S. cents per unit of the underlying currency. For instance a premium of 2.78 for a given option on British pounds is \$0.0278 per pound. Since each option contract is for 10,000 GBP, the total premium per contract is 0.0278 × 10,000 = \$278.00. Contract sizes for various currencies are shown in Table 12.4.

Table 12.4: Currencies and Contract Sizes.

Currency	Contract Size
Australian Dollar	10,000 AUD
British Pound	10,000 GBP
Canadian Dollar	10,000 CAD
Euro	10,000 EUR
Japanese Yen	1,000,000 JPY
Swiss Franc	10,000 CHF
New Zealand Dollar	10,000 NZD

All the above contracts are cash settled.

12.5.1 Arbitrage Restrictions

A foreign currency is like a stock paying a continuous dividend yield. The leakage of value in this case, takes place at a rate of r_f, which is the riskless rate of interest in the foreign currency. So the lower bounds for European call and put options may be expressed as:

$$C_{E,t} \geq \text{Max}[0, S_t e^{-r_f(T-t)} - Xe^{-r(T-t)}] \tag{12.24}$$

$$\text{and } P_{E,t} \geq \text{Max}[0, Xe^{-r(T-t)} - S_t e^{-r_f(T-t)}] \tag{12.25}$$

The put-call parity relationship for European options is given by:

$$C_{E,t} - P_{E,t} = S_t e^{-r_f(T-t)} - Xe^{-r(T-t)} \tag{12.26}$$

12.6 The Garman Kohlhagen Model

This model is an extension of the Black-Scholes model. According to it

$$C_E = S_t e^{-r_f(T-t)} N(d_1) - Xe^{-r(T-t)} N(d_2) \tag{12.27}$$

where

$$d_1 = \frac{ln\left(\frac{S_t}{X}\right) + \left(r - r_f + \frac{\sigma^2}{2}\right)(T-t)}{\sigma\sqrt{T-t}} \tag{12.28}$$

and $d_2 = d_1 - \sigma\sqrt{T-t}$. Example 12.3 shows the application of the Garman Kohlhagen model.

Example 12.3: Consider European calls on British pounds.

Let X = 200, and the spot rate be 185. The riskless rate of interest in the U.S is 4.5%, while the rate in the U.K is 6%. The time to expiration is six months, and the volatility of the spot rate is 30%.

$$d_1 = \frac{ln\left(\frac{185}{200}\right) + \left(0.045 - 0.06 + \frac{(0.30)^2}{2}\right)0.5}{0.30\sqrt{0.5}}$$

$$= -.2970$$

$$d_2 = -.5091$$

$$N(d_1) = 0.3832 \text{ and } N(d_2) = 0.3053$$

$$C_E = 185e^{-0.06\times0.5} \times 0.3832 - 200e^{-0.045\times0.5} \times 0.3053 = 9.0953$$

12.6.1 The Binomial Model with Given Parameters

Let's take the case of call options on British pounds. Let S_t be the spot exchange rate quoted as GBP/USD. Consider a portfolio consisting of a USD of riskless debt in the foreign currency, and B USD of riskless debt in the domestic currency. Example 12.4 illustrates the use of the binomial model to value the option.

Let $\mathbf{r}$ = 1 + domestic riskless rate, and $\mathbf{r_f}$ = 1 + foreign riskless rate.

In a given period, the spot rate can either go up to uS_t, or go down to dS_t.

If the spot rate were to increase, the portfolio will be worth

$$\frac{a}{S_t} r_f u S_t + Br \tag{12.29}$$

while, if it were to decline, it will be worth

$$\frac{a}{S_t} r_f d S_t + Br \tag{12.30}$$

Let's choose a and B such that

$$aur_f + Br = C_u \tag{12.31}$$

and

$$adr_f + Br = C_d \tag{12.32}$$

Therefore

$$a = \frac{C_u - C_d}{r_f(u-d)} \tag{12.33}$$

and

$$B = \frac{1}{r}\left[\frac{uC_d - dC_u}{u-d}\right] \tag{12.34}$$

Thus

$$C_t = a + B = \frac{pC_u + (1-p)C_d}{r} \tag{12.35}$$

where

$$p = \frac{\frac{r}{r_f} - d}{u-d} \tag{12.36}$$

and

$$(1-p) = \frac{u - \frac{r}{r_f}}{u-d} \tag{12.37}$$

Example 12.4: We will now compute the price of a call option on British pounds using a two period Binomial model. Let u = 1.2, d = .8, S_t = 185, r = 1.045, r_f = 1.06, and X = 200.

The spot exchange rate tree, may be depicted as shown in Figure 12.1.

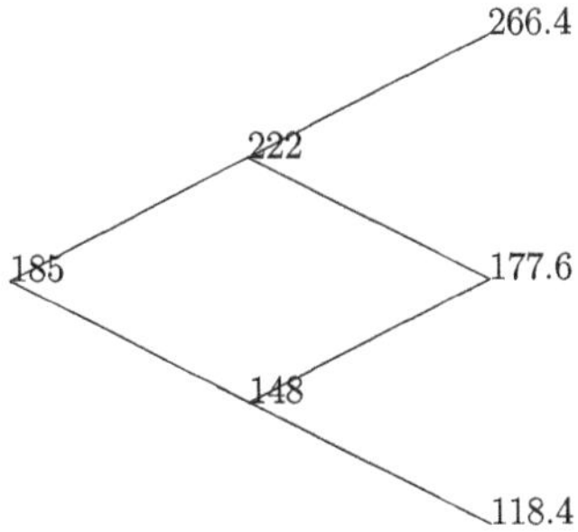

Figure 12.1: The Spot Exchange Rate Tree.

$$C_{uu,T} = 66.40, C_{ud,T} = 0, C_{dd,T} = 0$$

$$p = \frac{\frac{1.045}{1.06} - 0.8}{0.4} = 0.4646 \text{ and } (1 - p) = 0.5354$$

$$C_{u,T-1} = \frac{0.4646 \times 66.4 + 0.5354 \times 0}{1.045} = 29.5210$$

The intrinsic value at this node is 22.

$$C_{d,(T-1)} = \frac{0.4646 \times 0 + 0.5354 \times 0}{1.045} = 0$$

The intrinsic value at this node is zero.

$$C_t = \frac{0.4646 \times 29.5210 + 0.5354 \times 0}{1.045} = 13.1248$$

The intrinsic value at this node is zero. Thus the call will be worth 13.1248 cents.

Applying the Binomial Model for Given Value of Sigma

The formula for the option price using continuously compounded rates of interest r and r_f and the volatility of the exchange rate σ is similar to what we derived for a stock paying a continuous dividend yield. The only difference is that we replace δ with the riskless rate in the foreign currency r_f.

12.6.2 The Greeks

The greeks for foreign currency options are similar to those for a stock paying a continuous dividend yield. We have to once again replace δ with the foreign riskless rate r_f. In the case of Rho however we get two expressions, one for the partial derivative with respect to the domestic interest rate, ρ_r, and the other for the partial derivative with respect to the foreign riskless rate, ρ_{r_f}.

For a European call:

$$\rho_r = e^{-r(T-t)}X(T-t)N(d_2) \text{ and } \rho_{r_f} = -e^{-r_f(T-t)}S_t(T-t)N(d_1) \tag{12.38}$$

For a European put:

$$\rho_r = -e^{-r(T-t)}X(T-t)N(-d_2) \text{ and } \rho_{r_f} = e^{-r_f(T-t)}S_t(T-t)N(-d_1) \tag{12.39}$$

12.7 Futures Options

A futures option is an option on a futures contract. Such options are available on a number of successful futures contracts in many of the leading exchanges. Examples include options on index futures, interest rate futures, FOREX futures, and commodity futures.

12.7.1 Call Options

A call futures option gives the buyer the right to assume *a long position in a futures contract*. If and when the call holder decides to exercise, a long position will be established for him in the futures contract, and the contract will be immediately marked to market. Once the long position is entered into, the investor must either deposit adequate funds to meet the initial margin requirement of the futures contract, or else he must offset the futures position.

When the call holder exercises, a short position in the futures contract is established for the writer of the call. The writer's position will also be marked to market, and he must also deposit adequate margin for the futures position, or else, liquidate it. Example 12.5 is based on a call futures option.

Example 12.5: Consider a person who buys a call futures option on crude oil. Each contract is for 1,000 barrels of oil. We will assume that the current futures price of oil is $75.00 per barrel, and that the exercise price of the call is $72.50 per barrel.

If the call holder exercises, he will get a long position in the futures contract. At the same time, due to marking to market, he will receive an inflow of (75.00 − 72.50) × 1,000 = $2,500. How can we explain this inflow of $2,500? The futures option contract gives the holder the right to go long in a futures contract at a price of $72.50. If he exercises, and a long position is established for him, it will be at the prevailing futures price of $75.00. To ensure that he effectively gets a long position at $72.50, the difference between $75.00 and $72.50 must be paid to him. Notice, that if F_t is the current futures price, and X the exercise price, the call holder will exercise only if $F_t > X$. When he exercises, he will get an inflow equal to \$ $(F_t - X)$, which is the intrinsic value of the option.

12.7.2 Put Options

A put futures option gives the holder the right to go short in the futures contract at the exercise price. If the holder exercises, a long position in the futures contract will be established for the writer. Both the holder's and the writer's positions will be marked to market when the option is exercised, and they will both have to post the required margin for the futures contract, or else, liquidate their positions. Example 12.6 is based on a put futures option.

Example 12.6: Consider a person who owns a put futures option on crude oil. The exercise price is $75.00 per barrel, and the current futures price of oil is $72.00 per barrel.

If the holder chooses to exercise, he will get a short position in the futures contract. At the same time, due to marking to market, he will receive a cash inflow of (75.00 − 72.00) × 1,000 = $3,000. The rationale for this inflow should be obvious from the logic presented for call futures options. Notice, that if F_t is the current futures price, and X the exercise price, the call holder will exercise only if $F_t < X$. When he exercises, he will get an inflow equal to $ $(X - F_t)$, which is the intrinsic value of the option.

12.8 Arbitrage Restrictions

12.8.1 Lower Bounds for European Call Futures Options

It can be demonstrated that $C_{E,t} \geq \text{Max}[0, (F_t - X)e^{-r(T-t)}]$. As before we know that $C_{E,t} \geq 0$ and consequently that explains the first part of the expression. However, if $(F_t - X)e^{-r(T-t)} \geq 0$ then we can demonstrate that the option premium must be greater in order to preclude arbitrage.

Proof

Assume that $C_{E,t} < (F_t - X)e^{-r(T-t)} > 0$ or that $(F_t - X)e^{-r(T-t)} - C_{E,t} > 0$. Consider Table 12.5.

Table 12.5: Lower Bound for European Calls.

Action	Initial Cash Flow	Terminal Cash Flow	
		$F_T > X$	$F_T \leq X$
Buy a call	$-C_{E,t}$	$F_T - X$	0
Sell a futures contract	0	$F_t - F_T$	$F_t - F_T$
Borrow PV of $(F_t - X)$	$(F_t - X)e^{-r(T-t)}$	$-(F_t - X)$	$-(F_t - X)$
Total	$-C_{E,t} + (F_t - X)e^{-r(T-t)}$	0	$X - F_T$

In this table the cash flow at inception is positive by assumption and the subsequent cash flows are non-negative. Consequently this table reflects an arbitrage opportunity. Therefore, in order to preclude arbitrage it must be the case that

$$- C_{E,t} + (F_t - X)e^{-r(T-t)} \leq 0$$

$$\Rightarrow C_{E,t} \geq (F_t - X)e^{-r(T-t)} \tag{12.40}$$

We also know that $C_{E,t}$ must be greater than zero. Therefore, the lower bound is

$$C_{E.t} \geq \text{Max}[0, (F_t - X)e^{-r(T-t)}] \tag{12.41}$$

The lower bound for a European call on the underlying asset, with the same expiration date is

$$C_{E,t} \geq \text{Max}[0, S_t - Xe^{-r(T-t)}] \tag{12.42}$$

For an asset which does not make any payouts, $F_t = S_t e^{r(T-t)}$. Therefore, the lower bound for a European futures call option may be written as

$$C_{E,t} \geq \text{Max}[0, S_t - Xe^{-r(T-t)}] \tag{12.43}$$

Thus, the two lower bounds are equivalent. Hence, if the futures option, and the futures contract expire at the same time, a European call on the futures contract is equivalent to a European call on the spot commodity. The logic is that, at expiration, $S_T = F_T$. Hence $\text{Max}[0, S_T - X] = \text{Max}[0, F_T - X]$. If the payoffs from the two options are the same, the options must be equivalent.

What about American call futures options? An American option must always be worth at least its intrinsic value. So for an American futures option,

$$C_A \geq \text{Max}[0, F_t - X] \tag{12.44}$$

This is a tighter lower bound because $(F_t - X) > (F_t - X)e^{-r(T-t)}$. Hence an American option will be priced higher than a corresponding European option, and may be exercised early. Remember that for a stock which makes no payouts, we showed that American call options will never be exercised early. American calls on futures contracts are clearly different.

12.8.2 Lower Bound for European Put Futures Options

In the case of European puts, the no-arbitrage condition is:

$$P_{E,t} \geq \text{Max}[0, (X - F_t)e^{-r(T-t)}] \tag{12.45}$$

This condition has the usual interpretation. If $(X - F_t)e^{-r(T-t)} < 0$, then all that we can assert is that $P_{E,t} > 0$. However, if the expression is positive then we can demonstrate that $P_{E,t} \geq (X-F_t)e^{-r(T-t)}$. To prove it, consider the following strategy, shown in Table 12.6.

Table 12.6: Lower Bound for European Puts.

Action	Initial Cash Flow	Terminal Cash Flow	
		$F_T \geq X$	$F_T < X$
Buy a put	$-P_{E,t}$	0	$X - F_T$
Buy a futures contract	0	$F_T - F_t$	$F_T - F_t$
Lend PV of $(F_t - X)$	$-(F_t - X)e^{-r(T-t)}$	$(F_t - X)$	$(F_t - X)$
Total	$-P_{E,t} - (F_t - X)e^{-r(T-t)}$	$F_T - X$	0

Proof

To preclude arbitrage, we require that

$$-P_{E,t} - (F_t - X)e^{-r(T-t)} \leq 0$$
$$\Rightarrow P_{E,t} \geq (X - F_t)e^{-r(T-t)}$$

Thus, we can assert that

$$P_{E,t} \geq \text{Max}[0, (X - F_t)e^{-r(T-t)}]$$

For an asset which does not make any payouts, $F_t = S_t e^{r(T-t)}$. Therefore, the lower bound for a European futures put option may be written as

$$P_{E,t} \geq \text{Max}[0, Xe^{-r(T-t)} - S_t] \tag{12.46}$$

Thus the lower bound is equivalent to what we derived for a put option on the underlying asset. Hence, if the futures option, and the futures contract expire at the same time, a European put on the futures contract is equivalent to a European put on the spot commodity. The intrinsic value of an American put futures option is $\text{Max}(0, X - F_t)$, which provides a tighter lower bound. Hence American put futures options may be exercised early.

12.8.3 Put-Call Parity

The put-call parity condition for European options on a futures contract is:

$$C_{E,t} - P_{E,t} = (F_t - X)e^{-r(T-t)}$$

The proof is given in Table 12.7.

Table 12.7: Put Call Parity.

Action	Initial Cash Flow	Terminal Cash Flow	
		$F_T \geq X$	$F_T < X$
Sell a call	$C_{E,t}$	$-(F_T - X)$	0
Buy a put	$-P_{E,t}$	0	$(X - F_T)$
Buy futures	0	$F_T - F_t$	$F_T - F_t$
Lend PV of $(F_t - X)$	$-(F_t - X)e^{-r(T-t)}$	$(F_t - X)$	$(F_t - X)$
Total	$C_{E,t} - P_{E,t} - (F_t - X)e^{-r(T-t)}$	0	0

So to preclude arbitrage, we require that

$$C_{E,t} = P_{E,t} + (F_t - X)e^{-r(T-t)} \tag{12.47}$$

12.9 The Black Model

This model is a variation of the Black-Scholes model and is applicable for pricing European options on futures contracts. Assuming that the options and the underlying futures expire at the same time, Black showed that

$$C_{E,t} = e^{-r(T-t)}[F_t N(d_1) - XN(d_2)] \tag{12.48}$$

$$\text{and } P_E = e^{-r(T-t)}[XN(-d_2) - F_t N(-d_1)] \tag{12.49}$$

where

$$d_1 = \frac{ln\left(\frac{F}{X}\right) + \left(\frac{\sigma^2}{2}\right)T}{\sigma\sqrt{T-t}} \tag{12.50}$$

and $d_2 = d_1 - \sigma\sqrt{T-t}$. Example 12.7 demonstrates the application of the Black model.

Example 12.7: The price of a six months futures contract on crude oil is \$75. Options are available with an exercise price of \$70 and six months to expiration. The riskless rate is 8% per annum and the volatility is 30% per annum.

$$d_1 = \frac{ln\left(\frac{75}{70}\right) + \left(\frac{0.30 \times 0.30}{2}\right)0.5}{0.30\sqrt{0.5}}$$
$$= \frac{0.0915}{0.2121} = 0.4314$$
$$d_2 = 0.4314 - .2121 = 0.2193$$

N(0.4314) = 0.6669; N(0.2193) = 0.5868

$$C_{E,t} = e^{-0.08 \times .5}[75 \times 0.6669 - 70 \times 0.5868] = 8.5909$$
$$P_{E,t} = e^{-0.08 \times .5}[70 \times 0.4132 - 75 \times 0.3331] = 3.7870$$

12.9.1 The Binomial Model

We will now see as to how the binomial model can be used to price futures options. To start with we will focus on the one period model. Let the stock price follow a binomial model as described below in Figure 12.2.

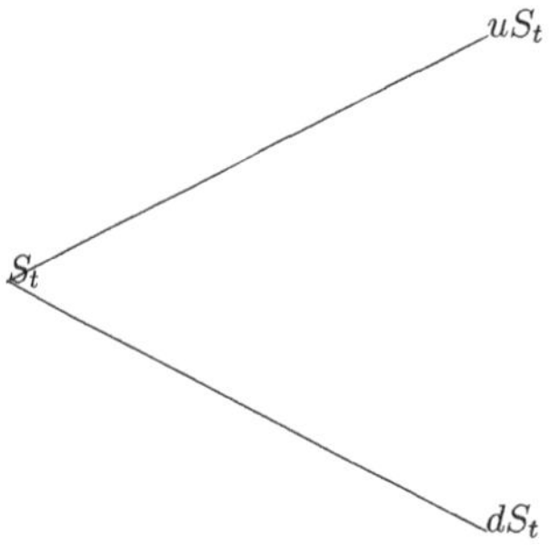

Figure 12.2: A One Period Stock Price Tree.

From the cost of carry model, the futures price at any node is given by $F = Sr^{(T-t)}$, where r is *1 + riskless rate* and $T - t$ is the number of periods left till the maturity of the futures contract.

Hence, the futures price can also be modeled using a binomial process as shown in Figure 12.3.

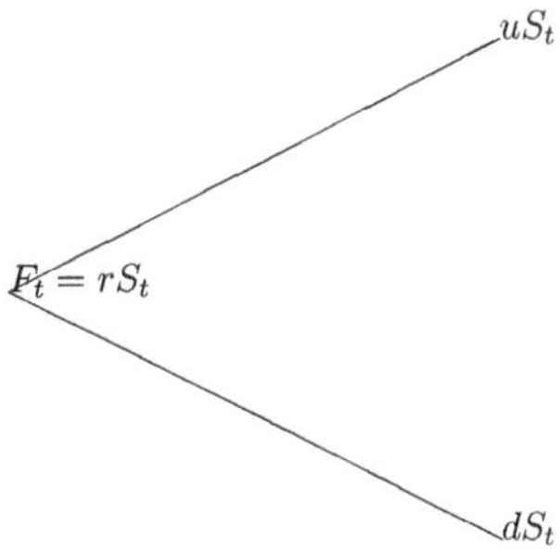

Figure 12.3: A One Period Futures Price Tree.

Let's form a hedge portfolio consisting of a long position in α futures contracts, and \$B in riskless debt. The initial investment = \$B, because it costs nothing to get into the futures contract. If this portfolio is to replicate the call, we require that

$$\alpha\left(\frac{u}{r}F_t - F_t\right) + Br = C_u \tag{12.51}$$

$$\text{and } \alpha\left(\frac{d}{r}F_t - F_t\right) + Br = C_d \tag{12.52}$$

Therefore

$$\alpha = \frac{C_u - C_d}{F_t\left(\frac{u}{r} - \frac{d}{r}\right)} \tag{12.53}$$

Let $u^* = \frac{u}{r}$ and $d^* = \frac{d}{r}$. Therefore

$$\alpha = \frac{C_u - C_d}{F_t(u^* - d^*)} \tag{12.54}$$

Substituting for α we get

$$B = \frac{1}{r}\left[\frac{1 - d^*}{u^* - d^*}C_u + \frac{u^* - 1}{u^* - d^*}C_d\right] \tag{12.55}$$

$$p = \frac{1 - d^*}{u^* - d^*} = \frac{1 - \frac{d}{r}}{\frac{u}{r} - \frac{d}{r}} = \frac{r - d}{u - d} \tag{12.56}$$

Thus p and $(1 - p)$ can be calculated using either u^* and d^* or u and d. Therefore

$$B = \frac{pC_u + (1 - p)C_d}{r} \tag{12.57}$$

Since the payoffs from the portfolio are the same as that from the call, $C_t = B$ Example 12.8 demonstrates the valuation of a call futures option with two periods to expiration.

Example 12.8: A stock is currently valued at $100. Every period the stock price may go up by 20% or go down by 20%. The riskless rate of interest is 5% per period. What is the value of a call futures option with two periods to expiration?

The stock price tree is depicted in Figure 12.4.

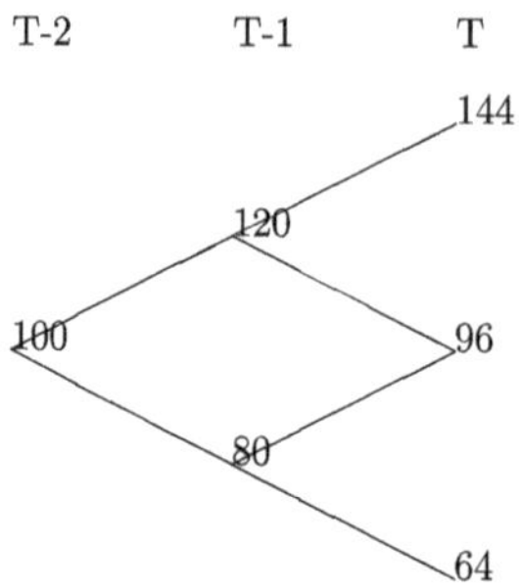

Figure 12.4: A Two Period Stock Price Tree.

The futures price tree is depicted in Figure 12.5, for a contract with two periods to expiration. As you can see, at expiration, the futures price is equal to the spot price.

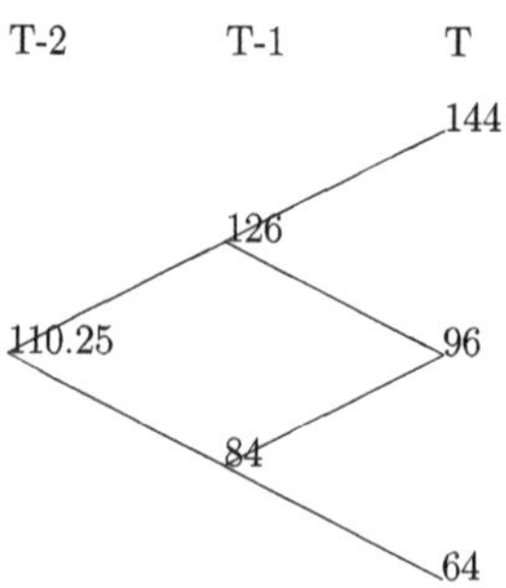

Figure 12.5: A Two Period Futures Price Tree.

If we assume that the futures contract and the option on the futures contract expire at the same time, then

$$C_{uu,T} = 44, C_{ud,T} = 0, \text{ and } C_{dd,T} = 0; p = 0.625 \text{ and } 1 - p = 0.375$$

$$C_{u,T-1} = \frac{0.625 \times 44 + 0.375 \times 0}{1.05} = 26.1905$$

If we are dealing with American options, we have to check and see as to whether this is less than the intrinsic value. The I.V at this node is 26, which is less. So the option will not be exercised early.

$$C_{d,T-1} = \frac{0.625 \times 0 + 0.375 \times 0}{1.05} = 0$$

The intrinsic value at this node is zero since the option is out of the money. Therefore

$$C_t = \frac{0.625 \times 26.1905 + 0.375 \times 0}{1.05} = 15.5896$$

Once again, we have to check for early exercise. The intrinsic value at 'T-2' is 10.25, so the option will not be exercised early. Thus the value of the American call futures option = $15.5896.

12.9.2 Applying the Binomial Model for a Given Value of Sigma

The binomial model can be used to value futures options using the following parameters.

$$u = e^{\sigma\sqrt{\Delta t}} \tag{12.58}$$

$$d = e^{-\sigma\sqrt{\Delta t}} \tag{12.59}$$

$$p = \frac{1 - d}{u - d} \tag{12.60}$$

12.10 Options on Futures versus Options on the Underlying

Futures options are often more actively traded than options on the underlying asset. One of the main reasons is that the underlying asset in the case of a futures option, namely the futures contract, is more liquid and consequently its prices are more reliable. In practice futures prices can be easily ascertained from the futures exchange, while the price of the underlying commodity may not be so transparent. This is particularly true for underlying assets like Treasury bonds which are largely traded over-the-counter.[1]

The other reason for the popularity of futures options is that the holder is not required to take possession of the underlying asset upon exercise, which is normally the case for options on the underlying asset. Since the exercise of a futures option leads to the establishment of a futures position for the holder, he has the option to offset and exit the market without taking delivery.

We have demonstrated earlier that a European futures option, whether a call or a put, must be worth the same as a European option on the underlying asset with the same time to maturity. However, if the European futures option were to expire before the expiration date of the underlying futures contract, then this would no longer be the case. In such a situation, the futures call will be worth more than a call on the underlying asset if the market is in contango, whereas it will be worth less than a call on the underlying asset if the market is in backwardation. For puts however, the case is the opposite. Puts

1 See Hull (2006).

on futures will be worth less than puts on the underlying if the futures market is in contango, whereas they will be worth more than puts on the underlying if the market is in backwardation. The same is the case for American futures options, irrespective of whether the futures contract expires at the same time as the option or after it.[2]

12.11 Portfolio Insurance

The term *portfolio insurance* refers to a strategy for protecting the principal value of a portfolio against a decline in the price. The strategy entails the acquisition of a put option, such that the floor value of the portfolio at the time of expiration of the put is the principal value of the portfolio.

This kind of a protective put strategy may be accomplished by acquiring an exchange traded put option, or by replicating a put option using positions in the underlying asset and the riskless asset, as we have demonstrated in our discussion of the Binomial model in the previous chapter. The first type of insurance may be termed as *static portfolio insurance* while the second may be considered as *dynamic portfolio insurance*.[3]

12.11.1 Dynamic Option Replication

We will assume in this illustration that we have more capital at the outset than our target insurance floor. More specifically, we are going to assume we have enough capital buy one unit of the underlying asset plus one put option on it.

Consider an asset that is currently valued at \$100. We will assume that every period the stock price may go up by 20% or go down by 20%. The riskless rate of interest is 5% per period. The evolution of the underlying asset over three periods is depicted in Figure 12.6.

Let's now consider a European put with an exercise price of \$100. The value of the put at each node can be computed using the binomial model. The risk neutral probabilities are:

$$p = \frac{1.05 - 0.80}{1.20 - 0.80} = 0.625 \text{ and } 1 - p = 0.375$$

$$P_{uuu} = 0; P_{uud} = 0; P_{udd} = 23.20; P_{ddd} = 48.80$$

P_{uu} is obviously zero. It can be shown that $P_{ud} = 8.29, P_{dd} = 31.24, P_u = 2.96, P_d = 16.09,$and $P_t = 7.51$. The evolution of the put price can consequently be depicted as shown in Figure 12.7.

2 See Hull (2006).

3 See Stoll and Whaley (1993).

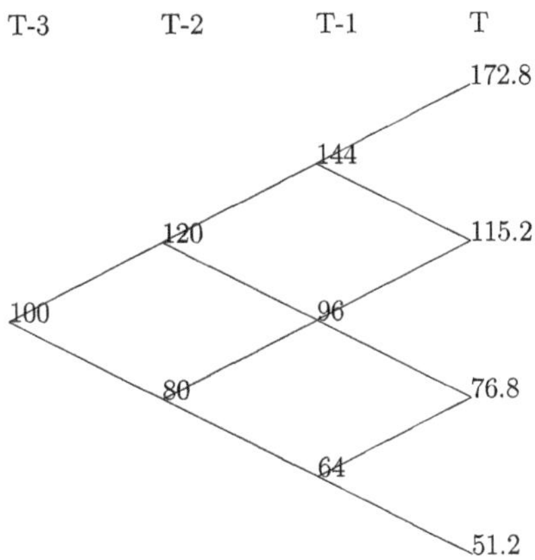

Figure 12.6: Evolution of the Asset Price.

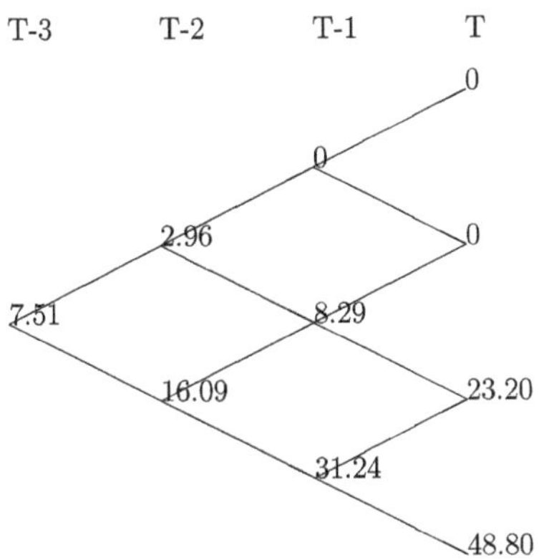

Figure 12.7: Evolution of The Put Option Premium.

So the insured portfolio consisting of one unit of the underlying asset and a put option follows the price process, shown in Figure 12.8.

As we have already seen from the study of the binomial model, a put option can be replicated by a combination of positions in the underlying asset and the riskless asset. We will denote the respective positions by α and B. For instance

$$\alpha_{T-3} = \frac{P_u - P_d}{S_{T-3} \times (u - d)} = \frac{2.96 - 16.09}{100 \times (1.20 - 0.80)} = -0.32825$$
$$B_{T-3} = \frac{uP_d - dP_u}{r \times (u - d)} = \frac{1.20 \times 16.09 - 0.8 \times 2.96}{1.05 \times 0.40} = \$40.3333$$

The composition of the replicating portfolios at the other nodes can be derived in a similar fashion. The insured portfolio consists of one unit of the underlying asset and a put option. Consequently, to replicate the insured portfolio, we need to start with a portfolio consisting of $1.0 - 0.32825 = 0.67175$ units of the underlying asset and \$40.3333 of

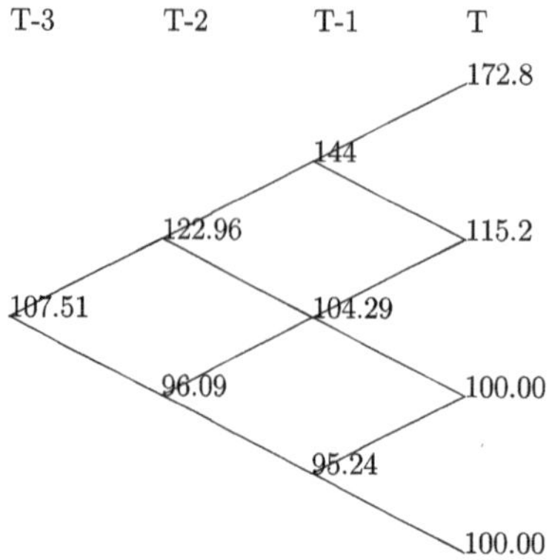

Figure 12.8: Evolution of the Value of the Insured Portfolio.

riskless debt. The composition of such a replicating portfolio at each node is depicted in Figure 12.9.

$\alpha = 1.0000$
$B = \$0.0000$

$\alpha = 0.8273$
$B = \$23.6857$

$\alpha = 0.67175$
$B = \$40.3333$

$\alpha = 0.3958$
$B = \$66.2857$

$\alpha = 0.2828$
$B = \$73.4667$

$\alpha = 0.0000$
$B = \$95.2381$

Figure 12.9: Changing Composition of the Replicating Portfolio.

As we have demonstrated in the previous chapter, this dynamic replication process is self-financing at each node.

12.11.2 The Cost of Insurance

One way of looking at the cost of insurance is by considering the price of the implied put option in the dynamic replication strategy. In our example we had to take out \$7.51 out of our initial capital of \$107.51 to insure the portfolio at a floor value of \$100.

Another way of looking at the cost of insurance is by considering the return foregone on the upside. In our case, by creating a put worth \$7.51, the manager is able to devote only $\frac{100}{107.51} \equiv 93\%$ of the total capital to the underlying asset. On the other hand, if he had not insured he would have been able to devote the entire \$ 107.51 to the underlying asset. The consequence is that, in the two states where the insurance is not required, namely $S_T = 172.80$ and $S_T = 115.20$, the insured portfolio is able to capture only 93% of the value that it could have captured had the insurance not been availed off.

12.11.3 Portfolio Insurance and the Black-Scholes Model

From put-call parity we know that:

$$\begin{aligned}
C_{E,t} - P_{E,t} &= S_t - \frac{X}{(1+r)^{T-t}} \\
\Rightarrow S_t + P_{E,t} &= C_{E,t} + \frac{X}{(1+r)^{T-t}} \\
&= S_t N(d_1) - \frac{X}{(1+r)^{T-t}} N(d_2) + \frac{X}{(1+r)^{T-t}} \\
&= S_t N(d_1) + \frac{X}{(1+r)^{T-t}} N(-d_2)
\end{aligned} \tag{12.61}$$

Thus in the Black-Scholes world, an insured portfolio can be created by investing in $N(d_1)$ shares and investing an amount of $N(-d_2)$ times the present value of the exercise price in the riskless asset. Thus, in this scenario, $N(d_1)$ or the delta of the call option plays the role of the hedge ratio for the insured portfolio.

From put-call parity

$$\Rightarrow S_t + P_{E,t} = C_{E,t} + \frac{X}{(1+r)^{T-t}} \tag{12.62}$$

Thus a portfolio consisting of a call option with an exercise price of \$100 plus an investment equal to the present value of the exercise price in the riskless asset, will behave in the same fashion as our insured portfolio consisting of positions in a share plus a put option. Thus this combination offers an alternative way of creating our insured portfolio.

12.12 Options on Volatility

The CBOE offers options on volatility computed using data for S&P500 index options. These trade under the symbol *VIX* where VIX is an acronym for volatility index. It is an estimate of expected volatility computed using the bid and ask quotes for options on the S&P500 index. The data spans a range of exercise prices. The computation is independent of any option pricing model.

The significance of VIX may be explained as follows. Option values are influenced by a number of variables, of which volatility is one factor. VIX isolates the expected volatility from the other factors, and allows investors to directly take a position on the volatility.

The contract multiplier is \$100, and the expiration date is the Wednesday thirty days prior to the third Friday of the calendar month immediately following the expiration month. The exercise style is European.

Suggestions for Further Reading

Chance D.M. *An Introduction to Derivatives & Risk Management.* Thomson;South-Western, 2004.

Dewynne J., Howison S., and P. Wilmott *The Mathematics of Financial Derivatives: A Student Introduction.* Cambridge University Press, 1999.

Hull J.C. *Options, Futures, and Other Derivatives.* Prentice Hall of India, 2005.

Kolb R.W. *Futures, Options, & Swaps.* Blackwell, 1999.

Stoll, H.R. and R.E. Whaley *Futures and Options: Theory and Applications*. South Western, 1993.

References

www.cboe.com

www.cftc.gov

www.cme.com

Chapter 13
Exotic Options

13.1 Introduction

Thus far we have dealt with standard European and American options, which are what a market professional would term as *plain vanilla products*. Most exchange traded products fall within this category. However, it is common for investment banks to offer options with non-standard features to their clients in the OTC markets. Such options have come to be known as *exotic options*. We will discuss some of the relatively more common exotic products. The list is by no means exhaustive, and options with more and more novel features are constantly being devised. From the standpoint of the investment banks, such derivatives not only pose a constant intellectual challenge to their so called *rocket scientists*, they also serve as an additional source of revenue in markets which are characterized by a constant shrinking of spreads due to enhanced competition.

13.2 Digital or Binary Options

There are two types of digital options, also known as binary options, which may be termed as *cash-or-nothing* and *asset-or-nothing* options. Let us first consider cash-or-nothing options.

13.2.1 Cash-or-Nothing

Consider a cash-or-nothing call option with an exercise price of X, and a time to expiration of T-t. Such an option will result in the holder receiving a payoff of $X from the writer, if $S_T > X$, that is if the option finishes in the money. Otherwise the option will simply expire worthless.

Similarly, in the case of a cash-or-nothing put option, the writer will pay $X to the holder if $S_T < X$. Obviously, if the option were to expire out of the money, it would simply expire worthless.

13.2.2 Asset-or-Nothing

An asset-or-nothing call option will result in one unit of the underlying asset being delivered to the holder by the writer if the terminal stock price is greater than the exercise price. Otherwise the option will expire worthless.

https://doi.org/10.1515/9783110746662-013

On the other hand, an asset-or-nothing put option will result in a unit of the underlying asset being delivered to the buyer by the writer if the terminal stock price is less than the exercise price. Else, the option will expire worthless.

The difference between asset-or-nothing and plain vanilla European options is that irrespective of whether it is a call or a put, an asset-or-nothing option does not require the holder to pay anything to the writer if and when he receives the underlying asset.

13.2.3 Equivalence with Plain Vanilla Options

Consider a long position in an asset or nothing call option with an exercise price of X and time to expiration T-t, and a short position in a cash or nothing call option with the same exercise price and time to expiration. If the terminal stock price were to be higher than the exercise price, such a position would result in the holder receiving the underlying asset from the writer in return for the payment of an amount equal to the exercise price. Thus, this portfolio is nothing but a standard European call option.

Similarly a European put option is equivalent to a long position in a cash-or-nothing put option plus a short position in an asset-or-nothing put option.

From the Black-Scholes formula

$$C_{E,t} = SN(d_1) - Xe^{-r(T-t)}N(d_2) \tag{13.1}$$

The first term, $SN(d_1)$ is the value of an asset-or-nothing call option with an exercise price of X and time to expiration equal to T-t. The second term, $Xe^{-r(T-t)}N(d_2)$, is the value of a cash-or-nothing call option with the same exercise price and expiration date. The minus sign before this term denotes a short position in such an option.

A European put option can be similarly analyzed in terms of its components. From the Black-Scholes formula

$$P_{E,t} = Xe^{-r(T-t)}N(-d_2) - SN(-d_1) \tag{13.2}$$

$Xe^{-r(T-t)}N(-d_2)$ is the value of a cash-or-nothing put option while $SN(-d_1)$ is the value of an asset-or-nothing put option.

13.3 Asian Options

An Asian option is a derivative in which the payoff is not based on the price of the asset at expiration but rather on the average price of the asset over the life of the option. Consequently such options are also known as *average price options*. Most Asian options can be exercised only at expiration. However, in certain cases early exercise may be permissible.

Let us denote the average asset price over the life of the option as $\bar{S}$. The payoff from an average price option, which cannot be exercised prior to maturity, may be defined as $\text{Max}[0, \bar{S} - X]$, in the case of call options, and as $\text{Max}[0, X - \bar{S}]$, in the case of put options. The strike price X in the case of such options is pre-defined like in the case of European and American options.

A variation of these options is known as the *average strike option*. In the case of such options the final payoff is based on the difference between the asset price at expiration and the average price over the life of the option. Thus, the exercise price in the case of such options is the average price of the underlying asset over the life of the option. The payoff from an average strike option, which cannot be exercised prior to maturity, may be defined as $\text{Max}[0, S_T - \bar{S}]$, in the case of call options, and as $\text{Max}[0, \bar{S} - S_T]$, in the case of put options.

The method of computing the average price needs to be specified in advance. There are two possibilities, arithmetic averaging and geometric averaging. If we have a vector of N stock prices the arithmetic mean may be defined as

$$\frac{1}{N} \times \sum_{i=1}^{N} S_i \tag{13.3}$$

and the geometric average as

$$\left[\prod_{i=1}^{N} S_i\right]^{\frac{1}{N}} \tag{13.4}$$

The advantage of using the geometric average, is that if the price of the underlying security is assumed to be lognormally distributed, then the average of the prices is also lognormal. However, such an assertion cannot be made in the case of an arithmetic average of the prices. In practice Asian options are usually defined in terms of the arithmetic average. For a given series of prices, the geometric average will always be lower than the arithmetic average, except in the trivial case where all the observations are equal.

In the case of a standard Asian option, all the observations are weighted equally while computing the average. However, options with unequal weights for the observations can be defined. The period during which the average is to be computed and the monitoring frequency have also to be specified. For instance, in the case of an option with one year to maturity, it is conceivable that the average price as per the terms of the option is computed using the observations for the first three or six months only. The monitoring frequency is also important. For instance, should the prices used for computing the average be based on the daily closing values or should they be sampled with a different frequency.

13.3.1 Average Price Options

We will use the two period Binomial model to compute the price of an average price call option. The illustration will first assume that the option has been defined in terms of the arithmetic average of prices. Subsequently, we will recompute the price using the geometric average of prices.

Consider the following data. The current stock price is $100. Every period the price may go up by 20% or may decline by 20%. An average price Asian option with two periods to expiration, and an exercise price of $100 is available. The riskless rate is 5% per period.

$$u = 1.2, d = .8, r = 1.05$$
$$\Rightarrow p = 0.625 \text{ and } (1 - p) = 0.375$$

The stock price tree for the two period case may be modeled as shown in Figure 13.1.

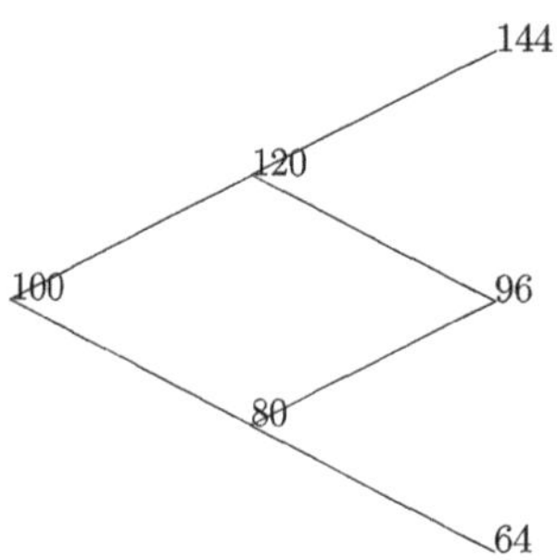

Figure 13.1: A Two Period Stock Price Tree.

As we can see, there are four paths to expiration. The average price attained along each path, and the probability of the asset price following that particular path, is given in Table 13.1. Both the arithmetic as well as the geometric average prices are given. We will illustrate the computation for the first path. Readers should be able to derive the remaining values. The data is summarized in Table 13.1.

Path 1: $100 \rightarrow 120 \rightarrow 144$

$$\text{Arithmetic average} = \frac{100 + 120 + 144}{3} = 121.33$$

$$\text{Geometric average} = (100 \times 120 \times 144)^{\frac{1}{3}} = 120$$

If the stock follows path 1 or path 2, the call option will be in the money, else it will be out of the money. Similarly the put will be in the money if the stock follows paths 3 or 4, else it will be out of the money.

We can compute the price of the option as the discounted value of the expected payoff at expiration, using the risk-neutral probabilities.

Table 13.1: Average Price for Each Path.

Path No.	Probability	Arithmetic Average	Geometric Average
1	0.390625	121.33	120.00
2	0.234375	105.33	104.83
3	0.234375	92.00	91.58
4	0.140625	81.33	80.00

The Case of the Arithmetic Average

$$C_t = \frac{1}{(1.05)^2} \times [.390625 \times (121.33 - 100) + .234375 \times (105.33 - 100) + .234375 \times 0 + .140625 \times 0]$$
$$= 8.6905$$

$$P_t = \frac{1}{(1.05)^2} \times [.390625 \times 0 + .234375 \times 0 + .234375 \times (100 - 92) + .140625 \times (100 - 81.33)]$$
$$= 4.0821$$

The Case of the Geometric Average

$$C_t = \frac{1}{(1.05)^2} \times [.390625 \times (120 - 100) + .234375 \times (104.83 - 100) + .234375 \times 0 + .140625 \times 0]$$
$$= 8.1130$$

$$P_t = \frac{1}{(1.05)^2} \times [.390625 \times 0 + .234375 \times 0 + .234375 \times (100 - 91.58) + .140625 \times (100 - 80)]$$
$$= 4.3410$$

Since the geometric average price is lower than the arithmetic average price, for a given value of the exercise price the call premium will be lower when the option is defined is terms of the geometric average while the put premium will be higher.

13.3.2 Average Strike Options

An average strike call will be in the money if the stock follows paths 1 or 3, else it will be out of the money. As before the price of the option can be calculated as the present value of the expected payoff at expiration. Thus, if the option is defined in terms of an arithmetic average

$$C_t = \frac{1}{(1.05)^2} \times [.390625 \times (144 - 121.33) + 0.234375 \times (96 - 92)] = 8.8825$$

However, if the option were to be defined in terms of the geometric average, then

$$C_t = \frac{1}{(1.05)^2} \times [.390625 \times (144 - 120) + 0.234375 \times (96 - 91.58)] = 9.4430$$

An average strike put will be in the money if the stock follows paths 2 or 4, else it will be out of the money. If the option is defined in terms of the arithmetic average

$$P_t = \frac{1}{(1.05)^2} \times [.234375 \times (105.33 - 96) + 0.140625 \times (81.33 - 64)] = 4.1939$$

However, if the option were to be defined in terms of a geometric average

$$P_t = \frac{1}{(1.05)^2} \times [.234375 \times (104.83 - 96) + 0.140625 \times (80 - 64)] = 3.9179$$

In the case of average strike options, the call premium is higher if the geometric average of the prices is taken, while the put premium is lower. This is because in the case of such options the average price is used in lieu of the exercise price, and the lower the exercise price the higher will be the value of a call and the lower will be the value of a put.

13.4 Lookback Options

Lookback call options allow the holder to acquire an asset for its lowest price during the life of the option, while lookback put options allow the holder to sell the asset for its highest price during the life of the option. That is, for a call option, the strike price at expiration is set equal to the minimum observed price of the asset during the life of the option, while for a put, the exercise price is set equal to the maximum asset price observed during the life of the option. Thus, for lookback options, the exercise price depends on the path taken by the asset price. Consequently, just like Asian options, lookbacks too are path dependent.

Let us denote the minimum and maximum prices attained during the life of the option by S_{Min} and S_{Max} respectively. The payoff from a lookback call at expiration is $\text{Max}[0, S_T - S_{Min}]$, while that from a put is $\text{Max}[0, S_{Max} - S_T]$. Hence, both call and put options are guaranteed to expire in the money or at the money.

Such options are also termed as *no-regrets* options because the holder will not have to face the ex-post regret of having sold or exercised the option at the wrong time. These options are also referred to as *hindsight options*.[1]

1 See Chance (1998).

We will once again use the risk neutral valuation technique to price such options. A risk neutral investor will calculate the expected payoff, and then discount it back at the riskless rate for the number of periods remaining, which we will denote by T-t. Therefore

$$C_t = \frac{1}{(r)^{T-t}} E[Max(0, S_T - S_{Min})] \tag{13.5}$$

and

$$P_t = \frac{1}{(r)^{T-t}} E[Max(0, S_{Max} - S_T)] \tag{13.6}$$

Now, by definition

$$S_T - S_{Min} \geq 0 \text{ and } S_{Max} - S_T \geq 0$$

Therefore

$$C_t = \frac{1}{(r)^{T-t}} E[S_T - S_{Min}] = \frac{1}{(r)^{T-t}} E(S_T) - \frac{1}{(r)^{T-t}} E(S_{Min}) \text{ and} \tag{13.7}$$

$$P_t = \frac{1}{(r)^{T-t}} E(S_{Max}) - \frac{1}{(r)^{T-t}} E(S_T) \tag{13.8}$$

For a risk neutral investor, the expected asset price at expiration is equal to the current stock price compounded at the riskless rate of interest. That is, $E(S_T) = S_t(r)^{T-t}$. Therefore

$$C_t = S_t - \frac{1}{(r)^{T-t}} E(S_{Min}) \text{ and} \tag{13.9}$$

$$P_t = \frac{1}{(r)^{T-t}} E(S_{Max}) - S_t \tag{13.10}$$

13.4.1 Computing the Value of a Call

We will use the same data as before. The stock price tree is as depicted in Figure 13.2. The minimum and maximum prices for each path, and the corresponding probability of the path are shown in Table 13.2.

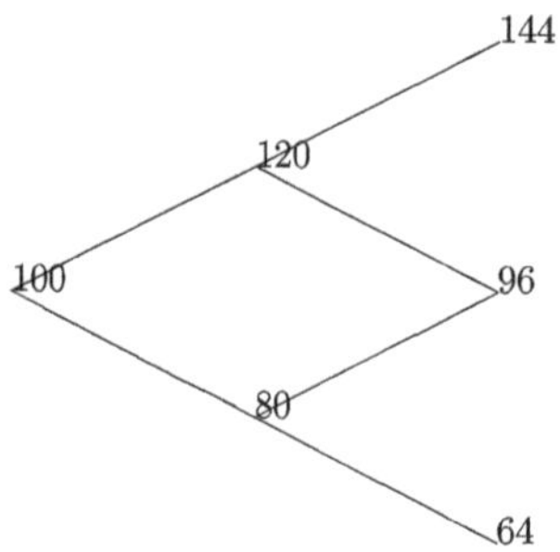

Figure 13.2: A Two Period Stock Price Tree.

Table 13.2: Minimum and Maximum Prices for Each Path.

Path No.	Probability	Minimum Price	Maximum Price
1	0.390625	100	144
2	0.234375	96	120
3	0.234375	80	100
4	0.140625	64	100

$$\begin{aligned} E(S_{Min}) &= 0.390625 \times 100 + 0.234375 \times 96 + 0.234375 \times 80 + 0.140625 \times 64 \\ &= 89.3125 \end{aligned}$$

Therefore, the call premium is given by

$$C_t = 100 - \frac{1}{(1.05)^2} \times 89.3125 = \$18.99$$

13.4.2 The Value of a Put

$$\begin{aligned} E(S_{Max}) &= 0.390625 \times 144 + 0.234375 \times 120 + 0.234375 \times 100 + 0.140625 \times 100 \\ &= 121.875 \end{aligned}$$

Therefore, the put premium is given by

$$P_t = \frac{1}{(r)^T} E(S_{Max}) - S_t$$

$$P_t = \frac{1}{(1.05)^2} \times 121.875 - 100 = \$10.54$$

13.4.3 Modified Lookback Options

In the case of a modified lookback option, the exercise price is specified at the outset. However, the payoff is based on the maximum price observed during the life of the option, if it is a call, and the minimum price observed during the life of the option if it is a put. We will illustrate such options with the help of Example 13.1.

Example 13.1: Consider a modified lookback call with an exercise price of \$100. We will continue to use the same stock price process that we have considered earlier. The payoff from a call option is

$$\text{Max}[0, S_{Max} - X]$$

while that from a put is

$$\text{Max}[0, X - S_{Min}]$$

The payoff from a call option and a put option, if the stock price follows a given path, is as shown in Table 13.3.

Table 13.3: Payoffs from Call and Put Options.

Path	Payoff From a Call	Payoff From a Put
1	44	0
2	20	4
3	0	20
4	0	36

The call option price is given by

$$\begin{aligned} C_t &= \frac{1}{(1.05)^2}[44 \times 0.390625 + 20 \times 0.234375] \\ &= \$19.8413 \end{aligned}$$

The put option price is given by

$$\begin{aligned} P_t &= \frac{1}{(1.05)^2}[4 \times 0.234375 + 20 \times 0.234375 + 36 \times 0.140625] \\ &= \$9.6939 \end{aligned}$$

13.4.4 Lookbacks versus European Options

If the stock price were to follow the process described above, it can be shown that a European call with an exercise price of \$100 will be priced at \$15.5896, while a European put with an exercise price of \$100 will be priced at \$6.2925. From these prices we can observe that standard lookback calls and puts are more expensive than standard European options. We will justify this by comparing the payoffs of the lookback options, both calls and puts, with the payoffs from European call and put options with an exercise price of \$100. Consider Table 13.4.

Table 13.4: Comparison of Payoffs from Lookback Options and European Options.

Path	Payoff From Lookback Call	Payoff From European Call	Payoff From Lookback Put	Payoff From European Put
1	44	44	0	0
2	0	0	24	4
3	16	0	4	4
4	0	0	36	36

As can be seen from Table 13.4, the payoff from a European call is less than or equal to that from a lookback call irrespective of the path taken by the stock price. The same is true for European puts. Consequently, both lookback calls and puts are valued higher than the corresponding European options.

In the case of modified lookback options, if the asset price at the outset is greater than or equal to the exercise price of the option, then a call option is guaranteed to expire in the money. Similarly, if the asset price at the outset were to be less than the exercise price of the option, a put option is guaranteed to expire in the money. If this condition is not satisfied, there is no guarantee that a modified lookback will finish in the money. Consequently, in such situations, modified lookbacks will be priced lower than standard lookbacks which are guaranteed to finish in or at the money.

However, modified lookbacks will always be valued higher than European options with the same exercise prices. Consider the case of modified lookback call options. The payoff is $\text{Max}[0, S_{Max} - X]$. Except for a situation where $S_{Max} = S_T$, where S_T is the asset price at expiration, the payoff from the modified lookback call will be greater than that of a European call. Consequently, the modified lookback will be priced higher. A similar line of argument applies to modified lookback put options. We will compare the payoffs from modified lookback calls and puts with those from the corresponding European options in order to substantiate our argument. As can be seen from Table 13.5, the payoff from both modified lookback calls as well as puts is greater than or equal to the payoff from the corresponding European options irrespective of the path taken by the stock price.

Table 13.5: Comparison of Payoffs from Modified Lookback Options and European Options.

Path	Payoff From Modified Lookback Call	Payoff From European Call	Payoff From Modified Lookback Put	Payoff From European Put
1	44	44	0	0
2	20	0	4	4
3	0	0	20	4
4	0	0	36	36

13.5 Compound Options

A compound option is an option on an option. There are four types of compound options. Let us take the case of calls first. We can have a call that gives the holder the right to buy a call if exercised or a call that gives the right to buy a put if exercised. Similarly we can have a put that gives the holder the right to sell a call if exercised or a put that gives the right to sell a put if exercised.

Take the case of a two period compound call on a call. If this call is bought at T-2, the investor would have acquired the right to acquire a one period call at T-1. Assume that the stock price tree is the same as what we have considered earlier, and that the option gives the right to acquire a call with an exercise price of $100 at T-1, by paying a premium of $20.

Let us value the one period call at T-1. $C_u = \frac{1}{(1.05)}[.625 \times (144 - 100) + .375 \times 0] = 26.1905$ and $C_d = \frac{1}{(1.05)}[.625 \times 0 + .375 \times 0] = 0$.

Thus if the up state is reached at T-1, the compound call is worth exercising because the holder gets a one period call worth $26.1905 for $20. However, if the down state is reached it is better to let the compound option expire worthless. Hence, the value of the compound option at T-2 is

$$\frac{1}{(1.05)}[.625 \times (26.1905 - 20) + .375 \times 0] = \$3.6848$$

13.6 Barrier Options

A barrier option is an option that gets activated or deactivated if the underlying asset price crosses a price barrier. There are two kinds of barrier options, *knock-in* options and *knock-out* options. In the case of knock-out options, an existing option will be deactivated if the barrier is breached. If the option is deactivated the holder may be entitled to a positive *rebate* in certain cases. If the barrier is not breached, then the option will be equivalent to a standard European option with the same exercise price, and will have an identical payoff at expiration. In the case of knock-in options, the option itself will come into existence if the barrier is breached. Once it is activated, it will subsequently behave like a European call with the same exercise price. However if it is not activated the holder may be given a positive rebate in certain cases.

Since the barrier can be either above or below the current stock price, knock-in options can be of two types, *up-and-in* or *down-and-in*.The word *up* denotes that the barrier is above the current stock price, while the word *down* implies that the barrier is below the current stock price. Similarly, knock-out options may be *up-and-out* or *down-and-out*. Of course every type of barrier options may be either a call or a put. Thus in all there can be eight types of barrier options.

The characteristics of the four kinds of barrier call options is summarized in Table 13.6. The same logic is applicable to put options.

Table 13.6: Features of Barrier Calls.

Nature of Option	Location of barrier B Relative to the Initial Stock Price S_t	Impact of Crossing/ Not Crossing the Barrier On the Option Payoff	
		If Crossed	**If Not Crossed**
Down and Out	Below	Rebate R ≥ 0	Standard Call
Down and in	Below	Standard Call	Rebate $R \geq 0$
Up and out	Above	Rebate $R \geq 0$	Standard Call
Up and in	Above	Standard Call	Rebate $R \geq 0$

Example 13.2 is based on an up and out barrier option, whereas Example 13.3, discusses an up and in barrier option.

Example 13.2: Assume that the current stock price is $100. Every period the stock may go up by 25% or go down by 25%. The riskless rate of interest is 10% per period. Consider a call option with an exercise price of $80 and a barrier of $110. We will assume that if the option is deactivated, then the holder will get a rebate of $10. The stock price tree is depicted in Figure 13.3.

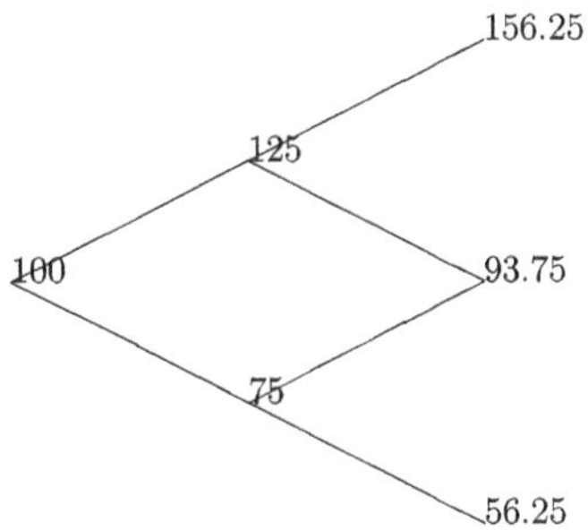

Figure 13.3: A Two Period Stock Price Tree.

$$p = \frac{1.10 - 0.75}{1.25 - 0.75} = 0.70; 1 - p = 0.30$$

We will inspect each possible path that the stock price can take.

Path 1: 100 → 125 → 156.25 The option will get deactivated when the price hits 125 at T-1. So the holder will get a rebate of $10 at expiration.

Path 2: 100 → 125 → 93.75 Once again the option will get deactivated. The holder will receive $10 at expiration.

Path 3: 100 → 75 → 93.75 The option will stay alive, and will pay off (93.75-80) = $13.75 at expiration.

Path 4: 100 → 75 → 56.25 The option will stay alive, but will finish out-of-the-money at expiration.

Using the risk-neutral valuation technique,

$$\begin{aligned} C_t &= \frac{1}{(1.10)^2}[(0.70)^2 \times 10 + 0.70 \times 0.30 \times 10 + 0.30 \times 0.70 \times 13.75 + (0.30)^2 \times 0] \\ &= 8.1715 \end{aligned}$$

Example 13.3: We will use the same data that we used in the previous example.

Path 1: 100 → 125 → 156.25 The option will get activated when the price hits 125 at T-1. The call will finish in the money at expiration, and the holder will consequently get (156.25-80) = $76.25.

Path 2: 100 → 125 → 93.75 Once again the option will get activated, and will finish in the money. The holder will receive (93.75-80) = $13.75.

Path 3: 100 → 75 → 93.75 The option will not come into existence. The holder will get a rebate of $10.

Path 4: 100 → 75 → 56.25 The option will once again not come into existence. Consequently the holder will receive a rebate of $10.

$$\begin{aligned} C_t &= \frac{1}{(1.10)^2}[(0.70)^2 \times 76.25 + 0.70 \times 0.30 \times 13.75 + 0.30 \times 0.70 \times 10 + (0.30)^2 \times 10] \\ &= 35.7438 \end{aligned}$$

13.6.1 Equivalence With European Options

It can be shown that an up and out call plus an up and in call is equivalent to a European option with the same exercise price, if the rebate for the barrier options is set at zero. We can see this by comparing the payoffs at expiration from a portfolio consisting of the two barrier options. Table 13.7 shows the payoffs from a portfolio of barrier options.

Table 13.7: Payoffs from a Portfolio of Barrier Options.

Path	Payoff from an Up and Out Call	Payoff from an Up and In Call	Payoff from the Portfolio
Path 1	0	76.25	76.25
Path 2	0	13.75	13.75
Path 3	13.75	0	13.75
Path 4	0	0	0

As can be seen from the last column of the above table, the payoff from the portfolio is identical to that of a European call. This is because while an up and out call has value only if the barrier is not breached an up and in call has value only if the barrier is breached. Since there are only two possibilities, that is, either the barrier is breached or it is not, it is but logical that a portfolio of the two barrier options should behave like a European option.

Similarly it can be shown that a portfolio consisting of a down and out call plus a down and in call is equivalent to a European call. The same holds true for put options.

13.7 Chooser Options

A chooser option allows the holder to decide whether he wants a call or a put option, by a specified choice date. Once the decision is made, the holder will get a conventional call or put option. Let us consider a three-period case where the holder has to make a choice after one period. That is, once the decision is made the option chosen will have two periods to expiration.

We will assume that the current stock price is \$100, and that every period the price may increase by 20% or decline by 20%. The risk-less rate is 5% per period. The exercise price of the option when chosen is \$100. The price evolution is shown in Figure 13.4. Consider the up state at T-2. The call value is given by:

$$0.625 \times \left[\frac{0.625 \times 72.80 + 0.375 \times 15.2}{(1.05)^2}\right] + 0.375 \times \left[\frac{0.625 \times 15.20 + 0.375 \times 0}{(1.05)^2}\right]$$
$$= \$32.2562$$

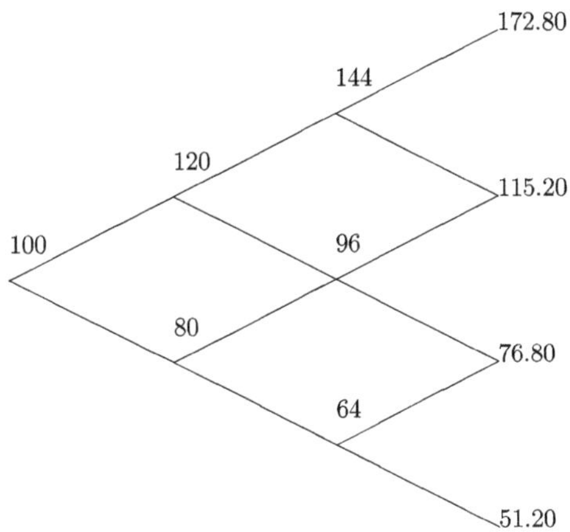

Figure 13.4: A Three Period Stock Price Tree.

The put value is given by:

$$0.625 \times 0 + 0.375 \times \left[\frac{0.625 \times 0 + 0.375 \times 23.2}{(1.05)^2}\right] = \$2.9592$$

Obviously the call will be chosen at this node.

Now let's consider the down state at T-2. The call premium is given by:

$$0.625 \times \left[\frac{0.625 \times 15.20 + 0.375 \times 0}{(1.05)^2}\right] + 0.375 \times 0 = \$5.3855$$

The put premium is given by:

$$0.625 \times \left[\frac{0.625 \times 0 + 0.375 \times 23.2}{(1.05)^2}\right] + 0.375 \times \left[\frac{0.625 \times 23.20 + 0.375 \times 48.80}{(1.05)^2}\right]$$
$$= \$16.0885$$

Thus the put will be chosen at this node.

The value of the chooser at T-3 may be computed as:

$$\left[\frac{0.625 \times 32.2562 + 0.375 \times 16.0885}{(1.05)}\right] = \$24.9460$$

13.8 Ladder Options

In the case of such options there are certain pre-specified price levels or 'rungs of a ladder'. If the asset price before expiration were to hit or breach a rung of the ladder, a minimum payoff will be locked in irrespective of what subsequently happens to the price.

Consider a call option with an exercise price of \$100, which assures a minimum payoff of \$20 if the asset price at any point in time prior to expiration were to breach the \$120 level. We will consider a two period case, where every period the asset price may go up by 20% or else decline by 20%. The risk-less rate is 5%, and the initial asset price is \$100. The price evolution is shown in Figure 13.5.

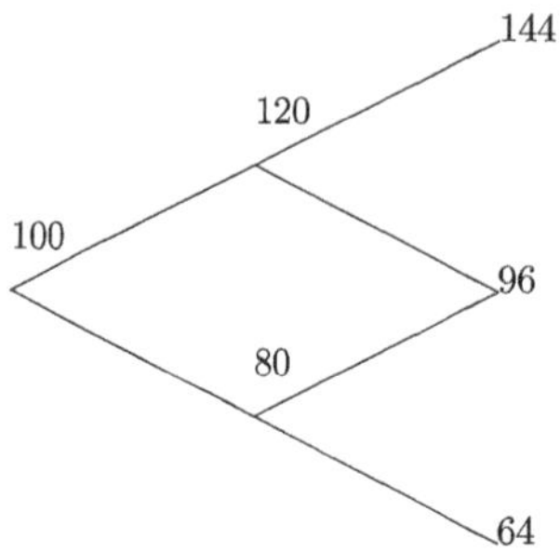

Figure 13.5: A Two Period Stock Price Tree.

The probability of each path, and the corresponding payoff at expiration is given in Table 13.8.

Table 13.8: Payoffs from a Ladder Option.

Path	Probability	Payoff
1	0.390625	44
2	0.234375	20
3	0.234375	0
4	0.140625	0

The initial value of the ladder option is:

$$\frac{(0.390625 \times 44 + 0.234375 \times 20)}{(1.05)^2} = \$19.8413$$

Suggestions for Further Reading

Arditti, F.D. *Derivatives*. Harvard Business School Press(1996).
De Weert, F. *Exotic Options Trading*. John Wiley, 2008.
Kolb, R.W. *Futures, Options, & Swaps*. Blackwell, 2000.
Exotic Options. Euromoney publications.

Chapter 14
The Valuation of Interest Rate Options

14.1 Introduction

At any point in time, an investor who is contemplating an investment in fixed income securities, will typically have access to a large number of bonds with different yields and varying times to maturity. It is common for investors and traders to frequently examine the relationship between the yields on bonds belonging to a particular risk class. A plot of the yields of bonds that differ only with respect to their time to maturity, versus their respective times to maturity is called a *Yield Curve*. The curve is an important indicator of the state of the bond market, and provides valuable information.

While constructing the yield curve it is very important that the data pertain to bonds of the same risk class, and having comparable degrees of liquidity. For example, a curve may be constructed for government securities or AAA rated corporate bonds, but not for a mixture of both. The primary yield curve in any domestic capital market is the government bond yield curve, for these instruments are free of default risk. In the U.S. debt market for instance, the primary yield curve is the U.S. Treasury yield curve.

14.2 Analyzing the Yield Curve

The yield curve is an indication of where the bond market is trading currently. It also has implications for the level of trading for the future or at least for what the market thinks will be happening in the future.

The yield curve sets the yield for all debt market instruments. First it fixes the price of money over the maturity structure. In practice the yields of government bonds from the shortest maturity instrument to the longest set the benchmark for yields on all other debt instruments. This would mean that if a 5 year government security is trading at a yield of 5%, all other 5 year bonds. irrespective of the issuer, will be trading at yields over 5%. The excess over the yield on the corresponding government security is called the *spread*. Thus issuers of debt in the market use the yield curve to price all debt securities.[1]

The yield curve also acts as an indicator of future yield levels. It assumes certain shapes in response to market expectations of future interest rates. Market participants therefore analyze the current shape of the curve in order to determine the direction of future interest rates. The curve is scrutinized in order to divine information about future rates by bond traders and fund managers.

1 See Choudhury (2004).

https://doi.org/10.1515/9783110746662-014

Central banks and government treasury departments also analyze the curve for its information content. This information is then used to set rates for the economy as a whole.

Portfolio managers use the curve to assess the relative values of investments across the maturity spectrum. The curve indicates the returns that are available at different points of time and is therefore important for fixed income fund managers who can use this information to assist them in assessing the points along the curve that offer the best returns. The curve can also be analyzed to determine which bonds are relatively cheap or costly.[2]

14.3 Spot Rates

The spot rate of interest for a particular time period is the discount rate that is applicable for a zero coupon instrument maturing at the end of the period.

For instance assume that the price of a six month zero coupon bond with a face value of $1,000 is $961.54. If we consider six months to be equivalent to one period, then the one period spot rate is given by

$$961.54 = \frac{1{,}000}{(1 + s_1)} \Rightarrow s_1 = 0.04 \equiv 4\%$$

Similarly if a one year or a two period zero coupon bond has a price of $873.44, then the two period spot rate is given by

$$873.44 = \frac{1{,}000}{(1 + s_2)^2} \Rightarrow s_2 = 0.07 \equiv 7\%$$

14.4 Relationship Between Spot Rates and the YTM

A plain vanilla bond consists of a series of cash flows arising at six monthly intervals. Thus such a bond is equivalent to a portfolio of zero coupon bonds, where each cash flow represents the face value of a zero coupon bond maturing at that particular instant.

The correct way to price a bond is by discounting each cash flow at the spot rate for the corresponding period.

Let's take the case of a bond with a face value of $1,000 and one year to maturity. Assume that it pays a coupon of 7% per annum on a semi-annual basis. Using the spot rates derived in the previous section, we can calculate the price of the bond to be

2 See Choudhury (2004)

$$P = \frac{35}{(1.04)} + \frac{1{,}035}{(1.07)^2} = \$\,937.66$$

The yield to maturity of this bond is given by

$$937.66 = \frac{35}{(1+\frac{y}{2})} + \frac{1{,}035}{(1+\frac{y}{2})^2}$$

$$\Rightarrow \frac{y}{2} = 0.069454 \equiv 6.9454\%$$

The yield to maturity is therefore a complex average of the spot rates. The problem with the yield to maturity is that it is a function of the coupon rate, for bonds with identical terms to maturity but with different coupons.

For instance let's take a 12% coupon bond with a face value of $1,000 and one year to maturity. Its price is given by

$$P = \frac{60}{(1.04)} + \frac{1{,}060}{(1.07)^2} = \$\,983.54$$

The yield to maturity of this bond is given by

$$983.54 = \frac{60}{(1+\frac{y}{2})} + \frac{1{,}060}{(1+\frac{y}{2})^2}$$

$$\Rightarrow \frac{y}{2} = 0.069092 \equiv 6.9092\%$$

Why is there a difference in the yields to maturity of the two bonds? After all they both have one year to maturity.

Let's take the 7% bond first. It has

$$\frac{\frac{35}{(1.04)}}{937.66} = 0.035891 \equiv 3.5891\%$$

of its value tied up in one period money and the balance 96.4109% tied up in two period money.

However, in the case of the 12% bond

$$\frac{\frac{60}{(1.04)}}{983.54} = 0.058658 \equiv 5.8658\%$$

of its value is tied up in one period money whereas the balance 94.1342% is tied up in two period money.

The one period spot rate is less than the two period spot rate, which implies that one period money is cheaper than two period money. Since the second bond has a greater percentage of its value tied up in one period money, its yield to maturity is less.

This is a manifestation of the *coupon effect*. In other words, the yield to maturity is a complex weighted average of spot rates where the weights depend on the pattern of cash flows receivable from a particular security. Consequently it tends to vary with the coupon rate on the bond, when comparisons are sought to be made among bonds with the same time to maturity. Thus a given measure of the YTM is specific to a particular security and cannot be used to estimate the fair value of another security.[3]

14.5 Yield Curve versus the Term Structure

Technically speaking, the term 'Yield Curve' is a graph depicting the relationship between the yield to maturity, which is plotted along the Y-axis, and the time to maturity, which is plotted along the X-axis. To reiterate, for the purpose of constructing the yield curve it is imperative that the bonds being compared belong to the same credit risk class. This is the most commonly used version of the yield curve for the simple reason that the YTM is the most commonly used measure of the yield from a bond.

The expression 'Term Structure of Interest Rates' on the other hand, refers to a graph depicting the relationship between spot rates of interest as shown along the Y-axis, and the corresponding time to maturity, which is plotted along the X-axis. Once again, to facilitate meaningful inferences, the data used to construct the graph should be applicable to bonds of the same risk class. The 'Term Structure of Interest Rates' is also referred to as the 'Zero Coupon Yield Curve' for obvious reasons. The zero coupon yield curve is considered to be the true term structure of interest rates because there is no reinvestment risk. The curve can be obtained from coupon bonds using the bootstrapping procedure as demonstrated below.

The YTM yield curve does not distinguish between different payment patterns that may result from bonds with different coupons - that is, the fact that low coupon bonds pay a higher portion of their cash flows in present value terms at a later date as compared to higher coupon bonds of the same maturity. To compensate for this bond analysts sometimes construct a coupon yield curve which plots the YTM against the term to maturity for a group of bonds with the same coupon.

The yield curve will be equivalent to the term structure if the term structure is flat, or in other words the spot rates are the same for all maturities. This is because, when the term structure is flat, the YTM which is a complex average of spot rates, will be equal to the observed spot rate.

3 See Babbel and Merill (1996).

14.6 Bootstrapping

In practice, we are unlikely to have data for the prices of zero coupon bonds maturing at regularly spaced intervals of time. Bootstrapping is a technique for determining the term structure of interest rates, given price data for a series of coupon paying bonds, and it works as follows.

Assume that we have the following data for four bonds, each of which matures at the end of the stated period of time, that is shown in Table 14.1. For ease of exposition we will also assume that the bonds pay coupons on an annual basis.

Table 14.1: Inputs for Determining the Zero Coupon Yield Curve.

Time to Maturity	Price in dollars	Coupon
1 Year	1,000	6%
2 Years	975	8%
3 Years	950	9%
4 Years	925	10%

The one year spot rate is obviously 6%. Using this information, the two year spot rate can be determined as follows.

$$975 = \frac{80}{(1.06)} + \frac{1080}{(1+s_2)^2}$$

$$\Rightarrow s_2 = 9.57\%$$

Similarly the three year spot rate can be determined as follows;

$$950 = \frac{90}{(1.06)} + \frac{90}{(1.0957)^2} + \frac{1090}{(1+s_3)^3}$$

$$\Rightarrow s_3 = 11.32\%$$

And finally, using the same logic

$$925 = \frac{100}{(1.06)} + \frac{100}{(1.0957)^2} + \frac{100}{(1.1132)^3} + \frac{1{,}100}{(1+s_4)^4}$$

$$\Rightarrow s_4 = 12.99\%$$

14.7 Practical Difficulties with Bootstrapping

In the above example we used the prices of four bonds, maturing after 1, 2, 3, and 4 years respectively. In some cases there may be several bonds of the same risk class, maturing at a given point in time. Usually each will have its own coupon. While estimating spot rates for a given maturity, obviously the coupon rates of the bonds being used is a factor. One of the other major issues while estimating the term structure using bootstrapping, is that a bond may not exist, or else it may not actively trade, for a particular maturity. And it is not necessary that we will always have access to a set of bonds whose maturity dates are conveniently spaced exactly one period apart.

Finally, all traded bonds may not be plain vanilla in nature. The U.S. Treasury has issued bonds which can be recalled after a point in time. This too has implications for the bootstrapping procedure.

14.8 Implied Forward Rates

Consider an investor who is contemplating a two period loan. He will be indifferent between a two-period spot rate of s_2 and a one period spot rate of s_1 with a forward contract to rollover his one period loan at maturity for one more period at a rate f_1^1, provided

$$(1 + s_2)^2 = (1 + s_1)(1 + f_1^1) \tag{14.1}$$

f_1^1 is the one period forward rate or the rate for a one period loan to be made one period later. It is known as the implied forward rate that is contained in the term structure. In general if we have an n period spot rate and an m period spot rate, where $m > n$, then

$$(1 + s_m)^m = (1 + s_n)^n (1 + f_n^{m-n})^{m-n} \tag{14.2}$$

where f_n^{m-n} is the m-n period implied forward rate for a loan to be made after n periods.

Forward rates are believed to convey information about the expected interest rate structure in the future. In fact, one school of thought called the *unbiased expectations hypothesis* believes that such rates are nothing but current expectations of future interest rates. Example 14.1 demonstrates the computation of forward rates.

Example 14.1: The one year spot rate is 8%; the two year spot rate is 10%, and the three year spot rate is 11.25%. Using this data what information can we deduce about implied forward rates?

$$(1 + s_2)^2 = (1 + s_1)(1 + f_1^1) \Rightarrow f_1^1 = 0.1204 = 12.04\%$$

Similarly

$$(1 + s_3)^3 = (1 + s_1)(1 + f_1^2)^2 \Rightarrow f_1^2 = 0.1291 \equiv 12.91\%$$

$$(1 + s_3)^3 = (1 + s_1)(1 + f_1^1)(1 + f_2^1) \Rightarrow f_2^1 = 0.1379 \equiv 13.79\%$$

14.9 Theories of the Term Structure

From observing yield curves in different markets at various points in time, an individual who studies the bond market will notice that the yield curve tends to adopt one of the three basic shapes.

- **Upward Sloping**: In the case of a yield curve with a positive slope, also termed as a rising yield curve, short term yields will be lower than long term yields.
- **Downward Sloping**: In the case of a yield curve with a negative slope, also termed as an inverted yield curve, long term rates will be lower than short term rates.
- **Humped**: A humped yield curve is characterized by lower rates at the short end of the spectrum. The curve then rises, reaching a peak at the middle of the maturity spectrum, and then gradually slopes downward at longer maturities.

A great deal of effort is expended by analysts and economists in analyzing and interpreting the yield curve, for there is often substantial information that is associated with the curve at any point in time. Various theories have been advanced that purport to explain the observed shapes of the curve. However, no theory by itself is able to explain all aspects of the curves that are observed in practice. So often, analysts seek to explain specific shapes of the curve using a combination of the accepted theories.

14.9.1 The Pure or Unbiased Expectations Hypothesis

The unbiased expectations hypothesis states that current implied forward rates are unbiased estimators of future spot rates. As per this theory long-term rates are geometric averages of expected future short-term rates, Thus a positively sloped yield curve would be consistent with the argument that the market expects spot interest rates to rise. If rates are expected to rise then investors in long term bonds will be perturbed for they face the specter of a capital loss. This is because rising interest rates will lead to declining bond prices, and long term bonds are more sensitive to rising interest rates than short term bonds. In such a situation investors will start selling long dated securities and buying short dated securities. This will lead to an increase in yields on long term bonds and a decline in yields on short term bonds. The overall result will be an upward sloping yield curve. On the contrary, an inverted yield curve would indicate that the market expects future spot rates to fall.

The hypothesis can be used to explain any shape of the yield curve. For instance a humped yield curve would be consistent with the explanation that investors expect short-term rates to rise and long-term rates to fall.

Expectations or views on the future direction of the market are a function mainly of the expected rate of inflation. If the market expects inflationary pressures in the future, the yield curve will be positively sloped, whereas if inflation is expected to decline then the slope of the yield curve will be negative.

14.9.2 The Liquidity Preference Theory (LPT)

Intuitively, most of us would feel that longer maturity instruments are more risky than those with a shorter maturity. An investor lending money for five years will usually demand a higher rate of interest than if he were to lend money to the same customer for a year. This is because the borrower may not be able to repay the loan over a longer term period. For this reason, long dated yields should be higher than short dated yields.

Take the case where the market expects inflation to remain fairly stable over time. The expectations hypothesis would postulate that this scenario would be characterized by a flat yield curve. However the liquidity preference hypothesis would predict a positively sloping yield curve. The argument would be as follows. Generally a borrower would like to borrow over as long a term as possible while a lender would like to lend over as short a term as possible. Thus lenders have to be suitably rewarded if they are to be induced to lend for longer periods of time. This compensation may be considered as a premium for the loss of liquidity from the standpoint of the lender. The premium may be expected to increase the further the investor lends across the term structure, so that the longest dated instruments will, all else being equal, have the highest yield.

As per this hypothesis, the yield curve should almost always be upward sloping, reflecting the bond holders' preference for liquidity. However inverted yield curves can still be explained by this theory by postulating that interest rates are likely to decline in the future, as a consequence of which, despite the liquidity premium, long term rates are lower than short-term rates.

14.9.3 The Expectations Hypothesis versus The LPT: A Mathematical Analysis

As per the expectations hypothesis forward rates are unbiased expectations of future spot rates. Thus

$$f_n^{m-n} = E_0[\,_nS_{m-n}] \tag{14.3}$$

In other words the **(m-n)** period forward rate, **n** periods from now, is the current expectation of the **(m-n)** period spot rate that is expected to prevail **n** periods from now. The expectations hypothesis can explain any shape of the term structure. For instance, an expectation that future short term interest rates will be above the current level would lead to an upward sloping term structure. Example 14.2 is based on an upward sloping term structure.

Example 14.2: Here is an illustration of an upward sloping term structure. Assume that $s_1 = 5.50\%$; $E[{}_1s_1] = 6.0\%$; $E[{}_2s_1] = 7.5\%$, and that $E[{}_3s_1] = 8.5\%$.

If so then

$$s_2 = [(1.055)(1.06)]^{\frac{1}{2}} - 1 = 5.75\%$$

$$s_3 = [(1.055)(1.06)(1.075)]^{\frac{1}{3}} - 1 = 6.33\%$$

$$s_4 = [(1.055)(1.06)(1.075)(1.085)]^{\frac{1}{4}} - 1 = 6.87\%$$

According to the expectations hypothesis, investors care only about expected returns and not about risk. Let's take the case of an investor who chooses to invest for two periods. He can buy a two period bond yielding a rate of s_2. Or else he can buy a one period bond that yields s_1 and then roll over into another one period bond at maturity. As per the hypothesis the investor will be indifferent between the two strategies if the expected returns in both cases are equal.

In other words the hypothesis predicts that the market will be in equilibrium if

$$(1 + s_2)^2 = E[(1 + s_1)(1 + {}_1s_1)] \tag{14.4}$$

But we know that if arbitrage is to be ruled out, then

$$(1 + s_2)^2 = (1 + s_1)(1 + f_1^1) \tag{14.5}$$

Thus as per the expectations hypothesis $f_1^1 = E({}_1s_1)$

Now let's focus on the liquidity preference theory. Take the case of an investor who has a one period investment horizon. He can buy a one period bond and lock in a rate of s_1. Or else he can buy a two period bond and sell it after one year. In the second case, the rate of return will be uncertain at the outset, for it will depend on the one period rate that will prevail one period from now.

Consider a two period zero coupon bond with a face value of $1,000. Its current price will be

$$\frac{1{,}000}{(1 + s_2)^2} = \frac{1{,}000}{(1 + s_1)(1 + f_1^1)} \tag{14.6}$$

The expected price of the bond after one period is

$$E\left[\frac{1{,}000}{(1 + {}_1s_1)}\right] \geq \frac{1{,}000}{1 + E({}_1s_1)} \tag{14.7}$$

How do we know that the expectation of the price after one year will be greater than or equal to the face value discounted by the expected one period spot rate one period from now. This conclusion arises from a result called Jensen's Inequality. It states that for a convex function, *the expectation of the function is greater than or equal to the function of the expectation.* That is:

$$E[f(X)] \geq f[E(X)] \tag{14.8}$$

In our case, $\frac{1{,}000}{1 + {}_1s_1}$ is a convex function because the second derivative is positive.

The expected rate of return from the two period bond over the first year will be:

$$\frac{E\left[\frac{1{,}000}{(1+{}_1s_1)}\right] - \frac{1{,}000}{(1+s_1)(1+f_1^1)}}{\frac{1{,}000}{(1+s_1)(1+f_1^1)}}$$

$$\geq \frac{\frac{1{,}000}{1+E({}_1s_1)} - \frac{1{,}000}{(1+s_1)(1+f_1^1)}}{\frac{1{,}000}{(1+s_1)(1+f_1^1)}}$$

$$\Rightarrow \frac{E\left[\frac{1{,}000}{(1+{}_1s_1)}\right] - \frac{1{,}000}{(1+s_1)(1+f_1^1)}}{\frac{1{,}000}{(1+s_1)(1+f_1^1)}}$$

$$\geq \frac{(1+s_1)(1+f_1^1)}{1+E({}_1s_1)} - 1$$

Obviously, the expected one period return from the two period bond will be greater than s_1 only if $f_1^1 > E({}_1s_1)$.

Now an investor with a one period investment horizon will obviously choose to hold a two period bond only if its expected return is greater than the assured return on a one period bond. This is because if he chooses to hold the two period bond, he will have to sell it after one period at a price that is unknown at the outset. From the above analysis this would imply that the forward rate must be higher than the expected one period spot rate. Thus if investors are risk averse, which is the normal assumption made in Finance theory, the forward rate will exceed the expected spot rate by an amount equal to the risk premium or what may be termed as the *liquidity* premium.

We know that

$$(1+s_2)(1+s_2) = (1+s_1)(1+f_1^1)$$

As per the LPT

$$(1+s_1)(1+f_1^1) > (1+s_1)[1+E({}_1s_1)]$$

Therefore

$$(1 + s_2)(1 + s_2) > (1 + s_1)[1 + E({}_1s_1)]$$

Consider a downward sloping yield curve. This would imply that $s_1 > s_2$. Therefore it must be the case that $E({}_1s_1)$ is substantially less than s_1. In other words the market expects spot rates to decline substantially. For instance if $s_1 = 7\%$ and $s_2 = 6\%$ then $f_1^1 = 5.01\%$ As per the expectations hypothesis $E({}_1s_1) = 5.01\%$. However as per the LPT, $E({}_1s_1) < 5.01\%$. If we assume that the liquidity premium is 0.50%, then $E({}_1s_1) = 4.51\%$

Now let's take the case of a flat term structure. As per the expectations hypothesis

$$s_1 = s_2 = f_1^1 = E({}_1s_1)$$

However according to the LPT $E({}_1s_1) < s_1 = s_2$. Thus while the expectations hypothesis would imply that the market expects spot rates to remain unchanged, the prediction according to the liquidity preference theory is that the market expects spot rates to decline. For instance if $s_1 = s_2 = 7\%$ then according to the expectations hypothesis $E({}_1s_1) = 7\%$. However according to the LPT, $E({}_1s_1) = 7 - 0.50 = 6.50\%$.

Finally let's take the case of an upward sloping yield curve. If $s_1 < s_2$ then for a slightly upward sloping yield curve the LPT would be consistent with the expectation that rates are going to marginally decline. However, if the curve were to be steeply upward sloping then the LPT would be consistent with the expectation that short term rates are going to rise. For instance, assume that $s_1 = 7\%$ and that $s_2 = 7.1\%$. If so

$$f_1^1 = 7.2\% \Rightarrow E({}_1s_1) = 7.20 - 0.50 = 6.70\%$$

However if $s_2 = 7.3\%$ then

$$f_1^1 = 7.6\% \Rightarrow E({}_1s_1) = 7.60 - 0.50 = 7.10\%$$

In both these cases however, the expectations hypothesis would predict that spot rates are likely to rise. In the first scenario, as per the expectations hypothesis, $E({}_1s_1) = 7.20\%$, whereas in the second case $E({}_1s_1) = 7.60\%$.

14.9.4 The Money Substitute Hypothesis

According to this hypothesis short-term bonds are substitutes for holding cash. Investors hold only short dated bonds because they are viewed as having low or negligible risk. As a result the yields on short dated bonds are depressed due to increased demand, and consequently long term yields are greater than short term yields. Borrowers on the other hand prefer to issue debt for long maturities and on as few occasions as possible to minimize costs. Thus the yields on long term securities are driven upward due to increased supply and lower liquidity.[4]

14.9.5 The Market Segmentation Hypothesis

This theory states that the capital market is made up of a wide variety of issuers, each with different requirements. Certain classes of investors will prefer short dated bonds while others will prefer long dated bonds. The theory argues that activity is concentrated in certain specific areas of the market, and that there are no interrelationships between these segments of the market. The relative amount of funds invested in each market segment causes differentials in supply and demand which leads to humps in the yield curve.

Thus, as per this theory the observed shape of the yield curve is determined by the supply and demand for specific maturity investments, and the dynamics in a particular market segment has no relevance for any other part of the curve. For example, banks concentrate a large part of their activity at the short-end of the curve as a part of daily cash management known as asset-liability management, and for regulatory purposes. On the other hand, fund managers such as pension funds and insurance companies are active at the long end of the market.[5] Few institutions however have a preference for medium dated bonds. This behavior leads to high prices and low yields at both the short and long ends of the maturity spectrum and to high yields in the middle of the term structure.

14.9.6 The Preferred Habitat Theory

This is a slightly modified version of the segmentation hypothesis. This suggests that different market participants have an interest in specified areas of the yield curve but can be persuaded to hold bonds from other parts of the maturity spectrum if they are provided with sufficient incentives. Hence, banks which typically operate at the short-end of the spectrum, may at times hold long dated bonds once the prices of these bonds fall to a certain level, thereby ensuring that the returns from holding such bonds is commensurate with the attendant risk. Similar considerations may persuade long-term investors to hold short term debt. So the incentive for an investor to shift out of his preferred habitat is the inducement offered by way of a higher rate of interest.

4 See Choudhry (2004).

5 See Choudhry (2004).

14.9.7 Short Rates

A short rate of interest is a future spot rate of interest that might arise over time. Usually it is denoted as a single period rate of interest, and is defined as the rate for the shortest period of time considered by a model.

At any point in time, if we consider a series of spot rates corresponding to different lengths of time, we will be able to derive a unique vector of forward rates. However, for any future point in time, there are an infinite number of short rates that may arise. Each possible value has a varying probability of occurrence. At the initial point in time, the one period spot rate will be equal to the one period forward rate, which will be equal to the one period short rate. However, if we look at a time horizon beyond the first period, these interest rate measures will in general not be equal to each other.

14.10 Issues in the Valuation of Interest Rate Derivatives

A Black-Scholes approach or a standard binomial model, which work well in the case of stock options, are inappropriate for interest rate dependent financial claims and their derivatives. For instance, let's take the case of a bond maturing after N years. Although the price before maturity is expected to evolve in a random fashion, as the time to expiration approaches zero, the price of the underlying security should tend towards its par value. Consequently, option pricing models based on lognormal or binomial outcomes for the price of the underlying asset are unsuitable for valuing a derivative like an option on an interest rate dependent asset such as a bond.

There is no standard model for pricing options on debt securities. However, almost all of the models that have been postulated are based on the following three-step approach.[6]

- The random character of interest rate movements is first modeled.
- The interest rate process is used to infer the distribution of prices of the underlying debt securities.
- The distribution of prices of the underlying asset is used to value the option.

Thus, the difference between competing models lies in the way they model the interest rate process.

6 See Rendleman (2002).

14.11 Equilibrium Models of the Term Structure

Such models derive a stochastic process for the evolution of the short rate by making a set of assumptions about economic variables. In a one-factor model, the stochastic process for the short rate is the only source of uncertainty. In general, short rates are assumed to follow an Ito process of the form:

$$dr = \mu(r)dt + \sigma(r)dZ \tag{14.9}$$

That is, the drift μ, and the variance rate σ^2 are assumed to be functions of the short rate, but are considered to be independent of time.

There is however a critical problem with this approach to the pricing of interest rate derivatives. In practice, it is usually the case that the prices of the underlying debt securities, which are inferred from the postulated interest rate process, are not equal to their observed market prices. It is obvious that if we are unable to correctly price the underlying security, it will be impossible for us to have faith in the derivative prices that are obtained from the same.

14.11.1 The Cox, Ingersoll, and Ross (CIR Model)

The CIR model may be specified as

$$dr = \alpha(\beta - r)dt + \sigma\sqrt{r}dZ \tag{14.10}$$

This model incorporates mean reversion. Mean reversion may be described as follows. When the short rate (r), is higher than the long-run rate (β), it will display a tendency to decline and will gradually tend towards β. On the other hand, if r is lower than beta, it will gradually rise and will once again tend towards β. In other words, when the short rate is high, the process will have a negative drift while when the short rate is low, it will be characterized by a positive drift. One of the appealing features of the CIR model is that it does not allow interest rates to become negative.

The long-run value for the short rate should not be misconstrued as a long-term rate of interest.[7] While the long-term interest rate in an economy is a variable that is expected to evolve stochastically, the long-run rate is a parameter to which the short rate may be expected to converge over a period of time. The parameter α determines the speed of adjustment of the short rate. If α is high the adjustment will be rapid. However if α is low, then the movement of the short rate to its long-run value will be more gradual.

7 See Ho and Lee (2005).

14.11.2 The Rendleman and Bartter Model

Rendleman and Bartter derived the following process for the short rate

$$dr = \mu r dt + \sigma r dZ \tag{14.11}$$

This is analogous to the process used by Black and Scholes to define the evolution of the stock price over time, and implies that the short rate follows geometric Brownian motion. One of the shortcomings of this model is that it does not incorporate mean reversion.

14.11.3 The Vasicek Model

Vasicek derived the following process for the short rate

$$dr = \alpha(\beta - r)dt + \sigma dZ \tag{14.12}$$

where $\alpha, \beta,$ and σ are constants. This process is referred to as the Ornstein-Uhlenbeck process, and it too incorporates mean reversion. That is, as per the model, the short rate displays a tendency to revert to its long-term mean of β. Vasicek obtained the prices of bonds of different maturities using a constant market price of risk.[8] The model has a drawback in the sense that it allows the short rate to become negative.

14.12 Arbitrage-Free Term Structure Models

This class of option pricing models takes the observed term structure of interest rates as an input, unlike the earlier class of models which generate the term structure as an output. The stochastic process for the short rate that is implied by the observed term structure is deduced and from it the values of the underlying debt securities are inferred. Finally, the price of the derivative security is obtained. The appealing feature of this approach is that the prices of the debt securities that are derived in this fashion are entirely consistent with the observed term structure.

We will now look at alternative models of the term structure.

8 We will shortly have more to say about the market price of risk.

14.12.1 The Ho and Lee Model

As per this model, the evolution of the short rate may be specified as

$$dr_t = \mu_t dt + \sigma dZ \tag{14.13}$$

14.12.2 The Hull and White Model

This model specifies the evolution of the short rate as

$$dr_t = [\mu_t - ar_t]dt + \sigma dZ \tag{14.14}$$

14.12.3 The Kalotay-Williams-Fabozzi Model

As per this model, the evolution of the short rate may be described as

$$dlnr_t = \mu_t dt + \sigma dZ \tag{14.15}$$

14.12.4 The Black-Derman Toy Model

The model may be stated as

$$dlnr_t = \mu_t dt + \sigma_t dZ \tag{14.16}$$

14.12.5 The Black-Karasinski Model

As per this model

$$dlnr_t = [\mu_t - alnr_t]dt + \sigma_t dZ \tag{14.17}$$

14.13 The Fundamental Bond Pricing Equation in Continuous Time

If P(t,T) is the price of a zero coupon bond maturing at time T, then the instantaneous return may be defined as

$$\frac{dP}{P} = \mu(t, T)dt + \sigma(t, T)dZ \tag{14.18}$$

where Z is a Wiener process.

Consider a portfolio of two bonds of different maturities, T_1 and T_2. Assume that we invest a proportion w of our wealth in the first bond and $1\text{-}w$ in the second bond. If we denote the portfolio by V, then the rate of return on this portfolio may be expressed as

$$\frac{dV}{V} = [w\mu(t, T_1) + (1 - w)\mu(t, T_2)]dt + [w\sigma(t, T_1) + (1 - w)\sigma(t, T_2)]dZ \tag{14.19}$$

Let's choose w in a way such that

$$w\sigma(t, T_1) + (1 - w)\sigma(t, T_2) = 0$$
$$\Rightarrow w = \frac{\sigma(t, T_2)}{\sigma(t, T_2) - \sigma(t, T_1)}$$

In such a case the portfolio return will be riskless and can be expressed as

$$[w\mu(t, T_1) + (1 - w)\mu(t, T_2)]dt = \left[\frac{\mu(t, T_1)\sigma(t, T_2)}{\sigma(t, T_2) - \sigma(t, T_1)} - \frac{\mu(t, T_2)\sigma(t, T_1)}{\sigma(t, T_2) - \sigma(t, T_1)}\right] dt$$

Since the portfolio is risk-less by construction, the rate of return must be equal to the riskless rate. Thus

$$\left[\frac{\mu(t, T_1)\sigma(t, T_2)}{\sigma(t, T_2) - \sigma(t, T_1)} - \frac{\mu(t, T_2)\sigma(t, T_1)}{\sigma(t, T_2) - \sigma(t, T_1)}\right] dt = r(t)dt$$
$$\Rightarrow \mu(t, T_1)\sigma(t, T_2) - \mu(t, T_2)\sigma(t, T_1) = r(t)[\sigma(t, T_2) - \sigma(t, T_1)]$$
$$\Rightarrow [\mu(t, T_1) - r(t)]\sigma(t, T_2)] = [\mu(t, T_2) - r(t)]\sigma(t, T_1)]$$
$$\Rightarrow \frac{[\mu(t, T_1) - r(t)]}{\sigma(t, T_1)} = \frac{[\mu(t, T_2) - r(t)]}{\sigma(t, T_2)} = \lambda(r, t) \tag{14.20}$$

$\lambda(r, t)$ is referred to as the market price of risk. Since μ is equal to $\lambda\sigma$, we can state that

$$\frac{dP}{P} = [r(t) + \sigma(t, T)\lambda(t, T)]dt + \sigma(t, T)dZ$$

A general form of a single factor model for the short rate is:

$$dr = \alpha(r, t)dt + \rho(r, t)dZ$$

Since $P = P(r, t)$ from Ito's lemma

$$dP = \left[\frac{\partial P}{\partial t} + \alpha \times \frac{\partial P}{\partial r} + \frac{1}{2} \times \rho^2 \times \frac{\partial^2 P}{\partial r^2}\right] dt + \rho \times \frac{\partial P}{\partial r} dZ$$

If we compare it with the earlier representation of dP, which is

$$dP = [r(t) + \sigma(t, T)\lambda(t, T)]P(t, T)dt + \sigma(t, T)P(t, T)dZ$$

we can state that

$$\left[\frac{\partial P}{\partial t} + \alpha \times \frac{\partial P}{\partial r} + \frac{1}{2} \times \rho^2 \times \frac{\partial^2 P}{\partial r^2}\right] = [r(t) + \sigma(t,T)\lambda(t,T)]P(t,T)$$

$$\text{and } \rho \times \frac{\partial P}{\partial r} = \sigma(t,T)P(t,T)$$

Thus

$$\frac{\partial P}{\partial t} + \alpha \times \frac{\partial P}{\partial r} + \frac{1}{2} \times \rho^2 \times \frac{\partial^2 P}{\partial r^2} = r(t)P(t,T) + \rho \times \lambda \times \frac{\partial P}{\partial r}$$

$$\Rightarrow \frac{\partial P}{\partial t} + [\alpha - \rho \times \lambda] \times \frac{\partial P}{\partial r} + \frac{1}{2} \times \rho^2 \times \frac{\partial^2 P}{\partial r^2} - rP(t,T) = 0 \tag{14.21}$$

This is the fundamental bond pricing equation.

14.14 The Binomial Tree Approach to The Term Structure

We will now illustrate no-arbitrage models of the term structure using a discrete time framework. Before we proceed we need to define certain variables.

We will denote the length of a time period in the binomial tree as Δt, where time is measured in years. Interest rates will consequently be specified as annual rates. s_n is the n-period spot rate at time 0, quoted as a percentage per annum, but compounded at an interval equal to Δt. Thus if a dollar is invested at time 0 for n periods, the future value will be

$$\text{F.V.} = (1 + s_n \Delta t)^n$$

We will define r_n as the short rate that will prevail n periods later. r_0 is obviously equal to the one period spot rate s_1. The time step in the binomial tree will be taken as six months for the purpose of illustration. Consequently, $\Delta t = 0.50$.

Consider a bond that pays \$1 after two periods. Its present value will be $\frac{1}{(1+\frac{s_2}{2})^2}$.

The short rate after one period will be either r_u or r_d. Thus the value of the bond after one period will be either

$$P_u = \frac{1}{\left(1 + \frac{r_u}{2}\right)} \text{ or}$$

$$P_d = \frac{1}{\left(1 + \frac{r_d}{2}\right)}$$

The present value of the one period bond will therefore be $\frac{P_u}{\left(1+\frac{S_1}{2}\right)}$ or $\frac{P_d}{\left(1+\frac{S_1}{2}\right)}$. Thus

$$\frac{1}{\left(1+\frac{S_2}{2}\right)^2} = \frac{q \times P_u}{\left(1+\frac{S_1}{2}\right)} + \frac{(1-q) \times P_d}{\left(1+\frac{S_1}{2}\right)}$$

$$\Rightarrow \frac{1}{\left(1+\frac{S_2}{2}\right)^2} = \frac{q}{\left(1+\frac{S_1}{2}\right)\left(1+\frac{r_u}{2}\right)} + \frac{1-q}{\left(1+\frac{S_1}{2}\right)\left(1+\frac{r_d}{2}\right)}$$

$$\Rightarrow \frac{\left(1+\frac{r_u}{2}\right)\left(1+\frac{r_d}{2}\right)\left(1+\frac{S_1}{2}\right)}{\left(1+\frac{S_2}{2}\right)^2} = q\left(1+\frac{r_d}{2}\right) + (1-q)\left(1+\frac{r_u}{2}\right)$$

$$\Rightarrow \frac{\left(1+\frac{r_u}{2}\right)\left(1+\frac{r_d}{2}\right)\left(1+\frac{S_1}{2}\right)}{\left(1+\frac{S_2}{2}\right)^2} - q\left(1+\frac{r_d}{2}\right) - (1-q)\left(1+\frac{r_u}{2}\right) \tag{14.22}$$

This is the fundamental equation that is used in no-arbitrage models to determine the short rates. To apply these models in practice one has to model r_u and r_d. The models differ in their approach to modeling these parameters.

14.14.1 Some Insights into the Ho-Lee Model

Let's depict a four-period interest rate tree. Each node will be denoted as $r_{k,j}$ where k represents the point in time that we are at and j represents the state. The tree may be modeled as shown in Figure 14.1.

Thus an up move from node $r_{k,j}$ is a move to node $r_{k+1,j}$ while a down move, is a move to node $r_{k+1,j+1}$. Notice that the above tree is recombining, that is, r_{ud} is the same as r_{du}. The recombination condition not only reduces the number of nodes at each point in time, and consequently makes computation relatively easier, it also has implications for σ as well shall shortly demonstrate.

Interest rates span time whereas prices do not. Consequently the above interest rate tree can be used to price bonds with up to four periods to maturity. That is, if we have a bond that pays \$1,000 at time t_4, the price tree corresponding to the above interest tree may be depicted as shown in Figure 14.2.

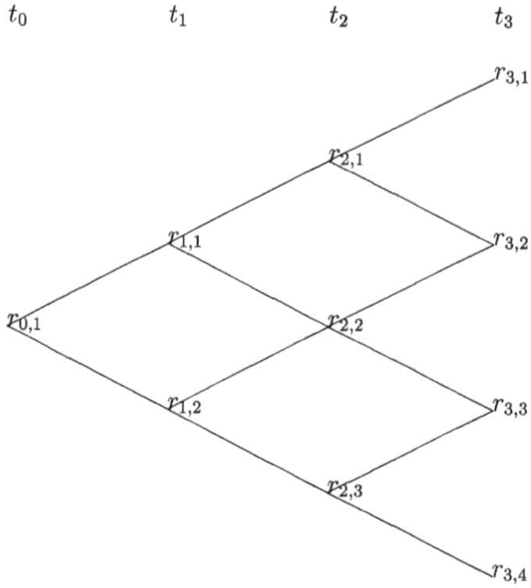

Figure 14.1: Interest Rate Tree.

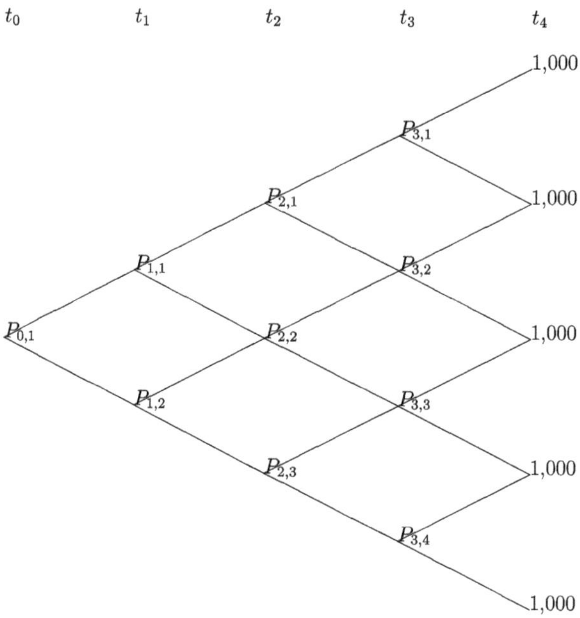

Figure 14.2: Price Tree.

Consider time point t_k where $t_k = k\Delta t$ and let r_k be the short rate at this point in time. For the process

$$dr = \mu_t dt + \sigma_t dZ$$

we can approximate dr as $r_{k+1,j+1} - r_{k,j}$ and can write

$$r_{k+1,j} = r_{k,j} + \mu_k \Delta t + \sigma_k \sqrt{\Delta t} \text{ and}$$
$$r_{k+1,j+1} = r_{k,j} + \mu_k \Delta t - \sigma_k \sqrt{\Delta t}$$

Thus

$$r_{1,1} = r_{0,1} + \mu_0 \Delta t + \sigma_0 \sqrt{\Delta t} \text{ and}$$
$$r_{1,2} = r_{0,1} + \mu_0 \Delta t - \sigma_0 \sqrt{\Delta t}$$
$$\Rightarrow r_{1,1} - r_{1,2} = 2\sigma_0 \sqrt{\Delta t}$$

Hence the spread between the upstate and the down state is a function of the volatility parameter. Similarly

$$r_{2,1} = r_{1,1} + \mu_1 \Delta t + \sigma_1 \sqrt{\Delta t}$$
$$r_{2,2} = r_{1,1} + \mu_1 \Delta t - \sigma_1 \sqrt{\Delta t} = r_{1,2} + \mu_1 \Delta t + \sigma_1 \sqrt{\Delta t}$$
$$r_{2,3} = r_{1,2} + \mu_1 \Delta t - \sigma_1 \sqrt{\Delta t}$$

Notice that $r_{2,2}$ can be expressed as a down-move from $r_{1,1}$ or as an up-move from $r_{1,2}$ because of the recombination requirement. Thus

$$r_{1,1} + \mu_1 \Delta t - \sigma_1 \sqrt{\Delta t} = r_{1,2} + \mu_1 \Delta t + \sigma_1 \sqrt{\Delta t}$$
$$\Rightarrow 2\sigma_1 \sqrt{\Delta t} = r_{1,1} - r_{1,2}$$
$$\Rightarrow \sigma_1 = \frac{r_{1,1} - r_{1,2}}{2\sqrt{\Delta t}} = \frac{2\sigma_0 \sqrt{\Delta t}}{2\sqrt{\Delta t}} = \sigma_0$$

Therefore if the interest rate tree is to recombine, then it must be the case that σ is a constant for all points in time. In other words, $\sigma_k = \sigma \forall k$.

14.15 Calibrating the Ho and Lee Model

We will now illustrate as to how the Ho and Lee model can be fitted to the observed term structure using the binomial tree approach. The parameters of the model will be chosen in a way such that the branches of the tree recombine. This, as you have already seen, implies that the standard deviation, σ, is constant for all points in time. In practice the value of σ is chosen arbitrarily. It is also assumed that given a state of nature, there is a 50% probability of an up move, and therefore obviously a 50% probability of a down move.

The movements in the short rate may be expressed as follows:

$$r_{t+1} = r_t + \mu_{t+1} + \epsilon_{t+1}$$

where $\epsilon_{t+1} = \sigma$ with a probability of 0.50 and is equal to $-\sigma$ with a probability of 0.50. Thus

$$r_{k+1,j} = r_{k,j} + \mu_{t+1} + \sigma$$

and

$$r_{k+1,j+1} = r_{k,j} + \mu_{t+1} - \sigma$$

The values of μ will be determined so as to generate the term structure that is observed in practice. Before we proceed to illustrate the calibration technique, let's first introduce the concept of an Arrow-Debreu security, a concept which we will use to subsequently value interest rate dependent securities.

14.15.1 Arrow-Debreu Securities

Such securities, also known as 'Pure Securities' will pay a dollar if a particular state of nature were to occur. However in all other states of nature, the payoff will be zero. Obviously each node of a binomial tree represents a particular state of nature. The value at time t_0, of a pure security that pays off \$1 in state (k,j), will be denoted by $q_{k,j}$.

Let's first consider a one period binomial tree, as shown in Figure 14.3. We will assume that the one period interest rate is 8% per annum. Each period represents a time interval of six months.

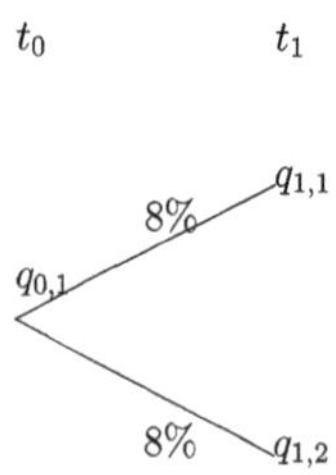

Figure 14.3: One Period Interest Rate & State Price Tree.

Thus the price of a security that pays off \$1 in the upstate is given by

$$q_{1,1} = 0.50 \times \frac{1}{(1 + 0.08 \times 0.5)} = \frac{1}{1.04} = 0.4808$$

$q_{1,2}$ or the price of a security that pays one dollar in the down state is obviously the same. The values of q that are calculated in this fashion are referred to as 'State Prices'.

A risk-less security in such an environment is obviously one that pays off a dollar irrespective of the state of nature after one period. Its price is obviously given by:

$$q_{1,1} + q_{1,2} = 0.4808 + 0.4808 + 0.9616$$

The risk-less rate of interest is therefore

$$\frac{1 - 0.9616}{0.9616} \equiv 4\%$$

which is what we would expect.

Now let's extend the model by a period, as shown in Figure 14.4. Assume that if the up state were to be reached after a period, the rate of interest will be 8.75% per annum, whereas if the down state were to be reached it will 7.25% per annum.

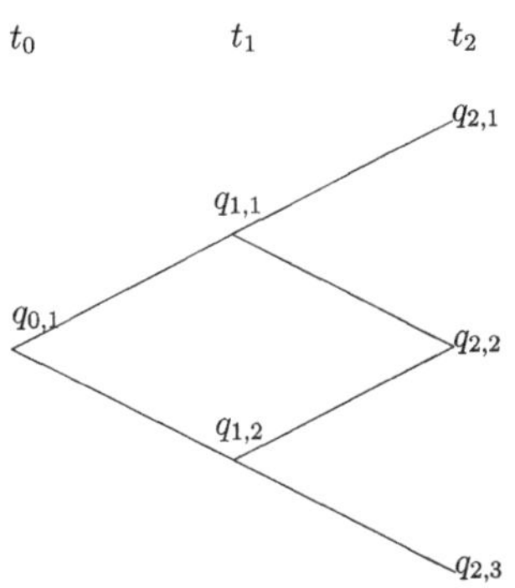

Figure 14.4: Two Period Interest Rate & State Price Tree.

At the end of two periods there will obviously be three states of nature. We can calculate the prices of the Arrow-Debreu securities as follows.

$$q_{2,1} = \frac{0.5 \times 0.5}{(1.04) \times \left(1 + \frac{0.0875}{2}\right)}$$

$$= q_{1,1} \times \frac{0.5}{1.04375} = 0.4808 \times \frac{0.5}{1.04375} = 0.2303$$

Let's analyze this expression. The value of an Arrow-Debreu security that pays off \$1 at state (2,1) is $\frac{0.5}{1.04375}$ at state (1,1). We know that the value of a pure security that pays off \$1 in state (1,1) is \$0.4808 as calculated at state (0,1). Consequently the value of a pure security that pays off \$1 in state (2,1), as calculated at state (0,1), is

$$0.4808 \times \frac{0.5}{1.04375} = 0.2303$$

Now let's consider a pure security that will pay off \$1 if state (2,2) were to occur. This state can be attained via two paths. Hence, using the same logic

$$q_{2,2} = q_{1,1} \times \frac{0.5}{\left(1 + \frac{0.0875}{2}\right)} + q_{1,2} \times \frac{0.5}{\left(1 + \frac{0.0725}{2}\right)}$$
$$= 0.4808 \times \frac{0.5}{1.04375} + 0.4808 \times \frac{0.5}{1.03625} = 0.4623$$

Similarly

$$q_{2,3} = q_{1,2} \times \frac{0.5}{1.03625} = 0.2320$$

Thus this approach enables us to price pure securities at various states of nature by working our way forward through the tree.

Now consider the term structure shown in Table 14.2.

Table 14.2: Vector of Spot Rates.

Period	Spot Rate
1	6.00%
2	5.80%
3	6.05%
4	5.90%

Assume that $\sigma = 1\%$. $r_{0,1}$ is obviously 6%. $q_{0,1} = 1$

We know that:

$$r_{1,1} = r_{0,1} + \mu_1 + 1 = 7\% + \mu_1$$

and

$$r_{1,2} = r_{0,1} + \mu_1 - 1 = 5\% + \mu_1$$
$$q_{1,1} = q_{1,2} = \frac{0.50}{\left(1 + \frac{0.06}{2}\right)} = 0.4854$$

The prices of the pure securities for the next period may be computed as follows.

$$q_{2,1} = q_{1,1} \times \frac{0.50}{\left(1 + \frac{0.07 + \mu_1}{2}\right)} = \frac{0.4854}{2.07 + \mu_1}$$

$$q_{2,2} = q_{1,1} \times \frac{0.50}{\left(1 + \frac{0.07 + \mu_1}{2}\right)} + q_{1,2} \times \frac{0.50}{\left(1 + \frac{0.05 + \mu_1}{2}\right)}$$

$$= \frac{0.4854}{2.07 + \mu_1} + \frac{0.4854}{2.05 + \mu_1}$$

$$q_{2,3} = q_{1,2} \times \frac{0.50}{\left(1 + \frac{0.05 + \mu_1}{2}\right)} = \frac{0.4854}{2.05 + \mu_1}$$

Obviously

$$q_{2,1} + q_{2,2} + q_{2,3} = \frac{1}{(1 + 0.5 \times s_2)^2} = \frac{1}{(1.029)^2} = 0.9444$$

Thus

$$\frac{2}{2.07 + \mu_1} + \frac{2}{2.05 + \mu_1} = \frac{0.9444}{0.4854} = 1.9456$$

This can be expressed as:

$$1.9456\mu^2 + 4.0159\mu + 0.0161 = 0$$

$$\Rightarrow \mu_1 = -0.4017\%$$

Thus $r_{1,1} = .07 - .004017 = .065983 \equiv 6.5983\%$ and $r_{1,2} = .05 - .004017 = .045983 \equiv 4.5983\%$
The prices of the pure securities are: $q_{2,1} = 0.2349$, $q_{2,2} = 0.4722$, and $q_{2,3} = 0.2372$.

Now let's proceed to the next point in time.

$$r_{2,1} = r_{1,1} + \mu_2 + 1 = 6.5983 + 1 + \mu_2 = 7.5983 + \mu_2$$

$$r_{2,2} = r_{1,1} + \mu_2 - 1 = 6.5983 - 1 + \mu_2 = 5.5983 + \mu_2$$

$$r_{2,3} = r_{1,2} + \mu_2 - 1 = 4.5983 - 1 + \mu_2 = 3.5983 + \mu_2$$

The prices of pure securities for the next point in time may be expressed as follows.

$$q_{3,1} = q_{2,1} \times \frac{0.50}{\left(1 + \frac{0.075983 + \mu_2}{2}\right)} = \frac{0.2349}{2.075983 + \mu_2}$$

$$q_{3,2} = q_{2,1} \times \frac{0.50}{\left(1 + \frac{0.075983 + \mu_2}{2}\right)} + q_{2,2} \times \frac{0.50}{\left(1 + \frac{0.055983 + \mu_2}{2}\right)}$$

$$= \frac{0.2349}{2.075983 + \mu_2} + \frac{0.4722}{2.055983 + \mu_2}$$

$$q_{3,3} = q_{2,2} \times \frac{0.50}{\left(1 + \frac{0.055983 + \mu_2}{2}\right)} + q_{2,3} \times \frac{0.50}{\left(1 + \frac{0.035983 + \mu_2}{2}\right)}$$

$$= \frac{0.4722}{2.055983 + \mu_2} + \frac{0.2372}{2.035983 + \mu_2}$$

$$q_{3,4} = q_{2,3} \times \frac{0.50}{\left(1 + \frac{0.035983 + \mu_2}{2}\right)} = \frac{0.2372}{2.035983 + \mu_2}$$

Obviously

$$q_{3,1} + q_{3,2} + q_{3,3} + q_{3,4} = \frac{1}{(1 + 0.5 \times s_3)^3} = \frac{1}{(1.03025)^3} = 0.9145$$

Thus

$$2 \times \frac{0.2349}{2.075983 + \mu_2} + 2 \times \frac{0.4722}{2.055983 + \mu_2} + 2 \times \frac{0.2372}{2.035983 + \mu_2} = 0.9145$$

$$\Rightarrow \mu_2 = 0.009364 = 0.9364\%$$

Therefore

$$r_{2,1} = 7.5983 + 0.9364 = 8.5347\%$$
$$r_{2,2} = 5.5983 + 0.9364 = 6.5347\%$$
$$r_{2,3} = 3.5983 + 0.9364 = 4.5347\%$$

The prices of the pure securities are:

$$q_{3,1} = 0.1126; q_{3,2} = 0.3413; q_{3,3} = 0.3446; q_{3,4} = 0.1160$$

Finally let's proceed to the penultimate point in time.

$$r_{3,1} = r_{2,1} + \mu_3 + 1 = 8.5347 + 1 + \mu_3 = 9.5347 + \mu_3$$
$$r_{3,2} = r_{2,1} + \mu_3 - 1 = 8.5347 - 1 + \mu_3 = 7.5347 + \mu_3$$
$$r_{3,3} = r_{2,2} + \mu_3 - 1 = 6.5347 - 1 + \mu_3 = 5.5347 + \mu_3$$
$$r_{3,4} = r_{2,3} + \mu_3 - 1 = 4.5347 - 1 + \mu_3 = 3.5347 + \mu_3$$

The prices of the pure securities at this point in time may be expressed as:

$$q_{4,1} = q_{3,1} \times \frac{0.50}{\left(1 + \frac{0.095347 + \mu_3}{2}\right)} = \frac{0.1126}{2.095347 + \mu_3}$$

$$q_{4,2} = q_{3,1} \times \frac{0.50}{\left(1 + \frac{0.095347 + \mu_3}{2}\right)} + q_{3,2} \times \frac{0.50}{\left(1 + \frac{0.075347 + \mu_3}{2}\right)}$$

$$= \frac{0.1126}{2.095347 + \mu_3} + \frac{0.3413}{2.075347 + \mu_3}$$

$$q_{4,3} = q_{3,2} \times \frac{0.50}{\left(1 + \frac{0.075347 + \mu_3}{2}\right)} + q_{3,3} \times \frac{0.50}{\left(1 + \frac{0.055347 + \mu_3}{2}\right)}$$
$$= \frac{0.3413}{2.075347 + \mu_3} + \frac{0.3446}{2.055347 + \mu_3}$$
$$q_{4,4} = q_{3,3} \times \frac{0.50}{\left(1 + \frac{0.055347 + \mu_3}{2}\right)} + q_{3,4} \times \frac{0.50}{\left(1 + \frac{0.035347 + \mu_3}{2}\right)}$$
$$= \frac{0.3446}{2.055347 + \mu_3} + \frac{0.1160}{2.035347 + \mu_3}$$
$$q_{4,5} = q_{3,4} \times \frac{0.50}{\left(1 + \frac{0.035347 + \mu_3}{2}\right)} = \frac{0.1160}{2.035347 + \mu_3}$$

Obviously

$$q_{4,1} + q_{4,2} + q_{4,3} + q_{4,4} + q_{4,5} = \frac{1}{(1 + 0.5 \times s_4)^4} = \frac{1}{(1.0295)^4} = 0.8902$$

Thus

$$2 \times \frac{0.1126}{2.095347 + \mu_3} + 2 \times \frac{0.3413}{2.075347 + \mu_3} + 2 \times \frac{0.3446}{2.055347 + \mu_3} + 2 \times \frac{0.1160}{2.035347 + \mu_3} = 0.8902$$
$$\Rightarrow \mu_3 = -0.010481 = -1.0481\%$$

Therefore

$$r_{3,1} = 9.5347 - 1.0481 = 8.4866\%$$
$$r_{3,2} = 7.5347 - 1.0481 = 6.4866\%$$
$$r_{3,3} = 5.5347 - 1.0481 = 4.4866\%$$
$$r_{3,4} = 3.5347 - 1.0481 = 2.4866\%$$

The prices of the pure securities are:

$$q_{4,1} = 0.0540; q_{4,2} = 0.2193; q_{4,3} = 0.3338; q_{4,4} = 0.2258; q_{4,5} = 0.0573$$

The no-arbitrage interest rate tree derived by us may be depicted as shown in Figure 14.5.
The state price tree may be depicted as follows as shown in Figure 14.6.

14.15.2 Valuation of a Plain Vanilla Bond

Consider a four period bond with a face value of $1,000, which pays a coupon of $40 every period. Using the state price tree, we can compute the value of this bond as follows.

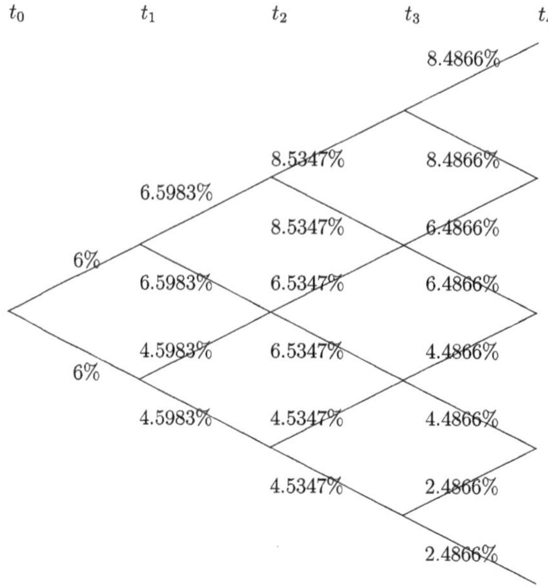

Figure 14.5: No Arbitrage Interest Rate Tree.

t_0	t_1	t_2	t_3	t_4
				0.0540
			0.1126	
		0.2349		0.2193
	0.4854		0.3413	
1.0		0.4722		0.3338
	0.4854		0.3446	
		0.2372		0.2258
			0.1160	
				0.0573

Figure 14.6: State Price Tree.

$$\begin{aligned} & 1{,}040 \times (0.3338 + 0.2193 + 0.2258 + 0.0540 + 0.0573) + 40 \\ & \quad \times (0.3413 + 0.3446 + 0.1126 + 0.1160) \\ & \quad +40 \times (0.2349 + 0.4722 + 0.2372) + 40 \times (0.4854 + 0.4854) \\ & \quad = 1{,}040 \times 0.8902 + 40 \times 0.9145 + 40 \times 0.9443 + 40 \times 0.9708 \\ & \quad = \$1{,}038.9920 \end{aligned}$$

14.15.3 Valuation of a Zero Coupon Bond

Consider a zero coupon bond that pays \$1,000 at time t_4. Its value at various nodes of the tree can be computed by working backwards.

At t_3, its value at node (3,1) is given by:

$$\frac{1{,}000}{\left(1+\frac{0.084866}{2}\right)} = \$959.2943$$

At node (3,2) the value is given by

$$\frac{1{,}000}{\left(1+\frac{0.064866}{2}\right)} = \$968.5859$$

Similarly at node (3,3), the value is

$$\frac{1{,}000}{\left(1+\frac{0.044866}{2}\right)} = \$978.0592$$

Finally at node (3,4), the value is

$$\frac{1{,}000}{\left(1+\frac{0.024866}{2}\right)} = \$987.7197$$

Working backwards we can calculate the prices at time t_2 as follows. At node (2,1) the value is:

$$0.5 \times \frac{959.2943}{\left(1+\frac{0.085347}{2}\right)} + 0.5 \times \frac{968.5859}{\left(1+\frac{0.085347}{2}\right)} = 924.4889$$

Similarly at node (2,2), the value is:

$$0.5 \times \frac{968.5859}{\left(1+\frac{0.065347}{2}\right)} + 0.5 \times \frac{978.0592}{\left(1+\frac{0.065347}{2}\right)} = 942.5269$$

Finally at node (2,3), the value is:

$$0.5 \times \frac{978.0592}{\left(1+\frac{0.045347}{2}\right)} + 0.5 \times \frac{987.7197}{\left(1+\frac{0.045347}{2}\right)} = 961.0980$$

Using the same logic, the value at (1,1) is:

$$0.5 \times \frac{924.4889}{\left(1+\frac{0.065983}{2}\right)} + 0.5 \times \frac{942.5269}{\left(1+\frac{0.065983}{2}\right)} = 903.6937$$

while the value at (1,2) is:

$$0.5 \times \frac{942.5269}{\left(1+\frac{0.045983}{2}\right)} + 0.5 \times \frac{961.0980}{\left(1+\frac{0.045983}{2}\right)} = 930.4207$$

At the starting node, the value is therefore:

$$0.5 \times \frac{903.6937}{\left(1+\frac{0.06}{2}\right)} + 0.5 \times \frac{930.4207}{\left(1+\frac{0.06}{2}\right)} = 890.3468$$

The bond prices may be depicted in a tree format as shown in Figure 14.7.

t_0	t_1	t_2	t_3
			959.2943
		924.4889	
	903.6937		968.5859
890.3468		942.5269	
	930.4207		978.0592
		961.0980	
			987.7197

Figure 14.7: Evolution of the Price of a Zero Coupon Bond.

14.15.4 Valuing a European Call

Consider a two period European call on the zero coupon bond with an exercise price of \$940. The payoff will be zero in node (2,1); \$2.5269 at node (2,2) and \$21.0980 at node (2,3). The value of the option at t_0 is

$$0.4722 \times 2.5269 + 0.2372 \times 21.098 = \$6.1976$$

14.15.5 Caps, Floors, and Collars

Before we go on to analyze caps and floors, let's first define *Caplets* and *Floorlets*.

A caplet is a call option on an interest rate, while a floorlet is a put option on an interest rate. To evaluate these options we will first reproduce a segment of the no-arbitrage interest rate tree that we derived earlier. Consider Figure 14.8.

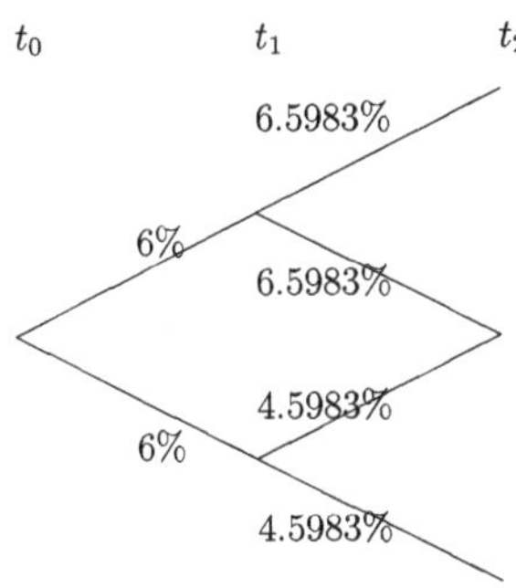

Figure 14.8: Segment of the No-arbitrage Interest Rate Tree.

Consider a one period caplet with an exercise price of 5%. Let the underlying principal be $1,000,000. Each time period is assumed to be of six months duration, and we will take it as 0.5 years in order to avoid issues regarding day-count conventions.[9]

At time t_1 if the node (1,1) were to be attained, the call will be in the money. The payoff will be

$$1{,}000{,}000 \times (0.065983 - 0.05) \times 0.5 = \$7{,}991.50$$

In the case of interest rate options, the payoff will occur not when the option expires, but at a point in time when the next interest payment is due. In the above case, the rate as determined at t_1 is applicable for computing the interest due at t_2. Consequently the caplet will payoff at t_2.

If however we were to attain node (1,2) at time t_1, the caplet will expire out of the money and the payoff will be zero.

Thus the value of the caplet at time t_0 may be computed as:

$$0.5 \times \frac{7991.50}{(1.03)\left(1 + \frac{0.065983}{2}\right)} = \$3{,}755.47$$

A floorlet is a put option on an interest rate. Let's consider a floorlet with the same exercise price and underlying principal as the caplet. The payoff will be zero in state (1,1).

9 In practice the length of the time period will have to be calculated as per the day-count convention that is applicable in the market in question.

However there will be a positive payoff at state (1,2), that is given by:

$$1{,}000{,}000 \times [0.05 - 0.045983] \times 0.5 = \$2{,}008.50$$

This payoff will obviously occur at time t_2. Consequently the value of the floorlet at t_0 is:

$$0.5 \times \frac{2{,}008.5}{(1.03)\left(1+\frac{0.045983}{2}\right)} = \$953.09$$

A cap is a portfolio of caplets, that can be acquired by a borrower who has availed of a floating rate loan, in order to protect himself against an increase in interest rates. Similarly, a floor is a portfolio of floorlets, that can be acquired by a lender, who has made a loan on a floating rate basis, to protect himself against a decline in interest rates.

Using the interest rate tree that we have derived (Figure 14.5) let's price a three period cap. It consists of three caplets, expiring after one, two and three periods respectively. The value of the two period caplet may be calculated as follows.

The payoff if state (2,1) is attained is:

$$1{,}000{,}000 \times [0.085347 - 0.05] \times 0.5 = \$17{,}673.50$$

The payoff at state (2,2) is given by:

$$1{,}000{,}000 \times [0.065347 - 0.05] \times 0.5 = \$7{,}673.50$$

The value at time t_0 of the first payoff is:

$$0.5 \times 0.5 \times \frac{1}{1.03} \times \frac{1}{1.032992} \times \frac{17{,}673.50}{\left(1+\frac{0.085347}{2}\right)}$$
$$= \$3{,}982.7226$$

Since there are two paths which lead to state (2,2), the value of the payoff if this state were to occur is given by:

$$0.5 \times 0.5 \times \frac{1}{1.03} \times \frac{1}{1.032992} \times \frac{7{,}673.50}{\left(1+\frac{0.065347}{2}\right)}$$
$$+ 0.5 \times 0.5 \times \frac{1}{1.03} \times \frac{1}{1.022992} \times \frac{7{,}673.50}{\left(1+\frac{0.065347}{2}\right)}$$
$$= \$1{,}745.9680 + \$1{,}763.0353 = \$3{,}509.0033$$

Thus the value of the caplet = 3,982.7226 + 3,509.0033 = \$7,491.7259

Similarly, the value of a three period caplet is given by:

$$0.5 \times 0.5 \times 0.5 \times \frac{1}{1.03} \times \frac{1}{1.032992} \times \frac{1}{1.042674} \times \frac{1}{1.042433}$$
$$\times 1{,}000{,}000 \times [0.084866 - 0.05] \times 0.5$$
$$+ 0.5 \times 0.5 \times 0.5 \times \frac{1}{1.03} \times \frac{1}{1.032992} \times \frac{1}{1.042674} \times \frac{1}{1.032433}$$
$$\times 1{,}000{,}000 \times [0.064866 - 0.05] \times 0.5$$
$$+ 0.5 \times 0.5 \times 0.5 \times \frac{1}{1.03} \times \frac{1}{1.032992} \times \frac{1}{1.032674} \times \frac{1}{1.032433}$$
$$\times 1{,}000{,}000 \times [0.064866 - 0.05] \times 0.5$$
$$+ 0.5 \times 0.5 \times 0.5 \times \frac{1}{1.03} \times \frac{1}{1.022992} \times \frac{1}{1.032674} \times \frac{1}{1.032433}$$
$$\times 1{,}000{,}000 \times [0.064866 - 0.05] \times 0.5$$
$$= \$4{,}341.6315$$

Thus the value of a three period cap is

$$\$\,3{,}755.47 + \$7{,}491.7259 + \$4{,}341.6315 = \$15{,}588.8274$$

The value of a three period floor can be computed in a similar fashion.

An interest rate collar is a combination of a cap and a floor. It requires the investor to take a long position in a cap and a short position in a floor.

Suggestions for Further Reading

Buetow G.W and J. Sochacki *Term-Structure Models Using Binomial Trees.* AIMR Research Foundation, 2001.
Chance, D.M. *An Introduction to Derivatives & Risk Management*. South Western, 2004.
Choudhry M. *An Introduction to Bond Markets.* Securities Institute, 2001.
Fabozzi F.J. *Bond Markets, Analysis, and Strategies.* Prentice-Hall, 1996.
Figlewski S., W.L. Silber, and M.G. Subrahmanyam *Financial Options: From Theory to Practice.* Irwin, 1990.
Garbade K.D. *Fixed Income Analytics.* The MIT Press, 1996.
Hull, J. *Fundamentals of Futures and Options Markets*. Prentice Hall, 2004.
Stigum M. and F.L. Robinson *Money Market & Bond Calculations.* Irwin, 1996.

References

Babbel D.F. and C.B. Merrill *Valuation of Interest-Sensitive Financial Instruments.* Society of Actuaries, 1996.
Choudhry M. *Analyzing & Interpreting The Yield Curve.* John Wiley, 2004.
Chourdakis K. *The Derivatives-on-Line Pages.*
Mohammed S. *Quantnotes.com*
Rendleman R.J. *Applied Derivatives: Options, Futures and Swaps.* Blackwell, 2002.
www.1728.com.

Chapter 15
Fundamentals of Swaps

15.1 Introduction

A swap is an exchange between two parties, of two payment streams that are different from each other. In the case of an interest rate swap, the two payments are denominated in the same currency, but are computed using different interest rates. On the other hand, in the case of a currency swap, the two counterparties are required to exchange streams of payments denominated in two different currencies. As we have explained earlier, in the case of an interest rate swap, both cash flow streams may be based on floating rates of interest, or else one stream may be based on a fixed rate while the other can be based on a floating rate. A fixed-rate to fixed-rate interest rate swap is infeasible for it would tantamount to arbitrage for the party who is making payments based on a lower rate of interest. That is, if such a swap were to exist, the party which is employing a lower rate to compute its payments, will always be receiving more than what it would have to pay to the counterparty. However, in the case of a currency swap, since the cash flow streams are denominated in two different currencies, all the three possibilities exist. That is, the swap may be fixed-fixed, fixed-floating or floating-floating.

15.2 Interest Rate Swaps

15.2.1 Contract Terms

The following terms must be explicitly stated while designing an interest rate swap contract.

- The identities of the two counterparties.
- The maturity of the swap. This is the date on which the last exchange of cash flows will take place between the two parties.
- The interest rate used by the first party to calculate its payments. It may be fixed or floating.
- The interest rate used by the second party to calculate its payments. It must be floating if the first party is making payments based on a fixed rate of interest.
- The day-count convention for the computation of interest.
- The frequency of payment.
- The notional principal. The principal is said to be notional because there is no need for the two parties to exchange the specified amount, considering the fact that all payments are denominated in the same currency. Nevertheless a principal amount is required to be specified in order to facilitate the computation of interest.

https://doi.org/10.1515/9783110746662-015

Example 15.1 demonstrates the mechanism of an interest rate swap.

Example 15.1: Consider a three year fixed-floating swap between HSBC and Barclays Bank. HSBC will be making payments based on an annual rate of 6%. Barclays will compute its liability based the six month SOFR. We will assume that every month consists of 30 days and that the year as a whole consists of 360 days. The exchange of payments will take place on a semi-annual basis. The notional principal amount is $5,000,000.

Assume that the six month SOFR, as observed at semi-annual intervals over the next three years are as shown in Table 15.1.

Table 15.1: Observed Values of the 6M-SOFR.

Time	6-M SOFR
Start	5.50%
After 6M	5.75%
After 12M	6.50%
After 18M	6.75%
After 24M	6.25%
After 30M	5.75%
After 36M	6.25%

Using this data, let's compute the payments to be made by the two parties every six months. This is shown in Table 15.2.

Table 15.2: Cash Flows In an Interest Rate Swap.

Time	Payment by HSBC	6-M SOFR	Payment by Barclays	Net Payment
Start	–	5.50%	–	–
6M	$150,000	5.75%	$137,500	$12,500
12M	$150,000	6.50%	$143,750	$6,250
18M	$150,000	6.75%	$162,500	$(12,500)
24M	$150,000	6.25%	$168,750	$(18,750)
30M	$150,000	5.75%	$156,250	$(6,250)
36 M	$150,000	6.25%	$143,750	$6,250
TOTAL	$900,000		$912,500	$(12,500)

Let's analyze the cash flows to be exchanged after six months. HSBC has to pay $150,000. This may be calculated as follows:

$$0.5 \times 0.06 \times 5{,}000{,}000 = \$150{,}000$$

Barclays has to pay $137,500. This may be calculated as follows.

$$0.5 \times 0.055 \times 5{,}000{,}000 = \$137{,}500$$

Notice the following. The fixed rate payment is constant because of two reasons. First the interest rate used by HSBC to compute its obligation is constant. Second we have assumed a 30/360 day count convention, as a consequence of which every semi-annual period is exactly one-half of a year. If we had assumed an ACT/360 convention, the payments to be made by HSBC would have varied across periods, despite the fact that it is paying a fixed rate.

The payments that are made by Barclays are based on the 6-M SOFR that is observed at the start of the period concerned. The interest itself is however payable at the end of the period. For instance, the payment made by Barclays at the end of the first period is based on a interest rate of 5.50%, which corresponds to the benchmark at the start of the period. This system of computation is known as determined in advance and paid in arrears.

Also, since the payments to be made by the two parties are denominated in the same currency, they can be netted, and the party which owes the larger amount can simply pay the difference to the other. For instance, after the first six months, HSBC owes $150,000 and in return is owed $137,500. Consequently all that it has to do is to make a payment of $12,500 to Barclays. This is shown in the last column of Table 15.2. Positive entries connote that HSBC has to pay the counterparty, whereas negative amounts indicate that the counterparty has to pay HSBC. The advantage of netting is that it reduces delivery risk. For instance, if Barclays were to pay the gross amount owed by it to HSBC, it is exposed to the risk that the payment of $150,000 owed by HSBC may never arrive. On the contrary, because of netting the risk for Barclays in this case is that the sum of $12,500 will not be received if HSBC were to renege.

15.2.2 Risk

An interest swap exposes both the parties to interest rate risk. In the case of HSBC, in the above illustration, the risk is that the 6-M SOFR rate may decline during the life of the swap. If so, the payments due to it may stand reduced, while the payments to be made by it are invariant to interest rate changes. On the other hand, the risk for Barclays is that the 6-M SOFR may increase over the life of the swap. If so, the quantum of payments to be made by it will increase. Obviously, the payments due to be received by it are invariant to rate changes.

15.2.3 Motivation For the Swap

Swaps may be used for speculation, hedging, or for arbitrage.

Speculation

Assume that HSBC expects interest rates to rise, whereas Barclays expects that rates will fall. In such a situation the swap that we have just illustrated can be used by both parties to speculate. If HSBC's view point were to be correct, and rates were indeed to rise, then the payments received by it, which are calculated on a floating rate basis, would be higher than the payments made by it, which are computed on a fixed rate basis. On the contrary, if Barclays were to read the movement of rates correctly, it would profit from the swap, for the payments made by it would be smaller in magnitude than what it receives from HSBC.

Hedging

Consider a situation where HSBC has taken a loan from Alpha Bank on a floating rate basis. Now after the loan has been made, it is worried that interest rates may rise. If so it can hedge by entering into a swap where it pays a fixed rate and receives payments based on a floating rate. If it is correct and rates do rise, then although it will have to pay more to the party from which it has borrowed, the extra funding cost will be mitigated by the profit from the swap.

On the other hand, Barclays too may use the swap to hedge. For instance, Barclays may have made a floating rate loan to Google. If interest rates were to fall, the payments from the borrower would stand reduced. However, in such circumstances, the bank would make a profit from the swap.

15.3 Terminology

- **Coupon Swap**: The type of interest rate swap that we illustrated, where one party makes payments based on a fixed rate while the other party makes payments based on a floating rate, is referred to as a coupon swap.
- **Basis Swap**: An interest rate swap where both the parties make payments based on floating rates is known as a basis swap. For instance, one party may commit to making payments on the basis of SOFR, while the other may agree to make payments based on the prime rate.
- **Payer and Receiver**: In a coupon swap, the party which agrees to make payments based on a fixed rate, is referred to as the 'payer'. The counterparty, which is committed to making payments on a floating rate basis, is referred to as the 'receiver'.

  Quite obviously, these terms cannot be used in the case of basis swaps, since both the cash flow streams are determined based on floating rates. Consequently, in order to be explicit and avoid ambiguities, it is a good practice to describe for each of the two parties, the rate on the basis of which it is scheduled to make payments, as also the rate on the basis of which it is scheduled to receive payments.

In the case of coupon swaps, some markets refer to the fixed rate payer as the 'buyer' and the fixed rate receiver as the 'receiver'.

- **Swap Rate**: The fixed rate of interest that has been agreed upon in a coupon swap is referred to as the swap rate. If the swap rate is quoted as a percentage, it is referred to as an 'all-in price' However in certain interbank markets the fixed rate is not quoted as a percentage. Instead, what is quoted is the difference, in basis points, between the agreed upon fixed rate and a benchmark interest rate. The benchmark that is chosen to compute this differential, is usually the government security whose remaining term to maturity is closest to the life of the swap in question. For instance, in the case of the HSBC-Barclays swap that we studied, the fixed rate was 6% per annum. If the swap rate were to be quoted as an all-in price, it would obviously be reported as such. However, in the second convention the rate would be quoted as follows. Assume that a three year T-note has a yield to maturity of 5.55%. The swap price will be quoted as 6% minus 5.55% or as 45 basis points.

15.4 Futures & Options versus Swaps

Swaps are exclusively traded OTC, unlike futures contracts that are traded on an organized exchange. Options of course may be traded OTC or on an exchange. Exchange traded contracts are accompanied by the intervention of a clearinghouse and the related requirement of margins. This ensures that default risk is considerably minimized. However, in the case of OTC instruments like swaps, default risk is definitely an issue. In this respect they are similar to forward contracts.

In practice, futures and exchange listed options contracts are usually available only for short to medium periods of time. However, swaps by virtue of being OTC instruments can be negotiated for any tenor and for any currency (in the case of currency swaps), provided of course that a suitable counterparty can be found.

15.4.1 Interpretation

Dealers quote two swap rates for each maturity. Why do we have two swap rates for each maturity? It must be understood that these rates are quoted by professional swap dealers and represent a 'paying' rate and a 'receiving' rate. The rationale is that the dealer should make a net profit if he were to undertake a fixed-floating swap with one party and offset it by doing a floating-fixed swap with another party. Thus, the lower rate or the 'bid' represents the rate that the dealer is willing to pay if he were to do a swap wherein he pays fixed and receives floating. Obviously, the higher rate or the 'ask' is the rate that he would like to receive in a swap where he receives fixed and pays floating.

When the swap market was at its nascent stage the normal practice was for investment banks to play the role of an intermediary. These banks would arrange the transaction by bringing together two counterparties, and in return would be paid an arrangement fee. Over a period of time the role of an intermediary evolved from that of an agent who facilitated a swap to that of a principal. One of the main reasons for this was that parties to swaps did not want their identities to be revealed to the counterparty. Second, as we have seen swaps expose both counterparties to default risk. For this reason, parties to a swap were more comfortable dealing with a bank, whose creditworthiness was easier to appraise.

Initially, the banks would do what are called 'reversals'. That is, they would agree to be the principal to a swap only if there was an equal and opposite swap that was immediately available. For instance assume that Google approaches Citibank for a swap where it pays fixed and receives floating. Citibank would agree only if it could simultaneously find another party with whom it could enter into an offsetting swap wherein the bank pays fixed and receives floating. A dealer who carries two offsetting swaps in his books, is said to be running a 'matched book'.

It must be understood that a dealer who maintains a matched book is exposed to default risk from both the parties with whom it has entered into swaps. These days market makers have become less fastidious about maintaining a matched book. That is, they are usually willing to accept a temporary exposure to an unmatched or naked position.

15.5 Valuing an Interest Rate Swap

In our illustration of a swap between HSBC and Barclays Bank, we arbitrarily assumed that the swap rate was 6%. We will now demonstrate as to how this rate will be determined in practice.

Assume that instead of entering into a swap, HSBC had issued a three year fixed rate note with a principal of $5MM on which it has to make semi-annual interest payments at the rate of 6% per annum. This money could have been used to acquire a three year floating rate note with the same principal, and which pays coupons semi-annually based on the benchmark observed at the start of the six-monthly period.

If we look at the cash flows of these two transactions, the result is equivalent to that on a three year fixed-floating swap. At the outset there will be an inflow of $5MM when the fixed rate note is issued. But this amount will be just adequate to purchase the floating rate loan. Thus the net cash flow is zero. Similarly, at the point of termination, that is after three years, HSBC will receive $5MM when the floating rate note matures. However this will be just adequate to retire the fixed rate note. The net result is that there is no exchange of principal, either at the outset or at the end, which is consistent with what we have seen for interest rate swaps.

Every six months, the floating rate note will pay a coupon based on the benchmark rate at the start of the period. HSBC will receive this amount and would be required to pay interest at the rate of 6% per annum to service the fixed rate note that it has issued. Consequently the cash flows every six months will be identical to that of the swap.

Thus, a long position in a floating rate note coupled with a short position in a fixed rate note, is equivalent to a swap which requires fixed rate payments in return for payments based on a floating rate. We will demonstrate as to how the fixed rate of a coupon swap can be determined.

Assume that the current term structure is as shown in Table 15.3.

Table 15.3: Observed Term Structure.

Time To Maturity	Reference Rate
6M	8.25%
12M	8.40%
18M	8.50%
24M	8.20 %
30M	7.80%
36M	7.50%

Since today, by assumption, is the start of the next six monthly period, the price of the three year floating rate note will be equal to its face value of $5MM. For, on a coupon reset date, the price of a floating rate bond will revert back to its face value. The question is, what should be the coupon rate for the fixed rate note, so that it too has a current price of $5MM.

Let's first determine the discount factors corresponding to the observed benchmark rates. The discount factor for a given maturity is the present value of a dollar to be received at the end of the stated period. The convention in the market is that if the number of days for which the rate is quoted is N, then the corresponding discount factor is given by $\frac{1}{\left(1+i\times\frac{N}{360}\right)}$. For instance, the discount factor for an investment of 18 months will be $\frac{1}{\left(1+i\times\frac{540}{360}\right)}$ where 'i' is obviously the quoted 18M rate. Thus the vector of discount factors for our example is as shown in Table 15.4.

Table 15.4: Discount Factors.

Time To Maturity	Discount Factor
6M	0.9604
12M	0.9225
18M	0.8869
24M	0.8591
30M	0.8368
36M	0.8163

If we denote the semi-annual coupon by $\frac{C}{2}$, it must be that:

$$\frac{C}{2} \times 0.9604 + \frac{C}{2} \times 0.9225 + \frac{C}{2} \times 0.8869$$
$$+ \frac{C}{2} \times 0.8591 + \frac{C}{2} \times 0.8368 + [\frac{C}{2} + 5{,}000{,}000] \times 0.8163$$
$$= 5{,}000{,}000$$
$$\Rightarrow 5.2282 \times \frac{C}{2} = 918{,}500$$
$$\Rightarrow \frac{C}{2} = 173{,}892.465 \Rightarrow C = 347{,}784.93$$

Thus the swap rate is:

$$\frac{347{,}784.93}{5{,}000{,}000} \times 100 = 6.96\%$$

15.5.1 Valuing a Swap at an Intermediate Stage

Assume that three months have elapsed since the above swap was initiated. Consider the term structure shown in Table 15.5.

Table 15.5: Observed Term Structure After Three Months.

Time To Maturity	Reference Rate	Discount Factor
3M	8.10%	0.9802
9M	8.20%	0.9421
15M	8.25%	0.9065
21M	8.10 %	0.8758
27M	7.90%	0.8491
33M	7.60%	0.8271

The value of the fixed rate note may be computed as follows.

$$\frac{C}{2} \times [0.9802 + 0.9421 + 0.9065 + 0.8758 + 0.8491 + 0.8271] + 5{,}000{,}000 \times 0.8271$$
$$= 173{,}892.465 \times 5.3808 + 5{,}000{,}000 \times 0.8271 = 935{,}680.58 + 4{,}135{,}500 = \$5{,}071{,}180.58$$

The value of the floating rate bond may be computed as follows. Three months hence it will pay a coupon based on the original six month rate which is 8.25%. The quantum of this coupon is:

$$0.5 \times 0.0825 \times 5{,}000{,}000 = \$206{,}250$$

Once this coupon is paid, the value of the bond will revert back to its face value of \$5,000,000. Consequently, its value today is:

$$5{,}206{,}250 \times 0.9802 = \$5{,}103{,}166.25$$

From the standpoint of the fixed rate payer, the swap is tantamount to a long position in a floating rate note that is combined with a short position in a fixed rate note. Thus the value of the swap is:

$$5{,}103{,}166.25 - 5{,}071{,}180.58 = \$31{,}985.67$$

For the counterparty the value will obviously be −\$31,985.67.

15.6 Terminating a Swap

Let's suppose that after three months have elapsed, the fixed rate payer in the above swap decides that it no longer wants to be a party to the swap. It could get out of the current situation in a variety of ways. One way is by way of a reversal. That is, it can enter into a swap with 33 months to maturity, wherein it is required to pay floating and receive fixed. The index for the floating rate payments must obviously be the same. In this case, there are two swaps which are in existence. So the party is exposed to credit risk in both swaps.

The second way to exit the swap would be by selling it to a new party. In this case, HSBC would receive \$31,985.67 from the acquirer since the swap has a positive value. If the value were to be negative, the acquirer would have to be paid to take over the swap. In this case, the original counterparty to the swap, that is Barclays, would have to agree to the deal.

Finally, Barclays itself may buy out the swap by paying HSBC the current value. This is known as 'buy-back' or 'close-out'.

15.7 Equivalence With FRAs

We have already established that a position in an interest rate swap is equivalent to a combination of a position in a fixed rate note and a position in a floating rate note. We will now show that a swap is equivalent to a series of *Forward Rate Agreements* also known as *FRAs*.

15.7.1 FRA

A forward rate agreement is a forward contract on an interest rate. Consider the case of an investor who has taken a long position in a FRA with two periods to maturity and a notional principal of \$5,000,000. As per the agreement the fixed rate of interest is 6%, while the floating rate is the 6M-SOFR. Assume that each period exactly corresponds to six months. If the interest rate at the end of two periods is 7%, the investor will receive:

$$5{,}000{,}000 \times (0.07 - 0.06) \times 0.5 = \$25{,}000$$

On the contrary, if the rate after two periods were to be 5%, then the investor will experience an outflow of

$$5{,}000{,}000 \times (0.05 - 0.06) \times 0.5 = -\$25{,}000$$

In practice, these cash flows have to be discounted to obtain the value at the time of determination of the interest rate. In the case of swaps, the payoff based on the reference rate, will be determined in advance and paid in arrears. Thus, the value of the payment, at the time of determination of the reference rate, is the discounted value of the payoff. Hence, the above payoffs have to be discounted using the relevant rates. Thus, if the 6M rate were to be 7%, the present value of the payoff from the FRA will be:

$$\frac{25{,}000}{\left(1 + \frac{0.07}{2}\right)} = \$24{,}154.59$$

In the second case, where the 6M happens to be 5%, present value of the outflow will be:

$$\frac{25{,}000}{\left(1 + \frac{0.05}{2}\right)} = \$24{,}390.24$$

15.7.2 Determining the Fixed Rate

In the above illustration we arbitrarily assumed a value of 6% for the fixed rate of interest. In practice it will depend on how the term structure is expected to evolve. Let's reproduce a segment of the no-arbitrage interest rate tree that we derived in the previous chapter using the Ho and Lee model. Consider Figure 15.1.

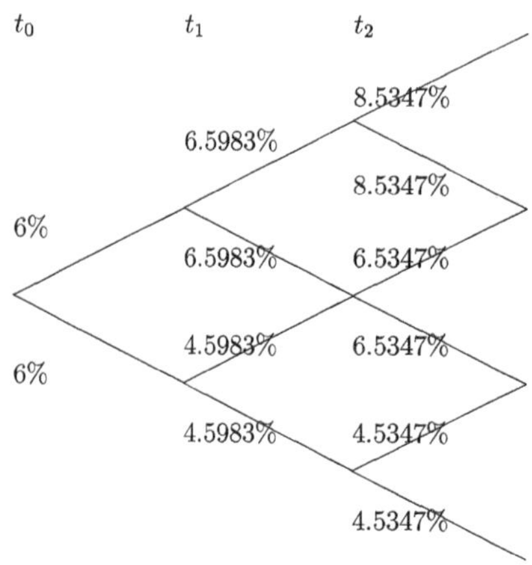

Figure 15.1: No Arbitrage Interest Rate Tree.

The payoff at node (2,1) is:

$$\frac{5{,}000{,}000 \times 0.5 \times (0.085347 - X)}{\left(1 + \frac{0.085347}{2}\right)}$$

The payoff at node (2,2) is:

$$\frac{5{,}000{,}000 \times 0.5 \times (0.065347 - X)}{\left(1 + \frac{0.065347}{2}\right)}$$

And at node (2,3)it is:

$$\frac{5{,}000{,}000 \times 0.5 \times (0.045347 - X)}{\left(1 + \frac{0.045347}{2}\right)}$$

The unknown fixed rate should be set in such a way that the risk-neutral expected payoff is zero. That is:

$$0.5 \times 0.5 \times \frac{5{,}000{,}000 \times 0.5 \times (0.085347 - X)}{\left(1 + \frac{0.085347}{2}\right)} + 2 \times 0.5 \times 0.5 \frac{5{,}000{,}000 \times 0.5 \times (0.065347 - X)}{\left(1 + \frac{0.065347}{2}\right)}$$
$$+ 0.5 \times 0.5 \frac{5{,}000{,}000 \times 0.5 \times (0.045347 - X)}{\left(1 + \frac{0.045347}{2}\right)} = 0$$
$$\Rightarrow X = 0.065251 \equiv 6.5251\%$$

The equivalence of swaps and FRAs may be demonstrated as follows. Consider the three year swap that HSBC did with Barclays. The very first payment due from Barclays is known at the very outset because the applicable benchmark rate is determined at the start of the period. Hence, the first transaction may be viewed as a spot transaction in which HSBC agrees to give Barclays $12,500 six months hence. The remaining five transactions are FRAs in which HSBC agrees to make payments based on a rate of 6% per annum, and receive payments based on the benchmark rate that prevails at the start of the corresponding period.

15.7.3 Off Market FRAs

In practice, if we consider a series of FRAs, each will have its own fixed rate, unless of course the term structure of interest rates is flat, in which case all the fixed rates will be equal. Thus, a swap may be viewed as a series of off-market FRAs, where the fixed rate remains constant, period after period.

15.8 Currency Swaps

A currency swap may be defined as a contract under which two parties commit themselves to exchange over a stated time period two streams of payments in two different currencies, each calculated using a different interest rate. They also agree to exchange, at the end of the stated time period, the corresponding principal amounts, at an exchange rate that is agreed upon at the outset.[1] Example 15.2 illustrates a currency swap.

Example 15.2: HSBC and JP Morgan Chase have entered into a contract wherein over a period of two years, the first party, namely HSBC, will pay interest in US dollars at a rate of 3% on a principal amount of $5MM, while the counterparty, namely JP Morgan Chase, will over the same period of time pay interest in British pounds at a rate of 4% on a principal amount of £3.125MM. The cash flows will be exchanged every six months over the period of two years. The interest rates to be used by the two parties will be fixed at the outset. As we explained earlier, since the payments are denominated in two different currencies, both parties may use fixed rates; or else one party may use a fixed rate while the other may use a variable rate such as SOFR; or else both may opt to use floating rates.

In this case the two banks also commit themselves to exchange, at the end of two years, the principal amounts of $5MM and £3.125MM on which the respective interest payments are being calculated. That is, HSBC will pay $5MM to JP Morgan Chase and in return will receive a payment of £3.125MM. The implicit exchange rate of 1.6000 GBP/USD is agreed upon right at the outset.

By definition, a currency swap requires an exchange of principal at the time of maturity. However, it is possible to structure the swap in such a way that there is an exchange of principal at inception as well. Such swaps are also referred to as 'cash swaps'.

Let's assume that the swap between HSBC and JP Morgan Chase is a cash swap. Such a swap would normally entail the following transactions.

---

1 See Geroulanos (1998).

- HSBC would borrow £3.125MM in London.
- JP Morgan Chase would borrow $5MM in New York.
- The two parties would then swap the principal amounts. The equivalent principal amount in the other currency is normally computed using the prevailing spot rate in the foreign exchange market. However this need not always be the case.
- At the end of two years, the principal amounts will be swapped back. The re-exchange is usually at the exchange rate that was used at inception. Thus HSBC would pay $5MM to JP Morgan Chase in return for a payment in sterling of £3.125. Such a swap where the same amount of principal is exchanged is known as a 'par swap'.[2]
- HSBC would use the pounds received by it to pay off its original loan.
- JP Morgan would use the dollars received by it to pay off its loan in New York.

Notice that during the life of the loan, HSBC would be receiving interest in pounds from JP Morgan, which will be used to service the loan that it has taken in London in British pounds. During the same period, JP Morgan Chase would be receiving interest in dollars from HSBC, which will be used to service the dollar denominated loan that it has taken in New York. Thus, the swap transaction enables each party to service the debt of the counterparty.

15.8.1 Cross-Currency Swaps

The term 'currency swap' strictly speaking should only be used for transactions between currencies that are on a fixed-rate to fixed-rate basis. Fixed-floating and floating-floating swaps involving two currencies are referred to technically as 'cross-currency' swaps. A cross-currency coupon swap is on a fixed-floating basis, whereas a cross-currency basis swap is on a floating-floating basis.

15.9 Inherent Risks

A currency swap, as we would expect, exposes both the parties to currency risk. Let's take the case where HSBC borrows and makes a payment in pounds to JP Morgan Chase in return for a payment in dollars. The exchange rate used was the prevailing spot rate of 1.600 GBP-USD.

At maturity HSBC would pay back $5MM USD to JP Morgan Chase and would receive £3.125MM from it. Now assume that in the intervening three years, the dollar has appreciated to 1.5000 GBP-USD. JP Morgan Chase would be benefited by the fact that the terminal exchange of principal is based on the original exchange rate. For, if £ 3.125MM were to be converted at the prevailing rate, it would receive only $4.6875MM USD. Thus, the counterparty which is slated to receive the currency that has appreciated during the life of the swap, stands to gain, while the other party stands to lose. In our illustration,

---

2 See Geroulanos (1998).

JP Morgan Chase avoids a loss of \$0.3125MM USD while HSBC foregoes an opportunity to save an equal amount.

15.10 Valuation

Let's consider the swap between HSBC and JP Morgan Chase. Assume that it is on a fixed-rate to fixed rate basis. The swap can be analyzed as follows. It is as if HSBC has issued a bond with a face value of \$5MM, converted the amount to £ 3.125MM at the prevailing spot rate and invested it in a bond denominated in pounds. From the perspective of the counterparty the transaction may be viewed as follows. JP Morgan Chase has issued a bond with a face value of £3.125MM, converted it to dollars at the prevailing spot rate and invested it in a bond denominated in US dollars. Thus, a currency swap between two parties is equivalent to a transaction in which each party issues a bond in one currency to the other, and uses the proceeds to acquire a bond issued by the counterparty. Consequently the fixed rate that is applicable in either currency, is the coupon rate that is associated with a par bond in that currency, as we have seen in the case of a fixed-floating interest rate swap. In this case, however we need to know the term structure for both currencies.

Consider the data shown in Table 15.6.

Table 15.6: Reference Rates for USD and GBP.

Maturity	USD Rate	Discount Factor	GBP Rate	Discount Factor
6M	2.50%	0.9877	3.30%	0.9838
12M	2.75%	0.9732	3.50%	0.9662
18M	2.60%	0.9625	3.40%	0.9515
24M	2.85%	0.9461	3.75%	0.9302

The value of the fixed rate for USD may be determined as follows. Consider a bond with a face value of \$1. Thus the coupon for a par bond denominated in USD is given by:

$$\frac{C}{2} \times .9877 + \frac{C}{2} \times 0.9732 + \frac{C}{2} \times 0.9625 + (1 + \frac{C}{2}) \times 0.9461 = 1$$

$$\Rightarrow \frac{C}{2} = 0.01393 \Rightarrow C = 2.7856\%$$

Similarly

$$\frac{C}{2} \times .9838 + \frac{C}{2} \times 0.9662 + \frac{C}{2} \times 0.9515 + (1 + \frac{C}{2}) \times 0.9302 = 1$$

$$\Rightarrow \frac{C}{2} = 0.01822 \Rightarrow C = 3.6433\%$$

for the British pound denominated par bond.

If the swap had been such that the rate in dollars was fixed while that in pounds was floating, the applicable rate would be 2.7856% for the dollar denominated payments and a floating rate for the pound denominated payments. On the other hand, if the rate were to be fixed for the payments in pounds and floating for the dollar denominated payments, the applicable rate would be the floating rate for the payment in dollars and 3.6433% for the payments in pounds. Finally, if payments in both currencies were to be on a floating rate basis, then we we would need the reference rates for both currencies.

15.11 Swaptions

A swaption is an option on a swap. Such an option requires the buyer to pay an up front premium, for the right to enter into a coupon swap. There are two possibilities. The holder of the option may either enter in into a coupon swap as a fixed rate payer or as a fixed rate receiver. Consequently there are two types of swaptions. In the case of a 'payer swaption' the option holder can exercise in order to enter into the swap as a fixed rate payer. On the other hand, a *'receiver swaption'* gives the holder the right to enter into a swap as a fixed rate receiver.

The exercise price specified in the swaption is an interest rate. The underlying asset is a swap with a specified term to maturity. A payer swaption will be exercised only if the prevailing rate for a swap with the specified maturity is higher than the exercise price of the swaption. Quite obviously, a receiver swaption will be exercised only if the prevailing swap rate is lower than the exercise price. Swaptions may be European or American in nature.

Suggestions for Further Reading

Chance, D.M. *An Introduction to Derivatives & Risk Management*. South Western, 2004.
Geroulanos P. *An Introduction to Swaps.* The Securities Institute, 1998.
Hull, J. *Options, Futures, and Other Derivatives*. Prentice Hall, 2006.

Chapter 16
Building Modern Markets: The Key Issues

16.1 A Brief History of Derivative Markets in Developed Economies

In the US organized futures trading first appeared in Chicago in the mid 19th century. The contracts were on agricultural products, and stemmed from the uncertainty regarding the prices of such products. Farmers, who were the producers, were perturbed with the possibility of bumper harvests, which had the potential to depress prices in the spot markets. Thus, they needed contracts, which would enable them to sell subsequently, at prices determined at an earlier point in time, so as to obviate the uncertainty. On the other hand, mills, who were the consumers, were confronted with the specter of high prices in between harvests, due to shortages in the market. Consequently, they sought contracts, which would enable them to lock in purchase prices in advance. A natural consequence was the evolution of commodity futures markets.

Derivative assets have been around for more than a century. Why is it that we hear so much about them these days? To better understand this issue, let's turn our attention to developments in the second half of the 20th century. There is a perception, among many market watchers, that developed capital markets, were always free and unfettered. But this was not the case.

Until the late 1960's, most of the activity in derivatives trading was restricted to commodities. Financial derivatives as a concept became significant only in the 1970's and 80's. The primary reasons for the rapid growth of derivatives trading over the past few decades are the following.

First, the Bretton Woods system of exchange rates was abandoned in the early 1970's, and the major economies of the world switched from fixed exchange rate regimes to floating rate mechanisms. Under the earlier system, all currencies had a fixed exchange rate with respect to the US dollar, and the US dollar had a fixed value in terms of gold. The US gave an undertaking, that on demand, it would convert dollars to gold and vice versa. Once, exchange rates became market determined, currency risk and its management became very important, leading to growth and innovations in the market for foreign exchange derivatives.

Second, there was a major war in the Middle East in 1973, after which petroleum prices became highly volatile and unpredictable. The rapidly oscillating crude oil prices, and the formation of a petroleum cartel, were products of this time. This had far reaching effects on the prices of all commodities, since the transportation costs of goods is directly linked to the price of crude oil. This gave a further impetus to the commodity derivatives markets.

Third, central banks, beginning with the U.S. Federal Reserve, led by Paul Volcker, began to abandon their policies of targeting interest rates, and shifted the focus to the levels of money supply. Central banks can implement policies in two ways. That is, they

https://doi.org/10.1515/9783110746662-016

can either focus on the price of money, namely interest rates, or on the quantity of money. Before 1979, the Federal Reserve focused on the price of money, by targeting the federal funds rate. To attain the target, the central bank bought and sold government securities, which is what is termed as open market operations. In October 1979, the FED switched its focus to the level of money supply in the economy. This, it believed was a more effective way of targeting inflation. As the FED believed, this change in approach lead to a greater volatility in interest rates. Starting with this period of time, interest rates in the US were substantially deregulated and became largely market determined, and hence, the market for interest rate derivatives developed and grew rapidly. This can be appreciated by the fact that most businesses thrive on borrowed money. Thus, interest rate volatility is a major source of concern for corporate treasurers.

16.2 Rebooting Capital Markets in Developed Nations

In October 1986, the London Stock Exchange (LSE) eliminated fixed brokerage commissions. This event came to be known as the *Big Bang* in financial circles. From February of the same year, the LSE had started admitting foreign brokerage firms as full members. These changes were intended to make London an attractive international financial market.[1] Until World War II, London was the major financial center in the world. After the war, all the attention shifted across the ocean to New York. But London, is ideally located geographically, and serves as a middle link between markets in the U.S and those in the Far East, thereby facilitating 24 hours trading in principle. Consequently, Britain was keen to restore the importance of London as a major market for financial securities.

Similar changes were effected in the United States in 1975 and in Japan in 1999. Today, in most countries commissions are negotiable between the broker and the client. There are however countries where government or exchange regulations specify fixed commission rates that ought to be charged by a broker. For instance, until early 2003 the minimum commission in Hong Kong was mandated to be 0.25% of the trade value.[2]

In a deregulated brokerage industry, commissions will vary substantially from broker to broker depending on the extent and quality of services provided. On one hand, we have *Full-service* brokers who charge the maximum commissions, but offer value added services and investment advice. On the other hand, there exist *Discount* and *Deep discount* brokers who charge the least by way of commissions, but whose only function is to execute trades. In other words they do not provide research reports or other investment advice to their clients.

There has been tremendous growth in *Information Technology*, which has been a key factor in the development of capital markets. From streamlining back-end opera-

1 See Resnick (1996).
2 See Harris (2003).

tions, to facilitating stock index arbitrage, computers have played a pivotal role in the growth of derivative markets. The advancement in telecommunication infrastructure, both voice as well as data related, has played a tremendous role in this transformation. From main frame computers to laptops, and from punch cards to USB drives, this world has indeed come a long way.

The developments in the field of telecommunications have been revolutionary in emerging markets. A few decades ago, a phone connection was a luxury in many of today's emerging markets. Today, most citizens in such countries have cellular phones. The Internet has transformed the financial landscape in such countries. Of late, the lag between an innovation in the developed nations, and its adoption in a developing nation, has narrowed considerably. Thus, online brokerages which provide access to modern exchanges have emerged in many countries, allowing people to trade from the comfort of home. The prices of electronic items have declined substantially. A few decades ago, desktop computers were priced exorbitantly. Laptops, of course, had not appeared on the horizon. Software was extremely primitive, and was primarily used for word processing. The economies of many of these markets were closed to global trades. So local manufacturers of such gadgets, sold sub-standard products at sky high prices. Today most of these economies are open. Global brands are available easily, and are often manufactured at local factories.

16.3 Electronic Trading

Until a few decades ago, stock trading was in rings, and derivatives trading was in pits. The system was opaque, and traders and investors, were often clue-less about the actual developments in the market. Electronic or screen based trading, has revolutionized capital markets. Using the services of an online broker, an individual operating from home or from office, can key in his or her orders, and execution can happen in seconds with the utmost transparency. The information highway is incredible. From New York to Hong Kong, and from Tokyo to London, everyone is getting the same information at the same point in time. This has largely mitigated facets of the asymmetric information problem, and created a level playing field. Electronic trading, coupled with the advent of online and discount brokers, has brought down trading costs substantially. This has drawn more people to the capital market, who are finding that lack of substantial capital or infrastructure, is no longer a barrier from the standpoint of accessing these markets.

Traditionally exchanges were owned by brokers, who had seats on them. Since the availability of seats was limited, entry was highly restricted. Today, in modern exchanges, any entity which has the threshold capital required, and satisfies other related criteria, can enjoy trading privileges. Exchanges have become demutualized, and membership and ownership have been separated. Exchanges, are owned by financial institutions, and members have trading privileges. Institutional linkages have been formed across geographies, primarily between the US and Europe, and the US and Asia.

Brokerage houses in developing economies have built partnerships with those in the developed countries. There was a time when the Dow Jones index was the only significant barometer of the health of capital markets. Today markets in other geographies have their own index, and have futures and options contracts based on such indexes.

Scripless or dematerialized trading, has been another revolution. Previously every transfer of a security, from one investor to another, was an operational nightmare. The process was slow, with a lack of transparency, and the physical documents were often plagued with forgeries and signature mismatches. It was not uncommon for a client to place an order, and then be told by his broker a few days later, that the order had gone through at a price of X. The client, had no way of ascertaining if this was indeed the true trade price. This problem, was extremely acute in developing countries. Today all securities are primarily held with depositories like the DTC in the US, and CREST in the UK. ICSDs, or international central securities depositories, like Euroclear and Clearstream, facilitate cross-border trading. Just the way traders can hold money electronically with commercial banks, they can hold securities electronically with depositories. Thus, depositories hold securities in safe custody, and clients can transfer securities electronically, without having to physically handle them, just the way commercial banks hold money electronically, and permit transfers without requiring clients to physically handle cash.

16.4 Advent Of Global Investors

It has been well accepted for many decades that investors should diversify, and not put all their eggs in one basket. But the question that people have been asking of late is, why should the basket consist of only domestic securities? In other words, why cannot a high net worth individual in the US, invest in European, Asian or Australian securities. Of course, if an investor were to invest across geographies, there is an additional element of risk, which is foreign currency risk. Institutions from the US, Japan and Europe have started investing heavily in emerging markets. These include mutual funds, pension funds, hedge funds, and insurance companies. Mutual feeder funds are available in the emerging economies, whereby their residents can invest in foreign securities.

American investors have access to Yankee bonds, ADRs, and ADDs. Yankee bonds facilitate exposure to the risk of a foreign issuer without having to face currency risk. ADRs and GDRs have facilitated the listing of companies of emerging economies, in the developed world. American investors, who seek to go the ADR route, can invest without fretting about currency related issues. They can use their regular brokers and trade the way they normally do.

16.5 Electronic versus Open Outcry Trading: Pros and Cons

The hallmark of a successful system is its ability to provide liquidity and reduce costs for market participants. Costs in this context, can take on two forms. First, there are the direct transactions costs or commissions. Second, there are indirect costs like lost revenues due to illiquidity or a lack of market depth.

In an oral-auction system, liquidity is supplied by traders called *locals* who constantly stand ready to buy and sell on their own account. However, the problem is that a local is restricted at any point in time to a single pit. In practice, futures contracts on different assets trade in different pits. A local obviously cannot keep running back and forth between pits. Consequently, he has little choice but to be present at his usual pit even when the trading activity there is considerably reduced.

In contrast, a trader who is using an electronic system can effectively switch to a different screen displaying the Limit Order Book (LOB) for a different asset, if he finds that activity in a particular futures contract is slackening. Thus, for relatively inactive contracts, electronic trading is clearly preferable. In the emerging economies, where derivatives trading is often characterized by low volumes, electronic systems are the preferred modes of trading. With the click of a mouse, traders can shift their attention from one asset to another.

Even in the advanced economies, exchanges are increasingly feeling the need to switch to electronic systems. In the earlier years, derivatives trading was characterized by high volumes in most contracts, because such instruments provided innovative features that were simply not available earlier. Consequently, although the underlying assets were not necessarily sophisticated, traders were nevertheless attracted to such derivative securities. However, as time has passed, the financial instruments that are now emerging tend to be highly specialized and are able to attract the attention of select professional clienteles only. The same is true for derivatives on such financial products. Consequently, derivatives on new products are characterized by relatively lower volumes, thereby encouraging established exchanges to switch over to screen based systems of trading. Some exchanges however, continue to use both types of trading platforms.

Traditional exchanges have also faced declining volumes in recent years due to enhanced competition from newly established exchanges. This is increasingly providing an impetus to them for embracing electronic systems. Electronic systems are also indispensable for cross-border trading, which is likely to increase steadily as the economies of the world integrate. From an operational standpoint, electronic systems can considerably reduce the probability of errors in recording and reporting trades.

Exchanges which are switching over to an electronic trading platform are finding that the operational costs for these systems are lower than the costs for the open-outcry systems which they are replacing. Screen based trading typically requires less labor, skill, and time. Open-outcry systems entail greater fixed costs due to the need to employ a greater number of personnel. Overheads in terms of buildings and back-office facilities also tend to be higher for such systems, as compared to electronic systems.

However, it is not as if the open-outcry system does not have any advantages of its own. Sarkar and Tozzi (1998) argue that highly active contracts are better traded on open-outcry systems. Traders on such exchanges are more accomplished at executing large and complex orders with a minimal impact on prices.

Traders in oral-auction systems also have the advantage of being able to get to know the trading behavior of competitors and counterparties with whom they interact on a regular basis. This kind of knowledge can be invaluable in predicting the response of others for a trader who is seeking to implement a particular trading strategy. In contrast, in a faceless electronic system, the counterparties remain unidentified.

Finally, in an open-outcry system, order revision is simpler because a quote is valid only for an instant. However, on an electronic system, a trader who seeks to modify or cancel an order issued earlier, has to give explicit instructions and hope that the original order does not get executed before it is canceled.

16.6 Developing Derivative Exchanges: Key Issues

Let's now discuss some of the salient features pertaining to the development of derivative exchanges, particularly from the standpoint of emerging markets. As Tsetsekos and Varangis (2000) point out, derivative exchanges tend to be established for sound economic reasons as well as for national pride. A well functioning derivatives exchange facilitates the correct allocation of resources and the transfer of risk from those who seek to avoid it, to those who want to take it on, that is, from hedgers to speculators. As Tsetsekos and Varangis (2000) point out, in many emerging markets, price discovery is difficult. Derivative markets tend to be more liquid and consequently information on supply and demand percolates faster into such markets. The result is more accuracy of prices in spot markets because as you have seen, spot and futures markets are inextricably linked by the process of arbitrage. Therefore, derivative markets have the potential to help economic agents in emerging markets to make better decisions about future production and trade.

However, in order to have an efficient derivatives exchange, it is imperative to have a cash market that is efficient and which attracts large volumes. It is also essential to have a sound legal system that facilitates enforcement of contracts between parties, as well as a well developed credit market.

A survey of derivatives exchanges undertaken by Tsetsekos and Varangis (1998), reveals that exchanges in emerging markets tend to introduce financial derivatives, rather than commodity derivatives. The main reason is that with liberalization and globalization, prices of commodities in the domestic markets of such countries are no longer insulated from international trends and price movements. Consequently, there tends to be a strong correlation between domestic spot prices in the emerging markets and futures prices on well established international exchanges in the developed countries. In other words, there is less basis risk while using derivative contracts on established exchanges to hedge, as compared to the pre-liberalization era. Hence, the need to develop domestic commodity derivatives exchanges is no longer being felt to the same extent.

Financial products like stocks and bonds, however, tend to be country specific and hence attract interest mainly from domestic investors. Similarly, for obvious reasons, currency derivatives are also country specific. Consequently, markets for financial derivatives have become popular in the emerging markets.

A thorough study of the feasibility of derivatives exchanges is a pre-requisite before trading is allowed to commence, if such exchanges are to succeed in the developing economies. Tsetsekos and Varangis (2000) list five important lessons based on research and the experiences of various countries.

1. The chances of success of derivatives exchanges are higher if stock index and interest rate derivatives are introduced first.

   Derivatives on agricultural commodities are more difficult to introduce, either because liberalization of agricultural markets in developing countries is more difficult than the liberalization of financial markets, or else because the post liberalization correlation between domestic and foreign markets is high enough to permit international exchanges to be used by domestic investors. In general, commodity exchanges have succeeded only in countries with a large domestic market for commodities, like Argentina, Brazil, China, and Malaysia.
2. It is very important to have a proper regulatory and legal framework in place. Uncertainty about the just and fair application of laws and regulations can keep potential investors away. Needless to say, a history of scandals and market failures can spell doom for a developing financial market.
3. Partnerships and joint ventures between new and existing exchanges may be mutually beneficial. Emerging exchanges stand to benefit from the experience and technological knowhow of established exchanges. At the same time, the growth of active trading in emerging markets is in the interest of traders in the developed countries, as the globalization process forges greater and closer links between economies.
4. Policymakers in emerging markets should permit domestic investors greater and relatively unfettered access to foreign markets and foreign investors access to domestic markets. If the barriers to trading abroad are removed, then it will facilitate arbitrage across borders, thereby making domestic exchanges more liquid.
5. Electronic trading, as we have discussed earlier, seems to be the preferred mode of trading in the new exchanges, as opposed to the open outcry system.

16.7 Emerging versus Established Markets

According to Upper and Valli, the economies and financial markets of emerging market economies tend to be more volatile than those of advanced economies. although there are exceptions. Given this volatility, and the anticipated consequences for hedging and speculation, we would expect derivative markets in such economies to be well developed. But, this is not always true. We would expected such markets to be characterized by high volumes of trading in both currency and interest rate derivatives, but such contracts, account for only about 10% of the global turnover of such contracts.

Upper and Valli point out that the desire to hedge need not result in liquid markets unless there is somebody willing to take the other side. For idiosyncratic risks that are easily diversifiable, a financial intermediary could sell the appropriate insurance. However, currency and interest rate risk are macroeconomic risks, and creating a liquid derivatives market is more challenging, unless there are economic agents who are exposed to such risk in opposite ways.

The low ratios of currency derivatives contract turnover to foreign trade in emerging markets, could be an indication that exporters and importers in these countries still find it relatively difficult to hedge the exchange rate risk associated with their transactions, although we cannot draw firm conclusions. However, derivatives trading in such economies is heavily geared towards currency contracts, which account for 75 – 90% in terms of volumes. It should be noted that currency derivative contracts outweigh interest rate derivative contracts in advanced economies as well, though by a smaller margin. Emerging derivatives markets tend to be smaller than markets in advanced economies, and they also feature less complex contracts. More sophisticated contracts, such as cross-currency swaps, currency options, interest rate swaps and interest rate options, account for a lower share in total turnover in emerging as compared to established markets.

A noticeable feature of some emerging derivatives markets is the prevalence of non-deliverable contracts. The prevalence of non-deliverable contracts reflects the fact that the currencies of many emerging economies are not fully convertible. Finally, most derivatives contracts in emerging markets are traded over the counter. OTC trading exceeds exchange-based trading considerably in most emerging markets, although in Brazil, derivatives exchanges account for a large fraction of turnover. Many emerging economies have active futures exchanges, but these tend to concentrate on stock index and commodity contracts rather than on currency and interest rate instruments.

Changes in exchange rates can cloud the perception of the performance of markets in emerging economies. Upper and Valli point out that the daily turnover in currency and interest rate derivatives, stood at 0.80 trillion USD in April 2016, which was approximately the same as the turnover recorded three years prior. But this does not portray the true picture since the domestic currencies had depreciated substantially with respect to the US dollar, over the same period. If the turnover is considered in local currencies, it turns out that the turnover increased by 25% in three years.

16.7.1 The Rationale: A Deeper Look

What is the rationale for the comparatively low level of activity in currency derivatives in emerging markets? Upper and Valli, argue that the development of a liquid derivatives market requires the existence of regular two-way flows. The first and most obvious hedging motive derives from international trade. The authors argue that the sum of the exports and imports of an economy is a suitable proxy. The second motive concerns the hedging of financial exposures. The authors use the size of the bond market in the domestic currency as a proxy. Investors in debt markets may want to hedge the interest rate risk associated with these securities, and so we would expect a vibrant bond market to be accompanied with a higher turnover in interest rate derivatives. Foreign portfolio investors may also want to hedge the currency risk associated with their bond holdings, so we would expect a vibrant domestic bond market to be associated with high turnover in the currency derivatives segment as well. The third motive, according to Upper and Valli, is related to the level of integration with global markets as measured by the size of external assets and liabilities. If a country has high external liabilities, we would expect a high demand for currency derivatives on the part of domestic borrowers. However, they argue that the impact of large external assets on currency derivatives turnover is more ambiguous. On one hand, the holders of external assets, may want to hedge the associated exchange rate risk in derivatives markets. Such hedgers therefore, act as natural counterparties to external borrowers. On the other hand, external assets holders may choose not to hedge, since the currencies of most emerging economies, tend to steadily depreciate with respect to convertible currencies such as the US dollar and the Euro. This can dampen the turnover of currency derivatives.

Upper and Valli conclude that, derivatives markets for currencies and interest rates in emerging economies tend to be much smaller than their advanced economy counterparts. Such derivatives markets are also limited to a narrower set of instruments, and a disproportionate part of trading takes place over the counter. The authors argue that there is reason to believe that residents of, and investors in, emerging markets find it more difficult and costly to hedge their exposures, as compared to market participants in advanced economies.

16.8 Focus on Korea and Turkey

Karagozoglu argues that the economic benefits that organized derivatives exchanges provide in developed countries are well documented. Peck (1985) the author argues, has demonstrated both theoretically and empirically the direct effect futures markets have on commodity prices. Peck also highlighted the relationship between derivative markets, and production, consumption and storage decisions in the economy. She also provides empirical evidence that seasonal and annual commodity prices are more stable in economies with vibrant futures markets. Futures markets fulfill an economic role by decreasing price volatility. Silber (1985) provides a sound explanation for the economic contribution of financial futures. He argues that increased liquidity and the availability of risk reduction tools, manifests itself as a reduction in the cost of capital to companies. This, ultimately translates into greater capital formation for the economy as a whole.

According to Bricheux, Savre and Tachon (1992), there are three important factors for developing a successful futures contract:

1. There should be required conditions for creating a futures market, from legal, regulatory, political and economic perspectives.
2. Conditions should exist for vibrant futures trading. Requirements include, presence of price volatility, and the presence of price risk factors pertaining to the underlying assets. There should exist large, mature and liquid cash markets. There should also exist a vibrant broker-dealer network in the markets.
3. Finally, the futures contracts should be well designed and exchanges should well developed.

In another paper, Karagozoglu (2003), along with Ersen, analyze the readiness of emerging markets for the establishment of derivatives trading. They report that, between 1989 and 2000, 183 derivatives contracts were introduced by 10 derivatives exchanges in emerging economies. The thrust was on futures contracts on financial assets, that is equity related products such as stock index and single stock futures, currency futures and interest rate futures. They found that 45 percent of the contracts launched by emerging country exchanges failed on an average, within 2.75 years after the launch date.

While the introduction of derivative contracts has its economic merits, studies show that there are perturbing features of such products. First, there could be a significant shift of trading from spot markets to derivatives markets, because the latter are less expensive with regard to trading costs and collateral requirements. High trading volumes result in low transaction costs. The ability to take positions by depositing relatively small amounts of collateral, further boosts trading volumes. Also, it is usually a lot easier to take a short position in the derivatives markets, than to short sell in spot markets. Should this shift occur from spot to futures, it can be argued that price volatility is likely to be transmitted from the futures to the cash market. The consensus appears to be that well-designed futures contracts help increase the efficiency of spot markets. Empirical evidence also seems to suggest that the introduction of futures contracts either brings stability to the underlying cash market or else has an insignificant effect on the latter's volatility.

Historically, exchanges have been membership organizations, and their success has been gauged by a focus on trading volumes. The key features of futures markets, are the facilitation of risk transfer from hedgers to speculators, and the impetus given to price discovery.[3] For a given underlying asset, if there is sufficient demand for from both hedges and speculators, and there is a perceived need for price discovery, a properly designed futures contract is likely to generate high trading volumes. This in turn will manifest itself as high revenues for the exchange members, in the form of commissions and exchange fees. Prior studies based on US derivative markets have shown that the factors contributing to the success of a futures contract can be both contract specific, as well as market specific. Silber (1985) argues that financial futures considerably reduce the cost of transacting; increase market liquidity as measured by trading volume; and facilitate risk reduction. Sandor (1973) states that price variability of the commodity, existence of a viable cash market, and proper contract specification are prerequisites for the creation of a successful futures market. Optimal contract design plays a key role in facilitating the success of derivatives contracts. While setting the contract size, as has been argued in earlier chapters, there will be a tradeoff between trading volume and transaction costs. Too small a contract size will increase the costs of transacting, whereas too large a contract size will make it difficult for small traders to enter the market. Margin requirements too play a key role. The lower the margin requirements are, the higher the larger trading volume is likely to be.

Ilyina too underscores the fact that despite rapid growth over the past several years, emerging market derivatives account for a relatively small fraction of the total outstanding notionals in global derivatives markets. Compared with established markets, the ratio of outstanding notional value of derivatives to the market capitalization of the underlying assets, is fairly small. Common problems that preclude the development of liquid derivative markets in emerging economies are:
1. Relatively underdeveloped markets for the underlying instruments
2. Weak and inadequate legal and market infrastructure
3. Constraints on the use of derivatives by local and foreign entities.

She points out that local entities with foreign exchange exposures, are typically among the most active users of derivatives in emerging markets. In most emerging markets the domestic financial markets are not deep enough for large local companies to borrow long term and in large size. Thus, domestic companies in such markets usually have to rely on international bond markets for this type of funding. Hence, in such economies, the local business sector has a positive net external financing requirement, and the use of currency derivatives becomes imperative.

Ilyina also notes that emerging derivative markets have grown rapidly over the past few years, in countries that have removed capital controls and have developed their underlying securities markets. The growing use of derivative products in such economies has also supported capital inflows and has helped investors to price and manage risks more efficiently. However, the use of derivatives has also arguably contributed to eco-

3 Peck (1985).

nomic crises, by accelerating capital outflows, amplifying volatility, and at times, by increasing the correlation between asset and currency markets.

16.9 Marketwise Historical Observations: A Summary

Ilyina makes the following observations about exchanges in derivatives markets.

- The most liquid OTC currency derivatives markets, are in Singapore, Hong Kong, and South Africa. In 1998, Singapore allowed foreign entities to issue bonds in Singapore dollars and swap the proceeds into foreign currencies, which could then be deployed outside the country. In 2002, a restriction, that foreigners could engage in cross-currency swap transactions, only if there was an underlying economic activity, was dispensed with. This too, provided an impetus to OTC currency derivatives in the country. In South Korea, till 1999, there was a legal requirement that forward contracts had to be used as hedges against future current account flows. Thus, most forward contract trades involving the Korean Won and the USD, took place outside the country. In South Africa, the central bank required market participants to provide evidence of an underlying trade flow for every forward contract or swap transaction. Consequently many foreign entities pulled out of the market.
- In Brazil a significant share of currency derivatives trading takes place at an organized exchange. In 1999, the Brazilian Real was allowed to float, and the domestic regulator authorized OTC derivatives on foreign exchange, interest rates, and price indices. Around this time there was a sharp increase in volatility of the real-dollar exchange rate, and the volatility of domestic interest rates. This facilitated the creation of a hedge culture in financial circles. On the other hand, the development of exchange traded derivatives in Mexico, has been slower. The primary reason is that both the Mexican market, and the CME Group in Chicago, are in the same time zone, and the CME Group offers derivative contracts on Mexican underlying items.
- Central European derivatives markets, have been slow to pick up. This was due to the lack of a supporting infrastructure, and the presence of restrictions on hedging activities by companies and pension funds. In Hungary, there has been de-regulation in the currency market, and relaxation of capital controls, and consequently there is a perceptible increase in trading activities. The Polish market is more active in comparison. In both countries, the legal framework has been substantially modernized.
- The most liquid fixed-income markets are in Singapore, Hong Kong, Brazil, Mexico, and South Africa. In both Latin America as well as Singapore, most interest rate derivatives are traded on organized exchanges. However, in Korea and South Africa, most of the trading is OTC. In Mexico, a combination of factors spurred derivatives trading. The issuance of government bonds increased, and restrictions were relaxed, that enabled banks and brokers to access derivatives markets. The derivatives exchange in Mexico launched many new products, which too boosted

trading activities. Falling interest rates and greater issuance of government bonds, were the prime drivers of interest rate swap transactions. In addition, the increasing use of structured products in Hong Kong and Taiwan, lead to greater demand for interest rate swaps.

The activities of institutional investors has also played a role in the increase in fixed income derivatives trading. In Singapore, insurance companies started using long-dated interest rate derivatives. In Taiwan, pension funds and insurance companies started using interest rate derivatives, due to a shift in focus from equity and real estate. In many countries, institutional investors are allowed to use only standardized exchange traded products, and not OTC derivatives. Consequently, the introduction of more instruments will facilitate the deepening of such markets.

Government bond futures have not been a major success in many emerging derivatives markets. Bond futures are used to hedge positions in the bonds themselves. If the market for the underlying bonds is not liquid, it is to be expected that bond futures will be thinly traded. Thus, in countries without a vibrant market for government bonds, it is to be expected that bond futures will not be actively traded. South Africa, on the contrary has an active market for government bonds, although bond futures are illiquid.

– Equity derivatives in Asian markets has seen steady growth over the past few decades. The growth is pronounced in Korea, which accounts for a substantial chunk of the global turnover in stock index derivatives. South Africa too, has an active market in equity derivatives, as do the major trading centers in Latin America. Local corporations are the main users of single stock options. Asset managers, use stock index futures and options, while pension funds prefer equity linked notes. In Korea and Taiwan, the bulk of the positions in single stock trades, are taken by retail investors. In Hong Kong and Taiwan, new products have been launched to cater to retail investors. These include small-sized equity index futures.

16.10 Emerging Derivatives Markets and Capital Flows

The rapid growth of derivatives across the globe has facilitated cross-border flows of capital. Investment vehicles, both debt and equity, expose lenders and borrowers to multiple risks, such as, interest rate risk, market risk, currency risk and liquidity risk. As Ilyina points out, derivatives can be used in various ways. Currency derivatives can be used to change the currency in which assets are denominated. This protects the hedger against changes in exchange rates. It has been observed that foreign entities use currency derivatives to hedge their long exposures in local currency, while domestic hedgers use these instruments to manage exchange risk associated with financing obtained from overseas. Hence, there is a connection between the amount of external fundraising by such entities, and the availability of tools for hedging such as futures and options.

Interest rate swaps are a useful tool for borrowers to convert floating rate liabilities to fixed rate liabilities. Thus, if an emerging market entity has a comparative advantage with respect to floating rate borrowings, it can raise funds abroad on a floating rate basis and use such derivatives to convert the liability to a fixed rate loan. This as can be appreciated, facilitates cross-border flows of capital.

Ilyina points out that local entities with exposure in foreign currencies, are the most active users of derivatives in emerging markets. In such economies, the local debt markets usually lack adequate depth, thereby compelling domestic entities to raise funds from abroad. Following the crisis in Asian markets, many countries in that region started sourcing funds in the local currencies. Also, many of these countries have recurring current account surpluses, due to booming exports, and consequently do not need to borrow abroad.

References

Bricheux B., Savre, J. M. and L. Tachon *Creation of futures: Conditions for success.* MATIF S.A., Development and Education Department Paper prepared for World Bank Workshop on Risk Management in Liberalizing Economies, Issues of Access to Futures and Options Markets, Paris, 1992.

Ersen, P., and A. Karagozoglu *Introduction of derivatives exchanges in emerging markets.* Hofstra University working paper, 2003.

Harris L. *Trading and Exchanges.* Oxford University Press, 2003.

Ilyina A. *The Role of Financial Derivatives in Emerging Markets.* International Monetary Fund.

Karagozoglu A. *Financial Derivatives in Emerging Markets: Experience of Korea and Turkey.* Hofstra News, May 2006.

Peck A.E. *The Economic Role of Traditional Commodity Futures Markets.* In Anne Peck (Ed.) Futures Markets: Their Economic Role. American Enterprise Institute for Public Policy Research.

Resnick B.G. *The Globalization of World Financial Markets.* In P.L. Cooley (Ed.), Advances in Business Financial Management, The Dryden Press, 1996.

Sandor R. L. *Innovation by an exchange: A case study of the development of the plywood futures contract.* Journal of Law and Economics, 1973, 16, 119-136.

Sarkar A. and M. Tozzi *Electronic Trading on Futures Exchanges.* Derivatives Quarterly, 1998.

Silber W.L. *The Economic Role of Financial Futures.* In Anne Peck (Ed.) Futures Markets: Their Economic Role. American Enterprise Institute for Public Policy Research.

Tsetsekos G.P. and P. Varangis *Structure of derivatives exchanges: Lessons from developed and emerging markets.* The World Bank Group, Working Paper No. 1887 (www.worldbank.org), 1998.

Tsetsekos G.P. and P.Varangis *Lessons in Structuring Derivatives Exchanges.* The World Bank Research Observer, February 2000.

Upper C. and M. Valli *Emerging Derivatives Markets.* BIS Quarterly Review, December 2016.

Chapter 17
India: The Crouching Tiger

17.1 The Big Bang Equivalent

The opening up of the London market to global traders in 1986, is known as the Big Bang in financial circles. In India, the equivalent, which may be termed as a tsunami or an earthquake, happened in 1991. Since independence, India had been a closed economy with stifling controls on private business enterprises. The government had a foot in almost every sector of the economy, and its companies, known as public sector enterprises, or PSEs, were notorious for their inefficiency, and had huge accumulated losses. Both the banking and insurance industries were dominated by state run institutions. There was a single mutual fund, known as the Unit Trust of India, which too was a government entity. There was one life insurance company, the Life Insurance Corporation of India (LIC), and one general insurance company, the General Insurance Corporation of India (GIC). The latter had multiple subsidiaries. Both the LIC and GIC continue to be owned by the government, although the shareholding of the government has been brought down substantially. Private companies are now allowed to operate in both the life and general insurance space. There were strict regulations regarding capital transfers from India, and foreign exchange transactions were tightly regulated. Some multinational corporations did exist, but had to comply with draconian regulations. Investment in business enterprises by MNCs, known as Foreign Direct Investment (FDI) was controlled, and Foreign Institutional Investment (FII), a term used for foreign acquisition of securities in the stock market, was prohibited.

In 1991 a new government was sworn in, and it became obvious that the system needed fundamental reforms. Under the leadership of Prime Minister Narasimha Rao, a professional economist, Dr. Manmohan Singh, who had earlier been the Governor of India's central bank, took over as the Finance Minister. FDI related regulations were substantially diluted, and foreign portfolio investment was allowed. The rupee was made largely convertible on the current account. The reform process has been gradual over the years, since the earth-shaking events of 1991. As someone said, "changes in Asian societies are evolutionary and not revolutionary." Today, India has modern, electronic stock and derivative exchanges. Private banks and insurance companies are allowed to operate in the country. Rates of both direct and indirect taxes has been reduced considerably. A landmark Goods and Services Tax (GST), which replaced a set of various taxes levied by the central and state governments, was launched, and has contributed considerably to the ease of doing business. Private mutual funds, and ETFs are allowed to operate in the country. Foreign exchange transactions, both inwards and outwards, have been substantially liberalized, although the Rupee is not fully convertible on the capital account.

https://doi.org/10.1515/9783110746662-017

Significant developments have taken place in allied areas. Credit rating agencies have come into existence, which rate various securities with respect to the default risk. Depositories have been set up, and consequently, most securities are held in electronic form. The banking, brokerage, and insurance sectors, are now fully computerized, and have made significant progress towards attaining global standards. The settlement system has moved from account period based settlement, to rolling settlement. Discount broking has come into existence, and competition has brought down transaction costs substantially.

17.2 Revival of Derivatives Trading In India

Financial sector reforms have been an integral part of the overall liberalization strategy for the Indian economy, which commenced in 1991. Before the introduction of relatively sophisticated instruments like derivatives, there was an urgent need to reform and revitalize the cash market for securities. Consequently, in the initial years, the focus was on the development of a modern, efficient and more transparent cash market. The most important developments in this regard may be summarized as follows.

1. A new *Electronic* exchange - The National Stock Exchange, was set up, backed by India's leading financial institutions. It commenced trading in equities in November of 1994. The NSE introduced screen based trading and linked up investors across the country using VSAT technology. This exchange provided healthy competition to the Bombay Stock Exchange (BSE) which was earlier India's premier stock trading platform. The consequences were soon apparent, for the BSE too chose to abandon the traditional open-outcry system of trading and switched to a screen-based system.
2. The National Securities Clearing Corporation (NSCCL) was set up to clear all trades. It has been subsequently renamed as NSE Clearing.
3. The National Securities Depository Limited (NSDL) was set up to facilitate trading of securities in the dematerialized mode. Subsequently a second depository, the Central Depository Services (India) Limited (CDSL), was set up.

As liberalization progressed, and the command economy was dismantled, it became obvious that market participants in India would face greater price risk. Liberalization brought in foreign capital, in the form of Foreign Direct Investment (FDI) as well as capital market investments by Foreign Institutional Investors (FIIs). However, capital does not flow across borders in isolation. Risk is an integral accompaniment. The next step, consequent to the streamlining of the cash market, was therefore the creation of a market for exchange traded derivatives. It was felt that derivatives were integral to the philosophy of economic reforms, because they give firms the freedom to decide as to what risks they are comfortable bearing and what they would rather hedge away.

However, there were legal barriers to the introduction of derivatives trading, that were a part of India's socialist legacy. The Securities Contracts (Regulation) Act, SC(R)A, prohibited trading in derivatives. Using the powers bestowed by this Act, the Government of India had prohibited all forward trading in securities in 1969. The first step was therefore to repeal some of the provisions of this Act. It must be pointed out that although forward trading in securities was proscribed, parties with legitimate foreign exchange transactions were permitted to protect themselves against currency risks by entering into forward contracts with commercial banks. Indian regulations also permitted the trading of futures contracts in certain commodities, although the volumes of trading in practice were insignificant.

The Securities Exchange Board of India (SEBI) set up a committee headed by Dr. L.C. Gupta in 1996, to develop an appropriate regulatory framework to facilitate derivatives trading. The committee, after extensive deliberations, submitted its report in March 1998. It recommended that derivatives be declared as securities so that the existing regulatory framework for the trading of securities could be extended to cover derivatives as well. Among its other recommendations, it suggested an automated screen based trading system for derivative securities. It mooted a separate clearing corporation and recommended strict eligibility criteria for brokers seeking to trade in the derivatives segment of an exchange.

Subsequently, the Securities Laws (Amendment) Bill was introduced in the Parliament, and was converted into an Act in December, 1999. The Government of India lifted the prohibition on forward trading in securities in March 2000. The SC(R)A post-amendment included derivatives as part of a broader definition of securities.

SEBI then gave approval to the BSE and the NSE to commence trading in approved derivative contracts, which included only index futures to begin with. The chronology of the introduction of equity derivatives is as follows. The BSE launched contracts on the Sensex which is a 30 stock index, and the NSE launched contracts on the Nifty, which is a 50 stock index. We will have more to say about the two indices later.

- On 9 June 2000 the BSE launched futures contracts on the Sensex.
- The NSE began trading futures contracts on the S&P CNX Nifty index from 12 June 2000.
- European options on the Sensex began trading from 1 June 2001.
- The NSE commenced trading in Nifty options (also European) on 4 June 2001.
- American options on individual stocks began trading on the NSE from 2 July 2001.
- The BSE introduced similar contracts on 9 July 2001.
- On 9 November 2001 the NSE launched single stock futures.
- Single stock futures were introduced by the BSE on 9 November 2002.

SEBI specified that stock futures and options were to be settled in cash. This means that if a call holder were to exercise the option, rather than paying the exercise price and receiving physical delivery of a share, he will receive the difference between the stock price at the time of exercise and the exercise price. Similarly, a put holder will receive the difference between the exercise price and the stock price, if he chooses to exercise. In the case of stock futures, all contracts are marked to market on the last day and all positions are declared closed. Index options, just like index futures, are cash settled, as is the global practice.

In 1998 SEBI constituted a committee under the Chairmanship of J.R.Varma, a Professor at IIM Ahmedabad, to formulate a risk management system for the proposed derivatives market. This committee designed a suitable margining system. It recommended the use of the Value at Risk methodology for computing margins, and suggested a procedure for computing the VaR. Considering the fact that even the best of statistical methods for computing potential losses cannot prevent the possibility of default in 100% of the cases, the committee recommended additional protection for preventing default, by requiring clearing members of the exchange to have a minimum liquid net worth.

17.3 Indian Derivative Exchanges

17.3.1 Securities Exchanges

The oldest stock exchange in India, is the Bombay Stock Exchange (BSE), which is located in Mumbai, the new name for the erstwhile city of Bombay. Subsequently the National Stock Exchange (NSE) was set up. Both these exchanges offer trading primarily in stock and stock index derivatives. Both these exchanges offer single stock futures and options, and stock index futures and options. There are two key indices in the Indian market. The Sensex, is based on 30 key stocks that are traded on the Bombay stock exchange. The NIFTY, is based on 50 key stocks that trade on the National Stock Exchange. Both indices are value-weighted and are based on the free-floating market capitalization approach. As of 31 March 2024, the level of the Sensex is around 73,000 and that of the NIFTY is around 22,000.

Currency derivatives are available on the NSE for four currency pairs - the USD-INR; the EUR-INR; the GBP-INR; and the JPY-INR. The NSE also offers derivatives on Government of India Bonds, and Government of India Treasury Bills.

The Bombay Stock Exchange was owned by the member brokers, and consequently there were a limited number of members at any point in time. The National Stock Exchange, was however set up as a demutualized, for profit exchange, right from the outset. In 2007, the Bombay Stock Exchange too was corporatized. The Bombay Stock Exchange had a trading ring for stocks, while the National Stock Exchange commenced operations as an electronic exchange. The advent of the latter, took equities trading to the smaller towns of India, and lead to the equity revolution. The NSE, has also been an outstanding success from the standpoint of trading in derivatives. The Bombay Stock Exchange, has now abandoned the trading ring structure, and moved completely to an electronic trading platform.

17.3.2 The Move to Rolling Settlement

Prior to the reforms in the markets in India, the exchanges were using account period settlement, which was a 14 day period. During this period, traders could buy or sell, without having to take delivery or give delivery. One of the major reforms was the transition to rolling settlement. In this, traders can buy or sell at any time during the day, and the net position at the end of the day is settled at the end of the settlement cycle. Currently the exchanges operate on a T+1 basis, and there are plans of transitioning to same day or T+0 settlement.

17.3.3 Commodity Exchanges

The Multi Commodity Exchange of India (MCX), and the National Commodities and Derivatives Exchange (NCDEX), offer derivatives on commodities. The MCX was established in 2003, and provides a platform for trading various commodities, including metals, energy products, and agricultural products. The exchange plays a vital role from the perspectives of price discovery and risk management for traders in commodity markets. The exchange is totally electronic. Products traded include gold, silver and copper in the metals category, crude oil and natural gas in the energy products category, and soybeans and cotton, in the agricultural products segment.

NCDEX is India's prominent commodity futures exchange. It too was established in 2003, and specializes in derivatives trading on agricultural commodities. It offers a platform for trading commodities like wheat, soybeans, and cotton. As an exchange, it facilitates the management of price risk by key segments of the economy, such as farmers, and traders in agricultural products. The exchange has brought in transparency and efficiency in the agricultural sector, which is important, because despite the tremendous growth in India' services sector, a significant percentage of the country depends on agriculture in some form or the other.

While both the exchanges are the major commodity futures trading platforms in India, they differ in various aspects. The basket of commodities on which contracts are offered is different. The regulatory structures of the two exchanges, also exhibit differences. MCX allows trading in a diverse spectrum of commodities, such as metals, energy products, and agricultural products. Thus, the range of underlying assets is much broader than just agricultural commodities. NCDEX, on the other hand, specializes in agricultural products.

Both MCX and NCDEX are regulated by the Securities Exchange Board of India, which is India's top cop, from the standpoint of regulating securities and commodities exchanges. MCX offers both physical delivery and cash-settled contracts for various commodities. This means that some contracts can result in the actual delivery of the underlying commodity, while others are settled by a fund transfer from the loser to the gainer. NCDEX, on the other hand, predominantly uses a delivery-based settlement system. This is important, because in the agricultural segment of the economy, many players may show keen interest in physical delivery.

Since MCX offers contracts on a wider array of products, contract specifications may vary widely across commodities. This is true from the standpoints of lot sizes, tick sizes, and expiration dates. On the other hand, contracts that are traded on the NCDEX are more standardized. Standardization across agricultural products facilitates trading for parties taking both long and short positions in agri-commodity futures. MCX is open for longer hours. Considering this, and due to the fact that contracts are offered on a wider basket, the trading volumes and levels of liquidity are higher.

17.4 Depositories

A depository is an institution that securely holds shares and other financial securities on behalf of investors in an electronic form. When securities are converted from physical form to electronic form, there are two possibilities. The original securities may be irrevocably replaced by electronic records, which is termed as dematerialization, or else the physical securities may be kept in safe custody, while traders transact in the electronic format. The latter method, is termed as immobilization. Investors need to open a demat account with a Depository Participant (DP), who acts as a link between the investors and the depository.

Thus, a depository is like a bank for securities. While banks hold funds in electronic form, depositories hold securities in electronic form. In the case of banks, parties can transfer funds from one entity to another, without physically handling cash. In the case of depositories, traders can transfer securities, without physically handling securities. When physical trading was the norm, there were various issues, like signature mismatches, and fraudulent versions of securities. Dematerialized trading has taken care of such issues. When a security is bought, the depository will debit the account of the seller and credit the account of the buyer. In the process, securities are transferred seamlessly from one party to another. A depository participant or DP, is an agent of the depository. When an entity wishes to raise a trade request, it needs to contact its DP. The DP will forward the instruction to the concerned depository.

There are two depositories in India National Securities Depository Ltd. (NSDL) and Central Depository Services India Ltd. (CDSL). NSDL was established in 1996, and the CDSL in 1999. Both have their headquarters in Mumbai. Both are regulated by the market regulator, SEBI. The depositories hold in safekeeping various financial securities like stocks, bonds, debentures, commercial paper and mutual funds. They facilitate record keeping of security ownership, and enable trading and transfer of securities in the market. They also offer clearing and settlement services. In addition to streamlining trading activities, depositories help credit corporate benefits to the shareholders. Equity shareholders are beneficiaries of corporate actions such as cash dividends, and stock dividends, which are termed as bonus shares in India. Depositories ensure that the security holders get the benefits to which they are entitled. At times, investors choose to use their shares held in demat accounts as collateral against loans. Both NSDL and CDSL provide a collateral account that holds the pledged securities till the loan is repaid.

NSDL primarily operates in the National Stock Exchange, while CDSL primarily operates on the Bombay Stock Exchange. As of January 2023, NSDL had in excess of 30 million demat accounts, while CDSL had close to 80 million accounts.

17.5 Badla: The Precursor to Exchange Traded Futures

Prior to the introduction of derivatives segments of the Indian stock exchanges, in the early part of this century, the exchanges offered an indigenous carry forward system known as Badla. In 1994 Badla was banned by the regulator, and there were growing expectations that it would be replaced with exchange traded derivatives products. In 1996 Badla was permitted once again, with a limit of Rupees 200 million per broker. The system was abandoned again in the middle of 2001, after exchange traded derivatives became available. Badla trading involved buying stocks with borrowed money. The cost of funds was determined by the demand for the underlying stocks.

In a normal stock market trade, the buyer of the stock is expected to take delivery by the end of the settlement cycle by paying the cost of acquisition. Sellers are expected to give delivery by the end of the same period, and accept cash in lieu. Badla offered traders, an avenue for carrying forward the transaction. The carry forward facility, permitted traders to defer their commitments from one settlement period to another. The exchanges had a list of securities called the *Specified List*. Securities on this list were also known as *forward securities*, *cleared securities*, or *Group A securities*. For securities on this list, transactions entered into during a trading period, were not required to be settled by delivery at the end of the period. Based on an agreement with the counterparty to the transaction, a broker could carry forward the transaction from one settlement period to the next. In India, the settlement period was of 14 days duration, and ended on alternate Fridays.

In the badla system, outstanding transactions at the end of a settlement period, could be carried forward through the clearinghouse, at prices known as *Makeup* or *Hawala* prices. The makeup prices were used by the exchange to compute the payments due from buyers, and the payments due to sellers. In this system, some brokers would receive less or more, than what was due to be received by them. This can be illustrated with the help of an example.

Gupta and Company, a broker, bought 200 shares of XYZ at Rs. 90 per share, from another broker called Mehta and Company. It also bought an additional 160 shares at Rs. 117 per share, from Chawla and Company, a third broker. Let's assume that on the settlement date, the make up price is fixed at Rs. 100 per share, and that the buyer, Gupta and Company, wishes to take delivery. In this case, Gupta and Company will pay Rs. 36,000 to the clearinghouse in exchange for 360 shares. Mehta and Company will deliver

200 shares and receive Rs. 20,000, while Chawla and Company will deliver 160 shares and receive Rs. 16,000. The amounts to be paid/received, are computed using the makeup price. Based on the transaction price, Gupta was required to pay Rs. 18,000 to Mehta and Company. Thus, Mehta has to pay Rs. 2,000 to Gupta. Similarly Chawla was required to be paid Rs. 18,720, and so Gupta has to pay Rs. 2,720 to Chawla. Thus Gupta will pay 36,000 − 2,000 + 2,720 = 36,720. This, amounts to a weighted average price of 102.

$$(200 \times 90 + 160 \times 117)/360 = 102$$

At the end of the settlement cycle, there will be traders with net long positions, and others with net short positions. Parties with net long positions, who wish to defer settlement, would have to locate other parties with net short positions, who are willing to carry the positions forward. Buyers of securities were usually not investors but speculators. They consequently had no intention of taking delivery. At the end of the delivery cycle, they could either pay and take delivery, or else arrange for funds. Most sellers were short sellers, who did not have securities to deliver. Thus, if called upon to give delivery, they could either buy the shares in the market, or else borrow the shares to cover their delivery obligations. This, as Gupta (1995) points out is the interdependence between buyers and sellers, and is the crux of carry forward trades.

The mechanics of a badla transaction may be demonstrated as follows. Ravi has bought shares through his broker, Ramdas and Company. If this transaction has to be carried forward, the broker has to find another broker, who has a net short position and is willing to carry it forward. If such a party cannot be found, then taking delivery is imperative. If a counterparty, who is net short, and wishes to carry forward is not available, the broker will arrange for a financier who was known as the badliwalla. The badliwalla would take delivery instead of Ravi. Ravi has to pay a financing charge called the *Contango* or *Seedha badla* charge. Assume that Rajesh, who has a net short position, is willing to carry it forward. In this case the payment will be made by Ravi to his broker, who will pay Rajesh's broker, who will in turn pay Rajesh. On the other hand, if the services of a financier are required, the payment will be made to the financier through Ravi's broker. The term *Contango*, refers to the interest on the principal, that is charged. If a party with a short position, agrees to carry forward the transaction by deferring the payment, it is effectively lending funds to the buyer for the duration of the settlement cycle. In the other case, where a financier is involved, the lending of money is a direct monetary transaction. The badla rate used to depend on the supply demand dynamics for the security concerned.

There could be cases where the number of buyers demanding delivery, is greater than the number of sellers who are in a position to make delivery. This is because parties who have gone short may be unable to locate securities. This is referred to as an oversold market. In such markets, the seller's broker will arrange for a party to lend securities. In practice, securities may not be easily available. The alternative is to persuade the buyer to carry forward the transaction. In this case, the seller has to pay a charge known as *backwardation* or *undha badla*. This charge may be perceived as a penalty levied on the seller for selling without having possession of the securities.

When a buyer is seeking funds, the process works as follows. He will be deemed to have sold his shares at the makeup price. At the same time, he will deemed to have bought the number of shares outstanding at the makeup price plus the badla charge. In the case of the seller, it would be deemed to have bought the shares at the makeup price and sold it at the same price plus the contango charge. In the case of an oversold market, the mechanics are similar, except that the transactions are deemed to be executed at the making up price less the backwardation charge.

Here is a detailed illustration of a hypothetical transaction, in Example 17.1

Example 17.1: Rohini has bought 200 shares of XYZ at 160 and sold 160 shares of DEF at 125. The exchange announces the following makeup prices. 172 for XYZ and 130 for DEF. The margin rates are Rs. 18 for long positions and Rs. 15 for short positions. The badla rates are Rs. 3.60 for XYZ and Rs. 2.80 for DEF. The amount due to be paid/received by Rohini may be viewed as the sum of three components: the transaction amounts, the carried forward transactions at the hawala rates, and the margin amount required to be deposited with the broker.

Rohini owes 32,000 for XYZ and is owed 20,000 for DEF. Thus the net amount due is 32,000 − 20,000 = 12,000. The carried forward transactions are 200 × 172 = 34,400 for XYZ and −160 × 130 = −20,800. The net amount to be received is equal to 34,400 − 20,800 = 13,600. The margin that is required to be deposited is 200 × 18 + 160 × 15 = Rs. 6,000. Hence, the total amount due to be deposited by Rohini is 12,000 − 13,600 + 6,000 = Rs. 4,400.

The carrying charges for the long position in XYZ and the short position in DEF, may be computed as follows. If the purchase of XYZ were to be settled in this period itself, the payable is the makeup price of 172. Since a margin of Rs. 18 has been deposited, the additional amount due is Rs. 154. The badla charge is 3.60. Thus, the monthly cost is

$$\frac{3.60}{154} \times \frac{30}{14} = 5\%$$

The annualized cost is 60%. In the case of the short position in DEF the amount receivable if the shares are delivered is 130. The margin deposited is Rs.15. Thus, the amount invested is Rs. 145. The badla receipt is Rs. 2.80. The income therefore is

$$\frac{2.80}{145} \times \frac{30}{14} = 4.14\%$$

The annualized income is 49.65%.

17.6 Clearing & Settlement on the NSE

We have four categories of exchange members in India. These are:

- Trading Members (TMs)
- Trading Members-Clearing Members (TM-CMs)

- Self Clearing Members (SCMs)
- Professional Clearing Members (PCMs)

Trading Members or TMs are the equivalent of non-clearing FCMs in the US. They can open accounts on behalf of their clients, but in turn, must clear through a clearing member. Trading Members Clearing Members or TM-CMs, are the equivalent of clearing FCMs. They can accept and clear trades on behalf of their clients, and can also clear trades routed through them by other TMs. Professional Clearing Members or PCMs are FCMs, whose only function is to clear and settle transactions routed through them by other TMs. They cannot accept trades. Finally, there is a category of brokers called Self Clearing Members (SCMs), who can clear trades on behalf of their clients, but are not authorized to clear trades routed through them by other trading members.

Professional Clearing Members are required to have a minimum net worth of Rs. 30 million, as are Trading Members-Clearing Members. Trading Members and Self Clearing Members are required to have a minimum net worth of Rs. 10 million.

The net worth of a member is calculated as the sum of his capital and free reserves less certain non-allowable assets.

Every clearing member is also required to maintain a base minimum capital of Rs. 5 million with the NSE Clearing. Of this, Rs. 2.5 million must be in the form of cash. The balance Rs. 2.5 million may be in or more of the following forms:

- Cash
- Fixed Deposit Receipts (in India Time Deposits are known as Fixed Deposits) issued by approved banks and deposited with approved custodians or NSE Clearing
- Bank Guarantee in favour of the NSE Clearing from approved banks
- Approved securities in demateralized form deposited with approved custodians

In addition, for every TM whose trades a clearing member undertakes to clear and settle, an amount of Rs. 1 million has to be maintained as Base Minimum Capital. Of this Rs. 200,000 should be in the form of cash and the balance Rs. 800,000 in one or more of the forms described above.

17.6.1 Client Level Margining

The National Stock Exchange follows a system of Gross or Client Level margining, as opposed to the Net or Broker Level margining systems that are used by many international exchanges.

As far as a clearing member is concerned, he is first required to classify a trade as either *Proprietary* (that is, on his own account), or as *Client* (that is, induced by a client). For proprietary trades, the open position is calculated as the total long position less the total short position. From the stand point of the clients, while the long and short positions for a particular client can be netted out in order to arrive at a net position, netting across clients is not permissible.

Similarly, as far as the trades of a trading member who is clearing through this clearing member are concerned, the trading member's proprietary trades will be netted, and the net position for each client of the trading member will be taken into account, once again without netting across the clients of the trading member.

We will illustrate these principles with the help of Example 17.2.

Example 17.2: Shadab Khan, a TM-CM, has placed the following orders on his own behalf, as well as on behalf of two of his clients, Suhasini Singh and Harita Reddy. In addition, Abraham Jacob, a TM, is also clearing his trades through Shadab.

Shadab's proprietary trades are as shown in Table 17.1.

Table 17.1: Shadab's Proprietary Orders.

Buy Orders		Sell Orders	
Price	**Quantity**	**Price**	**Quantity**
1020	600	1035	200

So from the standpoint of proprietary trades, Shadab has a net long position of 600 − 200 = 400 contracts.

Suhasini's and Harita's trades are summarized in Table 17.2.

Table 17.2: Shadab's Client Orders.

	Buy Orders		Sell Orders	
Client	**Price**	**Quantity**	**Price**	**Quantity**
Suhasini	1030	400	1015	200
Harita	1010	400	1025	800

Suhasini has a net long position of 400 − 200 = 200 contracts.

Harita has a net short position of 800 − 400 = 400 contracts.

Notice that we cannot net between Suhasini and Harita, since we are following a Client Level system and not a Broker Level system.

Now assume that Abraham Jacob's proprietary trades are as shown in Table 17.3.

So the net proprietary position for Abraham is short 600 contracts.

Also assume that two clients, Preeti Raghu and Sangeeta Shetty trade through Abraham. Their positions are as shown in Table 17.4.

So Preeti has a net short position of 600 contracts, while Sangeeta has a net long position of 600 contracts.

For the purpose of computing the initial margin, Shadab's total position will be determined as follows.

Long positions = 400 (his own) + 200 (Suhasini's) + 600 (Sangeeta's) = 1200 contracts.

Short positions = 400 (Harita's) + 600 (Abraham's proprietary trades) + 600 (Preeti's) = 1600 contracts.

Table 17.3: Abraham's Proprietary Orders.

Buy Orders		Sell Orders	
Price	Quantity	Price	Quantity
1020	600	1035	1200

Table 17.4: Abraham's Client Orders.

	Buy Orders		Sell Orders	
Client	Price	Quantity	Price	Quantity
Preeti	1030	1400	1015	2000
Sangeeta	1010	2400	1025	1800

Thus Shadab will be margined for 1200 long positions and 1600 short positions. Had a net margining system been in operation, he would have been margined for 400 short positions. A consequence of gross margining, is that brokers do not pay interest on margin deposits, unlike certain brokers in the US and elsewhere.

Initial margins have to be paid up front but need not be in cash. They could be in the form of cash, bank guarantees, fixed deposit receipts, or approved securities.

Initial margins are computed on a real time basis, that is, after every trade. During the day, if the required margin is such that it causes a member's liquid net worth to dip below Rs. 5 million at any point in time, it is considered a violation

At the end of each trading day, the required margin is once again computed. If the required amount exceeds what is currently being maintained by the member, then the shortfall is collected on the next business day.

In order to calculate the settlement price for the purpose of marking to market, the weighted average of futures prices observed during the last half hour of trading is taken. There could, however, be contracts which are illiquid or, in other words, trade infrequently. For such contracts a theoretical settlement price is computed according to the formula $F = Se^{rT}$, where S is the value of the underlying asset in the spot market, T is the time remaining to expiration, and r is the current value of MIBOR (the Mumbai Inter Bank Offer Rate).

On the expiration date, the open positions will be marked to market for the last time. On this day, the settlement price is set equal to the weighted average of the spot prices observed during the last half hour of trading. This procedure is legitimate since we know that spot and futures prices must converge at the time of expiration.

17.7 Rating Agencies

India has seven credit rating agencies.

1. Credit Rating Information Services of India Ltd, known by its acronym CRISIL. This is a wholly owned subsidiary of S&P Global.
2. Investment Information and Credit Rating Agency of India Ltd, known by its acronym ICRA.
3. Credit Analysis and Research Ltd., known by its acronym CARE.
4. Acuite Ratings and Research Ltd.
5. Brickwork Ratings India Private Ltd.
6. India Ratings and Research Private Ltd. This is a wholly owned subsidiary of Fitch.
7. INFOMERICS Valuation and Rating Private Ltd.

17.8 Derivative Products Traded on the National Stock Exchange

The National Stock Exchange started trading in the equities segment on November 3, 1994. It is currently the largest stock exchange in India, and the third largest stock exchange in the world, as per the World Federation of Exchanges. The market capitalization of listed companies, is currently about 4.5 trillion Rupees, which is approximately 55 billion USD. The daily turnover in the equity segment of the exchange is about 805 billion Rupees or 9.82 billion USD. The daily turnover in the derivatives segment for stock and stock index options is 567 billion Rupees or 6.92 billion USD. In the market for index futures and single stock futures, the daily turnover is 1.31 trillion Rupees which is roughly 16 billion USD.

The exchange provides futures and options contracts on four major indices and over 180 securities. These indices are the NIFTY 50 index, the NIFTY Bank index, the NIFTY Financial Services index, and the NIFTY Midcap Select index. Futures contracts have a maximum of three months to expiration at any point in time - the near month, the next month, and the far month. New contracts are introduced on the trading day following the expiry of the near month contracts. Contracts expire on the last Thursday of the expiry month. If the last Thursday is a trading holiday, the contracts expire on the previous trading day. Unlike in the US, where the contract size for stock futures and options is 100 shares, in India the contract size varies from stock to stock. The value of the options contracts on individual securities may not be less than Rs. 50 billion at the time of introduction for the first time at any exchange. The permitted lot size for futures contracts and options contracts shall be the same for a given underlying stock.

17.8.1 Risk Management

A sound risk management system is integral to an efficient clearing and settlement system. The National Stock Exchange was a pioneer in bringing global risk management techniques to the Indian market. Risk containment measures include capital adequacy requirements of members, monitoring of member performance, and track record, stringent margin requirements, position limits based on capital, online monitoring of member positions and automatic disablement from trading when limits are breached, etc. The exchange uses SPAN for risk management.

17.8.2 Liquid Net Worth

The purpose of collecting initial margins is to prevent default. However the VaR technique that is used for computational purposes is merely a statistical tool. There is always a possibility of a price move, however remote, that will lead to a loss in excess of the Initial Margin that is collected from an investor. It is for this reason that the Varma Committee mandated that a member ought to have a minimum liquid net worth at all times. This will serve as additional collateral in the event of losses exceeding the Initial Margin.

NSE Clearing collects initial margin up-front for all the open positions of a clearing member based on the margins computed by SPAN. A clearing member is in turn required to collect the initial margin from the trading members who clear through it, and from the clients of the former. The trading members should collect up front margins from their clients. Initial margin requirements are based on 99% value at risk (VAR) over a one day time horizon. However, in the case of futures contracts (on index or individual securities), where it may not be possible to collect mark to market settlement value before the commencement of trading on the next day, the initial margin is computed over a two-day time horizon, applying the appropriate statistical formula. A value at risk system does not provide protection in 100% of the cases. Consequently, an extreme value margin is collected. This is 2% of the notional value for index derivatives, and 3.5% of the notional value for stock derivatives.

17.8.3 Commodity Derivatives

While the NSE is not a commodities exchange, it does offer derivative contracts on bullion, energy products, and base metals. Energy products include WTI crude oil and natural gas; precious metals include gold and silver; and base metals include copper, aluminium, lead, zinc, and nickel.

17.8.4 Currency Derivatives

Futures and options contracts are available on the USD, EUR, GBP, and JPY. The contract size is 1,000 units for the first three currencies, and 100,000 for the Japanese Yen. Cross currency derivatives are available for the following currency pairs: EUR-USD; GBP-USD; and USD-JPY. The contract size is 1,000 Euros for the EUR-USD contract, 1,000 GBP for the GBP-USD contract, and 1,000 USD for the USD-JPY contract.

17.8.5 Interest Rate Derivatives

Futures and options contracts are available on Indian Government Securities, referred to as G-Secs in India, which are the equivalent of T-bond futures and options in the US. The underlying is a bond with a face value of 100, and a residual maturity ranging from 4-15 years, on the date of contract expiration. The lot size is 2,000 units, which means a face value of 200,000. At any point in time, six contract months are available, which include the three nearest months, and the next three months from the March quarterly cycle. Futures contracts are also available on 91-day T-bills, and on the Mumbai Interbank Offer Rate (MIBOR). Futures price for money market futures, are quoted as 100 - Interest Rate, as is the practice for SOFR futures on the CME Group.

17.9 Masala Bonds

Masala bonds are bonds denominated in Indian Rupees, which are issued outside India. Thus, they are technically Eurobonds. The first issue of such bonds was by the International Finance Corporation (IFC) in 2014. Since these bonds are denominated in Rupees, the holders in a foreign country stand to gain if their currency depreciates with respect to the Rupee, and stand to lose if their currency appreciates with respect to the Indian currency.

Thus, Masala bonds transfer exchange rate risk from Indian borrowers, to foreign investors. Traditionally, the only option to raise capital abroad for Indian entities, was to issue bonds in convertible currencies outside India. The Reserve Bank of India (RBI) has specified a maturity period of minimum three years for bonds with a face value with a rupee equivalent of 50 million US dollars or less, in a financial year. The maturity period is a minimum of five years for bonds with a face value in excess of the rupee equivalent of 50 million dollars.

The primary objectives of introducing Masala bonds was to fund infrastructure projects in India, and internationalize the Indian rupee. These bonds facilitate capital inflows into India, and help spur economic growth. Indian companies can issue ADRs to facilitate equity investments by foreign nationals. Masala bonds are a source of capital to obtain external funding in the form of debt.

17.10 Indian Depository Receipts (IDRs)

An Indian Depository Receipt (IDR) is a financial instrument denominated in Indian Rupees in the form of a depository receipt. It is an equivalent of the American Depository Receipts or ADRs, that are available for American investors. This facilitates the raising of equity capital from the Indian market by foreign companies. Like ADRs, every IDR is backed by a fraction of a foreign share or a multiple of a foreign share. Indian investors receive dividends in Indian rupees, and can trade using domestic brokers. If the foreign issuer were to take corporate actions such as cash dividends, stock dividends, or stock splits, the holders of the IDRs in India will be entitled to the benefits.

SEBI guidelines specify an issue process for IDRs, that is similar to that for the issue of domestic shares. The issuer company will file a draft red herring prospectus (DRHP), which will be examined by the regulator. Once the issuer obtains approval from the regulator, it sets the issue dates and files the document with the Registrar of Companies (ROC). Subsequently the marketing of the issue will begin. The DRHP will specify a minimum price for bids and a maximum price. The final price will be set after the closure of the issue. Indian investors who receive these receipts, with hold them with the Indian depositories, which is exactly the way in which they hold domestic equity securities.

17.11 MIBOR

MIBOR stands for the Mumbai Inter-Bank Offered Rate (MIBOR), which is similar to the LIBOR in London. It is the rate at which a bank in the Indian interbank market, can borrow on an unsecured basis, from a fellow bank. It is currently used as a reference rate for corporate bonds, term deposits, forward rate agreements, interest rate swaps, and floating-rate notes. The MIBOR is determined on a daily basis by the National Stock Exchange, in collaboration with FIMMDA, which is an acronym for the Fixed Income Money Market, and Derivative Association of India. The benchmark is set as a weighted average of the lending rates of all major banks in the country.

References

Gupta, Ramesh. *Badla Trading: A Primer and a Proposal.* Working Paper No. 1253, IIM Ahmedabad, May 1995.

Websites

www.bseindia.com
www.mcxindia.com
www.ncdex.com
www.nseindia.com

List of Figures

https://doi.org/10.1515/9783110746662-018

List of Tables

https://doi.org/10.1515/9783110746662-019

Index

https://doi.org/10.1515/9783110746662-020

www.ingramcontent.com/pod-product-compliance
Lightning Source LLC
Chambersburg PA
CBHW080938240926
51849CB00004BA/487
* 9 7 8 3 1 1 0 7 4 6 6 1 7 *